FOUNDATION PRESS

ADMINISTRATIVE LAW
STORIES

Edited By

PETER L. STRAUSS

Betts Professor of Law
Columbia University School of Law

FOUNDATION PRESS
2006

THOMSON
™
WEST

Cover Design: Keith Stout

Allegory of Good Government, detail of Justice inspired by Wisdom, and Allegory of Bad
Government, detail of Tyranny, 1338–40 (fresco); Lorenzetti, Ambrogio (1285–c.1348) / Palazzo
Pubblico, Siena, Italy, Alinari; Bridgeman Art Library

© 2006 By FOUNDATION PRESS
        395 Hudson Street
        New York, NY 10014
        Phone Toll Free 1–877–888–1330
        Fax (212) 367–6799
        foundation-press.com
Printed in the United States of America

ISBN–13: 978–1–58778–959–5
ISBN–10: 1–58778–959–0

 TEXT IS PRINTED ON 10% POST
CONSUMER RECYCLED PAPER

TABLE OF CONTENTS

*

FOUNDATION PRESS

ADMINISTRATIVE LAW STORIES

*

Editor's Note to Readers

What a privilege it has been to ask administrative law scholars whose work I greatly admire if they would contribute essays to this volume, and to have so many of them agree! However many of their essays you come to read, I know your appreciation for administrative law and administrative law practice will be deepened and concretized by them.

Administrative law, it is hardly necessary to remark, is a protean subject. It engages legislature, executive, agency and court. It extends from regulation of subtle and often hazardous activities affecting health, to regulation of complex economic behavior, to regulation of the incidents of daily living. It uses adjudication and rulemaking in various forms, as well as the persuasive techniques of politics. It occurs at the national, state and local levels in widely varying degrees of formality, before an extraordinary kaleidoscope of institutions. Both how we do it and how we think about it have changed considerably over the century or so it has been an important element in American law school curricula. And where you sit—in the chairs of bureaucrat, protected citizen or regulated industry—can have a great deal of influence over where you will stand on many of its pervasive issues.

In selecting essay subjects for this volume our general purpose has been to make more concrete, to set in context, a number of the issues you are likely to encounter in the standard law school course on Administrative Law by exploring a limited number of cases in depth. In general, these are the canonical cases, but that is not invariably the case. If David Vladeck of Georgetown Law School, one of the country's leading public interest litigators, could be persuaded to annotate his experiences trying to provoke the Occupational Safety and Health Administration into issuing a rule regulating a hazardous industrial chemical commonly used in hospitals (inter alia)—and thus to illustrate the course of a contemporary rulemaking and the political controls over it—the fact that the opinions resulting from his effort did not come from the Supreme Court was hardly a negative. Giving you a sense of what it means to practice administrative law is an important ambition of these pages.

The Table of Contents presents the essays in an essentially arbitrary order. This is the order in which they would come up, *if* you were taking Administrative Law with a professor using the casebook your editor has helped to create, and *if* his or her syllabus walked you straight through the book, not deviating from its organization. Every one of these essays will provide you with a depth of understanding about its subject that a casebook simply can't provide. They are all good stories.

Yet there are many other ways to organize your thinking about the supplemental values you can find here.

The back story of many administrative law disputes arises out of judicial encounters with extended legislative responses to social problems. A number of these essays explore the political background of the statutes whose administration was at issue in the cases they discuss. Thus, Congress's reactions to the Great Crash of 1929 (and the Crash itself) underlay the litigation that brought Administrative Law students not one, but two cases denominated *SEC v. Chenery Corp.*; and Roy Schotland's essay starts with an account of the financial manipulations to which some have attributed that cataclysm, and enactment of the Public Utility Holding Company Act of 1935. Elizabeth Garrett's essay on *Clinton v. New York* is a study of Congress's efforts to solve its enduring collective action problems when enacting budgetary and tax legislation in voluminous measures that too easily become "Christmas trees" for special interest provisions. Your editor's contribution on *Citizens to Preserve Overton Park* begins with a study of Congress's progressively more demanding efforts to structure consideration of highway location at the local, state and federal level, as the building of the Interstate Highway System revealed its disruptions, that eventually produced that litigation. Jerry Mashaw's account of *State Farm Mutual Auto Ins Co. v. Automobile Mfrs Ass'n* owes much to his understanding of the National Traffic and Motor Vehicle Safety Act and its changes over time.

Perhaps your interest lies in securing a concrete understanding how administrative law is practiced at the agency level, and/or how it is experienced by those who are engaged with it there. Most of these essays are revealing on this score—Professor Schotland's account of the "sporting proposition" that might have but did not resolve the *Chenery* dispute comes to mind—but for some this is a central focus: Professor Vladeck's account, already mentioned, of his client's effort to force rulemaking on OSHA; Craig Oren's account of the EPA rulemaking that underlay *Whitman v. American Trucking Ass'n;* Cynthia Farina's evocation of the dispute in *Mathews v. Eldridge*, in the perspective of applicant *and* state agency *and* federal administrators; your editor's similar effort respecting *Overton Park*; Gillian Metzger's close examination of the difficulties facing the Atomic Energy Commission and those who opposed its licensing nuclear power plants in *Vermont Yankee Nuclear Power Corp. v. NRDC*; Robert Kagan and Rachel VanSickel–Ward's revealing study of the problem of administrative inspections and the Fourth Amendment, at issue in *Marshall v. Barlow's, Inc.*; Professor Mashaw's evocation of the people involved in the struggles over automobile safety that eventuated in *State Farm*.

A third dimension concerns the litigating strategies of the lawyers who brought these cases to reviewing courts, perhaps especially the Supreme Court, and what we can know about the courts' actions in response. In addition to many of the essays already mentioned—your editor's and Professors Vladeck's and Metzger's, for example—you will find particular attention to these matters in Cynthia Farina's study of *Mathews*, Thomas Merrill's study of *Chevron U.S.A. Inc. v. NRDC* [and Ronald Levin's account of *Abbott Laboratories v. Gardner.*]

Then there is the after-life. What has been the continuing influence of the decisions studied? You will find this question substantially addressed in most of these essays; unsurprisingly, it is a principal focus of Professor Merrill's essay on *Chevron*, Professor Mashaw's consideration of *State Farm*, and Professor Levin's account of *Abbott Laboratories*.

Next, how can we place the decision studied in theoretical approaches to understanding government and its actors? Professor Garrett's essay reaches out to the perspectives of public choice; Professor Farina's "sees" the *Mathews* case through the eyes of several distinguished scholars as well as the many stakeholders in the dispute; Professor Mashaw brings his rich understanding of the political science literature to bear in his study of *State Farm*.

Introductions like these often include paragraph precis of each article. In this volume, those are placed at the beginning of each article. Instead, let us end these introductory notes with two tables suggesting other possible thematic organizations:

I.   Chronology

The classic cases of the New Deal	Schotland, SEC v. Chenery— A Sporting Proposition
The reformation of American Administrative Law in the '60's and '70's	Levin, Abbott Laboratories Strauss, Citizens to Preserve Overton Park Metzger, Vermont Yankee Kagan & Van Sickle–Ward, Marshall v. Barlow's
Standards transformed— the 1980's	Mashaw, State Farm Merrill, Chevron Farina, Mathews v. Eldridge Vladeck, ETO rulemaking
Recent developments	Oren, Whitman Garrett, Clinton v. New York

II. Procedural Focus of the Action

Informal agency action	Strauss, Overton Park
Enforcement and inspection	Kagan & Van Sickle–Ward, Marshall v. Barlow's Schotland, Chenery
Agency adjudication	Farina, Mathews v. Eldridge
Agency rulemaking	Vladeck, ETO rulemaking Mashaw, State Farm Oren, Whitman Metzger, Vermont Yankee Levin, Abbott Laboratories
Legislating	Strauss, Overton Park Mashaw, State Farm Oren, Whitman Garrett, Clinton v. New York
Presidential involvement	Vladeck, ETO rulemaking Garrett, Clinton v. New York
Judicial review	Schotland, Chenery Merrill, Chevron Mashaw, State Farm Levin, Abbott Laboratories

Peter Strauss
New York, NY June 2005

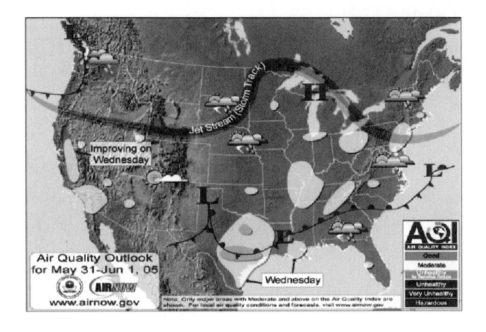

Professor Oren tells the story of the *Whitman* case, in which the Supreme Court refused to revive the delegation doctrine and instead upheld an Environmental Protection Agency rule requiring extensive efforts to reduce air pollution. His account depicts the rulemaking process to show the fierce political struggle that EPA's proposal evoked. The emphasis on delegation, Professor Oren shows, came less from the parties' litigating strategies than from the D.C. Circuit—indeed, once in the Supreme Court, the challengers to to the rule tried to move away from the D.C. Circuit's approach. Professor Oren also traces the post-Supreme Court history of EPA's rules, and predicts that the issues will likely recur.

1

Craig N. Oren*

Whitman v. American Trucking Associations—The Ghost of Delegation Revived . . . and Exorcised

Whitman v. American Trucking Associations[1] is a marvelous introduction to administrative law. The case demonstrates the breadth of the policymaking power that Congress can give to administrative agencies. More important, *Whitman*'s history shows how heated an administrative agency rulemaking becomes when it concerns a contentious and important issue of public policy. Administrative law, in other words, involves issues that go to the heart of public concern.

Whitman involved a challenge by industry groups to the United States Environmental Protection Agency (EPA)'s decision in 1997 to tighten the nation's air quality standards for two important air pollutants, ozone and particulate matter.[2] The Clean Air Act commands that such standards be set at the levels "that allowing an adequate margin of safety, are requisite to protect public health."[3] A divided D.C. Circuit panel held that this statutory language was too vague to satisfy the delegation doctrine, which requires that Congress lay down an "intelligi-

---

* Professor of Law—Rutgers (The State University of New Jersey) School of Law, Camden. The author wishes to thank all those who helped him, especially the lawyers who were willing to speak off-the-record about the case's history.

1. 531 U.S. 457 (2001).

2. The standard-setting decision was made by Carol Browner, administrator of EPA during both of President Bill Clinton's terms. The case bears Christine Whitman's name instead because, due to President George W. Bush's inauguration in 2001, Ms. Whitman succeeded Ms. Browner as administrator just weeks before the Supreme Court's decision.

3. Clean Air Act § 109(b)(1), 42 U.S.C. § 7409(b)(1) (2000). Unless otherwise indicated, all further statutory citations are to the Act.

ble principle" for an agency to follow,[4] and that EPA had to supply the principle.[5] In *Whitman*, the Supreme Court unanimously reversed.

Invocation of the delegation doctrine is so rare these days that it is extraordinary that any modern case should hinge on it. How did this happen? What was really at stake? This essay sets forth the case's history so that these matters can be better appreciated.

The Statutory Framework

The Clean Air Act directs EPA to set "national ambient air quality standards" for air pollutants that may endanger public health or welfare.[6] Health-based standards, like those involved in *Whitman*, must be achieved around the nation by specific deadlines.[7] These standards determine the amount of protection for people who suffer ill effects—asthma attacks, bronchitis, even premature death—from air pollution. The standards also impose regulatory burdens: the more stringent the air quality standards, the more control must be imposed by the states and by EPA on sources of air pollution—cars and trucks, power plants, industrial facilities, and even familiar consumer products like spray deodorant, hair spray, barbecues and paint. The air quality standards establish the total "budget" for air pollution emissions, and much of the remainder of the Act allocates the budget by stipulating what sources must do.

Ever since Congress commanded EPA in 1970 to set ambient air quality standards, the agency has asserted, with the support of the courts, that costs may not be considered in setting the standards' levels.[8] (This is known as the *Lead Industries* doctrine, after the D.C. Circuit decision that first announced it.) Rather, EPA must explain its decisions on the basis of public health alone. In this way, the sponsors of the Act tried to minimize the impact that costs would have on the standards' levels.

Deciding what protects public health is not easy. There is often uncertainty about the precise effects of air pollutants and the levels at which those effects occur. Scientists have not identified "threshold" levels at which there is no risk of harm. Rather, individuals vary greatly

---

4. See J. W. Hampton, Jr., & Co. v. United States, 276 U.S. 394, 409 (1928).

5. See American Trucking Ass'ns v. United States EPA, 175 F.3d 1027 (D.C. Cir.1999), *modified* 195 F.3d 4.

6. See Section 108(a)(1), 42 U.S.C. § 7408(a)(1) (2000).

7. See, e.g., Section 172(a)(2), 42 U.S.C. § 7502(a)(2) (2000).

8. See Lead Industries Ass'n v. EPA, 647 F.2d 1130, 1148 (D.C. Cir. 1980), *cert. denied* 449 U.S. 1042.

in the level that causes an effect. Nor is there any obvious way either to decide which effects constitute the kind of effects on health that the standards must protect against, or to calculate the "margin of safety" the statute requires. The agency must therefore make a policy decision about whom should be protected and from what.

Congress has given little guidance on these questions. The Senate Report accompanying the 1970 legislation stressed that the standards should protect "representative samples" of sensitive populations such as bronchial asthmatics.[9] But the report left unanswered how EPA was to decide whether a given group is a sensitive population.

Nor did Congress specify which effects should be considered to be effects on "health" that the standards should try to prevent. Rather, Congress left it to the EPA Administrator to make what Senator Edmund Muskie, the sponsor of the 1970 legislation, called a "pragmatic judgment" about how to cope with the absence of thresholds and with the disruption that would be caused if the standards were set at zero.[10] As Muskie acknowledged, the concept of a threshold was an "oversimplification" to allow the setting of standards on the basis of public health and so to force the development of better control technology.[11] The upshot, though, is that the standard-setting language grants EPA vast discretion to decide what will protect public health.

The difficulties of decision-making are great. In the early 1980s, a group of EPA staffers briefed then-Administrator William Ruckelshaus about the health and welfare damage caused by particulate matter. He asked how he should go about setting the air quality standards. A leading agency lawyer explained to him that he had broad discretion. Ruckelshaus was displeased. "I don't want to know what I can get away with, I want to know how to make the decision!"[12]

Control through Procedure

While EPA has broad substantive discretion, standard-setting decisions must run a complicated gauntlet. (EPA prepared in the late 1970s a 20-stage flow chart showing the process it followed for setting and revising the standards.)[13] A key role is played by the agency's Clean Air

---

9. S. Rep. No. 91–1196, at 10.

10. 123 Cong. Rec. 18643 (1977).

11. Senate Committee on Public Works, Subcommittee on Environmental Pollution, *Executive Branch Review of Environmental Regulations*, 96th Cong. 1st Sess 343 (1979).

12. Cf. R. Shep Melnick, Regulation and the Courts: The Case of the Clean Air Act 259 (1983) ("Explaining why the administrator chose a particular standard is as much a job for a psychologist as for a political scientist or physician.").

13. The chart is reprinted id. at 258.

Scientific Advisory Committee (CASAC).[14] Congress established CASAC in 1977 because of concern that the scientific basis for the agency's air quality standards was weak; the House committee sponsors said they believed that a firmer scientific foundation would cause the standards to become more stringent.[15] The sponsors also asserted that CASAC's existence would assist the courts in reviewing challenges to the air quality standards.[16]

CASAC consists of a seven-member committee that must include a member of the National Academy of Sciences, a physician and a representative of state air pollution control agencies.[17] (In practice, it tends to include two of each.)[18] Appointments are formally made by the Administrator, usually of candidates chosen by the staff of CASAC for their distinction in air pollution research. When CASAC is asked to review a particular standard, a panel is formed consisting of CASAC members and consultant members (either from the agency's overall Science Advisory Board or from the approximately three hundred consultants associated with it) to add additional expertise.[19] Panel members are selected to produce a balanced group, and members must file an exacting form designed to reveal financial interests.[20] In promulgating air quality standards, EPA must explain any departure from CASAC's recommendations—a task that is politically as well as technically difficult.[21] CASAC is not shy about critiquing EPA's approaches and conclusions, although relations between EPA and CASAC appear less confrontational than in CASAC's early years.[22]

The air quality standard-setting process begins with the preparation by EPA's National Center for Environmental Assessment (NCEA) of a "criteria document"—usually of multiple volumes—describing the pollutant's effects on health and welfare.[23] The staff who write criteria

---

14. For a brief history of CASAC and analysis of its roles, see SHEILA JASANOFF, THE FIFTH BRANCH: SCIENCE ADVISERS AS POLICYMAKERS 101–123 (1990).

15. H. REP. NO. 95–294, at 181–182 (1977) (report accompanying proposed Clean Air Act Amendments of 1977).

16. Id. at 182.

17. See Section 109(d)(2)(A), 42 U.S.C. § 7409(d)(2)(A) (2000).

18. For this and other details about CASAC, I am indebted to Fred Butterfield, the EPA staff official who works closely with the committee.

19. http://www.agiweb.org/hearings/epacat.html (link from the American Geological Institute describing CASAC and its workings).

20. See Science Advisory Board (SAB) Staff Office: Ad Hoc All–Ages Lead Model (AALM) Review Panel; Request for Nominations, 70 Fed. Reg. 9642, 9643 (2005).

21. See Section 307(d)(3), 42 U.S.C. § 7407(d)(3) (2000).

22. JASANOFF, supra note 14, at 12–13.

23. For information on the center, see http://cfpub.epa.gov/ncea/index.cfm.

documents are housed in Research Triangle Park, North Carolina, far from agency headquarters in Washington, and are part of the agency's Office of Research and Development rather than any of EPA's program or policy offices. Thus, the center is doubly isolated from day-to-day politics. Typically, the criteria document goes through several "external review drafts" available to the public before CASAC approves it.

CASAC is involved not only with the criteria document but also with ensuring that the state of the science is accurately described to decision-makers. CASAC approval is thus required of EPA's "staff paper." This is typically a book-length document for the EPA Administrator summarizing the science and advising on the range that should be considered for the standard. After approving the document, CASAC often polls itself on the members' individual preferences for the standard. This poll involves judgements about science policy questions (e.g., to what extent should the existence of scientific uncertainties counsel for or against a tight standard) as well as about the science itself. Like the approval of the staff paper, CASAC's poll is transmitted to the EPA Administrator.

The task of writing the staff paper typically falls upon a group of five to ten staffers within EPA's Office of Air Quality Planning and Standards (OAQPS). The directors of the group are senior staff who have been at EPA since the 1970s and are steeped in institutional history as well as environmental policy and science. While OAQPS is part of the agency's programmatic offices, its location in Research Triangle Park, North Carolina still distances it somewhat from Washington politics.

Lawyers for both industry and environmental groups participate actively. Representatives of groups meet with EPA staff to try to influence their policy views. These groups also typically submit voluminous comments on the proposed criteria document and staff paper, pointing out, for instance, studies that the agency may not have been considered or questioning the inferences that the staff draws from the studies. Sometimes a lawyer will try to convince a client to undertake or finance a study of health effects. A lawyer who works on these matters must become sufficiently adept in science to understand the studies and to convey critiques effectively.

Once the criteria document and staff paper are approved by CASAC, EPA then prepares a proposed rule for publication in the Federal Register, considers typically thousands of comments, and then promulgates a standard. The agency's senior management participates in the standard's consideration, and the final decision is typically made personally by the Administrator.[24] Both the Office of Management and Budget and other governmental agencies become involved; sometimes (as with

24. MELNICK, supra note 12, at 257–59.

the standards in *Whitman*), so too will the President or his immediate staff. Years are required to pass through the process; for instance, it took EPA ten years to revise its standard for particulate matter in the late 1980s.[25]

Starting the Process

EPA often drags its feet on changing the standards. Ozone—one of the pollutants involved in *Whitman*—is a good example. (Ozone is a prime constituent of summertime smog.) In 1982, the agency announced that it planned to begin reviewing the ozone standards it had set in 1978.[26] Six years later, CASAC approved the criteria document and staff paper. EPA took no action.

But environmentalists found a lever. The Clean Air Act requires that the agency review and, if necessary, revise its air quality standards every five years,[27] and allows individuals to bring suit in federal district court to force EPA to carry out this duty.[28] So in 1991, environmental groups brought suit to compel EPA to make a final decision on revising the ozone standards.

The district court gave EPA until March 1, 1993, to make up its mind. On that date, EPA announced it would not alter the ozone standards.[29] The American Lung Association promptly filed suit. The agency obtained a voluntary remand by promising to reconsider its decision. In February 1994, EPA announced that it planned a new revision of the ozone criteria document and the standards.[30] Perhaps EPA would have decided on its own to revisit the ozone standard, but the litigation at least gave agency advocates of revision the argument that "we have no choice," and thus a way to brush aside criticism of the revision. In this way, the ability of the environmental groups to bring suit allowed them to determine the agency's agenda.

---

25. See Revisions to the National Ambient Air Quality Standards for Particulate Matter, 52 Fed. Reg. 24,634, 24,636–637 (1987) (outlining the history of the standard's revision).

26. See Air Quality Criteria Document for Ozone and Other Photochemical Oxidants, 47 Fed. Reg. 11,561 (1982).

27. See Section § 109(d), 42 U.S.C. § 7409(d) (2000). See Env'tl Def. Fund v. Thomas, 870 F.2d 892, 900 (2d Cir. 1989).

28. See Section 304(d), 42 U.S.C. § 7604(d) (2000).

29. See National Ambient Air Quality Standards for Ozone—Final Decision, 58 Fed. Reg. 13,008 (1993).

30. See Review of National Ambient Air Quality Standards for Ozone, 59 Fed. Reg. 5164 (1994)

Assessing the Evidence: Ozone

Ozone is beneficial in the stratosphere, where it protects the Earth from ultraviolet radiation from the sun. Down at the surface where we breathe, ozone threatens health. EPA staff prepared in 1996 a staff paper, running 285 pages plus references and appendices, that attempted to summarize the evidence for the Administrator. There were nearly two hundred studies to consider. The staff found controversy about the effects ozone causes, and about, as the agency put it later, "who is to be protected and from what."[31]

Much of the evidence came from studies of children and adolescents playing sports at summer camps. The staff paper found that those sensitive to ozone—active children, outdoor workers, and those with preexisting respiratory disease as well as some otherwise normal individuals[32]—experience effects that range from short-lived irritation when breathing deeply to persistent uncontrollable cough and severe discomfort that is likely to limit activity.[33] Ozone, according to the paper, causes ten to twenty percent of all summertime emergency room visits related to respiratory problems,[34] although only about one percent of hospital admissions for asthma.[35]

The staff paper recommended that EPA set the standards in a range between 0.07 and 0.09 parts per million of air. The choice within that range, as narrow as it may seem, makes a huge difference in control costs. The range reflected uncertainty about the importance of the reductions in health effects that would be brought about by a tight standard. EPA believed, for instance, that a standard of 0.09 parts per million would allow over 1 percent of children, or 41,000 children, to experience on 220,000 occasions per year moderate or severe pain while breathing deeply outdoors. A standard of 0.08 parts per million—the standard EPA ultimately set—results in this effect occurring 120,000 times a year to 27,000 children, or 0.9 percent.[36] The uncertainty in these estimates makes it even more difficult to determine what standards are appropriate.[37]

---

31. National Ambient Air Quality Standards for Ozone, 62 Fed. Reg. 38,856, 38,867 (1997).

32. Id. at 38,859.

33. U.S. EPA, REVIEW OF NATIONAL AMBIENT AIR QUALITY STANDARDS FOR OZONE: ASSESSMENT OF SCIENTIFIC AND TECHNICAL INFORMATION: OAQPS STAFF PAPER [hereinafter OZONE STAFF PAPER] 67–72 (1996).

34. Alex Zacaroli, *Revising the PM. Ozone Standards: Major Questions Remain on Major Projects*, 27 Env't Rep.(BNA)—Current Developments 929 (1996).

35. See OZONE STAFF PAPER, *supra* note 33.

36. National Ambient Air Quality Standards for Ozone, 62 Fed. Reg. 38,856, 38,865 (1997).

37. Id. at 38,864 ("There are significant uncertainties in such quantitative estimates").

The staff took its handiwork to CASAC. The panel told Carol Browner, EPA's administrator during both Clinton administrations, that "there is no 'bright line' which distinguishes any of the proposed standards . . . as being significantly more protective of public health."[38] Instead, CASAC said that any standard within the 0.07 to 0.09 range would be appropriate. Ten panelists expressed personal preferences that divided between 0.09 and 0.08 ppm.

Particulate Matter: Assessing the Evidence

The same month that EPA agreed to start reviewing the ozone standards, the American Lung Association filed suit in federal district court in Arizona to compel EPA to do the same for particulate matter (the scientific name for particles like smoke and soot). The court ordered EPA to propose a decision by the end of November, 1996, and to take final action by the end of January, 1997[39]—later extended to the end of June, 1997. Hence EPA announced later in 1994 that it had begun to update the criteria document for particulate matter.[40]

This schedule caused a rushed review. For one thing, the agency had to produce the criteria document and the staff paper simultaneously rather than, as usual, in sequence. To quote the OAQPS staffer who managed development of the staff paper, "There are far more things it would be good to do than there will be time for."[41]

The key issue for particulate matter was how to cope with scientific uncertainty. Air pollution researchers have increasingly focused their studies on fine particles—those so tiny that they can easily be inhaled into the deep lung.[42] Data show that, as concentrations of these particles rise, so too do daily mortality and hospital admissions. One study, for instance, found that fine particles are associated with as many as a thousand deaths per year in Philadelphia.[43] Another study examined data from a half million Americans in 151 cities and found a consistent link between particle levels and death and disease.[44]

---

38. Ozone Staff Paper, supra note 33, at App. G.

39. See Am. Lung Ass'n v. Browner, 884 F. Supp. 345 (D. Ariz. 1994).

40. See Air Quality Criteria for Particulate Matter, 59 Fed. Reg.17,375 (1994).

41. *Two Agency Offices Synchronize Efforts to Meet Deadline on Particulate Rule*, 25 Env't Rep. (BNA)—Current Developments 1668 (1995).

42. See Particle Pollution and Your Health, available at http://epa.gov/airnow/particle/airborne.html.

43. U.S. EPA, Review of National Ambient Air Quality Standards for Particulate Matter: Policy Assessment of Scientific and Technical Information; OAQPS Staff Paper [hereinafter PM Staff Paper], IV, pp. 25–27 (1996).

44. *Agency Will Consider Particulate Study As It Moves to Revise National Standard*, 25 Env't Rep. (BNA)—Current Developments 2290 (1995).

But correlation does not prove causation. Sometimes an apparent correlation turns out to be caused by an unstudied factor. For instance, some researchers asserted that other pollutants caused the elevated morality.[45] This was possible because the levels of air pollutants often rise and fall together. Perhaps, as opponents of regulating fine particles argued, only a certain kind of fine particle was causing the effects so that it would be overinclusive to regulate all fine particles. Moreover, there were then doubts about whether there was a biological mechanism by which particulate matter could be causing the observed effects, thus further casting doubt on the correlation. It was even possible that the particle levels shortened lifespan by only a few days.

CASAC rejected these arguments and overwhelmingly endorsed the staff's view that the agency should, for the first time, set specific standards for fine particles. (An OAQPS staffer with two decades experience in the field hailed this decision as revolutionary).[46] But the panel splintered on whether EPA should pick standards at the stringent or lax end of the staff's suggested range. According to CASAC's chair at the time, this was due not only to the many scientific uncertainties but also to the court-imposed schedule for review which "did not allow adequate time to analyze integrate, interpret and debate the available data on this very complex issue."[47] There was only one thing that the panel agreed on: its wish not to be in the same position the next time the standard was reviewed.

The lack of data was, ironically, partly responsible for CASAC's view that fine particle standards should be set. Because such standards did not exist, states and cities had never been required to monitor fine particle levels in the air. Thus there was much doubt about what levels of particles were breathed by the populations that had been studied. According to its chair, CASAC wanted a fine particles standard to be set so that data would be gathered that could be used to judge whether such a standard is necessary and what its level should be.[48] Given the Clean Air Act's lengthy process for establishing control strategies, the standards could be revised before air pollution sources had to do anything to meet them. In other words, EPA was seeking to set fine particle standards to decide whether standards for fine particles were needed.

---

45. Oren, *Run Over by* American Trucking *Part I: Can EPA Revive Its Air Quality Standards*, 29 Env't L. Rep. (Env'tl L. Inst.) 10,653, 10660 (1999).

46. *CASAC Endorses Fine Particulate Standard, But Offers Wide Variety of Opinions on Form*, 27 Env't Rep. (BNA)—Current Developments 459 (1996).

47. PM Staff Paper, supra note 43 at App. H.

48. Oren, supra note 45, at 10660–61.

Proposing the Standards

Many fine particles are formed by air pollutants that also cause ozone. EPA therefore decided in mid-1996 to propose and promulgate the ozone and particulate matter standards together so that implementation strategies for the two could be coordinated.[49] This decision also provided a way to settle an additional law suit brought by the American Lung Association asserting that EPA had unreasonably delayed its revision of the ozone standard. Industry saw another motive: that EPA was trying to use the particulate matter standard as a way of buttressing the ozone standard, for which the scientific case was less strong.[50] Whatever the reason, both the ozone and particulate matter standards were now on a fast track for proposal and promulgation.

Industry and environmental groups sparred to influence EPA's proposed choices. The American Lung Association released studies on the damage caused by ozone;[51] the American Petroleum Institute issued reports asserting that the costs of implementing a new ozone standard would exceed the benefits by billions of dollars.[52] Industry voiced concern about whether the White House Office of Management and Budget would have a chance to review the standards before they were proposed. Some on Capitol Hill took the industry view. The Congressional conference report on EPA's budget "encouraged" the agency not to set a standard for fine particles until more data were available.[53]

During the summer of 1996, the agency held public hearings to garner the public's views on how strict EPA should be. The National Association of Manufacturers labeled these hearings a "kangaroo court" and urged members to appear.[54] At the Philadelphia hearing (attended by your author), a panel of scientists debated whether the standards should be revised. In the public hearing phase, industry and environmental representatives talked past each other. Industry representatives stressed all they had done to achieve the present air quality standards, and urged that they should not have to re-direct their efforts to meet a new standard. Environmentalists said repeatedly, to cheers from the

---

49. See National Ambient Air Quality Standards for Ozone and Particulate Matter, 61 Fed. Reg. 29,719, 29,721 (1996).

50. *Standard-Setting Process For Ozone, PM to be Coordinated Under New EPA Process,* 27 Env't Rep. (BNA)—Current Developments 372 (1996).

51. *Higher Ozone Levels Cause Increased Rates of Hospitalization, Lung Association Says,* 27 Env't Rep. (BNA)—Current Developments 497 (1996).

52. *Costs of Tightened Ozone Standard Exceed Benefits by Billions, API Claims,* 27 Env't Rep. (BNA)—Current Developments 589. (1996).

53. *Budget Bill Suggests EPA Retain Current PM Standard, Seek Better Science,* 27 Env't Rep. (BNA)—Current Developments 1219 (1997).

54. *Ozone Proposal Expected To Go To OMB Soon, Prompts Industry Concerns About Level Of Input,* 26 Env't Rep. (BNA)—Current Developments 779 (1996).

audience, that EPA's standards should protect public health. No one addressed what it meant to protect the public's health.

EPA had hoped to propose the standards by mid-summer 1996.[55] Instead, EPA did not propose standards until late November, 1996, about eight months before the court-ordered deadline for setting the final standard for particulate matter. EPA proposed ozone standards of 0.08 parts per million.[56] The agency said it had focused on whether to choose that number or 0.09.[57] Its selection of 0.08, EPA said, was based on the greater protection that level would give to children, on clinical studies reporting health effects at 0.08, and on the importance of giving protection to extremely sensitive individuals. The agency's rationale, though, gave virtually equal time to proponents of 0.09, summarizing their arguments that, for instance, the effects observed near 0.08 were transient and reversible. EPA also asked for comment on a 0.07 level, noting that such a standard could be justified as giving protection to the most sensitive and as providing a margin of safety against the possibility that the damage from low levels of ozone was more severe than thought.

Clearly EPA was on a slippery slope in setting the ozone standards. So too with particulate matter. EPA expressed its belief that the studies correlating fine particles with illness and death were consistent enough to justify setting a separate standard for them. The agency decided that limiting the level of particles averaged over a year was key to reducing health effects.[58] EPA proposed that this level be 15 micrograms per cubic meter. This, according to the agency, was below the concentrations that had been best correlated with health effects, and so it would offer a margin of safety.[59] The agency also proposed to limit average concentrations on any single day to 50 micrograms.

Administrator Browner announced the proposed new standards. She asserted that the scientific data supported the revisions, and cited estimates suggesting that perhaps twenty thousand deaths, sixty thousand cases of bronchitis, and 1.5 million instances of significant breathing problems would be prevented by the new standards. She also remarked that "the question is not one of science, the real question is one of judgment."[60] This statement caused a spasm of criticism among

55. *Proposed Changes to Ozone Standard Still Expected by Mid–1996, EPA Says,* 26 Env't Rep. (BNA)—Current Developments 1756 (1996).

56. National Ambient Air Quality Standards for Ozone: Proposed Decision, 61 Fed. Reg. 65,718 (1996).

57. Id. at 65,729.

58. National Ambient Air Quality Standards for Particulate Matter: Proposed Decision, 61 Fed. Reg. 65,638, 65,656–57 (1996).

59. Id. at 65,660.

60. *Agency Announces Proposals to Toughen Regulations for Ozone, Particulate Matter,* 27 Env't Rep.(BNA)—Current Developments 1571 (1996).

the standard's opponents. Browner retreated three months later, saying "I think it is not a question of judgment, I think it's a question of science."[61] The truth is that it was both. The standard could not be set intelligently without knowledge of the science. But, no matter how informed the decision-maker was about the science, ultimately the decision-maker had to make a policy judgment about the appropriate level of protection.

"The Mother of All Environmental Fights"

Environmental representatives promptly protested the agency's decision not to propose even tighter standards, such as a 0.07 level for ozone or a 10 microgram standard for particulate matter.[62] The major assault, though, came from those who argued that the proposed standards were too strict—or, in the words of one, "draconian and unnecessary."[63]

The latter group received an unexpected boost from Senator John Chafee, a long-time supporter of the Clean Air Act who chaired the Senate Committee on Environment and Public Works, which has jurisdiction over the Act. Chafee questioned whether the new standards would produce a health benefit and warned, "there is liable to be some kind of a backlash around [Capitol Hill]" if costs were not considered.[64] Chafee's concern was based on an EPA estimate that it would cost about $2.5 billion per year to achieve the new ozone standard, as compared with perhaps as much as $1.5 billion in annual benefits.[65]

Even before the standards were proposed, the National Association of Manufacturers formed an "Air Quality Standards Coalition" of five hundred corporate leaders to fight against them.[66] The coalition was co-chaired by C. Boyden Gray, formerly counsel to the Presidential Task Force on Regulatory Reform, chaired by Vice President George H. W. Bush during the Reagan Administration, and later White House counsel in Bush's presidential administration. Members included companies such

---

61. *Air Quality Standards: Science–Driven Ozone, PM Proposals Will Be Finished By July 19, EPA Says*, 27 Env't Rep (BNA)—Current Developments 2068 (1997).

62. *Agency Announces*, supra note 60.

63. Id.

64. John H. Cushman, Jr., *Surprise Senate Challenge to Air Pollution Plan*, N.Y. TIMES, Dec. 7, 1996, at A8.

65. *Cost of Ozone Standard May Outweigh Benefits, EPA Impact Analysis Concludes*, 27 Env't Rep. (BNA)—Current Developments 1603 (1996).

66. Joby Warrick & John E. Yang, *Stricter Air Quality Rules May Test Hill's New Veto; Several GOP Chairman Critical of EPA's Move*, WASH. POST, Nov. 28, 1996 at A1.

as Chevron, DuPont and PepsiCo's FritoLay Division. Trade associations chipped in as much as $100,000 each to pay for the effort.

The associations' activities included coaching governors on opposing the standards.[67] Opponents of the standards also ran radio and newspaper advertisements suggesting that the standards could "end up banning things like barbecue grills and lawn mowers," both contributors to emissions that help create ozone.[68] Other ads suggested that the standards would require prohibitions on Fourth of July fireworks displays and on agricultural plowing.[69] Opponents held a press conference in Chicago with the slogan "Don't Take My Barbecue Away," while environmental groups responded with a press conference in the same hotel featuring an eight-year old asthmatic who described his asthma attacks on smoggy days.[70] These groups accused industry opponents of "deliberately obfuscating the scientific evidence" and "vowed to match the industry coalition, blow for blow."[71] Medical experts were mobilized to defend the proposed standards.[72] Opponents of the standards warned they would be impossible to meet.[73] Representative Henry Waxman, a long-time defender of the Act, responded in an op-ed piece in the Washington Post that industry had a record of overestimating compliance costs.[74] Capitol Hill offices were "plastered . . . with pens and bumper stickers that read, 'Tell the EPA that barbecuing is not a crime.' "[75] In response, environmentalists staged rallies outside lawmakers' home offices displaying mock tombstones ("in memory of 15,000 Americans Who Will Die This Year from Air Pollution," read one) to dramatize potential health risks.[76]

---

67. Cindy Skrzychi, *EPA Finds a Way to Make the Grass Roots Grow*, WASH. POST, Nov 1, 1996 at F01.

68. Both kinds of sources have been regulated because of air pollution. But neither barbecues nor lawnmowers have been considered for a ban.

69. Joby Warrick, *Browner Defends Proposed Air Standards; EPA Administrator Says Fight is Not About "Barbecues or Lawn Mowers"*, WASH. POST, Feb. 13, 1997, at A03; Joby Warrick, *A Dust-up Over Air Pollution Standards*, WASH. POST, June 17 1997, at A01.

70. Joby Warrick, *Clean Air Standards Opponents Circle the Backyard Barbecues*, WASH. POST, Jan. 24, 1997, at A01.

71. Warrick & Yang, supra note 66.

72. Warrick, supra note 70.

73. Warrick, *Browner Defends*, supra note 69 (citing remarks of Sen. John Warner).

74. Henry A. Waxman, *False Alarms on Clean Air*, WASH. POST, March 5, 1997, at A21.

75. Joby Warrick, *Downwind States Welcome EPA Smog Plan; Northeast Coalition Wants Lower "Secondhand" Pollution*, WASH. POST, March 16, 1997, at A16.

76. Allan Freedman, *Key Hill Players Warily Await Decision on Clean Air Rules*, 55 CONG. Q. WEEKLY REP. 1312 (1997).

EPA tried to make one easy concession to the standards' critics; the agency asked the district court in Arizona for a sixty-day extension of the deadline for setting the particulate matter standards so that the comment period could be extended. The American Lung Association, the original plaintiff, objected,[77] perhaps thinking that more time would simply allow the standards' opponents additional opportunity to organize.[78] Instead, the court confined the extension to three weeks until July 19, 1997,[79] and made clear that no further extensions would be granted.[80]

The battle also raged on Capitol Hill. Representative Waxman warned that controversy over the new standards would become "the mother of all environmental fights."[81] He was right. The Senate Environment & Public Works Committee's subcommittee on clean air matters heard a panel of scientists, including two members of CASAC who could not even agree on whether the panel had concurred with the proposed particulate matter standards. Opponents of the standard—some of them wearing "fake glasses, lab coats and tangled wigs" showed placards reading "EPA–Show Me the Science!" while nearby proponents chanted "I want to breathe—dirty air stinks!" Subcommitee chairman James Inhofe, a conservative Republican, cracked that "we are shocked to find out that scientists don't agree."[82] Analyses done by EPA scientists of a long-term study of the health effects of particles were challenged as flawed.[83] EPA agreed to re-analyze, but, to the anger of opponents, refused to provide the raw data to outsiders for their assessment.[84] On the other side of Capitol Hill, the House Commerce Committee held a hearing at which three out of four current or former CASAC chairmen expressed opposition to the proposed fine particle standards.[85]

---

77. *Agency Asks Court for 60 More Days to Complete Standards on PM, Ozone* 27 Env't Rep. (BNA)—Current Developments 2021 (1997).

78. *Browner Bows to Requests, Will Seek Extension on PM, Ozone,* INSIDE EPA's CLEAN AIR REPORT, Feb. 6, 1997, at 1.

79. *Federal Court Gives Three–Week Extension to EPA for Completion of Ozone, PM Rules,* 27 Envt'l Rep. (BNA)—Current Developments 2067 (1997).

80. *Court Denies Ozone Petition For Two–Month Delay of PM Deadline,* INSIDE EPA's CLEAN AIR ACT REPORT, Feb. 11,1997, at 1.

81. *Legislative Efforts To Weaken Standards Would Undermine Air Act, Waxman Says,* 27 Env't Rep. (BNA)—Current Developments 1835 (1997).

82. Joby Warrick, *Panel Seeks Cease–Fire on Air Quality But Gets a War,* WASH. POST, Feb. 6, 1997, at A21.

83. *OMB, EPA Officials Deny Wrongdoing in Process of Proposing PM, Ozone Rules,* 27 Env't Rep. (BNA)—Current Developments 2631 (1997).

84. *Research Groups Prompting Reassessment of Key Health Data on Particulate Matter,* 28 Env't Rep. (BNA)—Current Developments 8 (1997).

85. *CASAC Chairmen Would Not Recommend EPA Proposal for Fine Particle Standard,* 27 Env't Rep. (BNA)—Current Developments 2800 (1997).

The procedure followed by the agency was also challenged. For instance, Senator Robert Byrd, the wily veteran West Virginia Senator, questioned whether other agencies were being given enough opportunity to critique EPA's proposal,[86] while Congressman Thomas Bliley, the chair of the House Committee on Commerce, attacked the Administration for allegedly withholding details of debate among Federal agencies over the proposed rules.[87] Other members of Congress urged that EPA had an obligation under the newly-enacted Small Business Regulatory Enforcement Fairness Act[88] to consider the effects of the proposed standards on small business—a demand, in effect, that EPA, for the first time, openly consider costs in its choice of air quality standards.[89] Similarly, some members called for the Clean Air Act to be amended to allow for cost consideration in standard-setting.[90] Several members of the House Commerce Committee demanded the phone records of Mary Nichols, the agency's assistant administrator for air and a long-time environmentalist, apparently to investigate whether she might be collaborating with environmental groups in their campaign for the standards.[91] In all, Browner, Nichols, and other agency officials spent scores of hours preparing for and testifying at hearings of the various committees and subcommittees that became involved.

The public comment period ended in mid-March, 1997, leaving EPA only four months to decide on the final standards. The agency's task was herculean. It had received 55,000 comments on the proposals, many in telephonic or web-based form.[92] More than half of the comments were form letters, but even so there was much in the comments that had to be summarized, sifted, and answered in the final rulemaking. Even more comments had come by way of several contentious public hearings.[93]

The agency's preambles for the ozone and particulate matter standards ultimately ran, respectively, 40 and 55 triple-columned small-type pages in the Federal Register. The standards and their rationales were

86. *Senator Seeks Independent Assessments of Ozone, PM Proposals From Agencies*, 27 Env't Rep. (BNA)—Current Developments 2301 (1997).

87. *House Panel to Look Into Communications Between OMB, EPA, Regarding Air Proposals*, 27 Env't Rep. (BNA)—Current Developments 2267 (1997).

88. Pub. L. 104–121 (1996), Subtitle D, § 244, 5 U.S.C. § 609 (2000).

89. *Two Senators Call for SBREFA Review of Proposals to Revise Ozone, PM Rules*, 27 Env't Rep. (BNA)—Current Developments 1899 (1997).

90. *Cost Issues Divide Parties in Early Talks on Congressional Review of Air Proposals*, 27 Env't Rep. (BNA)—Current Developments 1901 (1997).

91. *OMB, EPA Officials Deny Wrongdoing, supra* note 83.

92. *Nichols Assures Bliley EPA Review of NAAQS Comments is Thorough*, INSIDE EPA's CLEAN AIR REPORT, June 12, 1997, at 12.

93. *Industry, Environmental Groups Disagree on Need for Tighter Standards*, 27 Env't Rep. (BNA)—Current Developments 1947 (1997).

similar to those in the proposed standards. For ozone, the agency acknowledged that there was no bright line differentiating the final standard of 0.08 from either 0.07 or 0.09.[94] Because no CASAC member had supported 0.07, and because most of the effects observed at 0.07 were "transient and reversible," the agency focused on 0.08 and 0.09. The agency explained its choice of 0.08 as based on the lower amount of exposures to health effects that would occur at this level, the consistency of the evidence showing effects at 0.08, and the importance of protecting sensitive persons and of guarding against the possibility that ozone might cause unknown serious effects.[95]

As for particulate matter, the agency concluded that it should give special attention to fine particles because the correlation between fine particle levels and mortality was consistently found in many studies and existed even under widely varying levels of other pollutants.[96] The exact levels of the standards were described as striking an intermediate position between those who believed that little or no additional health protection was necessary, and those who thought the evidence for regulation was very strong.[97] Instead, the agency chose to promulgate its proposed annual average level of 15 micrograms because that was below the levels at which health effects had been observed.[98] Finally, in a concession to industry, EPA decided that the daily standard for particulate matter would be 65 micrograms rather than the 50 micrograms originally proposed.[99]

Yet having a technical rationale was far from enough. Rather, the agency had to attract the support of the Clinton Administration to sustain the proposed new standards against outside pressures. The issue posed a political conundrum for the White House because some Congressional Democrats opposed EPA's choices. Representative John Dingell, with over forty years experience in Congress as a strong and effective advocate of the economic interests of midwesterners, organized a group of over forty Democratic House members to seek a meeting with President Clinton to oppose the revisions.[100] The battle became regional; midwesterners feared the effects of the standards on utilities and other

---

94. See National Ambient Air Quality Standards for Ozone, 62 Fed Reg. 38,856, 38,864 (1997).

95. Id. at 38,865.

96. See National Ambient Air Quality Standards for Particulate Matter, 62 Fed. Reg. 38,652, 38,667–668.

97. Id. at 38,674–675.

98. Id. at 38,675–676.

99. For lengthier summaries, see American Trucking Ass'ns v. Environmental Protection Agency, 283 F.3d 355, 364–368, 375–378 (D.C. Cir. 2002).

100. *House Democrats Seek Talks with Clinton Over Proposed Changes to Ozone, PM Rules,* 28 Env't Rep. (BNA)—Current Developments 5 (1997).

industries in their region while northeasterners, including some Republicans, wanted to minimize emissions in the midwest that blow east with prevailing winds.[101] State and local government groups expressed fear over the effects of new standards on economic development. [102] Minority groups found themselves torn between protecting against damage to health in urban areas and promoting economic development to provide jobs.[103] Even in the Clinton Administration, some agencies testified on Capitol Hill against the agency's proposed standards.[104]

The administration decided to intervene early in the interagency battle about how stringent the final standards would be. The White House unnerved environmental groups by deciding that three agencies—none of them EPA, and two of them with an economic focus—would "coordinate deliberations" on the new standards.[105] Yet EPA Administrator Browner decided to urge, despite substantial opposition from White House aides, that she be allowed to promulgate her choice of standards.[106]

Environmental groups did their best to support her. For instance, public health groups announced that new studies justified EPA's proposals.[107] Environmentalists also attacked Vice President Al Gore, Administrator Browner's mentor and a well-known advocate of environmental protection. Gore was blasted for conducting a "silent spring" on environmental issues and for failing to publicly lead pressure on the Clinton Administration to adopt EPA's proposals. Environmental groups tried to lure Representative Richard Gephardt, Gore's rival for the 2000 Demo-

---

101. *Democrats Show Divisions On New Clean Air Rules*, 55 CONG. Q. WEEKLY REPORT 1512 (1997).

102. *Groups Fear Air Proposals Will Hamper Economic Development in Urban Areas*, 27 Env't Rep. (BNA)—Current Developments 2902 (1997); *see* John H. Cushman, Jr., *D'Amato Vows to Fight for E.P.A.'s Tightened Air Standards*, N.Y. Times, June 25, 1997, at 13. D'Amato's supporters included future Administrator Whitman, then governor of New Jersey. Id.

103. *Minority Groups Divided Over Air Proposals: Environmental Justice, Development at Issue*, 28 Env't Rep. (BNA)—Current Developments 303 (1997).

104. *No Obligation Found by EPA to Assess Impacts of Air Rules on Small Businesses*, 27 Env't Rep. (BNA)—Current Developments 2629 (1997) (recounting opposition to EPA by counsel for the Small Business Administration and by the Department of Agriculture).

105. Joby Warrick, *White House Taking a Hands-On Role in Writing New Clean Air Standards*, WASH. POST, May 22, 1997, at A10. To quote one environmentalist, "What does the National Economic Council know about health effects?" *EPA Delays PM/Ozone Review in Bid To Forge Interagency Consensus*, INSIDE EPA's CLEAN AIR REPORT, May 29, 1997, at 4.

106. John H. Cushman, Jr. *Top E.P.A. Official Not Backing Down on Air Standards*, N.Y. TIMES, June 1, 1997, at 1.

107. *Environmentalists Release New Studies Supporting PM/Ozone Proposal*, INSIDE EPA's CLEAN AIR REPORT, May 29, 1997, at 5.

cratic presidential nomination, into urging greater White House support for the environment.[108] In this way, Gore was forced to choose between his environmentalist allies and his desire to attract support in the midwest.[109]

Industry groups expressed confidence that EPA's standards would not survive White House review. One anonymous environmentalist replied that industry "pulled out the champagne and cigars a while ago, but we've beat [sic] the tar out of these polluters every time on clean air issues."[110] The environmentalist turned out to be right. In late June, after Vice President Gore had "jumped into the fray," President Clinton announced his support for Administrator Browner's choice of standards, saying that "kids ought to be healthy."[111] In return, EPA announced that it would be lenient in implementing the new standards, particularly in areas that complied with the old ozone standards but would exceed the new ones.[112] The White House took credit for this boon by publishing in the Federal Register, in a column of large type (rather than the conventional triple-column agate), a "Memorandum for the Administrator of the Environmental Protection Agency" prescribing how the agency would carry out the new standards.[113]

Critics of the proposed standards were not mollified. One industry representative charged that "the Administration lacked the courage to do what is right ... Those who worked hard to bring reason to the debate ... were simply ignored."[114] Within hours of the decision, Dingell called it "asinine" and vowed to have it overturned in Congress. He was joined by Congressman Bobby Rush, a former Black Panther, who called the decision "sick public policy."[115]

The vehicle for overturning the new standards became H.R. 1984, introduced by Congressman Ronald Klink, a Democrat from Pennsylva-

---

108. *Environmental Groups Say Gore Has Not Measured Up to the Job*, N.Y. Times, June 21, 1997, at 1.

109. James Gerstenzang, *Tougher Air Standards Pose Quandary for White House*, L.A. Times, June 7, 1997, at page 15A.

110. *Industry Sources Say White House Will Cave on PM, Ozone*, Inside EPA's Clean Air Report, June 12, 1997, at 7.

111. John H. Cushman, Jr., *Clinton Sharply Tightens Air Pollution Regulations Despite Concern Over Costs*, N.Y. Times, June 25, 1997, at A1.

112. See Craig N. Oren, *Run Over by* American Trucking *Part II: Can EPA Implement Revised Air Quality Standards?*, 30 Envtl. L. Rep. 10034, 10037 (2000). For a short summary of EPA's implementation policy, see Andrea Foster, *Highlights of the Revised Rules*, 55 Cong. Q. Weekly Rep. 1690 (1997).

113. Implementation of Revised Air Quality Standards for Ozone and Particulate Matter, 62 Fed. Reg. 38,721 (1997).

114. *Clinton Sharply Tightens*, supra note 111.

115. Democrats Show Divisions, supra note 101 at 1511.

nia. This bill sought a four-year moratorium on the establishment of new standards for ozone and fine particles and required that EPA decide in five years whether new standards should be promulgated. In the meantime, EPA would be required to monitor levels of fine particles to improve the scientific database.[116] Klink explained that his bill was necessary to prevent further job losses in Southwestern Pennsylvania,[117] an area where air pollution requirements are tight partly because pollution drifts there from Ohio.[118]

The bill was referred in the House to the Commerce Committee, which has jurisdiction over the Clean Air Act. But there the bill died. One reason was that the lenient implementation policy made the issue less urgent for many.[119] In vain did Representative Dingell argue that the policy was "entirely extra-legal,"[120] for environmental groups actually praised the policy.[121] For them, compromising on the schedule for meeting a standard was better than risking loss of the standard itself.

Some Republicans also helped to kill the Klink bill. Senator Chafee, during the weeks before the standards' promulgation, floated his own compromise to delay the proposed revisions.[122] But once the standards were released, Chafee opposed any attempt to undo them by legislation. Other northeastern Republicans joined him. Perhaps Chafee's most surprising supporter was Senator Robert Smith of New Hampshire, a perfervid conservative, who blamed his state's air pollution problems on midwestern states.[123]

The House Republican leadership was also reluctant to move. Bliley made clear that he would not bring up H.R. 1984 until Dingell and his allies produced one hundred Democratic Representatives in favor.[124] This

---

116. H.R. 1984, 105th Cong., 1st Sess. (1997).

117. 143 Cong. Rec. H3559 (1997).

118. See Southwestern Pennsylvania Growth Alliance v. Browner, 144 F.3d 984, 988 (6th Cir. 1998) (explaining objections to relaxation of air pollution requirements in Ohio.)

119. *Inhofe PM Ozone Repeal Encounters Skepticism From Both Sides*, INSIDE EPA: CLEAN AIR REPORT, August 7, 1997, at 10.

120. *House Democrats Opposed to Air Rules Mobilize Forces; Inhofe Offers Senate Bill*, 28 Env't Rep. (BNA)—Current Developments 812 (1997).

121. *Number of Counties Violating Air Rules Would More Than Double, Group Predicts*, 28 Env't Rep. (BNA)—Current Developments 430 (1997) (quoting David Hawkins of the Natural Resources Defense Council as calling the policy "a sensible approach.")

122. *Chafee Seeks "Deal" to Retain Ozone Rule, Delay Fine Particulate Matter Regulation*, 28 Env't Rep. (BNA)—Current Developments 69 (1997).

123. Allan Freedman, *Hill Foes of New Clean Air Bills Unite Behind Moratorium Bill*. 55 CONG. Q. WEEKLY REP. 1689 (1997).

124. *Industry Officials Attack Air Proposals, Call on Congress to Curb Agency's Power*, 28 Env't Rep. (BNA)—Current Developments 464 (1997).

was partly to offset, in the phrase of Majority Whip Tom DeLay, "greenie Republicans."[125] But DeLay also said that, without Democratic support, the Republican party would be "tarred as opposed to environmental protection."[126] Here DeLay was reacting to the party's perception, expressed by House Speaker Newt Gingrich, the GOP had lost public support for "overreaching" on environmental issues when the party first took control of the House in 1995.[127] Thus when Republican Senator Inhofe tried to attach a reversal of the standards to a fast-trade bill, the Republican leadership quickly disassociated itself from him.[128]

Dingell could not find the Democrats that Bliley demanded. Waxman, joined by two Republicans, gleefully announced that over one-third of the House had pledged to uphold a veto of the Klink bill.[129] At that point, the legislative battle was over, and the standards' opponents turned to the courts.

Challenging the Standards

The Clean Air Act requires that any challenge to the establishment of ambient air quality standards be brought in the D.C. Circuit within sixty days after publication of the standards in the Federal Register.[130] The American Trucking Associations and other industry groups filed suit the day the new standards were published.[131] Eventually, over ninety organizations joined the challenge or filed lawsuits of their own. The petitioners included the U.S. Chamber of Commerce, many electric utilities in the South and Midwest, the states of Michigan, Ohio and West Virginia, the United Mine Workers of America, as well as organizations representing small business, refineries, steel manufacturers, mining companies, chemical manufacturers and other industries.[132] Judy's

---

125.   Freedman, supra note 123 at 1690.

126.   Id.

127.   Warrick & Yang, supra note 66.

128.   *Ozone-PM Rules Survive Attack in Senate, Still Face Challenge In House This Year*, 28 Env't Rep. (BNA)—Current Developments 1369 (1997).

129.   *Backers of Air Rules Claim Enough Support To Uphold Veto of Bill to Block Standards*, 28 Env't Rep. (BNA)—Current Developments 654 (1997).

130.   See Section 307(b), 42 U.S.C. § 7607(b) (2000).

131.   *Spirit of Procedural Laws Followed in Revisions of Air Rules, GAO Finds*, 28 Env't Rep.(BNA)—Current Developments 655 (1997). The American Trucking Associations seeks to represent the interests of the trucking industry. http://www.truckline.com/aboutata/missionstatement Trucks, especially diesels, emit gases and particles that help form ozone and particulate matter in the air.

132.   For a full list of challengers, see Pet. for a Writ of Cert., Browner v. American Trucking Ass'ns, 519 U.S. 457 (2000) No. 99–1257, at ii., 2000 WL 33979605 (2000).

Bakery of Evanston, Illinois, also joined the challenge.[133] In contrast, only the American Lung Association and the States of Massachusetts and New Jersey intervened on EPA's behalf.

The briefs largely focused on whether EPA's explanation showed reasoned decision-making, and on whether the agency had violated any of the "regulatory reform" statutes of the 1980s and 1990s. But the delegation doctrine, requiring that Congress set out an intelligible principle when it confers power on administrative agencies, was mentioned in several of the challengers' briefs. One of these was submitted on behalf of "small business petitioners"—a group including not only Judy's Bakery and the National Indian Business Association, but also such groups as the Chamber of Commerce of the United States, the National Association of Manufacturers and American Trucking itself.

The brief argued that EPA had disobeyed the Small Business Regulatory Fairness and Enforcement Act by failing to consider the impacts of the standards on small businesses.[134] Edward W. Warren of the firm of Kirkland & Ellis, the lead attorney on the brief, added a twist toward the end. Warren had argued the *Benzene* case in the Supreme Court for the American Petroleum Institute over a decade before,[135] and well remembered being queried at oral argument about delegation.[136] There a plurality of the Court interpreted the Occupational Safety & Health Act as obligating OSHA to show that an occupational health standard addresses a "significant risk." This conclusion was partly based on the argument that the statute might otherwise constitute an excessive delegation of legislative power.[137]

Warren made a similar argument in the small business brief. His brief urged that, under EPA's approach, there was no intelligible principle. He noted that EPA had stated that its decision was "largely judgmental in nature," conformed to "no generalized paradigm," and "may not be amenable to quantification in terms of what risk is

---

133. Judy's Bakery had already jousted unsuccessfully with the Occupational Safety and Health Administration, thus becoming a folk hero to OSHA's conservative critics. See Sheila A. Moloney, *The Lady in Red Tape*, POL'Y REV. September–October 1996, Number 79, at 48, available at http://www.policyreview.org/sept96/moloney.html The former proprietor only dimly remembers being involved in *Whitman*. E-mail from Judy Hooper to Craig N. Oren (January 29, 2005) (on file with author).

134. Brief for Small Business Petitioners and Intervenor, American Trucking Ass'ns v. U.S. EPA, 175 F.3d 1027 (D.C.Cir. 1999), (No. 97–1441).

135. Industrial Union Dep't, AFL–CIO v. American Petroleum Institute, 448 U.S. U.S. 607 (1980).

136. E–Mail from Edward Warren to Craig N. Oren (Aug. 13, 2004) (on file with author).

137. *Industrial Union*, 448 U.S. at 646.

'acceptable' or any other metric."[138] Thus, he contended, the Clean Air Act or the Small Business Regulatory Fairness Enforcement Act had to be read narrowly to prevent EPA's "bid for unlimited standard-setting [authority]" and hence a violation of the delegation doctrine. This discussion took roughly a page of the 25-page brief.

The main body of challengers to the ozone standard gave delegation an equivalent share of their brief. This group was led by the utility industry, which anticipated that it would have to sharply cut emissions of air pollution to help meet the new standards. Henry V. Nickel of the Washington firm of Hunton & Williams, who had close to thirty years of experience representing the utility industry on environmental matters in the courts, at EPA, and on Capitol Hill was lead counsel. The utility-led group's brief urged that there were a number of standards that would satisfy the statutory mandate of protecting public health with an adequate margin of safety, and that it was arbitrary and capricious for EPA to pick one of those standards without having specific criteria for choice. Moreover, the brief continued, the standard-setting provisions of the Clean Air Act "should not be interpreted as a standardless delegation of legislation authority."[139] If, though, EPA could set a standard on the basis of "uncertain and inconclusive scientific evidence," then the Act would provide "no meaningful constraints on the Administrator's authority," thus obviating judicial review.[140] Rather, the Clean Air Act should be interpreted to provide "intelligible criteria" for the revision of air quality standards.[141] This delegation argument was meant, in the words of one utility lawyer, to act as an "exclamation point" but not a primary contention. At the very least, mentioning the delegation doctrine preserved its use on appeal if necessary.

The government brief responded that the statute contained an intelligible principle.[142] It noted that the D.C. Circuit had upheld, for instance "compelling public interest" as an intelligible principle,[143] and cited Supreme Court precedent (including *Benzene*) as approving agency policy discretion in choosing a standard. Thus, the government urged, the Clean Air Act's standard-setting language was well within the bounds of delegations approved in the past. Like the industry briefs, the

---

138. Brief for Small Business, supra note 134, at 20, citing NAAQS Ozone, 62 Fed. Reg. 38,856, 38,883 (1997).

139. Brief of Non–State Clean Air Act Petitioners and Intervenors, Am. Trucking Ass'ns v. United States EPA, 175 F.3d 1027 (D.C. Cir. 1999) (No. 97–1441) 46.

140. Id. at 47–48.

141. Id. at 48.

142. Final Brief for Respondent United States EPA, American Trucking Ass'ns. v. United States EPA, 175 F.3d 1027 (D.C. Cir. 1999) (No. 97–1440) 82.

143. Milk Indus. Found. v. Glickman, 132 F.3d 1467, 1473 (D.C. Cir. 1998).

government's brief paid little attention to the issue; it was largely devoted instead to answering the challengers' arguments that the agency had committed procedural error and failed to show that its scientific and policy choices were reasonable.

The D.C. Circuit panel consisted of Judges Stephen Williams and Douglas Ginsburg—both appointees of President Reagan—as well as David Tatel, appointed by President Clinton. Judge Williams was already on record as a skeptic about regulation.[144] Judge Tatel had written, and Judge Ginsburg had joined, the D.C. Circuit's recent *American Lung* decision.[145] There the court had remanded to EPA its decision not to set an air quality standard to control pollution levels that, according to the agency, caused significant health effects to approximately forty thousand asthmatics. The court ruled that the agency needed to explain its judgment that the effects did not amount to the kind of harm to public health that required an air quality standard.[146] While this decision was hardly pro-industry—the utilities had submitted a brief supporting the government's position—it seemed to signal a less accepting approach to EPA's standard-setting decisions and a greater insistence on explanation.

The oral argument in our case was grueling. It took four-and-one-half hours for the court to hear nine different lawyers representing the challengers, EPA, and environmental groups. One government lawyer comments that it felt like a week. Both E. William (Bill) Brownell, one of Nickel's partners, and Warren, representing the small business group, were among those who argued.

Unfortunately, neither a transcript nor a tape of the oral argument exists, and so we are dependent on the recollections of observers. Perhaps most worrisome to the government was a remark by Judge Tatel about *Lead Industries Ass'n v. EPA*, the D.C. Circuit precedent that first held that costs may not be considered in setting standards and that EPA has broad discretion in selecting the standards' levels.[147] Commented Judge Tatel, "the more I read the case, the less I understand it." Judges Williams and Ginsburg, though, took the lead in questioning, repeatedly challenging EPA on the quality of its explanation

---

144. See Stephen A. Williams, *Background Norms in the Regulatory State, (Review of Cass R. Sunstein, After the Rights Revolution: Reconceiving the Regulatory State)*, 58 U. CHI. L. REV 419 (1991) (critiquing Sunstein's defenses of the philosophical underpinnings of regulation); Stephen A. Williams, *Risk Regulation and Its Hazards: Review of Stephen Breyer, Breaking the Vicious Circle*, 93 MICH. L. REV. 1498 (1995) (urging that Breyer does not sufficiently consider the role of special interests in shaping environmental regulation.)

145. American Lung Ass'n v. EPA, 134 F.3d 388 (D.C. Cir. 1998).

146. Id. at 393. EPA, as of 2005, has not even proposed a response to the remand.

147. Lead Indus. Ass'n v. EPA, 647 F.2d 1130 (D.C. Cir.), cert. denied, 449 U.S. 1042 (1980) (upholding EPA's air quality standards for lead).

for its choices of standards. The lawyers' memories vary on how much delegation came up; Warren remembers that the panel pressed the point and so he threw away his notes, and devoted more time than he planned to delegation.[148] One lawyer for the government recollects that the delegation issue worried him, but that his colleagues assured him that there was no serious problem.

"Bizarre and Tortured"?

Delegation proved to be the court's focus.[149] Judge Williams, joined by Judge Ginsburg, concluded that EPA had construed the Act's provisions "so loosely as to render them unconstitutional delegations of legislative power."[150] EPA, the court believed, had identified factors that were relevant to choosing ambient air quality standards, but had not specified how they would be weighed. To quote the court:

> Here it is as though Congress commanded EPA to select "big guys," and EPA announced that it would evaluate candidates based on height and weight, but revealed no cut-off point. The announcement, though sensible in what it does say, is fatally incomplete. The reasonable person responds, "How tall? How heavy?"[151]

For instance, EPA had explained that, as concentrations of ozone diminish, the effects become more uncertain and more transitory, while, as pollution levels increase, more people are exposed to serious harms. Yet, said the court, this was no more than saying that the lower the standard, the lower the risk to health.[152] Nor could the agency defend a higher standard on the basis that uncertainty increases at lower concentrations because the agency had not developed a principle to say how much uncertainty is too much.[153] Instead, according to Judge Williams, "EPA's formulation of its policy judgment leaves it free to pick any point between zero and a hair below the concentrations yielding London's Killer Fog."[154]

---

148.   E-mail, supra note 136.

149.   There were important facets of the decision other than delegation—for instance, the challengers' arguments based on the Small Business Regulatory and Enforcement Fairness Act and other "regulatory reform" statutes were dismissed—but exploring those would take us far afield.

150.   American Trucking Ass'ns v. United States EPA, 175 F.3d 1027, 1034 (D.C. Cir. 1999).

151.   Id.

152.   Id. at 1035.

153.   Id. at 1036.

154.   Id. at 1037.

An equally surprising part of the opinion was the court's remedy. The court neither declared the statute unconstitutional nor narrowly construed it, as Warren and Nickel had urged, to solve the delegation problem. Instead the court directed EPA to develop an intelligible principle. Judge Williams relied here on his own opinion in *Lockout/Tagout I.*[155] There the court used the same approach to require that the Occupational Safety and Health Administration develop an "intelligible principle" describing how it selects workplace safety standards. But the court put an important limit on EPA; the court followed *Lead Industries* and held that the agency could not use cost as part of its principle.[156]

Judge Tatel dissented from the delegation holding, writing that the Act's delegation of authority "is narrower and more principled than delegations the Supreme Court and this court have upheld."[157] He pointed out that the Supreme Court had frequently upheld expansive delegations, and argued that an intelligible principle could be found in the Clean Air Act's command that health standards be set at levels "requisite" to protect public health and on the basis of air quality criteria describing the effects of the air pollutants.[158]

Judge Tatel and Judge Williams also differed on the significance of CASAC's endorsements of the standard's range. Judge Tatel argued that CASAC's participation showed that EPA's discretion was not unbounded and that the agency had acted reasonably in acting within its discretion.[159] Judge Williams responded that, despite the "undisputed eminence of CASAC's members, nothing in the committee's statements helps us discern an intelligible principle."[160]

The decision "sent shock waves through the [Clinton] White House and administration" as officials questioned whether governmental agencies would continue to be able to establish rules protecting the environment.[161] The New York Times denounced the decision as "bizarre and tortured," and criticized the court as threatening to "overturn a half-century of jurisprudence that has allowed Congress to delegate impor-

---

155. International Union, UAW v. OSHA, 938 F.2d 1310 (D.C. Cir. 1991). "Lockout/Tagout" regulations seek to prevent machinery from accidentally operating. Id. at 1312. OSHA's rather vague response was eventually approved by Judge Willliams. See International Union, UAW v. OSHA, 37 F.3d 665 (D.C.Cir. 1994).

156. Id. at 1040–1041.

157. Id. at 1057.

158. Id. at 1058.

159. Id. at 1059–60.

160. Id. at 1036.

161. Joby Warrick & Bill McAllister, *New Air Pollution Limits Blocked; Appeal Judges' Ruling May Curb Agencies' Powers*, WASH. POST, May 15, 1999, at A01.

tant rule-making powers to Federal agencies."[162] Similarly, Administrator Browner called the result "extreme, illogical and bizarre."[163]. By contrast, industry critics of EPA hailed the decision as "breathtaking,"[164] and some predicted it could be used "to begin to question all kinds of executive decisions."[165] Academics immediately began debating the scope and wisdom of the decision.[166]

Reviewing the Panel Decision

The government promptly petitioned for rehearing by the panel or by the D.C. Circuit en banc. The government's brief urged that "the majority's holding strays far from the path of the Supreme Court's nondelegation doctrine articulated over more than sixty years."[167] The brief cited, for instance, *Mistretta v. United States*,[168] in which the Supreme Court held that an intelligible principle exists if "Congress clearly delineates the general policy, the public agency which is to apply it, and the boundaries of this delegated authority."[169] The government argued that EPA had not, either in this case or any other, claimed the discretion to set standards "a hair below London fog," as suggested by the majority, and that the Clean Air Act sufficiently cabined EPA's decision-making authority.[170] Nor, according to the brief, had the panel adequately considered prior D.C. Circuit's decisions upholding EPA's choices of air quality standards.[171] Finally, the government urged (as it had in its original brief) that an intelligible principle could be found in

---

162.   *Bad Decision on Clean Air*, N.Y.Times, May 19, 1999, at A22.

163.   *Court Decision on Ozone, PM Rules Called "Extreme, Illogical" by Browner*, 30 Env't Rep, (BNA)—Current Developments 158 (1999).

164.   Robert Jackson & James Gerstenzang, *Air Quality Standards Rejected by Appeals Court*, L.A. Times, May 15, 1999, at A1 (quoting Robin Conrad, senior vice-president of the United States Chamber of Commerce).

165.   *Legal Doctrine Used to Strike Down EPA Rules Could Apply to Other Actions*, 30 Env't Rep. (BNA)—Current Developments 103 (1999).(quoting Jerry Taylor of the Cato Institute, a libertarian thinktank).

166.   Harvey Berkman, *Delegation Doctrine Revised: Dormant Rule Used to Void EPA Regs; Others in Potential Jeopardy*, National Law Journal, May 31, 1999 at 1. For examples, see Cass R. Sunstein, *Is the Clean Air Act Unconstitutional?*, 98 Mich. L. Rev. 302 (1999); Mark Seidenfeld, *The False Promise of the "New" Nondelegation Doctrine*, 27 Ecology L. Q. 549 (2000).

167.   Pet, for Reh'g and Pet. for Reh'g En Banc for the United States EPA, American Trucking Ass'ns v. EPA, 195 F.2d 4 (D.C.Cir. 1999) (No. 97–1440) at 6.

168.   488 U.S. 361 (1989).

169.   Id. at 371–372.

170.   Pet. for Reh'g, supra note 167 at 13–17.

171.   Id. at 11–12.

the Act's requirement that the standards be based on criteria documents, and in CASAC's approval of EPA's assessment of the science.[172]

In response, the utility-led defenders of the court's decision did their best to narrow it. To quote their submission, "the decision simply reflects the panel's application of long-standing rules of statutory construction to the record before it."[173] Thus industry, contrary to the public statements of some of its representatives, did its best to argue that the decision was not revolutionary and to minimize the importance of Judge Williams' rhetoric. In this way, the utility-led group showed its ambivalence over the panel decision.

The petition for panel rehearing was denied by the original breakdown of panel judges. But the petition for rehearing en banc came close to success.[174] Five of the nine judges hearing the petition voted to grant rehearing. The D.C. Circuit's rules, though, require a majority of all active judges, not merely those voting. Since the Circuit then had eleven sitting judges—one seat was vacant—the petition fell a vote short. The key may have been the choice by Judge Patricia Wald, who had already announced her retirement, not to participate.[175]

The division on the court was largely along partisan lines; the court's four Democratic appointees all voted to grant rehearing. The Republican appointees voted to deny rehearing, with one important exception. That was Judge Lawrence Silberman, a Reagan appointee, who wrote a statement dissenting from the denial. Judge Silberman questioned both the applicability of the delegation doctrine—"sad to say," he wrote, the doctrine remained "only a theoretical limitation" whose "boundaries ... remain only dimly perceivable"[176]—and the court's remand to the agency to develop an intelligible principle.[177] Rather than use the delegation doctrine, Judge Silberman argued, the court should have focused on whether the agency's decision satisfied the usual "arbitrary and capricious" test—something that Judge Silberman was "quite uncertain about."[178]

Going up to the Supreme Court

EPA immediately announced that it would seek Supreme Court

---

172. Id. at 13–14.

173. Resp. of Non–State CAA Petitioners to Pet. for Reh'g and Reh'g En Banc of United States EPA, American Trucking Ass'ns v. EPA, 195 F.3d 4 (D.C. Cir. 1999) 10.

174. American Trucking Ass'ns v. United States EPA, 195 F.3d 4 (D.C. Cir. 1999).

175. Oren, Part II, supra note 112 at 10035 n.6.

176. *Am. Trucking*, 195 F.3d at 14.

177. Id. at 14–15.

178. Id. at 15.

review.[179] The Solicitor-General's petition for certiorari asserted that the court of appeals decision "presents an important federal question with profound implications for the health of the American public and the effectiveness of the CAA.... The court of appeals' decision is a striking departure from this Court's nondelegation jurisprudence.... The court of appeals' decision marks a profound change in the ground rules that shape not only EPA's air quality and other programs, but also those of other federal agencies."[180] Like Judge Silberman, the Solicitor–General argued that the court should have confined itself to its traditional role of determining whether the agency had been arbitrary and capricious.[181]

Industry in response again tried to minimize the breadth of Judge Williams' decision. "All the court required here," wrote the utility-led challengers, "was that the agency explain its reasoning."[182] In addition, the utility-led and small business challengers each conditionally cross-petitioned on whether the D.C. Circuit was correct in its long-held position that costs may not be used in setting air quality standards.[183]

The Supreme Court granted the government's petition.[184] It also granted the small business group's conditional cross-petition—but not the utility-led group's. (Utility lawyers were miffed because they believed the cross-petition was their idea.) There is no easy explanation for the Court's action. It may have been simply because American Trucking, the lead named challenger, was part of the small business group. Whatever the reason, the Court's action strengthened the hand of the small business group in formulating strategy.

This became important as the standards' challengers turned to the task of trying to formulate their legal theories. Almost all of industry's lawyers thought that Judge Williams' delegation theory would not be

---

179. *Court Rejects Rehearing of NAAQS Case; Supreme Court Petition Next, EPA Says*, 30 Env't Rep.—Current Developments 1229 (1999).

180. Pet. for Writ, supra note 132 at 11, 19.

181. Id. at 19.

182. Brief in Response for the Respondents Appalachian Power, et al., Whitman v. American Trucking Ass'ns. 531 U.S. 457 (2000) (No. 99–1257). 2000 WL 33979493, at 12.

183. Id. at 1. To quote the utility-led group's formulation of the issue.

Whether Sections 101, 108, and 109 of the Clean Air Act require that the Environmental Protection Agency, in evaluating the adequacy of nationwide ambient air quality standards that address predicted "risks" to health, consider the overall societal consequences of managing such risks in determining whether and how to revise such standards?

Brief for Respondents Appalachian Power, et al., Whitman v. American Trucking Ass'ns, 531 U.S. 457 (2001) (No. 99–1426) 2000 WL 1010284, at i.

184. See Browner v. American Trucking Associations, 529 U.S. 1129 (2000) (granting the government's petition); American Trucking Associations v. Browner, 530 U.S. 1202 (2000) (granting American Trucking's cross-petition).

upheld by the Supreme Court. Most of the lawyers wanted to use the delegation theory in the Supreme Court, although perhaps not in Judge Williams' form.

Warren, the lead lawyer for the small business group, consulted with his long-time friend Charles Fried, professor of law at Harvard University. Fried was an ideal advisor on litigating the delegation doctrine because, as Solicitor-General in the 1980s, he had successfully argued in *Mistretta* that Congress had provided an intelligible principle when it authorized the United States Sentencing Commission to establish formulas for setting criminal sentences.

Fried suggested to the group that the key was to persuade the Court that EPA had to show that the benefits of its standards exceeded the costs. This could be an especially effective theory for challenging the ozone standard, for which EPA's own studies showed that costs exceeded benefits. In Fried's view, none of the contentions that could be made by the challengers stood alone as winning arguments, but the statutory and constitutional arguments could be melded together successfully.

Nickel's utility-led group and Warren's small business group took different approaches. The utility-led group's delegation brief focused on the need for the agency to set forth criteria for deciding between rival proposed standards. The brief emphasized the many scientific and policy uncertainties in determining what the risks were, and argued that the agency "had failed to articulate a principle based on the statute for managing those risks—i.e., a principle that explains why certain risks were 'sufficiently large' to require regulation or how much uncertainty is too much. The Agency did not articulate a principle that a court could use for assessing whether the resulting standard is reasonable."[185] The utility-led group argued that, even if the EPA had not violated the Constitution, such a principle was required under conventional judicial review doctrine.[186]

The group submitted a separate brief urging that the D.C. Circuit had erred in allowing the agency not to consider costs in setting the standards. This brief urged that EPA could not achieve the Act's purposes without using cost in helping to determine what is an adequate

---

185. Brief for Respondents Appalachian Power, et al., Whitman v. American Trucking Associations, 531 U.S. 457 (2001) (No. 99–1257), 2000 WL 1299500, at 18. (citation omitted) No. 99–1257.

186. Id. at 23. ("To be sure, there are several ways the lower court could have reached the same result: that the Agency's refusal to state a reason for its choice among alternative risk management options was 'arbitrary and capricious' under the Administrative Procedure Act ... that the Agency did not adequately explain its action; or that EPA misinterpreted the statute as providing no principle to guide its exercise of public health risk management judgment.") (citations omitted). In this way, the utility-led group again attempted to domesticate Judge Williams' opinion.

margin of safety.[187] The brief conceded, though, that EPA should not use costs in deciding what constitutes an adverse effect on health. In this way, the utility-led group tried to eschew a cost-benefit approach. That was in part because, to quote one utility lawyer puts it, "we never had much hope that a costs argument would win." Instead, the utilities were hoping to attract support from Justice Stephen Breyer, who has stressed the need for agencies like EPA to manage risks well and to find criteria for balancing the incremental benefits of tight regulation against high marginal costs.[188]

Fried and Warren submitted a brief for the small business group as co-counsel. The brief linked delegation and costs more tightly. The group argued that the delegation problem had been caused by the "frank irrationality" of *Lead Industries*'s rule prohibiting the use of costs, and urged that this "misbegotten" doctrine be overturned.[189] The brief contended that, if costs were excluded, no intelligible principle existed because such a principle had to provide for balancing competing considerations.[190] Thus, argued the small business group, the Court should accept the group's statutory claims that the Act required consideration of costs.[191]

The government's strategy was more straightforward. The Solicitor-General's brief as petitioner argued that the delegation doctrine did not require a determinate criterion to govern EPA's decisions, but only that there be standards to guide the agency.[192] Such standards, according to the Solicitor-General, could be found not only in the statute's "requisite to protect public health" language and its legislative history, but also in the complex procedure that the agency had to follow, including the requirement that it consult a body of experts.[193] Since EPA considered only the narrow range recommended by CASAC, there was simply no way, according to the brief, that Judge Williams' "Killer Fog" hypothetical could come true.[194]

---

187. Id. at 23. Cf. *Natural Res. Def. Council v. United States EPA*, 824 F.2d 1146 (D.C. Cir. 1987) (en banc) (taking this approach to another standard-setting provision of the Act.)

188. See STEPHEN BREYER, THE VICIOUS CIRCLE: TOWARD EFFECTIVE RISK REGULATION (1995).

189. See Brief of American Trucking Associations, Inc., Chamber of Commerce et al., Whitman v. American Trucking Ass'ns, 531 U.S. 457 (2001), 2000 WL 1299498, at 1.

190. Id. at 9, 13–14.

191. Id. at 23. These claims are presented in Brief of Cross–Petitioners, Whitman v. American Trucking Ass'ns, 531 U.S. 457 (2001), 2000 WL 1014021.

192. Brief for the Petitioners, Whitman v. American Trucking Ass'ns, 531 U.S. 457 (2001), 2000 WL 1010083, at 21–27.

193. Id. at 25.

194. Id. at 31–32.

The Solicitor-General separately sought to refute industry's claims that the agency had to consider costs in setting air quality standards. The brief included an extensive exegesis of the Act's language and legislative history. But it did not confine itself to strictly legal arguments. The brief also stressed that the new standards were based on "an extensive body of newly available scientific information ... that called for revision of the existing standards to address a wide range of adverse health effects."[195] CASAC's role was particularly emphasized to show that the standards had been chosen from a scientifically sound range.[196] In this way, the brief sought to prevent any impression in the Court's mind that the rules were unreasonable, and that existing doctrine needed to be stretched to prevent an improper regulatory burden. Finally, the brief cited an observation by Justice Scalia in a law review article that the air quality standards were based on health alone.[197] One government attorney still chortles at this.

With the briefs done, the industry challengers had to decide who would argue the cases before the Court, and hence which approach would be taken at oral argument. Initially the parties assumed that there would be only one hour for oral argument, and that Warren would argue because his group's cross-petition had been granted and because Warren had experience arguing before the Court. The Supreme Court then announced (to the surprise of at least some industry lawyers) that it would provide two hours for argument and hear each side's appeal separately. This meant that Warren could split time with Brownell, the utility-led group's oral advocate in the D.C. Circuit.

But instead Warren argued both cases. One argument in favor was that the Court might drive a wedge between two advocates. On the other hand, the utility-led group wanted very much to have its position represented. It seems surprising that the utility-led group did not prevail, since it accounted for most of the challengers to the standard

---

195. Respondent's Brief for the Federal Respondents, Whitman v. American Trucking Ass'ns, 531 U.S. 451, at 8.

196. Id. at 10–12.

197. Id. at 34 (citing The Honorable Antonin Scalia, *Responsibilities of Regulatory Agencies Under Environmental Laws*, 24 Hous. L. Rev.97, 102 (1987)). Justice Scalia had observed:

> By no means can the environmental laws be considered among those conferring the greatest amount of discretion upon the agencies. In fact, they are probably among those conferring the least ... [I]n some areas even cost-benefit analysis is excluded. For example, national primary ambient air quality standards are to be established not in light of what is "feasible" or "reasonable" (a formulation that would allow counterbalancing costs to be offset against the benefit of clean air) but rather on the sole basis of what is "requisite to protect the public health." [citation omitted]

This quotation also foreshadows Justice Scalia's view that including cost considerations would, if anything, increase the agency's discretion.

and had been, in one industry lawyer's phrase, "the moneybags." But Brownell, the utility group's choice for oral advocate, was needed by the Southern Company, one of Nickel's largest utility clients, to argue a case almost simultaneously in the 11th Circuit. (Ironically, that oral argument was postponed at the last minute.)[198] A prominent utility lawyer believes that the Chamber of Commerce persuaded the Southern Company to agree to have Warren alone argue the case, and speaks of the incident as "distasteful."

Oral argument was held on Election Day, November 7, 2000. Solicitor-General Seth Waxman began by presenting the government's appeal. Immediately Justice O'Connor asked him to state the intelligible principle behind the Act. Replied Waxman, "I believe I can say it in one sentence ... EPA must establish uniform national standards at a level that is requisite to protect public health from the adverse effects of the pollutant in the ambient air."[199] "Requisite" meant, according to Waxman, "sufficient but not more than necessary."[200] Justice Scalia joined the debate, asking for a criterion to judge whether the standard was set at the proper level. Waxman agreed that this was a matter for arbitrary and capricious review, but urged, with Scalia's apparent assent, that the delegation doctrine did not require such a criterion.[201]

Warren had a much more difficult time. He began by pressing the point that EPA needed a "generalized paradigm" for regulation to set standards validly. This paradigm existed in the Act, he asserted, if it was correctly interpreted to require the Administrator to weigh the costs of a standard against its benefits.[202] According to Warren, the Act's requirement to consider costs came from its use of the term "public health," a term that, he argued, connoted consideration of costs as well as benefits.[203]

Justice Scalia challenged the core of Warren's argument, asking how allowing consideration of costs would solve the delegation problem. Instead, Justice Scalia suggested, adding one more factor for the Administrator to consider would give the agency even more discretion.[204] After

----

198. E-mail from E. William Brownell to Craig N. Oren, (March 28, 2005) (on file with author). One informed lawyer reports that there was an unsuccessful effort to get the challengers to agree that the case would be argued by John Roberts, then in private practice and a frequent advocate before the Court.

199. Oral argument, Whitman v. American Trucking Ass'ns, 531 U.S. 457, 2000 WL 1674207, at 5.

200. Id. at 7.

201. Id. at 19–20.

202. Id. at 24–26.

203. Id. at 29–30.

204. Id. at 30–31.

all, if cost were relevant, then the range of possible outcomes would widen.

Warren responded that, since costs were a countervailing factor to health, including costs would narrow the range of outcomes. Both Justices Scalia and Breyer met this with skepticism.[205] Warren was finally asked if he was suggesting "that although the term . . . protect the public health [is] too vague and too standardless, it would be all right if it said, are requisite to protect the public health provided it doesn't cost too much?" Warren, with the red light on and the courtroom laughing, had time only to quickly deny it.[206]

Warren then had to stand up again to present his argument on the meaning of this statute. This went no better. One experienced observer thought that the Court had already had enough of the case. Warren repeatedly argued that the Act, by referring to public health, incorporated consideration of costs, and that *Lead Industries* and its progeny should be overruled. He ran into hostile questioning. At one point, Justice O'Connor expressed exasperation with Warren's attempt to formulate a clear definition of public health.[207] Warren seemed unwilling to advance any alternative argument, such as the utilities' contention that the Act's purposes could be accomplished only by allowing consideration of how the cost of compliance could affect health. Chief Justice Rehnquist challenged Warren to explain why *Lead Industries* should be overruled when it had proved workable for nearly twenty years.[208] This, to one prominent lawyer, spelled doom.

The Supreme Court's Decision

It took the Court less than four months after oral argument to reverse the lower court's decision.[209] Writing for the Court, Justice Scalia rejected industry's argument that the Act authorized consideration of costs in setting the air quality standards. Quoting the language of the statute, he remarked, "Were it not for the hundreds of pages of briefing [industry] respondents have submitted on the issue, one would have thought it fairly clear that this text does not permit the EPA to consider

---

205. Id. at 33–35.

206. Id. at 35–36.

207. Oral argument, Whitman v. American Trucking Ass'ns, 531 U.S. 457 (2001), 2000 WL 1674209, at 18–19 (quoting one Justice as telling Warren, "I've listened to a lot of vague language . . . [f]rom you . . . and I don't understand what it is you are saying.").Linda Greenhouse, "Attack on Clean Air Act Falters in High Court Argument," N.Y, Times, Nov. 8, 2000 at A20, identified Justice O'Connor as the questioner.

208. Id. at 20–21.

209. 531 U.S. 457 (2001).

costs in setting the standards."[210] Given the apparent clarity of the legislative language and statutory structure, Justice Scalia said, industry had to show a clear textual commitment to the use of costs; to quote the Justice, "Congress does not hide elephants in mouseholes."[211] Industry's various arguments, in Justice Scalia's view did not pass this test. Hence, according to Justice Scalia, even if the statutory language represented an excessive delegation, the statute could not be read to include costs.[212]

The opinion then upheld the standard-setting language under the delegation doctrine. Justice Scalia began by dismissing the lower court's holding that the agency should cure a nondelegation problem, calling it "internally contradictory." Were a court ever to conclude that Congress had failed to legislate sufficiently, only Congress could cure that defect.[213]

Justice Scalia conceptualized the delegation issue as whether the statute delegated legislative, rather than executive, power.[214] The power here was not legislative, according to Justice Scalia, because Congress had established an intelligible principle: the Solicitor-General's suggestion that the statute required standards that were "requisite, but not more than necessary" to protect public health.[215] As at oral argument, Justice Scalia suggested that the inclusion of costs would only detract from the intelligibility of the principle.[216] In this way, Justice Scalia's opinion made clear that the delegation doctrine would remain limited in scope. The only caveat came from Justice Thomas, who suggested that even statutes with an "intelligible principle" test might in some cases be defective.[217]

Justice Breyer took a different approach in concurring. He started from the premise that, in case of doubt, regulatory statutes should be interpreted to allow use of cost because this would make decision-making more rational.[218] Yet, according to Justice Breyer, the Clean Air Act's structure and legislative history (as usual, Justice Scalia did not mention legislative history) revealed that costs could not be considered. Justice

---

210. Id. at 464.

211. Id. at 468–69.

212. Id. at 471.

213. Id. at 473.

214. Justice Stevens, joined by Justice Souter, questioned this approach, arguing instead that the Constitution allows delegations of legislative power so long as there is an intelligible principle. But they did not argue that using their formulation would affect the result. Id. at 488–490.

215. Id. at 472–473.

216. Id. at 473–474.

217. Id. at 487–88.

218. Id. at 490.

Breyer particularly relied upon the desire of the Act's sponsors that the standards force the development of new technology.[219]

Justice Breyer gave special attention to the argument that, without some limit on the agency's discretion, EPA would have to set its standards at zero to eliminate all risk to health. Breyer pointed out the agency's discretion to consider which risks truly posed a threat to public health and to take into account comparative health risks.[220] He ended with the thought that, since preindustrial society was not a healthy society, "a standard demanding the return of the Stone Age would not be 'requisite to protect public health.' "[221]

Justice Breyer's opinion was, according to some industry lawyers, what they had hoped for. While Justice Breyer came out against the industry's claims, his opinion allowed cost to be indirectly considered. Although the Clinton Administration EPA could not be expected to use this authority, the seeds would be planted for its use by a more conservative administration. Moreover, Justice Breyer, by reciting considerations that the agency could use, arguably made it seem arbitrary for the agency not to have used any of them.

Still, it was Justice Scalia's opinion, not Justice Breyer's, that drew a majority of the Justices. In a paper he later published, Justice Breyer tried to explain his failure. Ordinarily, Justice Breyer said, costs should be disregarded in standard-setting. But, he continued, there might be exceptional instances in which ignoring costs could lead to a counterproductive result by creating health risks.[222] Justice Breyer believed that it was necessary in these instances to give the agency authority to consider costs. Such an approach, though, invited the question when the agency should have this authority. That would have involved an individualized approach. In contrast, the Court, in Justice Breyer's view, preferred a per se rule to make the law certain.[223]

---

219. Id. at 491–493.

220. Id. at 495–496.

221. Id. at 496.

222. Justice Breyer evidently based his view partly on studies suggesting that a wealthier society is a healthier society, and that regulation in the name of health can be counterproductive. *See* Stephen F. Williams, *The Era of "Risk–Risk" and the Problem of Keeping the APA Up to Date*, 63 U. CHI. L. REV. 1375 (1996) (contending that health increases with wealth); but see Lisa Heinzerling, *Regulatory Costs of Mythic Proportions*, 107 YALE L. J. 1981, 2070 (1997) (questioning the literature suggesting this result).

223. Stephen Breyer, *Economic Reasoning and Judicial Review*, AEI-Brookings Joint Center for Reg. Stud. 5–7 (2003), available at http://www.aei-brookings.org/admin/authorpdfs/page.php?id=840.

Back to the Appeals Court

The Court remanded the case to the D.C. Circuit to consider whether EPA had acted arbitrarily or capriciously in setting the standards.[224] Despite their loss in the Supreme Court, the challengers could feel reasonably confident. Much of the original appeals court decision could be recast as holding that EPA had not engaged in reasoned decision-making. For instance, Judge Williams' conclusion that EPA had no principle for distinguishing among proposed standards could be read as saying that EPA had not reasonably explained its choice of standards. (To quote one industry lawyer, "if these decisions weren't arbitrary and capricious, what would be? I defy anyone to explain EPA's basis for setting the standards at these levels!")[225] Moreover, the case was assigned to the same panel of Judges Williams, Ginsburg and Tatel that had handed down the first decision, thus giving industry challengers some room for hope. On the other hand, there had been some respects in which the original decision had found the standard-setting decisions to not be arbitrary, thus indicating that the panel would give EPA at least some deference.[226]

The utility-led group was the only industry participants in oral argument on remand, possibly because only they had the resources to continue the litigation. Brownell began by arguing that the prior decisions had established that EPA had not considered whether its standards were more stringent than necessary. Judge Williams ruefully acknowledged reversal: "Isn't the problem ... that apparently everybody in the world except Judge Ginsburg and I [sic] could see perfectly well that the word 'requisite' meant ... neither too much nor too little?"[227] Clearly, Judge Williams had no desire to try to revive the panel decision.

Matters went no better as Brownell began to argue that the ozone decisions had been arbitrary and capricious. Brownell found himself repeatedly interrupted by Judge Tatel, the dissenter on the original panel decision. Tatel and Brownell disputed whether EPA had shown sufficient reason to adopt a 0.08 standard rather than a laxer 0.09 standard. Both knew the record in great detail; both seemed frustrated that they could not make their position clear. At one point, Judge Tatel complained to Brownell, "you don't want to answer my question."[228]

---

224. *Whitman*, 531 U.S. at 476.

225. For a spirited argument that the standards were arbitrary and capricious, see Cary Coglianese & Gary E. Marchant, *Shifting Sands: The Limits of Science in Setting Risk Standards*, 152 U. Pa. L. Rev.1255 (2004).

226. See American Trucking Ass'ns. v. Whitman, 175 F.3d 1027, 1055–56 (D.C. Cir. 1999).

227. Transcript of Proceedings, American Trucking Ass'ns v. EPA, 283 F.3d 355 (D.C. Cir. 2002) (No. 97–1440) 7.

228. Id. at 29.

While this was going on, Judges Williams and Ginsburg, in the word of a utility lawyer, "sat there stone-faced." While the government's attempts to justify its line-drawing were also challenged by the court, Tatel seemed to observers to be sympathetic to EPA.

The court's opinion fulfilled industry's worst fears.[229] The court concluded, in an opinion by Judge Tatel, that EPA had reasonably exercised the discretion given to it in the Act.[230] For instance, the court held that the agency had rationally picked 0.08 rather than 0.07 or 0.09 for the ozone standards. The court found EPA's decision not to choose 0.07 reasonable, because there were no studies showing effects below 0.08, because no member of CASAC had endorsed 0.07, and because 0.07 approached natural background levels that would be nearly impossible to attain.[231] The court gave no express consideration to why 0.08 was a rational choice as compared to 0.09. Clearly the court, to borrow a phrase, chose to give a "soft glance" rather than a "hard look" at EPA's reasoning.[232] In fact, one commentator sees the court's decision as a missed opportunity for the D.C. Circuit to explicitly reject a "hard look" approach to reviewing agency exercises of judgment.[233]

The Aftermath

EPA is now implementing the 1997 air quality standards. The agency has classified 474 counties, with a population of nearly 160 million Americans, as violating the new ozone standards.[234] This compares with 235 counties, totaling about 110 million people, that violated the previous standards.[235] EPA has also designated 208 counties, with a population of 88 million, as not attaining the fine particle standards.[236]

---

229. American Trucking Ass'ns v. EPA, 283 F.3d 355 (D.C. Cir. 2002).

230. Id. at 364.

231. Id. at 379–380.

232. See William H. Rodgers, Jr., *The Most Creative Moments in the History of Environmental Law*, 39 WASHBURN L. J. 1, 2 (1999).

233. See Heath A. Brooks, *American Trucking Associations v. EPA: The D.C. Circuit's Missed Opportunity to Unambiguously Discard the Hard Look Doctrine*, 27 HARV. ENVTL. L. REV. 259 (2003).

234. See Eight–Hour Ozone Area Summary, available at http://www.epa.gov/oar/oaqps/green-bk/gnc.html For a map, see http://www.epa.gov/oar/oaqps/green-bk/naa8hr green.html.

235. See 1–Hour Ozone Area Summary, available at http://www.epa.gov/oar/oaqps/green-bk/onc.html For a map, see http://www.epa.gov/oar/oaqps/green-bk/onmapc.html.

236. See *EPA Adds 21 Counties in Nine States to Those Attaining Fine Particle Standard*, 36 Env't Rep. (BNA)—Current Developments 685 (2005). For a map of these

(Many of these counties also violate the new ozone standards). States are now preparing plans to demonstrate how they will achieve these standards by a complex set of deadlines.[237] EPA has established new rules requiring eastern and midwestern utilities to cut within ten years more than half of their emissions that contribute to the formation of fine particles and ozone.[238] Despite the cuts, the metropolitan corridor from New York to Washington, as well as urban areas such as Chicago and Houston, are not expected to reach the ozone and particulate matter standards by 2015.[239] Further reductions in emissions from sources of air pollution will be necessary.

Meanwhile, the air quality standards staff remains active in reviewing the science underlying the standards. Once again, EPA is under court deadlines to finish its review of the ozone and particulate matter standards. EPA has completed a new criteria document for particulate matter,[240] and has issued the second draft of the staff paper[241] concluding that, because of new data, the 1997 particulate matter standards should be tightened.[242] CASAC has concurred.[243]

Doubtless we will see more of the fierce controversy that surrounded the 1997 standards; perhaps the courts may have another chance to wrestle with reviewing EPA's air quality standards. That is another important aspect of administrative law: the work is steady.

---

areas, see Attainment and Nonattainment Areas in the U.S.-PM 2.5 Standards, http://www.epa.gov/pmdesignations/nonattaingreen.htm.

237. See, e.g., Final Rule To Implement the 8–Hour Ozone National Ambient Air Quality Standard—Phase 1, 69 Fed. Reg. 23,951 (2004). The deadlines for attaining the ozone standards are set forth at http://www.epa.gov/oar/oaqps/greenbk/gnc.html.

238. See EPA Issues Final Rule to Reduce Emissions From Power Plants in 28 States by 2015, 36 Env't Rep. (BNA)—Current Developments 461 (2005). For a summary of EPA's rules, see http://www.epa.gov/cair/basic.html.

239. See Ozone and Particle Pollution: CAIR, Together With Other Clean Air Programs, Will Bring Cleaner Air to Areas in the East: 2015, available at http://www.epa.gov/cair/pdfs/cairimp2015.pdf.

240. Air Quality Criteria for Particulate Matter, 69 Fed. Reg. 63,111 (2004).

241. Second Draft Staff Paper for Particulate Matter, 70 Fed. Reg. 5442 (2005).

242. *EPA Paper Recommends Consideration Of Stricter Standard for Fine Particles*, 36 Env't Rep.(BNA)—Current Developments 207 (2005).

243. See *Scientific Advisory Committee Endorses Stricter Standard for Fine Particulate Matter*, 36 Env't Rep. (BNA)—Current Developments 743 (2005).

AFP file

It is easy to dismiss the Line Item Veto Act of 1996 (LIVA) as a mere footnote in a larger tale of inter-branch dynamics. Effective for about a year before the Supreme Court declared it unconstitutional in *Clinton v. City of New York*, LIVA was part of the first plank in the Republicans' Contract with America, promises that brought them control of the House of Representatives in 1994. For Professor Garrett, the significance of its story lies in the congressional action, not in the court proceedings. LIVA exemplifies Congress's ability to delegate authority to the executive branch while retaining control over its exercise. The cancellation authority Congress delegated to the President in fact did not abdicate its responsibility for spending and tax policy, but crafted a structure providing legislators with continuing, significant influence. LIVA also provides a case study of congressional deliberation of thorny constitutional questions, a flawed deliberation that punted final resolution to the courts. This dimension of LIVA may make us wonder whether legislators can ever fulfill their responsibility to consider constitutional ramifications of their actions. Perhaps some shirk this duty hoping judicial abnegation of the statute will permit them to avoid blame for failing to deliver on promises their constituents wanted but they would just as soon not have made. Yet committee discussions and extended Senate debate suggest that members will spend time on constitutional issues, whether or not constitutional arguments will change minds.

2

Elizabeth Garrett*

The Story of *Clinton v. City of New York*: Congress Can Take Care of Itself

It is easy to dismiss the Line Item Veto Act of 1996 (LIVA)[1] as a mere footnote in a larger tale of inter-branch dynamics. Effective for about a year before the Supreme Court declared it unconstitutional in *Clinton v. City of New York*,[2] LIVA was part of the first plank in the Republicans' Contract with America, the policy agenda that propelled them into control of the House of Representatives in 1994. Even if LIVA had survived constitutional challenge, it probably would not have been used often by a President to block major congressional initiatives.[3] Under its authority, President Clinton canceled only 82 items in 11 laws, and Congress reinstated 38 of those cancellations over the President's veto. In the end, the savings to the federal government amounted to less than $600 million over five years—a trivial sum in an annual budget of over $1.5 trillion. This cursory chronicle, however, fails to recognize the value

* Sydney M. Irmas Professor of Public Interest Law, Legal Ethics, and Political Science, University of Southern California; Director, USC—Caltech Center for the Study of Law and Politics. I appreciate the outstanding research and drafting assistance of Alex Baskin (USC, '05) and comments from Louis Fisher, and Andrei Marmor.

1. Line Item Veto Act, Pub. L. No. 104–130, 110 Stat. 1200 (1996) (codified as amended at 2 U.S.C. §§ 621, 681, 691 to 691f, 692).

2. 524 U.S. 417 (1998).

3. The General Accounting Office (GAO) had predicted that the President would have used a line item veto authority to save a maximum of $70 billion over a six-year period (1984–1989). GAO, LINE ITEM VETO: ESTIMATING POTENTIAL SAVINGS (Jan. 1992). This report was criticized by Congressional Research Service constitutional expert Louis Fisher, and the Comptroller-General of the GAO responded by acknowledging that the actual savings over that period could have been "close to zero," and that the $70 billion figure contributed to a "misleading perception" of the potential effect of a federal line item veto. See LOUIS FISHER, CONGRESSIONAL ABDICATION ON WAR AND SPENDING, 142–43 (2000).

of the story behind LIVA's enactment and judicial challenge. The tale opens a window into the relationship among all three branches of government.

Legal scholars and law students may miss the significance of this story because it lies in the congressional action, not in the court proceedings. First, the story of LIVA and *Clinton v. City of New York* provides a clear understanding of how Congress can delegate authority to the executive branch while retaining a great deal of control over the exercise of delegated power. A close analysis of the structure of the cancellation authority delegated to the President shows that Congress did not use LIVA to abdicate its responsibility as the branch with the main authority over spending and tax policy. Instead, Congress crafted a structure that provided legislators with continuing and significant influence. The reality of the Act draws into question the claims of opponents that LIVA worked a fundamental change in the balance of power, severely weakening the legislature and substantially empowering the President. On the contrary, the ability of Congress to control the scope of any delegation justifies the Court's practice of allowing virtually all delegations to pass constitutional muster.[4] Congress needs no judicial protection because it has ample tools to protect itself in the political process, and it deploys those tools strategically.

Second, the story of LIVA provides a case study of congressional deliberation of thorny constitutional questions. Everyone expected a constitutional challenge to the Act because it purported to create a line item veto power by statute, which some saw as an end-run around the constitutional amendment process. The legislative history of LIVA clearly reveals, however, that Congress did not completely resolve the constitutional objections to the law. The most sustained discussion of constitutional issues occurred during the Senate debate on a version of the statutory line item veto that bore little resemblance to the LIVA that became law. In the end, Congress punted final resolution of these issues to the courts, providing in the statute an expedited process for any constitutional challenge to reach the Supreme Court.[5]

Congress' performance on this dimension of LIVA raises the question of whether legislators can fulfill their responsibility to consider constitutional ramifications of their actions. It may be the case that they shirk this duty not only because it takes time away from activity that constituents value more, but also because some hope the judiciary will strike certain laws down, allowing members of Congress to avoid blame for the failure to deliver on their promises in circumstances where they would prefer the status quo ante. On the other hand, the discussion in

---

4. See, e.g., Whitman v. American Trucking Assns., Inc., 531 U.S. 457 (2001).

5. 2 U.S.C. § 692(b), (c).

various committees and extended debate in the Senate demonstrate that
members will spend some time on constitutional issues, but that constitutional arguments do not necessarily change minds.

Putting LIVA into Context: The Federal Budget Process

The story of the modern federal budget process has two major
themes: one of inter-branch dynamics as Congress and the President
jockey for power, and a related one of a multi-member legislature facing
severe collective action problems. In some cases, Congress has delegated
power to the executive branch to reduce its collective action dilemmas,
but lawmakers are aware that such delegations may dangerously weaken
their institution's control over the power of the purse. So Congress
works to craft compromises that balance the need to retain ultimate
legislative control with the reality that the President and his agents
accomplish some budget objectives more successfully. For example, the
first modern comprehensive budget act, the Budget and Accounting Act
of 1921,[6] was primarily targeted at improving the presidential budget
process, but also contained provisions that strengthened congressional
oversight of appropriations.

The primary motivation behind passage of the 1921 Act was a series
of unprecedented budget deficits and the belief that Congress could not
restrain itself from profligate spending. Thus, stronger leadership from
the President was necessary. The 1921 Act, which still largely governs
executive branch budgeting, requires the President to develop and submit an annual budget to Congress, kicking off a process that then moves
to congressional committees and then to the House and Senate floors.
The Act also established the Bureau of the Budget in the Treasury
Department, which later became the Office of Management and Budget
(OMB) in the Executive Office of the President. OMB provides the
President with centralized, expert control over the budgets of the extensive executive branch agencies and departments, reinforcing the advantage that the President has relative to Congress. He is a unitary actor,
albeit one who must rely on his agents to help carry out his policies,
while Congress is a collective institution of 535 separate actors who may
pursue different goals and find coordination difficult to achieve and
enforce.

Although the 1921 Act strengthened the President in the hope that
he could restrain government spending which had skyrocketed after
World War I from $726 million in 1914 to $19 billion in 1919,[7] it also

---

6. Pub. L. No. 67–13, 24 Stat. 20 (1921) (codified as amended in scattered sections of
31 U.S.C.).

7. See ALLEN SCHICK, THE FEDERAL BUDGET: POLITICS, POLICY, PROCESS 14 (rev. ed. 2000).
During that time, public debt increased from $1 billion to $26 billion.

contained provisions to enhance congressional power over budgeting. Congress transferred the power to audit and account for expenditures from the Department of Treasury to a newly created entity, the General Accounting Office (GAO), that was controlled more by Congress than the President.[8] Congress also responded to the changes in the organization of executive branch budgeting by adopting new internal structures. As Congress passed the first version of the Act in 1920 (vetoed by President Wilson), lawmakers adopted internal rule changes that altered the congressional appropriations process. For example, the House created one large appropriations committee, thereby centralizing the legislative budget process in a move that mirrored the Act's centralization of the executive budget.[9]

The next wave of federal budget reform, leading to the adoption of the Congressional Budget and Impoundment Control Act of 1974,[10] similarly aimed to coordinate congressional budgeting and also to provide Congress with expert staff and detailed information about spending and taxing. This was partly a response to the perception that the executive branch's centralized budget apparatus, headed up by the President and OMB, was vastly superior to the legislative process in setting fiscal policy. Part of the problem that the 1974 Budget Act worked to solve is merely a coordination challenge as many committees in both houses work to produce a rational budget through the sequential enactment of different legislative vehicles, including more than a dozen appropriation bills and separate proposals dealing with tax revenues. Features of the congressional budget process put in place by the 1974 Budget Act to provide coordination include the annual concurrent budget resolution, a joint document of House and Senate that sets large budget goals and provides internal enforcement mechanisms to ensure that lawmakers conform to those objectives; the Congressional Budget Office (CBO), which provides expert assistance to lawmakers to counterbalance OMB; and the House and Senate Budget Committees, layered onto the existing budget structure with the primary role to oversee the congressional process.

The challenge of coordinating legislative action is one faced in many contexts, but the collective action problem is particularly intractable in the budget arena, because a legislature is also plagued by a prisoners'

---

8. AARON WILDAVSKY & NAOMI CAIDEN, THE NEW POLITICS OF THE BUDGETARY PROCESS 39 (4th ed. 2001); LUCIUS WILMERDING, THE SPENDING POWER: A HISTORY OF THE EFFORTS OF CONGRESS TO CONTROL EXPENDITURES 262–71 (1943). The GAO is now called the Government Accountability Office.

9. See CHARLES H. STEWART BUDGET REFORM POLITICS: THE DESIGN OF THE APPROPRIATIONS PROCESS IN THE HOUSE OF REPRESENTATIVES, 1865–1921 204–211 (1989).

10. Pub. L. No. 93–344, 88 Stat. 297 (1974) (codified as amended at 2 U.S.C. §§ 681–88).

dilemma when it works to control spending and reduce or eliminate deficits. Put simply, legislators who believe that the public interest is best served by reduced government spending know that, in the absence of coordination, most of their colleagues will not resist the temptation to spend, nor would it be rational for them to do so. The cost of government programs is spread among all taxpayers, while the benefits of spending can be concentrated on a few who will reward their supporters with votes and campaign contributions. If the government can fund spending through deficits, the temptation to spend is even greater because the burden of government debt is more diffuse than the tax burden—it extends across generations to the not-yet-born (and, more importantly, the not-yet-voting). Even if taxpayers who favor balanced budgets want to extract an electoral price from politicians who impose costs on them, voters are likely to hold all lawmakers responsible—not just the big spenders. If that is the case, no legislator will abstain from pork barrel politics. She is going to suffer consequences (if any) of her colleagues' actions so she might as well send some programs to her constituents as well. Moreover, an individual legislator can avoid responsibility for programs her constituents oppose by arguing that she had to vote for an omnibus spending bill in order to ensure passage of the special benefits her constituents want.

These problems became especially severe in the 1960s and 1970s and led to a showdown with the Executive Branch. Relations became so strained between the President and Congress that the period between 1966 and 1973 is called the "Seven-Year Budget War" by budget expert Allen Schick.[11] Budgeting during this period was an unusually difficult process because there was little additional money each year to fund new programs. Not only had President Johnson relied on deficit financing to fund the Vietnam War without compromising the funding for his domestic priorities, but more spending was occurring through entitlement programs like Social Security, welfare, unemployment compensation, and military and civilian retirement programs. These programs, once enacted, are essentially on automatic pilot and are sometimes referred to as "uncontrollable spending." They do not require annual appropriations to continue; their expenditures increase automatically as more people qualify for benefits; and many of them are indexed for inflation so that benefits increase with the cost-of-living. Each year, these entitlement programs had the first claim on federal revenues, leaving very little additional funds for other domestic or defense programs. Congress had responded to this budget reality by spending much more each year than it collected, leading to a string of deficits with no end in sight. Congress was primarily blamed for the budget disarray, with detractors citing its

---

11. See ALLEN SCHICK, CONGRESS AND MONEY: BUDGETING, SPENDING, AND TAXING ch. 2 (1980) (also providing details of the developments discussed in this paragraph).

apparent inability to produce a rational budget that met overarching objectives like reining in the escalating deficit.

Arguing that Congress was incapable of putting the country's fiscal house in order, President Nixon began to use policy impoundments to decrease spending and implement his own funding priorities. Nixon, citing an inherent constitutional right, refused to spend billions of dollars that Congress had appropriated. Such a refusal to spend money is called an impoundment. Although other Presidents had impounded funds, the scale and severity of Nixon's impoundments were unprecedented.[12] They were not routine decisions to achieve congressional objectives more efficiently, nor were they limited to appropriations for defense or foreign affairs, areas where the President as Commander-in-Chief had always asserted substantial discretionary authority. Instead, Nixon used impoundments to change domestic policy priorities of the Democratic Congress, and in some cases, he impounded money appropriated in bills enacted over his veto, ignoring a clear legislative signal that Congress wanted the money spent.[13] Thus, a budgetary crisis erupted into open inter-branch warfare.

When Nixon's impoundments were challenged in court, the President usually lost.[14] But Congress' legal victories came too late for spending to be effective, so it enacted the impoundment control measures in the 1974 Budget Act, requiring congressional approval for impoundments to go into effect. It thus explicitly denied the President the right to unilaterally withhold money Congress had appropriated. The same act restructured the congressional budget process, creating an expert staff in the CBO, Budget Committees in both houses to coordinate and centralize the process, and new internal process to structure the consideration of the many bills that make up the country's budget.

A more detailed discussion of the congressional budget process would take us far afield from the story of the Line Item Veto Act. But, as this brief tale of Nixon's showdown with Congress reveals, the budget arena is characterized by shifts of power between the two branches and the creation of new internal structures in Congress and other innovations to allow lawmakers to alter budgetary outcomes. Providing the President some power to trim or withhold appropriated funds has been a tool used frequently by Congress to enforce larger budgetary objectives.

---

12. See D. RODERICK KIEWIET & MATHEW D. MCCUBBINS, THE LOGIC OF DELEGATION: CONGRESSIONAL PARTIES AND THE APPROPRIATIONS PROCESS 217 (1991) (calling Nixon's constitutional assertions "radical, aggressive, and erroneous").

13. See LOUIS FISHER, PRESIDENTIAL SPENDING POWER 175–77 (1975).

14. See Ralph S. Abascal & John R. Kramer, *Presidential Impoundment Part II: Judicial and Legislative Responses*, 63 Geo. L.J. 149 (1974). See also Train v. City of New York, 420 U.S. 35 (1975) (unanimous Court holding that the President was required to spend money authorized by Congress to decrease water pollution).

For example, in the mid-1980s, Congress delegated to the Director of the OMB the power to sequester funds—or to make pro rata cuts in federal programs—necessary to ensure that federal spending conformed to previously-established deficit targets.[15] The development of sequestration as a deficit-reduction tool demonstrates the tension inherent in the federal budget process: Congress first delegated the sequestration power to the Comptroller-General of the GAO, an agent of Congress, and only grudgingly gave the power to an executive branch official after the Supreme Court struck the first arrangement down as a violation of constitutional separation of powers.[16]

Toward a Federal Line Item Veto: Extrapolating from the State Experience

Pro-rata sequestration leaves little discretion to the executive branch, but other impoundments, including Nixon's policy impoundments, can operate like a line item veto, a power allowed to governors by most state constitutions in addition to the power to veto an entire bill. Forty-three states grant the governor the power with respect to items in appropriation bills, and one of those states, Washington, also allows the governor to eliminate items from any kind of legislation.[17] When a governor uses a line item veto, he removes the disfavored item from the bill and then by signing the bill completes the process of enacting the remaining provisions; the vetoed items are never enacted unless the legislature overrides the veto. Most states require a supermajority vote of the legislature to override.

The state line item veto is seen as an adjunct to a balanced budget requirement because it provides the governor a way to enforce the mandate.[18] The line item veto is a mechanism designed to ameliorate the results of the prisoners' dilemma described above that is faced by a legislature in the budget context. The line item veto is one way to solve the collective action problem because it vests the power to rein in spending to a single actor—the governor, who can be more easily held

---

15. For a description of budget process acts in the 1980s, see Wildavsky & Caiden, supra note 8, at 126–33; Kate Stith, *Rewriting the Fiscal Constitution: The Case of Gramm-Rudman-Hollings*, 76 Cal. L. Rev. 593 (1988).

16. Bowsher v. Synar, 478 U.S. 714 (1986).

17. BRUCE WETTERAU, CONGRESSIONAL QUARTERLY'S DESK REFERENCE ON THE STATES 43 (1999) (the only states without line item veto provisions in their constitutions are Indiana, Maine, Nevada, New Hampshire, North Carolina, Rhode Island, and Vermont). For one of the best discussions of the state line item veto, see Richard Briffault, *The Item Veto in State Courts*, 66 Temple L. Rev. 1171 (1993).

18. For discussions of state balanced budget requirements—and their limitations— see RICHARD BRIFFAULT, BALANCING ACTS: THE REALITY BEHIND STATE BALANCED BUDGET AMENDMENTS 15–30 (1996); Louis Fisher, *The Effects of a Balanced Budget Amendment on Political Institutions*, 9 J. Law & Pol. 89, 91–92 (1992).

responsible by the voters and may be less susceptible to pressure from narrow special interests since he represents all taxpayers. The line item veto thus moves important budget decisions to an elected official who cannot disclaim responsibility on the ground either of being one of a collective decision maker or of being faced with an all-or-nothing choice.

Notwithstanding the conventional view of the line item veto as a tool of fiscal discipline, it need not necessarily lead to reduced spending for two reasons. First, lawmakers may pass more spending to pander to their constituents, knowing that the governor will use his line item veto to keep the state's fiscal house in order. It is not clear, however, that legislators have much to gain by this tactic. It is hard to believe that voters will be particularly grateful at Election Day for projects that are never funded because the governor slashes them out of the appropriation bills. They are more likely to question the lawmaker's effectiveness, wondering why the champion of the program was unable to convince the governor to support it.

Second, the line item veto may increase the aggregate amount of spending because it introduces a new dynamic into budget bargaining. The item veto provides the chief executive a more credible threat in the budget process because he has a scalpel to slice out spending he disfavors while still allowing the rest of the appropriation bill to go into effect. Unlike the President, a governor with a line item veto need not take the bitter to get the sweet. Knowing that, legislators will bargain with the governor to ensure that their pet projects do not fall victim to the line item veto. This strategy may actually increase the amount of total spending if the price of the governor's forbearance is enactment of programs he favors along with the legislators' projects.[19]

Empirical work on the effect of this state constitutional tool bears out the conclusion that it will not inevitably lead to lower state spending. Most studies conclude that the state item veto has very little impact on the amount of spending and has not led generally to lower state appropriations. The item veto does affect the mix of spending programs, however, because it empowers the governor relative to the legislature, granting the chief executive more influence over the contours of state spending.[20] In other words, the main consequence of the line item veto is

---

19. For an excellent analysis of the effect of the line item veto on inter-branch bargaining, see Maxwell L. Stearns, *The Public Choice Case Against the Item Veto*, 49 Wash. & Lee L. Rev. 385 (1992). See also, DANIEL SHAVIRO, DO DEFICITS MATTER? 291–92 (1997) (describing these dynamics).

20. See, e.g., George Abney & Thomas P. Lauth, *The Line-Item Veto in the States: An Instrument for Fiscal Restraint or Partnership?*, 45 Pub. Admin. Rev. 372 (1985); James A. Dearden & Thomas A. Husted, *Do Governors Get What They Want?: An Alternative Examination of the Line-Item Veto*, 77 Pub. Choice 707 (1993); Douglas Holtz-Eakin, *The Line Item Veto and Public Sector Budgets: Evidence from the States*, 36 J. Pub. Econ. 269

on the allocation of money among programs, not on the level of spending. This effect is more pronounced during times of divided government, when the preferences of the two branches are likely to be further apart.

Georgia and Texas were the first states to adopt the line item veto in 1865, and since that time Presidents have requested that Congress propose a constitutional amendment to allow them a similar power.[21] Presidents have coveted the ability to excise particular items from spending bills, rather than being faced with the all-or-nothing decision required by the veto allowed by Article I, Section 7 of the Constitution. Ronald Reagan's advocacy of the line item veto began the push that ended in the adoption of the Line Item Veto Act of 1996. In his 1986 State of the Union address, Reagan called for a constitutional amendment granting him the line item veto power like he had as Governor of California. "Give me the authority to veto waste, and I'll take the responsibility," he said, "I'll make the cuts, I'll take the heat."[22]

Modern Presidents have been particularly eager for a line item veto power because Congress has increasingly done its work through omnibus bills, legislation "that addresses numerous and not necessarily related subjects, issues, and programs, and therefore is usually highly complex and long."[23] As President Clinton wrote in a letter advocating "a strong version of the line item veto," the omnibus structure empowers "special interests, who too often are able to win approval of wasteful projects through manipulation of the congressional process, and bury them in massive bills where they are protected from Presidential vetoes."[24] A President pays a high price when he vetoes an omnibus law that likely contains provisions that are vital to his policy agenda; he would be in a more powerful bargaining position if, like most governors, he could extract offending portions and enact only the remaining portions that he supports.

Although Congress objected to Nixon's attempts to use unilaterally-imposed impoundments as a *de facto* line item veto authority, lawmakers

(1988). For work theorizing that the line item veto would have a similar effect at the federal level, see Nolan M. McCarty, *Presidential Pork: Executive Veto Power and Distributive Politics*, 94 Am. Pol. Sci. Rev. 117 (2000).

21. Only Presidents Taft and Carter opposed giving the line item veto power to the President, while at least ten presidents since the Civil War explicitly requested the power. See S. Rep. No. 104–9, at 6 (1995).

22. State of the Union Address, 22 Weekly Comp. Pres. Doc. 135, 136 (Feb. 4, 1986).

23. Barbara Sinclair, Unorthodox Lawmaking: New Legislative Processes in the U.S. Congress 71 (2d ed. 2000). For an argument that the increase in omnibus legislation has not eroded the traditional federal veto power or the President's power relative to Congress, see Neal E. Devins, *In Search of the Lost Chord: Reflections on the 1996 Item Veto Act*, 47 Case Western Res. L. Rev. 1605, 1621–23 (1997).

24. S. Rep. No. 104–13, at 5 (1995) (quoting President Clinton).

have considered proposals to delegate to the President line-item-veto-like power over spending as a way to better enforce fiscal discipline. Several times between Reagan's call to action and the Contract with America, Congress considered proposals to provide the President different kinds of rescission power. When the President rescinds, he withholds the funding that has been appropriated by Congress, thereby blocking federal funds directed at particular programs. This statutory power is similar to the governors' line item veto authority because it can be used in a targeted way against individual programs and projects. In budget terminology, there are many words used to describe the power of the President to decline to spend appropriated money: rescission, cancellation, impound-ment—all synonyms for the same authority to withhold federal funds permanently.

Congressional rescission proposals are typically drafted as amend-ments to the impoundment provisions of the Congressional Budget and Impoundment Control Act of 1974. Under the provisions of this law, enacted to stop Nixon's practice of policy impoundments, the President is required to submit to Congress a list of rescissions, or cancellations of spending enacted in appropriation bills. Congress must approve the rescissions before they take effect. Congress has forty-five days to consider a rescission request; if it does nothing in that time period, the money must be spent. Because lawmakers enacted the appropriations that the President seeks to rescind, it is not surprising that few of the President's recommendations pass, and that the rescission bills that do come out of Congress are often dominated by rescissions that the President did not request.[25] Schick reveals that in the first twenty-five years after enactment of the 1974 Budget Act, Presidents were forced to spend more than $50 billion of the $76 billion in spending they had recommended for rescission.[26]

Congressional proposals to strengthen the President's rescission power have usually taken one of two forms: expedited rescissions and enhanced rescissions. An expedited rescission bill speeds up the time in which Congress has to act, and often includes special procedures that require the President's rescission request to be discharged from commit-tee and that protect it from filibuster on the Senate floor. Expedited rescission proposals require that Congress actually vote on the Presi-dent's package; it cannot avoid the issue by inaction, although it can still fail to pass the rescission and effectively mandate the previously-enacted spending. An enhanced rescission bill works an even more significant change in the budget process. Once the President submits his list of

---

25. For example, President George H.W. Bush proposed $8 billion in rescissions in 1992; Congress enacted only $2 billion of those and added its own group of more than $22 billion in rescissions from programs Bush supported. Schick, supra note 7, at 254.

26. Id.

proposed rescissions, Congress has a certain period of time to disapprove them, and if the legislature fails to act, the President is authorized to withhold spending. Because any disapproval bill is subject to the President's veto, and he is likely to exercise his veto since he prefers to cancel the appropriations, Congress must muster a two-thirds vote in each house to force the President to spend the money. Thus, under an enhanced rescission regime, the effect of legislative inertia is reversed; inaction means that the spending will not occur, and therefore the President's power is enhanced.

For more than a decade, various enhanced and expedited rescission proposals traveled down the path to enactment but were killed at some point in the legislative process.[27] Congress also considered but did not pass joint resolutions to amend the Constitution to include a line item veto. In the mid-1990s, however, a unique set of political circumstances dramatically propelled our story forward. The momentum of the Contract with America and the desire of the new Republican House of Representatives to deliver on campaign promises, along with the strong support of a Democratic President who had repeatedly requested the power, set the stage for enactment. With insufficient support for a two-thirds vote in each house to amend the Constitution, advocates of a federal line item veto had to travel the perilous statutory route.

The Enactment of the Line Item Veto Act of 1996

As a former governor from a state with a line item veto, Bill Clinton staunchly supported a federal line item veto in his 1992 campaign for the presidency, describing it as a tool "to eliminate pork-barrel projects and cut government waste."[28] In his first budget document, *A Vision of Change for America*, Clinton requested a "modified line-item veto" as a tool to restrain unnecessary spending. The document seems to describe an expedited rescission process where the President would propose rescissions and Congress would then "cast a separate vote on those items."[29] The clear and longstanding preference of Chief Executive notwithstanding, Clinton's proposal probably would not have gotten very far in the legislature without other political developments.

After the election of a Republican House in 1994, the 104th Congress, led by Speaker Newt Gingrich (R–GA), sought to deliver quickly on its Contract with America, which had included an enhanced rescission proposal, called a line item veto, as part of its proposed Fiscal Responsi-

---

27. Mark T. Kehoe, *History of Line-Item Veto Effort*, Cong. Q., Mar. 30, 1996, at 867.

28. BILL CLINTON & AL GORE, PUTTING PEOPLE FIRST: HOW WE CAN ALL CHANGE AMERICA 23 (1992).

29. EXECUTIVE OFFICE OF THE PRESIDENT, A VISION OF CHANGE FOR AMERICA 113 (Feb. 17, 1993).

bility Act. Helping to get the bandwagon rolling in the Senate was Bob Dole (R–KS), Majority Leader in the Senate, the frontrunner to challenge Clinton in the 1996 election. A top congressional leader might be expected to oppose delegating enhanced rescission authority to the chief executive—indeed, the most outspoken opponent of the legislation was Senator Robert Byrd (D–WV), a legendary defender of congressional prerogatives and former majority leader. But Dole had competing interests: he needed to appear to be an effective Senate leader in the run-up to the presidential election, and he wanted to augment the power he could wield if he won. When he declared his support for the bill because "[i]f we cannot control ourselves—maybe the Chief Executive can help,"[30] he was probably not thinking of Bill Clinton as Congress' savior. Given the Republicans' strong showing in the 1994 mid-term elections, a second term for President Clinton was by no means certain. This not only meant that Dole himself hoped to benefit from the delegation of enhanced rescission authority, but also that the Republican Congress believed there was a good chance that the power would be used by a Republican president.

The first ten bills introduced by the majority party at the beginning of each session of Congress highlight the key aspects of its policy agenda. In the 104th Congress that began in January 1995, the Line Item Veto Act was H.R. 2 in the House, sponsored by Rep. William Clinger (R–PA) with 160 cosponsors, and S. 4, introduced by Dole with 28 cosponsors. The House bill was referred to the Committee on Government Reform and Oversight and the Committee on Rules, and the Senate bill was jointly referred to the Committee on the Budget and the Committee on Governmental Affairs, with instructions that once one of the committees reported the bill out, the other had thirty days to report or the bill would be automatically discharged to the floor.

Much of the ensuing congressional debate focused on the form of the statutory power. Competing visions included an expedited rescission bill that would still require congressional action before any rescissions took effect, supported by Senator Pete Domenici (R–NM), chair of the Senate Budget Committee; the enhanced rescission bill that was reflected in H.R. 2 and S. 4; and a separate enrollment bill, which was ultimately the version that passed the Senate. We have previously seen the differences between expedited and enhanced rescission proposals. Under separate enrollment procedures, Congress divides an omnibus spending bill, formally enrolling as a separate bill each provision that allocates funds to particular programs. The entire group of bills is then passed by Congress, using a procedure that would not require separate votes on each bill but would deem them all passed as a group. The President can use

---

30.   141 Cong. Rec. S4483 (daily ed. Mar. 23, 1995).

his constitutional power to veto as many of the separate bills as he wishes, and Congress has the opportunity to override any veto with a supermajority vote. For example, rather than one bill with 350 sections, Congress would pass 350 separately enrolled bills, and the President would sign only the bills that provide money to programs he supports.

The advantage of separate enrollment over enhanced rescission, supporters argued, is that the former technically complies with all the constitutional requirements. Dozens, even hundreds, of bills are enacted separately, enrolled, presented to the President, and then signed or vetoed using the traditional power given the President by the Constitution. Separate enrollment has its own set of problems, however, as would become clear in the Senate deliberations on this method. The logistics of dividing one bill into hundreds pose practical and perhaps constitutional problems, and separate enrollment requires that Congress put the details of spending in statutes rather than appropriating in lump sums and using legislative reports to earmark funds to particular projects. The latter practice, long used by Congress in appropriations, allows agencies and Congress more flexibility to redirect funds throughout the fiscal year.

When introduced in the 104th Congress, both versions of the Line Item Veto Act were enhanced rescission proposals. The proposals delegated to the President the power to cancel budget authority[31] in discretionary spending bills without any further action by Congress. Discretionary spending bills are the laws that are enacted annually through the appropriation process. They require yearly enactment by Congress, in contrast to entitlement programs like Social Security or Medicare, which authorize spending indefinitely according to legislative formulas without any further action by Congress. Under the first versions of LIVA, before the President could cancel an item of discretionary spending, he had to determine that the rescission would not "impair any essential Government functions" or "harm the national interest."[32] The House version also required that the rescission "help reduce the Federal budget deficit," while the Senate version required that the President determine that the rescission would "help balance the Federal budget, reduce the Federal budget deficit, or reduce the public debt."[33] The President had 20 days after a bill was enacted to cancel items, a period shortened by the House committee to 10 days. Unless Congress passed a disapproval bill reinstating the spending items, the President's cancellations would

---

31. Budget authority is the technical term for the legal authority to enter into obligations that will result in the spending of federal money. An appropriation bill provides an agency or other executive branch entity with budget authority, which allows it to commit to the spending (an obligation) and to actually spend the money (an outlay).

32. H.R. 2, 104th Cong. § 2(a) (1995).

33. Compare H.R. 2, § 2(a)(1)(A), with S. 4, § 1101(a)(1)(A).

take effect. In other words, congressional inaction would lead to cancellation, but the proposals included a fast-track procedure to make it easier for Congress to act on disapproval bills. Because the President would presumably veto any disapproval bill, Congress would need to muster a two-thirds majority in each house to ensure that the previously appropriated spending take place.

The primary difference between the initial enhanced rescission bills introduced in the House and Senate was that the House version extended the President's cancellation authority beyond appropriation bills and allowed him to "veto any targeted tax benefit" as well.[34] In this first incarnation of LIVA, a targeted tax benefit was defined as a tax subsidy that benefited five or fewer taxpayers.[35] In the House committee, this definition was expanded so that a tax provision benefiting 100 or fewer taxpayers would be eligible for the President's cancellation authority. This provision aimed at tax subsidies sometimes referred to as "rifle shots" because they provide tax relief to a very narrow group of taxpayers. These provisions are more likely to be special interest giveaways, providing a subsidy to a small group of influential people or businesses, rather than good public policy. Because they are relatively inexpensive, narrowly targeted tax benefits can be slipped into omnibus revenue legislation and provoke little opposition; the concern is that, in the aggregate, targeted tax subsidies can transfer significant money from all taxpayers to a handful of taxpayers with political clout.

Including tax benefits in LIVA reflected a recognition that lawmakers can "spend" money on programs through the tax code; thus, a cancellation bill limited to annual appropriation bills would be incomplete. Indeed, tax provisions that provide favorable treatment for certain behavior by taxpayers through credits and deductions are often called "tax expenditures" to link them explicitly to other more conventional federal expenditures.[36] For example, if Congress wants to encourage home ownership, it has several options. It can work to enact a program that gives people grants of federal money when they purchase a home, and fund such a spending program through annual appropriations ("discretionary spending") or an entitlement that continues to allow disbursements of money without annual legislation ("direct spending"). Or Congress can likewise encourage home buying by providing all taxpayers a deduction for the interest they pay on their mortgages ("tax expenditure").

---

34. H.R. 2, § 2(a).

35. Id. at § 4(3).

36. See STANLEY S. SURREY, PATHWAYS TO TAX REFORM: THE CONCEPT OF TAX EXPENDITURES (1973).

Not all members of Congress accept the notion of tax expenditures, so including them in LIVA's coverage was controversial. The most adamant opposition to inclusion can be found in the arguments of Senator Spencer Abraham (R–PA), otherwise a strong supporter of LIVA. He contended that "the general concept of 'tax expenditures' is fundamentally flawed because it assumes that taxpayers' income belongs to the Federal government first. ... Tax dollars belong to American people first. Many of the so-called 'tax expenditures' simply allow people to keep more of their own hard-earned tax dollars." Although he would in the end support LIVA even though it applied to certain tax benefits, he emphasized his belief that "our Nation's budget deficit is caused by overspending, not undertaxation."[37]

Including tax expenditures in the House version of LIVA, and ultimately in the Senate version, was mostly compelled by practical politics, not ideological debate over the notion of tax expenditures. Members of the Appropriations Committees insisted that other committees with jurisdiction over spending programs also be vulnerable to the President's cancellation power. The federal budget process involves many different committees with jurisdiction over some aspect of federal spending or revenue.[38] The Appropriations Committees, divided into 13 subcommittees at the time Congress was considering LIVA, oversee the annual appropriation process that provides discretionary funds to federal programs. The House Ways and Means Committee and the Senate Finance Committee have jurisdiction over tax bills, including tax expenditures, and some of the most expensive entitlement programs, like Social Security and Medicare. The Budget Committees in both houses coordinate the congressional budgeting process, but they cannot dictate the details of appropriation or revenue bills except in extraordinary circumstances.

Thus, the congressional budget process is always at least in part a story of jurisdictional turf wars among all these committees; LIVA is simply an example. Before LIVA, impoundments had been limited to programs funded through the annual appropriation bills, but the appropriators were determined that any new cancellation authority would include all the methods of federal spending. They argued that any proposal concentrated solely on discretionary spending was a very limited tool; only about one-third of all federal spending (a figure which does not include tax expenditures resulting in foregone revenue) occurs through discretionary spending; the majority of federal spending is related to entitlement programs and other direct spending. Neither of

---

37. S. Rep. No. 104–10, at 19–20 (1995).

38. For an account of the functioning of committees in the budget process, see Elizabeth Garrett, *Rethinking the Structures of Decisionmaking in the Federal Budget Process*, 35 Harv. J. on Legis. 387, 397–401 (1998).

the introduced bills attempted to constrain entitlement spending, but H.R. 2, in contrast to S. 4, for the first time included certain tax benefits as possible targets for presidential cancellation. Thus, the House version set the stage for the final version of LIVA which applied to discretionary spending, targeted tax benefits, and entitlement programs.

Statutory language played an important role in the story of LIVA. When describing the power delegated to the President, the bills used the term "veto" in addition to the more familiar budget terms for impoundment such as "cancel" and "rescind." For example, H.R. 2 provided that "any provision of law *vetoed* under this Act ... shall be deemed *repealed*" unless a disapproval bill was enacted to require the spending.[39] This language was dangerous; the more the proposal looked like an attempt to enact through statute a new constitutional line item veto power without following Article V's requirements to amend the Constitution, the more likely the resulting bill would be successfully challenged in court. As Justice Scalia, writing in dissent in *Clinton v. City of New York*, observed, the "title of the Line Item Veto Act, which was perhaps designed to simplify for public comprehension, or perhaps merely to comply with the terms of a campaign pledge, ... succeeded in faking out the Supreme Court."[40] Scalia was comparing LIVA, which the Court struck down, to other laws allowing presidential rescissions, which were more likely to be considered constitutional delegations of power to the executive branch.[41] In fairness to the majority in *Clinton v. City of New York*, ambiguous terminology abounded. Beyond the title's likely-fatal statement that the Act established a line item veto, language used both in the final version and earlier incarnations was not carefully crafted to avoid constitutional red flags. Instead, the bills used language such as "veto," "repeal," and "prevent ... from having legal force or effect," interchangeably with the traditional terminology of "impound," "rescind" and "cancel."

House Consideration of H.R. 2: Modifying Enhanced Rescission

Action on the enhanced rescission authority began in the House, which was eager to deliver on its Contract that had been signed during the 1994 campaign by more than 300 Republican candidates. At the crest of his powers, Speaker Gingrich adroitly guided the bill through the House. The House Committee on Government Reform and Oversight,

---

39. H.R. 2, § 3(a)(2) (emphasis added). See also id. at § 4(a)(B) (using "veto" to describe cancellation of targeted tax benefit).

40. *Clinton*, 524 U.S. at 469 (Scalia, J., dissenting).

41. Indeed, in *Bowsher v. Synar*, the Court had found the delegation of sequester authority to the Comptroller-General of the GAO unconstitutional because it allowed a legislative agent to exercise an executive power. This case characterized rescission authority delegated by Congress as executive in nature, not legislative. 478 U.S. 714 (1986).

chaired by the author of H.R. 2, Representative Clinger, reported the bill out favorably after making a few modifications. The period for the President to cancel items was shortened from 20 to 10 calendar days and the definition of targeted tax benefits was expanded to include subsidies benefiting 100 or fewer people (rather than five or fewer). It was left to the President to determine whether a tax benefit was a targeted one and thus susceptible to his cancellation power. There would be attempts on the House floor to broaden the definition of limited tax benefits beyond the 100-taxpayer cut-off.[42] All these amendments were defeated, diluting the effect of LIVA on tax expenditures relative to appropriation items eligible for cancellation, which had no limitation on the number of potential beneficiaries.

The Government Reform and Oversight Committee Report on LIVA made clear that the legislation was part of a broader strategy to reduce federal spending and balance the budget. "Enhanced presidential [cancellation] authority will be one method, used in concert with others, to move the nation toward a balanced budget."[43] The problem of omnibus legislation policed only through the blunt instrument of the constitutional veto power led to "outlandish projects and tax benefits [being] concealed in appropriation bills and revenue measures. On their own it is unlikely that these items would survive scrutiny either in Congress or when the bill reached the President's desk. Tucked away in omnibus bills, however, they survive." Targeted tax benefits were singled out for particular attack. The report described a tax bill designed to create enterprise zones in the aftermath of the Los Angeles riots. This bill emerged with several targeted tax benefits, such as "special exemptions for certain rural mail carriers, special rules for Federal Express pilots, deductions for operators of licensed cotton warehouses, exemptions for some small firearms manufacturers, and exemptions for certain ferry operators." LIVA was intended to allow the President to get rid of spending programs—in appropriation bills and through the tax code—designed for "narrow, parochial purposes." In addition, the Committee believed that the process would bring visibility to these special interest giveaways, forcing Congress to be more accountable and reducing the number of wasteful projects through increased transparency.

The Committee Report on H.R. 2 clarified that the Act did not limit the President to canceling only items in the text of the spending bills themselves; instead, the President could look through a bill to its legislative history and cancel items delineated in committee reports or joint explanatory statements that accompanied conference reports of

---

42. 141 Cong. Rec. H1116 (daily ed. Feb. 2, 1995) (Slaughter Amendment); 141 Cong. Rec. H1168 (daily ed. Feb. 3, 1995) (Spratt Amendment).

43. H.R. Rep. No. 104–11, pt. 2, at 8–10 (1995) (for all quotes in text).

appropriation bills. In this way, the enhanced rescission proposals did not require that Congress change its practice of enacting bills with lump sum appropriations and directing the money to particular programs and projects in the committee reports that accompanied the bills. Congress had long appropriated in relatively large lump sums, with more detailed instructions in the legislative documents associated with the laws, so that "agencies are able to make adjustments and shift funds within large appropriations accounts" without the need for additional legislation.[44] Allowing the President to cancel items identified in the legislative history meant that congressional practice could remain the same, but the President's power could be used with precision to eliminate only particular projects and programs that he considered wasteful or unnecessary.

The House Committee on Rules also reported H.R. 2 favorably and recommended passage of LIVA. Its changes were minimal, focusing on the special procedures in the House for consideration of a disapproval bill responding to any presidential cancellation. The amendments were designed to make sure that the disapproval bill included all the President's cancellations relating to a particular appropriation or tax bill so that lawmakers couldn't "cherry-pick" and disapprove only a few of the cancellations.[45] Instead, Congress would be limited to voting up-or-down to disapprove all the cancellations relevant to a spending bill or to allow them all to go into effect. In addition, the changes ensured that lawmakers could not add unrelated items to a disapproval bill. Generally, disapproval bills would receive expedited consideration in the House and Senate, and floor consideration could not be blocked by the committee with jurisdiction. The Rules Committee report contained a brief discussion of the constitutionality of this enhanced rescission bill, quoting from a Congressional Research Service ("CRS") Memorandum. This CRS Memo had concluded the Supreme Court's delegation jurisprudence set forth a practical doctrine that allowed virtually all congressional delegations of power to the executive branch to survive judicial scrutiny. It concluded that the delegation of cancellation authority in H.R. 2 would be no exception.[46]

The enhanced rescission bill was considered on the House floor for three days in early February, under an open rule. In the House, the Rules Committee determines the procedures for the floor debate of each piece of legislation; each bill is considered under a "rule" shaping the deliberation and voting. Under the Democrats, the Rules Committee had

---

44. Id. at 12.

45. H.R. Rep. No. 104–11, pt. 1, at 6 (1995).

46. Id. at 8–9 (quoting CRS, Memorandum Regarding Constitutional Questions Respecting Bill to Grant President Enhanced Rescission Authority over Appropriations and Targeted Tax Benefits (Jan. 9, 1995)).

relied on rules that often prohibited any amendments that the majority party did not support or set procedures so that disfavored amendments were unlikely to be adopted. These rules are called "closed" because they allow little change of the bill on the floor; "open" rules permit longer debate and more opportunity for members to propose amendments.[47] The Republicans had chafed under the regime of closed rules and had promised to open debate substantially when they gained control. After experiencing life under open rules, however, the Republicans would eventually revert to the practice of using more closed procedures; they learned quickly that much of the advantage of being the majority party consists in the ability to set the rules of debate and deliberation so that they favor particular outcomes. But LIVA was an early bill considered when the Republican leadership was still committed to "wide open rules," so the House debate was much more robust than had been the case in past Democratic Congresses and would soon be the case in Republican Congresses.[48]

Two amendments that were adopted unanimously by the House clarified that the President could only cancel amounts of funding and could not use his authority to veto substantive legislation or non-funding language often included in appropriation bills. Chairman Clinger, for example, proposed an amendment to require that the items subject to cancellation had to be identified specifically in legislative history or text language, not in documents produced by the executive branch. As with much of the design of LIVA, this amendment ensured that Congress retained a great deal of its power, here to define the scope of each item that might be canceled. As Clinger said in floor debate, his amendment made certain that Congress did not allow "a broad-ranging, free-wheeling President to go around changing all kinds of things, so it is a limited thing."[49] Clinger's amendment also stated that the rescission authority could not be used to cancel "bill language" but could only be used against "dollar amounts."[50] Another amendment by Rep. Nancy Pelosi (D–CA) prohibited the President from canceling "any prohibition or limitation of discretionary budget authority set forth in any appropriation Act," thereby insulating appropriation riders and other substantive provisions from cancellation.[51]

---

47. For discussion of the various rules, see WALTER J. OLESZEK, CONGRESSIONAL PROCEDURE AND THE POLICY PROCESS 123, 126–30 (6th ed. 2004).

48. Rep. Gerald Solomon (R–NY), Chairman of the Rules Committee, noted that the bill was considered under an open rule, in contrast to other statutory line item veto bills in Congress' recent history, where Democrats had crafted rules disfavoring strong versions. 104 Cong Rec. H1080–81 (daily ed. Feb. 2, 1995).

49. 141 Cong. Rec. H1107 (daily ed. Feb. 2, 1995).

50. 141 Cong. Rec. H1105 (daily ed. Feb. 2, 1995).

51. 141 Cong. Rec. H1107 (daily ed. Feb. 2, 1995).

Another amendment accepted unanimously by the House set in place a judicial review mechanism allowing members of Congress to challenge the constitutionality of the Act before a three-judge district court panel, with direct appeal to the Supreme Court and a requirement for expedited consideration. The author of the amendment, Representative Nathan Deal (R–GA), argued that "we are proceeding in a statutory form for a line item veto and not a constitutional amendment, [so] it should be obvious that until that constitutionality is clarified, it will be under a cloud."[52] Other members of Congress viewed this mechanism as setting up a way to send a "test case" to the courts for a decision before any presidential exercise of the authority.[53] Thus, rather than trying to resolve the constitutionality of enhanced rescission—or to more carefully craft a bill so that it was clearly an impoundment authority rather than a presidential power to "veto" or "repeal" enacted legislation, the House adopted a review procedure that itself was constitutionally questionable. The process edged dangerously close to asking the Court for an advisory opinion,[54] and the question of congressional standing to bring such a challenge was not clear at the time. Indeed, the Court used the first case concerning LIVA, *Raines v. Byrd*,[55] to make clear that congressional standing to bring constitutional challenges to enacted legislation was a very limited doctrine and not sufficient to allow this sort of preliminary "test case" before any actual cancellation decision.

The battle between those who supported the more aggressive enhanced rescission embodied in H.R. 2 and those who advocated only an expedited rescission authority that would still require congressional approval for any cancellation to take effect began on the House floor. Representatives Robert Wise (D–WV), Charles Stenholm (D–TX), and John Spratt (D–SC) offered an amendment in the nature of a substitute to replace the enhanced rescission approach with an expedited rescission process. They justified their preference for expedited rescission on the ground that it delegated less power to the executive branch. As Stenholm posed the decision to his colleagues: "The only question is, how much power do you wish to cede to a President. That is it."[56] Other supporters of expedited rescission voiced concerns about the constitutionality of enhanced rescission, arguing that granting a power like the line item veto to the President required a constitutional amendment. Representa-

---

52. 141 Cong. Rec. H1138 (daily ed. Feb. 2, 1995).

53. 141 Cong. Rec. H1139 (daily ed. Feb. 2, 1995) (statement of Rep. Collins (D–IL)).

54. See Neal Devins & Michael A. Fitts, *The Triumph of Timing:* Raines v. Byrd *and the Modern Supreme Court's Attempt to Control Constitutional Confrontations*, 86 Geo. L.J. 351 (1997) (criticizing such expedited review provisions).

55. 521 U.S. 811 (1997) (declining to hear Senator Byrd's challenge to the Act before the President had canceled any spending item because Byrd did not have standing to sue).

56. 141 Cong. Rec. H1176 (daily ed. Feb. 3, 1995).

tive Dellums (D–CA) argued that an enhanced rescission bill empowered "one-third plus one" of the Congress to make policy along with the President because unless a veto-proof supermajority of the Congress passed a disapproval bill, the President's cancellation of a previously-enacted spending item would go into effect. Thus, he warned of governance by a minority of lawmakers, suggesting that this would violate the Constitution's requirement that laws be made by a majority of each house and the President.[57]

The Committee on Government Reform and Oversight had considered and rejected the expedited rescission approach as "too weak to yield significant budget savings and too weak to discourage wasteful legislative habits."[58] Chairman Clinger reiterated this theme in the floor debate: "[W]e want to make it as difficult as possible, as difficult as possible, for this House, which has proven in the past not to be able to restrain itself, to in fact deny the President the ability to cut spending."[59] Although 342 Members of the House had voted for expedited rescission in 1994 and the approach was unquestionably constitutional, lawmakers were ready in 1996 to delegate more authority to the President and to get closer to the constitutional line. The amendment was defeated 167–246.

Finally, after three days of debate, the House passed an enhanced rescission bill by a comfortable margin of 294 in favor and 132 opposed. Final passage occurred on February 6, 1995, Ronald Reagan's 84th birthday, a fitting gift, in the eyes of House Republicans, for the President who had placed the issue on the national agenda. The stage was set for Senate consideration.

Senate Consideration of S. 4: Transforming Enhanced Rescission into Separate Enrollment

The duel between enhanced and expedited rescission bills was prominent during the Senate consideration of LIVA; the surprise was that the Senate floor ultimately discarded both approaches in favor of separate enrollment. At the same time that S. 4, the enhanced rescission proposal that was the counterpart to H.R. 2, was referred to the Senate committees, an expedited rescission bill, S. 14, was also sent to those committees for joint consideration. S. 14 was very similar to the substitute proposal that Representatives Wise, Stenholm, and Spratt had offered on the House floor. In the Senate, it had a particularly powerful backer in the

---

57.   141 Cong. Rec. H1178 (daily ed. Feb. 3, 1995). See also INS. v. Chadha, 462 U.S. 919 (1983) (holding that legislative action, under Art. I, § 7, requires passage by both houses of Congress and then approval by the President).

58.   H.R. Rep. No. 104–11, pt. 2, at 10 (1995).

59.   141 Cong. Rec. H1175 (daily ed. Feb. 3, 1995).

respected chair of the Budget Committee, Pete Domenici. Domenici's committee had jurisdiction over both proposals, and he preferred the less sweeping delegation because it would disrupt inter-branch relations less severely. As he stated, S. 14 would "guarantee the President a vote on his rescission proposals while maintaining the delicate balance of power between the two branches on spending authority."[60] The expedited rescission approach also had more Democratic support than did S. 4, with Minority Leader Tom Daschle (D–SD) an outspoken advocate of this approach because it preserved more congressional power, was more clearly constitutional, and undermined the Republican push to enact a key provision of the Contract with America.

The Budget Committee took the lead in the Senate, holding hearings on S. 4 and S. 14. At the same time, the Subcommittee on the Constitution, Federalism, and Property Rights of the Senate Judiciary Committee held the only sustained inquiry into the constitutionality of the various statutory approaches, although in the context of a hearing on constitutional amendments to establish a federal line item veto. The discussion in the hearing included analysis of constitutional issues raised by statutory proposals, as well as competing formulations for a constitutional amendment. At this point only the enhanced and expedited rescission bills were pending in committee, but Senator Joseph Biden (D–CT), Ranking Member of the Judiciary Committee, strenuously supported separate enrollment. So this method was on the table as well, although few of the witnesses addressed it.

Walter Dellinger, the Assistant Attorney General in charge of the Office of Legal Counsel, reaffirmed President Clinton's preference for a strong statutory cancellation authority—enhanced rather than expedited rescission power. He assured the Senators that "S. 4 in my view is clearly constitutional. It does not raise a Presentment Clause issue, because the President would sign the omnibus bill into law. . . . What S.4 really is is a very strong delegation of authority to the President."[61] Although he acknowledged that the expedited rescission bill was even more clearly constitutional, he, like the CRS experts cited by the House, analyzed the bill under delegation principles, a doctrine that was unlikely to convince the Supreme Court to nullify an enhanced rescission law. He did warn lawmakers that the language of "veto" and "repeal" in the current version of H.R. 2 was problematic and should be replaced with terms like "suspend" so it would not appear that the President was unilaterally making law. Even Louis Fisher, a CRS expert on the

---

60. See S. Rep. No. 104–9, at 15 (1995) (additional views of Sen. Domenici).

61. The Line-Item Veto: A Constitutional Approach: Hearings before the Subcomm. on the Constitution, Federalism, and Property Rights of the Comm. on the Judiciary, U.S. Senate, 104th Cong., 1st Sess. 34 (1995). See also id. at 44–49 (Dellinger's prepared statement's analysis of delegation).

Constitution who had grave doubts about the wisdom of enhanced rescission, agreed that the Court would likely uphold S. 4 as a constitutional delegation of power to the executive branch.[62]

At the end of February, the Senate Budget Committee reported S. 4 out of committee, but without recommendation. This procedural move allowed the bill to move to the next committee, and then to the floor.[63] But the absence of a positive recommendation from the committee signaled that the Act still faced significant problems and lacked the support of some key Republicans like Domenici. The significant sticking point remained the disagreement between enhanced rescission supporters, with Dole and John McCain (R–AZ) at the forefront, and expedited rescission advocates, led by Domenici and supported by many Democrats. The committee adopted two amendments to S. 4. First, Domenici added a sunset to the legislation so that it expired on September 30, 2002, and would have to be re-enacted if Congress wished to continue to delegate cancellation authority to the President. Supporters of the amendment understood that unless the Act included a sunset provision, a repeal of LIVA would presumably be vetoed by the President who would not willingly cede the statutory line item veto power that his predecessors had sought for decades. Thus, if Congress changed its mind and wished to retrieve the power it delegated to the President under LIVA, it would be required to do so with a two-thirds vote of each house. A termination date, however, ensured that it would require an affirmative act of only a majority of both houses to continue the delegation, and the vote would occur after some experience with the new arrangement.

Second, Senators Kent Conrad (D–ND) and Olympia Snow (R–ME) clarified that any money saved by cancellations would be placed in a "lockbox" for deficit reduction. A budgetary lockbox is a method to ensure that any savings effected by a rescission actually reduce the deficit rather than freeing up money for additional spending. The purpose behind delegating cancellation authority to the President was not to change the allocation of money among federal programs, but to allow the President to eliminate special interest and pork-barrel spending so that overall federal spending would be reduced. Using the mechanism of a budgetary lockbox concretely demonstrated that LIVA was a tool to force deficit reduction and lower federal spending.

The Committee on Governmental Affairs also quickly passed S. 4 out of committee, also without recommendation. Democrats on the committee strongly objected to the Chair's decision, supported by the

---

62. Id. at 86.

63. 141 Cong. Rec. S4192 (daily ed. Mar. 20, 1995) (remarks of Sen. Domenici) (noting that had the bill not made it out of Committee, it would have needed 60 votes in order to defeat a point of order, a number it would have been hard-pressed to obtain).

Republican committee members, to oppose all amendments in committee.[64] At this point, Senate leaders were focused on getting the bill to the floor and demonstrating that they could deliver on their promise to enact some sort of line item veto power just as Newt Gingrich's House Republicans had. The two versions of the enhanced rescission bill—the House-passed version and the Senate Budget Committee's version—were very similar except that the House bill included targeted tax benefits in the items eligible for presidential cancellation. Interestingly, S. 14, the expedited rescission bill, which was also reported out of both Senate committees without recommendation, applied to targeted tax benefits that affected 100 or fewer taxpayers.

Days before both bills were to be considered on the Senate floor, the Senate defeated a constitutional amendment to balance the budget by one vote—that of Republican Mark Hatfield (R–OR).[65] Immediately, unflattering comparisons were drawn between Speaker Gingrich, who seemed to be moving the Republican agenda effortlessly through his chamber, and Majority Leader Dole, who did not manage to hold his party together to pass a key part of the Republican agenda—the balanced budget amendment—and could not get his party members to stop squabbling about what form the Line Item Veto Act should take.[66] As one Republican flatly acknowledged, "Bob Dole had to have a victory; he could not lose another one."[67] Dole also faced the threat of a filibuster by Democrats who favored expedited rescission over stronger versions of the line item veto and who knew that, even though both proposals had emerged from committee, Senate leadership would bring S. 4 to the floor first. Not only was Daschle threatening a filibuster, which would require 60 votes to end, but the long-winded Senator Byrd signaled his support of delaying tactics to force compromise.

In a surprise move, Dole chose to discard both forms of rescission and immediately offered on the floor an amendment in the form of a substitute that turned S. 4 into a separate enrollment bill.[68] Under this amendment, after an omnibus bill had been passed, the enrolling clerk would divide the bill into its separate spending items, enroll each of these items into separate bills, and the package of separately-enrolled items would be "deemed" to have been enacted by Congress. They would

64. S. Rep. No. 104–13, at 11–13 (1995) (additional views of Senators Glenn (D–OH), Nunn (D–GA), Pryor (D–AR), and Akaka (D–HI)).

65. S.J. Res. 1, 104th Cong. (1995) (Amendment); 141 Cong. Rec. S3314 (daily ed. Mar. 2, 1995) (vote).

66. Louis Fisher, supra note 3, at 148.

67. Helen Dewar, *Senate Approves Line-Item Veto Bill, 69–29*, Wash. Post, Mar. 24, 1995, at A1.

68. 141 Cong. Rec. S4188 (daily ed. Mar. 20, 1995) (Amendment No. 347).

be presented as individual bills to the President to sign or veto. Dole portrayed his amendment as the product of "the efforts of those on both sides of the aisle to reach a consensus after all these years of arguing."[69] Its main objective, however, was to unite Republicans behind one proposal so that Dole could begin to work to gain the additional votes he needed to head off a filibuster. With only 52 Republicans in the Senate, he would need some Democratic support to ensure passage, a prospect that seemed likely since separate enrollment had been advocated by Biden and others and had received Democratic support when it was considered in 1985.[70] Dole's separate enrollment substitute succeeded in his goal of party unity; for example, Senator Domenici, who had opposed enhanced rescission, supported the compromise. Domenici noted approvingly that "this bill is built around conventional, ordinary vetoes that Presidents have had the authority to do forever." He argued that Dole's approach "significantly expands the President's authority over spending without unduly disrupting this delicate balance of power" between the two branches.[71]

Although separate enrollment had been mentioned by Biden in the hearing on constitutional issues in the Judiciary Subcommittee, there had been no committee hearings on the proposal, nor were there any committee reports to explain the substitute. But Dole argued that the Senate had been considering various versions of a statutory line item veto for nearly a decade and that the deliberations had included discussion of separate enrollment. To this, Senator Byrd responded: "No printed hearings. No committee report. The amendment comes before us much like Minerva, who spring from the brain of Jove, or Aphrodite, who sprang from the ocean foam. It is the product of a collective fertile mind, and from it will flow fertile confrontations, fertile vetoes and, in all likelihood, it will undoubtedly prove to be a fertile field for exploitation by the lawyers of this country."[72] Byrd later referred to separate enrollment as a "hybrid monstrosity."[73] During the course of the Senate debate, the substitute amendment went through significant change so that the bill sent to the conference committee for reconciliation was written in substantial part on the floor rather than through the traditional committee process.

The main objections to the separate enrollment procedure were practical. Congress did not tend to itemize in appropriation bills, a

---

69. 141 Cong. Rec. S4189 (daily ed. Mar. 20, 1995).

70. 141 Cong. Rec. S4194 (daily ed. Mar. 20, 1995) (statement of Sen. Lott (R–MS)) (noting the past support of current Democrats for line item veto legislation).

71. 141 Cong. Rec. S4193 (daily ed. Mar. 20, 1995).

72. 141 Cong. Rec. S4228 (daily ed. Mar. 21, 1995).

73. 141 Cong. Rec. S4412 (daily ed. Mar. 23, 1995).

reality which had led drafters of the enhanced rescission alternative to allow the President to look through the statute to cancel items identified in legislative documents like conference committee reports. But separate enrollment would require that itemization appear in the statute so that a clerk could break the bill into separate paragraphs and sections, making each of these a separately-enrolled bill for the President to sign or veto. Not only was this a daunting logistical task for the clerks, but it also would reduce the flexibility of agencies to transfer money over the course of the year between various programs and activities. If bills were sufficiently detailed for separate enrollment to be meaningful, then any change in the use of money by an agency would require new legislation. Under current practices where itemization appeared in legislative documents but not statutes, reprogramming of funds occurred more informally, typically through agreement between the relevant committees and the agency. This sort of re-allocation of money was controversial, and some supporters of separate enrollment claimed a byproduct of its enactment would be greater congressional involvement in reprogramming decisions.

Senator McCain answered some of the practical objections to separate enrollment by describing an experiment with the previous year's longest appropriation bill. Using a computer program, his staff had divided the bill into 500 separate bills in about four hours.[74] Byrd responded that other appropriation bills would have been divided into 2,000 bills (Energy and Water Development Appropriation Act), 800 bills (VA/HUD Appropriation Act); 757 bills (Agriculture Appropriation Act); and so on. He proposed to call them "act-lettes" or "mini-bills" and claimed that in the preceding year, there would have been 9,625 such "law-lettes" had separate enrollment been in effect.[75] Senator Levin (D–MI) worried that when larger acts were divided into parts by a computer program or the enrolling clerks, some of the individual bills would be nonsensical. For example, many provisions refer back to other provisions in the same act, a drafting convention that makes sense when each provision is part of a larger bill but one that would lead to incomprehensible laws when each provision is enacted separately.[76]

Although supporters of separate enrollment like Senator Biden thought it more likely to be constitutional because it complied with the formal constitutional requirements, others thought the Court might look through the form to the substance of the procedure and hold it circumvented Article V's requirements to adopt a constitutional line item veto.[77]

---

74.   141 Cong. Rec. S4157 (daily ed. Mar. 20, 1995).

75.   141 Cong. Rec. S4231 (daily ed. Mar. 21, 1995).

76.   141 Cong. Rec. S4251 (daily ed. Mar. 21, 1995).

77.   141 Cong. Rec. S4160 (daily ed. Mar. 20, 1995) (statement of Sen. Reid (D–NV)) (objecting primarily to Congressional delegation of bill division to enrolling clerks). See 131

A supporter of the separate enrollment amendment, Senator Dan Coats (R–IN), included in the *Congressional Record* a lengthy analysis of its constitutionality of prepared by Johnny Killian, an analyst with the CRS.[78] The key constitutional question was whether the deeming provision in the separate enrollment bill was constitutional. "How is it, then, it may be asked, that separate bills, which in their subsequent form have not passed both Houses, may be deemed bills that have passed both Houses and are then properly presented to the President?" This report noted the traditional judicial deference to Congress when a house has exercised its authority under the Constitution's rulemaking provision,[79] and it observed that the courts might well use the political question doctrine to avoid looking behind the formal appearance of enrollment that all the separate bills would exhibit and thus avoid questioning the manner in which they were actually enacted.

The CRS report also examined the merits of any constitutional arguments, both because courts might not defer and because Congress is supposed to exercise independent judgment on the propriety of legislation. It noted that the way the omnibus bills were broken into parts was the most problematic aspect of the process. Each separate bill had to conform to some part of the omnibus bill so that the smaller bills were identical to the bill previously passed. That would require Congress to change the way it appropriated, eschewing lump sum appropriations for more detailed bills. Leaving too much to the discretion of enrolling clerks might be viewed as an unconstitutional delegation of lawmaking power to an agent of the legislature.[80] The report concluded that because there were not many applicable precedents, a conclusion about the constitutionality of separate enrollment could not be confidently reached. "In the end, Congress must exercise a constitutional judgment when deciding on passage of the proposal." A great deal of the debate over the six days of Senate deliberation focused on the constitutional issues raised by separate enrollment, providing both the views of the Senators themselves and views of legal scholars who had provided their assessments of the constitutional issues.[81]

Cong. Rec. S4232, 4245 (daily ed. Mar. 21, 1995) (Senator Byrd's reference to Walter Dellinger's statement before the Judiciary Subcommittee).

78. 141 Cong. Rec. S4214–17 (daily ed. Mar. 21, 1995) (providing all quotes from the CRS document in text).

79. U.S. Const., Art. 1, § 5, cl. 2. The deeming provision of the separate enrollment provision was an internal matter, "subject to alteration by simple resolution at any time in either House." 141 Cong. Rec. S4216 (daily ed. Mar. 21, 1995).

80. See Bowsher v. Synar, 478 U.S. 714 (1978) (requiring that Congress delegate only to executive branch officials power to execute laws that it passes).

81. See, e.g., 141 Cong. Rec. S4445–50 (daily ed. Mar. 23, 1995) (Sen. Moynihan (D–NY) inserting letter of Professor Michael J. Gerhardt and Report of the Association of the Bar of the City of New York into the *Record*).

The details of Dole's substitute amendment reflected some of the deliberation in the House and Senate committees on the enhanced rescission proposal. First, his separate enrollment proposal allowed the President to veto targeted tax benefits and also new direct spending programs, an addition targeted at changes in entitlement programs that would increase federal spending.[82] His substitute defined "targeted tax benefit" more broadly than the House version. A targeted tax benefit was a provision that lost revenue and had "the practical effect of providing more favorable tax treatment to a particular taxpayer or limited group of taxpayers when compared with other similarly situated taxpayers."[83] Supporters of this broader language argued it would reduce games by sophisticated taxpayers, aided by their wily tax lawyers, to make sure that any tax provision benefited at least 101 taxpayers and thus escaped the scope of the House's version of LIVA. Second, Dole retained a sunset provision, although he moved the expiration forward to September 30, 2000.[84] This would allow five years experience with LIVA before Congress would consider whether or not to re-enact it.

Dole still had to fight off an amendment on the floor to change the proposal back to an expedited rescission, this time made by Senator Daschle. Daschle defended his amendment as simpler than separate enrollment, clearly constitutional, and more consistent with majority rule than enhanced rescission because a majority of Congress would have to agree to a cancellation before it could take effect. Hard-liner McCain dismissed Daschle's amendment as an unprincipled alternative that represented "some kind of sham or charade or false line-item veto."[85] Supporters of Dole's approach also noted that the Democratic President had indicated that he wanted the strongest power possible, thereby undermining the Democrats' attempt to characterize the choice between the two versions of the statutory line item veto as a partisan issue. Ultimately, the expedited rescission amendment was tabled by a vote of 62–38, a parliamentary move that effectively kills a proposal. No Republican voted in favor of the expedited rescission proposal, even though it was based on Domenici's S. 14; ten Democrats crossed over to oppose Daschle's amendment. This vote was noteworthy not only because it defeated the Democratic alternative, but also because it demonstrated that Dole had the 60 votes necessary to cut off a filibuster.

---

82. 141 Cong. Rec. S4484 (daily ed. Mar. 23, 1995) (§ 2(b) of the substitute).

83. 141 Cong. Rec. S4485 (daily ed. Mar. 23, 1995) (§ 5(5)(B) of the substitute). The final version slightly changed the revenue loss requirement but maintained the definition of targeted tax benefits.

84. 141 Cong. Rec. S4301 (daily ed. Mar. 22, 1995) (Amendment No. 403).

85. 141 Cong. Rec. S4154 (daily ed. Mar. 20, 1995).

The Senate agreed to several amendments of the Dole substitute. Perhaps most importantly, the Senate adopted an expedited judicial review section very similar to the one adopted on the House floor. Its author, Paul Simon (D–IL), explained that the Congress should not "live in limbo. We have people like John Killlian of CRS and Prof. Larry Tribe of Harvard who believe it is constitutional. You have others like Louis Fisher of CRS and Walter Dellinger, who believe it is not constitutional. I do not know who is right. The courts have to make that determination."[86] At Senator McCain's urging, a severability clause was also added to the Act so that if a minor provision was declared unconstitutional, the rest of LIVA would remain in effect.[87] This expedited judicial review section was added notwithstanding the relatively lengthy Senate debate about constitutional issues—a debate that in included legal opinions from CRS and other constitutional law experts, as well as extended analysis from senators such as Byrd, Coats, and Biden. In the end, there were sufficient reservations about separate enrollment, and a majority voted in favor of the Simon amendment.

After the defeat of Daschle's expedited rescission substitute, everyone knew that the Senate would pass separate enrollment, and the two very different approaches to LIVA would have to be reconciled in conference committee. A few other amendments were added to Dole's substitute before its inevitable passage. The Senate accepted a lockbox amendment offered by Senator Exon (D–NE) that would ensure money saved by cancellations be used for deficit reduction not new spending.[88] This amendment, as well as the debate, reflected the view that LIVA was designed as a tool to rein in spending and reduce the deficit. Like their counterparts in the House, Senators did not view LIVA as encouraging the President to cancel large spending items. Rather, they viewed this budget weapon as one mainly designed to reduce pork-barrel spending and tax subsidies that benefited the few at the expense of all taxpayers. McCain argued that the President would "take a sterner view of public expenditures—be they in the form of appropriations or tax concessions—which serve the interests of only a few or which cannot be reasonably argued as worth the expense given our current financial difficulties," but he did not expect the line item veto authority to solve the country's deficit problem.[89] As in the House, supporters hoped LIVA would make tax and spending provisions benefiting organized special interests more visible because they could be singled out by the President.

---

86. 141 Cong. Rec. S4244 (daily ed. Mar. 21, 1995).

87. 141 Cong. Rec. S4259 (daily ed. Mar. 21, 1995).

88. 141 Cong. Rec. S4326 (daily ed. Mar. 22, 1995) (acceptance of Exon lockbox amendment).

89. 141 Cong. Rec. S4474 (daily ed. Mar. 23, 1995).

Even though most lawmakers clearly understood that the authority given to the President could not be used to implement sweeping changes in spending, some supporters characterized LIVA as a way, in the words of Fred Thompson (R–TN), to "change fundamentally the way we make decisions and the way we spend taxpayers' dollars." In the same breath, Thompson acknowledged that the bill was aimed at "targeted items, specifically designated items that go to provide a benefit for a particular class of individuals, small group of individuals, which cannot be defined in any sense in the national interest."[90] The rhetoric about fundamental change was, like the title of the Act, doubtlessly designed for public consumption, particularly because the Senate had failed to deliver on the plank in the Contract with America that would have represented significant change in budget practice, the constitutional amendment requiring a balanced budget. Senator Coats acknowledged that LIVA was hardly the extensive change that the balanced budget amendment would have been. "The line-item veto is a pale shadow in comparison to the balanced budget, but it is the only other game in town—the only other game in town other than what we have been doing for 25 straight years, and that is running deficits."[91]

Nonetheless, some opponents of LIVA seized on the rhetoric characterizing separate enrollment as a monumental change in budgeting and governance. As the debate drew to a close, Senator Byrd and other Democrats continued to object to the Act as an unprecedented shift in the balance of power. Byrd's oration was lengthy and dramatic. The old warrior, fighting a cold, began by declaring: "Oh, that my voice would carry to the hills or the mountains, and though I had to be brought into this Chamber on a stretcher, I would still fight for this Constitution and its system. This is not a process. Process. This is the Constitution that we are talking of here. This is the constitutional system that we are about to imperil."[92] In the end, Bryd, in a speech full of references to Rome, the Founders, and his own book on the Constitution, concluded that the great leaders of the Senate would be "ashamed, ashamed, to see the Senate without a fight, and a long fight, accept a piece of junk like this."[93] Despite his rhetoric, on March 23, S. 4, now called The Separate Enrollment and Line Item Veto Act of 1995, passed the Senate with a decisive vote of 69 in favor and 31 opposed; all the Republicans and 17 Democrats supported the Senate's version of LIVA. Byrd's impassioned opposition suggested that the fight was not over: he would continue to

---

90. 141 Cong. Rec. S4220 (daily ed. Mar. 21, 1995).

91. 141 Cong. Rec. S4230 (daily ed. Mar. 21, 1995).

92. 141 Cong. Rec. S4226 (daily ed. Mar. 21, 1995).

93. 141 Cong. Rec. S4472 (daily ed. Mar. 23, 1995).

rail against whatever emerged from Congress, and he signaled that he would resort to the courts if he lost in the legislature.

Conference Committee: Choosing Enhanced Rescission

The bicameralism requirement of the Constitution mandates that a bill pass both houses in the same form before it can be sent to the President for his signature. Conference committees, made up of members from both the House and the Senate, work to reconcile two versions of a bill and send a consensus proposal, explained in a conference report, to each house for passage. The conference committee for the Line Item Veto Act faced a daunting task. The two versions of the bill were very different, and enhanced rescission, the approach taken by the House, had been discarded in the Senate because it faced some Republican opposition and was vulnerable to a filibuster threat. On the other hand, the House had not considered separate enrollment, and many were dubious that the process could work given longstanding congressional practice of enacting bills with lump sum appropriations and leaving the details to the legislative materials.

Chairman Clinger made clear that he expected a difficult conference. In a statement on the House floor, he referred to the Senate version as a "weaker bill" and a logistical challenge because it "would require the enrollment of thousands of bills to pass appropriations in discrete line items requiring thousands of signatures and guaranteeing future Presidents an amazing case of writer's cramps as they deal with this as well as creating some significant amount of paperwork."[94] But he acknowledged that the House version was vulnerable to a potential constitutional challenge, so neither bill was unproblematic. Clinger would serve as Chairman of the conference committee and lead the House side of negotiations with Dole and the Senate leadership.

It took five months just to appoint members to the conference committee. The delay was caused by the distance between the two bills, as well as the worry of some Republicans that whatever they passed would empower a Democratic President with different budget priorities. Some congressional observers theorized that Republicans were particularly hesitant to hand President Clinton the line-item veto in time for him to use it during the fiscal year 1996 appropriation cycle.[95] In August, Senate Democrats tried to turn up the heat by forcing a vote on a nonbinding sense-of-the-Senate resolution that they attached to the Energy and Water Development Appropriations Act. The amendment observed that "the line item veto was a major plank in the House majority's

---

94. 141 Cong. Rec. H5091 (daily ed. May 17, 1995).

95. Andrew Taylor, *GOP Renews Drive on Line-Item Veto*, Cong. Q., Aug. 5, 1995, at 2346.

'Contract with America' and has received strong bipartisan support,"
but that the House had failed to ask for a conference or appoint
conferees once the Senate demanded a conference. It strongly hinted
that the delay was designed to deprive the President of the tool until
after the enactment of all budget legislation for fiscal year 1996 and even
noted that "the House majority leadership has publicly cast doubt on the
prospects for a conference on S.4 this year."[96] Unresolved gridlock was
unacceptable, however. Dole needed the legislation for his presidential
bid; Republican Senators wanted to pass a piece of budget reform
legislation to regain ground after having killed the balanced budget
amendment; and Gingrich and his House Republicans were increasingly
under pressure to deliver on a plank of their Contract.

By September, a conference committee had been appointed, chaired
by Clinger for the House and led by Ted Stevens (R–AK) for the Senate.
OMB Director Alice Rivlin wrote to Senator Dole that the President
preferred the House's enhanced rescission proposal to the Senate's
separate enrollment. She provided recommendations to improve the
legislation, some of which were reflected in the final version. Rivlin
supported the Senate's decision to apply the line item veto power to
direct spending as well as discretionary spending and targeted tax
benefits; she urged that lawmakers be careful in their use of terminology, avoiding words like "veto" and "repeal" and using traditional words
of impoundment like "suspend"; and she urged inclusion of a severability provision.[97]

Negotiations between the two houses did not move quickly. Although presidential politics played a role in the slow pace of bargaining,
the rift between Senate Republicans also made the conference unusually
challenging. On one side, Senators Stevens and Domenici had long
opposed expedited rescission, while, on the other side, Senators McCain
and Coats, supported by Dole and the leadership, thought enhanced
rescission was too weak.[98] The logjam broke in November when House
Republicans offered a compromise based largely on the enhanced rescission model of H.R. 2, but accepting some elements of the Senate proposal
such as including direct spending within the Act's scope and the lockbox
amendment.[99] The Joint Committee on Taxation (JCT), a committee
with members from the Senate Finance Committee and House Ways and
Means Committee, had also drafted a more workable definition of

---

96. H.R. 1905, 104th Cong., § 512 (1995).

97. Joint Appendix, at 91, Raines v. Byrd, 521 U.S. 811 (1997) (Letter from Alice
Rivlin, to Robert Dole (Sept. 11, 1995)), *available at* 1997 WL 33487254.

98. Interview with Monty Tripp, former counsel to House Government Reform and
Oversight Committee (Apr. 11, 2005).

99. See VIRGINIA A. MCMURTRY, CONGRESSIONAL RESEARCH SERVICE ISSUE BRIEF FOR CON-
GRESS: ITEM VETO AND EXPANDED IMPOUNDMENT PROPOSALS 7 (Mar. 1, 2001).

targeted tax benefit. Stevens, under pressure from Senate leadership, announced he would support enhanced rescission as long as the conference agreement included a sunset provision.[100]

Despite Stevens' concession, the conference report was not immediately forthcoming. After weeks of inaction, President Clinton called for passage of LIVA in his January 1996 State of the Union address.[101] Negotiations resumed seriously once Congress returned to work later that month, and Republicans reached a compromise in mid-March. Not only did the Senate Republicans accede to the House version, but Clinton and Dole agreed to delay the effective date of the Act until January 1, 1997, after the elections and at the end of Clinton's first term. That held out the prospect (although increasingly unlikely as the 1996 campaign developed) that Dole would be the first President to use cancellation under LIVA. The conference report that provided the terms of the agreement and the final legislative language was filed on March 21, 1996, nearly a year after the Senate passed its version of LIVA.[102] Representative Robert L. Ehrlich, Jr. (R–MD) explained the agreement to adopt enhanced rescission, " 'We're one team, one team' that's all we hear these days. It kind of happened overnight. There's obviously been some kind of meeting of the minds between our top leaders in the House and Dole."[103] A one-time Senate opponent of enhanced rescission and member of the conference committee that adopted the approach, Thad Cochran (R–MS), summarized his group's retreat as a decision to agree to "[w]hatever Bob Dole wants to do."[104]

The conference report revealed the purpose of LIVA: "to promote savings by placing the onus on Congress to overturn the President's cancellations of spending and limited tax benefits."[105] In some ways, the scope of LIVA was broader than any other impoundment authority previously delegated to the President. He could cancel discretionary spending items, new limited tax benefits, and new direct spending. Items of discretionary spending could be identified in an appropriation law or in accompanying committee reports or joint explanatory statements, eliminating the need for statutory line itemization that separate enroll-

---

100. Andrew Taylor, *Senate May Give In on Line-Item Veto*, Cong. Q., Nov. 11, 1995, at 3446.

101. President William J. Clinton, State of the Union Address, Jan. 23, 1996, reprinted in 1 Public Papers of the Presidents of the United States: William J. Clinton 79, 85 (1997).

102. H.R. Conf. Rep. No. 104–491 (1996).

103. Karen Hosler, *Dole Unites GOP Forces in Congress with One Goal; Leadership Retools for White House Bid*, Balt. Sun, Mar. 24, 1996, at 1A.

104. Andrew Taylor, *GOP Negotiators Agree on Line-Item Veto*, Cong. Q., Mar. 23, 1996, at 779, 780.

105. H.R. Conf. Rep. No. 104–491, at 16.

ment demanded. The conference committee adopted an entirely new method to identify limited tax benefits. They were defined as revenue-losing provisions that provided a benefit to 100 or fewer beneficiaries, unless all similarly-situated taxpayers received the same treatment. Unlike discretionary and direct spending items, the President could only cancel limited tax benefits that were identified as such in a list of eligible provisions assembled by the Joint Committee on Taxation and accompanying the conference report of any revenue bill. The JCT also had the option of issuing a report stating that a revenue bill contained no limited tax benefits, in which case the President could not cancel anything. Only if the JCT failed to issue any report at all could the President use his discretion to determine which provisions were limited under LIVA and therefore eligible for cancellation.

The President could exercise his cancellation power only after signing and thereby enacting the bill containing items. He could cancel only dollar amounts of discretionary spending, direct spending items (a specific provision of newly-enacted law that would increase the deficit), or limited tax benefits (identified as such by the JCT). He had five days to exercise his authority, and he had to determine that each cancellation would reduce the deficit, "not impair any essential Government functions" and "not harm the national interest."[106] He was to inform Congress of all cancellations of items contained in a particular law in one special message that would identify the canceled items in that law, explain the cancellations, and provide "all facts, circumstances, and considerations relating to or bearing upon the proposed rescission[s] or the reservation[s]."[107]

The conference report is replete with discussions of the cancellation authority clearly designed to deflect judicial challenge of the delegation. For example, it noted that the definition of items susceptible to cancellation "make clear that the President may only cancel the entire dollar amount, the specific obligation to pay, or the specific tax benefit. ... This means that the President cannot use this authority to modify or alter any aspect of the underlying law, including any restriction or condition on the expenditure of budget authority.... If the President desires a broader result, then the President must either ask Congress to modify the law or exercise the President's constitutional power to veto the legislation in its entirety."[108] In another passage, the conferees described the power delegated as "narrowly defined and provided within specific limits."[109] Finally, the report noted that the definitions it drafted

---

106.   2 U.S.C. § 691(a)(3)(A).

107.   2 U.S.C. § 683(a)(5).

108.   H.R. Conf. Rep. 104–491, at 20.

109.   Id. at 19.

signaled the intent of the conferees that "the President may use the cancellation authority to surgically terminate federal budget obligations."[110]

Heeding the advice of Dellinger and Rivlin, the conference report was more careful in the language used to define the cancellation power. It did not include terms like "repeal" or "veto" in anything other than the title of the Act and instead relied as much as possible on terms long used in the budget context. That strategy was possible in the case of discretionary spending because this had been the traditional target of impoundment authority in the past. The conference report noted that in this context, to cancel means "to rescind. . . . The term rescind is clearly understood through long experience between the Executive and Legislative branches with respect to appropriated funds."[111] Unfortunately, there was no long experience with respect to cancellations of direct spending or limited tax benefits, and there it was defined as preventing the provisions from "having legal force or effect." The conference report clarified that these definitions were intended to ensure that the power given to the President was "very narrow" and that he could not use it to "change, alter, or modify any other aspect" of the underlying law.[112]

The conference agreement retained the Senate's addition of a sunset, but set it at January 1, 2005. The report noted that "[g]iven the significance of this delegation, the conference report includes a sunset of [the cancellation] authority."[113] Pursuant to the agreement reached by the two presidential candidates, President Clinton and Majority Leader Dole, the Act would not take effect until January 1, 1997. The effective and termination dates meant that the Act would be effective for eight years, if it survived any judicial challenge. Another Senate provision retained in the conference agreement was the lockbox provision to ensure any savings from the cancellations would reduce the deficit and not become available for new spending or tax benefits.

Just as in the House version, cancellations would take effect unless Congress passed a disapproval resolution within 30 days of receiving the President's special message. Since the President would undoubtedly veto the disapproval bill, the money would be spent or the tax benefit would take effect only with two-thirds support in each house. LIVA provided for expedited procedures to consider disapproval bills, including time limits for debate in the Senate, and it severely reduced the ability to amend the disapproval bills in either chamber. If Congress failed to pass a disapproval bill within the 30 days allowed, the items in the Presi-

---

110. Id. at 20.
111. Id. at 29.
112. Id.
113. Id. at 19.

dent's special message would be canceled, effective on the date the special message had been received by the House and Senate.

Finally, the conference report version of LIVA included an expedited judicial review provision, although, unlike the House version, it did not require a three-judge panel to hear the initial challenge. Any member of Congress or any individual adversely affected by the statute could challenge its constitutionality in the U.S. District Court for the District of Columbia. The Act authorized a direct appeal of the district court decision to the Supreme Court and instructed both courts to expedite their consideration. The severability clause added in the Senate was not part of the conference agreement, and none of the official documents include an explanation for the omission. A staffer who was involved in the conference committee negotiations explained that Senator Stevens was the main supporter in the conference committed of the severability provision, and he backed away from insisting on its inclusion when legislative lawyers provided an opinion that such clauses were "irrelevant" in litigation.[114]

The Senate moved first on the conference report, taking it up on March 27, 1996. One of the first speakers, Senator Domenici, had opposed enhanced rescission a year before when the Senate had first considered the line item veto proposal in the 104th Congress. Although he clearly understood that the conference report "essentially adopts the House's enhanced rescission approach," he indicated that he had changed his position and decided that "the time is now to give line item veto a chance, to get it over to the President who will sign it."[115] His speech and other by Republicans who had opposed enhanced rescission in the past signaled that Republican resistance in the Senate to enhanced rescission had crumbled, so the only remaining question was whether Byrd and the Democrats had the strength to filibuster the compromise.

Byrd spoke at length, but he lacked the support to mount a filibuster. After an unsuccessful motion to recommit the bill (a parliamentary tactic to kill the conference report and force renegotiation), the result in the Senate was a foregone conclusion. The conference report passed 69 to 31. A day later the House followed suit, a less surprising outcome because the conference report so closely followed the House-passed version of LIVA. Again, there was an unsuccessful motion to recommit

---

114. Interview with Monty Tripp, supra note 98. See also WILLIAM N. ESKRIDGE, JR., PHILIP P. FRICKEY & ELIZABETH GARRETT, CASES AND MATERIALS ON LEGISLATION: STATUTES AND THE CREATION OF PUBLIC POLICY 888–89 3d ed. (2001) (discussing judicial approach); Israel E. Friedman, *Inseverability Clauses in Statutes*, 64 U. Chi. L. Rev. 903, 904–07 (1997) (student note discussing same).

115. 141 Cong. Rec. S2932–3 (daily ed. Mar. 27, 1996).

the conference report, followed almost immediately by final passage of LIVA by a vote of 328 in favor and only 91 voting against it.

On April 9, 1996, President Clinton signed the Line Item Veto Act into law, characterizing it as a bipartisan accomplishment long sought by Presidents. He stated: "For years, presidents of both parties have pounded this very desk in frustration at having to sign necessary legislation that contained special interest boondoggles, tax loopholes and pure pork. The line item veto will give us a chance to change that, to permit presidents to better represent the public interest by cutting waste, protecting taxpayers and balancing the budget. . . . This law gives the president tools to cut wasteful spending, and, even more important, it empowers our citizens, for the exercise of this veto or even the possibility of its exercise will throw a spotlight of public scrutiny onto the darkest corners of the federal budget."[116] He would not be able to immediately use the new cancellation power because it took effect only the next year, a compromise he said he had accepted without hesitation in order to gain the power for the Executive Branch. In the end, President Clinton would be the only President to exercise cancellation authority under LIVA before the Supreme Court struck it down as unconstitutional.

LIVA: Hardly an Unprecedented Shift of Power

The main theme sounded by opponents of the stronger versions of LIVA—enhanced rescission and separate enrollment—was that the budget reform would shift substantial power from Congress to the President. Byrd sounded the alarm in the final debate on the conference report: "The legislative branch sleeps but there stands the President at the head of the executive branch, ever ready . . . to seize upon every advantage which presents itself for the extension and expansion of the executive power. And now, we are preparing here in the Senate to augment the already enormous power of an all-powerful chief executive [by shifting power to him] that will be used against the legislative branch, to be used against the elected representatives of the people. . . . It is as if the legislative branch has been seized with a collective madness."[117] Surely even Senator Byrd knew that this rhetoric was hyperbole. LIVA was not a sign of legislative madness; on the contrary, the design of the enhanced rescission bill demonstrates that lawmakers can be coolly rational when they delegate power to the executive that might weaken their relative clout in the long run. LIVA was constructed so that Congress kept great control over the President's future use of the cancellation power, al-

---

116. William J. Clinton, Statement on Signing the Line Item Veto Act, 1 PUB. PAPERS 559 (Apr. 9, 1996).

117. 142 Cong. Rec. S2940 (daily ed. Mar. 27, 1996).

though not through the traditional mechanism of substantive standards set forth in the statute.[118]

One way for Congress to control the extent of a delegation is to set out "intelligible principles"[119] in the statutory text that constrain the executive branch's discretion. Congress then relies on third parties, like the courts, to police the executive branch by applying the standards provided in the substantive law. LIVA provided little by the way of intelligible principles. The text of the statute required only that the President find that a cancellation would reduce the deficit (which all cancellations necessarily did, at least as long as the country was running a deficit), would "not impair any Government functions," and would "not harm the national interest." This directive boils down to "Don't do anything terrible." It provides no positive guidance to the President during the five days he considers which items in a spending or tax bill to cancel.

The statutory standards can be supplemented by the congressional purposes behind enactment that are revealed in the legislative history and the context of enactment. Mirroring the debate, the conference report cited the growing public outcry for "greater fiscal accountability" and indicated that the cancellation authority should be used "to eliminate wasteful federal spending and to cancel special tax breaks."[120] The main target seemed to be pork-barrel programs or rifle shot tax subsidies. But there is no generally accepted or objective definition of pork barrel spending. One person's "pork" is another person's vital federal program aimed at meeting important public policy goals. Although the statutory definition of limited tax benefit in the House version and the conference report, as well as the debate surrounding the meaning of spending "items," suggested that Congress was focused mainly on narrowly targeted programs, not all such spending is necessarily unjustified. For example, tax subsidies for the blind, while limited to a relatively small, discrete group of taxpayers, might be universally acknowledged as good public policy, while some large public works projects, such as spending for particular weapons systems, might be considered wasteful. Although LIVA directs the President to consider "the legislative history, construction, and purposes of the law which contains [the spending items, and] any specific sources of information referenced in such law or

---

118. Some of this discussion is drawn from Elizabeth Garrett, *Accountability and Restraint: The Federal Budget Process and the Line Item Veto Act*, 20 Cardozo L. Rev. 871 (1999).

119. See J.W. Hampton Jr. & Co. v. United States, 276 U.S. 394, 409 (1928) (requiring Congress to lay down "an intelligible principle to which the person or body authorized to fix such rates is directed to conform").

120. H.R. Conf. Rep. No. 104–491, at 15 (1996).

... the best available information,"[121] it is very unlikely that congressional materials relating to an appropriation or revenue bill will label particular items as wasteful, unnecessary, or pork-barrel. On the contrary, the legislative history is likely to contain explanations for each item designed to characterize it in its best light. In the end, the guidance from legislative history adds very little to the relatively empty statutory standards.

LIVA also required that the President provide reasons for his cancellations in his special message. Although the Supreme Court subsequently ruled that delegation concerns cannot be answered by standards adopted by the executive branch to limit its discretion,[122] the requirement that the President justify his decisions could reduce the chance of arbitrary determinations. In addition, the explanations could aid Congress in exercising its oversight of the cancellation authority. Indeed, there was evidence that lawmakers used the information provided in President Clinton's special messages when they considered disapproval bills. In the one year that LIVA was in force, Clinton canceled 82 items in eleven laws. Thirty-eight of these cancellations, totaling $287 million, related to items in the Military Construction Appropriations Act of 1998.[123] In his special message, Clinton informed Congress that these projects met three additional substantive criteria: they would not improve the quality of life for members of the military; they had not been requested by the military; and they did not contribute to national defense. When Congress overrode these rescissions by veto-proof majorities in both houses,[124] members stated that they had applied these standards to the canceled items and found that all passed muster.

Nothing in the Act required the President to set forth additional standards to constrain his use of the cancellation authority, and after Clinton's experience with the military construction bill cancellations, a President might think twice about fuller explanations. So substantive standards—whether provided in the Act, the legislative history, or subse-

---

121. 2 U.S.C. § 691(b)

122. Whitman v. American Trucking Assns., Inc., 531 U.S. 457, 472–73 (2001). At the time LIVA was enacted, some influential administrative law scholars had long argued that the executive branch could respond to constitutional delegation concerns by providing more specific guidance to constrain discretion. See, e.g., KENNETH C. DAVIS, ADMINISTRATIVE LAW TREATISE 1 211–12 (2d ed. 1978). *Whitman* decisively rejected this argument, at least as it pertains to the constitutional nondelegation doctrine. But see Lisa Schultz Bressman, *Beyond Accountability: Arbitrariness and Legitimacy in the Administrative State*, 78 N.Y.U. L. Rev. 461, 529–33 (2003) (arguing that the Administrative Procedure Act, which would not apply to presidential action like LIVA's cancellation authority, should be interpreted to require executive branch specification under some circumstances).

123. See Cancellation Nos. 97–4 to–41, 62 Fed Reg. 52,452 (1997).

124. See H.R. 2631, 105th Cong. (1997) (disapproving the cancellations transmitted by the President on October 6, 1997, regarding Pub. Law 105–45).

quently in special messages—were not the main tool through which
Congress exercised control over the delegated power. Congress retained
continuing control, however, because it could always exempt spending or
tax bills from the President's cancellation power, and, even more importantly, Congress retained the power to determine what provisions would
be considered items susceptible to rescission. Moreover, House amendments retained by the conference committee clarified that the cancellation power could not be used to suspend conditions of spending or nullify
substantive legislation sometimes included in spending bills. Congress
presumably learned these techniques from state legislatures, which had
long manipulated the scope of "items" in order to reduce the vitality of
the Chief Executive's line item veto.[125]

Because the President had to sign, and thereby enact, any bill before
he could cancel items in it, Congress could effectively specify in the
spending bill itself that particular projects could not be canceled or even
that the entire bill was "cancellation-proof." Such a straightforward
waiver of LIVA by Congress was probably unlikely, however. First, most
such bills could have been filibustered by LIVA supporters in the Senate.
All appropriation bills can be filibustered, and some tax and direct
spending bills are subject to the filibuster, although many of those
vehicles now take the form of budget reconciliation bills which are
governed by time limits on Senate debate.[126] Thus, a determined minority of fiscal conservatives could block most, but not all, explicit waivers.
Second, the political costs of waivers might be substantial. A waiver
would only highlight any exempted project or bill, and voters might
perceive a waiver as inconsistent with fiscal discipline and accountability. Of course, even explicit waivers might be overlooked in some of the
massive omnibus appropriation bills passed hurriedly in the final days of
a legislative session. Furthermore, waivers attached to large projects that
lawmakers believed could be persuasively portrayed to voters as important policy and not pork might provoke very little political fall-out.[127]

But lawmakers did not have to rely only on high-profile waivers of
LIVA to insulate spending programs or tax subsidies. They had more
subtle tools at their disposal. With respect to discretionary spending
items, LIVA required that the President cancel the dollar amount of an
item entirely; he could not reduce an appropriation. Congress could not
defeat the cancellation authority by appropriating in large lump sums,
because LIVA allowed the President to look through a lump sum in a

---

125. See Briffault, supra note 17, at 1181; LOUIS FISHER, STATE TECHNIQUES TO BLUNT THE
GOVERNOR'S ITEM-VETO POWER (1996) (CRS Report No. 96–996 GOV).

126. See SARAH A. BINDER & STEVEN S. SMITH, POLITICS OR PRINCIPLE: FILIBUSTER IN THE
UNITED STATES SENATE 192 (1997).

127. See Robert D. Reischauer, *Line Item Beef: Little Beef and Mostly Bun*, Wash.
Post, Apr. 10, 1996, at 1C.

statute and identify particular items listed in managers' joint explanatory statements and committee reports. To understand how this look-through provision worked, consider an appropriation bill that provided budget authority of $50 million for agricultural research. The committee report might instruct the Department of Agriculture to allocate $400,000 of this lump sum to wheat utilization research at the University of Oklahoma. In that case, the President could cancel the $400,000 project without canceling the rest of the research projects funded by the lump sum. The ability to use legislative materials to delineate items was a major consideration in the conference committee's decision to discard the Senate's separate enrollment format for the enhanced rescission mechanism favored by the House.

The problem with this look-through mechanism, designed to facilitate the use of the cancellation authority, is that Congress could legislate in lump sums and specify funding for particular projects in ways that would be immune from rescission. For example, the committee report could instruct in one sentence that $4 million of the lump sum should go to wheat utilization research conducted by universities in several states. This strategy would force the President to cancel more projects with wider consequences, thereby irritating more members of Congress and their constituents. Or Congress could dispense with detailed instructions in the committee reports or joint explanatory statements in the *Congressional Record* and communicate its preferences on itemization through means not listed in LIVA. If the committee wanted to assure that the Agriculture Department allocated $400,000 of the lump sum to O.U. but protect that project from cancellation, it could send a letter, signed by all committee members, to the relevant agency official. If backed by enough lawmakers, such a letter could provide virtually the same incentive to the agency to comply with congressional wishes as does a committee report. Neither has the force of law. Executive branch officials follow committee instructions, in whatever their form, because they know they must return to the same committee for funding in the next fiscal year and because some of the lawmakers also sit on the committees with oversight responsibilities. As Senator Sam Nunn (D–GA) observed during debate on separate enrollment, "The likely effect of the [Dole] substitute will be to drive pork into underground shelters where it will be hidden from scrutiny. ... [T]he really egregious earmarks will no longer be set forth in committee reports. The earmarks will be described in ... letters from committees, or even phone calls from committee chairmen to the heads of agencies."[128] This observation is true of the enacted LIVA as well.

---

128. 141 Cong. Rec. S4344 (daily ed. Mar. 22, 1995).

Congress' continuing control over cancellation of limited tax benefits was even stronger. First, with respect to both tax benefits and direct spending programs, the President could only cancel new items. Unlike appropriations which must be re-enacted each year, tax laws and entitlement programs do not have to be revisited each year but continue to operate without further action by Congress. The President was not given authority to re-assess existing programs and cancel items that were already part of the law. Second, the conference committee adopted new language concerning limited tax benefits that severely circumscribed the President's cancellation power over tax expenditures. The President was restricted to canceling only provisions that the JCT had expressly identified during the legislative process. While Congress was considering a tax bill, the JCT had two options: It could state that LIVA would apply to specifically-identified limited tax benefits, or it could state that LIVA would not apply to any provision in the Act. In the latter case, the President could not cancel any provision in the bill even if it met the definition of a "limited tax benefit." In short, any provision that JCT did not list was immune from cancellation.[129] Only if the Committee failed to produce any statement at all could the President independently determine whether the bill contained limited tax benefits and then choose to cancel some or all of those provisions.

In the only experience with the cancellation authority in the context of tax bills, JCT exercised its authority to list limited tax benefits vulnerable to cancellation. With respect to the Taxpayer Relief Act of 1997, the Joint Committee on Taxation listed eighty of the provisions as limited tax benefits,[130] a miniscule number in a law requiring 550 pages of general explanation.[131] Among this relatively small universe of tax benefits eligible for rescission, presumably there were some that the President supported and thus were not likely targets for cancellation. In the end, the President canceled only two of the eighty eligible benefits, describing the disfavored subsidies as "opportunities for abusive tax planning" and likely to result in "tax-haven abuses."[132] One of these cancellations, a tax benefit permitting preferential capital gains treat-

---

129.   Again, lawmakers were aware of the impact of this provision. See 141 Cong. Rec. S2992 (daily ed. Mar. 29, 1996) (statement of Sen. McCain) ("The JCT declaration is more than a piece of paper. It is a declaration of immunity for what could very well be a limited tax benefit. It is an inoculation against a Presidential line-item veto. It is the magic bullet for tax lobbyists.").

130.   See Conference Report on H.R. 2014, Taxpayer Relief Act of 1997, 142 Cong. Rec. H6623, 6640–43 (Memorandum of Kenneth J. Kies to Members of the Conference Committee Regarding Provisions in H.R. 2014 Which Are Subject to the Line Item Veto).

131.   See Staff of Joint. Comm. on Taxation, 105th Cong., General Explanation of Tax Legislation Enacted in 1997 (Comm. Print 1997) (JCS–23–97).

132.   See Cancellation Notices 97–1 and 97–2, H.R. Doc. No. 105–116 (1997).

ment to sales of certain stock to farmers' cooperatives, provided the basis for one of the challenges heard in *Clinton v. City of New York*.

Congress self-consciously protected itself in another way. The conference committee, following the lead of the Senate, provided that LIVA would terminate after eight years and would continue only if Congress re-enacted the authority. This sunset provision ensured that a majority of Congress could reclaim the authority it had delegated if it determined that LIVA caused an undesirable shift in the balance of power. As the debate in the Senate reveals, Congress was well aware that a sunset was required to protect its power; otherwise, any attempt to repeal LIVA would require a two-thirds majority in each house to overcome a certain presidential veto. Although LIVA passed both houses by a substantial margin, suggesting that re-enactment would have been a foregone conclusion, lawmakers began to complain about the Act once Clinton actually canceled a few programs. Senator Robert Bennett (R–UT) told reporters, "I was a proponent. I campaigned for it vigorously. But when I saw the way that President Clinton abused the line-item veto, I ate crow publicly."[133]

Given Clinton's relatively restrained use of cancellation, it is hard to imagine how Bennett would approve of any President's exercise of his delegated power—or at least, of any Democratic President's use of it. Representative Jose Serrano (D–NY) observed of his colleagues, "I've never seen a vote taken where more people wanted their vote back."[134] Congress' ability to refuse to extend LIVA would have depended on the deficit situation at the time; current projections of historically large deficits suggest that lawmakers would have found it difficult to avoid re-enacting LIVA when it would have expired in 2005. But their willingness to let LIVA die, or to cut it back, would have primarily turned on the inter-branch dynamics that would have played out over the eight years of experience. At least the sunset allowed them the ability to judge whether the costs of LIVA were worth its fiscal and political benefits.

The story of LIVA does not prove that Congress always protects itself when it delegates authority to the President, but it does demonstrate that Congress has ample tools at its disposal to retain its influence vis-à-vis the executive branch when it drafts legislation and that it knows how to use them. Thus, the story supports the current state of the delegation doctrine in courts, where judges do not overturn broad delegations as unconstitutional abdications of congressional authority but apply a pragmatic doctrine that seeks to limit the scope of delegation

---

133. Lyle Denniston & Jonathan Weisman, *Line-Item Veto Voided by Justices*, Balt. Sun, June 26, 1998, at A1.

134. Guy Gugliotta & Eric Pianin, *Line-Item Veto Tips Traditional Balance of Power; Capitol Hill Plots Strategy to Counter President's Pen*, Wash. Post, Oct. 24, 1997, at A1.

where possible but essentially leaves the policing of the nondelegation doctrine to Congress itself. It is interesting that Congress built into LIVA so many safeguards because the Act did not delegate to the President a particularly robust authority to radically transform spending priorities or substantially reduce the size of government. Thus, it is not clear that all the protections were necessary in this particular law. The total savings from Clinton's cancellations during the fiscal year in which LIVA was effective were only $600 million over five years; even if all 82 cancellations had gone into effect (rather than 44 which remained after the enactment of the disapproval bill relating to the military constructions projects), the total amount saved over five years would have been just under $1 billion.[135] Moreover, the purpose behind LIVA—to allow the President to go after narrowly targeted programs—suggests that the rescissions would necessarily be limited in size.

Perhaps Congress feared that the President would grow bolder over time, and it was certainly possible for him to aggressively wield the cancellation power with respect to discretionary spending items because they did not have to be limited to only a few beneficiaries in the same way that eligible tax expenditures were. Moreover, Congress might not have been able to muster a two-thirds vote to reinstate the rescissions relating the military construction appropriation bill had the Clinton administration not revealed that it had made eighteen mistakes in applying the President's own standards. The budget staff did not reveal which of the 38 cancellations were mistakes, which made it easier for Congress to pass a disapproval bill relating to all of them by a veto-proof majority.[136]

Certainly, Congress had experience with a President willing to make sweeping rescissions. The 1974 Budget Act had been prompted, after all, by President Nixon's use of policy impoundments to undermine congressional priorities relating to the environment, housing and other domestic programs. President Clinton may have used cancellation sparingly in the first year to try to avoid provoking a judicial challenge of a law that even its drafters were not convinced was constitutional; perhaps he would have changed his tactics if it became apparent that a judicial challenge was either unlikely or unsuccessful. If his strategy was to avoid a judicial showdown, however, he would have been advised to cancel only items in appropriation bills, where the power of impoundment was relatively uncontroversial. It is not accidental that the cancellations giving rise to *Clinton v. City of New York* were related to a tax benefit and a direct

---

135. Line Item Veto Act After One Year: Hearings before the Subcomm. on Legislative and Budget Process of the Comm. on Rules, U.S. House of Representatives, 105th Cong. 6 (1998) (statement of June E. O'Neill, Director, Congressional Budget Office), *available at* http://www.cbo.gov/ftpdocs/3xx/doc365/031198.pdf.

136. See Garrett, supra note 118, at 899 n.125.

spending program. The well-established presidential power of congressionally-sanctioned impoundment was limited to rescissions of discretionary spending; the use of the power was more suspect when it was aimed at tax benefits or entitlement programs. On the other hand, Clinton's wariness may have been more a consequence of the need for congressional reauthorization than his worry about judicial challenge. How strong a moderating influence the sunset provision would have exerted is unclear; LIVA would not have expired until January 1, 2005, long after Clinton left office.

Although the story of LIVA shapes the way we think about the nondelegation doctrine and the judiciary's hands-off approach to broad congressional delegations, the Court's majority opinion in *Clinton v. City of New York* did not view this case as posing a delegation question. Rather it framed the constitutional issue more formally, asking whether the President's power to cancel tax benefits and direct spending programs was a power to repeal a law without congressional involvement. Answering that question "yes" meant that the Constitution's requirement of bicameralism was violated and LIVA was unconstitutional. This decision, and the fact that the case took place pursuant to special expedited judicial review provisions, raises the second important aspect of our story: Did Congress adequately consider the constitutional issues presented by LIVA and work to avoid those difficulties, or did it just punt the hard questions to the courts?

LIVA: A Mixed Story of Congress' Ability to Analyze Constitutional Issues

It did not surprise members of Congress that LIVA was challenged in court soon after enactment, and it probably did not surprise many that the Act did not survive the second challenge in *Clinton v. City of New York*. The congressional debate clearly demonstrates that members knew the Act was close to the constitutional edge, if not over it, and the expedited judicial review provision invited challenge and ensured speedy resolution. After all, Congress was trying to use a statute to create a power similar to the constitutional line item veto authority exercised by most governors. The task itself was explicitly designed to circumvent Article V's onerous requirements to amend the Constitution and to adopt a solution less durable than a constitutional change. Moreover, throughout the 1980s, lawmakers had adopted a variety of creative responses to the conflicting pressures to send pork home and to reduce the deficit, and a few of these devices had been struck down on separation-of-powers grounds.[137]

---

137. See Bowsher v. Synar, 478 U.S. 714 (1978) (striking down provision in Gramm-Rudman-Hollings Act that allowed Comptroller-General of the GAO to implement a

Although many have indicted Congress as insufficiently attentive to constitutional issues or institutionally incapable of serious constitutional analysis,[138] the debate concerning LIVA reveals that members spent time in committee and on the floor talking about constitutional concerns. There was relatively extensive discussion, certainly in the Senate which held a hearing in a Judiciary subcommittee and which engaged in substantial debate on the constitutionality of its separate enrollment approach, and also in the House where the Rules Committee received an analysis by CRS and some members highlighted concerns in floor debate. Members also referred to discussion in past Congresses about the constitutionality of various statutory approaches to the line item veto, indicating that some members had thought about these issues before. Despite the recognition of a serious question of constitutionality, however, neither house seems to have confidently resolved it.

There could be many reasons for the failure to continue the deliberation, and more than one could have been operating. Lawmakers might have believed the Court would not be influenced by more substantial debate and analysis; getting a rough sense of the right answer was the best they could do, and then judges would independently resolve the question. Further discussion might not have changed minds or eliminated constitutional doubts for some members; after all, this was a close constitutional question. Or perhaps they did not care what happened to LIVA once it left the House and Senate chambers because they mainly wanted credit for delivering on the Contract with America and for enacting a symbolic, but not very potent, law to appear responsive to public concerns about out-of-control spending. In that case, they did not value more constitutional discussion for its own sake and only engaged in the some constitutional discourse for strategic reasons or to appear to constituents to be taking their responsibilities seriously. The debate might also have been a way to communicate to voters that the main obstacle to achieving this part of the Contract with America was not legislative, but judicial, so Congress could shift the blame to the courts if LIVA was blocked.

Although there is ample reason to be cynical about congressional deliberation on constitutional arguments, Congress could be genuinely interested in constitutional issues for several reasons. First, anticipating possible constitutional attacks allows lawmakers to craft a bill more likely to survive challenge if they actually want to enact a change in

---

sequester). In addition, budget laws contained legislative vetoes, an oversight mechanism ruled unconstitutional by INS v. Chadha, 462 U.S. 919 (1983).

138. Abner Mikva, a former member of Congress and then federal appellate judge, scathingly attacked Congress' ability to consider constitutional issues thoughtfully and well. See Abner J. Mikva, *How Well Does Congress Support and Defend the Constitution?*, 61 N.C. L. Rev. 609 (1983).

policy.[139] Certainly, some lawmakers did want to establish a stronger rescission power and thus to devise a law that would withstand judicial attack. The constitutional concerns about enhanced rescission were two-fold. First, members wondered whether the delegation to the President contained sufficient standards. The House Rules Committee received an opinion from the American Law Division of CRS that characterized the judicial nondelegation doctrine as requiring "the most minimal of policy direction and statement of goals" and concluded that H.R. 2 was "constitutionally permissible."[140] Witnesses before the Senate Judiciary Subcommittee reached the same conclusion. Accordingly, Congress never amended LIVA to provide more specific guidance than the three, relatively empty criteria discussed above. In fairness to the CRS and other legal analysts, had the Court analyzed LIVA under delegation principles, as did the dissenters in the case, it seems likely that LIVA would have survived judicial challenge. Congress' failure was in predicting accurately which approach the Court would take.

The second concern, and the one that ultimately convinced the majority of the Supreme Court to strike LIVA down, was that the President's cancellation effected a repeal of law without congressional involvement. This constitutional argument is based on the Court's assessment of the legislative veto in *INS v. Chadha*.[141] The legislative veto, a process whereby one house of Congress or sometimes one committee could block regulatory action, had been found unacceptable because it allowed a part of Congress to make law, bypassing bicameralism and presentment. The President's cancellation could be attacked on similar grounds; if cancellation was the equivalent of repealing a law, then the President was making law without the involvement of Congress.

The record clearly shows that legislators knew of this possible constitutional infirmity. Democratic representatives had sounded the alarm in the House Government Reform and Oversight Committee's report, worrying that enhanced rescission shifted power to the President and a "one third plus one" minority in each house (the number needed to block enactment of a disapproval bill over the President's veto). In debate on the floors of both houses on the expedited rescission substitutes offered by Democrats, supporters of the amendments argued that they were more clearly constitutional than any of the other statutory line item veto alternatives because they did not raise the specter of a

---

139. See J. MITCHELL PICKERILL, CONSTITUTIONAL DELIBERATION IN CONGRESS: THE IMPACT OF JUDICIAL REVIEW IN A SEPARATED SYSTEM 23 (2004) (noting that constitutional issues appear on the legislative agenda when members fear a law may be struck down).

140. H.R. Rep. No. 104–11, pt. 1, at 8–9 (1995).

141. 462 U.S. 919 (1983).

Chadha-like challenge.[142] In the Senate, where the debate on constitutional issues was more substantial than in the House, *Chadha* concerns were raised during consideration of the conference report.[143]

Particular attention was paid to the testimony of Assistant Attorney General Walter Dellinger before the Senate Judiciary Subcommittee. He argued that words like "veto" and "repeal" in the original H.R. 2 set off alarms that the Act violated "the plain textual provision of Article I, clause 7 of the Constitution, governing the manner in which federal laws are to be made and altered."[144] The conference committee eliminated these particularly problematic words from the final version of the bill, although for political and symbolic reasons, it left the troublesome title of the bill unchanged. Senator Levin argued that eliminating the words that raised red flags without altering the underlying process would not solve the constitutional problem.[145] As it turned out, he was right, and his analysis was similar to that used by the Court.

One reason given for Dole's decision to substitute separate enrollment for enhanced rescission on the Senate floor was to respond to concerns that enhanced rescission was unconstitutional. Indeed, the consideration of constitutional issues in the Senate was much more extensive than that in the House, although on the floor it was mainly focused on separate enrollment, a method killed in conference committee. The more extended debate in the Senate may reflect the reality that separate enrollment was really no less constitutionally problematic than enhanced rescission, and, given its deeming provision that allowed all the little bills to pass without separate votes on each, its constitutionality was perhaps more dubious.

Senators had ample outside analyses of the constitutional issues to inform their debate, and these assessments were available to House members as well. The testimony about constitutional issues raised by expedited and enhanced rescission proposals before the Subcommittee on the Constitution, Federalism, and Property Rights in the Senate Judiciary Committee occurred in January 1995, early in the legislative process. In addition, the American Law Division of CRS produced a memo on the constitutionality of separate enrollment that members frequently referred to.[146] This CRS document suggests that separate enrollment would

---

142. See, e.g., 141 Cong. Rec. H1185 (daily ed. Feb. 3, 1995) (statement of Rep. Spratt); 142 Cong. Rec. S4249 (daily ed. Mar. 27, 1996) (statement of Sen. Byrd) (raising *Chadha* concern about separate enrollment); 142 Cong. Rec. S4353 (daily ed. Mar. 22, 1995) (statement of Sen. Daschle).

143. 142 Cong. Rec. S2944–45, 48–49 (daily ed. Mar. 27, 1996) (statement of Sen. Byrd and letter by Prof. Gerhardt).

144. 141 Cong. Rec. H1174 (daily ed. Feb. 3, 1995) (quoting Dellinger).

145. 142 Cong. Rec. S2964–65 (daily ed. Mar. 27, 1996).

146. See, e.g., 141 Cong. Rec. S4156 (daily ed. Mar. 20, 1995) (statement of Sen. McCain).

either escape judicial review because of the political question or other related doctrine of deference; it is less definite on the issue whether the deeming process in separate enrollment is consistent with the Constitution's requirements to enact a bill. Senator-lawyers provided their own views of separate enrollment, most notably Senator Biden, a high-ranking member of the Judiciary Committee, who believed it constitutional,[147] and Senator Byrd, an author of a book on the Constitution,[148] who vehemently contested that conclusion.[149] Finally, Senators on both sides of the issue had gathered the views of various constitutional law scholars, primarily again on separate enrollment[150] but also on the enhanced rescission bill that was ultimately enacted.[151]

Non-strategic debate on constitutional issues is relevant in a second way to legislative decision making. Some lawmakers may make up their minds to support or oppose a law based on their views of its constitutionality. They do so because their constituents want them to act consistently with constitutional mandates, because they take an oath to support the Constitution, because they value the Constitution, or because of some combination of these factors.[152] In that case, we might expect to find lawmakers stating that although they favored or disfavored LIVA on policy grounds, they were nonetheless voting in the opposite way because of their views on constitutionality. In our story, it is impossible to find such statements in committee reports or *Congressional Record*. Certainly, members of Congress appear to change their minds over the course of the debate. Senator Domenici consistently opposed enhanced rescission in committee and on the floor of the Senate until the conference committee sent its enhanced rescission proposal to the floor. Although some of Domenici's early statements hinted that part of his initial

---

147. See, e.g., The Line-Item Veto: A Constitutional Approach, Hearing Before the Subcomm. on the Constitution, Federalism, and Property Rights of the Comm. on the Judiciary, U.S. Senate, 104th Cong. 8–9 (Jan. 24, 1995).

148. ROBERT C. BYRD, THE SENATE OF THE ROMAN REPUBLIC: ADDRESSES ON THE HISTORY OF ROMAN CONSTITUTIONALISM (1995).

149. See, e.g., 141 Cong. Rec. S4228–29, 4232–44 (daily ed. Mar. 21, 1995).

150. 141 Cong. Rec. S4160 (daily ed. Mar. 20, 1995) (Iowa Law Review); 141 Cong. Rec. S4238–9 (daily ed. Mar. 21, 1995) (Judith Best), S4232 (Dellinger); S4248 (Fisher); S4249 (Mikva and Flanagan); 141 Cong. Rec. S4445, et seq. (daily ed. Mar. 23, 1995) (Gerhardt, etc.).

151. 142 Cong. Rec. S2974 (daily ed. Mar. 27, 1996) (additional references to Prof. Gerhardt's letter); 142 Cong. Rec. S2965–66, 2971 (daily ed. Mar. 27, 1996) (references to Prof. Laurence Tribe's letter to Sen. Bill Bradley (D–NJ)).

152. See Elizabeth Garrett & Adrian Vermeule, *Institutional Design of a Thayerian Congress*, 50 Duke L.J. 1277, 1288–89 (2001) (discussing why lawmakers could value constitutional lawmaking). See also Paul Brest, *The Conscientious Legislator's Guide to Constitutional Interpretation*, 27 Stan. L. Rev. 585 (1975) (discussing the way lawmakers should approach constitutional questions raised by legislative proposals).

position was driven by constitutional concerns,[153] he discussed the balance of power as the primary reason for his positions, and he does not explicitly link that argument to constitutional mandates.

Senator Exon came closest to articulating a gap between his constitutional views and policy preferences. He clearly favored some line item veto with relatively sharp teeth, but in the floor debate he sounded constitutional concerns about any method other than expedited rescission.[154] Was he convinced to change his mind on the constitutional issues? It does not appear so. When he stated that he would vote for the conference report, he also noted that he has "some possible constitutional questions and concerns."[155] Even those senators who mainly focused on constitutional aspects of LIVA, such as Senator Levin[156] and Senator Thompson,[157] appeared also to reach the same conclusions on policy grounds, so it is difficult to determine how much of an independent role constitutional issues played.[158]

Perhaps the expedited judicial review provision added to LIVA by Nathan Deal in the House and Paul Simon in the Senate made it easier for lawmakers to vote their policy preference despite any lingering concerns about constitutionality. Both houses eagerly adopted these provisions as amendments on the floor, and a version was retained in the conference report. Interestingly, Senator Simon recognized one likely problem with the Senate's provision, that only allowed a member of Congress to challenge the Act in Court, and counseled the conference committee also to provide standing to bring a "test case" to "any person adversely affected by the act."[159] The conference committee wisely adopted this suggestion in the final version. Simon's concerns about congressional standing were well-founded; the Court dismissed the first challenge to LIVA brought by members of Congress before the President had exercised his cancellation authority on the ground that members of Congress lacked a concrete injury and thus did not have standing to sue.[160] Only when individuals and entities adversely affected by presidential cancellations brought a challenge did the Court reach the merits of the case. The Court did not discuss in either case, nor did Congress find

---

153. S. Rep. No. 104–9, at 14 (1995); 141 Cong. Rec. S4193 (daily ed. Mar. 20, 1995).

154. 141 Cong. Rec. S4330–32 (daily ed. Mar. 22, 1995); 141 Cong. Rec. 4411 (daily ed. Mar. 23, 1995).

155. 104 Cong. Rec. S2991 (daily ed. Mar. 27, 1996).

156. 142 Cong. Rec. S2964 (daily ed. Mar. 27, 1996).

157. 141 Cong. Rec. S4475 (daily ed Mar. 23, 1995).

158. See Pickerill, supra note 139, at 135, 144 (finding, based on interviews with members and staff, that constitutional issues play little if any role in policy positions).

159. 141 Cong. Rec. S4476 (daily ed. Mar. 23, 1995).

160. Raines v. Byrd, 521 U.S. 811 (1997).

problematic, that this expedited review provision could essentially ask the Court for an advisory opinion—a possibility hinted at in statements by lawmakers that cases brought under the provision would serve as "test cases." Because *Clinton v. City of New York* concerned actual cases—a hospital in New York would suffer financial hardship because of the cancellation of a change in the Medicaid law, and a farmer would lose the ability to take advantage of a targeted tax benefit—the Court was not faced with the possibility that it was being asked to give an advisory opinion.

Did the expedited review provision encourage lawmakers to shirk their responsibility to make independent judgments about LIVA's constitutionality? Some certainly argued that was the case. Senator Byrd contended, "We should be resolving these questions on our own. All of us take an oath of office to support and defend the Constitution. During the process of considering a bill, it is our duty to identify—and correct constitutional problems. ... It is irresponsible to punt to the courts."[161] The general tone of the Senate debate, however, suggests that most members had reached some conclusion about the constitutionality first of separate enrollment and then of enhanced rescission, based on opinions of outside experts, CRS lawyers, and the debate of their colleagues. Nonetheless, they acknowledged uncertainty about their legal conclusion by supporting a provision allowing early judicial resolution.

Did the expedited review also allow those with doubts to vote for the bill? Probably. Senator Exon supported Simon's amendment because, although he thought Congress should make an independent constitutional judgment when voting, he acknowledged that the availability of speedy judicial review would ease the concerns of those with lingering constitutional doubts. Would Congress have engaged in more searching constitutional analysis without the provision? That seems unlikely, particularly in the Senate, because there was a great deal of debate devoted to such arguments. Did the provision allow those who secretly hoped the Act would be struck down to cast a politically convenient vote for LIVA? It is hard to answer that question with confidence. As the previous analysis suggested, LIVA was crafted so it could not substantially shift power away from Congress and to the executive branch, so the additional protection of expediting any judicial challenge of a statute close to the constitutional borderline might not have been a deciding factor for many lawmakers. Furthermore, even with the expedited review provision, parties adversely affected by a cancellation could have challenged the constitutionality of the Act in court, although they would not have been guaranteed direct and speedy appeal to the Supreme Court.

---

161. 142 Cong. Rec. S2943 (daily ed. Mar. 27, 1996). See also Louis Fisher, *Congressional Abdication: War and Spending Powers*, 43 St. Louis U. L.J. 931, 1003 (1999).

Although academic criticism of Congress' constitutional performance with respect to LIVA and the expedited review provision has been pointed,[162] a close reading of the debate does not necessarily reflect unfavorably on lawmakers. However, the debate also does not demonstrate that constitutional concerns are the deciding factor in any lawmaker's vote, nor do constitutional arguments appear to change the decision that members would have made on policy or partisan grounds. Constitutionality loomed as a concern, and the conference committee made many changes to respond to input by legal experts, but the Republicans were unwilling to change the problematic title of the bill. As some wished and others feared, the Court ultimately decided the fate of LIVA. With a divided vote and strongly worded opinions that demonstrated that the justices also found *Clinton v. City of New York* to be a close case, the Court struck down LIVA, at least to the extent it allowed cancellation of limited tax benefits and new direct spending programs.[163]

Conclusion

After *Clinton v. City of New York*, the Line Item Veto Act of 1996 was no long part of the federal budget process, but the story of its enactment should not be forgotten. In fact, the story may yet have a sequel. Since the Supreme Court struck down the President's use of cancellation directed toward tax expenditures and entitlement programs, the President has continued to request some sort of line item veto power in the Budget he sends each year to Congress. President George W. Bush has sometimes asked for a constitutional amendment to give him the same power that state governors have; in other years, he has asked Congress to delegate him some sort of enhanced rescission power that would act like a line item veto. It is possible that Congress could still comply with his second request either by using the Senate's separate enrollment mechanism that has not been considered by the Court, or by applying enhanced rescission authority only to annually appropriated items which are the traditional targets of presidential cancellation power and were not explicitly considered by the Court.

Whether Congress will pass such a bill now is unclear; it is certainly more likely in a period of substantial federal deficits. Moreover, Congress is apt to seriously consider this sort of delegation to the executive branch

---

162. See, e.g., Devins & Fitts, supra note 54; Fisher, supra note 161.

163. No cancellation of discretionary spending was challenged in court, and the Supreme Court did not take a position on this part of the Act. McCain's severability clause, which the Senate had attached to Simon's judicial review amendment, was dropped without explanation in conference committee. The Supreme Court explicitly did not consider whether cancellation of discretionary spending was severable from the rest of the statute. *Clinton*, 524 U.S. at 448 n.43. All have assumed, however, that LIVA in its entirety was struck down.

when the same party controls both houses of Congress and the presidency. The story of the first LIVA will provide guidance about the possible obstacles in such a bill's way. At the very least, Congress has probably learned a valuable lesson in choosing titles for its budget process innovations: any new enhanced rescission bill should be named something other than "The Line Item Veto Act." Beyond that, the end of the federal line item veto story is yet to be written.

Click on your region of interest

Adapted from the OSHA website, http://www.osha.gov

The American legal and political tradition, suspicious of possible misuse of governmental power, has been to restrict law enforcement officials from intruding on private property without having first obtained a judicial search warrant, issued only if they can show probable cause to believe that evidence of a legal offense will be found. Governmental regulatory programs seek to make private property more open to public scrutiny, often authorizing regulatory compliance officers to inspect business facilities on a routine basis, without probable cause or a judicial warrant. In their account of *Marshall v. Barlow's, Inc.*, built around a feisty Idaho businessman's challenge to an OSHA inspector, Professor Robert Kagan and Rachel VanSickle-Ward tell us how the U.S. Supreme Court has struggled to reconcile the demand for control of government power and the demand for prevention of the harms that can flow from modern technology. It also shows how these legal issues reflect broader political struggles about regulation, which, along with the Court's decisions, have contributed to the evolution and legitimation of regulatory enforcement in American society.

3

Robert A. Kagan*

Rachel VanSickle-Ward**

Marshall v. Barlow's Inc.: Legitimizing Regulatory Enforcement

Introduction

Every day, squadrons of governmental inspectors fan out across the United States, enforcing the legal rules of the contemporary regulatory state. We count on this white collar police force to help protect us from leaking gas mains, air and water pollution, workplace hazards, contaminated foods, substandard care in nursing homes, and much more. In the name of the law, therefore, regulatory inspectors explore the operations of private enterprises. They walk factory floors, interview personnel, pore through business records, sample effluent, and inspect furnaces and railroad tracks. They can order an airliner to be grounded, block the shipment of food products, close a mineshaft, and gather information for prosecuting recalcitrant business owners.

Regulatory inspectors' powers of intrusion and control raise the specter of possible misuse. An overly-cautious inspector could embargo food that is not in fact dangerous. An officious inspector, annoyed at not being treated with the deference he deserves, could deliberately harass an enterprise that is in fact operating within the law. A venal inspector could learn and sell trade secrets, extort bribes, engage in blackmail, or favor one firm while imposing heavier regulatory burdens on its competitors. In recent decades, there have been remarkably few stories of that kind of malfeasance. But in American legal culture, the possibility of misuse of power generates the demand for legal controls on the law

---

* Professor of Political Science and Law, University of California at Berkeley.

** Ph.D. candidate, University of California at Berkeley

enforcers themselves. In a 1978 case, *Marshall v. Barlow's, Inc.*,[1] the United States Supreme Court debated one such control: the constitutional limits on regulatory inspectors' authority to enter and inspect privately-owned business facilities at will.

The Fourth Amendment of the U.S. Constitution proclaims that "The right of the people to be secure in their persons, houses, papers, and effects, against unreasonable searches and seizures shall not be violated ..." It goes on to say that "no warrants shall issue, but upon probable cause ... particularly describing the place to be searched, and the persons or things to be seized." In ordinary criminal law enforcement, the Supreme Court has held, those two clauses are linked: in order to search a private place, law enforcement officers, absent exigent circumstances (and certain other exceptions), must first obtain a targeted search warrant from a judicial officer, based on pre-existing evidence that the search would probably produce evidence of a legal offense. But does a homeowner's or apartment dweller's right to insist on a valid search warrant before letting a police officer through the door also apply in the case of an entrepreneur or a corporate executive who finds a regulatory inspector in his office, demanding access to potentially hazardous business operations?

To Bill Barlow, an air conditioning, ventilation and electric contractor in Pocatello, Idaho, the answer was "Yes, indeed!" Barlow had worked hard all his life. He had built a business that employed 35 workers. And Barlow mistrusted government. He was a member of the hyper-conservative John Birch Society.[2] In 1975, when an inspector from the Idaho office of the U.S. Occupational Safety and Health Agency (OSHA) showed up at Barlow's Inc. and asked to inspect the working areas of the enterprise, Bill Barlow responded with some questions of his own.[3]

Why was the "young fellow" there? Had his neighbors complained? Had his workers complained? The compliance officer answered that no complaints had been filed by Barlow's employees or neighbors. "Well why are you here then?" Barlow repeated. The inspector said, "Well your name came up." Barlow made it clear that he "didn't think that was right" and said something like "It sounds to me like it's a fishing expedition." The inspector pulled out a plastic card which contained a

---

1.   436 U.S. 307 (1978).

2.   "Watt Report," The Nation 17 January 1981: 5.

3.   The quotes, and the bulk of this account of Barlow's initial encounter with the OSHA inspector, are from our interview with John Runft, the Boise attorney who represented Barlow through all the stages of the case (phone, October 12, 2004). Runft says that his account of the initial inspection is based on a meeting he had with the OSHA inspector about two weeks later, in which he sought to "nail the facts down."

copy of the relevant provisions of the Occupational Safety and Health Act of 1970, in which Congress had authorized the agency to conduct surprise inspections of any workplace.[4] Bill Barlow studied the card and then played his own trump. Pointing to a copy of the U.S Constitution hanging on his office wall, he said "This is a higher law than your card."

Ten days later, the inspector was back in Pocatello with a court order. It threatened to hold Barlow in contempt of court if he didn't let the inspector in. Barlow's response was to find himself a lawyer, John L. Runft. Runft petitioned the U.S. District Court for Idaho to enjoin the contempt order. He also demanded a three-judge panel to consider Barlow's constitutional claim: that the government simply could not search Barlow's business without a warrant and without probable cause to believe that a violation of the OSHA regulations had occurred there. Before we follow the struggle between Bill Barlow and OSHA to the US Supreme Court, however, it will be helpful to take a look at the political context in which the dispute arose and at the legal precedents that would frame the debate once it got into the hands of lawyers and judges.

Political Background

There is nothing new about government regulation. For centuries, government inspectors have poked into business enterprises to uncover and deter fraudulent, harmful, or unfair behavior. In the colonial era, a Massachusetts law required each town to appoint a "gager or packer" to ensure that "the best be not left out" in sealed packages of beef or pork.[5] By the last decades of the 19th Century, state governments were sending inspectors into mines and factories to enforce ventilation and accident-prevention measures. Municipal inspectors enforced more detailed housing and sanitation codes, and Federal inspectors scrutinized railroad compliance with regulations governing switching equipment and track-maintenance. In 1906, Congress enacted the Food and Drug Act and the

---

4. 29 U.S.C. § 657(a) of the Act provides that an OSHA inspector:

(a) ... upon presenting appropriate credentials to the owner, operator, or agent in charge, is authorized—

(1) to enter without delay and at reasonable times any factory, plant, establishment, construction site, or other area, workplace or environment where work is performed by an employee of an employer; and

(2) to inspect and investigate during regular working hours and at other reasonable times, and within reasonable limits and in a reasonable manner, any such place of employment and all pertinent conditions, structures, machines, apparatus, devices, equipment, and materials therein, and to question privately any such employer, owner, operator, agent or employee."

5. EUGENE BARDACH & ROBERT A. KAGAN, GOING BY THE BOOK: THE PROBLEM OF REGULATORY UNREASONABLENESS 8 (Transactions Books, 2002).

Meat Inspection Act, launching systematic government inspection of processing plants for signs of poor sanitation or adulterated meat.

The 1960s and early 1970s, however, saw a dramatic upsurge in the reach and intrusiveness of protective regulation. Congress enacted an unprecedented wave of ambitious regulatory statutes. It forbade discrimination based on race, gender, and age. It mandated far tougher nationwide restrictions on air and water pollution, and compelled state governments to enforce them more vigorously. Demanding federal regulatory programs were created to advance occupational safety and health, motor vehicle safety, the safety of other consumer products, and the control of toxic chemicals.

Yet the new legislation, even as it expanded federal regulatory authority, reflected distrust of concentrated governmental power. Pro-regulation activists and their allies in the Democratic Party feared that agencies would succumb to the political influence of business and would be too lenient. The business community and its Republican allies feared that regulatory agencies would be permeated by leftist ideologues who would be hostile or indifferent to the legitimate concerns of economic enterprise. This mutual distrust generated a new, more prescriptive type of regulatory law, designed to constrain the discretion of regulatory officials and regulated businesses alike. The statutes expanded both regulated businesses' and pro-regulation advocacy groups' legal rights to demand judicial review of new regulations and agency decisionmaking.

In the 1960s and '70s, statutes and regulations became not only more detailed but much more expensive for regulated businesses to comply with. Manufacturing enterprises were compelled to make costly investments in pollution control technologies, monitoring equipment, record-keeping and reporting systems. Facilities had to be re-engineered to reduce the risk of harm to workers, consumers, and neighbors. Personnel decisions had to be subjected to systematic, ostensibly more objective standards and procedures. At the same time, regulation became much more threatening. In many programs, statutes called for large monetary penalties for violations and authorized potentially costly private lawsuits against violators.

In the mid-1970s, as petroleum prices soared, inflation accelerated, and economic growth stagnated, complaints from the business community about the new legal requirements mounted. The complaints did not focus, by and large, on the sheer economic cost of intensified regulatory requirements. Nor did they focus on regulatory inspectors' power to enter business premises and examine company records. Rather, the complaints focused on "regulatory unreasonableness"—the legalistic enforcement of detailed regulations regardless of whether a literal violation had actually caused any harm, and regardless of the degree to which the regulated enterprise had been working in good faith to reduce the risk of harm or injustice. Put another way, the business community, by and large, was not complaining about being victimized by "lawless" intrusions or focused harassment by regulatory inspectors—a problem that might be ameliorated by requiring enforcement officials to get search warrants from the judiciary. The complaint, instead, was that inspectors had been compelled to follow the law too mechanically, rather than being allowed to exercise discretion in citing and punishing violations and in shaping remedial orders.

The federal Occupational Safety and Health Administration (OSHA), established in 1970, was an especially prominent target of such complaints. In its first years, OSHA issued large numbers of detailed "technology standards," requiring prescribed types of guards on machinery, railings of particular heights, warning signs of specified sizes, use of protective clothing, and so forth. Such rules often were over-inclusive: they probably made sense overall, but they did not make sense in many particular situations where alternative safety measures existed and where the main risks of injury stemmed from other factors. Thus academic studies of OSHA calculated that even perfect compliance with OSHA safety regulations probably would reduce injury rates by only 15 or 25 percent.[6]

By the mid-to-late 1970s, OSHA had become a symbol of regulatory unreasonableness, the butt of jokes about governmental nitpicking and rigidity. Congress held numerous oversight hearings in which business representatives presented horror stories of legalistic enforcement. OSHA and its supporters barely averted passage of a series of bills that sought to strip the agency of its jurisdiction over small businesses or rescind its powers to issue citations against "first instance" violations.[7] Political counter-attack was accompanied by case-specific legal resistance. When the Occupational Safety and Health Review Commission was first formed in the early 1970s, it estimated that is caseload of appeals by employers seeking review of OSHA citations would be about 100 or 200 cases per year. By the mid-1970s, it was receiving 300 or 400 appeals each *month*.[8]

---

6. The relevant research is summarized in Lawrence Bacow, Bargaining for Job Safety and Health (MIT Press, 1980) at pp. 39–40. John Mendeloff, a leading analyst of OSHA, observed "Most workplace injuries are not caused by violations of standards, and even fewer are caused by violations that inspectors can detect." Mendeloff, "Costs and Consequences: A Political and Economic Analysis of the Federal Occupational Safety and Health Program" (Ph.D. dissertation, University of California, Berkeley (1977), p. 555). See also John Mendeloff, Regulating Safety: A Political and Economic Analysis of the Federal Occupational Safety and Health Program (MIT Press, 1979).

7. Steven Kelman, "Occupational Safety and Health," in James Q. Wilson, ed., The Politics of Regulation (Basic Books, 1980).

8. Steven Kelman, "Regulating Job Safety and Health," Ph.D. dissertation, Harvard University, 1978, p. 595. See also Steven Kelman, Regulating America, Regulating Sweden: A Comparative Study of Occupational Safety and Health Regulations (MIT Press, 1981).

Disgruntlement about particular citations, fines or regulatory requirements usually did not extend to outright resistance to the regulatory inspection process. Both big business and the U.S. Chamber of Commerce (representative of smaller firms) recommended cooperation with regulatory inspectors.[9] To turn an inspector away, in the minds of most business officials, was only to invite further and more suspicious scrutiny in the future.[10] Thus Bill Barlow's "don't tread on me" stand toward the OSHA inspector, while not unprecedented, was far from typical. But in "standing up" to an agency that had acquired a reputation for regulatory unreasonableness, Barlow became a hero to many small businesses in the mid-1970s.

His fame was triggered when the three-judge federal court panel in Boise ruled in his favor on December 30, 1976, holding that the Occupational Safety and Health Act, in authorizing warrantless searches of workplaces throughout the nation, was unconstitutional and enjoining the Secretary of Labor from implementing that portion of the Act.[11] Ray Marshall, the Secretary of Labor, immediately appealed to the U.S. Supreme Court, and a small Idaho businessman's challenge to the machinery of the regulatory state became a nationwide news story. Calls of support and donations to Barlow's legal cause flooded in from around the country. Similar challenges to warrantless inspections were filed by small businesses in other judicial districts. *Foundry Management and Technology*, a trade magazine ordinarily devoted to technical production issues, published an article entitled "What To Do When OSHA Knocks," discussing the unconstitutionality of warrantless inspections.[12]

Legal Background

It was not at all clear how the U.S. Supreme Court would decide Bill Barlow's case. In several previous cases, the tension between business rights of privacy and the public interest in prompt regulatory inspections had left the justices divided. The 1959 case of *Frank v. Maryland*,[13] for example, arose when a Baltimore health inspector, responding to a neighbor's complaints about rats, found rodent feces amidst the piles of trash in the back yard of a dilapidated house. When he sought to inspect the basement, however, the homeowner, Mr. Frank, refused to allow him in. Baltimore's municipal code, incorporating an ordinance first enacted

---

9.   Bardach & Kagan, note 5 supra, at 115.

10.   On the rationality of cooperation versus conflict, for both regulatory enforcement officials and regulated enterprises, see John Scholz, *Cooperation, Deterrence, and the Ecology of Regulatory Enforcement*, 18 Law & Society Review 179 (1984).

11.   424 F. Supp. 437 (D.Idaho 1976).

12.   Bardach & Kagan, note 5 supra, at 115.

13.   359 U.S. 360 (1959).

in 1801, authorized a health inspector to demand entry to houses "in the daytime" if he had cause "to suspect that a nuisance exists." Appealing Frank's conviction for refusing the inspector entry, the defense lawyer argued that the municipality's code conflicted with the U.S. Constitution's prohibition of unreasonable searches and seizures and its warrant requirement.[14] The homeowner, it was argued, had a right to insist on a search warrant issued by a judge or magistrate.

A five-justice majority of the Supreme Court decided in favor of the government. To assess the constitutional need for a warrant, Justice Frankfurter's majority opinion said, required close attention to "the nature of the demand being made upon individual freedom in a particular context and the justification of social need on which the demand rests" (359 U.S. at 363). And in this context, he argued, the threat to the homeowner's liberty was extremely minimal. The government was conducting an *administrative* search, authorized by law and aimed not at criminal prosecution but at the detection and abatement of threats to public health. These kinds of regulatory searches are not the kind of threatening law enforcement actions that the 4th Amendment's privacy protections and warrant requirement had been established to control. "Here was no midnight knock on the door, but an orderly visit in the middle of the afternoon ..." (359 U.S. at 366). The inspector's purposes were remedial, not punitive. He wished "merely to determine whether conditions exist which the Baltimore Health Code proscribes. If they do appellant is notified to remedy the infringing conditions. No evidence for criminal prosecution is sought to be seized." (Ibid). Conversely, in Frankfurter's opinion, the social need for inspections was great:

> Time and experience have forcefully taught that the power to inspect dwelling places, either as a matter of systematic area-by-area search or, as here, to treat a specific problem, is of indispensable importance to the maintenance of community health; a power that would be greatly hobbled by the blanket requirement of the safeguards necessary for a search of evidence of criminal acts. (359 U.S. at 372).

Justice Douglas, in a dissenting opinion joined by Chief Justice Warren, and Justices Black and Brennan, took a much more literal—and libertarian—view of the Fourth Amendment, arguing that the majority opinion had watered down the right against arbitrary intrusion "to embrace only certain invasions of one's privacy" (359 U.S. at 375). To the dissenters (who made reference to government's "search for subversives" in the preceding decade), there was an ever-present risk of

---

14. In Wolf v. Colorado, 338 U.S. 25 (1949), the Court had decided that the Fourth Amendment's prohibition of unreasonable searches and seizures applies to states and local governments through the Due Process Clause of the Fourteenth Amendment.

governmental abuse of power. Douglas argued that if the social benefits of catching dangerous criminals did not justify setting aside the warrant requirement, neither did the social desirability of regulation:

> One invasion of privacy by an official of government can be as oppressive as another. Health inspections are important. But they are hardly more important than the search for narcotics peddlers, rapists, kidnappers, murderers, and other criminal elements. . . . (359 U.S. at 382).

The warrant requirement was an essential check, the dissenters wrote, because "The official's measure of his own need often does not square with the Bill of Rights." (Ibid).

But wouldn't the Fourth Amendment's insistence that warrants issue only on "probable cause" undermine the systematic inspection processes of municipal health agencies, whose purpose was not merely to wait for complaints but to actively search for hazards that homeowners and neighbors might not be aware of? Douglas responded:

> "This is not to suggest that a health official need show the same kind of proof to a magistrate to obtain a warrant as one must who would search for the fruits of instrumentalities of crime. Where considerations of health and safety are involved, the facts that would justify an inference of 'probable cause' to make an inspection are clearly different. . . . Experience may show the need for periodic inspections of certain facilities without further showing of cause to believe that substandard conditions dangerous to the public are being maintained." (359 U.S. at 383).

Justice Frankfurter's majority opinion labeled Douglas's suggestion of a different, less demanding standard for administrative inspections an endorsement of "synthetic search warrants." A warrant authorizing "periodic inspections", he wrote, was neither constitutionally warranted nor sensible:

> If a search warrant be constitutionally required, the requirement cannot be flexibly interpreted to dispense with the rigorous constitutional restrictions for its issue. A loose basis for granting a search warrant for the situation before us is to enter by way of the back door to a recognition of the fact that . . . [administrative searches] do not offend the protection of the Fourteenth Amendment (359 U.S. at 373).

Thus in *Frank v. Maryland,* both the majority and the dissenters agreed on a fundamental point: the governmental and public interest in proactive, systematic inspection meant that to enter a building, a government inspector (unlike a police officer) should not need prior evidence ("probable cause to believe") that he would find a regulatory violation inside. To support that view, the five-justice majority held that administrative searches were not really covered by the Fourth Amendment. To get to the same position, the four-justice minority said that a warrant was required, but the traditional probable cause standard didn't really apply.

Eight years later, in *Camara v. Municipal Court*, 387 U.S. 523 (1967) the Court revisited the same issue and did an about-face, essentially overruling *Frank*. By a 6:3 vote, the Court held that Mr. Camara was justified in refusing to let a San Francisco housing inspector into his leased premises without a search warrant.[15] The arguments of the Court's majority and minority were essentially the same as in *Frank*, but three things had changed. First, two justices on the *Frank* majority (including Frankfurter) had retired; the two justices who now occupied their seats—White and Fortas—joined the Douglas-Warren-Black-Brennan group to create a 6-justice majority in *Camara*. Second, the intervening eight years had been astonishingly turbulent: the country had been shaken by the marches and clashes of the civil rights movement, by mounting pressures for racial integration in the schools, by riots in urban ghettos, by war in Vietnam and the associated mass anti-war protests, and, perhaps most relevant for our purposes, by increased distrust of the police and of government in general. Third, the Warren Court had accelerated its use of the Fourteenth Amendment and the Bill of Rights to enhance judicial oversight of law enforcement. To that end, the Court had insisted in several criminal cases that police compliance with the 4th Amendment's warrant and probable cause requirements were crucial in establishing the "reasonableness" of a search and seizure.

The majority opinion in *Camara* reflected the general national mood of distrust of government and the Court's growing emphasis on the warrant requirement. Rejecting the *Frank* majority's argument, Justice White, writing for the Court, said:

> But we cannot agree that the Fourth Amendment interests at stake in these inspection cases are merely "peripheral." ... For instance, even most law-abiding citizen has a very tangible interest in limiting the circumstances under which the sanctity of his home may be broken by official authority, for the possibility of criminal entry

---

15. The inspector had entered a multi-storey building to make a routine annual inspection for possible violations of the city's Housing Code. The building manager told the inspector that Camara was using the rear of his ground-floor leasehold as a personal residence, which was forbidden by the Housing Code. Camara twice refused to let the inspector in, because he didn't have warrant. As in Baltimore, San Francisco's Code provided that authorize city employees "shall, upon presentation of proper credentials, have the right to enter, at reasonable times, any building, structure, or premises in the City to perform any duty imposed on them by the Municipal Code." 387 U.S. at 523.

under the guise of official sanction is a serious threat to personal and family security. And ... [l]ike most regulatory laws, fire, health and housing codes are enforced by criminal processes ... Even in cities where discovery of a violation produces only an administrative compliance order, refusal to comply is a criminal offense, and the fact of compliance is verified by a second inspection, again without a warrant. (387 U.S. at 530–31).

Yet the *Camara* Court (like the dissent in *Frank*) was willing to relax the 4th Amendment's "warrants only on probable cause" standard to accommodate the needs of regulatory programs. Here Justice White stressed the non-criminal, preventive nature of administrative inspections and indicated—ironically, echoing Frankfurter's balancing test in *Frank*—that "In determining whether a particular inspection is reasonable—and thus in determining whether there is probable cause to issue a warrant for that inspection—the need for the inspection must be weighed in terms of [the] reasonable goals of code enforcement." (387 U.S. at 535). A systematic search of all properties in an area of a city, the opinion asserted, is a "reasonable" search, and probable cause to issue a warrant exists if there are reasonable administrative standards for conducting an area inspection. In sum, the 4th Amendment's warrant clause applies to administrative searches, but the test for issuing a warrant is whether the inspection is pursuant to a "reasonable" systematic administrative inspection plan—not on whether there is probable cause to believe a violation will be found in any particular business. The homeowner's privacy right is to insist that she is not being arbitrarily singled out for inspection, and to have a magistrate assess the reasonableness of the agency's inspection program.

The next issue before the Court was whether that warrant requirement applied to administrative searches of business enterprises. Business establishments, it might be argued, have a lesser interest in privacy than householders, thus obviating the need for a warrant. *See v. City of Seattle*, raising that question, was argued before the Supreme Court on the same day as *Camara*, decided on the same day, and decided in the same way. Mr. See had been convicted of refusing to allow a fire marshal to enter and inspect his locked commercial warehouse[16] as part of a routine, city-wide inspection program designed to ensure compliance with the Seattle Fire Code. See complained to the Supreme Court that the fire marshal did not have a search warrant or probable cause. The Court reversed his conviction, reaffirming that an administrative search is "presumptively unreasonable" if conducted without a warrant, and

---

16. See's warehouse apparently was not widely accessible to his customers but was, according to the lower court opinion, "maintained as a locked premises and ... [was] inaccessible to anyone except the defendant." Seattle v. See, 67 Wash.2d 475, 408 P.2d 262, 263 (1965).

further asserting that "The businessman, like the occupant of a residence, has a constitutional right to go about his business free from
unreasonable entries upon his private commercial property."[17]

On the other hand, the Court's opinion in *See v. Seattle*, also by
Justice White, noted in passing that regulation of business enterprises
may be different in some ways, entailing a lower degree of privacy
protection than dwelling places:

> We do not in any way imply that business premises may not
> reasonably be inspected in many more situations than private
> homes, nor do we question such accepted regulatory techniques as
> licensing programs which require inspections prior to operating a
> business or marketing a product. (387 U.S. at 545–46).

Indeed, in some subsequent cases, the Court held that for certain
"pervasively regulated" types of businesses, long subject to governmental licensing and close scrutiny, warrantless, no-probable-cause searches
did not offend the Fourth Amendment. For example, in *United States v.
Biswell*, 406 U.S. 311 (1972), the Court upheld the warrantless inspection of a licensed gun dealer's storeroom by a federal agent looking for
possible violations of the reporting and record-keeping requirements of
the Federal Gun Control Act. Surprise inspections, Justice White observed, are essential to enforcement of that Act, and they would be
impeded by a warrant requirement. Similarly, the court upheld warrantless searches of liquor storerooms in *Colonnade Catering Corp. v. United
States*[18] on the grounds that the liquor business was, as Justice Douglas
argued, a "closely regulated industry ... long subject to close supervision and inspection." The centrality of unannounced inspections to the
enforcement of the Occupational Health and Safety Act would later be
stressed by the federal government in *Marshall v. Barlow's*, in arguing
that no warrant should be required of OSHA inspectors.

The precise boundaries of the "pervasively regulated business"
exception, however, remained unclear in 1975, when Mr. Daniel T.
Sanger of the OSHA office in Boise, Idaho arrived at the door of Barlow's
Inc. As noted earlier, since the mid-1960s, almost every substantial
business in the United States had become pervasively regulated in a
colloquial sense. They were subject to detailed OSHA regulations designed to protect the health and safety of their workers, along with equal
employment reporting requirements, wage and hour regulations, federal
regulations governing the integrity of employee pension funds, and
detailed permits requiring reporting of all their emissions to air and
water and sewer systems. Given these mandated increases in the transparency and social responsibilities of business, did it make still make

---

17.   387 U.S. 541, 543 (1967).

18.   397 U.S. 72 (1970).

sense, as the Court had stipulated in *Seattle v. See,* to allow business managers to insist that inspectors obtain a warrant—or were almost all businesses now "pervasively regulated," little different from the gun dealers in the *Biswell* case? Conversely, could it not be argued that the increased intrusiveness and powers of the regulatory state, in which business facilities were subjected to ever more inspections each year by different agencies, as well as to tougher legal penalties for violations, suggest that business's Fourth Amendment protections, including the warrant requirement, should be maintained or strengthened?

The three-judge federal court convened to hear Barlow's complaint concluded that the issue was governed by the precedents in *Camara* and *Seattle v. See.* Barlow's establishment, the Court said, was not a "pervasively regulated business" in the same sense as a gun dealership or liquor store. Hence Barlow was indeed entitled to demand a search warrant before granting the OSHA inspector admission, and Congress had acted unconstitutionally in authorizing OSHA inspectors to conduct warrantless searches in the 1970 Occupational Safety and Health Act[19] (enacted *after* the Court had decided *Camara* and *See*).

Mr. Barlow's Case in the Supreme Court

The Department of Labor and the Department of Justice did have some grounds to hope they might persuade the Supreme Court to reverse the lower court decision. By the time the case was decided by the Supreme Court, there were several decisions by U.S. District Courts and Courts of Appeals on the same issue, and several appeals still pending. Although some lower federal court judges had agreed that *Camara* and *See* dictated the result for OSHA inspections, others had taken a different position.[20] In *Brennan v. Buckeye Industries,*[21] for example, a U.S. District Court judge held that an OSHA official did not need a warrant or probable cause to inspect a clothing manufacturing plant in Wrightsville, Georgia. Such a requirement, the judge asserted, would "destroy the object" of the federal workplace safety protection program, adding "Buckeye Industries is, constitutionally speaking, marching to the beat of an antique drum."[22]

---

19. Barlow's, Inc. v. Usery 424 F.Supp. 437 (D. Idaho 1976).

20. No warrant needed: Usery v. Godfrey Brake and Supply Service, 545 F.2d 52 (8th Cir. 1976); Lake Butler Apparel v. Secretary of Labor, 519 F.2d 84 (5th Cir. 1975); Bloomfield Mechanical v. OSHA, 519 F.2d 1257 (3d Cir. 1975); Brennan v. Buckeye Industries, 374 F.Supp. 1350 (S.D. Ga. 1974); Usery v. Northwest Orient Air, 1977 WL 22362 (E.D. N.Y. 1977). Warrant needed: Brennan v. Gibson's, 407 F.Supp. 154 (E.D. Tex. 1976), Dunlop v. Hertzler Enterprises, 418 F.Supp 627 (D.N.M.1976); Usery v. Rupp Forge, 1976 WL 16638 (N.D. Ohio 1976); Usery v. Centrif–Air, 424 F.Supp. 959 (N.D. Ga. 1977).

21. 374 F.Supp. 1350 (S.D. Ga.1974).

22. 374 F.Supp. at 1356.

In addition, *amicus curia* briefs urging reversal of the lower court decision in Barlow's case were filed by the attorneys general of Michigan, New Jersey, New Mexico, North Carolina, Pennsylvania, South Carolina, Vermont, Virginia, and Wyoming, as well as by the American Federation of Labor and the Sierra Club (which was concerned that the warrant requirement would inhibit inspections by environmental agencies).[23] And by January 1978, when the U.S. Supreme Court heard arguments in *Marshall v. Barlow's*, 20 years after the *Camara* and *See* decisions, personnel changes had nudged the Court in a more conservative direction.[24]

Since *Camara* and *See*, the Court had found that certain kinds of limited searches—such as a police officer's "frisk" of a criminal suspect to check for weapons,[25] or routine motor vehicle stops at checkpoints near the Mexican border to discourage illegal immigration[26]—entailed only limited intrusions on privacy, and hence passed the Fourth Amendment's "reasonableness" test even if the law enforcement officers had no warrant and were acting only on suspicion, with less than "probable cause." Thus the government's brief in *Marshall v. Barlow's* argued that employers like Barlow had only a "diminished expectation of privacy" in the work areas that OSHA inspectors sought to examine,[27] and hence the warrant and probable cause requirements of the Fourth Amendment should not be deemed applicable. The government also argued that in this respect Barlow's case was distinguishable from and should not be bound by the Courts' opinion in *Seattle v. See*, which involved a locked warehouse not ordinarily accessible to anyone but See himself.

Indeed, the government argued, OSHA inspections are more like the inspections of "pervasively regulated businesses," such as the gun deal-

---

23. On the other hand, briefs supporting Barlow's demand for a warrant were filed by the attorney generals of other states, as well as by the American Chamber of Commerce, the American Conservative Union, the National Federation of Independent Businesses, and the American Civil Liberties Union. Interestingly, The ACLU brief only represented one chapter. National ACLU representatives came down on both sides of the debate and hence decided not to file a brief. However, the Chicago chapter filed a brief in support of Barlow.

24. Warren, Black, Douglas, and Fortas, all in the *Camara* and *See* six-judge majority, had retired. So had Clark and Harlan, who had been two of the three dissenters, but of the newer justices, five (Chief Justice Burger, Blackmun, Powell, Rehnquist, and Stevens) had been appointed by Republican Presidents Nixon and Ford, and only one (Thurgood Marshall) by a Democrat, President Johnson.

25. Terry v. Ohio, 392 U.S. 1 (1968).

26. U.S. v. Martinez–Fuerte, 428 U.S. 543 (1976).

27. "The areas and equipment within appellee's workplace that the Secretary seeks to inspect are routinely occupied and used by appellee's employees. This critical fact serves to diminish appellee's claims of privacy with respect to the work areas of his business premises, especially vis-à-vis the inspectors who are charged with the responsibility of insuring the health and safety of the employees whom appellee has assigned to such areas." Appellants Brief, p. 13.

erships in the *Biswell* case, where the Court had held no search warrant was required. Finally, the government also pointed out that the OSHA regulatory scheme, as designed by Congress, emphasized surprise, unannounced inspections as essential to maintain constant pressure for compliance. Thus, as in Frankfurter's "balancing" analysis in *Frank v. Maryland,* the government's brief contended that a warrant requirement would significantly impede OSHA's important injury-reduction mission, while not protecting any significant privacy interest.

The Supreme Court disagreed. By 5–3 vote,[28] the Court affirmed the lower court decision. Justice White's majority opinion declined to extend the "pervasively regulated business" exemption from the warrant requirement to OSHA inspections—and by implication, most multi-industry regulatory and inspection programs, such as those enforced by the US Environmental Protection Agency and its state-level counterparts. The fact that the OSHA inspector sought to enter rooms in which Barlow's employees routinely worked did not mean that Barlow had no significant privacy interests at stake, Justice White reasoned:

> The Government inspector ... is not an employee. Without a warrant he stands in no better position than a member of the public. ... The owner of a business has not, by the necessary utilization of employees in his operation, thrown open the areas where employees alone are permitted to the warrantless scrutiny of Government agents. (436 U.S. at 315).

Justice White also rejected the government's claim that the warrant requirement should be inapplicable because it would enable employers to turn away surprise visits from OSHA inspectors. Based on past experience, he argued, "the great majority of businessmen can be expected ... to consent to inspection without warrant" (436 U.S. at 316). OSHA regulations, he added, already provide that when an employer refuses to admit an inspector, the agency can seek an appropriate court order—and that provision, by allowing an employer to buy time, does not seem to have crippled OSHA's effectiveness (436 U.S. at 319). Further, White's opinion asserted that if the inspector is sent away and succeeds in getting a warrant, he or she can regain the advantages of surprise by reappearing at the premises at a random time. Ibid.

---

28. Justice Brennan, who had voted for the warrant requirement in *Camara* and Seattle v. See, did not participate in the decision of Marshall v. Barlow's. White was joined by Justices Stewart (who had voted with him in the majority in *Camara* and Seattle v. See), Marshall and two Nixon appointees, Powell and Chief Justice Burger. The dissenters, all new to the Court since Seattle v. See, were Justices Stevens (appointed by President Ford), Blackmun (appointed by Nixon) and Rehnquist (Nixon). It is hard to see how political ideology dictated the pattern of decision in this case, as the four Nixon–Ford appointees split 2–2.

But as in *Camara* and *Seattle v. See*, the Court was quick add that while a warrant was required for administrative searches, "Probable cause in the criminal law sense is not required." (436 U.S. at 320). Rather:

> A warrant showing that a specific business has been chosen for an OSHA search on the basis of a general administrative plan ... derived from neutral sources such as, for example, dispersion of employees in various types of industries across a given area, and the desired frequency of searches in any of the lesser divisions of the area, would protect an employer's Fourth Amendment rights. (436 U.S. at 321).

What, then, has been accomplished, asked Justice Stevens's dissenting opinion? A watered-down warrant requirement, allowing inspectors to enter premises as long as the employer was selected on the basis of neutral administrative criteria (in response to an employee complaint, or according to systematic visits to all facilities of a particular type, systematic follow up of previous remedial orders) protects business's privacy only with respect to non-routine, arbitrary inspections, as when an inspector decides on his own to give special attention to (or harass) a particular employer whom he is "out to get." Justice Stevens noted, however, that protection against the harassing inspection is already provided by the OSHA Act and regulations; these empower employers to ask to see an OSHA's inspector's credentials and to make toll-free telephone calls to the inspector's field office supervisor. And an employer can still refuse admission, in which case OSHA regulations tell the inspector to go away and get his office to seek a court order requiring the employer to admit him. An inspector who would like to conduct a nonroutine search for indefensible reasons, Stevens argued, is just as likely to be deterred by having to inform his superiors of his desire to get a court order and defend his reasons to the judge he asks for a court order as by having to go to court to ask for a search warrant. (436 U.S. at 333).

Far better, the dissenting opinion argued (in terms much the same as Frankfurter's majority opinion in *Frank v. Maryland*) to recognize that regulatory searches under systematic administrative systems such as OSHA's do not implicate the kind of privacy interests that the Fourth Amendment was aimed at protecting. "Fidelity to the original understanding of the Fourth Amendment ... leads to the conclusion that the Warrant Clause has no application to routine, regulatory inspections of commercial premises." (436 U.S. at 328). They should be regarded as "reasonable" within the meaning of that Amendment without a warrant and without probable cause. (436 U.S. at 326).

The Consequences of *Marshall v. Barlow's, Inc.*

Mr. Barlow's principled stand against the OSHA inspector had been vindicated by the U.S. Supreme Court. But as the dissent argued, it is hard to see what he really accomplished in terms of affecting the day-to-day interactions between regulated enterprises and the governmental inspectorate. The next time an OSHA inspector would come to Barlow's Inc. or any other workplace on a routine inspection, it would be both fruitless and needlessly alienating for the business manager to insist that he first get a search warrant. Within weeks of the decision, OSHA and other regulatory agencies had revised their enforcement manuals to instruct inspectors how to get a warrant, the key to which was to simply to show the court that the enterprise to be inspected had been selected according to a pre-existing, systematic plan for deploying scarce enforcement resources. Enforcement agencies already had been in the business in making and revising such plans constantly.[29] Not surprisingly, therefore, when we asked about *Marshall v. Barlow's* long-term effect on the regulatory inspection process in the United States, it was difficult to find any significant impact.

For example, the Assistant Administrator for Enforcement of the Environmental Protection Agency at the time *Barlow's* was decided determined that the decision *applied* to "all current inspection programs of EPA, including inspection conducted by State personnel and by contractors." But he also noted that "*Barlow's* should only have a limited effect on EPA enforcement inspections."[30] That seems to have been the case for OSHA, too. Table 1 shows the percentage of OSHA inspections, from 1970–2001, in which an inspector's initial request for entry was denied.[31] Except for a brief flurry of Bill Barlow imitations in the first years after the Court decision, only a tiny percentage of regulated enterprises have insisted that an OSHA inspector first get a search warrant. After a peak of refusals in 3.7 percent of inspections in 1982, the numbers declined sharply. In 2001 (the last year for which

---

29. Thus an April 1978 Memorandum from the EPA enforcement office to enforcement officials around the country summarized the Supreme Court's standard for an administrative warrant (a general administrative plan based on neutral criteria) and then noted:

> "Every program enforced by the Agency has such a scheme by which it prioritizes and schedules its inspections. For example, a scheme under which every permit holder in a general program is inspected on an annual basis is a satisfactorily neutral administrative scheme. Also, a scheme in which one of every three known PCB transformer repair shops is inspected on an annual basis is satisfactory." Memorandum on Entry Procedures, U.S. Environmental Protection Agency, 11 April 1978.

30. Ibid.

31. OSHA's integrated management system.

data is available), 257 OSHA inspections were initially refused out of 72,836 inspections—a mere 0.35 percent of the total.[32]

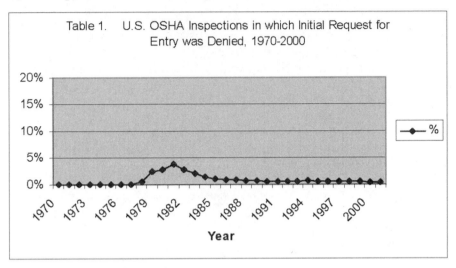

Table 1.   U.S. OSHA Inspections in which Initial Request for Entry was Denied, 1970-2000

This aggregate data is reinforced by anecdotal evidence. Representatives of the Boise Area OSHA office told us in 2005 that warrant requests are very rare, maybe one or two a year out of 500 or so inspections.[33] OSHA inspectors there were not even familiar with the *Barlow's* ruling. Mike Horowitz, a district manager at the California OSHA Enforcement Unit, recalls only a handful of warrant requests in his eleven years with the agency.[34] One such request was from Yellow Freight, a transport company with an "institutional policy" of insisting on warrants. Such cases are highly unusual, however; out of approximately 10,000 or so CAL-OSHA inspections, warrant requests occur ten or twenty times a year.[35]

Inspectors at other agencies give similar accounts: Pat Kennelley, chief of the Food and Drug branch in the California Department of Health Services, estimates that inspectors in that office need to obtain a

---

32. This number does not tell us how many times warrants were required (OSHA does not keep data on this), but rather how inspections were originally turned away (which could have been for pragmatic reasons related to business schedules, rather than for Barlow-type reasons of principle). Many of these cases may have been resolved without the need for a warrant.

33. Interview by author, phone, April 1, 2005.

34. Interview by author, phone, April 11, 2005.

35. Michael Mason, Cal OSHA legal department, interview by author, phone, April 11, 2005.

search warrant maybe twice a year, out of more than 4000 yearly inspections—and those are in the rare *criminal* investigation, rather than routine administrative compliance-oriented inspections.[36] Initial refusals are more common, perhaps one out of every 300, but many of these are resolved within five minutes.[37] Wil Bruhns, a public relations officer for the San Francisco Bay Regional Quality Control Board, which performs about 500 inspections a year[38], has obtained a warrant twice in the past 28 years.[39] In one of those cases (an inspection of the IT corporation in Benicia) the warrant was secured preemptively and turned out to be unnecessary.[40]

However infrequent conflicts about inspections have become, a handful of determined businesses have forced the courts continue to wrestle with the scope of the legal doctrine announced in *Marshall v. Barlow's, Inc.* In a 1984 U.S. Court of Appeals case, the Fifth Circuit held that New Orleans Public Service officials could insist that the Office of Federal Contract Compliance first seek a search warrant before examining company employment records to check compliance with an Executive Order forbidding employment discrimination.[41] On the other hand, the Ninth Circuit held that commercial fishing boats fell within the "closely regulated business" exception, and upheld a regulation issued under the Marine Mammal Protection Act that made issuance of a commercial fishing permit contingent on agreeing to allow federal inspectors on board upon request without a warrant.[42] Shortly after the *Barlow's* decision a California appeals court held that, since CAL-OSHA allowed for criminal sanctions (not at issue with Federal OSHA), a probable cause standard was legitimate.[43] However, a 1989 case[44] signifi-

36. Interview by author, phone, October 12, 2004.

37. Ibid.

38. Permits issued by the Board include a consent-to inspect provision, giving the agency authority to inspect all licensed industries. Nevertheless, inspectors have been informed by legal advisors that they may still need to secure an administrative warrant. Many regulatory agencies include such "right of entry" provisions in their permits. Although this does not necessarily override the regulated firm's right under *Marshall v. Barlow's* to insist on a warrant before admitting the inspector, it may dissuade most permit holders from doing so.

39. Interview by author, phone, April 11, 2005.

40. Ibid.

41. United States v. New Orleans Public Service, 723 F.2d 422 (5th Cir.1984). According to the decision: "Executive Order (E.O.) 11,246 prohibits employment discrimination by contractors with the federal government. The order requires that all covered government contracts contain a nondiscrimination clause and that contractors agree to take affirmative action to ensure the equal employment opportunity goals of the order are attained."

42. Balelo v. Baldrige, 724 F.2d 753 (9th Cir.), cert. denied, 104 S.Ct. 3536 (1984).

43. Salwasser Manufacturing Co. v. The Municipal Court for the Fresno Judicial District of Fresno County, 94 Cal. App. 3d 223 (1979).

cantly vitiated California's requirement of criminal probable cause, in effect endorsing the compromise standard put forth in *Barlow's*.

Consequences for Bill Barlow[45]

Bill Barlow, capitalizing on his newfound fame as protagonist in a U.S. Supreme Court case, was elected to the Pocatello City Council. His subsequent run for the Idaho state senate was unsuccessful, but he became enmeshed in other legal struggles against state authority. After an altercation with the Idaho Tax Commission, the State Attorney General's office charged Barlow with tax evasion and he was convicted. However, the trial judge threw out the verdict due to allegations that a Tax Commission auditor had misled the jury. The state appealed and the Idaho Supreme Court reinstated the conviction, remanding the case to the trial judge for sentencing. According to his son Wayne, who took over Barlow's Inc. shortly after his father's death in 1992, the trial judge sentenced Bill Barlow to pay a $5 penalty.

Barlow's success in the courts made him a hero to small business interests and conservative activists. On Wayne's desk there are several plaques awarded Barlow, including those bestowed by the Idaho Chapter of the Associated Builders and Contractors, and the Conservative Activists Award. The latter bears the inscription "for proving that American citizens can, by standing steadfast for their freedoms, successfully combat the excesses of bureaucracy." In addition to the awards for Bill Barlow's moxie in taking on the system, his son proudly displays the Industrial Company Safety Award bestowed on Barlow's Inc. for outstanding accident prevention. Says Wayne Barlow, "They picked on the wrong guy."

But of course OSHA didn't "pick on" Barlow's Inc. They merely picked it. That alone was the nub of Barlow's resistance. Bill Barlow had really wanted not merely the right to turn away (for a while) random regulatory searches, but the right to tell government to let him alone entirely. What bothered his father in the aftermath of the Supreme Court case, Wayne told us, was simply the endurance of OSHA. Bill Barlow, said Wayne, had hoped to "put them out of business." Instead they are "much worse now than they were in '75 ... [The ruling] wounded but it didn't kill. They used to have teeth, now they have fangs." Even aside from the questionable accuracy of that assessment,[46]

---

44. Salwasser Manufacturing Co. v. Occupational Safety and Health Appeals Board, 214 Cal. App. 3d 625 (1989).

45. The quotes, and the biographical account of Barlow after the Supreme Court case, are from our interview with Wayne Barlow, Bill Barlow's son (phone, April 1, 2004).

46. In fact, the Occupational Safety and Health Act provides for the imposition of far weaker criminal sanctions and far smaller fines than those authorized by the statutes defanging OSHA was something Barlow simply could not expect from the courts. His complaint was at bottom a political one. And the struggle over the optimal intrusiveness and enforcement methods of the growing regulatory state would evolve in the realm of politics, not of courts.

Conclusion

In 1975, when Bill Barlow asserted that he had a constitutional right to exclude a regulatory inspector, his stance might be seen as part of the birth pangs of a rapidly intensifying regulatory order. Business people in industries that had not previously been closely regulated were suddenly subjected to demanding new regulations concerning nondiscrimination, workplace safety and health, pollution control, waste disposal, quality control, employee benefit plans, consumer protection, and much more. In the 1970s, the regulatory inspector was often greeted with trepidation and resentment—not necessarily because of his agency's demands but because he symbolized a whole cadre of regulatory officials from a variety of agencies. The inspector symbolized not a serious imposition on the business manager's *privacy* but a serious reduction in his *autonomy and power*. The regulations were detailed and complex, and it was easy to be found to be out of compliance. Regulated businessmen—middle class people who thought of themselves as law-abiding and responsible members of their communities—complained that regulatory inspectors treated them as if they were criminals or potential criminals.

By the first decade of the 21st Century, however, a quarter-century after the Supreme Court decided *Marshall v. Barlow's*, both regulation and the regulated community have evolved. In cross-national perspective, American regulation continues to be more prescriptive, complex, and legalistically enforced than parallel regulatory programs in other economically advanced democracies.[47] But decades of political complaints by regulated businesses have had a significant impact.

---

enforced by the U.S. Environmental Protection Agency, the Food and Drug Administration, the Securities and Exchange Commission and many other federal regulatory bodies—and criminal prosecution by OSHA have been few and far between. THOMAS McGARITY & SIDNEY SHAPIRO, THE FAILED PROMISE OF THE OCCUPATIONAL SAFETY AND HEALTH ADMINISTRATION (1993); Orly Lobel, Interlocking Regulatory and Industrial Relations: The Governance of Workplace Safety Administrative Law Review (forthcoming, 2005). Budgetary cuts have left OSHA with a smaller staff than it had in the 1970s, and its corps of inspectors is widely regarded as inadequate. PETER STRAUSS, TODD RAKOFF & CYNTHIA FARINA, GELLHORN & BYSE'S ADMINISTRATIVE LAW 286–290 (10th Ed. 2003). Furthermore, OSHA's enforcement style currently tends to be less legalistic than it was in the 1970s.

47. See Kazumasu Aoki & John Cioffi, *Poles Apart: Industrial Waste Management Regulation and Enforcement in the United States and Japan* 21 Law & Policy 213–45 (1999); John Braithwaite, "The Nursing Home Industry," in BEYOND THE LAW: CRIME IN COMPLEX ORGANIZATIONS, Michael Tonry & Albert J. Reiss, Jr., ed., (1993); Marco Verweij, (2000) *Why is the River Rhine Cleaner than the Great Lakes (Despite Looser Regulation)*, 34 Law & Society Review 1007 (2000); ROBERT A. KAGAN & LEE AXELRAD, EDS., REGULATORY

Regulatory officials usually are adept at reading the tenor of their political environment and at shaping enforcement methods accordingly.[48] Comparing OSHA enforcement activities in 30 counties in the state of New York, 1976–1985, political scientist John Scholz and colleagues found that OSHA inspectors imposed more penalties and larger penalties in counties whose legislative representatives were liberal Democrats.[49] In the late 1970s, as Barlow was arguing that business needed the judiciary to guard against over-reaching OSHA inspectors, the ongoing political complaints about OSHA's legal enforcement style induced President Carter to urge OSHA to reduce citations and small penalties for "nonserious" regulatory violations. President Reagan, elected after a campaign denouncing "excessive government regulation," appointed a new OSHA chief who promised a less legalistic approach. OSHA's propensity to imposed fines declined significantly,[50] as did the proportion of fines that employers contested.[51]

The business community changed too. In the contemporary regulatory state, the overwhelming majority of business firms accept the legitimacy of regulatory inspections. They no longer (if they ever did) have the same expectations of privacy concerning their business operations that they do concerning their dwelling places. Sociolegal research indicates that most contemporary business managers generally regard compliance with most laws and regulations as a social and political necessity as well as a legal responsibility.[52] Noncompliance that results in legal penalties often generates adverse publicity, which can alienate

ENCOUNTERS: MULTINATIONAL CORPORATIONS AND AMERICAN ADVERSARIAL LEGALISM (Berkeley, CA: University of California Press, 2000).

48. Nancy Frank & Michael Lombness, *Gaining Regulatory Compliance: Law Enforcement and Power in an Interactionist Perspective*, 20 Administration and Society 71 (1988); David Hedge, Donald Menzel & George Williams, *Regulatory Attitudes and Behavior: The Case of Surface Mining Regulation*, 41 Western Political Quarterly 323 (1988).

49. John Scholz, Jim Twombly and Barbara Headrick, *Street Level Political Controls over Federal Bureaucracy*, 85 American Pol. Sci. Rev. 829 (1991).

50. John Scholz & Feng Heng Wei, *Regulatory Enforcement in a Federal System*, 80 Am. Pol. Sci. Rev. 1249 (1986). Similar declines in the use of penalties occurred in other federal regulatory agencies during Reagan's first term, although they returned to their previous trajectory during his second term, after angry oversight hearings by Congressional Democrats forced the President to restore agency enforcement budgets and appoint new agency leaders who promised more vigorous enforcement. Dan Wood & Richard Waterman, *The Dynamics of Political Control of the Bureaucracy*, 82 Am. Pol. Sci. Rev. 213 (1988).

51. The proportion of OSHA fines formally contested by employers dropped from 21 percent in 1979 to 3 percent in 1983. Thomas Kniesner & John Leeth, *Improving Worker Safety*, Regulation, Fall 1991 pp. 64–70.

52. M. Vandenberg, *Beyond Elegance: A Testable Typology of Social Norms in Corporate Environmental Compliance,* 22 Stanford Environmental Law Journal 55 (2003); NEIL GUNNINGHAM, ROBERT A. KAGAN & DOROTHY THORNTON, SHADES OF GREEN: BUSINESS, REGULATION AND ENVIRONMENT (2003).

employees, local communities, business partners, and family members.
Business managers also have become accustomed to complying with a
broad array of governmental reporting requirements that make various
aspects of their operations more transparent. A recent survey indicates
that managers often applaud news that a serious regulatory violator in
their industry has been punished (for that reassures them their own
compliance efforts have not been foolish).[53] Hence most business people
simply accept the authority of the regulatory inspector who appears in
the front office, just as almost all motorists accept the authority of the
highway patrol officer who orders them to halt and show him their
license and registration, and almost all taxpayers accept the authority of
the IRS agent who asks them to produce documents that would support
the statements on their income tax return.

Meanwhile, regulatory agency leaders appointed by Democratic governors and presidents as well as by Republicans have come to put a very
high premium on developing more flexible, cooperation-seeking ways of
implementing regulatory norms. Regulators' acceptance of the site-
specific knowledge, problem-solving skills, and legitimate interests of
regulated business thus has been the complement of growing business
acceptance of regulation. That is not to say that business-government
cooperation is universal, that deterrence is not necessary,[54] or that
serious political and legal conflict over particular regulatory enforcement
actions are uncommon. It does mean, however, that the battle Mr.
Barlow fought, which was about keeping the regulatory inspector at bay,
has become increasingly outmoded.

Was *Marshall v. Barlow's* important in this evolution of business
and government attitudes about regulation and regulatory inspection?
Probably not. The forums for that evolution were not in the courts but
in business complaints to politicians, legislative hearings, presidential
campaigns, trade association meetings, and the constant interaction

---

53. Dorothy Thornton, Neil Gunningham & Robert A. Kagan, *General Deterrence
and Corporate Environmental Behavior*, 27 Law & Policy 262 (2005); Gunningham,
Thornton & Kagan, *Motivating Management: Corporate Compliance in Environmental
Protection* 27 Law & Policy 289 (2005). Of course, notwithstanding the general trend
toward stronger commitments to regulatory compliance, there are still many regulatory
violations and, in some industries, firms that heedlessly disregard regulatory responsibilities. For a vivid example in the field of workplace safety, see David Barstow and Robin
Stein, "When Workers Die," The New York Times (December 21, 22 and 23, 2003).

54. Empirical studies demonstrate that "regulatory inspections work." OSHA inspections that result in the imposition of penalties, for example, typically result in reductions in
workplace injuries in those establishments. Wayne Gray & John T. Scholz, *Analyzing the
Equity and Efficiency of OSHA Enforcement*, 13 Law & Policy 185 (1991); John Mendeloff
& Wayne Gray, *Inside the Black Box: How do OSHA Inspections Lead to Reductions in
Workplace Injuries?* 27 Law & Policy 219 (2005). Similar results have emerged from studies
of environmental inspections. See Wayne Gray & Ronald Shadbegian, *When and Why do
Plants Comply? Paper Mills in the 1980s*, 27 Law & Policy 238 (2005).

between regulatory officials and regulated businesses. *Marshall v. Barlow's* struck a compromise that meant it would have little effect on day-to-day regulatory enforcement and hence little effect on the attitudes of either regulators or business people.

But *Marshall v. Barlow's* does symbolize the responsiveness of the American legal system. It demonstrated once again that on occasion, a person of conviction and determination like Bill Barlow (who has a committed lawyer like John Runft) can take his complaint to the highest court in the land and receive not only a respectful hearing but actually win his case. And it demonstrated the Supreme Court's tendency to combine both legalism and pragmatism—as the justices insisted, rather legalistically, that the Fourth Amendment's protections against arbitrary law enforcement apply to business entities as well as to households, but at the same time sought, quite pragmatically, to protect the public interest by ensuring that the warrant requirement would not really impose any burdens on the administration of regulatory programs.

In her contribution, Professor Metzger explores the puzzle of *Vermont Yankee v. NRDC*. *Vermont Yankee* stands as a definitive rejection of judicial efforts to control burgeoning informal rulemaking by adding to the procedural requirements contained in the Administrative Procedure Act. Yet judicial expansion of the APA's procedural requirements has continued apace, and the Court's simultaneous sanction of searching substantive scrutiny sits oddly with its excoriation of the D.C. Circuit for that court's perceived procedural excesses. To understand *Vermont Yankee*, Professor Metzger puts the decision in its administrative and judicial context, exploring the case law and practical dilemmas facing administrators, advocates, and judges as the case unfolded. As her story tells it, *Vermont Yankee* is very much a creature of its time, when dramatic expansions in congressionally-mandated regulation led to multiple political and institutional struggles—between advocates and agencies, between agencies and courts, and between the Supreme Court and the D.C. Circuit. But the cautionary tale of *Vermont Yankee* has broader significance, and the decision's simultaneous centrality and practical irrelevance demonstrate the challenges facing judicial review in the modern administrative state.

4

Gillian E. Metzger*

The Story of Vermont Yankee: A Cautionary Tale of Judicial Review and Nuclear Waste

Tucked into Vermont's southeast corner, the small town of Vernon might seem an unlikely backdrop for one of the most important decisions interpreting the Administrative Procedure Act ("APA"). But in 1966 the Vermont Yankee Nuclear Power Corporation applied for a permit to start building a nuclear reactor along the banks of the Connecticut River in Vernon, and three years later applied for an operating license to run it. Thus were set in motion the agency proceedings that ultimately culminated, in 1978, in the Supreme Court's decision in *Vermont Yankee Nuclear Power Corporation v. Natural Resources Defense Council*.[1]

What follows here is the story of *Vermont Yankee*. To give a brief preview: The Atomic Energy Commission (AEC), in response to challenges raised against Vermont Yankee's operating license application, issued a rule addressing the environmental effects of the nuclear fuel cycle for use in assessing a reactor's environmental impact. The rule then came before the U.S. Court of Appeals for the District of Columbia Circuit, increasingly becoming the nation's central administrative law court and subjecting agency decisionmaking to assertive review. The D.C. Circuit concluded the AEC had failed to "thorough[ly] ventilat[e]" the issues of long-term storage and reprocessing of nuclear waste, and remanded the fuel cycle rule to the agency. In *Vermont Yankee*, the Supreme Court in turn reversed the D.C. Circuit, using the decision as

---

* Assoc. Prof., Columbia Law School. Special thanks to Ella Campi, Alan Lewis, and Nick McQuaid for excellent research assistance.

1. 435 U.S. 519 (1978).

an occasion to clip that court's wings and sternly rebuking it for suggesting the procedures utilized by the agency were deficient.

Vermont Yankee is a milestone in the development of judicial review in the modern regulatory state. In the late 1960s and early 1970s, the courts were faced with burgeoning federal regulation at a time when public confidence in agency expertise and impartiality was at low ebb. A debate reigned about what was the appropriate judicial response to this development. The main protagonists in this debate were two judges on the D.C. Circuit, Chief Judge David Bazelon and Judge Harold Leventhal. On many issues, the two were in accord; both accepted the need for enhanced judicial scrutiny of agency decisionmaking and for expansive readings of the APA's requirements for informal rulemaking. Where they disagreed was over whether the courts should impose procedural requirements on rulemaking beyond those listed in the APA or required by other statutes, agency regulations, or due process. Bazelon advocated such judicial procedural impositions, believing that courts were not competent to address the merits of the complex technological issues often involved, while Leventhal contended that courts should limit themselves to rigorous substantive scrutiny of agency decisionmaking.

Vermont Yankee stands as a rejection of Bazelon's proceduralist approach, with the Supreme Court ostensibly restricting judicial development of administrative procedure to the rarest of circumstances. The Court instructed federal judges in no uncertain terms that they should not embellish on the informal rulemaking procedures contained in the APA and codified at 5 U.S.C. § 553. Yet the lower courts continued to do exactly that, avoiding a direct confrontation with *Vermont Yankee* by rooting their procedural demands (however implausibly) in the text of § 553. In addition, even in *Vermont Yankee* itself, the Court affirmed the importance of careful judicial scrutiny to ensure that agencies provide an adequate record to justify the substance of the rules they adopt. The pressure of such substantive judicial review of agency decisionmaking led agencies to undertake additional deviations from the APA's minimal procedural blueprint for informal rulemaking—in particular, dramatically expanding the record and explanatory basis of their decisions.

On the other hand, it would be wrong to view *Vermont Yankee* as simply a toothless tiger. The decision limited the arsenal that judges could call upon to ensure agency accountability, arguably with poor or at least mixed results. After *Vermont Yankee*, agencies had less reason to explore new procedural formats as a means of addressing accountability concerns in-house, while courts were encouraged to engage in close substantive review of agency decisions for which they were often ill-equipped. At a minimum, the need to base procedural requirements in the APA's text limited courts' ability to overtly assess the policy benefits of procedural innovations or take into account the changed landscape of federal regulation.

The one thing *Vermont Yankee* clearly did not do, however, was resolve the growing debate over nuclear power and the problem of nuclear waste. Nearly thirty years after *Vermont Yankee* the nation still lacks a means for long-term storage of high-level nuclear waste. Moreover, as Yogi Berra famously said, it's deja vu all over again, as a recent D.C. Circuit decision has put on hold government efforts to develop a long-term waste repository at Yucca Mountain, Nevada.[2]

Vermont Yankee at the AEC

With the Atomic Energy Act of 1954, the federal government embarked on a policy of fostering commercial uses of nuclear power.[3] Prior to this point, nuclear plants in the United States were government-owned and operated under the aegis of the AEC. But the 1954 Act instructed the AEC to "encourage widespread participation in the development and utilization of atomic energy for peaceful purposes to the maximum extent consistent with the common defense and security and with the health and safety of the public."[4] Even with the impetus of the 1954 Act, it was only in the 1960s that significant numbers of commercial plants began to be built. By the late 1960s, however, a "great bandwagon market" for commercial nuclear power was underway, with utilities seeking permission to build new and larger nuclear power plants.[5]

Perhaps given the limited number of plants then in existence, for many years the AEC did not devote substantial attention to the question of how to deal with the wastes generated by nuclear power. The most noxious waste products generated by nuclear power plants are the highly radioactive and toxic elements contained in spent nuclear fuel, such as plutonium. Many of these elements not only are extremely harmful to humans, but in addition retain their toxicity for very long periods,

---

2. See Nuclear Energy Inst., Inc. v. EPA, 373 F.3d 1251, 1266–73 (D.C. Cir. 2004), rehearing and rehearing en banc denied (Sept. 1, 2004).

3. This discussion of issues surrounding nuclear waste and the federal government's response is drawn largely from the following sources: J. Samuel Walker, Containing the Atom: Nuclear Regulation in a Changing Environment, 1963–71 (1992); Joel Yellin, *High Technology and the Courts: Nuclear Power and the Need for Institutional Reform*, 94 Harv. L. Rev. 489 (1981); Charles H. Montange, *Federal Nuclear Waste Disposal Policy*, 27 Nat. Resources J. 309 (1987); American Physical Soc'y, Study Group on Nuclear Fuel Cycles and Waste Management, Report to the American Physical Society, 50 Mod. Rev. Physics 1 (1978); *Nuclear Energy Inst.,* 373 F.3d at 1258–62.

4. Atomic Energy Act of 1954, Pub. L. No. 83–703, § 3d, 68 Stat. 919, 922, (codified at 42 U.S.C. § 2013(d)).

5. Walker, supra note 3, at 18.

ranging from 600 to millions of years. Disposing of such waste thus requires either some form of long-term storage or reprocessing, through which plutonium and uranium are recovered from spent fuel. Each of these methods of disposal presents difficulties. Long-term storage requires identifying a site that is sufficiently geologically stable to prevent dissipation of the radioactive elements for the lengthy periods involved— and a community willing to have such a storage facility nearby. Reprocessing reduces the amount of high-level waste requiring disposal but creates substantial security concerns, because it becomes necessary to control access to the plutonium that reprocessing produces.

By the early 1970s, the problems involved in dealing with high-level waste were gaining public attention. Indeed, commercial use of nuclear power generally was becoming increasingly contentious, as public concerns grew about the health and safety risks posed by nuclear power plants.[6] Under the Atomic Energy Act and AEC regulations, licensing of nuclear reactors is a two-stage event; reactor operators first apply for a construction permit and then after the plant is built, apply for a license to operate it.[7] Any interested person affected by grant of a construction permit or operating license can request a hearing on the application and intervene as a party in the proceeding. Such license hearings are considered formal adjudications, and thus trigger the trial-type procedures set out in the APA.[8] Initially, the statutory right to a hearing was rarely invoked, but as the number of licenses issued and public concerns about nuclear power increased, environmental and citizen groups started to seek intervention to oppose new plants. And these plant opponents began raising nuclear waste concerns as part of their arguments against the government licensing proposed facilities.

Their challenges on this score were buttressed by enactment of the National Environmental Policy Act of 1969 (NEPA), which required federal agencies to issue a detailed environmental impact statement on

---

6. *See* Steven Ebbin & Raphael Kasper, *Citizen Groups and the Nuclear Power Controversy: Uses of Scientific and Technological Information* 10–21 (1974) (discussing growth of contested AEC license proceedings in the 1960s and early 1970s); Walker, *supra* note 3, at 387–422 (detailing changes in public views of nuclear power and effect of rise of environmentalism on the AEC); Richard Goldsmith, *Regulatory Reform and the Revival of Nuclear Power*, 20 Hofstra L. Rev. 159, 161–77 (1991) (describing increasing public skepticism of the AEC).

7. See Power Reactor Dev. Co. v. IUEW, 367 U.S. 396 (1961); see also 10 C.F.R. part 50 (2004) (Domestic Licensing of Production and Utilization Facilities); Goldsmith, supra note 6, at 186–91 (describing the NRC's more recent development of a combined license option).

8. *See* 5 U.S.C. §§ 556–557, 42 U.S.C. § 2239(a). However, such licensing hearings differ from formal adjudication under the APA in that they are presided over by three-member atomic safety and licensing boards, as authorized by the Atomic Energy Act. See 42 U.S.C. § 2241(a).

major federal actions affecting the quality of the environment.[9] NEPA's enactment created a substantial dilemma for the AEC. After some initial debate, the AEC's General Counsel's office came to the view that NEPA applied to the agency's licensing and rulemaking decisions. A harder problem was what to do about nuclear plants under construction, or already constructed but not yet licensed. Licensing proceedings on these plants would take place after NEPA's effective date of January 1, 1970. But particularly for plants authorized and constructed without attention to environmental issues, application of NEPA had a retroactive aspect, and might necessitate significant retrofitting or perhaps (in extreme cases) cancellation of planned facilities. At a minimum, application of NEPA would lead to substantial delays in plant licensing and construction, to allow for preparation of impact statements and hearings.[10]

The AEC's response was to postpone NEPA's enforcement. Expressing concerns about the need for "an orderly transition . . . and to avoid unreasonable delays in the construction and operation of nuclear power plants urgently needed to meet the national requirements for electric power," the AEC prohibited consideration of environmental issues at hearings officially noticed before March 4, 1971. In addition, the agency stated it would delay assessment of environmental factors for plants granted a construction permit before NEPA became effective until the plant applied for an operating license.[11] This timing decision, as well as the AEC's reluctance to independently assess environmental effects of proposed plants other than by having staff promulgate impact statements, provoked great ire on the D.C. Circuit. In *Calvert Cliffs' Coordinating Committee v. AEC*, the D.C. Circuit castigated the AEC for a "crabbed interpretation of NEPA [that] makes a mockery of the Act," and characterized the agency's timing proposal as a "shocking" delay that "seems to reveal a rather thoroughgoing reluctance to meet the NEPA procedural obligations in the agency review process."[12] Under the 1971 *Calvert Cliffs'* decision, the AEC was required to consider the environmental impact of all facilities for which license proceedings were still pending when NEPA became effective, as well as to assess promptly the environmental impact of facilities under construction to determine if construction changes were available that might lessen environmental harm caused by the facilities. Despite *Calvert Cliffs'* disruptive effects, the AEC decided not to seek further review, in part out of concern to

9. Pub. L. No. 91–190, 83 Stat. 852, (codified at 42 U.S.C. § 4331, § 4332(2)(c)); Robert L. Rabin, *Federal Regulation in Historical Perspective*, 38 Stan. L. Rev. 1189, 1279–90 (1986).

10. For a description of this debate, see Walker, supra note 3, at 363–86.

11. See *Implementation of the National Environmental Policy Act of 1969*, 35 Fed. Reg. 18,469, 18,470 (Dec. 4, 1970).

12. 449 F.2d 1109, 1117, 1119–20 (D.C. Cir. 1971).

improve the agency's public image on environmental issues and in part because the potential for judicial or legislative reversal seemed slim.[13]

Calvert Cliffs' also led to the emergence of a more coordinated opposition to nuclear plant licensing. The attorney for the Calvert Cliffs' Coordinating Committee was Anthony Roisman, a partner at a new public interest law firm in Washington D.C.[14] Roisman worked closely with the National Resources Defense Council (NRDC), a national environmental law group founded the year before and funded by the Ford Foundation,[15] as well as other environmental law groups springing up at the same time. Roisman's work on *Calvert Cliffs'* got his name circulating as an attorney who would represent citizen groups opposing nuclear plants before the AEC; up to this point most such groups participated in AEC hearings without benefit of counsel.[16] In particular, Roisman subsequently represented the New England Coalition on Nuclear Pollution, a group started in 1971 by citizens and scientists from Vermont and western Massachusetts. Along with NRDC, the New England Coalition took a lead role in opposing award of Vermont Yankee's operating license.

Only one environmental group had sought to intervene in the hearing the AEC held on Vermont Yankee's application for a construction permit in 1967. But, as a sign of the changing climate for nuclear power, seven such organizations intervened when Vermont Yankee subsequently applied for an operating license for the plant in 1969.[17] Vermont Yankee was one of the plants that would have been exempted from NEPA under the AEC's proposed policy, as the hearing on its operating license was noticed in February, 1971. As a result of *Calvert Cliffs'*, however, NEPA now applied. Indeed, NEPA formed the basis for the intervenors' main challenge to award of Vermont Yankee's operating license: that the environmental effects associated with the "back end" of the nuclear fuel cycle—the transportation, reprocessing, and storage of spent fuel from a plant[18]—had to be considered in determining whether

---

13. See Walker, supra note 3, at 383–84.

14. The firm, Berlin, Roisman and Kessler, was started by Edward Berlin and Gladys Kessler, in addition to Roisman, in 1969. Telephone Interview with Anthony Z. Roisman, Founding Partner, Berlin, Roisman, and Kessler (Nov. 23, 2004) [hereinafter Roisman Interview]. For a discussion of their decision to start a public interest law firm, *see* Edward Berlin, Anthony Z. Roisman, & Gladys Kessler, *Public Interest Law*, 38 Geo. Wash. L. Rev. 675 (1969).

15. For a history of the origins of the NRDC, *see* ROBERT GOTTLIEB, FORCING THE SPRING: THE TRANSFORMATION OF THE AMERICAN ENVIRONMENTAL MOVEMENT 140–43 (1993).

16. Roisman Interview, *supra* note 14.

17. See In re Vermont Yankee Nuclear Power Corp., 4 A.E.C. 776, 777 (Mar. 14, 1972); In re Vermont Yankee Nuclear Power Corp., 4 A.E.C. 36, 37 (Dec. 8, 1967).

18. The nuclear or uranium fuel cycle refers to the chain of activities associated with production and ultimate disposal of nuclear fuel. The "back end" activities are those that

to award Vermont Yankee's license and included in the environmental impact statement on the reactor.

Unfortunately for the intervenors, the atomic safety and license board conducting the hearing on Vermont Yankee's operating license took a different view of the scope of NEPA's application, and refused to require the AEC staff to include fuel cycle environmental effects. The appeal board that reviewed the licensing board's decision agreed, stating there was "no way of ascertaining now which of the various reprocessing plants now in existence or to be constructed will from time to time receive some irradiated fuel elements from [the Vermont Yankee] plant," and new methods of reprocessing might be developed during the Vermont Yankee plant's projected forty-year life. As a result, the appeal board concluded that individual reactor licensing proceedings should address environmental issues connected to transportation of spent fuel and other waste from the plant, but not issues related to reprocessing, storage, and disposal of spent fuel; the latter should instead be addressed in reprocessing plant license proceedings. Rejecting the intervenors' other challenges, the appeal board affirmed the licensing board's decision to award Vermont Yankee a temporary operating license.[19]

[handwritten margin note: Board said didn't have to address reprocessing]

The AEC's commissioners declined to grant further review. But in November 1972, shortly after the appeal board's decision in *Vermont Yankee*, the AEC proposed issuing a rule on the question of whether—and how—environmental effects of the nuclear fuel cycle should be considered in individual reactor proceedings. According to the AEC, a generic rule addressing the environmental effects of the fuel cycle was needed because of the frequency with which the fuel cycle issue was arising in individual license proceedings. Vigorous judicial enforcement of NEPA no doubt also spurred the agency to action. Prior to NEPA's enactment, the AEC's position had been that it was statutorily precluded from considering environmental concerns unrelated to radiation. In 1969, the First Circuit upheld the AEC's position in a case involving the Vermont Yankee reactor, rejecting New Hampshire's claim that the AEC should have considered the effect that discharge of boiling water from Vermont Yankee would have on the Connecticut River.[20] But under

---

occur after the fuel is burnt in the reactor, the "front end" those that occur beforehand. For a light-water reactor such as Vermont Yankee's, front end activities include: mining and milling uranium ore; converting uranium oxide to uranium hexafluoride; enriching uranium; reconversion of uranium hexafluoride to uranium oxide; and fabricating nuclear fuel.

19. See In re Vermont Yankee Nuclear Power Corp. (Vermont Yankee Nuclear Power Station), 4 A.E.C. 930, 933–34 (AEC, Atomic Safety & Licensing App. Bd., 1972); In re Vermont Yankee Corp., 5 A.E.C. 297 (AEC, Atomic Safety & Licensing App. Bd., 1972); see also Ebbin & Kasper, supra note 6, at 89–121 (describing Vermont Yankee licensing proceedings).

20. See New Hampshire v. AEC, 406 F.2d 170, 175 (1st Cir. 1969).

NEPA, consideration of environmental effects became part of every federal agency's mandate, and the D.C. Circuit's *Calvert Cliffs'* decision made clear that court would vigorously enforce that mandate.

In its November 1972 notice of proposed rulemaking, the AEC sought comment on two regulatory alternatives. The first expressly followed the approach outlined in the appeal board's *Vermont Yankee* decision and excluded any consideration of environmental effects of the fuel cycle in individual reactor proceedings, other than those connected to transportation of fuel to and wastes from the plant. The second established preset numeric values for environmental effects associated with different stages of the fuel cycle that the AEC's regulatory staff would include in the environmental impact statement on light water nuclear reactors. These values were listed in what became the infamous Table S–3 of a lengthy AEC staff report, *Environmental Survey of the Nuclear Fuel Cycle*, that was made publicly available at the same time as the notice of proposed rulemaking and represented the primary database for the proposed rule. To compile Table S–3, the AEC's regulatory staff first calculated the annual fuel requirement for a model light water reactor with a 30–year life, and then normalized the land use, water use, fossil fuel use and effluent releases for each activity (other than transportation) involved in fabricating and disposing of this amount of fuel. To give an example: the estimate release of liquid uranium or uranium daughters associated with the model reactor's annual fuel requirement was 2.4 curies, with 2 curies released during uranium milling, .33 curies released during uranium hexafluoride production, and .02 curies released during both fuel enrichment and fuel fabrication.[21]

The AEC billed the rulemaking an informal proceeding, and thus subject only to the requirements for informal rulemaking contained in § 553. Informal rulemaking was one of the APA's central innovations.[22]

---

21. See AEC, Environmental Survey of the Nuclear Fuel Cycle S–2 to S–18 & Table S–3A (November 1972).

22. *See* KENNETH CULP DAVIS, ADMINISTRATIVE LAW TREATISE § 6.15, at 283 (1st ed. Supp. 1970) (terming informal rulemaking "one of the greatest inventions of modern government"); George P. Shepherd, *Fierce Compromise: The Administrative Procedure Act Emerges from New Deal Politics*, 90 Nw. U. L. Rev. 1557, 1650–51 (1996).

TABLE S-3

SUMMARY OF ENVIRONMENTAL CONSIDERATIONS

FOR NUCLEAR FUEL CYCLE

(NORMALIZED TO MODEL LWR ANNUAL FUEL REQUIREMENTS)

Natural resource use	Total	Effluents — Chemical (MT)	Total
Land (acres):		Gases (including entrainment): [1]	
		SO_x	4400
Temporarily committed	63	NO_x [2]	1170
Undisturbed area	45	Hydrocarbons	11.3
Disturbed area	18	CO	29.7
		Particulates	1156
Permanently committed	4.6		
		Other gases:	
Overburden moved ($MT \times 10^{-6}$)	2.7	F-	1.9
Water (gallons $\times 10^{-6}$):		Liquids:	
		$SO_4^=$	5.8
Discharged to air	163	NO_3-	5.2
Discharged to water bodies	11,091	Fluoride	0.4
Discharged to ground	123	Ca^{++}	5.4
		Cl-	5.2
Total	11,238	Na	13.5
		NH_3	5.4
Fossil fuel:		Fe	0.4
Electrical energy (mw.-hr. $\times 10^{-3}$)	317	Tailings solutions ($\times 10^{-3}$)	240
Equivalent coal ($MT \times 10^{-3}$)	118		
Natural gas (s.c.f. $\times 10^{-6}$)	102	Solids	91,000

Effluents—Radiological (curies)	Total	Maximum effect per annual fuel requirement of model 1000 MWe LWR
Gases (including entrainment):		
Rn-222	83	Principally from mills — Maximum annual dose rate <4
Ra-226	.02	percent of average natural background within 5 miles of
Th-230	.02	mill. Results in 0.06 man-rem per annual fuel require-
Uranium	0.6	ment. Due to dilute concentration and short half-life of
Tritium ($\times 10^{-3}$)	12	principal component, exposure beyond a 5-mile radius is
Kr-85 ($\times 10^{-6}$)	130	minuscule relative to natural background.
I-129	.002	Principally from fuel reprocessing plants—Whole body dose
I-131	.02	is 4.4 man-rem for population within 50-mile radius. This
Fission products	1.0	is <0.005 percent of average natural background dose to
Transuranics	.004	this population.
Liquids:		
Uranium and daughters	2.4	Principally from milling—included in tailings liquor and
		returned to ground—no effluents; therefore, no effect on
		environment.
Ra-226	.077	From UF_6 production—concentration <5 percent of 10 CFR
Th-230	.27	20 for total processing of 27.5 model LWR annual fuel
		requirements.
Th-234	.001	From fuel fabrication plants—concentration <1 percent of
Other uranium daughters	.001	10 CFR 20 for total processing 26 annual fuel requirements
		for model LWR.
Ru-106	4	From reprocessing plants—maximum concentration <4 per-
Tritium ($\times 10^{-6}$)	6.2	cent of 10 CFR 20 for total reprocessing of 26 annual fuel
Solids (buried):		requirements for model LWR.
Other than high level	1,300	From mills—included in tailings returned to ground—no
		significant effluent to the environment.
Thermal (B.t.u. $\times 10^{-9}$)	3,370	

[1] Estimated effluents based upon combustion of equivalent coal for power generation.
[2] 1.2 percent from natural gas use and process.

While providing a formal rulemaking procedure that embodied many of the procedural requirements of traditional agency adjudication, the APA additionally authorized a new, more informal and flexible approach to rulemaking. Known also as "notice and comment" rulemaking and codified at § 553, informal rulemaking was modeled more on legislation than adjudication and by its text was subject to notably few constraints.[23] According to the APA, agencies have to provide a "[g]eneral notice" that, in addition to giving logistical information and identifying the governing legal authority for the proposed rulemaking, need only include "either the terms or substance of the proposed rule or a description of the subjects and issues involved."[24] Although agencies must receive comments, they can choose whether to hold an oral hearing or limit participation to written form. And in promulgating their final rules agencies only have to "incorporate in the rules adopted a concise general statement of their basis and purpose."[25]

Even though not required to do so by § 553, the AEC opted to hold an oral hearing on the fuel cycle rule at which interested persons could submit oral or written testimony. The Commission created a three-member hearing board to preside over the hearing, and authorized it to question witnesses on their testimony. It further provided that the rulemaking record would stay open for 30 days after the hearing for supplemental written comments, thereby providing an opportunity to respond to testimony and issues that arose at the hearing.[26] Critically, however, the Commission decided not to allow discovery or cross-examination by participants at the hearing, nor were parties allowed to propose questions for the hearing board to ask.[27] This represented somewhat of a deviation from the AEC's recent practice; in two other major rulemakings initiated in 1971—one on emergency core cooling systems for reactors, the other on whether reactors should be required to keep the radioactivity in effluents as low as practicable—the AEC had allowed fuller use of adversarial procedures, including cross-examination. One result, however, was that these earlier rulemakings were very lengthy and resource-intensive proceedings; the cooling systems rulemaking, for example, involved more than 100 days of hearings.[28] That

---

23. See Rabin, supra note 9, at 264–66; Martin Shapiro, *APA: Past, Present, Future*, 72 Va. L. Rev. 447, 452–54 (1986).

24. See 5 U.S.C. § 553(b).

25. See id. § 553(c).

26. See Environmental Effects of the Uranium Fuel Cycle, 38 Fed. Reg. 49, 49–50 (1973).

27. See Vermont Yankee Nuclear Power Corp. v. NRDC, 435 U.S. 519 (1978) (Nos. 76–419, 76–528) app. at 659–60, 950 [hereinafter *Vermont Yankee* Appendix].

28. *See* Michael A. Bauer, *The Development of Rulemaking Within the Atomic Energy Commission: The Nuclear Regulatory Commission's Valuable Legacy*, 27 Admin. L. Rev.

experience had surely soured the agency on the idea of using adjudicatory proceedings for its rulemakings.

On the other hand, greater adversarial procedures would be available if issues involving the fuel cycle's environmental effects were addressed in individual reactor hearings, as these hearings are subject to the formal adjudication requirements of the APA.[29] This difference led two groups, the Consolidated National Intervenors (CNI) and Union of Concerned Scientists (UCS), to challenge the rulemaking procedures. CNI was an umbrella group that included numerous environmental and citizen organizations. Along with UCS, CNI was represented at the fuel cycle rulemaking by Roisman. CNI/UCS contended that in order for the fuel cycle rule to be legally valid, the rulemaking had to employ the same full adjudicatory procedures used to address safety and environmental issues in individual reactor hearings, and more particularly had to allow discovery and cross-examination. Although CNI/UCS repeatedly requested a hearing on the fuel cycle's environmental effects where rights of cross-examination and discovery would be provided, for the most part these groups did not identify specific testimony at the hearing that required further exploration.[30] Instead, motivating CNI/UCS' demand for cross-examination and discovery was their belief, derived from their experience with the recent cooling systems rulemaking, that only through these means could they uncover potential concerns raised by second-level staff which were not included in the *Environmental Survey* or in the testimony of top AEC officials.[31]

A two-day hearing on the fuel cycle rule was held in February 1973.[32] Presiding over the hearing was a three-member hearing board consisting of Max Paglin, Dr. Martin Steindler, and Dr. John Geyer. Two of these, Steindler and Geyer, were scientists with expertise on the nuclear fuel cycle and radioactive waste management; Steindler, for

---

165, 170–73 (1975); Goldsmith, supra note 6, at 171–77; see generally Note, *The Use of Generic Rulemaking to Resolve Environmental Issues in Nuclear Plant Licensing*, 61 Va. L. Rev. 869 (1975).

29. See 5 U.S.C. §§ 554, 556–557.

30. *Vermont Yankee* Appendix, supra note 27, at 837, 842–45, 933. The closest they came to such an identification was Roisman's remarks in passing on the need for further clarification regarding AEC assurances that nuclear wastes could be safely stored permanently. Id. at 837. This lack of specification led industry representatives to argue, both at the rulemaking and before the D.C. Circuit, that CNI/UCS had waived their request for cross-examination, a charge the D.C. Circuit rejected. See id. at 983–84; NRDC v. NRC, 547 F.2d 633, 643 n.25 (D.C. Cir. 1976).

31. *See Vermont Yankee* Appendix, supra note 27, at 946–49; Roisman Interview, supra note 14. For a description of cooling systems rulemaking, *see* Ebbin & Kasper, supra note 6, at 122–38.

32. A preliminary hearing to go over logistical details of the hearing was held on January 17, 1973. *Vermont Yankee* Appendix, supra note 27, at 655–99.

example, subsequently served on advisory committees on nuclear wastes for both the National Academy of Science and the Nuclear Regulatory Commission (NRC). Steindler, who worked at the AEC's Argonne National Laboratory, had served as an AEC consultant in the past, while Geyer, located at John Hopkins, had sat on numerous AEC atomic safety and licensing boards.[33] Paglin, in turn, was an experienced administrative lawyer—a former General Counsel and Executive Director of the Federal Communications Commission—who served as a permanent member and chairman of atomic safety and licensing boards for the AEC and NRC from 1972–75.[34] A broad range of organizations and interests testified at the hearing, including representatives of the AEC, the Environmental Protection Agency (EPA), state governments, environmental and citizen groups, and the nuclear power industry. The hearing generated a lengthy record; testimony and selections of the written comments comprise over five hundred pages of the appendix submitted to the Supreme Court.[35] At times, the hearing board engaged in active questioning, in particular asking the AEC official in charge of producing the *Environmental Survey*, S. H. Smiley, detailed questions about how the AEC's regulatory staff derived the values listed in Table S–3.

From the perspective of the subsequent judicial decisions, the most important testimony at the hearing was that of Dr. Frank Pittman, director of the AEC's waste management and transportation division. As originally issued, *Environmental Survey* did not include discussion of techniques for disposing of high-level wastes, and thus Pittman's testimony constituted the main support for the fact that Table S–3 assigned no environmental effects to waste storage and disposal other than the permanent commitment of land for a storage facility.[36] Indeed, his testimony provided the most detailed statement yet issued of the AEC's plans for dealing with such wastes. As outlined by Dr. Pittman, the AEC's assumption, in line with federal policy at the time, was that spent nuclear fuel from reactors would be reprocessed. Its plan was to construct a surface facility for storing high-level waste generated by reprocessing until a permanent geologic waste disposal site could be developed. Pittman provided schematic drawings of what the surface facility would look like and described how wastes would enter the facility and be stored.

---

33. *See* John C. Geyer, *ASCE Honorary Member, Dies at 89*, Civ. Engineering, Oct. 1985, at 72–73; Who's Who in America 4985 (58th ed. 2004) (biography of Martin Steindler); Comm. on Mixed Wastes, Nat'l Research Council, The State of Development of Waste Forms for Mixed Wastes 125–26 (1999) (same).

34. See The Communications Act: A Legislative History of the Major Amendments, 1934–1996 xxiii (Max D. Paglin ed., 1999).

35. *Vermont Yankee* Appendix, supra note 27, at 647–1186.

36. See *Environmental Survey*, supra note 21, at S–17 to S–19 (Table S–3A).

Even so, Dr. Pittman offered few specifics regarding key aspects of the facilities. For example, he provided little explanation of how a failure of the cooling system in the surface facility would be prevented or rectified, other than to claim that it would take over a week for the cooling water to boil away, allowing any of "[v]arious corrective actions" to be taken. More notably, he provided few details about the AEC's plans for a permanent facility, other than stating that the Commission expected to develop a site containing salt-beds and describing a plan for a pilot facility once a site was identified. Nonetheless, Pittman was confident that the safety and environmental impact of the proposed facilities was minimal. In his words, concerns raised regarding management of nuclear wastes were a "bugaboo" that "cannot logically be used as a rationale for delays in the progress of an essential technology." He argued that the AEC's plan assured "commercial high-level waste will be managed safely," characterizing the possibility of a meltdown at the surface facility as "incredible," and concluding the probability that the AEC would be able to develop an acceptable long-term bedded-salt facility was "very high." Indeed, the presumption that wastes could be permanently stored without any release of radioactivity was incorporated into Table S–3, which contained no entry for the environmental impact of such releases.[37]

Although the hearing board asked Dr. Pittman some questions regarding operation of and need for the surface facility, they did not seek further details on the permanent facility.[38] Greater concerns with Pittman's testimony and the problems of waste storage were raised by CNI/UCS. Anthony Roisman, who began his testimony immediately after the board finished questioning Dr. Pittman, stated "we are not satisfied with Mr. Pittman's well intentioned, but, we think, not at all well explained position with regard to the ability to handle nuclear waste for thousands of years. He has . . . referred to it as a program of perpetual management. . . . I think the public deserves the right to ask the question, What does that mean?"[39] Roisman additionally noted prior problems the AEC had encountered with waste disposal, as did a subsequent CNI/UCS witness, Dr. Henry Kendall of MIT. Kendall also testi-

---

37. See Statement of Dr. Frank Pittman, Director of Waste Management and Transportation, AEC, reprinted in *Vermont Yankee* Appendix, supra note 27, at 777–78, 782–83, 791; see also Baltimore Gas & Elec. Co. v. NRDC, 462 U.S. 87, 91–94 (1983) (discussing the incorporation of this zero-release assumption in Table S–3); *Environmental Survey*, supra note 21, at S–19 (Table S–3A).

38. *Vermont Yankee* Appendix, supra note 27, at 830–35. Dr. Pittman's initial testimony was in the first morning session of the hearing, but the board postponed its questioning of him until the afternoon. See id. 801, 827, 829–30. This delay may explain why the D.C. Circuit erroneously stated that the hearing board had not subjected Dr. Pittman to any questioning. See infra note 91.

39. *Vermont Yankee* Appendix, supra note 27, at 837–38.

fied to security risk of diversion associated with transportation of highly enriched uranium and plutonium.[40]

As instructed by the Commission, the hearing board produced a report identifying the issues raised by the hearing.[41] One main issue identified by the board was CNI/UCS' procedural challenge. According to CNI/UCS, existing case law supported their claim for an adjudicatory proceeding providing rights of cross-examination and discovery. At the time of the fuel cycle hearing in February 1973, this was a debatable proposition.[42] In a 1966 decision, *American Airlines v. Civil Aeronautics Board*, the en banc D.C. Circuit had noted that procedures in addition to those set out in § 553 at times might be necessary to ensure a fair hearing. But this language was dictum as the court refused to require additional procedures in that case, emphasizing that the Civil Aeronautics Board "did not limit itself to minimum procedures" in issuing the cargo service rule there at issue, and in particular had provided opportunity for oral argument.[43] More importantly, *American Airlines* upheld an agency's power to issue rules without providing full adjudicatory procedures, even if the issues addressed by the rules would otherwise be dealt with in a hearing where such procedures would apply.[44] The D.C. Circuit subsequently required use of procedures beyond those required by § 553 in two 1973 cases involving informal rulemaking, *Mobil Oil Corp. v. FPC*[45] and *International Harvester Co. v. Ruckelshaus*.[46] *International*

---

40. See id. at 843, 888–97, 904–05. UCS elaborated on these criticisms in supplemental comments submitted after the oral hearing was complete, describing the discussion of waste storage in the *Environmental Survey* (amended to include Dr. Pittman's testimony) as "replete with bland reassurances that problems can be solved even though the full extent and seriousness of these problems are not presented and explored." *Id.*, at 1069, 1081–98.

41. See Environmental Effects of the Uranium Fuel Cycle, 6 A.E.C. 539, 541 (July 6, 1973) [hereinafter Hearing Board Report].

42. For a detailed discussions of the relevant D.C. Circuit precedent, *see* Antonin Scalia, *Vermont Yankee: The APA, The D.C. Circuit, and the Supreme Court*, 1978 Sup. Ct. Rev. 345, 348–52; Stephen F. Williams, *"Hybrid Rulemaking" under the Administrative Procedure Act: A Legal and Empirical Analysis*, 42 U. Chi. L. Rev. 401, 425–36 (1974).

43. 359 F.2d 624, 632–33 (D.C. Cir. 1966) (en banc), cert. denied, 385 U.S. 843 (1966); see also Walter Holm & Co. v. Hardin, 449 F.2d 1009, 1016 (D.C. Cir. 1971) (invoking *American Airlines* and statutory requirement of notice and hearing to support conclusion that fairness required opportunity for cross-examination on the crucial issues involved in tomato marketing regulation); Marine Space Enclosures, Inc. v. FMC, 420 F.2d 577, 589 & n.36 (D.C. Cir. 1969) (also suggesting in dictum that in some cases "brief and oral argument" might not be sufficient to air certain issues).

44. *American Airlines*, 359 F.2d at 628–32.

45. 483 F.2d 1238, 1251–54, 1260 (D.C. Cir. 1973) (requiring "some sort of adversary, adjudicative-type procedures" and describing APA's provisions for informal and formal rulemaking as creating a spectrum of possible procedures rather than either-or procedural requirements).

Harvester in particular had held that at least some limited right of cross-examination might be needed to ensure fair ventilation of the issues.[47] The *International Harvester* court also expressed approval for the technique of having a hearing officer screen and ask questions submitted in advance by participants,[48] but the AEC had not employed that procedure in the fuel cycle rulemaking. Neither *Mobil Oil* or *International Harvester*, however, mandated additional procedures in every informal rulemaking, and the AEC had already gone beyond the requirements of § 553 in formulating the fuel cycle rule. Moreover, both decisions were potentially distinguishable, as the D.C. Circuit had emphasized provisions of the underlying organic statutes in mandating additional procedures.[49]

Thus, by the time the AEC addressed CNI/UCS' procedural complaint in April 1974, the D.C. Circuit had displayed its willingness to mandate rulemaking procedures beyond those required by § 553, and in particular its support for giving participants some opportunity to participate in questioning. On the other hand, agency counsel had a basis for advising the AEC that precedent did not demand procedures beyond those the AEC had provided, and accepting CNI/UCS' procedural challenge at that point would have required reopening the rulemaking, with substantial potential for delay. Perhaps not surprisingly, therefore, the Commission rejected CNI/UCS' argument. Concluding that the procedures used were "more than adequate," it emphasized that no proffered evidence was excluded and that CNI/UCS did not "make an offer of proof—or even remotely suggest—what substantive matters it would develop under different procedures."[50] The Commission also underscored

---

46. 478 F.2d 615, 630-31 (D.C. Cir. 1973). Similarly, in a January 1974 decision, O'Donnell v. Shaffer, the D.C. Circuit upheld a rule promulgated using § 553 procedures but stated "[t]his Court has long recognized that basic considerations of fairness may dictate procedural requirements not specified by Congress. Oral submissions . . . and cross-examination may be necessary if critical issues cannot otherwise be resolved." 491 F.2d 59, 62 (D.C. Cir. 1974).

47. *Int'l Harvester*, 478 F.2d at 649.

48. Id. at 631.

49. See id. at 629–31, 648–49 (discussing statutory requirement of "public hearing" on applications for suspension of auto emission standards and justifying additional procedures on the ground that "[t]he procedures followed in this case . . . have resulted in a record that leaves this court uncertain, at a minimum, whether the essentials of the intention of Congress [in authorizing suspensions] were achieved."); *Mobil Oil*, 483 F.2d at 1258–59 (emphasizing statutory requirement of substantial evidence review, which it read as entailing that "the proceedings must provide some mechanism for introduce adverse evidence and criticize evidence introduced by others"). *Mobil Oil* is further distinguishable by the fact that the court expressed doubt that the Federal Power Commission had even met the notice requirements of § 553. See id. at 1251 n.39.

50. *See Environmental Effects of the Uranium Fuel Cycle*, 39 Fed. Reg. 14,188, 14,189 (Apr. 22, 1974).

that the regulatory staff had made various drafts and notes used in preparing the *Environmental Survey* publicly available.

The remaining issues identified by the hearing board were more substantive. In particular, the *Environmental Survey* was challenged as inadequate, due to its failure to include analysis of the environmental effects associated with waste reprocessing and storage.[51] As the CNI/UCS witnesses noted, at the time of the hearing the AEC had already encountered difficulties in dealing with nuclear wastes. Other countries, in particular France, had active reprocessing plants. But in the United States only one commercial reprocessing plant had been built, and that plant shut down in 1972—six years after it began operations—because of technical and financial problems. In 1970, the AEC announced plans to develop a long-term geologic storage repository in salt-beds in Lyons, Kansas. However, by 1972 the agency was forced to acknowledge that the site was unsuitable for a long-term facility, due to abandoned gas and oil drill holes in the area and a neighboring mine that used large amounts of water to remove salt, all of which raised the danger that the facility might be breached, allowing radioactive wastes to escape.[52] In addition, sizeable leaks of stored high-level waste had occurred at the AEC's facility in Hanford, Washington.[53]

Given these problems and the lack of detail in Dr. Pittman's testimony, the D. C. Circuit's description of his remarks "as vague, but glowing" seems not only fair but overly kind.[54] Whether agency counsel could have predicted that the D.C. Circuit would find Pittman's testimony so inadequate as to necessitate a remand is a closer call, as the D.C. Circuit had only recently begun to tighten scrutiny of agency rulemaking.[55] On the other hand, it did not require prescience to predict that the

---

51. See Hearing Board Report, supra note 41, at 542–543. Additional issues involved, inter alia, the possibility of sabotage, the treatment of pending license cases, the feasibility of the proposed alternatives, and access to the background materials and calculations used by the AEC's regulatory staff in generating the Survey. *See id.* at 544–45.

52. See Walker, supra note 3, at 24–25; Philip M. Boffey, *Radioactive Waste Site Search Gets Into Deep Water*, 190 Science 361 (1975). By mid-1975, a subsequent effort to develop a long-term storage facility in salt-beds in New Mexico had also proved unsuccessful. *See id.*

53. See Yellin, supra note 3, at 535–36.

54. See NRDC v. NRC, 547 F.2d 633, 648 (D.C. Cir. 1976); infra text accompanying notes 139–44 (describing process leading to development of Yucca Mountain site). For similar assessments of Dr. Pittman's testimony, *see* Scalia, supra note 42, at 353; Richard B. Stewart, Vermont Yankee *and the Evolution of Administrative Procedure*, 91 Harv. L. Rev. 1805, 1809–10 (1978). For a more favorable view, *see* Stephen Breyer, Vermont Yankee *and the Courts' Role in the Nuclear Energy Controversy*, 91 Harv. L. Rev. 1833, 1841–42 (1978).

55. See infra p. [141]ff (discussing the D.C. Circuit's emerging administrative law jurisprudence).

D.C. Circuit might look askance at agency acceptance of Dr. Pittman's conclusory assurances. Arguably, therefore, agency counsel should have advised the Commission to supplement the record on waste storage or to heed the D.C. Circuit's admonition in *International Harvester* and engage in "candid discussion" of weaknesses in Pittman's testimony.[56] Perhaps indeed the AEC's General Counsel did suggest such measures, but if so the Commissioners ignored counsel's advice. Instead, both the hearing board and the Commission viewed Pittman's testimony in highly positive terms. The hearing board described Dr. Pittman as having offered "an extensive presentation" on waste disposal options and their environmental effects, and subjected him to minimal questioning.[57] The Commission agreed, stating that "considerable information was presented at the hearing on high level waste storage." It dismissed concerns that estimates of the storage facilities' effects were unreliable because the facilities did not yet exist on the grounds that the proposed facilities would use already existing technology.[58] It also found that the now-revised *Environmental Survey*, amended in response to the hearing to among other things include Dr. Pittman's written testimony on waste storage, provided an adequate basis for the values listed in the Survey's Table S-3.

In its final fuel cycle rule, the AEC opted for the second proposed alternative, inclusion of predetermined values in the environmental impact statements issued for individual reactors. The agency thus ultimately adopted an approach to the fuel cycle's environmental effects that differed from the approach outlined by the appeal board in the *Vermont Yankee* proceeding, and it stated that the *Vermont Yankee* decision would have "no further precedential significance." However, the AEC also decided not to apply the new rule to previously issued environmental impact statements, on the ground that the fuel cycle's environmental effects were "relatively insignificant." As a result, Vermont Yankee was allowed to retain its operating license, which had become permanent in February 1973, without further proceedings.[59]

---

56. 478 F.2d 615, 632–33 (D.C. Cir. 1973); see also Portland Cement v. Ruckelshaus, 486 F.2d 375, 393–94 (D.C. Cir. 1973) (faulting the EPA for, on prior remand, not responding to comments criticizing data the agency had used to formulate emission standards under the Clean Air Act and instead simply including the comments in the rulemaking record on the standards).

57. See Hearing Board Report, supra note 41, at 543; *Vermont Yankee* Appendix, supra note 27, at 830–351.

58. See *Environmental Effects of the Uranium Fuel Cycle*, supra note 50, at 14,189.

59. See id, at 14,188, 14,190–91; see also In re Vermont Yankee Nuclear Power Corp., 6 A.E.C. 358, 358 (AEC, Atomic Safety & Licen. App. Bd., 1973) (upholding award of Vermont Yankee's permanent operating license).

Similarly exempted from the new rule was the grant of a construction permit to Consumers Power Company to build two nuclear reactors
in Midland, Michigan. The proposed reactors were across a river from a
major Dow Chemical facility, which had agreed to purchase steam
generated by the plants. Indeed, proximity to the Dow facility was the
reason why Consumers chose Midland as the site for the reactors. Most
Midland residents strongly favored the project; Dow was Midland's
biggest employer and supported a wide range of cultural and charitable
activities in the city.[60] The few who disagreed faced significant community ostracism. One was Mary Sinclair, who organized the Saginaw Valley
Nuclear Study Group to oppose the reactors. Her mailbox was bombed,
her children were harassed in school, and she was forced out of her
church. But Sinclair gained one key ally, the eldest daughter of Dow
Chemical's founder, who provided the funds Saginaw needed to hire
Myron Cherry. Cherry was a Chicago lawyer with an abrasive style who,
like Roisman, was gaining a reputation as a fierce opponent of nuclear
power plants. Cherry had played a lead role in the AEC core cooling
systems rulemaking, and also participated in the fuel cycle rulemaking.
Represented by Cherry, Saginaw and several other groups intervened in
the Consumers Power proceeding, as did a group of residents from
nearby Mapleton, Michigan, led by a local businessman named Nelson
Aeschliman.[61]

Cherry's strategy was to strongly contest license applications and
draw out licensing proceedings as long as possible, thereby inflicting
costly delays on plant operators.[62] He pursued this strategy to the hilt in
the Consumers Power proceeding: Consumers filed its construction permit application in January 1969, and the proceeding was not resolved
until May 1973. Part of the reason for the length of the proceeding was,
again, *Calvert Cliffs'*. That decision was issued on the last day of the
hearing on Consumers Power's construction permit, July 23, 1971,
necessitating holding a supplemental fourteen day hearing in May–June
1972 devoted solely to environmental issues.[63] As a whole, the Consumers Power proceeding was extremely contentious, with Saginaw attacking the chair of the licensing board as biased because of comments he

---

60. Public support was also fueled by a rumor that failure to construct the reactors
would cause Dow to leave Midland. *See* Ebbin & Kasper, supra note 6, at 21–22.

61. See Ron Winslow, *Woman Helps Sink Nuclear Power Plant That Cost $4
Billion—Mary Sinclair's 15–Year Drive In Midland, Mich., Ends in Ostracism—and
Victory*, Wall St. J., July 18, 1984, at 1; Jerry M. Flint, *Midland, Mich., Wants Nuclear
Plant*, N.Y.Times, Dec. 3, 1971, at 24.

62. See John R. Emshwiller, *Nuclear Nemesis: Using the Law's Delay, Myron Cherry
Attacks Atomic–Power Projects*, Wall. St. J., Mar. 10, 1978, at A1, 35.

63. See *In re Consumers Power Company (Midland Plant, Unit 1 and 2)*, 5 A.E.C.
214, 216 (AEC, Atomic Safety & Licensing Bd., 1972).

made in a law review article.[64] In turn, the AEC castigated Saginaw for failing to provide evidence to support many of its environmental challenges, including Saginaw's claim that alternatives such as energy conservation made the proposed reactor unnecessary.[65] In the end, the AEC rejected the intervenors' challenges and awarded Consumers Power its construction permit, with the appeal board again reaffirming its refusal to consider most environmental aspects of the nuclear fuel cycle in an individual reactor licensing.[66]

Vermont Yankee at the D.C. Circuit

The next step in all three proceedings—the individual license proceedings for the Vermont Yankee and Consumers Power reactors and the fuel cycle rulemaking—was review before the D.C. Circuit. The D.C. Circuit at the time was something of a first among equals, composed of legal luminaries such as David Bazelon, Harold Leventhal, Skelly Wright, and Carl McGowan, to name just a few; Chief Justice Warren Burger had also been a member before his elevation to the Supreme Court.[67] Bazelon, the Circuit's longtime Chief Judge, was renowned for his commitment to using the law as a tool of social change, writing influential decisions that expanded the rights of criminal defendants and developed the insanity defense. In the words of one of his colleagues, "[a] restrained judge he was not."[68] Judge Bazelon was also famous for the lunches he organized in a backroom of Milton Kronheim's liquor warehouse, where liberals from across Washington would gather.[69]

The D.C. Circuit's stature as the nation's administrative law court developed in the late 1960s and 1970s. Congress chose to make the D.C.

---

64. The law review article in question was Arthur W. Murphy, *The National Environmental Policy Act and the Licensing Process: Environmentalist Magna Carta or Agency Coup de Grace?*, 72 Colum. L. Rev. 963 (1972).

65. Indeed, Saginaw failed to participate in the hearing on Midland's environmental effects. Cherry explained this absence as stemming from his need to attend the ongoing cooling systems rulemaking, and the conflict in hearing dates was another bone of contention in the Midland proceedings. See In re Consumers Power Co. (Midland Plant, Units 1 and 2), 6 A.E.C. 331, 332–33, 352–53 (AEC, Atomic Safety & Licensing App. Bd., May 18, 1973).

66. See id. For a detailed description of the Midland proceeding, see Ebbin & Kasper, *supra* note 6, at 59–89.

67. For general discussions of the D.C. Circuit during this period and its role in developing judicial review of agency action, see Christopher P. Banks, *Judicial Politics in the D.C. Circuit Court* 1–50 (1999); Jeffrey Brandon Morris, *Calmly to Poise the Scales of Justice: A History of the Courts of the District of Columbia Circuit* 194–235, 279–315 (2001).

68. Patricia M. Wald, *Ghosts of Judges Past*, 62 Geo. Wash. L. Rev. 675, 681 (1993).

69. See Fred Barbash, *Judge Bazelon's Network: The Salon of the Ultimate Liberal*, Wash. Post, Mar. 1, 1981, at A2; Abner J. Mikva, *The Real Judge Bazelon*, 82 Geo. L. J. 1 (1993); Patricia M. Wald, *Lessons Amid Losses*, Am. Lawyer, Mar. 9, 1993 at 9.

Circuit the center for challenges to administrative regulations issued under new federal environmental and health statutes, such as the Clean Air Act (CAA) and the Occupational Safety and Health Act. In addition, sparked by the Nixon administration's opposition to its liberal criminal and poverty law decisions, Congress ended the D.C. Circuit's appellate jurisdiction over local D.C. courts, giving it more time to focus on administrative cases.[70] As its administrative docket grew, the D.C. Circuit began to develop new administrative law doctrines and expand the scope of judicial review, particularly of informal rulemaking.

Only in the late 1960s and early 1970s did use of informal rulemaking become widespread, in part because many of the new statutes mandated that agencies issue standards and generally applicable regulations. This move to informal rulemaking was generally hailed as a salutary development. It allowed agencies to develop policy in a more coherent and consistent manner that provided greater opportunities for public comment than individualized adjudications, while avoiding the heavy resource burdens and delays that accompanied formal rulemaking.[71] Yet the growth in informal rulemaking also raised concerns about loss of procedural protections and agency accountability. The substantial economic and social impact of the new regulations meant that arbitrary agency decisionmaking could exert significant harm, while the complex factual questions and issues of scientific and technical uncertainty underlying the regulations provided ample room for debate about the correctness of agency determinations.[72] The fuel cycle rulemaking was a good case in point: Determining the values to include in Table S–3 required the Commission to make factual estimates about the environmental impact of waste storage, notwithstanding the uncertainty regarding how wastes ultimately would be stored. The Commission's erring too much towards either conservatism or laxity in its estimates could have serious effects on society and commercial nuclear power.

---

70. The discussion in this and subsequent paragraphs on developments in administrative law and the debate over judicial review on the D.C. Circuit draws heavily on the following sources: Rabin, supra note 9, at 1278–1315; Scalia, supra note 42; Richard B. Stewart, *The Development of Administrative and Quasi-Constitutional Law in Judicial Review of Environmental Decisionmaking: Lessons from the Clean Air Act*, 62 Iowa L. Rev. 713, 725–40 (1976); Peter L. Strauss, *Changing Times: The APA at Fifty*, 63 U. Chi. L. Rev. 1389 (1996); and *The Contribution of the D.C. Circuit to Administrative Law*, 40 Admin. L. Rev. 507 (1988) (remarks by Chief Judge Wald).

71. See, e.g., American Airlines v. CAB, 359 F.2d 624, 630–31 (D.C. Cir. 1966) (en banc); KENNETH CULP DAVIS, ADMINISTRATIVE LAW IN THE SEVENTIES § 6:04–1, at 217–19 (1976); Henry J. Friendly, *Some Kind of Hearing*, 123 U. Pa. L. Rev. 1267, 1305–15 (1975); see generally Robert W. Hamilton, *Procedures for the Adoption of Rules of General Applicability: The Need for Innovation in Administrative Rulemaking*, 60 Cal. L. Rev. 1276 (1972).

72. See Paul Verkuil, *Judicial Review of Informal Rulemaking*, 60 Va. L. Rev. 185, 205–214 (1974).

Moreover, at the same time as agencies were engaging in greater use of informal rulemaking and regulating in new areas, suspicion was growing about willingness of agencies to take public interests seriously. Agencies increasingly were seen not as the embodiment of impartial expertise, but as entities that had become captured by the industries they regulated.[73] The AEC was a particular target for such concerns about agency capture. The Atomic Energy Act had given the agency the incompatible responsibilities of both regulating and promoting the commercial nuclear industry. Concern that the AEC had sacrificed public health and safety in order to foster commercial uses of nuclear power led Congress in 1974 to abolish the AEC. Its regulatory duties were transferred to an independent agency, the NRC, while its research and promotional activities were first assigned to the Energy Research and Development Administration and subsequently given over to the Department of Energy.[74]

The D.C. Circuit's response to these concerns was to subject agency decisionmaking to more intensive scrutiny. Enhanced judicial review was seen as the means by which agency accountability would be preserved; in the words of the *Calvert Cliffs'* decision, it fell to the courts to ensure that "important legislative purposes, heralded in the halls of Congress, are not lost or misdirected in the vast hallways of the federal bureaucracy."[75] In this scheme, "agencies and courts together constitute a partnership in furtherance of the public interest."[76] The D.C. Circuit was not alone in thus expanding the role of the courts in regulation. Indeed, the Supreme Court seemed to signal that change was afoot with its 1971 decision in *Citizens to Preserve Overton Park v. Volpe*, which—while stating that courts should not substitute their views for those of an agency—also required that judicial review be "searching and careful."[77] But it was the D.C. Circuit that most clearly developed a new approach to informal rulemaking. The new climate of judicial review extended to decisions of the AEC. That agency previously had received gentle treat-

---

73. See Thomas Merrill, *Capture Theory and the Courts*, 72 Chi.-Kent L. Rev. 1039 (1997).

74. See Energy Reorganization Act of 1974, Pub. L. No. 93–438, 88 Stat. 1233, (codified in scattered sections of 42 U.S.C.); 42 U.S.C. § 7151 (transferring responsibilities of the Energy Research and Development Administration; to the newly created Department of Energy); see also Walker, supra note 3, at 417–25 (describing criticisms of the AEC as too soft on the nuclear industry); ROBERT J. DUFFY, NUCLEAR POLITICS IN AMERICA 103–22 (1997) (describing origins and enactment of the 1974 legislation).

75. Calvert Cliffs' Coordinating Comm. v. AEC, 449 F.2d 1109, 1111 (D.C. Cir. 1971).

76. Greater Boston Television Corp. v. FCC, 444 F.2d 841, 851–52 (D.C. Cir. 1970).

77. 401 U.S. 402, 416 (1971); *see also* Peter Strauss' comment on *Overton Park* in this volume.

ment at the hands of the D.C. Circuit,[78] but *Calvert Cliffs'* signaled that those halcyon days were largely over.

Although the D.C. Circuit was in agreement on the need for greater judicial oversight of agency decisionmaking, a deep debate raged on that court about the form this oversight should take. According to Judge Bazelon, courts lacked the technical competence to assess the scientific evidence underlying many of the new regulations. As a result:

> [T]he best way for courts to guard against unreasonable or erroneous administrative decisions is not for the judges themselves to scrutinize the technical merits of each decision. Rather, it is to establish a decision-making process that assures a reasoned decision that can be held up to the scrutiny of the scientific community and the public.[79]

But several of his colleagues argued that courts lacked authority to impose procedural mandates not based in statutes or the Constitution, and worried that imposition of additional procedures would undermine informal rulemaking's advantages. Instead, they argued courts must undertake searching substantive review of agency decisionmaking. The most prominent advocate of this view was Judge Leventhal, who also coined the phrase "hard look" review by which such substantive scrutiny came to be known. Leventhal insisted courts could undertake such scrutiny without intruding on agencies' policy prerogatives. Regardless, they had no choice but to steep themselves in the substantive details of the underlying subject matter:

> [W]hile giving up is the easier course, it is not legitimately open to us at present. Our present system of review assumes judges will acquire whatever technical knowledge is necessary as background for decision of the legal questions.
>
> . . .
>
> . . . Better no judicial review at all than a charade that gives the imprimatur without the substance of judicial confirmation that the agency is not acting unreasonably.[80]

---

78. See, e.g., Siegel v. AEC, 400 F.2d 778, 783–84 (D.C. Cir. 1968) (describing AEC as unique in the breadth of its discretion and in close supervision by Congress through the Joint Committee on Atomic Energy).

79. International Harvester Co. v. Ruckelshaus, 478 F.2d 615, 650, 652 (D.C. Cir. 1973) (Bazelon, C.J., concurring in result); see Ethyl Corp. v. EPA, 541 F.2d 1, 66–68 (D.C. Cir. 1976) (Bazelon, C.J., concurring); see generally David L. Bazelon, *Coping with Technology through the Legal Process*, 62 Cornell L. Rev. 817 (1977).

80. *Ethyl Corp.*, 541 F.2d at 68–69 (Leventhal, J., concurring); see generally Harold Leventhal, *Environmental Decisionmaking and the Role of the Courts*, 122 U. Pa. L. Rev. 509 (1973). Judge Wright took a similar view. See J. Skelly Wright, *The Courts and the Rulemaking Process: The Limits of Judicial Review*, 59 Cornell L. Rev. 403 (1973).

The D.C. Circuit's debate between procedural and substantive review was carried out over several years in the pages of the F.2d, without a clear victor emerging. In some decisions, such as *International Harvester*, the D.C. Circuit appeared to opt for the proceduralist approach, requiring the agency to employ some form of cross-examination on remand even though such procedure was not required by § 553.[81] In others, however, the court justified its procedural impositions as stemming from § 553 itself. *Portland Cement Association v. Ruckelshaus*, a 1973 decision, demonstrates this approach of putting a heavy interpretive gloss on the procedures actually required by § 553; the D. C. Circuit there read § 553's minimal notice demand as requiring publication of material on which an agency is relying.[82] But at the same time, several D.C. Circuit decisions instead based their procedural demands on the prerequisites for adequate judicial review. Thus, in *Kennecott Copper Corp. v. EPA*, a 1972 decision, the court held that the EPA satisfied § 553's concise and general statement requirement in setting standards for sulfur oxide. Yet it nonetheless remanded the standard to the agency for fuller explanation, emphasizing that "the provision for statutory judicial review contemplates some disclosure of the basis of the agency's action."[83] And many decisions justified the demands put on agencies on multiple grounds. In *Portland Cement*, for example—a Leventhal decision—the court relied not only on § 553's requirements but also on the courts' responsibility to steep themselves in technical matters so as to ensure agencies have undertaken reasoned decisionmaking.[84] However justified, the bottom-line effect of these D.C. Circuit decisions was the same: the development of "hybrid rulemaking," which engrafted more

---

81.   See 478 F.2d at 649 (requiring "some opportunity for cross-examination" on remand); Mobil Oil Corp. v. Federal Power Corp., 483 F.2d 1238, 1260 (D.C. Cir. 1973) (emphasizing the importance of adversarial procedures to providing substantial evidence to support agency decisions); American Airlines v. Civil Aeronautics Bd., 359 F.2d 624, 631–33 (D.C. Cir.), cert. denied, 385 U.S. 843 (1966) (noting court's willingness to require oral hearings in rulemakings even where not required by Congress); see also Scalia, supra note 42, at 348–52; Williams, supra note 42, at 425–36 (arguing that D.C. Circuit decisions seeming to require additional cross-examination in fact had a minimal impact on agency practice).

82.   486 F.2d 375, 392–94 & n.67 (D.C. Cir. 1973). Other examples of this approach to § 553 are United States v. Nova Scotia Foods Corp., 568 F.2d 240, 252–53 (2d Cir. 1977) (adopting similar approach to § 553's notice and concise general statement requirements); Automotive Parts & Accessories Ass'n v. Boyd, 407 F.2d 330, 338 (D.C. Cir. 1968) (warning against agencies reading § 553's requirement of "a concise general statement of [the rule's] basis and purpose" too literally).

83.   See 462 F.2d 846, 849–50 (D.C. Cir. 1972); see also Greater Boston Television Corp. v. FCC, 444 F.2d 841, 851–53 (D.C. Cir. 1970) (describing agency obligation to "articulate with reasonable clarity its reasons for decision and identify the significance of the crucial facts," thereby ensuring for the court that it has taken "a hard look at the salient problems") (internal quotations omitted).

84.   See 486 F.2d at 402.

formal procedural elements, including often greater participation rights
but at a minimum a substantial paper hearing, onto informal rulemaking
under § 553.

Many of these decisions, in particular *Portland Cement*, *Kennecott
Copper*, and *International Harvester*, involved the CAA. That statutory
context might, at least in theory, help explain these decisions, as the
court emphasized that the CAA imposed greater record and explanation
requirements than contained in the APA.[85] Perhaps more importantly,
the 1977 Amendments to the CAA imposed detailed procedural requirements that essentially codified and expanded on the D.C. Circuit's hybrid
rulemaking precedent.[86] This suggests that these decisions could have
been read as limited to the CAA context. On the other hand, the D.C.
Circuit never indicated that it viewed these decisions as so limited, and
on the contrary alluded to § 553 as well as the CAA. Nor have commentators, at the time or historically, viewed the decisions as CAA-specific.[87]
What the 1977 CAA amendment do demonstrate, however, is that in
some instances Congress was the source of such hybrid rulemaking
requirements, expressly mandating that agencies provide detailed notice,
hold oral hearings on proposed rules, and (more rarely) requiring cross-
examination.[88]

The D.C. Circuit's decisions on the fuel cycle rule and the two
licensing proceedings reflected its turn to more searching review of
informal rulemaking and agency decisionmaking more generally. In
Natural Resources Defense Council v. NRC, an opinion written by Judge
Bazelon, the court held those portions of the fuel cycle rule addressing
waste disposal and reprocessing to be arbitrary and capricious, and
remanded the rule to the agency.[89] The court found Dr. Pittman's

---

85. For example, in holding that the EPA was not subject to NEPA's environmental
impact statement in promulgating standards under section 111 of the CAA, the *Portland
Cement* the court emphasized that "an EPA statement of reasons for standards and criteria
[under the CAA] require a fuller presentation than the minimum rulemaking requirement
of the [APA]." Id. at 386.

86. See 42 U.S.C. § 7607(d), historical and statutory notes; Clean Air Act Amendments of 1977, H. Rep. 294, 95th Cong., 1st Sess. at 318–25 (1977).

87. See, e.g., *Portland Cement*, 486 F.2d at 393 n. 67; Stewart, supra note 70, at 762–
67; see generally Williams, supra note 42.

88. See, e.g., 42 U.S.C. § 7607(d) (imposing detailed record, notice, and justification
requirements on rulemaking under the CAA, including requiring that interested persons be
given an opportunity for oral hearing and that promulgated rules respond to significant
comments, criticisms, and new data submitted during the comment period); The Occupational Safety and Health Act of 1970, 29 U.S.C. § 655 (providing right to require Secretary
of Labor to hold an oral hearing on proposed safety or health standards); 1 Administrative
Law Treatise § 7.7 at 485–92 (Richard J. Pierce, Jr., ed., 2002) (describing other statutes
with hybrid rulemaking requirements).

89. See 547 F.2d 633, 655 (D.C. Cir. 1976).

testimony conclusory and his optimistic assessments of the risks posed by nuclear waste unexplained, adding that the NRC (substituted as the defendant for the now defunct AEC) compounded the problem by ignoring these deficiencies.[90] "Without a thorough exploration of the problems involved in waste disposal, including past mistakes, and a forthright assessment of uncertainties and differences in expert opinion, this type of agency action cannot pass muster as reasoned decisionmaking."[91] Moreover, "[m]any procedural devices for creating a genuine dialogue on these issues were available to the agency." Although purporting "not to intrude on the agency's province by dictating to it which, if any, of these devices it must adopt to flesh out the record," the opinion concluded that "[w]hatever techniques the Commission adopts, before it promulgates a rule limiting further consideration of waste disposal and reprocessing issues, it must in one way or another generate a record in which the factual issues are fully developed."[92]

The question left hanging by the D.C. Circuit's opinion was precisely where the court thought the NRC had gone astray. Was it the failure to provide opportunity for "genuine dialogue," through cross-examination, discovery, or other procedures, that would have ensured a "thorough ventilation of the issues"?[93] Was it instead the agency's failure to produce a record that demonstrated such ventilation, however obtained? The opinion is a masterpiece of obfuscation on this point.[94] In support of the latter view is the fact that, despite frequent references to the value of additional adversarial procedures, the opinion repeatedly describes its

---

90. Although identifying reprocessing as another area where "detailed explanation and support for the staff's conclusions was noticeably absent from the Environmental Survey," id. at 647, the opinion did not provide further discussion of why the agency's treatment of reprocessing issues was inadequate.

91. Id. at 647–53. The court initially identified the hearing board's failure to question Dr. Pittman as an example of the agency's insufficient probing. Upon being notified by the NRC that in fact the hearing board had questioned Dr. Pittman, the court simply deleted these references but did not otherwise alter its opinion. See Petitioner's Supplemental Brief & Supplemental Appendix, No. 76–419, at 1–2, app. 1–2. The original decision is reprinted in the appendix to Vermont Yankee's petition for certiorari, see Petitioner's Brief for Certiorari, app. 1–59, Vermont Yankee Nuclear Power Corp. v. NRDC, 435 U.S. 519 (1978) (Nos. 76–419).

92. *Natural Resources Defense Council*, 547 F.2d at 653–54.

93. Id. at 644.

94. The opinion is also unclear as to whether, to the extent additional procedures are required, they stem ultimately from NEPA, the APA, due process, or a generalized common law requirement of reasoned decisionmaking. Although noting at the outset that under NEPA agencies must consider contrary scientific opinion on adverse environmental effects, and that the public interest intervenors' primary complaint was that the procedures used denied their due process right to participate meaningfully in the proceedings, see id. at 643, 646, most of the opinion either refers to APA requirements or speaks in more general terms.

ultimate concern as being to ensure the agency adequately considered the issues at stake.[95] Yet it is hard to read the opinion except as demanding the NRC provide greater opportunities for public participation on remand, even if not specifying the exact shape these procedures must take. One member of the panel, Judge Tamm, took such a view, and therefore concurred only in the result even though he agreed that the record was inadequate to sustain the rule.[96] Judge Tamm criticized the majority for issuing a procedural mandate, leading to the oddity of Judge Bazelon issuing a separate statement to his own opinion, in which he urged agencies to adopt "innovat[ive] procedural formats" that better ensure accurate factfinding on complex scientific and technical issues or in areas where formal adjudicatory procedures traditionally were the norm.[97] Judge Bazelon's separate opinion reinforces the impression that the majority did indeed intend the NRC to provide additional adjudicatory procedures on remand.

The court also remanded the individual licensing decisions. Although affirming the NRC's authority to treat the environmental effects of the fuel cycle issue through generic rulemaking, the court rejected the appeal board's claim that it was impossible to assess such environmental effects in the context of an individual reactor proceeding. Ruling that these environment effects must be adequately considered at some point—either in generic or individual proceedings—the court also remanded the grant of Vermont Yankee's operating license.[98] Moreover, in a decision again written by Judge Bazelon, but for a different panel, the D.C. Circuit found that the AEC had erred in granting Consumers Power a construction permit for its Midland plant. The AEC's exclusion of any consideration of the environmental effects of the fuel cycle in evaluating the proposed reactors' environmental impact was one reason for the reversal. But the D.C. Circuit additionally faulted the Commission for failing to seek greater clarification of a statutorily-mandated independent safety report and for not investigating energy conservation as an alternative to the proposed reactors. According to the court, NEPA required agencies to investigate any colorable alternatives and energy conservation was such an alternative, despite the intervenors' failure to do much more than simply assert that conservation could render the proposed reactors unnecessary.[99]

---

95. See, e.g., id. at 644, 654.

96. See id. at 658–61.

97. Id. at 656.

98. See id. at 641 n.17.

99. See Aeschliman v. NRC, 547 F.2d 622, 627–31 (D.C. Cir. 1976); see also id. at 631 (instructing the NRC to take into account changes in Dow Chemical's need for process steam in redoing the cost-benefit analysis for the environmental impact statement to include fuel cycle environmental effects).

The D.C. Circuit's handling of these cases seems inordinately slow; even the court acknowledged that its decision in *Aeschliman* was "long delayed."[100] The petition for review of the grant of the Consumers Power construction permit was filed in 1973, and for review of the fuel cycle rule and the award of Vermont Yankee's operating license in 1974. Yet the D.C. Circuit did not issue its decisions until two years later, in July 1976.[101] Vermont Yankee was already operating, and therefore the impact on it of this delay was fairly minimal. But for Consumers Power, the wait meant a multi-year delay in commencing construction, which could (and did) prove very costly to the Midland project. Perhaps recognizing this impact, the court subsequently refused the intervenors' request that it set aside the Consumers Power's construction permit, allowing construction of the Midland reactors to proceed.[102]

The most significant effect of all, however, was the impact on nuclear licensing generally. The decisions called into question not only all licenses in which the now-vacated Table S–3 values were used to assess a reactor's environmental impact, but in addition all licenses which the AEC determined should not be reopened for application of Table S–3 and the fuel cycle rule. Moreover, until the rule was amended to address the D.C. Circuit's concerns, no reactors could be licensed without consideration of the fuel cycle's environmental effects in the individual license proceedings. Hence, in response to the decision the NRC put all nuclear licensing on hold until the *Environmental Survey* could be revised and an interim rule issued.[103]

Vermont Yankee at the Supreme Court

The stage then shifted to the Supreme Court. Both Vermont Yankee and Consumers Power petitioned for writs of certiorari. On the face of it, the odds of getting the Court to grant cert would seem poor. Not only was the exact nature of the D.C. Circuit's holding on the fuel cycle rulemaking ambiguous, but appellate reversal of two discrete and largely factbound agency licensing proceedings, even if erroneous, rarely triggers further review. Indeed, the ambiguities of the D.C Circuit's decision led to the novelty of the government submitting a "Janus-like" brief that

---

100. Id. at 624 n.4.

101. The decision in *Aeschliman* was held by the court first for the AEC to consider motions to reopen and then pending the decision in the fuel cycle rulemaking. See id.

102. See Aeschliman v. NRC, Docket Sheet, No. 73–1776 (noting petitioner's first emergency motion to enforce mandate filed on Oct. 6, 1977 and denied by the court on Oct. 27, 1977, and second motion filed on Mar. 20, 1978).

103. See *Environmental Effects of the Uranium Fuel Cycle*, 41 Fed. Reg. 34,707, 34,708 (1976). The NRC subsequently resumed licensing shortly after it issued a revised *Environmental Survey* and proposed interim fuel cycle rule. See *Environmental Effects of the Uranium Fuel Cycle*, 41 Fed. Reg. 49,898, 49,899 (1976).

simultaneously argued for *and* against a grant of certiorari.[104] The NRC read the D.C. Circuit as holding the rulemaking to be procedurally defective, albeit in compliance with § 553, and argued that the question of a court's authority to impose procedural requirements beyond those contained in § 553 merited Supreme Court reversal. The Solicitor General's position, on the other hand, was that the D.C. Circuit had simply held that the record in the fuel cycle rulemaking was inadequate—an erroneous decision but not one that merited Supreme Court review.[105] The Solicitor General agreed, however, that the D.C. Circuit's errors were more significant if the decision were read as reversing the Commission on procedural grounds.[106]

The contrasting positions of the NRC and the Solicitor General on the need for Supreme Court review merits note, because it underscores the different perspective of attorneys whose responsibility is to represent the government generally in court and those who provide counsel to specific agencies. From the Solicitor General's point of view, the ideal response to the D.C. Circuit's decision would be for the NRC on remand to supplement the record to provide additional support for its conclusions, but not change its procedures. If the appellate court again reversed, the question of the propriety of judicial imposition of procedures in excess of § 553's requirements would then be cleanly presented, and the government would have an ideal test case with which to take this issue to the Court. The NRC and its lawyers, however, had no interest in developing an ideal test case; their focus was instead on devising a response to the decision that would allow licensing to resume as quickly as possible. It was for this reason that the NRC reopened the fuel cycle rule for further proceedings even while the petitions for certiorari were pending. But rather than risk a second reversal, the NRC wanted to fashion this supplemental rulemaking to ensure that it would meet the

---

104. See *Vermont Yankee*, 438 U.S. at 540 n.15.

105. See Brief for the Federal Respondents on Petition for Certiorari at 5–10, Vermont Yankee Nuclear Power Corp. v. NRDC, 435 U.S. 519 (1978) (Nos. 76–419, 76–528, 76–548 and 76–745). The Solicitor General's willingness to go ahead and file such a brief stemmed in part from the fact that the government needed to respond to the cert petitions filed by Vermont Yankee and Consumers Power, but also may have reflected a desire to avoid debate over whether agencies that have statutory authority to represent themselves in court can appear before the Supreme Court without Solicitor General approval. See Interview with Peter L. Strauss, General Counsel to the NRC 1975–77, in New York, N.Y. (Aug. 29, 2004) [hereinafter Strauss Interview]. For a discussion of issues raised by Solicitor General control over independent agencies' access to the Court, see generally Neal Devins, *Unitariness, Independence, and Solicitor General Control over Independent Agency Litigation*, 82 Cal. L. Rev. 215 (1994).

106. See Brief for the Federal Respondents, supra note 105, at 9; Brief for the Federal Respondents at 37, Vermont Yankee Nuclear Power Corp. v. NRDC, 435 U.S. 519 (1978) (Nos. 76–419, 76–528).

D.C. Circuit's procedural as well as substantive concerns.[107] Hence, although the agency adopted an interim rule using only § 553's notice and comment procedures, it planned to hold oral hearings on the final revised fuel cycle rule at which participants could propose questions for the hearing board to ask.[108]

Of course, that the NRC intended to go forward with additional proceedings on the fuel cycle rule was another factor making grant of certiorari unlikely. But the Court seems not to have focused on the fact that agency proceedings were ongoing at the certiorari stage. As a result, much of the discussion at oral argument addressed the status of the rulemaking and Vermont Yankee's license, and after argument there was supplemental briefing on whether the case had become moot.[109] Moreover, the D.C. Circuit decision clearly was having a significant effect on nuclear licensing. Previously, the Court had been willing to review appellate court decisions having a major impact on the nation's nuclear program notwithstanding the presence of similar factors counseling against a grant of certiorari.[110] For this reason, neither Richard Ayres, who argued the case at the Court on behalf of the NRDC, nor Anthony Roisman was surprised that the Court decided to take the case.[111]

In any event, grant the Supreme Court did. Acknowledging that "the matter is not entirely free from doubt," the Court read the D.C. Circuit as invalidating the fuel cycle rule because of procedural deficiencies. It then soundly reversed the D.C. Circuit in a unanimous decision, written by then-Justice Rehnquist, in which seven justices participated.[112] The Court left open the possibility that judicial procedural impositions might be warranted in some contexts, for example when needed to satisfy due process in quasi-adjudicatory proceedings or when an agency departs without justification from "well-settled agency procedures of

---

107. See Strauss Interview, supra note 105.

108. See *Uranium Fuel Cycle Impacts from Spent Fuel Reprocessing and Radioactive Waste Management*, 42 Fed. Reg. 13,803, 13,805–06 (1977); Transcript of Oral Argument 23, Vermont Yankee Nuclear Power Corp. v. NRDC, 435 U.S. 519 (1978) (Nos. 76–419, 76–528).

109. See Transcript of Oral Argument, supra note 100, at 5–6, 13–18, 17–24, 34–36, 54; see also Motion to Dismiss and Suggestion of Mootness, Vermont Yankee Nuclear Power Corp. v. NRDC, 435 U.S. 519 (1978) (Nos. 76–419, 76–528) (Dec. 1, 1977) and responding briefs.

110. See, e.g., Duke Power Co. v. Carolina Envtl. Study Group, Inc., 438 U.S. 59 (1978) (reversing on the merits lower court determination that the Price–Anderson Act, capping plant operators' liability for nuclear accidents, was unconstitutional despite serious questions regarding whether the citizen groups that brought the suit had standing).

111. Telephone Interview with Richard Ayres, Richard Ayres, principal of the Ayres Law Group and co-founder NRDC (November 30, 2004); Roisman Interview, supra note 14.

112. *Vermont Yankee*, 435 U.S. at 540–41. Justices Powell and Blackmun did not participate.

long standing." However, "such circumstances, if they exist, are extremely rare,"[113] and this was not one of them. Lest there be any doubt about its bottom line, the Court stated: "[T]his much is absolutely clear. Absent constitutional constraints or extremely compelling circumstances the administrative agencies should be free to fashion their own rules of procedure and to pursue methods of inquiry capable of permitting them to discharge their multitudinous duties."[114]

According to the Court, its prior decisions had rejected the view that the APA only set out the procedural minima to which an agency must adhere, with courts free to amplify procedural requirements due to the complexity or importance of the substantive issues involved. On the contrary, the Court read the APA as "generally speaking ... establish[ing] the maximum procedural requirements which Congress was willing to have the courts impose on agencies" in rulemaking. The procedural requirements of the APA were, in the Court's view, "a formula upon which opposing social and political forces ha[d] come to rest," and not intended to evolve over time through judicial innovation.[115] Instead, under the APA, discretion to impose additional procedures lay in the agencies, not in the courts.[116] Judicial second-guessing of agency procedural choices was not only precluded by the APA, but also unwise on policy grounds. Faced with unpredictable judicial procedural mandates and "Monday morning quarterbacking" based on how well their chosen procedures actually functioned, agencies "would undoubtedly adopt full adjudicatory procedures in every instance, ... [and] the inherent advantages of informal rulemaking would be totally lost."[117]

Strong words, but the Court saved its harshest language for its assessment of the D.C. Circuit's decision in the Consumers Power proceeding. According to the Court, the appellate court's decision reversing the grant of Consumers Power's construction permit "borders on the Kafkaesque":

> Nuclear energy may some day be a cheap, safe source of power or it may not. But Congress has made a choice to at least try nuclear energy.... The fundamental policy questions appropriately resolved in Congress and in the state legislatures are *not* subject to reexamination in the federal courts.[118]

---

113. Id. at 524, 542.

114. Id. at 543.

115. Id. at 523–24 (quoting Wong Yang Sung v. McGrath, 339 U.S. 33, 40 (1950)).

116. Id. at 524, 545–46.

117. Id. at 546–47.

118. Id. at 557–58.

The Court could not have made plainer its view that the D. C. Circuit had overstepped its proper role and illegitimately used its judicial review function to advance its judges' own policy preferences. This harsh tone prompted a protest by senior D.C. Circuit Judge Fahy, who had sat on the *Aeschliman* panel. In a memo to the other circuit judges, which he also sent to Chief Justice Burger, Judge Fahy remarked that while he expected reversal, he "was surprised ... by the severity" and "the unseemly character of the criticism heaped upon us"—criticism he argued was unfair and rested on the Court's failure to recognize that the D.C. Circuit had not stopped construction of the Consumers Power reactors.[119]

Given its unsparing condemnation of the D.C. Circuit, outright reversal would seem to follow as a matter of course. But instead the Court remanded to the D.C. Circuit for further review. Noting that "[t]here are also intimations in the majority opinion" suggesting that the judges believed the administrative record was inadequate to support the fuel cycle rule, the Court remanded to let the lower court rule expressly on the record's adequacy. Moreover, the Court emphasized that it was taking no position on this question. "Upon remand, the majority of the panel of the Court of Appeals is entirely free to agree or disagree with Judge Tamm's conclusion that the rule pertaining to the back end of the fuel cycle under which petitioner Vermont Yankee's license was considered is arbitrary and capricious" even if not procedurally faulty.[120] In other words, despite its stern language, the Court made clear that its decision might not affect the result in the case, as the lower court was free to remand the fuel cycle rule to the agency provided it did so on substantive rather than procedural grounds.

Judge Fahy was right to expect reversal once the Court granted review. As the Court itself and then-Professor Antonin Scalia argued, the D.C. Circuit's willingness to impose procedural requirements not based in statutes was, if not directly at odds, certainly in strong tension with prior Supreme Court decisions.[121] In particular, two lines of precedent presaged the result in *Vermont Yankee*. The first was the Court's willingness to allow agencies to forego formal adjudicatory or formal rulemaking procedures, even in contexts where it was originally expected such procedures would be used. Fairly early on in the life of the APA, in *United States v. Storer Broadcasting Company*, the Court ruled that a statutory requirement of a full hearing did not preclude an agency from

---

119. Memorandum to All Circuit Judges and Judge Justice From Judge Fahy, Supreme Court Decision in Consumers Power Co. v. Aeschliman, at 1–2 (Apr. 5, 1978), (on file with the Biddle Library, University of Pennsylvania Law School, Papers of Judge David L. Bazelon (Box 48, Folder 2)).

120. 435 U.S. at 535 n.14; see also id. at 549 (same).

121. See id. at 524–25, 542–45; Scalia, supra note 42, at 356–57, 359–75.

using informal rulemaking to issue rules that significantly limited the scope of adjudicatory hearings.[122] In two decisions issued in the early 1970s, *United States v. Florida East Coast Railway Company* and *Allegheny-Ludlum Steel Corporation*, the Court also took a narrow view of when agencies are required to use the APA's formal rulemaking procedures, holding that a statutory provision authorizing an agency to issue rules only "after hearing" was insufficient on its own to trigger formal rulemaking.[123] As the Atomic Energy Act included a similar hearing requirement, providing that the Commission must provide a hearing if requested "[i]n any proceeding for the issuance or modification of rules and regulations dealing with the activities of licensees," *Vermont Yankee*'s unsubstantiated statement that nothing in the NRC's statutory mandate required additional procedures rests on the *Florida East Coast/Allegheny–Ludlum* holdings.[124] *Vermont Yankee* thus represents affirmation of agencies' power to use informal rulemaking in a broad array of contexts in lieu of the APA's more formal procedures.

The second line was the Court's decisions upholding an agency's discretion to control its mode of procedure in the absence of statutory (or constitutional) mandates. In *SEC v. Chenery Corporation*, a decision issued shortly after the APA became effective, the Court held that the choice to proceed by adjudication or rulemaking "is one that lies primarily in the informed discretion of the administrative agency."[125] The Court reaffirmed this view that an agency must have discretion to determine which procedures best serve its purposes just three years before the

---

122. 351 U.S. 192, 203–05 (1956); see also Federal Power Comm'n v. Texaco, 377 U.S. 33, 39 (1964). No doubt as a result of this clear precedent, none of the intervenors argued to the D.C. Circuit or the Supreme Court that the NRC lacked authority to address the environmental effects of the fuel cycle through generic rules and instead had to consider this issue on a case-by-case basis in individual licensings. See *Vermont Yankee*, 435 U.S. at 535 n.13.

123. See *Florida East Coast*, 410 U.S. 224, 234–38; U.S. v. Allegheny-Ludlum, 406 U.S. 742, 757–58 (1972).

124. 42 U.S.C. § 2239(a)(1)(A); *Vermont Yankee*, 435 U.S. at 548; see also Siegel v. AEC, 400 F.2d 778, 785–86 (D.C. Cir. 1968) (holding § 2239(a) did not trigger formal rulemaking requirements under the APA). Section 2239(a) seems to authorize the fuel cycle rule awkwardly at best, as the rule addresses the Commission's activities in issuing licenses more than the activities of licensees themselves. The Commission also has general rulemaking authority under 42 U.S.C. § 2201(p), but judicial review in the Court of Appeals under the Hobbs Act, the apparent basis for jurisdiction over the fuel cycle rule, is tied to orders made under § 2239. Although § 2239(b) similarly provides only for judicial review of any "order" entered in "any proceeding" under § 2239(a), and under the APA orders are generated through adjudication rather than rulemaking, by its text § 2239(a) includes some rulemaking proceedings. See also Nathaniel Nathanson, *The* Vermont Yankee Nuclear Power *Opinion: A Masterpiece of Statutory Misinterpretation*, 16 San Diego L. Rev. 183, 189–95 (1978) (critiquing the Court for reading the Atomic Energy Act as not requiring formal procedures for rulemaking undertaken under § 2239).

125. 332 U.S. 194, 203 (1947).

Vermont Yankee decision, in *NLRB v. Bell Aerospace Company*,[126] as well as in *Florida East Coast Railway*.[127] The Court also expressed this insistence on agency procedural discretion in decisions such as *Federal Power Commission v. Transcontinental Gas Pipe Line Corporation*, where it faulted an appellate court for "dictating to the agency the methods, procedures, and time dimensions" which would govern agency proceedings on remand. Having found the agency's record inadequate to sustain its decision, the proper course was instead for the court "to remand to the agency in order that it can exercise its administrative discretion in deciding how . . . it may best proceed to develop the needed evidence."[128] Indeed, this was exactly the approach the Court ultimately took in *Vermont Yankee*, when it left the D.C. Circuit free to hold that the fuel cycle record as it currently stood was inadequate.

A third trend that sealed the D.C. Circuit's fate was broader and more ideological. Loss of faith in apolitical agency expertise and concerns about agency capture affected the Supreme Court as well as the D.C. Circuit in the 1960s and 1970s. One manifestation was the Court's dramatic relaxing of standing and ripeness rules, another its willingness to engage in searching substantive scrutiny of agency decisions under the APA's "arbitrary and capricious" standard. The effect of both developments was to foster far greater and earlier judicial review of agency action than the APA's drafters would have envisioned, thus calling into serious question the assertion in *Vermont Yankee* that courts should adhere to the specific terms of the APA so as not to deviate from the careful political compromise that the statute represented.[129] But by the 1980s, changes were afoot. Public choice theory, with its skepticism about judicial impartiality and conception of statutes as political compromises, buttressed growing opposition to judicial policymaking on separation of powers grounds. The result was a turn towards formalism and textualism in statutory construction and away from more open-ended

---

126. 416 U.S. 267, 292–95 (1974).

127. 410 U.S. at 242–45.

128. 423 U.S. 326, 331–34 (1976) (per curiam); see also FCC v. Schreiber, 381 U.S. 279, 290–91 (1965) (reasserting "the established principle that administrative agencies 'should be free to fashion their own rules of procedure and to pursue methods of inquiry capable of permitting them to discharge their multitudinous duties' ") (quoting FCC v. Pottsville Broad. Co., 309 U.S. 134, 143 (1940)); see also *Vermont Yankee*, 435 U.S. at 524–25, 543–45 (discussing *FPC, Schreiber,* and *Pottsville*).

129. See, e.g., Scalia, supra note 42, at 377–81; Stewart, supra note 54, at 1814–15; Strauss, supra note 70, at 1401–05, 1407–08; see also Kenneth C. Davis, *Administrative Common Law and the* Vermont Yankee *Opinion*, 1980 Utah. L. Rev. 3, 7–12 (1980) (arguing Supreme Court has always taken a more common law approach to administrative law and the APA's framers expected it to do so). But see Clark Byse, Vermont Yankee *and the Evolution of Administrative Procedure: A Somewhat Different View*, 91 Harv. L. Rev. 1823, 1829 (1978) (arguing ripeness and standing doctrines are distinguishable from other provisions of the APA).

judicial development of administrative law.[130] *Vermont Yankee* is not a clear exemplar of this change; the decision was issued in the late 1970s and invokes policy concerns to justify its conclusions.[131] Nonetheless, with its resistance to judicial inventiveness and its originalist approach to interpreting the APA, *Vermont Yankee* signaled this coming trend in administrative law.

But while the Court's rejection of judicial procedural impositions was to be expected, the unanimity of the *Vermont Yankee* decision *is* surprising. Joining the Court's decision without reservation were Justices Brennan and Marshall, hardly thought of as opponents of judicial activism. While the animosity between Chief Justice Burger and Judge Bazelon was well-known, Justices Brennan and Marshall were good friends with Bazelon; indeed, Justice Brennan was a regular at the Kronheim lunches.[132] Their acquiescence in the Court's harsh criticism of the lower court is thus hard to explain. Particularly given that the Court ended up remanding rather than reversing the D.C. Circuit, and that NRC was committed to revising the fuel cycle rule regardless of the Court's decision, it seems odd that none of the Justices who participated in the case challenged the Court's decision to reach the merits.

In fact, however, they did. Justice Brennan led the charge, quickly drafting an opinion that would dismiss the grant of certiorari as improvidently granted (or DIG, in the Court's parlance) once it became apparent after oral argument and supplemental briefing that the NRC intended to go forward with a new rulemaking.[133] Like the Court's published opinion, Justice Brennan's draft stated that the Court of Appeals had erred "[i]f the Court of Appeals had decided that NEPA requires procedures in rulemaking in excess of those expressly required by the [APA]" and that the occasions for judicial imposition of hybrid rulemaking procedures are "severely limited." However, Justice Brennan was far more generous in his reading of the D.C. Circuit's opinion, rejecting the procedural interpretation advocated by Vermont Yankee and the NRC: "Instead, we understand the Court of Appeals to have held only that the original

---

130. See Merrill, supra note 73, at 1043–48, 1067–74; William N. Eskridge, Jr., *The New Textualism*, 37 UCLA L. Rev. 621, 646–66 (1990); Philip P. Frickey, *From the Big Sleep to the Big Heat: The Revival of Theory in Statutory Interpretation*, 77 Minn. L. Rev. 241, 244–56 (1992); see generally Strauss, supra note 70 (discussing changes in the Court's approach to interpreting the APA).

131. See John Duffy, *Administrative Common Law in Judicial Review*, 77 Tex. L. Rev. 113, 139–46, 184–89 (1998) (noting change in statutory interpretation but arguing that *Vermont Yankee* should be viewed as an instance of administrative common law).

132. See Barbash, supra note 69, at A2.

133. See Memorandum from Justice Brennan to the Conference, Vermont Yankee Nuclear Power Corp. v. NRDC, 435 U.S. 519 (1978) (Nos. 76–419, 76–528) (Jan. 12, 1978) (on file with the Library of Congress, Manuscript Room, Papers of Justice Thurgood Marshall (Box 201)).

spent fuel rule was inadequately supported by the rulemaking record."
And review of this determination—unlikely to warrant Supreme Court
consideration in any event—was particularly inappropriate given that
the NRC was committed to revising the rule.[134]

Justice Brennan's efforts proved unavailing. In a responding memorandum, Justice Rehnquist made clear he would dissent from any effort
to dismiss the grant of certiorari, stressing the continuing impact of the
D.C. Circuit's decision on the licenses of the two plants involved and
reactor licensing generally.[135] His views carried the day, with Chief
Justice Burger, Justice White and Justice Stevens also voting against
dismissal.[136] Justice Brennan then turned his attentions to trying to
temper Justice Rehnquist's proposed draft. He again urged that the
better course was to read the D.C. Circuit decision as simply holding the
fuel cycle rule was inadequately supported by the record, with an aside
to the effect that judicial imposition of procedures would be plainly
improper here. And he also argued against remanding, stating "[w]heth-
er or not a remand [for further consideration] could be said to 'border[]
on the Kafkaesque,' I do think it simply wastes everyone's time."[137] But
here too, Justice Brennan's renowned powers of persuasion fell short,
with Justice Rehnquist refusing to accept a non-proceduralist reading of
the lower court's decision.[138] Although at first threatening to write

---

134. See Brennan First Printed Draft at 8–9, Vermont Yankee Nuclear Power Corp.
v. NRDC, 435 U.S. 519 (1978) (Feb. 17, 1978) (on file with the Library of Congress,
Manuscript Room, Papers of Justice Thurgood Marshall (Box 201)). Justice Brennan even
included a footnote specifically defending Judge Bazelon against the charge that he had
sanctioned imposition of additional procedures in his separate opinion below. See id. at 9
n.15.

135. See Memorandum from Justice Rehnquist to Justice Brennan, Vermont Yankee
Nuclear Power Corp. v. NRDC, 435 U.S. 519 (1978) (Nos. 76–419, 76–528) (Jan. 17, 1978)
(on file with the Library of Congress, Manuscript Room, Papers of Justice Thurgood
Marshall (Box 201)).

136. See Memorandum from Justice Rehnquist to Justice Brennan, Vermont Yankee
Nuclear Power Corp. v. NRDC, 435 U.S. 519 (1978) (Nos. 76–419, 76–528) (Feb. 10, 1978)
(on file with the Library of Congress, Manuscript Room, Papers of Justice Thurgood
Marshall (Box 201)).

137. See Memorandum from Justice Brennan to Justice Rehnquist Vermont Yankee
Nuclear Power Corp. v. NRDC, 435 U.S. 519 (1978) (Nos. 76–419, 76–528) (Feb. 27, 1978)
(on file with the Library of Congress, Manuscript Room, Papers of Justice Thurgood
Marshall (Box 201)). Justice Marshall also suggested a few modifications "to soften some of
the language just a bit," which Justice Rehnquist took. Justice Marshall's suggestions were
minor language tweakings that left more room for the possibility that additional procedures might be judicially required. Memorandum from Justice Marshall to Justice Rehnquist, Vermont Yankee Nuclear Power Corp. v. NRDC, 435 U.S. 519 (1978) (Nos. 76–419,
76–528) (Mar. 3, 1978) (on file with the Library of Congress, Manuscript Room, Papers of
Justice Thurgood Marshall (Box 201)).

138. See Memorandum from Justice Rehnquist to Justice Brennan, Vermont Yankee
Nuclear Power Corp. v. NRDC, 435 U.S. 519 (1978) (Nos. 76–419, 76–528) (Feb. 27, 1978)

separately, Justice Brennan ultimately signed onto Justice Rehnquist's opinion in full, remarking to Justice Rehnquist "you are a damned good fisherman. Indeed, so good that I now give up the sporting fight and 'acquiesce' in your catch in these cases."[139]

The Impact of *Vermont Yankee*

Vermont Yankee sparked extensive commentary when it was issued, as well as extensive briefing when it was before the Court.[140] Its unqualified and stern language reinforces the impression that it is an administrative law decision of major import, and the opinion is a leading case in every administrative law casebook. But how significant was *Vermont Yankee* really, in the end?

One reason to question its importance is evident on the face of the decision itself, in the fact that the Court remanded for the D.C. Circuit to determine whether the fuel cycle rule was adequately supported by the record. As several commentators remarked, if the Court meant to leave substantive judicial review unaffected and only curb judicial imposition of procedural requirements, then the decision's actual import would be far more limited than might at first appear.[141] Judge Leventhal would be crowned the victor in his battle with Judge Bazelon—which was indeed how the former viewed the decision[142]—but in practice little

(on file with the Library of Congress, Manuscript Room, Papers of Justice Thurgood Marshall (Box 201)) ("I do not think it can be fairly said that the Court of Appeals did not review the procedures employed by the agency and remand because it considered the procedures inadequate.").

139. See Memorandum from Justice Brennan to Justice Rehnquist, Vermont Yankee Nuclear Power Corp. v. NRDC, 435 U.S. 519 (1978) (Nos. 76–419, 76–528) (Feb. 28, 1978) (on file with the Library of Congress, Manuscript Room, Papers of Justice Thurgood Marshall (Box 201)); Memorandum from Justice Rehnquist to Justice Brennan, Vermont Yankee Nuclear Power Corp. v. NRDC, 435 U.S. 519 (1978) (Nos. 76–419, 76–528) (Mar. 20, 1976 [sic]) (on file with the Library of Congress, Manuscript Room, Papers of Justice Thurgood Marshall (Box 201)).

140. For academic commentary, *see* articles cited in supra notes 42, 54, 124, & 129 and infra note 141. For discussion of the briefing in *Vermont Yankee*, *see* Strauss, supra note 70, at 1408–11.

141. See, e.g., Paul R. Verkuil, *Judicial Review of Informal Rulemaking: Waiting for* Vermont Yankee III, 55 Tul. L. Rev. 418, 418–19 (1981); see also Byse, supra note 129, at 1826–30 (1978) (supporting decision in *Vermont Yankee* but arguing that courts retain power to adequately oversee agency procedures through substantive review); Davis, supra note 129, at 16 (criticizing the *Vermont Yankee* decision but arguing that the Court's retention of substantive scrutiny may limit its impact); William H. Rodgers, Jr., *A Hard Look at* Vermont Yankee: *Environmental Law Under Close Scrutiny*, 67 Geo. L.J. 699, 713–15 (1979) (arguing *Vermont Yankee* unlikely to effect hard look review, but will discourage agencies' procedural innovations).

142. See Strauss, supra note 70, at 1412 & n.68.

would change. Courts would remain active in policing and overseeing informal rulemaking.

Over time, it has become apparent that the Court did intend to draw such a distinction between procedure and substance in judicial review. To be sure, the Court at times has taken a highly deferential stance in scrutinizing an agency's substantive conclusions—a prime example being the decision in *Baltimore Gas & Electric Company v. NRDC*, when the fuel cycle rule made its next (and final) appearance before the Court. On remand from *Vermont Yankee*, the D.C. Circuit first stayed the proceeding to allow the NRC to issue its revised fuel cycle rule and then, in a lengthy decision, held the new rule was inadequately supported by the record. In the D.C. Circuit's view, the NRC's continuing refusal to take the uncertainties involved in long-term storage and disposal of nuclear waste into account in balancing the costs and benefits of nuclear reactors violated NEPA and was arbitrary and capricious.[143] Once more, however, the Court disagreed. In an opinion written by Justice O'Connor, it held that where, as here, an agency is "making predictions, within its area of special expertise, at the frontiers of science[,] . . . . a reviewing court must generally be at its most deferential."[144] Particularly important for the Court was the NRC's openness regarding the uncertainties that underlay its approach (an openness that contrasted with the AEC's earlier uncritical acceptance of Dr. Pittman's testimony).

But notwithstanding such deference to agency decisionmaking under conditions of uncertainty, the Court has continued to adhere to *Overton Park*'s emphasis on judicial responsibility to engage in close scrutiny of agency decisionmaking. In *Motor Vehicle Manufacturers Association v. State Farm Mutual Auto Insurance Company*, a decision issued less than three weeks after *Baltimore Gas*, the Court described the judicial task as being to ensure that agencies "examine the relevant data[,] articulate a satisfactory explanation for [their] actions," consider "the relevant factors" and not ignore "an important aspect of the problem."[145] The APA supports requiring agencies to compile administrative records adequate to explain their decisions, authorizing courts to "set aside agency action, findings, and conclusions found to be . . . arbitrary, capricious, [or] an abuse of discretion."[146] However, the level of agency explanation and

---

143. See NRDC v. NRC, 685 F.2d 459, 478–85 (D.C. Cir. 1982).

144. Baltimore Gas & Elec. Co. v. NRDC, 462 U.S. 87, 103–04 (1983). It is worth noting that Justice Brennan again tried to mitigate criticism of Judge Bazelon and the D.C. Circuit, prompting Justice Blackmun to write in his personal notes on the case that Brennan "is protecting his friend, and with difficulty." *See* Conference Sheet, Baltimore Gas & Elec. Co. v. NRDC, 462 U.S. 87 (1983) (Nos. 82–524, 82–545, 82–551) (on file with the Library of Congress, Manuscript Room, Papers of Justice Harry Blackmun (Box 386)).

145. See 463 U.S. 29, 42–43 (1983).

146. 5 U.S.C. § 706(2)(A).

factual basis that courts often require goes beyond that mandated the mild language of this provision. Thus, such rigorous substantive scrutiny would seem to contradict the holding of *Vermont Yankee*.[147]

In *Pension Benefit Guaranty Corp. v. LTV Corporation*, the Court attempted to diffuse this charge of inconsistency. According to the Court, its decisions upholding searching substantive review at most impose a "general procedural requirement of sorts ... that an agency take whatever steps it needs to provide an explanation that will enable the court to evaluate the agency's rationale." By contrast, "*Vermont Yankee* stands for the general proposition that courts are not free to impose upon agencies specific procedural requirements that have no basis in the APA."[148] In practice, however, this distinction between general and specific procedural mandates may offer little comfort to agencies. Whether a court phrases its complaint in terms of the general inadequacy of the record or specific procedural deficiencies, the net result is a remand. Moreover, on *Vermont Yankee*'s own reasoning, the rational administrative response to searching substantive review is to act preemptively by developing an exhaustive record, responding to every possible later judicial objection, which imposes delay and limits the flexibility of informal rulemaking in the same way as does judicial procedural scrutiny.

Equally important, *Vermont Yankee* has not called into question lower court decisions adopting expansive accounts of the terse and minimal requirements of § 553. As noted, this practice is evident in several decisions issued prior to *Vermont Yankee*, such as *Kennecott Copper* and *Portland Cement*, and it continued unabated after the *Vermont Yankee* decision came down. For example, courts have held that agencies violate § 553's minimal demand that an agency provide notice of "either the terms or substance of the proposed rule or a description of the subjects and issues involved" if the rule ultimately adopted is not adequately foreshadowed by the agencies' original proposal. They have also read § 553 as requiring that the agency provide notice of the data and studies on which the proposed rule is based.[149] Neither the Court nor the participants in *Vermont Yankee* ever called into question these decisions adopting expansive readings of § 553's requirements, and the Court has not seen fit to do so since.

It is interesting to puzzle over why these decisions interpreting § 553 were unaffected by *Vermont Yankee*, despite their seeming tension. The answer that these paper hearing requirements are rooted in the text

---

147.   See Stewart, supra note 54, at 1816.

148.   496 U.S. 633, 654–55 (1990).

149.   See, e.g., Black Media Coalition v. FCC, 791 F.2d 1016 (2d Cir. 1986); see generally 1 ADMINISTRATIVE LAW TREATISE, supra note 88, § 7.3 at 430–41.

of the APA is implausible; like searching substantive scrutiny, these requirements go far beyond the minimal language of the APA and its framers' original understandings. Instead, the explanation may lie in the disconnect between *Vermont Yankee*'s dictate and contemporary administrative reality. Allowing agencies to provide only vague and general information on their proposed actions became untenable in light of the expansion and import of informal rulemaking, as well as changing norms regarding openness in government incorporated in the Freedom of Information Act and other statutes. The need to preserve mechanisms for ensuring agency accountability led courts to read *Vermont Yankee* in the narrowest of terms, as disavowing ad hoc procedural review of the kind advocated by Judge Bazelon but not challenging the fundamental image of courts and agencies as partners in the quest for reasoned decisionmaking. Moreover, it is not surprising that courts would continue to rely on procedural requirements in particular as a means of reining in agencies, giving their familiarity and comfort with adjudicatory process.[150]

Vermont Yankee thus had fairly minimal effect on the courts' transformation of informal rulemaking procedures and the development of paper hearing requirements.[151] Yet it is also important not to ignore the impact that the decision did have. Notwithstanding the creative judicial interpretations of § 553's text, *Vermont Yankee* limited judges' ability to constrain agencies through procedural means. Further, the Court's remand for the D.C. Circuit to determine the adequacy of the fuel cycle rulemaking record conveyed its evident sanction of substantive review of agency decisionmaking. The net result was to give a green light to the hard look doctrine and close judicial scrutiny of rulemaking records, an approach the Supreme Court even more expressly sanctioned in *State Farm*. Much administrative law scholarship has since condemned such searching substantive review as creating major problems for informal rulemaking. According to these critics, courts lack the scientific and technical knowledge to distinguish the wheat from the chaff, and have held up or reversed major rulemaking efforts because of minor errors. Moreover agencies, fearing reversal, have felt obliged to respond in detail to minor issues, transforming rulemakings into lengthy, resource-intensive proceedings and destroying their promise as a means of efficient and coherent regulation.[152]

---

150. See PETER L. STRAUSS ET AL., GELLHORN AND BYSE'S ADMINISTRATIVE LAW, 510–15, 549 (10th rev. ed., 2003); Edward Rubin, *It's Time to Make the Administrative Procedure Act Administrative*, 89 Cornell L. Rev. 95, 111 (2003).

151. See Strauss, supra note 70, at 1410–11; see also Stewart, supra note 54, at 1812–14 (expressing concern that *Vermont Yankee* jeopardized decisions developing idea of paper hearing).

152. For a classic accounts of this argument, see JERRY L. MASHAW & DAVID L. HARFST, THE STRUGGLE FOR AUTO SAFETY, (1990); Thomas O. McGarity, *Some Thoughts on "Deossify-*

Of course, these criticisms of the hard look doctrine may be misguided, and in any event judicial procedural review might well have had a similar effect. Certainly, the benefits of greater adversarial procedures are easy to exaggerate.[153] But it is worth noting that despite the D.C. Circuit's greater affection for cross-examination and other adversarial mechanisms, not even that court advocated employing full-scale adjudicatory proceedings such as are laid out in the APA's requirements for formal rulemaking. The Court's predictions in *Vermont Yankee* of dire effects from Monday-morning procedural quarterbacking may therefore have been somewhat overblown. True, the possibility of reversal on procedural grounds might well lead agency counsel to advise widespread use of procedures, such as oral hearings or perhaps some opportunity for questioning, that clearly go beyond what § 553 requires and could seriously hamper rulemaking. But it is also possible that, over time, courts and agencies might have come to general agreement on when additional procedures are needed and what form those procedures should take.[154] Indeed, one clear message of the D.C. Circuit's decision in *Vermont Yankee* is that agency acceptance of conclusory and unsubstantiated statements is likely to provoke courts to think greater procedural protections were necessary. Notably, in its opinion the D.C. Circuit stated that "the procedures the agency adopted in this case, if administered in a more sensitive, deliberate manner, might suffice."[155] Thus, had the hearing board subjected Dr. Pittman to more probing questions or the AEC been more acknowledging of the weaknesses of his testimony, perhaps the D.C. Circuit would have ruled differently.

---

ing" *the Rulemaking Process*, 41 Duke L.J. 1385, 1387–96, 1410–26 (1992). Others take a more positive view of the hard look doctrine. See, e.g., Mark Seidenfeld, *Demystifying Deossification: Rethinking Recent Proposals to Modify Judicial Review of Notice and Comment Rulemaking*, 75 Tex. L. Rev. 483, 503–524 (1997); Patricia M. Wald, *Judicial Review in the Time of Cholera*, 49 Admin. L. Rev. 659, 662–63 (1997); see also Strauss et al., supra note 150, at 1017–26 (providing additional samplings of the debate).

153. For arguments regarding the limited benefits from greater adversarial procedures in rulemakings that address complex scientific issues, see Thomas O. McGarity, *Substantive and Procedural Discretion in Administrative Resolution of Science Policy Questions: Regulating Carcinogens in EPA and OSHA*, 67 Geo. L.J. 729, 749–53, 776–80 (1979); Yellin, supra note 3, at 505–08, 552–53.

154. The evolution of procedural due process may be instructive here. In the procedural due process context, the Court has insisted on independently assessing the constitutional adequacy of procedures once it determines that a protected property interest is at stake. See Cleveland Bd. of Educ. v. Loudermill, 470 U.S. 532, 539–41 (1985). Yet over time, the Court in practice has become increasingly deferential to governmental procedural choices, even when the only procedure supplied by the government is a post-deprivation judicial remedy. See, e.g., Lujan v. G & G Fire Sprinklers, Ltd., 532 U.S. 189, 195–99 (2001); Walters v. National Ass'n of Radiation Survivors, 473 U.S. 305, 321–34 (1985).

155. NRDC v. NRC, 547 F.2d 633, 653–54 (D.C. Cir. 1976).

Another effect of *Vermont Yankee* is that it precluded courts from engaging agencies in a more honest dialogue regarding the flaws courts perceive in agency decisionmaking and the benefits of different procedures. A court that believes an agency should have employed additional procedures now can only express its objections in substantive terms, perhaps leading the agency to misunderstand the real basis of the court's concerns.[156] In addition, rather than justify their procedural impositions (such as detailed notice requirements) on straightforward policy grounds, courts must now root these mandates in the terms of § 553, making it harder for agencies and others to refute the appropriateness of these measures. In this light, the main effect of *Vermont Yankee* was not to preclude courts from imposing procedural controls on agencies, but to force courts to do so *sub rosa*, with openness and rationality of judicial decisionmaking suffering in the process.

As for *Vermont Yankee*'s impact on nuclear power, both Vermont Yankee and Consumers Powers received their licenses. Other than occasional safety shutdowns, Vermont Yankee has been operating since 1972. However, Vermont Yankee faces a growing problem of what to do with its spent nuclear fuel, given the lack of any fuel reprocessing or long-term disposal facilities in the country. Vermont Yankee stores its spent fuel on-site, but space in its spent-fuel pool is now at a premium, and the plant was already given permission to re-rack the pool to higher density in 1997—absent that permission, it would have had to shut down. Sold to Entergy Nuclear Corporation in 2002, Vermont Yankee is also in the midst of a new licensing battle at the NRC as it seeks permission to expand its energy generating capacity.[157] The state of Vermont has intervened, choosing none other than Anthony Roisman to assist it in the proceedings.[158]

Consumers Powers was not so lucky. Its Midland Plant was plagued with construction problems, including the need to add a new foundation when the plant began to sink. These problems, combined with lengthy regulatory proceedings and Consumers Power's lack of capital, led to substantial delays in the plant's construction. Dow Chemical eventually pulled out of the project in 1983, when the plant was nearly ten years late and still unfinished. Consumers ultimately stopped work on the plant one year later, with only one reactor near completion and the

---

156. See CHRISTOPHER F. EDLEY, JR., ADMINISTRATIVE LAW: RETHINKING JUDICIAL CONTROL OF BUREAUCRACY 228 (1990).

157. See Matthew L. Wald, *Safety of Adding to Nuclear Plants' Capacity Is Questioned*, N.Y. Times, Jan. 26, 2004, at A15; David Gram, *Nuclear Waste: Meltdown of Vermont Harmony*, L.A. Times, May 24, 1987, at 26. For stories of occasional problems at Vermont Yankee, see *Nuclear Plant Faces NRC Fine in Vermont*, Wall St. J., Aug. 26, 1996, at B8; *Fine Proposed for Errors at Yankee Nuclear Plant*, N.Y. Times, Oct. 16, 1982, at A6.

158. Roisman Interview, supra note 14.

company already having spent $4.2 billion—over a ten-fold increase from
the original estimated cost of $359 million for two reactors. In the end,
the plant was reconfigured and came on-line in 1987 as a cogeneration
facility that burns natural gas to produce steam for Dow as well as
electricity. This allowed Consumers Powers to avoid bankruptcy, although Michigan ratepayers bore substantial costs as a result of the
failed nuclear power effort.[159]

Most importantly, the problem of what to do about nuclear waste
has continued to plague the nuclear power industry. Concerns about
expanding access to plutonium led President Carter to impose a moratorium on licensing any fuel reprocessing plants in 1977.[160] While this
removed the difficult issues of nuclear proliferation and how to secure
plutonium produced by reprocessing from the nuclear waste debate, it
heightened the need to develop a long-term storage facility. Spent
nuclear fuel has continued to pile up in temporary storage pools at
nuclear facilities across the country, with the total amount of such fuel
being estimated at 49,000 metric tons in 2003.[161] But developing a long-
term storage facility, and more specifically determining where to locate
it, has been a major political minefield. Recognition of the growing
nuclear waste problem led to enactment the Nuclear Waste Policy Act of
1982 (NWPA), which set up a detailed system for identification and
approval of a site for a long-term disposal facility.[162] Ongoing political
and legal battles over selecting a depository site proved expensive and
time-consuming, and in 1987 Congress directed the federal agencies
involved to focus their efforts on developing a facility at Yucca Mountain,
Nevada, located on the federal government's Nevada Test Site.[163] Not
surprisingly, the selection of Yucca Mountain was vigorously opposed by
Nevada, as well as other states along the train routes on which nuclear
waste would be transported. Over the ensuing years, Nevada (along with
several environmental groups) brought numerous legal challenges, and

---

159. See John R. Emshwiller, *Nuclear Fallout: Utility Plant Delays in Michigan Spur
Rift with Major Customer*, Wall St. J., Mar. 24, 1977, at 1; Ron Winslow, *Chain of Problems
at Nuclear Site Threatens Consumers Power's Plan to Finish Facility*, Wall St. J., Oct. 28,
1983, at 33; *Michigan Utility Says It Will Close Midland Project*, Wall St. J., July 17, 1984,
at 1; Thomas W. Lippman, *Rescue of a Failed Nuclear Plant; Mothballed for Years,
Michigan Facility Operates on Natural Gas*, Wash. Post, Apr. 10, 1990, at D1.

160. See 1 PUBLIC PAPERS OF THE PRESIDENTS OF THE UNITED STATES: JIMMY CARTER 581,
582–83 (1977); *see also* Frank N. von Hippel, *Plutonium and Reprocessing of Spent Nuclear
Fuel*, Science, Sept. 28, 2001, at 2397 (describing changes in approach to reprocessing in
subsequent administrations).

161. See Nuclear Energy Inst., Inc. v. EPA, 373 F.3d 1251, 1258 (D.C. Cir. 2004).

162. Pub. L. No. 97–425, 96 Stat. 2201 (1982) (codified as amended at 42 U.S.C.
§ 10101–10270).

163. For criticism of NWPA and its subsequent amendments, see GREGORY JACOB, SITE
UNSEEN: THE POLITICS OF SITING A NUCLEAR WASTE REPOSITORY, 95–163 (1990).

in July 2004 one of these challenges proved successful before the D.C. Circuit. That court, again entering the nuclear waste fray, held that the EPA's use of a 10,000 year time period as the standard for assessing the facility's environmental impact was not a reasonable interpretation of the 1992 Energy Policy Act.[164]

Even prior to the D.C. Circuit's decision, Yucca Mountain was not expected to be operating before 2010 at the earliest, and the continuing delay in opening a waste depository means that the federal government owes nuclear plant operators millions, and potentially billions, to cover the costs for storing waste. While Congress could overturn the D.C. Circuit's decision, quick legislative action to get Yucca Mountain back on track seems unlikely, and the success of efforts to issue acceptable regulations is uncertain.[165] But what is clear is that, nearly 30 years after the decision in *Vermont Yankee*, the courts are still making their voices heard on questions of nuclear waste disposal and nuclear policy.

---

164. See *Nuclear Energy Inst.*, 373 F.3d at 1258–62, 1273.

165. See Matthew L. Wald, *U.S. Settles Nuclear Case over Burial of Waste*, N.Y. Times, Aug. 10, 2004, at A5; Matthew L. Wald, *Ruling on Nuclear Site Leaves Next Move to Congress*, N.Y. Times, July 14, 2004, at A20. On September 1st, 2004, the D.C. denied rehearing and rehearing en banc, and the period for seeking certiorari at the Supreme Court expired without a petition being filed.

Riva Ridge wins the Kentucky Derby.

Our experience with the 1990s' financial bubble adds a special edge to Professor Schotland's tale about a pair of cases that stemmed from an earlier financial bubble, built on the 20th century's first great new technology—electric power. The technology was sound but the financial and corporate structure were not. That structure, viewed as a main cause of the Crash, led to the New Deal's "most bitterly contested" statute, the Public Utility Holding Company Act, an unusually potent and challenging regulatory program. The two *SEC v. Chenery* decisions give us two fundamental propositions of Administrative Law, which doubtless would have emerged even if these cases had not arisen. But the cases would not have arisen if a settlement proposed by the SEC had been accepted. The tale, interesting for revisiting dramatic developments of several generations ago, memorably underlines the need to take settlement possibilities seriously. An unrelated part of the tale involves the unusually heated dissent in 1947's *Chenery II* and helps solve a puzzle about whether that decision was inconsistent with 1943's *Chenery I*. Last, a happy ending: Mr. Chenery, two-time loser at the Court, later enjoyed a historic win in a very different forum.

5

Roy A. Schotland*

A Sporting Proposition—*SEC v. Chenery*

*"You got to know when to hold 'em. Know when to fold 'em."***

Setting the Scene

During the first quarter of the 20th Century, electric power generation was an extraordinary engine of the American economy. From 1902 to 1922, the industry grew a stunning 13 times in generating capacity and nine times in value, and then by 1927 it again more than doubled in value. The number of kilowatt-hours of electric power used in 1929 was 36 times greater than in 1902.[1]

With this growth came an industrial structure that many would subsequently view as a major cause of the 1929 Crash. The public utility companies generating this electricity were controlled by holding companies ("PUHCs") with uniquely arcane, complex, and problem-laden structures that effectively concentrated power over the utilities and the streams of income they generated in the hands of a very few. Shortly after the Crash, a high-level National Power Policy Committee[2] would report to the Congress that, using these pyramid-like structures, "it [was frequently] possible for relatively small but powerful groups with a disproportionately small investment . . . to control and to manage solely

---

* Professor of Law, Georgetown University.

** "The Gambler," by Kenny Rogers: "You got to know when to hold 'em. Know when to fold 'em. Know when to walk away and know when to run. You never count your money when you're sittin' at the table. There'll be time enough for countin' when the dealing's done." Provided by Lyrics XP.com Song Search.

1. Comment, *Federal Regulation of Holding Companies: The Public Utility Act of 1935*, 45 Yale L.J. 468, at 469, n. 4.

2. The Committee was chaired by Secretary of Interior Harold I. Ickes, with seven other members including David E. Lilienthal, who in 1936 became chairman of the Tennessee Valley Authority and later the first chairman of the Atomic Energy Commission.

in their own interest tremendous capital investments of other people's money."[3] "The pyramiding process allowed the holding companies to make extremely large gains on very small increases in operating company profits."[4]

The PUHCs' structural complexity was compounded by intricate arrays of different kinds and classes of securities. And the PUHCs controlled not only large numbers of operating utilities, but also affiliated companies from which the utility subsidiaries bought goods like coal and services like construction; obviously, the webs of affiliates that surrounded the utilities precluded arms-length bargaining. The resulting complexity made it difficult (to understate it) for investors in these securities and for state utility regulators to understand the reality of the utilities' operations. And although the PUHC structures brought economies of scale, they also assured that the savings would be directed to the holding company owners, not other investors.

Further, actual "practices ... added positive abuses"[5]: the PUHCs employed high leverage and unsound, even manipulative practices, that made their public investors acutely vulnerable to adverse economic developments. Thus, in 1932, when one major holding company's gross operating revenues fell 11% below the prior year's, the income applicable to the common stock held by public investors fell 96%; another holding company's common stock, which in 1931 had enjoyed a pitiful 15% of the consolidated holding company income, got less than 1% in 1932.[6]

All those problems were exacerbated by two more: highly concentrated ownership, and absentee control of operating utilities. As of 1929, "sixteen holding company groups controlled 92% of the power produced by private companies in the United States"; more than 40% was held by the three largest groups (and they were not independent of each other).[7] The largest single PUHC controlled utilities in 36 States, and eight other systems had operating units in 11 to 29 States.[8]

After the 1929 Crash, 53 holding companies went into bankruptcy.[9] A number of the individuals who controlled the tops of the pyramid-

---

3. Printed as Appendix to Senate Rpt. 621, Public Utility Act of 1935, Committee on Interstate Commerce, 74th Cong. 1st Sess., at 55 (1935).

4. Department of Energy, Energy Information Administration, Public Utility Holding Company Act of 1935: 1935–1992 (1993), 2.

5. Yale Comment, n. 1 above, at 474.

6. Norman S. Buchanan, *The Public Utility Holding Company Problem*, 25 Calif.L.Rev. 517, 524–25 (1937).

7. Yale Comment, n. 1 above, at 471.

8. Power Policy Committee Report, n. 3 above, at 57.

9. PacifiCorp, Integrated Resource Planning Report (2003), at 164. Available at http://www.pacificorp.com/File/File25687.pdf.

structures left the United States, many of them for countries which had no extradition treaty with us. The most notorious expatriate was Samuel Insull, who controlled the third largest PUHC system, Middle West Utility Co, and—fairly or not[10]—was one of the main figures blamed for the 1929 crash.[11] From 1925 to 1929, his company's stock price rose from $83 to $570; as the market was moving to its peak before the October

---

10. Insull's biography opened as follows:

An old man leaned against the rail of the S.S. "Exilona," staring blankly into the early morning fog off the New Jersey shore, as the pilot and quarantine boats hove into view and Ambrose Light drew slowly abeam. The twenty-four-day crossing had done little to relieve his aching, exhausted body and had only partially mended his broken spirit. With a sigh born partly of reflection and partly of resignation, Samuel Insull turned and spoke to his State Department guard.

"Berry," he said, "if two men had walked down Fifth Avenue a year ago"—that would have been May, 1933—"and one of them had a pint of whiskey in his pocket and the other had a hundred dollars in gold coin, the one with the whiskey would have been called a criminal, and the one with the gold an honest citizen. If these two men had, like Rip van Winkle, slept for a year and again walked down Fifth Avenue, the man with the whiskey would be called an honest citizen and the one with the gold coin a criminal. I find myself somewhat in this sort of situation. What I did, when I did it, was honest; now, through changed conditions, what I did may or may not be called honest. Politics demand, therefore, that I be brought to trial; but what is really being brought to trial is the system I represented."

Forrest McDonald, Insull, 1–2 (1962).

11. Both anti-business people and pro-business people needed scapegoats, and Insull headed the list. In 1932, Insull was indicted for embezzlement, using the mails to defraud investors, etc.; that was followed by an 18-month chase to catch him in a country that would extradite him. Finally he was brought home, tried and acquitted of all charges (as were his 16 co-defendants), then went back to Europe and later died in a Paris Metro station.

But he probably was more scapegoat than villain. For a strong defense of Insull ("who started as Thomas Edison's gofer at 21 and helped build the company that became General Electric"), see Sir Harold Evans, Follow the Money (review of Steve Fraser, Every Man a Speculator), N.Y. Times Book Review, 14–15 (Mar. 13, 2005).

As for his start: far from being a mere "gofer," he was so gifted that as soon as he started with Edison he became his "financial factotum": e.g., he created and carried out a plan to free Edison of the "leaden collar" that Edison's lenders had imposed, which had kept Edison from developing central plants—later known as public utilities—to generate electric power. In doing that, the 22-year-old Insull overcame J.P. Morgan, leader of the lenders. See McDonald, n. 10 above, at 22, 31–32 (1962).

Insull was a remarkable innovator. At what became General Electric, he headed sales and manufacturing and established what became the model national sales program for American manufacturers. Later, at the Chicago utility he started, he established the pattern for ratemaking throughout the world. McDonald, 42, 68. Most pertinent for the regulatory domain was his proposal in 1898, as president of the utilities' trade association that is now the Edison Electric Institute, that utilities were "natural monopolies" and should be under government regulation. Richard D. Cudahy and William D. Henderson, From Insull to Enron: Corporate (Re)Regulation after the Rise and Fall of Two Energy Icons, 26 Energy L.J. 35, 46 (2005).

crash, insider trading in these shares moved the price from $159 in May to $364 in end-July.[12]

Our tale starts with another of those who went abroad, Floyd Ostrum. Before 1929, he had pledged his PUHC shares at the Chase Bank as collateral for a loan. After the crash and the nonpayment of that loan, the bank had foreclosed on that collateral and then sold the shares to Christopher Chenery. Chenery, who had founded and headed one PUHC, Federal Water & Gas, and eventually chaired several others, was an engineer who had "practiced on most of the frontiers of America, ranging from Alaska to Wall Street [and encountering] black bears and brown bears [and] more recently . . . the even wilder inhabitants of the financial markets."[13]

In the wake of the Crash, these financial difficulties for ordinary investors, and the apparent skullduggery of at least some PUHC financiers, Congress moved to adopt the Public Holding Company Act of 1935, now a near-relic but originally one of the New Deal's major, hardest-won statutes.[14] It created so large a regulatory challenge that for many years it constituted the main task of the new Securities and Exchange Commission.

The legislative struggle over PUHCA was "the most bitterly contested of the New Deal."[15] As one Senator described it: "The people of this Nation have been regaled with stories of the railroad manipulation of politics, but in their palmiest days the railroad kings were cheap pikers compared to the clever, ruthless, and financially free-handed political manipulators of the Power Trust. Compared to them, all the so-called 'lobbyists and political fixers' of all time are as moonlight unto sunlight and water unto wine."[16] One indicator of how heated was the struggle over PUHCA is that an amendment to the bill became the first federal regulation of lobbying.[17] That amendment stemmed from an effort led by the populist Senator from Alabama, Hugo Black, even before the major hearings held on the public utility industry's lobbying, by a Special Committee to Investigate Lobbying that he chaired.[18]

---

12. Department of Energy, n. 4 above, at 6.

13. Washington & Lee Alumni Magazine (August 1927), 39. He was a trustee there from 1950 to 1970, and such a devoted alumnus that he borrowed the school's colors for his racing stable.

14. 49 Stat. 803 (1935), 15 U.S.C. § 79.

15. Cudahy and Henderson, n. 11 above, at 76.

16. Senator Homer Bone (D–Wash), 79 Cong.Rec. 8683 (1935), borrowing ("moonlight . . . wine") from Tennyson, Locksley Hall, see ALFRED LORD TENNYSON, POEMS (Boston, 1842).

17. Section 12 of PUHCA, 15 U.S.C. Sec. 79l(I).

18. See John F. Kennedy, *Congressional Lobbies: A Chronic Problem Re-examined*, 45 Geo. L. J. 535, 543 (1957). In 1937, Senator Black would become President Roosevelt's first appointee to the Supreme Court.

PUHCA's opening section enumerated the "abuses" that had been found, that they had "become persistent and wide-spread", and so were "unless regulated ... injurious to investors, consumers, and the general public.... Upon the basis of facts disclosed by the reports of the Federal Trade Commission [and] the reports of the [House] Committee and otherwise disclosed and ascertained ... it is hereby declared that the national public interest, the interest of investors in the securities of holding companies ... and the interest of consumers of electric energy ... are or may be adversely affected—

"(*l*) when such investors cannot obtain the information necessary to appraise the financial position or earning power of the issuers ...;

"(2) when subsidiary public-utility companies are subjected to excessive charges for services, construction work, equipment, and materials, or enter into transactions in which evils result from an absence of arm's-length bargaining ...;

"(3) when control of subsidiary public-utility companies affects the accounting practices and rate, dividend, and other policies of such companies so as to complicate and obstruct State regulation...."

The Act applied to all PUHCs. Its most dramatic and controversial provision was the "death sentence," requiring that the complex structures be collapsed and replaced by corporate structures that would be simple, and with capital structures that would "fairly and equitably" distribute the stockholders' voting power.[19] The legislative struggle over this provision was the most intense battle in the war over the bill. The Senate bill included the "death sentence," but the House bill delegated to the SEC the question of what changes, if any, should be made in the PUHCs. Delegating that issue to the agency would have been excessive, if not in terms of constitutionality then certainly as a matter of administrative manageability. This was memorably described by James Landis, a leading scholar of Administrative Law who in 1934 was one of the SEC's initial members, and then became its second Chairman, 1935–37:

> As passed by the Senate, the bill called for the abolition of all holding companies [with narrow specific exceptions]. On the other hand, as passed by the House, the bill required the Commission to take such action as would have the effect of confining each holding company organization, in its operations, to a single integrated system. But the House bill also authorized the Commission to exempt any holding company from this requirement if such exemption was found to be consistent with the public interest. We have here two radically different approaches. Putting aside any question as to the merits of the so-called "death sentence" of the Senate bill, it did

---

19. Quoting PUHCA Sec. 11(a).

indicate a definite line of action for the Commission to undertake. The House amendment, however, turned over the whole burning issue of the future of the holding company in the public utility field to the Commission itself without any indication of what it should do with it other than that the public interest should be the guide for Commission action. It was obvious at once that, for the Commission, this was an impossible responsibility. It meant nothing less than that the Commission, rather than the Congress, would become the focal point for all the pressures and counter-pressures that had kept the Congress and the press at a white heat for months. Instead of the controversy being concluded, it would have been protracted interminably with the rooms of the Commission the place of debate rather than the halls of the Congress. Some determination as to the place, generally, of the holding company in the public utility field had first to be made by the Congress before the problem was defined sufficiently for an administrative approach.[20]

The Senate prevailed, but that led to the question how the "death sentence" provision would be implemented. The Commission would "require by order, after notice and opportunity for hearing," that such action be taken by each PUHC as the SEC found necessary "to ensure that the corporate structure or continued existence of any company in the holding company system does not unduly or unnecessarily complicate the structure, or unfairly or inequitably distribute voting power among security holders...."[21] Every PUHC was entitled to submit "a plan" to comply with those requirements, which the Commission would approve if the plan was found "fair and equitable to the persons affected [and] appropriate to effectuate" the Act. If no plan was submitted or approved, the SEC could sue to enforce simplification, and the courts were empowered to take possession of the PUHC and its assets and to appoint a trustee; the SEC might be appointed as sole trustee.[22]

This was a remarkable regulatory scheme for its time, affording as much initiative as it did to the regulated industry—albeit under the controlling hand of regulatory authority. " 'People forget about it, but it really was epochal,' said Jonathan Katz, secretary of the [SEC, in 2004]. 'Imagine today if Congress gave a government agency the authority to study the entire high-tech industry and the responsibility to reorganize it.' "[23] And the responsible agency, the brand new Securities and Ex-

---

20. From JAMES M. LANDIS, THE ADMINISTRATIVE PROCESS 55–57 (1938).

21. Sec. 11(b)(2). The Commission could exempt any PUHC from any provision, in specified circumstances, Sec. 3.

22. Sec. 11(e).

23. Quoted in an obituary for Milton Cohen, who in the 1940's became head of the SEC's division implementing PUHCA and was later a leader of the SEC bar and a visiting

change Commission, enjoyed a status few federal agencies, before or since, have attained. Its first chairman was Joseph Kennedy, a multimillionaire who had been one of President Roosevelt's few business supporters; he would become Ambassador to Great Britain, and during his time in London his son would prepare for the presidency, writing his senior thesis on why Great Britain was unprepared for war.[24] Its second chairman was James Landis, one of the intellectual fathers of the administrative state; when Landis left the SEC to become Dean of Harvard Law School he was succeeded by one of the young intellectual stars of the Legal Realist movement, William O. Douglas, 38—who had been a law professor at Columbia at 29, at Yale at 30, and was subsequently the longest sitting Justice of the Supreme Court. Douglas was succeeded as Chairman by one of his colleagues on the Commission, Jerome N. Frank, later one of the Second Circuit's immortals. And one of Douglas's assistants was Abe Fortas, much later a Supreme Court Justice. The SEC was the place to be.

Direct responsibility for PUHCA administration was in the hands of the SEC's largest division. Milton Cohen, the head of that Division for many years, would later recount his experience for an oral historian:

MC: "[The PUHCA Division's] job was to examine each holding company system separately and decide whether it met the [PUHCA] standards of being geographically integrated and corporately simplified.

Interviewer: "[T]he Commission was beset with all kinds of litigation challenging the Constitutionality of the Act, the administrative process, and just about anything else that the lawyers could dream up. Did the work ... carry forward during that litigation or was the litigation disruptive?

MC: "We never had to interrupt because of pending litigation. We were never enjoined from proceeding."[25]

A unanimous Supreme Court sustained PUHCA against constitutional challenges in 1936—in the shadow of its then-recent decisions finding unconstitutional delegations under other New Deal statutes and well before FDR's failed effort at Court-packing and the famous "switch in time that saved nine."[26] After the remand ordered by that decision,

---

professor at Harvard Law School. *Milton Cohen, 93, A Lawyer Who Inspired Market Reform*, N.Y. Times, Nov. 14, 2004, 44.

24. John F. Kennedy, Why England Slept (1940).

25. Transcript, Interview with Milton Cohen, Nov. 29, 2001, pp. 5–7, Securities and Exchange Commission Historical Society. Online: http://www.sechistorical.org/museum/oralhistories/pdf/Cohen_interview_NOV_29_01. See n. 23 above.

26. Landis v. North American Co., 299 U.S. 248 (1936)(unanimous, with Justice McReynolds concurring in the result).

plaintiffs—two of the principal PUHCs—withdrew their suit and registered under the statute.[27]

The Chenery Application

Among those filing for registration was the PUHC headed by Christopher Chenery, briefly introduced above as the "white knight" who had bought the shares of émigré Floyd Ostrum after he had failed to meet payments on his bank loans. Particularly pertinent to this story, as becomes clear soon, is the fact that Mr. Chenery in 1936 bought The Meadow Farm and as an avocation started breeding thoroughbreds, with his first winners sired by a stallion he had bought for $125. By 1950, one of his horses was Horse of the Year (Hill Prince), but Chenery's natural ambition was to win the Kentucky Derby, which his horses tried several times without success.[28]

In November 1937, Chenery and his group submitted to the SEC its proposed plan for simplification of the Federal Water Service Company, a PUHC holding securities of subsidiary water, gas, electric, and other companies in thirteen states and one foreign country. Like a great many submissions, it was rejected because the SEC was not satisfied that the proposed new structure adequately distributed shareholder voting power. Over the following two years, Chenery submitted two amended plans, also rejected. Finally in March 1940, a further-amended plan was submitted. During that considerable period of submissions and informal negotiations, Chenery and some others in his control group had been adding to their holdings of their PUHC's preferred stock.

As anyone familiar with securities law knows, since 1934 there has been a statutory provision regulating the purchase or sale of securities by "insiders" (directors, officers and holders of 10% or more of the shares). Insiders have been required to report all their buying and selling to the SEC, and forbidden to profit from short-term buying and selling within a six-month period. Chenery and his group were insiders and were complying completely with these requirements. They were only buying, not selling, and they were reporting these transactions. But once upon a time records were not computerized: the "insider" reports went to a different division of the SEC, not the PUHCA division. No one in either division had thought of looking into whether any PUHC insiders were filing such reports. However, the reports have always been public

---

27. N.Y.Times, *Two Utility Groups Agree to Register*, Feb. 10, 1937, at 33; and see Note, *The Discretionary Stay as a Strategic Device in Constitutional Litigation*, 46 Yale L.J. 897 (1937). See also Electric Bond & Share Co. v. SEC, 303 U.S. 419 (1938)(opinion by Hughes, C.J. for six Justices including Justice Black, two not participating, and McReynolds dissenting without opinion); North American Company v. SEC, 327 U.S. 686 (1946)(unanimous, three Justices including Douglas not participating).

28. Red Smith, *The Good Horses of Chris Chenery*, N.Y. Times, Feb. 16, 1973, 27.

information and someone outside the agency found them and wrote to the PUHCA division about the Chenery insiders' buying. After the SEC division staff looked into the matter, they called in Mr. Chenery to discuss it. He came, of course with counsel (from a leading New York firm, Hughes, Hubbard Blair and Reed), to meet with division head Joseph Weiner. And many years later, Mr. Weiner told the author what had happened at that meeting.[29]

Mr. Chenery explained why they had been buying: someone else, they did not know who, had been steadily accumulating preferred shares, and they feared it was the former owner Ostrum, probably trying to reacquire control of the PUHC. Chenery and his group were buying only to make sure they did not lose control—they had no intention or even thought of profiting from their knowledge of the negotiations with the SEC. The SEC staff completely accepted that explanation, but still saw a considerable problem: even if in fact there was no connection between the Chenery group's inside knowledge of their negotiations and their transactions, the same might not—indeed, probably would not—be true generally. If any PUHC insiders did try to trade on their inside knowledge of pending negotiations, that might jeopardize the whole PUHCA program.

As the officials explained their problem, Mr. Chenery said that was all understandable and reasonable. Then Mr. Weiner, having heard Chenery's explanation, said

> Mr. Chenery, we know you're a sporting man. We understand what's happened and we agree that there's no improper conduct here. But we can't allow [PUHC] executives to be in here negotiating a simplification plan and at the same time trading in their shares. I'll bet we can settle this. You weren't trying to make a profit on those shares, you were just trying to safeguard your control of the company. How about this: your group sells to your company the shares you've recently bought, the company buys them as treasury shares—and so they stay in your control—with the company paying you just what you'd paid, plus interest. Won't that do the job for you?

Mr. Chenery responded: "You're right, I'm a sporting man and that sounds to me like a sporting deal, that sounds fair"—at which point his counsel angrily pounded the table and said "That's unconstitutional!"

Mr. Chenery said simply that he'd follow his lawyer's advice—and so, off they went to two Supreme Court cases. If the settlement offer had been accepted, not only would the Chenery group have avoided nine

---

29. Much of the explanation that follows is found also in Mr. Chenery's testimony set forth in the SEC's opinion after remand from the first Supreme Court decision, see In the Matter of Federal Water Service Corp., 18 S.E.C. 231, 241–43 (1945).

years of litigation costs, but the value of having taken that step would
have appreciated, according to Joe Weiner's estimate years ago, to about
$20,000,000 as of 2005.

To the Courts

The SEC's final decision had been that it would not approve the
March 1940 plan "so long as the preferred stock acquired by the
respondents would be permitted to share on a parity with other preferred stock," because (the agency concluded) the PUHC's managers
"were fiduciaries and hence under a 'duty of fair dealing' not to trade in
the securities of the corporation while plans for its reorganization were
before" the agency.[30] The Commission then approved the plan with an
amendment incorporating the settlement offer; the Chenery group objected to that amendment and went to the United States Court of
Appeals for the District of Columbia Circuit. That court, by a split
decision, held for the Chenery group:[31] they had complied with all
existing law, which included no such requirement of such a "duty of fair
dealing."

The SEC then took the case to the Supreme Court to protect its
ability to prevent "the possibilities of abuse" that would arise if the
lower court decision became the law. "Frequently, through control of
timing, control of the provisions of the [reorganization] plan, or through
possession of information which is not fully or generally known by the
security holders, [the management] could realize profits at their expense
if permitted to deal in the securities."[32] The Supreme Court granted
certiorari "because the question presented looms large in the administration of the Act" and, after an opinion that remains important to
administrative law practice but has receded from administrative law
classrooms, remanded to the agency.[33] As you are unlikely to have
already to have encountered much about this first *Chenery* case, it is
worth spending a few paragraphs on it here. To telegraph the main
point, which importantly endures: judicial review of agency action must
limit itself to the basis on which the agency acted—the reviewing court
cannot itself substitute a more satisfying rationale (even one suggested
by the agency's attorneys) for the one the agency has chosen, as it *could*
do in reviewing a district court's judgment. "[T]he Supreme Court
established the proposition that when an agency gives the wrong reason

---

30. Securities and Exchange Comm'n v. Chenery Corp., 318 U.S. 80, 85 (1943),
commonly known as *Chenery I*, referring to the SEC's lengthy decision, which had been
unanimous on this issue although divided on others, In the Matter of Federal Water
Service Corp., 8 S.E.C. 893 (1941).

31. 128 F.2d 303 (1942), remanding for proceedings in conformity with that opinion.

32. Petition for certiorari, at 16.

33. Securities Exchange Comn'n v. Chenery Corp., 318 U.S. at 81.

for a decision of policy or law, the reviewing court will send the case back for reconsideration, even though the court might have upheld the order if a different reason had been assigned."[34]

Justice Frankfurter had been the country's leading scholar of administrative law before his appointment to the Court. Now, for Justices Stone, Roberts and Jackson (with Justice Douglas not participating and one vacancy on the Court), he wrote in sympathy with both administrative action generally and also the ambitions and projects of the New Deal. The four-Justice majority agreed with the SEC that the managers were "fiduciaries," but "to say that a man is a fiduciary only begins analysis.... What obligations does he owe as a fiduciary?" The agency had found "[i]n its own words [that] 'honesty, full disclosure, and purchase at a fair price' characterized the transactions," and had "dealt with this as a specific case, and not as the application of a general rule formulating rules of conduct for reorganization managers." Instead, the agency had analogized " 'to the same standards as other fiduciaries ... dealing with the property which is the subject matter of [a] trust' ... merely applying 'the broad equitable principles enunciated' in ... cases" which had relied upon "principles of equity announced by courts" in bankruptcy and express trust matters, not involving "persons in control of a corporate enterprise toward its stockholders.... "

> If an order is valid only as a determination of policy or judgment which the agency alone is authorized to make and which it has not made, a judicial judgment cannot be made to do service for an administrative judgment. For purposes of affirming no less than reversing its orders, an appellate court cannot intrude upon the domain which Congress has exclusively entrusted to an administrative agency.

> If, therefore, the rule applied by the Commission is to be judged solely on the basis of its adherence to principles of equity derived from judicial decisions, its order plainly cannot stand. ... [T]he Commission did not in this case proffer new standards reflecting the experience gained by it in effectuating the legislative policy. On the contrary, it explicitly disavowed any purpose of going beyond those which the courts had theretofore recognized....[35]

> [The SEC's] argument lays stress upon the 'strategic position enjoyed by the management in this type of reorganization proceed-

---

34. Henry J. Friendly, Chenery *Revisited: Reflections on Reversal and Remand of Administrative Orders*, 1969 Duke L.J. 199.

In Citizens to Preserve Overton Park, Inc. v. Volpe, 401 U.S. 402, 420 (1971), *Chenery I* is cited supporting this: "[L]itigation affidavits were merely *'post hoc'* rationalizations ... which have traditionally been found to be an inadequate basis for review."

35. 318 U.S. at 86–89.

ing. . . .' It contends that these considerations warrant the stern rule
applied in this case since the Commission 'has dealt extensively with
corporate reorganizations, both under the Act, and other statutes
entrusted to it' . . . and that the situation was therefore 'peculiarly
within the Commission's special administrative competence.'

[T]he Commission could take appropriate action for the correction of
reorganization abuses found to be 'detrimental to the public interest
or the interest of investors or consumers.' But . . . the considerations urged here in support of the Commission's order were not
those upon which its action was based. The Commission did not rely
upon 'its special administrative competence'; it formulated no judgment upon the requirements of the 'public interest or the interest of
investors or consumers' in the situation before it. Through its
preoccupation with the special problems of utility reorganizations
the Commission accumulates an experience and insight denied to
others. Had the Commission, acting upon its experience and peculiar
competence, promulgated a general rule of which its order here was
a particular application, the problem for our consideration would be
very different. . . . But before transactions otherwise legal can be
outlawed or denied their usual business consequences, they must fall
under the ban of some standards of conduct prescribed by an agency
of government authorized to prescribe such standards—either the
courts or Congress or an agency to which Congress has delegated its
authority. Congress itself did not proscribe the respondents' purchases. . . . Established judicial doctrines do not condemn these
transactions. Nor has the Commission, acting under the rule-making
powers delegated to it . . . promulgated new general standards of
conduct. It purported merely to be applying an existing judge-made
rule of equity. . . .

Judged, therefore, as a determination based upon judge-made rules
of equity, the Commission's order cannot be upheld. Its action must
be measured by what the Commission did, not by what it might have
done. It is not for us to determine independently what is 'detrimental to the public interest or the interest of investors or consumers'
or 'fair and equitable' within the meaning of [PUHCA]. The Commission's action cannot be upheld merely because findings might
have been made and considerations disclosed which would justify its
order as an appropriate safeguard for the interests protected by the
Act. There must be such a responsible finding. There is no such
finding here.

Congress has seen fit to subject to judicial review such orders of the
[SEC] as the one before us. That the scope of such review is
narrowly circumscribed is beside the point. For the courts cannot
exercise their duty of review unless they are advised of the consider-

ations underlying the action under review. If the action rests upon an administrative determination—an exercise of judgment in an area which Congress has entrusted to the agency—of course it must not be set aside because the reviewing court might have made a different determination were it empowered to do so. But if the action is based upon a determination of law as to which the reviewing authority of the courts does come into play, an order may not stand if the agency has misconceived the law. 'The administrative process will best be vindicated by clarity in its exercise.' All we ask of the [agency] is to give clear indication that it has exercised the discretion with which Congress has empowered it. . . . We merely hold that an administrative order cannot be upheld unless the grounds upon which the agency acted in exercising its powers were those upon which its action can be sustained.[36]

The matter was remanded, Justice Black dissenting in an opinion joined by Justices Reed and Murphy. Not so far from his participation in the Senate's consideration of PUHCA, Justice Black did not disagree that review of the Commission's judgment must occur on its own terms—the proposition for which *Chenery I* has long stood. His dissent argued principally that the facts and the Commission's opinion sufficiently expressed its rationale, which on his reading rested not on existing judicial doctrine, but on the Commission's own experience and understanding. Perhaps because he saw the Commission's action in this way, in concluding passages he expressed a concern that something else might be in the wind:

A judicial requirement of circumstantially detailed findings as the price of court approval can bog the administrative power in a quagmire of minutiae. Hypercritical exactions as to findings can provide a handy but an almost invisible glideway enabling courts to pass "from the narrow confines of law into the more spacious domain of policy." Phelps Dodge Corp. v. Labor Board, 313 U.S. 177, 194. . . .

That the Commission has chosen to proceed case by case rather than by a general pronouncement does not appear to me to merit criticism. The intimation is that the Commission can act only through general formulae rigidly adhered to. In the first place, the rule of the single case is obviously a general advertisement to the trade, and in the second place the briefs before us indicate that this is but one of a number of cases in which the Commission is moving to an identical result on a broad front. But aside from these considerations the Act gives the Commission wide powers to evolve policy standards, and this may well be done case by case, as under the Federal Trade

---

36. Id. at 90–96.

Commission Act. Federal Trade Commission v. Keppel & Bro., 291
U.S. 304, 310–312.[37]

Upon remand, the SEC reached the same decision as before, this time
unanimously on all issues with lengthy consideration of "[t]he powers of
a holding company management under the Act" and the "conflicting
interests arising from Stock Purchase Program by Management During
Reorganization under the Act."[38] Unlike the 1941 opinion's heavy reliance on judicial precedent, this opinion noted only one precedent, an
English ruling in 1802 to support the proposition that "Passing judgment on the personal integrity and will-power of the individual fiduciary
in particular cases, where conflicts of interest are shown to exist, is a
function that is traditionally avoided by courts of equity."[39]

> The Supreme Court read our former opinion in this case as contain-
> ing a determination by us that "in [our] own words, 'honesty, full
> disclosure and purchase at a fair price' characterized the transac-
> tions." Our counsel, in briefs and arguments upon appeal, also
> assumed this for the purpose of argument. However, we made no
> finding to this effect, but said only that "honesty, full disclosure and
> purchase at a fair price do not take the case outside the rule." We
> said this in the course of stating that equity precedents forbid a
> trustee to trade for profit even at a fair price and without fraud at a
> public sale. We meant merely to indicate that what we deemed to be
> the inflexible rule of equity did not even permit inquiry into the
> question whether the transactions of the reorganization managers in
> this case were marked by honesty, full disclosure and purchase at a
> fair price. . . .
>
> Moreover in this case the interveners, when they bought the pre-
> ferred stock of Federal, were not acting wholly in a legal vacuum. As
> reasonable men they must at least have known that they were
> running some risk that their purchase program might not achieve
> its purpose . . .
>
> The interveners urge that we have no alternative but to act first by
> general rule or published statement of policy if we are to act at all in
> a matter of this kind. The Supreme Court indicated the advisability
> of promulgating a general rule, though we do not understand its
> opinion to hold that the absence of a pre-existing rule is fatal to the
> decision we have reached. Now that we have had the question
> sharply focused in this and other cases before us, and have had an
> extensive period in which to consider the problems involved, we may

---

37. Id. at 99–100.

38. In the Matter of Federal Water Service Corp., 18 S.E.C. 231, 248, 251, 257–58
(1945).

39. Id. at 254 n. 27.

well decide that a general rule, with adequately flexible provisions, would be both practicable and desirable; but we do not see how the promulgation of such a rule now or later would affect our duty to act by order in this case in deciding whether this plan is fair and equitable and meets the other standards of the Act. We therefore reserve for further consideration the question whether or not a rule should be adopted. [F]urther, without flexibility the rule might itself operate unfairly....[40]

Once more, the SEC brought the case to the Supreme Court—a Court whose membership had now changed, and which produced the opinion you doubtless have encountered in taking Administrative Law. Now Justice Murphy, one of the *Chenery I* dissenters, wrote the majority opinion, and he found that the SEC had now successfully

avoid[ed] the fatal error of relying on judicial precedents which do not sustain it. This time, after a thorough reexamination of the problem in light of the purposes and standards of [PUHCA], the Commission has concluded that the proposed transaction is inconsistent with the standards of ... the Act. It has drawn heavily upon its accumulated experience in dealing with utility reorganizations. And it has expressed its reasons with a clarity and thoroughness that admit of no doubt as to the underlying basis of its order.[41]

Joined by the two other *Chenery I* dissenters and new Justice Wiley Rutledge,[42] he rejected the Chenery group's contention that the agency could not proceed against them adjudicatively, but only by a general rule "with no retroactive effect upon the instant situation."[43]

We reject this contention, for it grows out of a misapprehension of our prior decision and of the Commission's statutory duties. We held no more and no less than that the Commission's first order was unsupportable for the reasons supplied by that agency....

It is true that our prior decision explicitly recognized the possibility that the Commission might have promulgated a general rule dealing with this problem under its statutory rule-making powers, in which

---

40. Id. at 256–60.

41. Securities and Exchange Comm'n v. Chenery Corp., 332 U.S. 194, 199 (1947) (*Chenery II*).

42. Two other Justices were new to the Court. Justice Burton concurred in the judgment without opinion and Chief Justice Vinson joined Justice Douglas in not participating. Douglas, of course, had been Chairman of the SEC during the pendency of the *Chenery* applications; presumably Chief Justice Vinson did not participate because he had been on the D.C. Circuit panel that had decided the first round in the *Chenery* litigation there (he had been in the majority). Of the original *Chenery I* majority, this left only Justices Frankfurter and Jackson to dissent.

43. Id. at 200.

case the issue for our consideration would have been entirely different from that which did confront us. But we did not mean to imply thereby that the failure of the Commission to anticipate this problem and to promulgate a general rule withdrew all power from that agency to perform its statutory duty in this case. To hold that the Commission had no alternative in this proceeding but to approve the proposed transaction, while formulating any general rules it might desire for use in future cases of this nature, would be to stultify the administrative process. That we refuse to do.[44]

More than three months later and at the beginning of a new Term of Court—in itself an unusual event[45]—Justice Jackson filed an unusually heated dissent, that you have probably encountered in your readings. Author in important respects of the APA,[46] he had been one of the majority of four in *Chenery I*, and his dissent now was joined by Justice Frankfurter, the author of that first opinion. For Justice Jackson, the intimations Justice Black had feared, seem to have been the point of *Chenery I*.

The reversal of the position of this Court is due to a fundamental change in prevailing philosophy....

As there admittedly is no law or regulation to support this order, we peruse the Court's opinion diligently to find on what grounds it is now held that the Court of Appeals, on pain of being reversed for error, was required to stamp this order with its approval. We find but one. That is the principle of judicial deference to administrative experience. ... The Commission must be sustained because of its accumulated experience in solving a problem with which it had never before been confronted!

Of course, thus to uphold the Commission by professing to find that it has enunciated a "new standard of conduct" brings the Court squarely against the invalidity of retroactive law-making.[47] But the

---

44. Id. at 200–202.

45. The decision came down June 23, the dissent was filed October 6.

46. You may have encountered his opinion in Wong Yang Sung v. McGrath, 339 U.S. 33 (1950), at this time still years in the future.

47. Justice Jackson's phrasing, "the invalidity of retroactive law-making," is strikingly broad. See, on some of "The Problematics of 'Retroactivity,' " William V. Luneburg, *Retroactivity and Administrative Rulemaking*, 1991 Duke L.J. 106, 109–10.

With respect to adjudication by courts: "Mere absence of precedent directly in point cannot be deemed an assurance of no liability in the Anglo-American common law system (and, in view of the impossibility of pre-ordained rules covering all future variations of human conduct, probably not in any system.)." PAUL J. MISHKIN AND CLARENCE MORRIS, ON LAW IN COURTS, 123 (1965). See also Background Notes on Judicial Enforcement of Primary Obligations Not Previously Recognized as Enforceable Legal Obligations, HENRY M. HART,

Court does not falter.... Now I realize fully what Mark Twain meant when he said, "The more you explain it, the more I don't understand it."

... Whether, as matter of policy, corporate managers during reorganization should be prohibited from buying or selling its stock, is not a question for us to decide. But it is for us to decide whether, so long as no law or regulation prohibits them from buying, their purchases may be forfeited, or not, in the discretion of the Commission. ...

The truth is that in this decision the Court approves the Commission's assertion of power to govern the matter *without* law.... It is the first encouragement this Court has given to conscious lawlessness as a permissible rule of administrative action. This decision is an ominous one to those who believe that men should be governed by laws that they may ascertain and abide by, and which will guide the action of those in authority as well as of those who are subject to authority.

I have long urged, and still believe, that the administrative process deserves fostering in our system as an expeditious and nontechnical method of *applying law* in specialized fields. I can not agree that it be used, and I think its continued effectiveness is endangered when it is used, as a method of *dispensing with law* in those fields.[48]

Still one more time, Chenery lost. After *Chenery II*, his reorganized PUHC applied to the SEC for permission to dissolve. Permission was granted—but the Chenery group's motion to share equally with other stockholders was denied. Back to court, now arguing that there was no substantial evidence to support the SEC's refusal. The district judge, noting that

the facts, admittedly, do not disclose either fraud or double dealing [and the] SEC in its arguments [retreated] to the formalistic defense of *res judicata*. [I]f I did not think I were foreclosed by the Supreme Court [holding], I would have no hesitation in holding that there is no substantial evidence to support the Commission's finding that Chenery should be penalized and limited to cost plus interest for its preferred stock purchases.[49]

And this despite Chenery's argument, with which the district judge agreed, that the limitation on the Chenery group "was never followed by the Commission, except in the instant case ..." In two other agency

---

Jr. and Albert M. Sacks, The Legal Process 450 (William N. Eskridge, Jr. and Philip P. Frickey, eds., 1994).

48. 332 U.S. at 209, 210–18.

49. In re Federal Water & Gas Corp., 87 F.Supp. 289, 292–93 (D.Del.1949), aff'd on the res judicata ground, 188 F.2d 100 (3d Cir.), cert. denied 341 U.S. 953 (1951).

decisions in 1947, "the SEC did not limit the owners of stock purchased during pendency of reorganization notwithstanding the new stock carried voting rights and obviously was purchased for profit. In short, although both power and profit were present, the Commission did not again apply the *Chenery* 'policy'."[50] Thus, on res judicata, the SEC won again. But as the SEC official had said, Chris Chenery was "a sporting man."

Years ago, Administrative Law classes spent substantial time arguing about both *Chenery I* and *Chenery II*. Justice Frankfurter's opinion in *Chenery I* that the agency must clearly give a sound explanation was itself unclear: had the Frankfurter majority required nothing more than what *Chenery II* said, a supportable explanation? Or had *Chenery I* required a general rule that would operate only prospectively? Did the fact that Justice Frankfurter joined the Jackson dissent show that he (and his other co-signers) had originally shared the view Justice Jackson would later so forcefully express? How, it was argued, could Frankfurter—one of the pioneer professors of Administrative Law—have intended a constraint that would so hamper agency action, just as *Chenery II* explained?

In the 1960s, the author had a talk with Judge Henry Friendly, another Second Circuit immortal and a close friend of Justice Frankfurter. In response to the simple question, "Why did FF join Jackson?" he gave a simple if surprising answer. "Jackson was so upset, and FF just didn't want him to be alone. After all, what difference whether it was 6–1 or 5–2?" Doubtless that is accurate. But why was Jackson so upset? All we know is that the dissent was not filed until over three months after the decision came down, as noted above. Judge Friendly could say no more. But, speculate: why might Jackson have been so upset about retrospective lawmaking? It was 1947, he had just returned from the Nuremberg Trials, where (on leave from the Supreme Court) he had been Lead Prosecutor, representing the United States. Chief Justice Stone had called the Trials "Jackson's high grade lynching party in Nuremberg."[51] Stone was not alone in having strong doubts about

---

50. Id. at 292.

51. In a 1946 letter to professor Charles Fairman, see Alpheus Thomas Mason, *Extra-Judicial Work for Judges: The Views of Chief Justice Stone*, 67 Harv.L.Rev. 193, 212 (1953).

Jackson answered that in his introduction to a book about the trials, published in 1954. After noting other objections or alternatives to the trials (like "Stalin, according to Churchill's account, proposed to line up and shoot fifty thousand high-ranking German leaders."), Jackson wrote the following:

"Chief Justice Stone, who had his own personal reasons for disliking the trial, writing about 'the power of the victor over the vanquished' said, 'It would not disturb me greatly if that power were openly and frankly used to punish the German leaders for being a bad lot,

whether the trials were improper because, it was argued, they were retroactive lawmaking. Perhaps Jackson too had doubts?

Epilogue

Mr. Chenery's luck turned, though it took 20 years. In the spring of 1971, Chenery's horse Riva Ridge won the Belmont Stakes, was named the year's Champion Two-Year-Old Colt—and so, as recounted below, saved his stable. A year later, with Chenery fatally ill, Riva Ridge won the Kentucky Derby. Mr. Chenery was hospitalized and unable to speak, "but his nurse turned on the television for the race, and later said that she wiped tears from the old man's cheek as his daughter accepted the trophy."[52]

And in 1973, a few months after Mr. Chenery's death, Riva Ridge's stable-mate Secretariat won the Triple Crown: Kentucky Derby (track record), Preakness Stakes (track record), and Belmont Stakes (world record for the distance). In the last of those, he beat the second horse by 31 lengths, "one of the most memorable [victories] in sports history."[53]

Last notes about Mr. Chenery. His son Hollis, co-owner of Secretariat, was an economist and Director of Research at the World Bank.[54] And Chenery's daughter Helen "Penny" Tweedy, who succeeded her father as head of Meadow Farm, in her second term as president of the Thoroughbred Owners and Breeders Association became one of the first

---

but it disturbs me some to have it dressed up in the habiliments of the common law and the Constitutional safeguards to those charged with crime.' It is hard to find a statement by a law-trained man more inconsistent with the requirements of elementary justice. When did it become a crime to be one of a 'bad lot'? What was the specific badness for which they should be openly and frankly punished? And how did he know what individuals were included in the bad lot? Can it be less right to punish for specific acts such as murder, which has been a crime since the days of Adam, than to punish on the vague charge always made against an enemy that he is 'bad'? If it would have been right to punish the vanquished out-of-hand for being a bad lot, what made it wrong to have first a safeguarded hearing to make sure who was bad, and how bad, and of what his badness consisted?

"[N]o sound and general foundation of public information about the trial was laid. This has made it easy for those hostile to the policy of holding a trial to stigmatize it with slogans which required no information to utter and none to understand."

Jackson, Robert H. "Introduction," in, WHITNEY R. HARRIS, TYRANNY ON TRIAL xxix, xxxiii–xxxvi (1954).

52. Unofficial Thoroughbred Hall of Fame, Riva Ridge, at 3 (available at http://sky.prohosting.com/spiletta/UTHOF/rivaridge.html).

53. Secretariat.com, available at http://www.secretariat.com/past_performance.htm, at 2; and http://www.secretariat.com/races/belmont.htm, at 1. See also WILLIAM NACK, BIG RED OF MEADOW STABLE: SECRETARIAT, THE MAKING OF A CHAMPION (1975).

54. Paul A. Samuelson, in a letter to his former student David Dorsen: "[W]hat intrigued me most was to learn that you had evolved into an owner of thoroughbreds. [Samuelson went on, after describing his friend Hollis Chenery and Secretariat's greatness:] That was as near as I ever got to contacting 'greatness.'" Letter of May 19, 2004.

three women admitted to The Jockey Club (which registers thorough-breds and keeps the American Stud Book) after "89 years as an all-male bastion." The two admitted with her were Allaire duPont and Martha Gerry.[55] Penny Chenery Tweedy had saved Meadow Farm when, with her father dying and bills mounting, she persuaded her siblings to keep the farm and the horses by the then-innovative step of syndicating Riva Ridge—for $5,120,000. After Secretariat's Triple Crown, when he and Riva Ridge ran in a match race and Riva Ridge lost, she said "I have the greatest admiration for Secretariat, but I love Riva Ridge."[56] Not many two-time losers at the Supreme Court end up such historic winners.

Nor was Christopher Chenery the last or the most unlucky in losing a settlement offer "bet." As this essay goes to press, Morgan Stanley, having turned down a $20 million settlement offer, has been found liable for $1.45 billion, including $845 million in punitive damages.[57]

*

---

55.   N.Y. Times, *Sports People*, Nov. 17, 1983, B20. The Chenerys owned Secretariat because, in 1970, Penny Chenery had lost a coin-toss to Jockey Club Chairman Ogden Phipps, leaving her stuck owning a horse who was pregnant—with Secretariat. Red Smith, n. 28 above.

56.   Unofficial Thoroughbred Hall of Fame, Riva Ridge, n. 52 above, at 1, 2, 5 (available at http://sky.prohosting.com/spiletta/UTHOF/rivaridge.html).

57.   Mark A. Stein, *A Bad Week for Morgan Stanley*, N.Y. Times, May 21, 2005, at B3.

Sisyphus Copyright © 1992 by Kent Lew

Professor Vladeck reveals a seven-year war to force OSHA to protect workers from excessive exposure to ethylene oxide (EtO)—a hazardous yet common industrial chemical. The war was waged over two recurrent issues: (a) when, if ever, courts may force agencies to take action they would not take on their own, and (b) whether the President may direct the work of agencies in promulgating regulations. Vladeck offers a behind-the-scene look at how litigators enlist the courts in provoking agency action. Although courts rarely do compel agencies to act, Vladeck suggests that the possibility places an important discipline on agency behavior. He also challenges the reader to consider the legitimacy and wisdom of the Office of Management and Budget's (OMB) central role in rulemaking. As Vladeck sees it, OMB's cost-benefit focus is generally anti-regulatory—is a one-way ratchet pressing agencies to do less (not more) to protect the public health. Others contend that the President should ensure that the Executive Branch is unified on regulatory matters.

6

David C. Vladeck*

Delay, Unreasonable Intervention: The Battle to Force Regulation of Ethylene Oxide

Introduction

Ethylene oxide (EtO) is one of the most widely used chemicals in the United States. Nearly 7 *billion* pounds are produced annually. EtO is used as a sterilizing agent, fumigant, pesticide, and intermediate in the manufacturing of products including antifreeze, textiles, films, bottles and detergents. Hospitals and medical device manufacturers use EtO to sterilize heat sensitive medical equipment. Over 100,000 workers in the United States are exposed to EtO every day on the job. But exposure to EtO causes cancer, chromosome damage, spontaneous abortion, and serious neurological damage in humans.

In 1971, the Occupational Safety and Health Administration (OSHA) set a permissible exposure limit (PEL) of 50 parts of EtO per million parts of air (ppm) as a time-weighted average (TWA) over an eight-hour working day.[1] This standard was taken from voluntary indus-

* Associate Professor of Law and Co-Director, Institute for Public Representation, Georgetown University Law Center, and Scholar, Center for Progressive Regulation. I would like to thank my long-time colleague, Alan B. Morrison, the founder and my predecessor as director of Public Citizen Litigation Group, and now Senior Lecturer in Law at Stanford Law School, who provided helpful comments based, in part, on his participation as co-counsel in the ethylene oxide litigation.

1. The Occupational Safety and Health Act of 1970 (OSH Act), 29 U.S.C. §§ 651 et seq., created OSHA, as part of the Department of Labor, to establish standards and enforce the Act, and the National Institute of Occupational Safety and Health (NIOSH), as part of the Department of Health and Human Services, to "develop and establish recommended occupational safety and health standards" to assist OSHA. 29 U.S.C. § 671. OSHA's 1971 EtO standard was not adopted pursuant to rulemaking. It was instead a "national

try standards, which, in turn, were based on animal studies showing no acute health effects at this level. In 1977, the National Institute of Occupational Safety and Health (NIOSH) recommended that OSHA adopt a "ceiling limit," restricting short-term high concentration exposures to 75 ppm over fifteen minutes, based on concerns EtO might be mutagenic. In 1979, the Environmental Protection Agency (EPA) reported its preliminary risk assessment on EtO, concluding that there was a 23% likelihood that someone continuously exposed to even 1 ppm of EtO would develop cancer. In 1979, two studies found unexpectedly high cancer rates among workers exposed to EtO at levels well under OSHA's 50 ppm limit. Then, in January 1981, NIOSH published a study showing that exposure to EtO at levels between 30–35 ppm caused leukemia and other cancers in rats.

Reacting to these new studies, on August 13, 1981, Public Citizen Health Research Group (HRG) and the American Federation of State, County and Municipal Employees (AFSCME), a union representing over 100,000 hospital workers, petitioned OSHA to issue immediately an emergency temporary standard lowering the allowable worker EtO exposure from 50 ppm to 1 ppm as an 8 hour TWA, and imposing a maximum (peak) exposure of 5 ppm.

The filing of the petition was the signal event that triggered seven years of proceedings before OSHA, three trips to the federal courts resulting in four published opinions, a contentious congressional hearing, and almost constant behind-the-scenes maneuvering to obstruct the rule-making by the White House's Office of Management and Budget (OMB).

What follows is the story of the battle to regulate EtO—a battle that was the regulatory equivalent of hand-to-hand combat. No one chapter can do justice to a case intensely fought for seven years. This chapter concentrates on two issues that formed the core of the dispute: (a) may courts force an agency to take action it would not undertake on its own, or to accelerate agency action that would otherwise proceed at a much slower pace, and (b) may the President, through his appointees at OMB, direct the work of regulatory agencies in the promulgation of regula-

consensus standard" adopted pursuant to Section 6(a) of the Act, which set up a summary procedure for implementing consensus standards that would establish minimum levels of health and safety protection for workers while the agency developed more protective standards through the Act's standard-setting provisions. 29 U.S.C. § 655(a). Congress understood that these consensus standards were stop-gap measures. As the Senate Report put it, "a large proportion of the voluntary standards are seriously out-of-date. Many represent merely the lowest common denominator of acceptance by interested private groups. Accordingly, it is essential that such standards be constantly improved and replaced as new knowledge and techniques are developed." S. Rep. No. 91–1282, at 6 (1970).

tions. Novel at the time the EtO battle was joined, these questions remain controversial today.

In the interest of candor, let me acknowledge at the outset that this is not a dispassionate review of an important case. It is instead a first-hand account of a case that I handled at every stage and count as one of the most challenging cases I worked on during my nearly thirty-year career as a lawyer.[2] Although I try to be fair to the capable lawyers who represented OSHA, I make no pretense of objectivity. I remain appalled at the delay in regulating EtO. Obstructionism, with the health and well-being of over 100,000 workers hanging in the balance, is hard to countenance. Nor do I believe that OMB's intervention in the EtO rulemaking was an isolated or aberrational occurrence. Particularly in an administration committed to deregulation, OMB's institutional responsibilities to ensure that regulations meet data quality and cost-benefit standards virtually ensure that health and safety safeguards will be delayed, weakened, and even derailed at OMB's behest.

Setting the Stage—The Reagan Deregulatory Efforts

The petition for emergency rulemaking on EtO was filed barely eight months after the inauguration of President Ronald Reagan. Deregulatory fervor was high. President Reagan campaigned on a promise to get government "off the back" of American business, and often invoked OSHA as the poster child of an out of control federal agency. He appointed Thorne Auchter as the Assistant Secretary of Labor for Occupational Safety and Health. Auchter, a thirty-six year old with a business degree from Jacksonville University, was the vice president of his family's construction company; he had run special events for President Reagan's Florida campaign.[3] After his confirmation, Auchter an-

---

2. To put my role in perspective, a brief explanation is in order. Prior to joining the faculty of Georgetown University Law Center, I spent more than twenty-five years as a staff attorney at, and then director of, Public Citizen Litigation Group, a Washington, D.C., public interest law firm founded by Ralph Nader and Alan Morrison. One mission of the Litigation Group was to use the courts to force administrative agencies to better protect the public. I was assigned to help Public Citizen Health Research Group—a sister organization within Public Citizen—prepare and file the petition for an emergency standard, with the understanding that I would handle the litigation that was certain to follow. Among the important administrative law cases handled by the Litigation Group are Cheney v. United States Dist. Court, 124 S. Ct. 2576 (2004); INS v. Chadha, 462 U.S. 919 (1983); Bowsher v. Synar, 478 U.S. 714 (1986); Raines v. Byrd, 521 U.S. 811 (1997); Mistretta v. United States, 488 U.S. 361 (1989); Public Citizen v. Department of Justice, 491 U.S. 440 (1989); Critical Mass Energy Project v. NRC, 975 F.2d 871 (D.C. Cir. 1992) (en banc).

3. THOMAS MCGARITY & SIDNEY SHAPIRO, WORKERS AT RISK: THE FAILED PROMISE OF THE OCCUPATIONAL SAFETY AND HEALTH ADMINISTRATION, at 60 (Praeger 1993); see also DAVID BOLLIER & JOAN CLAYBROOK, FREEDOM FROM HARM: THE CIVILIZING INFLUENCE OF HEALTH, SAFETY AND ENVIRONMENTAL REGULATION 140 (Public Citizen 1986).

nounced to a group of business leaders, "We're here to do what the President was elected to do—provide regulatory relief."[4]

President Reagan's appointees were carefully screened for their deregulatory credentials. But the White House was nonetheless worried that entrenched pro-regulatory bureaucrats would sabotage the Administration's deregulatory agenda. To protect Auchter and other regulators from this fate, the White House ramped up the centralized regulatory review process under OMB that had first appeared in Richard Nixon's administration and had continued to grow through the administrations of Presidents Gerald Ford and Jimmy Carter. Just a month after his inauguration, President Reagan replaced Jimmy Carter's Executive Order with Executive Order 12,291. This Executive Order, for the first time, required agencies to prepare detailed Regulatory Impact Analyses (RIAs) specifying the costs and benefits of *all* proposed "major" rules.[5] The Order provided that, unless otherwise forbidden by law, an agency could not undertake rulemaking unless "the potential benefits to society ... outweigh the costs," and the agency selected the regulatory option "involving the least net cost to society." The Order also directed that no regulatory initiatives could be proposed or finalized until OMB had approved the agency's RIA. Lest there be any doubt about the Order's purpose, its implementation was overseen by the newly-formed Presidential Task Force on Regulatory Relief, actively led by Vice President George H.W. Bush. The Executive Order gave OMB a powerful weapon to control the regulatory output of all federal agencies, including OSHA.

Filing The Petition

On August 13, 1981, HRG and AFSCME filed their petition, but with little reason to believe that OSHA would grant it. The petition began with a description of OSHA's 1971 EtO standard and EtO's impact on worker health.[6] While requiring employers to assure that employee exposure did not exceed 50 ppm determined as an 8-hour time TWA, that standard placed no short-term exposure limit (STEL) for relatively brief exposures.[7] Workers might be exposed to concentrations in excess of 50 ppm for intervals of an hour or more. The exposure

---

4. Lublin, *New OSHA Chief Tries to Please Business and Labor, but Rule Cutback Riles Unions,* Wall St. J., 25 (Nov. 23, 1981).

5. Exec. Order 12,291, §§ 1(b), 7(g)(2); 3 C.F.R. 127 (1981), reprinted in 5 U.S.C. § 601, at 431 (1982).

6. See Petition Requesting a Reduced Tolerance for Ethylene Oxide Through an Emergency Temporary Standard Issued Under the Authority of the Occupational Safety and Health Act (Aug. 13, 1981). The petition is reproduced in the Joint Appendix filed in Public Citizen Health Research Group v. Auchter, No. 83–1071, at 1907 (filed on February 11, 1983) (hereinafter "Auchter JA").

7. 29 C.F.R. 19100.1000 Table Z–1 (1981).

patterns in the health care and medical products industries, where workers were especially at risk, made the omission of a STEL critical. Those industries use EtO to sterilize heat-sensitive products. Objects being sterilized are placed into sealed vessels, like autoclaves, which are then flooded with EtO. At room temperature, EtO is a gas somewhat heavier than air. After the sterilization process is complete, the EtO should be vented; because the heavy EtO tends to cling to the items, the sterilized items also need to be "aerated." However, if the equipment leaks, or the gas is not fully vented, workers operating the sterilizing equipment will be exposed to the residual gas—often in concentrations up to twelve times (600 ppm) the level OSHA then allowed—until the gas dissipates. Exposure also occurs as a result of failure to educate workers on how to use the equipment safely. Workers cannot smell EtO until it reaches concentrations of 800 ppm or greater, at which point prolonged exposures can be fatal.

The petition also canvassed the serious dangers workers face from exposure to EtO. The available data demonstrated that EtO is a potent carcinogen and causes chromosomal abnormalities (which also suggest a cancer-link), infertility and spontaneous abortion. The data on EtO was particularly compelling because not only was there considerable *animal* evidence showing it to be carcinogenic and mutagenic, but there was also substantial evidence linking EtO to cancer and genetic damage in *humans*.[8] Recent epidemiological studies had found significant increases in leukemia, overall mortality, and chromosome damage in workers exposed to EtO at levels far below OSHA's standard. These findings were consistent with numerous animal studies, which had found significant increases in leukemia, peritoneal mesotheliomas (cancers of the lining of the abdomen), and mortality in rats breathing EtO for as little as fifteen months at 30–35 ppm.[9] Based on this evidence, the EPA had estimated that there was a 23% likelihood that someone exposed continuously to even 1 ppm of EtO would develop cancer.[10] The petition asked OSHA to issue a rule that provided that "no employee shall be exposed to concentrations of EtO above 5 ppm over 15 minutes or to an 8-hour time-weighted average (TWA) above 1 ppm." It urged that standard be

---

8. At the time the petition was filed, it was rare that epidemiological evidence was available for regulatory purposes. Most of OSHA's health standards, based on animal studies alone, had been upheld by reviewing courts. See, e.g., Dry Color Manufacturers Ass'n v. Department of Labor, 486 F.2d 98 (3d Cir. 1973); Synthetic Organic Chemical Manufacturers Ass'n v. Brennan, 506 F.2d 385 (3d Cir. 1974), cert. denied, 420 U.S. 973 (1975).

9. See, e.g., SNELLING, ET AL., FINAL REPORT ON ETHYLENE OXIDE TWO YEAR INHALATION STUDY ON RATS, Bushy Run Center (1981) (Auchter JA 305) (the "Bushy Run Study"). Earlier reports from this study formed the basis for the EPA's 1979 risk assessment.

10. See EPA, THE CARCINOGEN ASSESSMENT GROUP, PRELIMINARY RISK ASSESSMENT ON ETHYLENE OXIDE, REPORT TO THE EPA (Oct. 16, 1979) (Auchter JA 1058).

issued on an emergency basis and remain in effect while the agency
engaged in a rulemaking to finalize a permanent standard.

History of the Occupational Safety and Health Act

The Occupational Safety and Health Act is an ambitious statute. It
was designed to level, at least in part, the unequal playing field between
employers and workers when it comes to workplace safety.[11] The drive
for better workplace protection was launched in January 1968 when
President Lyndon Johnson delivered his Manpower Message to Congress
proposing a federal occupational safety and health program. Certainly
the statistics drove home the need for reform. According to 1970 congressional findings, "14,500 persons are killed annually as a result of
industrial accidents" and by "the lowest count, 2.2 million persons are
disabled on the job each year, resulting in the loss of 250 million man
days of work."[12] A 1972 Labor Department study estimated that 100,000
workers died each year from occupationally-related diseases and that
another 390,000 suffered from some job-related illness.[13]

The OSH Act declares that its purpose is "to assure as far as
possible every working man and woman in the Nation safe and healthful
working conditions."[14] To achieve this lofty goal, Congress gave the
Secretary of Labor broad power to promulgate occupational safety and
health standards.[15] To establish permanent rules, the Secretary must
undertake a time-consuming hybrid rulemaking process, adding the
demand of a public hearing to the ordinary requirements of notice and
comment rulemaking under 5 U.S.C. § 553.[16]

---

11. For an overview of OSHA's pre-history, see generally JOSEPH PAGE & MARY-WIN
O'BRIEN, BITTER WAGES (Grossman, 1972); McGarity & Shapiro, n. 3 supra, at 1–27.
Historically, employers alone had determined the safety of their factories and offices. Id.
Although by the mid-1960s labor unions had made some inroads on improving safety, the
employer still had the upper hand, and many of the most dangerous workplaces were not
unionized. *Id.* Low levels of compensation under state-imposed worker compensation
schemes did little to force safety improvements, and may have even sapped whatever
incentives employers might otherwise have had to provide workers a safe and healthful
workplace. Id.

12. S. Rep. No. 91–1282, at 2 (1970), referring to the Testimony of George P. Schultz,
Secretary of Labor, to the U.S. Senate Comm. on Labor and Public Welfare, Subcomm. on
Labor, hearings on the Occupational Safety and Health Act, S. 2193 and S. 2788, Part I, at
77 (quoting NATIONAL SAFETY COUNCIL, ACCIDENT FACTS, 1971).

13. THE PRESIDENT'S REPORT ON OCCUPATIONAL SAFETY AND HEALTH, GPO Document No.
2915–011, at 111 (May 1972).

14. 29 U.S.C. § 651(b).

15. Id. § 655.

16. Id. §§ 655(b)(1)–(b)(4). See generally Stephen Williams, *"Hybrid Rulemaking"*
Under the Administrative Procedure Act: A Legal and Empirical Analysis, 42 U. Chi. L.
Rev. 401 (1975).

Congress understood, however, that swift regulatory action would be needed when workers face grave danger, and therefore provided for emergency standards. The Act provides that the Secretary "shall" issue an emergency standard when "workers are exposed to grave danger from exposure to substances or agents determined to be toxic or physically harmful or from new hazards," and "such [an] emergency standard is necessary to protect employees from such a danger."[17]

PCHRG v. Auchter—Round I—District Court Proceedings

As HRG's scientific staff was preparing the petition, I was preparing the lawsuit that we anticipated would be needed to force OSHA to act on it. The first question I had to resolve was what court— the district court or the court of appeals—had subject matter jurisdiction over a case complaining about an agency's failure to act? The D.C. Circuit eventually settled that question in the *TRAC* case[18] (holding that where an agency's statute commits final review of agency action to the court of appeals, that court has exclusive jurisdiction to hear "any suit seeking relief that might affect" its future statutory review power). But there was no clear answer in 1981. The OSH Act specifies that any person adversely affected by an adopted standard may file a petition challenging its validity in the court of appeals.[19] But we were not expecting to challenge the *validity* of a standard, we expected to be faced with OSHA's failure to answer our petition or, perhaps, its refusal to *issue* a standard. Initial appellate review of a final standard—accompanied by a preamble setting forth the agency's reasons for promulgating it and supported by a comprehensive record—makes sense. But the same cannot be said of a challenge to review agency *inaction*, where there may be neither an explanation nor a record. Nor did the OSH Act address denials of petitions for rulemaking. The default rule in the APA is that, unless

---

17. Id. § 655(c)(1). Congress intended that this provision would be invoked only when there was an "obvious need for quick responses to new health and safety findings." S. Rep. No. 91–1282, 7 (1970), *reprinted in* Legislative History of the Occupational Safety and Health Act of 1970, at 147 (1970) (Comm. Print). By 1981, although this provision had been invoked sparingly, OSHA's authority to issue emergency standards had been upheld by the courts. See, e.g., Synthetic Organic Chemical Mfrs. Ass'n v. Brennan, 506 F.2d 385 (3d Cir. 1974), cert. denied, 420 U.S. 973 (1975) (affirming emergency temporary standard for dichlorobenzidine and chloromethyn methyl ether); Dry Color Mfrs. Ass'n v. Department of Labor, 498 F.2d 98 (3d Cir. 1973) (affirming emergency temporary standard on ethyleneimine).

18. Telecommunications Research and Action Project (TRAC) v. FCC, 750 F.2d 70, 75–76 (D.C. Cir. 1984). Many circuits have adopted TRAC. See, e.g., Wellesley v. Federal Energy Regulatory Comm'n, 829 F.2d 275 (1st Cir. 1987); Oil, Chem., & Atomic Workers Union v. OSHA, 145 F.3d 120, 123 (3d Cir. 1998); George Kabeller, Inc. v. Busey, 999 F.2d 1417 (11th Cir. 1993).

19. 29 U.S.C. § 655(f).

there is a statutory directive to bring suit in the court of appeals, cases must be filed in the district court.[20]

We decided we would file in the district court. The few cases that had been brought to challenge agency inaction had been filed in the district court. And we thought that a district court would give the case closer supervision if we needed discovery to develop a record. But the choice was pure guesswork.

We also went back and forth over how long we should give OSHA to respond to our petition before we filed suit. Our clients wanted to file suit as soon as possible; I thought that we should wait at least sixty days or so to avoid any claim that we had failed to exhaust administrative remedies or acted with unseemly haste. Ultimately, we decided that one month after we filed the petition Dr. Sidney Wolfe, Director of HRG, would telephone Mark Cowan, Auchter's special assistant, to emphasize the need for swift agency action. If Dr. Wolfe thought that OSHA had decided to stall on the petition, he was to tell Cowan that we would be compelled to sue immediately. Dr. Wolfe called Cowan on September 16, 1981, and was told that OSHA would not be able to respond to the petition for months because OSHA had been directed by the Task Force on Regulatory Reform to focus on deregulatory priorities.

On September 22, 1981, we filed a complaint in the district court in Washington, D.C., asking the court to direct OSHA to respond to our petition and to issue an emergency temporary standard immediately.[21] Our legal theory was simple: OSHA's failure to "act promptly on plaintiffs' petition and issue an emergency temporary standard contravenes section 6(c)(1) of the [OSH] Act, is arbitrary and capricious, and constitutes agency action unlawfully withheld, *see* 5 U.S.C. §§ 706(1) & (2)(A), because the evidence of grave and irreparable danger to thousands of workers is so overwhelming as to leave no room for doubt as to the necessity for issuance of an emergency temporary standard."[22] The case was assigned to the Honorable Barrington J. Parker. We thought this was a lucky draw. Judge Parker was a smart, highly-respected, slightly cantankerous, judge who had seen it all. He would not be troubled—if he agreed with us—about issuing a decision that compelled OSHA to act.

---

20. 5 U.S.C. § 703.

21. Complaint for Preliminary and Permanent Injunctive Relief, Public Citizen Health Research Group v. Auchter, Civil Action No. 81–2343 (filed Sept. 22, 1981).

22. Id. at ¶ 10. Section 6(c)(1) of the Act is the Emergency Temporary Standard provision. 29 U.S.C. § 655(c)(1). In subsequent unreasonable delay cases, we also relied on 5 U.S.C. § 555(b)'s mandate that agencies decide matters "within a reasonable time," but did not do so here because the court might have construed that reference as one that went only to OSHA's duty to rule on our petition, not to issue an emergency standard.

Five days after we filed our complaint, OSHA denied the petition. OSHA acknowledged "important new health data on the carcinogenic risk" of EtO, but said that an emergency standard "is not 'necessary' for employee protection under existing circumstances."[23] OSHA also assert-ed that it had no jurisdiction to regulate EtO's use as a sterilizing agent (that is, in hospitals and health care facilities), because the EPA had regulatory jurisdiction over pesticides. OSHA did hold out an olive branch: it noted that "the current OSHA standard of 50 ppm may not be sufficiently protective," and it would undertake a rulemaking at some future time to revise the standard. OSHA's letter had the effect of mooting our claim challenging OSHA's failure to respond to the petition. But by acknowledging the health risks posed by EtO and the need to revise its standard, we thought OSHA's letter fortified our claim that OSHA should be compelled to issue a standard.

Even though our petition had been denied, we thought we were still properly in the district court. To move the litigation along, we had to build a record the court could review. OSHA contended that it had no obligation to certify a record or do anything to help. Accordingly, we served on OSHA requests for the production of all documents relating to EtO the agency had before it when it considered our petition. Although it slowed the litigation, the requests eventually resulted in the release of virtually all of the agency's EtO records.[24] But OSHA withheld a few documents under the "deliberative process" privilege, which protects advice given by subordinates to agency decision-makers. One withheld document—an "options memorandum" to Thorne Auchter from OSHA's senior scientists (including John Martonik, who was in charge of devel-oping health standards)—piqued our interest.[25] We had a hunch that OSHA withheld the memo because its scientific staff agreed with us about EtO's health risks and perhaps urged swift action—points that would be damning to the agency in litigation. We moved to compel its release, contending that it was not privileged because it addressed technical scientific issues, not policy questions, but even if its recommen-dations were privileged, the factual portions of the memo had to be

---

23. Letter of September 28, 1981, from Assistant Secretary of Labor Thorne Auchter to Sidney M. Wolfe, M.D., Director, Public Citizen Health Research Group.

24. The discovery requests were made under Rule 24, Fed.R.Civ.P. Discovery is generally unavailable in APA cases, where judicial review is based on the "record" before the agency at the time it acts. Citizens to Preserve Overton Park v. Volpe, 401 U.S. 402 (1971). Here, of course, there was no formal record, and Judge Parker made it clear that he would permit us discovery to compile a record to facilitate judicial review.

25. The memo was described as a 13-page document dated September 11, 1981, from John Martonik, the Acting Director of the Directorate of Health Standards (the unit within OSHA responsible for producing health standards) and R. Hays Bell, Director of the Directorate of Technical Support, to Thorne Auchter. See, e.g., Defendants' Opposition to Plaintiffs' Motion to Compel the Production of Documents, filed on December 10, 1981.

disclosed.[26] As a general matter, intra- and inter-agency communications that contain frank discussions of policy options are not available either in ordinary civil litigation against the government or under the Freedom of Information Act ("FOIA").[27] The deliberative process privilege does not, however, cover purely factual material or expert opinion where the material can reasonably be segregated.[28]

One morning about ten days before Christmas, and just a few days after I filed our motion to compel, I got to work early and found a manila envelope on my desk, with no postage, no return address, and no markings, other than my name, misspelled. The envelope had been slipped under the office door and a colleague had put it on my desk. I thought it might be an early Christmas present. Curious, I opened the envelope and found a present of a different sort—a copy of the options memo, or something that met its description. No cover letter, no card, just the memo. I read the memo, and then I read it again. It was dynamite.

For the most part, the memo reviewed the scientific evidence on EtO and, without exception, confirmed that EtO posed an extraordinary danger to workers. The memo also revealed that, before denying our petition, OSHA had performed a quantitative risk assessment and concluded that "lifetime risk estimates vary from 450–643 [excess cancer deaths] per 1,000 workers after 45 years of occupational exposure [to EtO] at the present OSHA permissible exposure limit (PEL) to 12–20 per 1,000 workers for exposure to a 1 ppm PEL."[29] These risk numbers were

---

26. Memorandum in Support of Plaintiffs' Motion to Compel, filed on November 20, 1981.

27. See generally Jordan v. Department of Justice, 591 F.2d 753 (D.C. Cir. 1978) (en banc) (FOIA case); Coastal States Gas Corp. v. Department of Energy, 617 F.2d 854 (D.C. Cir. 1980) (FOIA case); Carl Zeiss Stiftung v. V.E.B. Carl Zeiss, Jena, 40 F.R.D. 318, 324 (D.D.C.1966), aff'd per curiam, 384 F.2d 979 (D.C. Cir.), cert. denied, 389 U.S. 952 (1967) (civil discovery).

28. Id.

29. The memo laid out a chart of the findings of the risk assessment:

TABLE I

Lifetime Excess Risk of Cancer Per 1000 Workers
After 45 Year Occupational Exposure to Ethylene Oxide

Exposure level (PPM)	Range of Estimates*
50	450–643
25	258–403
10	113–186
5	58–98
1	12–20
.5	6–10

*95% upper confidence limits on the estimates.

stratospheric, exceeding even EPA's estimate. Equally important, the memo addressed a number of options, but emphasized that:

> It is the conclusion of the health scientists and technical staff conducting this review that the recent and accumulated toxicity data on EtO exposure document a serious health hazard for workers and that the current Federal PEL of 50 PPM is inadequate to protect worker health. We recommend that the Agency proceed with rulemaking by Agency option (1) Issue an Emergency Temporary Standard (ETS) followed by an immediate Section 6B Rulemaking or (2) Begin Regular Section 6B Rulemaking, but decline to issue an ETS. If option (2) is chosen, then we recommend that Agency efforts in the 6B rulemaking be expedited.

Auchter, of course, had chosen neither of these options, but had instead said only that the agency would initiate permanent rulemaking sometime in the future.

The memo must have been a gift from a senior official who disagreed with the OSHA's decision to deny our petition. But the memo also posed a dilemma. For one thing, it might not be authentic. For another, even if it were authentic, using it might spawn time-consuming satellite litigation over how the memo came into our possession and might trigger a witch-hunt at OSHA to find the person responsible for the leak. Nonetheless, the memo undoubtedly bolstered our case. The question was how to use it without revealing that we had a copy.

We still had a reply brief to file on our motion to compel. We again pressed for disclosure, but we now also urged the court to review the options memo in camera. When Judge Parker heard argument, he seemed skeptical of my submission that the factual portions of the memo were not privileged. But one ray of sunshine broke through the clouds. At the end of the argument Judge Parker directed the government to submit the memo for in camera review—a standard procedure under FOIA.[30] Months later, Judge Parker denied our motion to compel the memo's release.[31] Now that he had a copy of the options memo, however, the ruling was hardly significant.[32]

The 45-year period comes from the requirement in the OSH Act that OSHA set standards to ensure that "no employee will suffer material impairment of health or functional capacity even if such employee has regular exposure to the hazard dealt with by such standard for the period of his working life." 29 U.S.C. § 655(b)(5).

    30.   See 5 U.S.C. § 552(a)(4)(B) (authorizing in camera review under FOIA); Carter v. Department of Commerce, 830 F.2d 388, 392–94 (D.C. Cir. 1987).

    31.   Order, Public Citizen Health Research Group v. Auchter (May 20, 1982).

    32.   On January 26, 1982, while our motion to compel was still pending, OSHA published an Advanced Notice of Proposed Rulemaking (ANPRM) in the Federal Register,

The parties then turned to briefing the case, focusing on two issues—(1) whether the risks from EtO were "grave," and if so, was OSHA then legally obligated to issue an emergency standard and (2) whether EPA's registration of EtO as a pesticide precluded OSHA's regulation of EtO as a sterilizing agent. On the first question, our brief laid out the scientific evidence linking EtO to cancer, chromosome damage and spontaneous abortion. It then addressed the OSHA and EPA risk assessments, which drove home the unprecedented magnitude of the cancer risk workers faced. This risk, we claimed, was heightened because many of the nation's over-100,000 EtO-exposed hospital and health care workers were subjected to levels at or near OSHA's 50 ppm PEL. For these reasons, we argued, both requirements of the Act's emergency standard provision were met: workers faced "grave" risks, and emergency action was "necessary" to protect them from those risks.[33] As the brief put it, "Congress gave the Secretary little latitude but to issue an emergency standard where, as here, there is overwhelming, uncontradicted evidence of a clear danger to workers, which, unless remedied, seriously imperils their health."[34]

Our brief also addressed OSHA's preemption argument. We pointed out that EPA only required EtO's registration as a pesticide, and both EPA and OSHA had for over a decade consistently said that OSHA, not EPA, was responsible for the protection of workers in hospitals and production sites.

For its part, OSHA argued that its regulation of EtO as a sterilizing agent was preempted by EPA's action, and that OSHA and EPA's prior views were simply wrong. OSHA's principal argument, however, was that the court should not second-guess its judgment about whether an emergency standard should be issued, particularly since that judgment was a discretionary one fraught with scientific and technical complexity. OSHA also submitted an affidavit from John Martonik, the head of OSHA's standard-setting division, questioning the gravity of the risks posed by EtO and asserting that "average" workplace exposures were 10 ppm or lower. These factors, Martonik claimed, justified a cautious approach to rulemaking.

Martonik's affidavit differed considerably from the options memo he had written only a few months earlier. But we were stuck. We could not use the memo to attack Martonik's affidavit without admitting that we

---

47 Fed. Reg. 3566, soliciting information and comments on EtO. The ANPRM could give no indication of OSHA's timetable, and nothing in it suggested that OSHA was committed to expediting the rulemaking process.

33.   See 29 U.S.C. § 655(c)(1).

34.   Plaintiffs' Memorandum of Law in Support of Plaintiffs' Motion for Summary Judgment, at 14.

had a copy. We had to find some other approach. In the end, we argued that the affidavit should be stricken because it constituted an impermissible *post hoc* justification for the agency's decision. As a fallback, we suggested that if the court accepted the affidavit, it should also release the options memo so the two documents could be compared. The motion was denied, but it soon became clear that the court understood the memo's significance.

Argument took place on October 22, 1982, before a courtroom packed with union and OSHA staff. Arguing before Judge Parker was daunting: he was always well prepared; he always dominated the argument; and he rarely concealed his judgments about the case. He could be short-tempered with lawyers he thought were unresponsive, ill-prepared, or disrespectful.

There is no transcript of the argument, but I did write a detailed memo to my clients immediately afterwards. I wrote: "The argument went well. The judge is quite troubled by the Department's inaction." He was also "skeptical" of the agency's scientific justification and wondered why, in the face of all of this evidence, the agency had decided "to take its time rather than to move quickly?" Judge Parker's questions to me focused on the statute, particularly on what factors come into play with emergency temporary standards, and "whether any court has ever required OSHA to issue an emergency standard when it did not want to?" He also asked "why should I be the one telling OSHA what to do?" I was not confident that he was reassured by my answers.

John D. Bates, a senior lawyer in the U.S. Attorney's office (later appointed by President George H.W. Bush to be a federal district court judge), argued for the government. Judge Parker asked a number of questions that were plainly based on the options memo, probing the grounds for OSHA's claims in its briefs (but not in the options memo) that the risks from EtO exposure were uncertain. Bates responded by emphasizing the complexities and uncertainties inherent in regulating toxic substances, and urged Judge Parker to defer to OSHA's expertise, but he tried to steer clear of the specific evidence on EtO. As Bates' argument was winding down, Judge Parker pressed him on the agency's rulemaking timetable for EtO. When Bates could not answer the questions with sufficient specificity to satisfy Judge Parker, the Judge requested that OSHA submit a schedule to the court, and adjourned the argument. OSHA submitted a timetable that contemplated the publication of a proposed rule in late-1983 with a final rule to follow by the end of 1984, with extensive periods blocked out for OMB review. A few weeks later, we filed a supplemental brief to bring to the court's attention the results of the study by Hemminki *et al.*, for the Finnish government, finding a three-fold increase in miscarriage among hospital workers exposed to very low (1 ppm or less) background levels of EtO, but peak exposures as high as 250 ppm.[35] All we could do now was wait.

Judge Parker issued his decision on January 5, 1983, ruling in our favor entirely.[36] Judge Parker found that OSHA's decision not to issue an emergency standard "could not have been based upon a proper assessment of the relevant considerations" because "the record before the agency presented a solid and certain foundation showing that workers are subjected to grave health dangers from exposure to EtO at levels within the currently permissible range. An immediate adjustment in the existing standard is necessary to protect those workers." The judge also found that "OSHA's authority to regulate exposure to EtO is not preempted" by EPA. He ordered OSHA to "promulgate within 20 days from this date an appropriate emergency temporary standard addressing worker exposure to ethylene oxide."[37]

PCHRG v. Auchter—Round II—On to the D.C. Circuit

Judge Parker's ruling was a tremendous victory. But it brought to mind the wisdom of the famous Chinese proverb "be careful what you wish for." We had asked that OSHA be directed to issue an emergency standard immediately. But we did not expect that the agency would be given only twenty days to do so. As far as we could tell, no court had ever ordered the government to do so much in so little time. We were certain OSHA would appeal. As expected, OSHA filed its notice of appeal and asked Judge Parker for a stay on January 13, 1983.

---

35. Plaintiffs' Notice of Filing, November 24, 1982, attaching Hemminki, K., et al., [Insitute of Occupational Health, Finland], *Spontaneous Abortion in Hospital Staff Engaged in Sterilising Instruments with Chemical Agents,* British Med. Journal 285:1461–3 (Nov. 20, 1982). Of 545 pregnancies in women exposed to EtO while pregnant, 15.1% ended in miscarriage, compared to a miscarriage rate of only 4.6% in 605 women also employed in hospitals but not exposed to ethylene oxide. No correlation between miscarriage and exposure to two other frequently used sterilizing agents, formaldehyde and glutaraldehyde, was found. Id.

36. Public Citizen Health Research Group v. Auchter, 554 F. Supp. 242 (D.D.C. 1983). The ruling generated considerable press attention, in part because it was seen as a set-back to President Reagan's regulatory roll-back efforts. See, e.g., Shabecoff, *Judge Bids US Act on Gas Carcinogen,* N.Y. Times, A10 (Jan. 7, 1983); Barringer, *Judge Orders OSHA to Toughen Standard on Exposure to Gas,* Washington Post, A17 (Jan. 7, 1983); Barringer, *Chemicals that Cause Cancer Getting "Benefit of the Doubt,"* Washington Post, A4 (Jan. 26, 1983).

37. Judge Parker's ruling contained a minor personal victory. He ordered OSHA to release the options memo because of the "the Martonik Affidavit's selective description" of the options memo's contents. 554 F. Supp. at 249 n.16. Months later, John Bates, the Assistant U.S. Attorney representing OSHA, sent me the options memo with a cover letter with a gentle barb: "[a]t this point, I am confident that the contents will not surprise you." Letter of John D. Bates, Asst. U.S. Attorney, to David C. Vladeck, June 29, 1984.

With Judge Parker's January 25th deadline looming, OSHA could not wait for Judge Parker to act, and so it asked the Court of Appeals to enter a stay. On January 20, 1983, with our consent, the Court granted a brief administrative stay to consider the stay papers, warning that its order "should not be taken as an indication of how the Court will ultimately rule on the merits of the motion for stay." On February 3, the court ordered the parties to file supplemental merits briefs by February 11, and scheduled argument for February 16. The court also directed the parties to address whether EtO should be given priority over other pending OSHA rulemakings. I had a mixed reaction to the court's order. The panel's willingness to hear OSHA's appeal immediately signaled that it understood the case's importance, but the order also reflected concern that the district court had usurped the agency's priority-setting authority.

In their supplemental briefs, the parties fine-tuned the arguments they had made to the district court.[38] OSHA's brief repeated its preemption argument.[39] But the brief's theme was that the district court had improperly "refused" to defer to OSHA's construction of its "narrowly circumscribe[d]" authority to issue emergency standards and had engaged in a "blatant substitution of judgment in evaluating the record." Worse, OSHA claimed, the district court was trying to take on the constitutional and legal responsibility of the executive branch—an activist judge overstepping his appropriate bounds. On the merits, OSHA argued that the health risks of exposure to EtO at low levels are uncertain and that voluntary industry practices had, on average, driven workplace exposures down to acceptable levels.

Our brief focused on worker health: "Absent action by this Court, 100,000 American hospital and health care workers, and manufacturers of medical devices ... will continue to be exposed to dangerously high levels of ethylene oxide" despite "overwhelming evidence establishing that ethylene oxide is a potent carcinogen and causes chromosome damage at levels far below OSHA's current standard."[40] We of course relied heavily on Judge Parker's detailed description of the options

---

38. Filing the briefs was a nightmare. A fierce snow storm had gripped Washington, D.C., on February 10, shutting the city down. Public transportation stopped running and government employees were told to go home. I finished the plaintiffs-appellees brief midday on February 11, but the copying shop that ordinarily produced our appellate briefs had closed. I ran off several copies of our brief on the office copying machine and walked the two miles or so from my office at Dupont Circle to the Court of Appeals, where a security guard logged in the briefs, and the Labor Department, where I left service copies with another guard. I was not served with OSHA's brief until the afternoon of February 14.

39. Brief for the Appellants, No. 83–1071 (D.C. Cir.), filed on February 15, 1983, at 34–41.

40. Brief of Appellees, No. 83–1071 (D.C. Cir.), filed on February 11, 1983, at 19.

memorandum and the other evidence before OSHA.[41] Based on this
evidence, the brief challenged OSHA's claims that the risks of EtO
exposure at levels below 10–15 ppm did not warrant regulation and
argued that OSHA's use of averages obscured the fact that, although
some workers were exposed to low levels of EtO, tens of thousands of
workers were still exposed to EtO levels at or near the 50 ppm PEL. We
also chided OSHA for relying on voluntary industry efforts to reduce
exposures. "Non-enforceable voluntary standards, which can be violated
or abandoned at any time . . . are no substitute for federally-set"
enforceable standards. And the brief explained that OSHA's preemption
theory made no sense because, if it were correct, then *no* agency could
protect hospital and health care workers from EtO.

Argument was held in the packed fifth floor courtroom in the E.
Barrett Prettyman Courthouse in Washington, D.C., that is home to the
D.C. Circuit. The judges on the panel—Chief Judge Spottswood Robinson, and Judges Malcolm Wilkey and Ruth Bader Ginsburg—were
primed for the case. Because OSHA lost below, it argued first.[42] Representing OSHA was Dennis K. Kade, the agency's senior appellate lawyer.
From the moment Kade took the podium, he was barraged with questions, mostly about the health risks of EtO, the agency's regulatory
timetable, and the agency's priority-setting process. The judges were
skeptical of Kade's effort to downplay the health risks of EtO, referring
repeatedly to the Hemminki study, OSHA's risk assessment, and the
options memo.[43] The judges were, however, especially interested in how
the risks associated with EtO compared with the risks posed by other
substances OSHA was regulating.

As I rose to take the podium, I too was peppered with questions
from the bench; the questions for me focused on whether the district
court had overstepped the proper bounds of judicial authority, not EtO
health risks. The judges' questions explored the limits of a court's power

---

41. Although the options memorandum was submitted to the district court *in
camera*, it was nonetheless part of the district court's record that was provided to the court
of appeals. Thus, although we had not yet been formally provided a copy of the memo by
the government, we nonetheless argued that the courts of appeals should review it, and
pointed to the extended passages in Judge Parker's opinion summarizing the memo's
findings. *See* 554 F. Supp. at 249–50.

42. I have not been able to obtain a transcript of this argument, but once again, I
have detailed argument notes that reflect what transpired. See also BARBARA CRAIG, COURTING
CHANGE: THE STORY OF PUBLIC CITIZEN LITIGATION GROUP 269 (PC Press 2004).

43. More than any other study in the record, the Hemminki study highlighted the
need for immediate action on EtO. Because of long latency periods, cancer risks rarely are
imminent, and the risks added by a few months of exposure are uncertain. But for
pregnant women, the Hemminki study showed that a few months of exposure to EtO could
sharply increase their risk of miscarriage. We had pushed this point in our briefs, and it
appeared that the court understood this argument.

to direct an agency to take a serious, perhaps extraordinary, regulatory action when the agency claimed that to do so would be improper. They were also worried about the prospects of generalist judges telling an expert agency how to order its affairs. I responded by arguing that in this case, there was no real disagreement over the science—scientists from OSHA, NIOSH and EPA shared our view about the gravity of the risks posed by EtO. The real question, I maintained, was whether OSHA, when faced with a substance posing a risk of this magnitude, could delay issuing a standard to protect workers. The OSH Act, I said, made clear that the answer to that question was "no." I was not sure my answers reassured the court. I was, I thought, better able to persuade the court that none of OSHA's other rulemakings was as important as EtO. Judge Ginsburg then asked questions about the scientific evidence—particularly EtO's reproductive effects—and I was relieved to finally address the health risks posed by EtO.

Towards the end of the argument, Judge Wilkey asked whether the plaintiffs would be satisfied with a ruling that directed OSHA to issue a proposed rule promptly and to complete rulemaking within a year. This question had been raised at my moot court, and it was a difficult one. We estimated that, without a court order, OSHA would likely take two years or more to issue a permanent EtO standard. If we were going to lose the case, Judge Wilkey's proposal would save us at least a year. But if we were going to win, it would cost us nearly a year. I paused for a moment and said: "Well your honor, I'd rather just win my case," trying to signal that we could live with his compromise, but would not be thrilled with it. Everyone in the courtroom cracked up, and to his credit, so did Judge Wilkey. After the question, I tried to emphasize the importance of getting a meaningful EtO rule in place as soon as possible. But the argument was over.

The court ruled just a month later.[44] "This [is a] difficult case," the court began, "which we must decide under pressing circumstances." The court first overturned the district court's decision requiring OSHA to issue an emergency standard. "While it is a close question, our review of the record indicates that, in ordering an emergency standard, the most drastic measure in the Agency's standard-setting arsenal, the district court impermissibly substituted its evaluation for that of OSHA." In light of Judge Wilkey's question, this was no surprise.

But the court did not let OSHA off the hook. The court said that due to the "significant risk of grave danger" posed by EtO, "we fully agree with the district court that 'OSHA has embarked upon the least responsive course short of inaction.'" The court emphasized that "[t]hree

---

44. Public Citizen Health Research Group v. Auchter, 702 F.2d 1150 (D.C. Cir. 1983) (per curiam).

years from announced intent to regulate to final rule is simply too long,"
and that "[d]elays that might be altogether reasonable in the sphere of
economic regulation are less tolerable when human lives are at stake."
Accordingly, "OSHA must expedite the rulemaking in which it is now
engaged." "To assure that OSHA will give due regard to the need,
urgent for some workers, for a new EtO standard ... we direct the
Assistant Secretary to issue a notice of proposed rulemaking within
thirty days ... and we expect the Agency to bring this matter to a close
within a year."

Although the court of appeals ruling was a set-back when measured
against Judge Parker's order, it was as much as we could have hoped for
when we filed the complaint. Courts are understandably reluctant to
impose "hammers" requiring agencies to act by a date-certain, because
courts are worried about usurping an agency's power to set its own
priorities. Moreover, action-forcing orders are at least arguably in tension with the long-standing rule that courts may not order agencies to
take enforcement actions, since those decisions are committed to agency
discretion.[45] While we would have preferred to see the court of appeals
affirm Judge Parker, we understood that *Auchter* was a considerable
victory.

The Development of OSHA's Final Rule Part I—Ex Parte Meetings With Industry

On April 15, 1983, exactly thirty days after the D.C. Circuit's March
15 ruling, Thorne Auchter signed OSHA's Notice of Proposed Rulemaking on Ethylene Oxide.[46] The good news was that OSHA proposed to
reduce the PEL from 50 ppm to 1 ppm, as we had requested. The bad
news was the draft had no STEL. Instead, OSHA posed a series of
questions about the necessity and feasibility of a STEL, with comments
due by June 19, and a hearing set for July 19.

The July 1983 hearing focused mainly on the need for a STEL.
Another chapter could be written about the complexities of an OSHA
hearing, and the EtO hearing would be a textbook illustration. Spanning
nine full hearing days, the OSHA hearing permitted OSHA's EtO team—
the scientists, physicians, industrial hygienists, policy analysts and lawyers working on the standard—to hear over a hundred witnesses discuss
virtually every facet of the proposed rule, although much of the testimony focused on the STEL issue. Among the witnesses were experts OSHA
brought in to advise the agency. Industry groups called witnesses in an
attempt to build a case—both scientific and economic—against the
STEL. With my clients playing a coordinating role, labor unions and

---

45.   See Heckler v. Chaney, 470 U.S. 821 (1985).

46.   48 Fed. Reg. 17,284 (1983).

public health organizations also called in experts and workers affected by EtO to testify in support of the STEL. Throughout the hearing, I and other lawyers made sure that our witnesses were able to get their points across and that the industry witnesses were cross-examined.[47]

This was the public side of the debate on the STEL question. In November 1983, a highly publicized and contentious congressional hearing on OSHA's handling of the STEL question[48] would suggest that Dr. A. Leonard Vance, the head of OSHA's Directorate of Health Standards, after extensive, off-the-record meetings with industry officials, had tried to sabotage OSHA's fact-finding about the STEL. Here is what happened.

Because the necessity of a STEL question was a major concern, Dr. Robert Beliles, the leader of OSHA's EtO team, decided to prepare a risk assessment based on the Hemminki study linking EtO to spontaneous abortion. The assessment would quantify the risk, not from cumulative exposures, but from intermittent, high-levels exposures of the kind that are common in work settings but would be uncontrolled by a PEL. If the risk assessment showed significant risks of spontaneous abortion, then OSHA would be obligated under the OSH Act to impose a STEL to address that risk. Ultimately, Dr. Theodora Tsongas, an OSHA epidemiologist, was directed to perform the assessment. Before she could do so, Vance countermanded Beliles' order, and no assessment was prepared. These facts are undisputed.

Here the story gets murky. According to his testimony before Congress, Beliles was at work on June 19, 1983—just after the comment period on the proposed rule closed and a month before the EtO hearing—when Mr. Arlin Voress arrived to meet with Vance. Voress was the head of occupational safety at Union Carbide, a major producer and user of EtO; he was also chair of the Ethylene Oxide Industry Council (EOIC), the lead trade group of EtO producers. According to Beliles, Vance was busy when Voress arrived, so Vance asked Beliles to meet with Voress until Vance could do so. Beliles claims that, despite his efforts to keep Voress from discussing EtO, Voress told Beliles that while the EOIC had no objection to the 1 ppm PEL, "a ceiling [STEL] would be a problem" due to cost, and would be opposed by the EOIC.[49] Vance

47. Participants in OSHA hearings have no right to cross examine adverse witnesses, but an Administrative Law Judge presides over the hearings and, as a matter of discretion, generally permits participants to question other witnesses, within strict time limits. As a result, there are opportunities to ensure that witnesses are asked the hard questions if the OSHA panel fails to do so.

48. *Hearings on the Use and Control of Ethylene Oxide*, Before the Subcomm. on Labor Standards of the House Comm. on Education and Labor, 98th Cong., 1st Sess. (Nov. 1, 1983).

49. Id. at 254. The EOIC wanted to address the risks from short duration exposures by requiring EtO-exposed workers to wear respirators. Workers generally object to wearing

and Voress then met for "at least an hour," according to Beliles. Beliles placed a memo of his meeting with Voress in the EtO public docket, Vance did not.[50] Vance acknowledged that he met with Voress several times, but denied discussing the specifics of the EtO rulemaking. Voress sent a letter to Congress confirming that he discussed the EtO rulemaking with both Vance and Beliles, but he gave no details of the meetings. Vance promised Congress that he would furnish the daily logs he kept of each meeting which would, he said, corroborate his testimony.

Vance's meetings with Voress take on importance in light of two events. First, several OSHA scientists testified—and Vance did not deny—that, shortly after Vance's June 1983 meeting with Voress, Vance, who had no prior involvement in the EtO rulemaking, ordered Dr. Tsongas not to produce the risk assessment on spontaneous abortion. Ultimately, the absence of this risk assessment was cited by STEL opponents, including OMB, as a fatal flaw in the record. Making matters worse, Beliles testified that Vance ordered him not to ask questions at the hearing that would support the adoption of a STEL, a story corroborated by other OSHA staff. Vance denied giving Beliles "a direct order" to avoid questions on the STEL, but during the EtO hearings the OSHA team was oddly quiet on matters relating to the STEL.[51]

Did Vance deliberately try to scuttle a STEL? What became of Vance's allegedly exculpatory logs? Here is part of the *Washington Post*'s account:

respirators, which are hot, uncomfortable, and notoriously ineffective because of the difficulties in getting a sufficiently tight fit to ensure that workers are not exposed to toxic gases. Employers often favor respirator use as a substitute for instituting more expensive engineering controls to reduce emissions. See, e.g., Christopher H. Schmitt, et al., *Secrets Behind the Mask*, U.S. News & World Reports, at 37 (Aug. 9, 2004).

50. When agencies commence rulemakings, they create "dockets" which are public repositories for all material filed with, or by, the agency in connection with the rulemaking. As material is filed, it is entered on a master list or docket that provides an index of all documents submitted to the agency. We generally looked at OSHA's EtO docket at least once a week, and often more frequently. Increasingly, this task is eased by agencies making their dockets available on line. But at the time, it required sending an attorney to OSHA's reading room to review the master index of all dockets filed since the attorney's last visit. The attorney would then request any document that appeared interesting from the docket clerk, who would pull the document from OSHA's files, just as a librarian might retrieve a book from a closed library stack. Documents could be examined in the docket office, and a copying machine was available to copy relatively short (ten to twenty page) documents for a modest fee. Longer documents were sent to a special copying facility and it was often several days before the documents were available.

51. Because of the significance of Vance's actions on the EtO rulemaking, the Committee staff asked me to testify at the hearing. I declined, fearing that my participation might complicate what appeared to be inevitable litigation over OSHA's failure to adopt a STEL. I did, however, provide background materials to the Committee and helped several of my clients prepare for their appearances at the hearing.

R. Leonard Vance, director of health standards at the Occupational Safety and Health Administration, last week told the House Education and Labor subcommittee on labor standards that he was unable to provide three of the four logbooks it is seeking because they were ruined by his dogs.

Vance said he had carried the books in the back of his pickup truck when he went hunting recently, and that the dogs had become sick and threw up on them. Vance told the subcommittee staff that the books were in such bad shape that he had no choice but to throw them out at the closest dump.[52]

As we will see, Vance's effort to sabotage the STEL—if that is what it was—ultimately backfired. Although the STEL opponents invariably pointed to the absence of the risk assessment as a fatal gap in the record, the hearing transcript made it apparent that OSHA's scientific staff strongly believed that the Hemminki study (and a risk assessment based on it, had one been prepared) demonstrated the serious risks posed by short-term, high-level exposures that would be uncontrolled by a PEL. Thus, the transcript of the November 1983 congressional hearings became an effective substitute for the never-prepared risk assessment in arguing in favor of a STEL.

The Development of OSHA's Final Rule Part 2—EtO Meets OMB

By June 14, 1984, OSHA had completed its work on the standard, which was to be released the following day.[53] That standard contained provisions for a 1 ppm PEL and a 10 ppm STEL, although OMB intervention changed that. OSHA sent its EtO standard to the Office of the Federal Register on June 15, where it was to be posted for public inspection and then published in the Federal Register. Once again, an anonymous OSHA employee came to our aid. OSHA sent two versions of the June 14 document to the Federal Register on June 15th, both reflecting changes made at OMB's behest. One had a thin pencil mark drawn through the portions of the document to be deleted, so the text earmarked for excision could easily be read. The other copy had been edited with a thick black marker, making it impossible to read the

---

52. Early, *Logbooks Dog-Gone, He Says*, Washington Post, A22 (March 27, 1984); see also *Precision, Excision & Excuse*, N.Y. Times, A30 (April 3, 1984); BNA, *Occupational Safety and Health Reporter*, 13 (Nov. 3, 1983). In a feature article entitled *The Puke Stops Here*, Esquire awarded Dr. Vance one of its annual "Dubious Achievement" awards. *Dubious Achievements of 1984: The Annual Report*, Esquire Magazine, at 66 (Jan. 1985).

53. In spite of the Court of Appeals' unmistakable directive that OSHA complete the rulemaking within a year of its order, it became clear by March 1984 that OSHA would not meet the deadline. To avoid litigation over the propriety of the delay, the parties to the initial lawsuit, which was still pending in the district court, entered into a stipulation requiring OSHA to complete its rulemaking by June 15, 1984.

deleted material. About lunch-time on June 15th, someone called my office and left a message urging that I immediately go to the Office of the Federal Register "to review the new EtO rule." The caller did not leave a name or phone number. Acting on the tip, I went to the Office of the Federal Register and was permitted not just to see, but also to make a copy, of the legible copy of the edited June 14 document.[54]

In the original June 14 document, OSHA concluded that a STEL was necessary because a 1 ppm PEL would not, in itself, reduce the cancer risk posed by EtO to acceptable limits.[55] Even with a 1 ppm in force, "an excess EtO-related cancer mortality risk of 12 to 23 deaths per 10,000 workers persists." A STEL would be the most "effective way of addressing the serious risk of chromosome damage," and was "essential" to reduce the risk of spontaneous abortion. However, in the edited versions of the document released on June 15th, the 1 ppm PEL and OSHA's justifications for it remained unchanged, but all references to the STEL had been deleted.[56]

Why? Because on June 14, OMB delivered a letter to OSHA objecting to the inclusion of a STEL on cost-effectiveness grounds, which OSHA immediately placed in its public docket. OMB took the position that the STEL was too expensive. OMB was unwilling to place any value on avoiding cases of spontaneous abortion and genetic harm—the principal function of the STEL—because it questioned the evidence on these harms and because OSHA had failed to quantify the number of these cases a STEL might prevent, a clear reference to the missing risk assessment. Strikingly, in places OMB's objections were drawn word-for-word from objections filed by industry groups, a fact we discovered simply by comparing OMB's June 14th letter with the comments industry groups had previously submitted to OSHA. OMB's letter asserted that its review of the draft standard had been ongoing "for several weeks," but nothing relating to that review had been placed in OSHA's EtO docket or otherwise made public. Nor was it possible to learn whether OMB had been meeting with industry representatives.

In response to OMB's objection, OSHA did what it was told. It dropped the STEL and sanitized (or tried to sanitize) all references to it in the final standard. The STEL's deletion put OSHA in a difficult position. It could not issue a final standard that was silent on the STEL.

---

54. I never learned how two versions of the same document ended up at the Office of the Federal Register. My guess is that an OSHA official opposed to the agency's decision to delete the STEL made sure that the legible copy of the marked up June 14th document was sent to the Federal Register just so it would end up in our hands. While OMB and OSHA were dismayed that we submitted the legible version of the June 14th document to the court of appeals, there was nothing they could do about it.

55. Tyson JA 178, 227–29.

56. 49 Fed. Reg. 25,734 (1984).

But the radical surgery performed to transform the June 14 document into a final, STEL-less standard had done just that. To buy time, OSHA announced that it would embark on another round of rulemaking on the STEL, which it hoped to conclude within six months. We immediately went back to Judge Parker, arguing that OSHA's additional rulemaking violated the Stipulation requiring the completion of the EtO rulemaking by June 15. At an August 23, 1984 hearing, Judge Parker called OSHA's delay "atrocious," but he declined to interfere with OSHA's new proceeding. He did require OSHA to keep the plaintiffs informed of its progress.

As part of its renewed STEL proceeding, OSHA solicited comments from other agencies, industry groups, and the public. Predictably, because its prior proceeding had just ended, the comments added nothing new. Two submissions, however, bear mention. First, NIOSH submitted comments emphasizing the importance of a STEL and demonstrating that OMB's objections "conflict with substantial scientific evidence." Second, OSHA's entire EtO team—scientists, doctors, and lawyers—took the unprecedented measure of placing a memo in the docket objecting to the STEL's deletion. They warned that if OSHA decides "to go along with OMB's reservations" it will have reversed its position "without having any new substantive information to support such a change."

None of this moved OSHA. On December 29, 1984, the agency announced that it would not promulgate a STEL because of the lack of definitive data linking adverse health effects to short-term exposures.[57] We promptly filed a petition in the D.C. Circuit challenging OSHA's deletion of the STEL; industry groups intervened to defend OSHA's determination. And the Association of Ethylene Oxide Users (AEOU), the lead trade association of EtO users (mostly hospitals), filed its own challenge to the 1 ppm PEL.

Court of Appeals Round 2—Public Citizen Health Research Group v. Tyson

Like many challenges to complex rules, *Tyson* involved the submission of hundreds of pages of briefs and an appendix nearly as hefty as a side of beef. But the legal issues were discrete and tightly focused: the AEOU argued that the evidence did not support a 1 ppm PEL; we argued that the STEL's deletion was neither supported by the evidence nor consistent with the agency's mandate to set the most worker-protective standard possible. We also argued that Executive Order 12,291 did not justify OMB's displacement of OSHA's decisional authority.

The dynamics of the litigation worked against AEOU. It was the only party challenging the 1 ppm PEL, it had no support from interve-

---

57. 50 Fed. Reg. 64 (1985).

nors or amici, and the D.C. Circuit's ruling in *Auchter* made regulation of EtO inevitable. On the other hand, the STEL question was the focal point of the parties' briefs, with the EOIC and AEOU supporting OSHA, and the Chairman of the five House committees having jurisdiction over regulatory agencies supporting us on the OMB interference point.[58] Accordingly, we skip over AEOU's objections and concentrate on the STEL litigation.

We argued that the deletion of the STEL violated the OSH Act. As noted earlier, the "purpose and policy" of the Act is "to assure every working man and woman in the Nation safe and healthful working conditions."[59] This general mandate is given substance in section 6(b)(5) of the Act, which says that the Secretary "shall set the standard which most adequately assures, to the extent feasible, on the basis of the best available evidence, that no employee will suffer material impairment of health or functional capacity."[60] This language is not hyperbole. As the Supreme Court put it, the Act "place[s] pre-eminent value on assuring

---

58. This was a roster of important Democrats in Congress. Representative John Dingell was chair of the Committee on Energy and Commerce and its legendary Subcommittee on Oversight and Investigations; Representative Peter Rodino was chair of the Committee on the Judiciary, as well as its Subcommittee on Administrative Law and Governmental Relations; Representative Jack Books headed the Government Operations Committee, which had oversight jurisdiction over the entire Executive Branch and the Paperwork Reduction Act, which is administered by OMB; Representative Augustus Hawkins was chair of the Education and Labor Committee, which had jurisdiction over OSHA; and Representative William D. Ford chaired the Committee on Post Office and Civil Service. Congressional interest in the case was strong because it was the first court challenge to the legality of OMB's intervention in agency rulemaking to reach the court of appeals. Congress was troubled by OMB's increasing dominance in rulemakings. During 1982–83, the House alone held no fewer than seven hearings to examine health and safety rules weakened by OMB's intervention. See, e.g., *OMB Control of OSHA Rulemaking*, Hearings before the Subcomm. on Manpower and House of the House Comm. on Gov't Operations, 97th Cong., 2d Sess. (1982); *Infant Formula: The Present Danger*, Hearings before the Subcomm. on Oversight and Investigations of the House Comm. on Energy and Commerce, 97th Cong., 2d Sess. (1982); *EPA: Investigation of Superfund and Agency Abuses (Part 3)*, Hearings before Subcomm. on Oversight and Investigations of the House Comm. on Energy and Commerce, 97th Cong., 1st Sess. (1983). Given Congress' concern over OMB's role, it was not difficult to persuade key congressional staffers that an amici brief would assist our case. Arnold & Porter, a high-powered Washington, D.C. firm, volunteered to write the brief; the brief's authors included Merrick D. Garland, now a judge on the D.C. Circuit, and Jack Quinn, who later became Vice President Gore's legal counsel.

59. 29 U.S.C. § 651(b).

60. Id. § 655(b)(5). This requirement is reinforced by the command, also in section 6(b)(5), that the Secretary set standards geared toward "the attainment of the highest degree of health and safety protection for the employee," and section 6(a), 29 U.S.C. § 655(a), which directs the Secretary to promulgate standards "which assure the greatest protection of safety or health of the affected employees" within the limits of feasibility.

employees a safe and healthful working environment, limited only by the feasibility of achieving such an environment."[61]

Our first argument was that, when measured against the Act's worker-protection requirements, the deletion of the STEL was indefensible. An EtO standard lacking a STEL did not assure workers a "healthful working environment." OSHA recognized that the 1 ppm PEL did not adequately protect workers from the risk of cancer, chromosome damage and spontaneous abortion,[62] and it "must, if it is feasible, seek to reduce [the cancer] risks below those estimated by the risk assessment to persist at a PEL of 1 ppm." Thus, once OSHA determined that a STEL was feasible and would enhance worker protection, the Act compelled it to include a STEL in the final standard.

Our second argument was that by removing the STEL the Secretary of Labor improperly surrendered his decisional responsibility to OMB. There was no question that, if left to its own devices, the Labor Department would have included the STEL in the final standard. The agency's scientific staff strongly supported a STEL, and there is no evidence that, until OMB formally objected, the top officials at the Department had reservations about the STEL.

The removal of the STEL at OMB's behest, we argued, violated the OSH Act. Congress assigned the Secretary of Labor responsibility for promulgating health standards—not OMB. The Act does not mention OMB, let alone give it power to override the Secretary's determinations as to what measures are necessary to protect worker health. Under the Act, once the Secretary determines that a standard is necessary to safeguard worker health and is feasible, he is bound to act.

We also contended that Executive Order 12,291 did not justify the Secretary's action. An Executive Order cannot override Congress' judgment that a specific statutory responsibility must be carried out by a particular office-holder. This point takes on special force where Congress has entrusted decision-making responsibility to an office-holder because of his agency's technical expertise and institutional competence.[63] We

---

61. American Textile Manufacturers Institute (ATMI) v. Donovan, 452 U.S. 490, 540 (1981). *ATMI* is a pivotal case in OSHA law. In *ATMI*, industry challenged OSHA's cotton dust standard on the ground that the Secretary of Labor had failed to show "that the costs of the standard bear a reasonable relationship to its benefits." 452 U.S. at 506. The Court "reject[ed] the argument that Congress required cost-benefit analysis in § 6(b)(5)," *id.* at 512, holding instead that OSHA is obligated to set the most worker-protective standard possible, constrained only by feasibility concerns. *Id.* at 512–14.

62. Brief for Petitioners Public Citizen Health Research Group, et al., No. 84–1252, et seq., at 36 (filed March 1, 1985) ("PCHRG Br.") (citing 49 Fed. Reg. at 25,738).

63. We further argued that, to the extent that the Administration claimed that the Executive Order authorized OMB to override the Secretary's determinations, such a claim would be wrong. We said that "nothing in the Executive Order can override the express

also argued that the Executive Order could not lawfully be applied because the OSH Act forbids application of cost-benefit principles in formulating worker protection standards.

In ordinary OSHA cases, Labor Department lawyers draft the briefs and argue the cases, with minimal coordination with the Justice Department. But this was no ordinary case. The government brief was written mainly by Justice Department lawyers charged with defending OMB's participation in the rulemaking. As a result, the brief spent only eight pages on the decision to drop the STEL, contending that the deletion was required because there was no solid data showing that low-dose exposures to EtO harm workers.

Most of OSHA's brief was devoted to defending the facial constitutionality of Executive Order 12,291—even though we had not claimed that the Order was unconstitutional as written. But the brief also argued that, in enacting the OSH Act, Congress implicitly granted the President, and his appointees at OMB, the authority to exercise "supervisory" power over OSHA rulemakings. This power emanates both from the President's constitutional duty to "take care that the laws be faithfully executed," and from the President's power of removal—a power intended "[t]o insure the President's control and supervision over the Executive Branch."[64] The brief asserted that in "the face of statutory silence, it must be assumed as a principle of statutory construction that Congress, by assigning duties to a member of the Executive Branch subject to the

mandate of Congress in the OSH Act, which assigns exclusive authority for the formulation of health and safety standards to the Secretary of Labor, and thus necessarily forbids OMB from exercising what amounts to veto power over such standards. Youngstown Sheet & Tube Co. v. Sawyer, 343 U.S. 579, 587–89 (1952); see also id. at 637–39 (Jackson, J., concurring)." PCHRG Br. at 56. We also pointed out that "whatever the scope of OMB's authority to play a role in the formulation of agency regulatory policy as a general matter, it surely does not extend to the formulation of the kind of complex scientific and technical judgments OSHA was called on to make regarding the need for a STEL. Indeed, in defending the constitutionality of the Executive Order, the Department of Justice recognize[d] that Myers v. United States, 272 U.S. 52, 135 (1926), the case on which it chiefly relies, expressly noted that 'there may be duties so peculiarly and specifically committed to the discretion of a particular officer as to raise a question whether the President may overrule or revise the officer's interpretation of his statutory duty in a particular instance.'" Id. The Justice Department had conceded that this language from Myers "is based on the view that Congress may constitutionally conclude that some statutory responsibilities should be carried out by particular officers without the President's revision, because such officers head agencies having the technical expertise and institutional competence that Congress intended the ultimate decisionmaker to possess." Department of Justice, Office of Legal Counsel, Memorandum of February 13, 1981, reprinted in *Presidential Control of Agency Rulemaking: An Analysis of Constitutional Issues That May Be Raised By Executive Order 12291*, Report of the House Committee on Energy and Commerce, 97th Cong., 1st Sess. at 81 (June 15, 1981) (Comm. Print).

64. Respondents' Brief at 80 (quoting Sierra Club v. Costle, 657 F.2d 298, 405 (D.C. Cir. 1981)).

President's power of removal, intended these duties to be discharged pursuant to the President's supervisory authority."[65]

Our reply brief accused OSHA of "ignoring petitioners' principal arguments and discussing at length matters not at issue."[66] OSHA had not addressed our argument that the Act compelled the restoration of the STEL. Nor did OSHA defend its decision to wait for definitive dose-rate evidence before imposing a STEL, even though the OSH Act directs the agency to act on the basis of the "best *available* evidence"[67] because Congress did not want "workers [to] suffer while it awaits the Godot of scientific certainty."[68]

On the OMB interference point, we challenged the claim that the President had the power to "supervise" OSHA rulemakings. After all, Congress had repeatedly rejected efforts to centralize power in OMB and "no court ha[d] ever held that the President's supervisory power is so limitless that it empowers him to direct the outcome of an administrative rulemaking." Finally, we said that OSHA "asks this Court to shut its eyes to political reality." OSHA was not "free to ignore OMB's objections and . . . go ahead with the STEL." Not only was that option foreclosed by the Executive Order, but OMB holds too much power over agencies for an agency head to disregard OMB's objections.[69] As then-OMB Director James Miller put it, "[i]f you're the toughest kid on the block, most kids won't pick a fight with you. The executive order establishes things quite clearly."[70]

These arguments were supported by the House Chairmen's brief, which set forth a blistering critique of OMB review:

> The amici Congressmen object to the systematic usurpation of legislative power by OMB pursuant to Executive Order 12,291. * * * Executive Order 12,291 is the cornerstone of a steadily growing Presidential apparatus, the effect of which is to contravene explicit Congressional delegations of authority, to subvert meaningful public

---

65. Cf. Elena Kagan, *Presidential Administration,* 114 Harv. L. Rev. 2245, 2251, 2319 (2001) (a later-written analysis of the same issue by a lawyer for the Clinton White House, who has since become Dean of Harvard Law School).

66. Petitioners' Reply Brief, Public Citizen Health Research Group v. Tyson, No. 84–1252 et seq., at 2 (filed July 12, 1985).

67. Id. at 13 (citing 29 U.S.C. § 655(b)(5) (emphasis added)).

68. Id. (quoting United Steelworkers of America v. Marshall, 647 F.2d 1189, 1266 (D.C. Cir. 1980), cert. denied, 453 U.S. 913 (1981)).

69. Id. OMB has control over agency budgets, personnel requests, and the testimony of agency staff before Congress. See generally Erik Olson, *The Quiet Shift of Power: Office of Management and Budget Supervision of Environmental Protection Agency Rulemaking Under Executive Order 12291,* 4 Va. J. Nat. Res. L. 1 (1984).

70. *Deregulation HQ,* Regulation 19 (March/April 1981).

participation in and judicial review of federal regulations, and to impose substantive standards on decisionmakers foreign to the statutes they administer. Unless it is checked, the program embodied in Executive Order 12,291 will fundamentally damage the administrative process by which our laws are implemented, the legislative system by which our laws are enacted and monitored, and the separation of powers upon which our system of government rests.

Because the Chairmen's *amici* brief was filed after OSHA's, the court gave OSHA the last word.[71] OSHA's reply acknowledged that OMB review is neither "innocuous" nor "ineffectual," and that "OMB can be expected to provide an independent perspective which may often assist agency heads in conforming their agency's actions to the President's policies." But "OMB has no authority to require an agency to conform to its views," and "OMB has done no more here than what the Order permits—it has reviewed Labor's proposed final rule and expressed its views on the matter." The filing of OSHA's reply brought briefing to a close.

Argument was held on January 22, 1986. A standing-room-only crowd, including many members of the Administration, braved frigid temperatures to attend. The panel hearing the case was a distinguished one: Chief Judge Robinson, who had been on the *Auchter* panel, joined by Judges Skelly Wright and Carl McGowan.

I went first. I began my argument with the straightforward claim that the deletion of the STEL violated the OSH Act. I was concerned that, if I started with the OMB interference point, I might not get an opportunity to address the health concerns that lay at the heart of the case. But the panel—especially Judge McGowan—was plainly steeped in the record, and I spent most of my time explaining the evidence on the health effects and very little of my time on OMB. That is, until my yellow light signaled that I was nearly out of time. Just as I asked to save my remaining few minutes for rebuttal, Judge Robinson asked me two questions: first, why shouldn't the court take the Secretary's word that the decision to delete the STEL was his, not OMB's, and second, if the President may remove the Secretary, why shouldn't the President be able to make it clear how he expects the Secretary to carry out his responsibilities?

I wished I had sat down a moment earlier, but I tried to answer Judge Robinson's questions. The first question, I said, was best answered by the record in the case. None of the objections OMB raised to the STEL were new—indeed, OMB literally cribbed its objections word-for-word from industry comments to OSHA. Thus, it was not the *force* of

---

71. Respondents' Reply Brief, Public Citizen Health Research Group v. Tyson, No. 84–1252 (filed Aug. 5, 1984).

OMB's comments that persuaded OSHA; rather, it was the *source* of the comments. I also pointed out that, given the timing of events and the pending court order requiring OSHA to issue a rule by June 15, it was not credible to suggest that the Secretary had not approved the June 14 draft. On the removal point, I said that there was a vast difference between a President discharging a subordinate from office—and taking whatever political heat might flow from that decision—and telling a Cabinet Secretary how to exercise discretion Congress committed to the Secretary, not the President. When agencies promulgate rules, they are exercising essentially legislative power, and Congress has a right to select the office-holder it wants to make those decisions. At that point, Judge Robinson signaled that my time had ended, and I sat down.

Alfred Mollin, a senior Justice Department lawyer, argued for the government. I'm over six feet tall, but Mollin is massive—maybe 6'6" or more. Not realizing that I had raised the podium as high as it would go, Mollin spent a few moments trying to raise the podium even higher. Ultimately, he gave up and began an elegant, if somewhat combative, defense of the Executive Order and OMB's participation in the rulemaking. But the court was far more interested in the science and bored in with questions about the implications of the Hemminki study, the residual risks to workers even with the 1 ppm PEL in place, and the legal requirements of the OSH Act. Time and again, Mollin would try to address the OMB issue and time and again, the court would press him on the health questions. I took this as a good sign.

The court handed down its decision on July 25, 1986. It was a complete win.[72] Judge McGowan's opinion for a unanimous court painstakingly went through all of the scientific evidence before OSHA and, as we expected, upheld the 1 ppm PEL. But the court found OSHA's reasons for rejecting the STEL "insufficient to warrant affirmance." The court bought our interpretation of the OSH Act, finding that "if, in fact, a STEL would further reduce a significant health risk and is feasible to implement, then the OSH Act *compels* the agency to adopt it."[73] The court directed OSHA to "ventilate the issues on this point thoroughly and either adopt a STEL or explain why empirical or expert evidence on exposure patterns makes a STEL irrelevant to controlling long-term average exposures." But the court specified no timetable for the completion of a rulemaking that had already taken five years.

The court's disposition of the STEL question on statutory grounds permitted it to avoid our challenge to OMB's actions. As the court said, because "OSHA's decision on the STEL cannot withstand our statutory

---

72. Public Citizen Health Research Group v. Tyson, 796 F.2d 1479 (D.C. Cir. 1986).
73. 796 F.2d at 1505 (emphasis in original).

review, we have no occasion to reach the difficult constitutional questions presented by OMB's participation in this episode."

Court of Appeals Round 3—Waiting for Godot

Given the D.C. Circuit's clear direction in *Tyson*, we assumed that OSHA would finally issue a STEL and bring the EtO rulemaking to a close. After all, the court had imposed a hurdle that OSHA could not overcome. Unless a STEL would be "irrelevant" to improving worker protection, OSHA had to add one to the EtO rule. Nonetheless, months passed with no discernable action to finalize the STEL. We made every effort to track what was going on within OSHA on the STEL—we wrote letters to agency counsel, checked the docket, and had members of Congress make inquiries. None of these efforts bore fruit, only fueling our suspicion that OSHA was again dragging its heels. Finally, more than six months after the remand order, OSHA announced that it hired a contractor to collect and interpret exposure data from employers, and that it hoped to complete the STEL proceeding by March 1988—nearly *two years* after the *Tyson* remand, and nearly *four years* after the *Auchter* remand.

We immediately filed a motion with the court of appeals charging that OSHA had "contemptuously and unreasonably delayed" promulgation of a STEL in violation of the order in *Tyson*. We argued that nothing in the remand contemplated yet another round of rulemaking, that OSHA had already compiled all evidence relevant to a STEL, and that this additional, lengthy proceeding was a sham to again delay the imposition of a STEL, which OMB still opposed. OSHA responded by pointing to the court's language in *Tyson* directing it to "ventilate" the STEL issues "thoroughly," and arguing that it would be remiss if it did not collect and review the most up-to-date information.

The court (the same judges who had heard *Tyson*) acted quickly on our motion, and this time, it spoke in no uncertain terms:

> We cannot countenance maneuvering that merely maintains a facade of good faith compliance with the law while actually achieving a result forbidden by court order. We understand that technical questions of health regulation are not easily untangled. We understand that an agency's limited resources may make impossible the rapid development of regulation on several fronts at once. And we understand that the agency before us has far greater medical and public health knowledge than do the lawyers who comprise this tribunal. But we also understand, because we have seen it happen time and time again, that action Congress has ordered for the protection of the public health all too easily becomes hostage to bureaucratic recalcitrance, factional infighting, and special interest politics. At

some point, we must lean forward from the bench to let an agency know, in no uncertain terms, that enough is enough.

At issue here, then, is whether that point has been reached. We conclude that it has, but that the court's proper role within the constitutional system counsels caution in fashioning a remedy.[74]

Although the court was unwilling to hold OSHA in contempt, it found that OSHA had engaged in "unreasonable delay." As a remedy, the court decreed that OSHA would have to make its final decision on the STEL "no later than March 1988" or face "liability for contempt."

True to form, OSHA waited until the last possible day to issue the STEL. On March 31, 1988, Assistant Secretary John A. Pendergrass signed the final rule adding a 5 ppm STEL averaged over fifteen minutes to the EtO rule, which is precisely the STEL we had asked for seven years earlier, and stricter than the 10 ppm STEL in the June 14 document.[75] As the preamble to the final STEL makes clear, OMB and the hospitals represented by AEOU remained opposed to the STEL, arguing that its costs outweighed its benefits, notwithstanding OSHA's finding that the incremental cost of the STEL would be modest, if not zero, because compliance with the 1 ppm PEL would, in most cases, drive short-term exposures down to levels below the STEL. Mercifully, there were no further appeals.[76]

---

74. Public Citizen Health Research Group v. Brock, 823 F.2d 626, 627 (D.C. Cir. 1987).

75. 53 Fed. Reg. 11414 (April 6, 1988).

76. OMB's involvement in the EtO rule did not end with the issuance of the STEL. Under Section 5 of Executive Order 12,866, agencies are required to review periodically their regulations to ensure that they have not "become unjustified or unnecessary as a result of changed circumstances" or "inappropriately burdensome," and that they are "consistent with the President's priorities and the principles set forth in this Executive Order." Section 5(c) of the Executive Order empowers OMB to "identify for review" any "existing regulation." *See also* 5 U.S.C. § 610 (provision of the Regulatory Flexibility Act, also requiring agencies to review periodically existing rules). OSHA recently concluded a comprehensive reexamination of the EtO rule, which may have been mandated by OMB. OSHA's finding are important, and they underscore the success of protective health and safety regulation. The OSHA report found, among other things, that "[t]here is a continued need for the rule," that EtO-exposed workers "would continue to be at risk of cancer, genetic changes and other adverse health effects, without the rule," and that the rule "has been effective in reducing exposures to EtO thereby achieving the predicted health benefits." As to OMB's concerns about the cost-effectiveness of the rule, the report concluded, perhaps ironically, that the rule in fact saved employers a good deal of money in the long run. According to OSHA, the rule "encouraged the development of improved sterilizers, which achieved compliance" at a "cost about half the cost of the older equipment." See OSHA, *Notice of Availability of the Regulatory Flexibility Act Review of the Occupational Health Standard for Ethylene Oxide*, 70 Fed. Reg. 20807–08 (Apr. 22, 2005).

Epilogue

What conclusions can be drawn from the battle to regulate EtO? Perhaps most important, hospital and health care workers are better off with a full EtO standard in place. New scientific evidence on EtO has reinforced the conclusion that EtO exposure causes leukemia, birth defects, and miscarriages at alarmingly high rates. Regulation can save lives and prevent harm. Timely regulation would have better protected the health and well-being of EtO-exposed workers.

Unreasonable delay litigation, a novelty when we first sued, has become a viable option in cases where agencies disregard their statutory duties. *Auchter* set the template for cases brought to challenge an agency's unreasonable delay.[77] Courts understandably remain cautious about granting relief in these cases to avoid upsetting an agency's prerogative to set priorities.[78] But, as the D.C. Circuit said in *Brock*, sometimes an agency's delay is so protracted and so inexplicable that it becomes necessary for a court to say that "enough is enough" and order an agency to take action by a date-certain.

OMB's participation in rulemaking also remains controversial, although litigation over the legality of OMB's participation has died down. The reason, I suspect, is perhaps a lesson taught by *Tyson*: When OMB's interference leads an agency to take action that is contrary to the statutory directive that the agency is required to enforce, or is otherwise arbitrary or irrational, a reviewing court will set aside the action for that reason alone and will not wade into the briar patch of the constitutionality of OMB's participation in agency rulemaking.[79]

---

77. See, e.g., In re International Chem. Workers Union, 958 F.2d 1144 (D.C. Cir. 1992) (finding OSHA had unreasonably delayed issuing a standard for cadmium); Public Citizen Health Research Group v. Commissioner, FDA, 740 F. 21 (D.C. Cir. 1985) (challenging FDA's delay in putting warning labels on aspirin products for Reyes Syndrome): Public Citizen Health Research Group v. Chao, 314 F.3d 143 (3d Cir. 2002) (finding OSHA had unreasonably delayed issuing a standard for hexavalent chromium).

78. See, e.g., UAW v. Chao, 361 F.3d 249 (3d Cir. 2004) (rejecting unreasonable delay claim against OSHA). In Norton v. Southern Utah Wilderness Alliance, 124 S. Ct. 2373 (2004), the Court made clear that cases challenging an agency's failure to take action may be brought only where the agency is under a statutory duty to act. *Southern Utah* thus leaves undisturbed the *Auchter* line of cases. As discussed earlier, *Auchter* and similar cases are brought to compel non-discretionary agency action.

79. Nor is it clear that a constitutional challenge to OMB's intervention would prevail. There are scholars who defend OMB's role on what is termed the "unitary executive" theory. See, e.g., Steven Calabresi, Christopher Yoo, & Anthony Colangelo, *The Unitary Executive During the Modern Era: 1945–2004*, 90 Iowa L. Rev. 601 (2005); Steven Calabresi & Christopher Yoo, *The Unitary Executive During the Second Half Century*, 26 Harv. J.L. & Pub. Pol'y 667 (2003); Steven Calabresi & Kevin H. Rhodes, *The Structural Constitution: Unitary Executive, Plural Judiciary*, 105 Harv. L. Rev. 1153 (1992). See also Elena Kagan, *Presidential Administration*, n.65 supra.

Tyson also shows in stark terms the dangers of OMB review. OMB's participation is a one-way ratchet—OMB presses agencies to do less to protect the public health, not more, and to focus on lower cost options, not more protective ones. OMB's job is to ensure that rules meet a cost/benefit litmus test, and many experts claim that cost/benefit analysis is inherently anti-regulatory.[80] EtO is a good illustration of their point. OMB contended that the STEL was not cost-effective. But OMB was unwilling to assign any value to the health protections a STEL would provide, beyond the value of cancer deaths avoided. Economists have placed values on human lives, but they struggle with other health valuations: How much is it worth to avoid genetic damage to a woman of child-bearing age or a miscarriage? While the anticipated *costs* of regulations are generally easier to estimate (and easy to overstate), the *benefits* of regulation—avoided cancers, miscarriages, genetic damage that might cause infertility or birth defects, kidney failures requiring dialysis and transplant, to name just a few—are notoriously difficult to quantify and are often downplayed or ignored by OMB.

There is also the question of transparency. At the time of the EtO litigation, OMB conducted most of its work behind closed doors, with no public record of its meetings with agency staff or with industry.[81] OMB secrecy fueled the suspicion that in many cases it was serving simply as a conduit for industry objections. Measures imposed since then have added some accountability to the process. OMB contacts with industry are supposed to be docketed and written exchanges between OMB and an agency are supposed to be made public once a rule is published in final form (assuming the rule ever reaches that stage).[82] But these requirements are easily evaded and it remains difficult to track OMB's involvement in many rulemakings.

Finally, there is the question of expertise. As *Tyson* shows, health and safety rulemakings involve enormously complex questions often at the frontiers of scientific knowledge. OMB intervention, although generally driven by OMB's mission to reduce regulatory costs, is often based on scientific and technical grounds in which OMB's economists and

---

80. See generally FRANK ACKERMAN & LISA HEINZERLING, PRICELESS: ON KNOWING THE PRICE OF EVERYTHING AND THE VALUE OF NOTHING (New Press 2004); Lisa Heinzerling, *Regulatory Costs of Mythic Proportions*, 107 Yale L.J. 1981, 2060–63 (1998).

81. OMB's practice was to deliver criticisms to agencies orally, so as not to "leave fingerprints" in the administrative record. See Behr, *If There's a New Rule, Jim Tozzi Has Read It*, Washington Post, A21 (1981) (quoting OMB Deputy Administrator Jim Tozzi).

82. See Executive Order 12,866, §§ 6(b) & (c), 58 Fed. Reg. 51,735 (1993), as amended by Executive Order 13,258, 67 Fed. Reg. 9,385 (Feb. 26, 2002); see also http://www.whitehouse.gov/omb/inforeg/regpol.htm (website of OMB's Office of Information and Regulatory Affairs); http://www.regulations.gov (website providing gateway to all agency regulatory initiatives).

policy analysts have little or no expertise. Nonetheless, OMB wields enormous and often decisive influence, at times overriding the judgment of expert agencies.[83]

One might ask: What is the harm? After all, when OMB interference forces an agency down the wrong path, the courts will step in and require the agency to correct its misjudgment. That answer, however, is far from satisfactory. Delays in instituting important health and safety protections exact a real toll on the lives, health and well-being of those who are the regulation's beneficiaries. Additional rounds of rulemaking drain scarce agency resources and undermine the morale of agency personnel. And it is wrong to count on courts to correct agency error, regardless of fault. Many agency actions favoring industry go unchallenged because there is no party with the economic incentive, or the financial wherewithal, to sue. The seven year battle over EtO shows that forcing a recalcitrant agency to act is like fighting a medieval siege battle; years of constant bombardment are needed before the walls of resistance begin to crumble. Few organizations without a financial stake in the outcome have the resources or staying-power to take on such an endeavor. For this reason, while cases like *Tyson* shine a light on the OMB process, the courts cannot realistically serve as a check on OMB's participation in the regulatory process.[84]

---

83. In a recent interview, Dr. Peter Infante, formerly a senior OSHA scientist and member of the EtO team, talked about the dominating influence OMB had on OSHA rulemakings. Dr. Infante said: "OMB always had the last word in the rulemaking process. What was frustrating about the OMB review process is that OMB policy analysts fought with us constantly about highly technical matters relating to epidemiology and risk assessment—even though they had no expertise in these fields. None of these discussions was on the record. Most of the time they were simply repeating what they had been told by industry representatives who had made the same arguments to OSHA. At OSHA, of course, we rejected these arguments because they weren't scientifically sound. But when they were made by OMB, we had to do business with them and we often were overruled by OMB, even on technical matters." According to Dr. Infante, "the EtO STEL was a perfect example. Everyone at OSHA thought that a STEL was essential to control EtO, which is a very dangerous and toxic substance. We had been given clearance for the STEL by the Assistant Secretary of OSHA and by the Department of Labor's policy review board, which spoke for the Secretary of Labor. But OMB objected to the STEL because industry did not want it, and we simply caved in. There was no scientific justification for dropping the STEL. The staff was up in arms. But the Secretary of Labor was not going to do battle with OMB over one provision of an OSHA rule—no matter how important that provision was to the health of workers. The staff was just demoralized." Interview with Dr. Infante, Aug. 27, 2004 (notes on file with the author).

84. *Tyson* is hardly an aberrational case. Consider Public Citizen v. Mineta, 340 F.3d 39 (2d Cir. 2003), where the Second Circuit set aside a rule issued by the National Highway Traffic Safety Administration (NHTSA) that had been substantially weakened by OMB. NHTSA proposed to require automobile manufacturers to install devices that would detect under-inflated tires; OMB insisted that NHTSA permit the installation of not only the highly effective devices NHTSA selected, but far less effective devices favored by industry for cost reasons. The Second Circuit found that the final rule did not meet Congress'

These concerns have sparked an ongoing and spirited debate over the legality and wisdom of presidential control over the regulatory process. Many experts defend the OMB review process as a brake on overly zealous, pro-regulatory bureaucrats and as a way for an Administration to manage and rationalize its regulatory policy.[85] As they point out, since President Gerald Ford, every U.S. President has employed some form of centralized review. And since President Reagan, every President has relied on OMB to spearhead regulatory policy, as well as engage in regulatory review. When President Clinton came into office in 1992, he entertained the idea of moving away from centralized OMB review. He instead embraced it, issuing an Executive Order carrying forward the core elements of Executive Order 12,291, but adding provisions to make OMB review more transparent.[86] President George W. Bush has further solidified OMB's hold on the regulatory process.[87]

On the other hand, many scholars believe that, while presidents understandably want to consolidate their power, and that centralized control over the regulatory process permits them to so do, presidential control of the regulatory process is both unconstitutional and unwise.[88]

---

requirements and was arbitrary and capricious. But the introduction of this important safety feature will be delayed for several years as a result of OMB's interference. See also Public Citizen v. FMCSA, 374 F.3d 1209 (D.C. Cir. 2004) (setting aside on safety grounds rule *extending* the hours truck drivers may drive after OMB intervened on behalf of trucking companies to reverse agency's proposal *reducing* the hours).

85. See, e.g., Stephen Croley, *White House Review of Agency Rulemaking: An Empirical Investigation*, 70 U. Chi. L. Rev. 821 (2003).

86. See Executive Order 12,866, supra n.79; see also Elena Kagan, *Presidential Administration*, 114 Harv. at 2319 (explaining and defending the Clinton Administration's approach to regulatory review, but acknowledging that the President's power to intervene in regulatory matters stems not from Article II of the Constitution, but rather from the general intent and understanding of Congress).

87. See, e.g., Joel Brinkley, *Out of Spotlight, Bush Overhauls U.S. Regulations,* N.Y. Times, A1 (Aug. 13, 2004) (reporting Administration's "pro-business tilt" and that the "overall regulatory record shows that the Bush administration has heeded the interests of business and industry" by dismantling existing rules industry disfavors); Amy Goldstein & Sarah Cohen, *Bush Forces a Shift in Regulatory Thrust: OSHA Made More Business Friendly,* Washington Post, A1 (Aug. 15, 2004) (reporting OMB's key role in easing OSHA regulation on business); Marc Kaufman, *Lobbyists' Role in Food Rules Questioned,* Washington Post A23 (Sept. 30, 2004) (reporting OMB's role in weakening FDA food safety rules).

88. See, e.g., Peter L. Strauss, *Presidential Rulemaking,* 72 Chi.-Kent L. Rev. 965, 985–86 (1997) (arguing that "[f]or [the President] to make the bureaucrats believe that they are his is precisely to tear down the structures of law and regularity Congress has built up in relation to the presidency," and that presidential control of rulemakings threatens to alter the "psychology of government."); see also Robert V. Percival, *Presidential Management of the Administrative State: The Not-So-Unitary Executive,* 51 Duke L. J. 963 (2001); Thomas O. McGarity, *Presidential Control of Regulatory Agency Decisionmaking,* 36 Am. U. L. Rev. 443 (1987); Alan B. Morrison, *OMB Interference With Agency Rulemaking: The Wrong Way to Write a Regulation,* 99 Harv. L. Rev. 1059 (1986).

These scholars argue that OMB intervention forces agencies to disregard the policy directions set by Congress in legislation. OMB control also distorts lines of authority within government. No longer does an OSHA employee get marching orders just from the agency; OSHA's views are always subject to revision at OMB's direction. And they argue that OMB review blurs political accountability for important regulatory decisions.

This debate is unlikely to be resolved any time soon. But the stakes are enormous, implicating the most basic principles of separation of powers. At bottom, the real question is whether the White House or agencies will make the policy decisions that Congress entrusted to the agencies, not to the President. These decisions may seem mundane in the abstract, but in fact they are breathtaking in their scope and importance: affecting, among other things, the purity of the air we breathe, the food we eat, and the water we drink, the safety of our drugs, medical devices, cars, airplanes, trains, and ships, and the security of our nation's airports, refineries, nuclear power plants, chemical plants, and even our nation's border. At the moment, the pendulum has swung in favor of the White House, with OMB control of the regulatory process perhaps at its zenith. But pendulums rarely remain in place for long.

Rashomon

In the tradition of the Japanese film *Rashomon*, Professor Farina tells the story of George Eldridge's claim for an oral hearing, before termination of his disability benefits, from the perspective of several of the participants: Eldridge, the Social Security Administration, the Government arguing the case in court, and a variety of external consultants. Like the viewer of Kurosawa's classic, the reader is invited to speculate about whether this is a situation in which all the stories are true and none of them are true. The nature of adjudication, however, requires the Court to endorse only one story, and it announces the now-famous *Mathews* calculus as the method of finding the truth for purposes of due process. After reviewing the universal criticism the calculus received, Prof. Farina suggests that, viewed from the vantage point of thirty years of "new due process" jurisprudence, the *Mathews* methodology may have served us better than we have appreciated.

7

Cynthia R. Farina*

Due Process At Rashomon Gate: The Stories of Mathews v. Eldridge

It was a tale worthy of Akira Kurosawa.[1]

Six years earlier, *Goldberg v. Kelly* had radically rewritten the groundrules of social-welfare program administration by interpreting the Constitution to require an oral evidentiary hearing before New York City could suspend welfare benefits.[2] Due process was not satisfied, the Court held, by existing administrative procedures that offered an informal give-and-take with front-line agency personnel and internal agency review prior to termination, with a full hearing (and, if appropriate, retroactive benefits) available after payments had been stopped. The companion case of *Wheeler v. Montgomery* applied this principle to California's old-age benefits program.[3] Significant changes in the size, composition, and decisional protocols of the welfare bureaucracy had resulted.[4]

---

* Professor of Law and Associate Dean of the University Faculty, Cornell University.

1. For those not movie buffs, Kurosawa was one of Japan's greatest directors—perhaps one of the 20th century's greatest directors. His 1951 film *Rashomon* brought him international acclaim, and remains the topic of critical interest and debate. Seeking shelter from a downpour in the ruins of the massive Rashomon gateway to ancient Kyoto, a woodcutter and a Buddhist priest try to understand the meaning of an incident of great concern to the local community—an incident that has just been the subject of a trial in which both testified. The film then retells the event from the perspective of each of four persons who were present, one of whom was the woodcutter. The four stories coincide, and conflict, in essential details. See text following n. 75 infra.

2. 397 U.S. 254 (1970).

3. 397 U.S. 280 (1970).

4. See, e.g., JERRY L. MASHAW, DUE PROCESS IN THE ADMINISTRATIVE STATE 33–34 (1985); Cesar A. Perales, *The Fair Hearings Process: Guardian of the Social Service System*, 56 BROOKLYN L. REV. 889 (1990); William H. Simon, *The Rule of Law and the Two Realms of Welfare Administration*, 56 BROOKLYN L. REV. 777 (1990).

Year by year as the 1970s proceeded, the Due Process Clause reshaped the procedural design of other kinds of regulatory programs as well. *Bell v. Burson* refused to allow the Georgia Department of Public Safety to postpone the hearing to determine liability for an automobile accident until after suspension of an uninsured motorist's driver's license, so long as the statutory scheme had chosen to make liability relevant.[5] *Morrissey v. Brewer* required Iowa to provide a preliminary hearing "reasonably prompt[ly]" after arrest to determine the existence of probable cause to believe a parole violation has occurred, followed by a more elaborate hearing "within a reasonable time" after the parolee is taken into custody.[6] *Gagnon v. Scarpelli* extended these requirements to the Wisconsin Department of Public Welfare's system of probation revocation.[7] *Wolff v. McDonnell* rejected the Nebraska Department of Correction's argument that the process for disciplining prison inmates for serious misconduct is "a matter of administrative policy rather than constitutional law," and recast the procedures by which the Adjustment Committee withdrew good-time credits.[8] *Goss v. Lopez* told the Columbus, Ohio Public School System that the short-term suspension of public school students must be preceded by an informal oral hearing which, if it now seems a paltry measure of process compared with *Goldberg's* plenary hearing rights, was then an astounding insertion of the Constitution into routine public school administration.[9] The entire line of cases echoed in varying degrees the sentiments of *Bell v. Burson*:

> While "[m]any controversies have raged about ... the Due Process Clause," it is fundamental that except in emergency situations ... due process requires that when a State seeks to terminate an interest such as that here involved, it must afford "notice and opportunity for hearing appropriate to the nature of the case" *before* termination becomes effective.[10]

And, although civil-libertarian Justice Brennan had written *Goldberg* and *Bell*, the others cases in the series reflected a broader authorship that included Justice Powell, Justice White, and Chief Justice Burger.

Now, however, the Court was to determine the role of the Constitution in administration of the largest and most vexing social welfare program in existence: the Social Security disability program. Decision about the procedures required to terminate benefits of current recipients

---

5. 402 U.S. 535 (1971).

6. 408 U.S. 471 (1972).

7. 411 U.S. 778 (1973).

8. 418 U.S. 539, 555 (1974).

9. 419 U.S. 565 (1975).

10. 402 U.S. at 542, quoting Mullane v. Central Hanover Bank & Trust Co., 339 U.S. 306, 313 (1950) (emphasis in original).

had been avoided once when, shortly before oral argument, the Court was advised that the Social Security Administration had revised its termination procedures.[11] Even the revised procedures deferred the right to an oral evidentiary hearing until well after suspension of benefits. The government nonetheless insisted that the revisions satisfied SSA's due process obligations. The claimants, unsuprisingly, condemned the new procedures as still palpably unconstitutional given existing precedent. A majority of the Court put off decision, remarking—with sublime disregard of probability, inasmuch as the case was a class action—that if the claimants were found to be still eligible under the new procedures, resolution of the constitutional challenge would become unnecessary.

Meanwhile, the number of disability recipients continued to rise faster than anyone had anticipated. As both claim backlogs and program costs increased, Congress unabashedly berated the SSA for both being unresponsive to claimants and being too easy on them.[12] And George Eldridge's case was one of more than 150,000 working its way through the system.[13]

A. The Actors

George Eldridge[14]

I'm George Eldridge and until my back got so bad I couldn't carry soda pop cases any more, I drove a truck for a soda distributor. I had worked on the railroad a long time before that and I always paid into the Social Security and so I applied for disability in Richmond when I got so I couldn't work. That was back in March of 1967. But they turned me down. I had to go to a hearing and the Examiner gave a decision that I was disabled because of my back and because of the diabetes and "chronic anxiety."[15] All this took till June of 1968, that's 15 months for

---

11.   Richardson v. Wright, 405 U.S. 208 (1972).

12.   See Jerry L. Mashaw, Bureaucratic Justice: Managing Social Security Disability Claims 19–20 (1983) [hereinafter "Bureaucratic Justice"].

13.   More precisely, 160,627determinations of whether disability continued were made during 1973, the year following the termination of George Eldridge's benefits. See Staff of House Comm. on Ways & Means, 93d Cong., 2d Sess., The Disability Insurance Program, at 347 (July 1974) [hereinafter "Cong. Staff Report"](cited in Government's Brief in the Supreme Court).

14.   The story told here contains a little—but only a little—artistic license. All the facts, and much of the actual phrasing, can be found in the following parts of the Supreme Court record: Appendix 11–12 (Affidavit of Bernard Popick, Director, Bureau of Disability Insurance, SSA); Appendix 13 (May 25, 1972 letter of George Eldridge); Transcript of Oral Argument 39, 47–48; Respondent's Brief 2, 6.

15.   "One of every two applicants for Social Security disability benefits is denied them. Of those denied, about 40 percent request that SSA reconsider their case, about half

me to start getting any benefits with me not able to work with six children to take care of.

I thought everything was finally settled but then in February 1970 I got a letter from Richmond saying that my disability had ceased as of January and my checks would stop in February. What did they know? Nobody came to see me, nobody asked me anything, nobody gave me a chance to say anything about it. They just stopped my checks. I had to get an attorney and he filed papers to Richmond asking for reconsideration but nothing happened until we took them to court. The court made them start my checks again and keep sending them until they gave me a hearing on my case. It took them till March of 1971 to give me a hearing. God knows what my family would have done if we had been without my checks all that time. The Examiner took only a week make his decision wholly in my favor and stated in his decision for my checks to continue without interception.

Then a year later, March of 1972, I got another letter asking a lot of questions about my condition. I told them nothing was improved and gave them my doctors' names. In May, they told me I had to be examined by another psychiatrist. So I went. Four days later, I got a letter that I wasn't disabled any more and that I could work and my checks would be stopped unless I submitted additional evidence.

All they do is harass me. If I was able to work I would work because if I was able to work I could make more money than the Social Security paid me. I know they already had enough evidence in my files to prove the disability. They didn't even read what they had. I wrote to them, "if you will check my reports a little closer I think you will find that I have arthritis of the spine rather than a strained back as you stated in your letter." What it comes down to is this. The people at the Disability Section in Richmond have never made a yes decision in my case, I have always had to have a hearing in order to get the decision made properly.

I got so tired and fed up with being harassed and having to spend money I didn't have to get my rights. All those years I paid into the Social Security while I was able to work. "So go ahead and make your own decision in the case," I wrote them, "I know I'm not able to work, if I ever get able to work again I will, I will get by someway without the Social Security." And do you know what they did, those government lawyers who grind a man down by harassing him and twisting a man's words. They told the Supreme Court of the United States that I said I didn't need the benefits, I said I could "get by" without the Social Security![16]

of which are eventually awarded benefits during the appeals process." General Accounting Office Study of Disability Denials, quoted in Cong. Staff Report, supra note 13, at 439.

16.   See Government's Brief at 38 and Supplemental/Reply Brief at 16 fn. 8, selectively quoting George Eldridge's letter.

Do you know how my family got by? We got by sleeping in one bed, me and my six children now that my wife passed on. That was after they repossessed the furniture. They foreclosed the house. All those years I worked on the railroad and then driving a soda truck and paying into the Social Security and it's all gone.

You tell me, is that fair? Is that due process?

The Disability Determination Section of the Virginia Department of Vocational Rehabilitation (the State Agency)[17]

People are used to having Social Security deducted from their paycheck and they think that if they get sick or hurt and have trouble working, they just have to come in and file a claim and get "their" money. But it's not that easy. In fact, anyone who knows anything about the disability benefit provisions of the Social Security Act will tell you that it's a hard statute.

First, there's the definition of disabled. According to 42 U.S.C. § 423(d)(a)(A), "disability" means not only that you are unable to perform your own job for a period "expected to last for a continuous period of not less than 12 months." It also requires a that the worker "cannot, *considering his age, education, and work experience*, engage in *any other kind* of substantial gainful work which exists in the *national* economy." Consider, for a moment, how difficult *that* determination is to make. And that's not all: the statute goes on to say, "*regardless* of whether such work exists in the immediate area in which he lives, or whether a specific job vacancy exists for him, or whether he would be hired if he applied for work." In other words, for this program, it's not enough to show that you have medical problems and cannot find work on account of them. Instead, you have to show that you have medical problems, you cannot find work on account of them, *and* they are so severe that they render you unable to work. A worker with a demonstrable health problem, but who also has the *capacity* to do some job in the national economy is not "disabled" even if we know that employers have access to a pool of healthy workers from which they will hire in preference to hiring this worker. Congress deliberately set it up that way. It isn't unemployment insurance, after all.

In this program, there aren't degrees of disability. Either you meet the standard, or you don't. If you don't, you get no benefits even if it's obvious that a substantial amount of functioning has been lost. It is the

---

17. This account represents the greatest fictional license, for the state agency did not appear at all in the litigation. All the factual statements, however, are sound and can be verified in a number of sources including the Government's Brief at 14–27 and ROBERT G. DIXON, JR., SOCIAL SECURITY DISABILITY & MASS JUSTICE: A PROBLEM IN WELFARE ADJUDICATION (1973) [hereinafter DIXON].

worker's responsibility to prove disability. And the disability must be "by reason of any *medically determinable* physical or mental impairment." Finally, even for a fully qualified, provable disability, the statute usually requires a wait of five months before benefits can begin. 42 U.S.C. § 423(c).

If all this isn't enough to stack the deck against the worker, there's the way internal agency review works. Although state agencies make the initial determinations of original and continuing disability, the federal agency is ultimately in control. The case file and our initial determination is forwarded to SSA. Whenever we initially decide someone is disabled (or still disabled), SSA can reject that decision, but if we decide someone is *not* disabled (or that a disability has ceased), SSA does not have the power at this point to reach the opposite conclusion. The statute was deliberately set up so that, at this stage, the SSA can only make a determination *less* favorable to the worker than the state agency makes.[18] Instead, benefits are denied (or terminated), and if the worker wants to fight it he has to request and go through the reconsideration process, which takes another 2–4 months. Congress called provisions like this "protecting the Trust Fund." Economists talk about "controlling for moral hazard." But, from the perspective of a worker looking for disability benefits, it just adds up to a hard statute.

From the beginning we tried to explain to Mr. Eldridge that we have to check on him regularly to see whether his disability is continuing.[19] The initial award of benefits told him that we would be examining his claim a year later for possible medical improvement. Similarly, when we sent the questionnaire in 1972, we reminded him of the review requirement and offered help in answering the questions. When he responded that he didn't think his condition had improved, we explained why the evidence in the file appeared to indicate medical recovery. Our team, which includes a physician and a trained disability examiner, reviewed the evidence we had. The diabetes was now under control with no complications noted; there was no medical evidence of significant continuing motion limitation from the back strain, and the psychiatric examination we requested concluded that his current anxiety level did not preclude all work for which he was qualified. We asked if he had additional information he wanted us to consider and offered him additional time if he needed it to get such information. He refused to give us anything else.

---

18. 42 U.S.C. § 421(c). See Government's Brief at 16, 29. SSA could informally suggest that the state agency change its denial decisions, and indeed frequently did so—at least through the mid-1970s. However, as the decade progressed and political pressure to tighten eligibility mounted, SSA increasingly exercised one-way review to reverse state worker-favoring determinations. See BUREAUCRATIC JUSTICE, supra note 12, at 174–75.

19. See SSA Claims Manual §§ 6700–02, Appendix B to Government's Brief.

We had no choice but to recommend termination of benefits.

The Social Security Administration[20]

This agency, through its Bureau of Hearings and Appeals ("BHA"), operates the largest single adjudicative system in the western world.[21] More than 90% of its caseload involves the disability program.[22] Four years ago, the Administrative Conference of the United States published a study of administration of the disability program subtitled, "A System in Crisis."[23] That subtitle ruffled some feathers here[24] but, in the end, it wasn't far from the truth.

In the mid-1960s, we were handling fewer than 400,000 disability claims a year; by the end of 1973, more than two million disabled workers were receiving benefits annually. From a staff of 278 in 1970, our corps of hearing examiners had grown to well over 500 by the end of 1975[25]—most of whose time is spent handling disability appeals. In mid-1971, our median processing time from request for a hearing to decision was 118 days; by mid-1975, it had risen to 217 days.[26] Why? Because requests for hearings in that period increased 300% but hearing officers and support staff increased only 200%.[27] The program's rampant growth and the resulting backlog have so alarmed and frustrated various constituencies, including Congress, that we have been the object of numerous hearings and studies to examine and suggest improvements for the program's administration.

---

20. The story here takes its facts from the Petition for Certioriari, the Government's original and Supplemental/Reply Briefs and, occasionally, from DIXON, supra note 17, which was cited in the Government's brief. The tone, however, differs significantly from the briefs filed by the Solicitor General on behalf of the Government; rather, the tone here owes far more to the picture of the agency that emerges from the work of Robert Dixon and from the study by Jerry Mashaw, Charles Goetz, Frank Goodman, et al., SOCIAL SECURITY HEARINGS AND APPEALS: A STUDY OF THE SOCIAL SECURITY ADMINISTRATION HEARING SYSTEM (1978)[hereinafter MASHAW, GOETZ, GOODMAN, ET AL.] This study, commissioned by the Bureau of Hearings and Appeals of SSA at the request of the Subcommittee on Social Security of the House Ways and Means Committee, was getting under way just at the time *Mathews* was being decided.

21. MASHAW, GOETZ, GOODMAN, ET AL., supra note 20, at xi.

22. Id. at 1.

23. ROBERT G. DIXON, JR., THE SOCIAL SECURITY DISABILITY SYSTEM: A SYSTEM IN CRISIS (ACUS 1971).

24. Id. at vi.

25. See DIXON, supra note 17, at 4; Government's Brief at 22 fn. 23 & Supplemental/Reply Brief at 18 fn. 9.

26. MASHAW, GOETZ, GOODMAN, ET AL., supra note 20, at 1.

27. Id. BHA's budget grew from $21.8 million in 1970 to $43 million in 1974; staff in the same period grew from 1278 employees to 2044 employees. Government's Brief at 49 fn. 56.

If SSA were required to offer a hearing prior to benefit termination to all who request it, the results would be devastating. We presently terminate the benefits of approximately 33,600 disability claimants annually because their disabilities are determined to have ceased. Of these, fewer than 1900 now proceed to a post-termination hearing.[28] Yet even with this relatively small percentage of total terminations seeking hearings, we currently have a 10–11 month backlog for hearing requests. Our efforts to increase the number of hearings officers have been hampered by difficulty in finding sufficient qualified candidates who meet the Civil Service requirements. Adding a hearing requirement prior to all terminations would overwhelm existing personnel and further erode effective administration of the program. Moreover, because the procedures now used in the disability program are similar to those used in other programs administered by SSA, including old age and survivors insurance benefits, a holding that pretermination hearings are required here would likely be extended to these other areas.

Then there is the cost of continuing to pay benefits while the hearing is pending. The Social Security trust fund already faces an actuarial deficiency that is being worsened by the economic situation. Prolonged unemployment resulting from the current period of inflation has produced both increased claims for benefits and decreased revenues from payroll taxes.[29] Indeed, a recent Congressional study expressed concern that any further enlargement of Social Security responsibilities may be "the straw that breaks the camel's back."[30] If pretermination hearings are required, benefits will have to be paid during the entire backlog period and, inevitably, many of these payments will turn out to have been unjustified. Yet these losses will be largely unrecoupable. 42 U.S.C. § 404(b) prohibits us from recouping overpayments if the recipient is "without fault" and recovery "would be against equity and good conscience." In many cases, beneficiaries will meet this standard. Even when they don't, recoupment is unlikely as a practical matter. Most terminated beneficiaries will not be receiving other payments that we could withhold; for those who don't voluntarily return overpayments, the only alternative is legal action likely to cost more than it would be worth.

---

28. These figures are adjusted down significantly from those in the Petition for Certiorari. Compare id. at 8 with Government's Brief at 11A and Supplemental/Reply brief at 14 fn. 7.

29. Government's Brief at 53. In the three calendar years proceeding the *Mathews* decision, inflation as measured by the CPI rose 6.2%, 11% and 9.1% respectively. Bureau of Labor Statistics available at ftp://ftp.bls.gov/pub/special.requests/cpi/cpiai.txt. The national unemployment rates for those years were 4.9%, 5.6%, and 8.9% respectively. Bureau of Labor Statistics available at http://www.bls.gov/cps/cpsaat1.pdf.

30. Government's Brief at 55. See Cong. Staff Report, supra note 13, at 9.

Thus the likely result is large losses that will further compromise the trust fund.

It is important to remember that we are not dealing here with government action that finally deprives a person of a property interest, but rather only with a *provisional* determination. This determination is subject to de novo review and, if appropriate, retroactive correction after a full evidentiary hearing. Equally important, the procedures for making the preliminary determination already include the elements that Judge Friendly, in a recent article, has identified as essential to a "fair hearing."[31] The claimant gets notice of the action taken and the grounds asserted for it. He gets an opportunity to present reasons why the action should not be taken. He is entitled to know the evidentiary basis for the action, to present additional evidence, and to have the termination decision based only on the evidence in the file. He has a right to be represented by counsel if he chooses. The decision is made by an unbiased tribunal, which gives a statement of its reasons. In sum, a great deal of process already precedes even the provisional decision that the disability has terminated, and in no way can those procedures be said to be fundamentally unfair. We continue to review the accuracy of our program administration and to experiment with ways to improve the quality and speed of decisionmaking.[32]

As Judge Friendly has aptly observed, "It should be realized that procedural requirements entail the expenditure of limited resources, that at some point the benefit to individuals from an additional safeguard is substantially outweighed by the cost of providing such protection, and that the expense of protecting those likely to be found undeserving will probably come out of the pockets of the deserving."[33]

B.   The Calculus

Mathews is now famous (perhaps, infamous) for specifying the multi-part calculus that, in modern procedural due process analysis, determines what process is due. A court is to consider

> first, the private interest that will be affected by the official action; second, the risk of an erroneous deprivation of such interest through the procedures used, and the probable value, if any, of additional or substitute procedural safeguards; and finally, the Government's interest, including the function involved and the fiscal and adminis-

31.   See Henry Friendly, *Some Kind of Hearing*, 123 U. PA.L.REV. 1267, 1279–1295 (1975), cited in Government's Supplemental/Reply Brief at 11–12.

32.   See DIXON, supra note 17, passim.

33.   Friendly, supra note 31 at 1276, quoted in Government's Supplemental/ Reply Brief at 19–20.

trative burdens that the additional or substitute procedural requisites would entail.[34]

"First, The Private Interest That Will Be Affected by the Official Action"

Under 42 U.S.C. § 423(a), a disability claimant whose benefits are being terminated is entitled to two months of benefits from the time that the disability has ceased. In theory, this eases the transition back to the working world. In fact, according to the government, in about half the terminations, this time has already expired when the claimant learns that the agency believes his disability has ceased, so benefits stop immediately. At this point, the claimant can request reconsideration by the state agency (with internal review by BHA). This process takes 2–4 months from receipt of the claimant's request. Assuming the decision is still negative, the claimant can then request a de novo evidentiary hearing at BHA. Decision comes 10–11 months later.[35]

Hence, if the claimant acts *immediately* to request reconsideration on receiving the initial notice, and again *immediately* to request a hearing on being denied reconsideration, he would still experience 9–15 months without benefits, assuming eventual success at the hearing. What is the private interest in avoiding this interim deprivation?

Social Security Administration[36]

Disability benefits are significantly different than the welfare benefits involved in *Goldberg v. Kelly*. The disability program is neither designed nor operated to take account of recipient need. Congress made a deliberate choice to structure it as an insurance program—triggered by meeting the statutory conditions of a specified minimum payroll contribution plus disability—not a welfare program. Hence, workers or their families may have assets or other sources of income that do not affect their receipt of disability benefits, and that will be available if benefits are terminated during the pendency of a hearing.[37] If they do not have other assets, then the welfare system should come into play.

---

34. Mathews v. Eldridge, 424 U.S. 319, 335 (1976).

35. All the figures in this paragraph come from the Government's Brief at 29–30.

36. This argument was made in the Government's Brief at 37–39 and Supplemental/Reply Brief at 16–17.

37. The Government did admit that the statute explicitly provides for a partial offset of any workers compensation benefits received, see 42 U.S.C. § 424a—although its suggestion that workers' resources could include "private insurance" (see Government's Brief p. 18) failed to point out that the pages of the Staff Report it cited for this proposition were in fact expressing concern that private disability insurance contracts typically provide for an offset of statutory disability benefits.

Eldridge's Lawyer[38]

SSA argues that disability benefits are unrelated to need. A widower shown to be twice totally and permanently disabled, and with dependent children, could hardly be in more need. The agency urges that a worker should avail himself to welfare benefits if he is truly needy. It is submitted that one should not force himself to indigency due to the procedures selected by the Secretary, which procedures he has twice found to be unreliable.

AFC-CIO, Amicus Curiae[39]

Workers who do the hard and dirty jobs, and who are typically among the lowest paid, are most likely to draw upon the Social Security disability system. To be sure, because Congress chose to preserve "the self reliance, the dignity and the self-respect of disabled workers,"[40] it did not establish a financial needs test for benefits. But "the ... system is structured to provide benefits in part according to presumed need."[41] SSA's own data support this presumption. The government's most accurate, complete and recent statistics "indicate that the mean income of the family unit of a disabled worked was $3,803.00. The median income for a similar grouping was $2,836.00."[42] At the time, the official government poverty line was an income of $3,223 a year. According to the same data, the median liquid assets of disabled workers' family units was $940. Given the statutory mandatory 5-month waiting period for receipt of benefits, it is all but inconceivable that the typical recipient would have enough assets to last through the 12–15 month period during which he must wait for a post-termination evidentiary hearing.

It is simply not true that a recipient terminated from the program will be able reliably to obtain support through welfare programs. The welfare system for the disabled (Supplemental Security Income) employs the identical definition of "disability," so terminated disability recipients are automatically barred from that program. Locally operated and financed welfare programs ("general assistance" or "poor relief") do not exist in many areas and, where they are present, they rarely provide

---

38. The language here is taken almost directly from Respondent's Brief at 6–7.

39. "The individual members of the AFL-CIO constitute the largest single class of beneficiaries of the Social Security disability system." AFL-CIO Statement of Interest, Brief at 2. The union appeared as amicus on behalf of the claimants in this and the companion class action case, Green v. Weinberger. The account here follows the argument, and draws heavily on the phrasing, of the union's brief in the Supreme Court.

40. H.R. Rep. No. 1189, 84th Cong., 1st Sess, 4–5 (1955), quoted in AFL-CIO Brief at 14.

41. Weinberger v. Wiesenfeld, 420 U.S. 636 (1975), quoted in AFL-CIO Brief at 14.

42. Letter from Office of the Gen. Counsel, Dep't of Health, Educ. & Welfare., Mar. 7, 1975, AFL-CIO Brief at App. 5a–6a.

even a bare subsistence level of support. See President's Comm. on Income Maintenance Programs, Background Papers, 279 (1969) (average payment of such programs is $11.00/week)[43]

The General Accounting Office[44]

We conducted a statistical sampling of individuals who were denied disability benefits from 1967–1971 to see what happened to those individuals. One of the several notable areas of concern that have surfaced from our review is the following: Many people denied disability benefits are still earning little or no income. About 50% of the people in our sample were earning $1,680 a year or less. Another 10% were earning between $1680 and $2400 a year.[45]

The Solicitor General[46]

All that's at stake here is the loss of the use of the money. These people do have alternative welfare systems or alternate forms of income, and they recapture retroactive benefits at the end of the hearing if they are found still disabled. We can calculate, from the total benefits awarded during 1973, that the average monthly benefit per claimant in this period was $184. So, at 8% interest on that stream of monthly benefits, about $147 per worker was lost from the delay.[47]

Mashaw, Goetz, Goodman, et al.—Consultants in a Study Commissioned by SSA[48]

If the claimant were able to borrow, the loss of the use of the money during the period in which the claim is pending could be compensated simply by including interest in the award of retroactive benefits. It seems unlikely, however, that disability claimants are able to borrow

---

43. Cited at AFL-CIO Brief at 17.

44. The General Accounting Office provides research and assessment of government programs to Congress. The information in this paragraph comes from a response to a question posed by the House Committee on Ways and Means. See CONG. STAFF REPORT, supra note 13, at 439–40.

45. These results were consistent with an earlier study conducted by SSA itself. See Phoebe H. Goff, The Post-Denial Experience of Disability Insurance Applicants, 1957–62 at 55–56 (Dep't of Health, Educ. & Welfare, SSA, Off. of Research & Statistics, Sept. 1970) (of a random sample of applicants 5 years after denial, 2/3s had no work in any year; fewer than 20% averaged $1200 in earnings in any year; only 10% averaged $3000 in earnings in any year.) In 1962, the poverty line for an individual was $1519. (See http://www.census.gov/hhes/poverty/histpov/hstpov1.html.).

46. This account of the individual interest at stake comes not from the Government's Brief, but rather from the oral argument of Solicitor General Robert Bork, who offered it much as phrased here. See Tr. of Oral Arg. 7, 21–23.

47. The Solicitor General used 11 months of delay, apparently failing to add the 2–4 months of delay attributable to the mandatory reconsideration period. Hence, his calculation should be adjusted upward by approximately $25–$50.

48. See note 20 supra. This account comes from MASHAW, GOETZ, GOODMAN, ET AL., supra note 20, at 29–31.

against the contingency of a successful claim, or indeed against any other security. Accordingly, the loss is a function of the individual claimant's personal discount rate (i.e., how valuable it is for the particular individual to have the money now rather than later). If disability claimants are poor—as is generally the case—they will have a high discount rate and consequently suffer great damage from delay. Also, uncertainty about whether the claim will ultimately be allowed appears likely to impose high psychic costs on disability claimants, who often have severe emotional problems and lack the capacity to adapt to unusual or difficult situations. These costs would be very difficult to monetize accurately.

Moreover, although in theory the claimant should be proceeding to attempt to acquire new skills, seek information about alternative employment and/or get additional treatment while awaiting hearing, in fact it is unlikely that claimants will be in a position, psychologically, to take new initiatives in terms of rehabilitation or employment until an authoritative determination of their case. Delay, therefore may have serious consequences.

"Second, the Risk of an Erroneous Deprivation of Such Interest Through the Procedures Used . . ."

The following data were derived from SSA's answers to interrogatories in a companion case and, for K, from the Government's brief:[49]

	Stage reached	Number	Percent of "A"
A.	Initial determination disability had ceased	33,595	100%
B.	Adverse initial determination accepted w/o challenge	24,843	73.9%
C.	Requests for reconsideration	8,752	26.1%
D.	Reconsiderations favorable to worker	2,987	8.9% (34.1% of C)
E.	Reconsiderations unfavorable to worker	5,765	17.2% (65.9% of C)
F.	Adverse reconsiderations accepted w/o challenge	3,887	11.6% (67.4% of E)
G.	Requests for evidentiary hearing	1,878	5.6% (32.6% of E)
H.	ALJ decisions favorable to worker	1,101	3.3% (58.6% of G)
I.	ALJ decisions unfavorable to worker	777	2.3% (41.4% of G)
J.	Total adverse initial determinations subsequently reversed at administrative level(D plus H)	4,088	12.2% (46.7% of C)
K.	Appeals Council reversals of ALJ decisions unfavorable to worker (I)	[93]	0.28% [12% of I]

---

49. See Government's Supplemental/Reply Brief at 14 fn. 7; Government's Brief at 31.

What *is* the relevant risk of error?

Eldridge's Lawyer[50]

George Eldridge's own case shows and emphasizes the unreliability of the SSA's termination procedures. Twice he was denied benefits, or his benefits were terminated, and twice did evidentiary hearings reveal this decision to be inaccurate. It may be true that "he who giveth may taketh away," but the taking should be done only after the beneficiary has been afforded an opportunity for an evidentiary hearing of equal status as the two prior hearings at which his benefits were awarded.

The Government, in its Brief[51]

The crucial error rate is the overall error rate for all denials of benefits, which this Court has previously recognized as an important part of a "complete assessment" of a system of procedure.[52] That rate is only 12.2 percent, and is the best measure of the fairness and reliability of the initial determination process. Indeed, in many of these cases, the different ultimate result reflects either (1) merely different judgments, made in the subsequent de novo administrative review, about the effect of physical limitations or discomfort on ability to work in borderline cases; or (2) the submission of new evidence, which the claimant is permitted to do. Therefore, many of these should not be regarded as "reversals" in the usual sense.

Even a high reversal rate would not imply that the existing procedures lack fundamental fairness. But this is not an unreasonably high rate of error.

---

50. This account follows the relatively brief argumentation, and adopts much of the phrasing, of Respondent's Brief.

51. This account comes principally from the Government's Supplemental/Reply Brief, although the non-numerical parts of the argument are developed in the initial Brief as well. In its initial Brief, the Government argued an overall error rate of 15%, using inaccurate data that it derived by misreading charts in the CONG. STAFF REPORT. See Brief at 43 (citing CONG. STAFF REPORT data on initial applications; data on continuing disability cases is listed in the cited charts as "Not available"). The Supplemental/Reply Brief uses data from SSA's interrogatories—which in fact yields the lower overall error rate of 12.2%—with no mention of the conflicting data or acknowledgment of the earlier error.

52. Government's Supplemental/Reply Brief at 14, quoting Fusari v. Steinberg, 419 U.S. 379, 383 n. 6 (1975), which remanded a case challenging termination of unemployment benefits without a prior evidentiary hearing for reconsideration in light of intervening changes in relevant law.

The AFL-CIO[53]

The present procedures are less accurate than flipping a coin: In 1973, 58.6% of appealed decisions were reversed when an evidentiary hearing was held.[54] (In fact, the "reformed" procedures, which led the Supreme Court to stay its hand in *Richardson*, actually have a higher error rate than those previously in effect!) This reversal rate is higher than those produced by the procedures found unconstitutional in *Goldberg v. Kelly* (36%). Recently the Court, in remanding a case challenging the procedures for terminating unemployment benefits, characterized a reversal rate ranging from 19.4% to 26.1% as "significant."[55] These figures, which the Court described as the "the reversal rate of appealed denials," were seen as the measure of the system's reliability.[56] This is the sensible measure to use rather than a figure that includes the vast percentage (almost 3/4) of termination decisions that are not appealed. Those decisions are simply not germane to the present inquiry. The relevant question is whether workers who *request* an evidentiary hearing are to be granted one before their benefits are cut off. Therefore the only relevant benchmark is the percentage of workers who currently prevail in an evidentiary hearing.

If the high reversal rate at hearing were attributable to the claimant's ability to place new evidence in his file and the fact that this is de novo review, then we would expect to see a comparable rate of reversal at the next stage: appeals to the Appeals Council—for, as the Govern-

---

53. This account follows the argument at pp. 7–10 of the AFL-CIO's Brief.

54. As the AFL-CIO pointed out, the Government did not reveal this particular reversal rate in any of its filings. It emerged only when the Union submitted the Answers to Interrogatories as an Appendix to its amicus brief. Then, the Government as part of its Supplemental/Reply Brief compiled the table that appears after note 49.

55. Fusari v. Steinberg, 419 U.S. at 383.

56. Id. The *Fusari* opinion could be said to encourage both the Government and the AFL-CIO in their view of the relevant error rate. What the Court actually said was:

The District Court's findings of fact provide some indication of the actual operation of the Connecticut system. The findings reveal that the reversal rate of appealed denials of benefits was significant, ranging from 19.4% to 26.1% during the periods surveyed. [footnote]

[text of footnote:] During the period July 1971 to June 1972, there were 6,534 appealed denials, of which 26.1% were reversed. The reversal rate for July to October 1972 remained at approximately 26%, but fell to 19.4% during the three-month period from January to March 1973. The director of the Waterbury office testified that the reversal rate had fallen to 18.8% by May 1973.

A more complete assessment of the operation of the Connecticut system might be obtained by attempting to determine the overall error rate for all denials of benefits. The District Court made no finding on this point.

Id. & n. 6. (citations omitted)

ment's Brief explains, at this stage as well, the decisionmaker "may review the record de novo and may receive additional evidence." Here, however, the reversal rate is only about 12%, which is considerably different than the 58.6% at the trial stage. The difference in the two rates simply confirms a central proposition of Anglo-American jurisprudence: An evidentiary hearing is more likely than the available alternatives to produce a determination of contested fact issues that will stand up on review.

Moreover, the Court has also said that "the rapidity of administrative review is a significant factor in assessing the sufficiency of the entire process," and has characterized a system which produced a 126-day delay as "torpid."[57] Disabled workers must wait 12–15 months for an evidentiary hearing during which they receive no benefits even though, if they are among the over half who are wrongfully cut off, they are so disabled as to be unable "to engage in any substantial gainful activity." 42 U.S.C. § 423(d)(1)(A).

Mashaw, Goetz, Goodman, et al. Consultants in a Study Commissioned by SSA[58]

It has become common to attribute much of the variance between the state agency determination and the hearing outcome to differences in the record from the open-file concept and to progressive worsening of the claimant's condition. However, a recent study by SSA itself casts some doubt on the importance of those factors in explaining the high reversal rate at hearing.

Alternatively, if one assumes that the cases appealed to hearing are the borderline cases, then a reversal rate close to 50% on de novo review would be expected. By hypothesis, these are cases that could reasonably go either way, and such a reversal rate would not indict the process as grossly inaccurate. Surprisingly, however, our study did not support the conventional wisdom that the group of appealed cases typically comprised the "close" cases.

Therefore, the critical fact in evaluating the meaning of the reversal rate at hearing remains unknown: What are the characteristics of the denied claims that are *not* appealed? If the medical and vocational characteristics of those who do not appeal are similar to those who do, then—given the medical and vocational difficulties of most claimants—it would be extremely difficult to rationalize the current system by arguing

---

57.   AFL-CIO Brief at 8, quoting Fusari, 419 U.S. at 386.

58.   The content here comes from MASHAW, GOETZ, GOODMAN, ET AL., supra note 20, at 18–20.

that the failure to request a hearing represents claimant self-selection and presumed satisfaction with the denial.

The Solicitor General in Oral Argument[59]

I've been looking at the briefs, and I think they're all unrealistic about what the relevant error rate is, including our own (i.e., the Government's). Really we should be looking at the reconsideration stage, because the worker can get reconsideration quickly and any impact he might feel to that stage is almost de minimis. Also, reconsideration is the same kind of paper record determination that occurs at the initial determination stage. So, the relevant reversal rate is the one from there, to the oral hearing. That reversal rate—1101 workers who succeeded at the oral hearing, having lost at the initial stage—out of about 35,000 [sic] terminations decisions is 3.5%. So we have an oral hearing that cured mistakes at a 3.5% reversal rate. And, if you measure that against all determinations concerning disability made in the system that year— about 150,000—you get a harmful error rate of only seven-tenths of one percent!

Now, it would be nice to say, I suppose, that the system must be perfect. But I don't think any legal process or any chemical process or any industrial process ever can afford to remove the last bit of impurities in that process.

The Nagi Study[60]

A Type 1 error occurs when a true hypothesis is rejected—here, when a disabled applicant is denied benefits. A Type 2 error occurs when a false hypothesis is accepted—here, when someone not meeting the statutory definition is granted benefits. It is not at all obvious that the two types of errors should be regarded as equally problematic. For example, the criminal law is deliberately designed to minimize Type 1 error—i.e., the error of rejecting true innocence. The reason is that the individual is seen as weak and defenseless relative to society, and therefore less able to sustain the consequences of an erroneous decision. By contrast the rule in medicine, although less explicit and more flexible, is "When in doubt, continue to suspect illness." Doctors are trained to prefer Type 2 errors, because rejecting the hypothesis of pathology when

---

59. If you believe that I have taken artistic license in constructing this account, I invite you to look at the transcript of oral argument, pp. 19–20.

60. A landmark assessment of the disability program, the Nagi study took nearly 2500 disability cases that had been processed through the initial determination by the state agency in Louisiana, Minnesota and Ohio, and had them reassessed for ability to work by specially trained clinical teams comprised of medical, psychological, social service and vocational personnel. See SAAD Z. NAGI, DISABILITY AND REHABILITATION: LEGAL, CLINICAL AND SELF-CONCEPTS AND MEASUREMENT, 162, 51(1969). See also BUREAUCRATIC JUSTICE, supra note 12, at 132. The study is discussed in the CONG. STAFF REPORT, supra note 13, at 356.

present can be dangerous to the patient and, in the case of communicable diseases, to others.

How one ought to view these two sorts of errors in disability decisions raises many important questions. Consciousness of public funds and taxpayers money tend to influence decisions more toward Type 1 errors: denial of benefits when in doubt. Moreover, resolving doubts in favor of a conclusion of disability may cause individuals to assess their own medical situation as more hopeless than it is in fact, inducing unwarranted illness behavior. On the other hand, it is much more difficult for an individual, as compared with society, to sustain the economic consequences of an erroneous decision. This suggests a preference for Type 2 errors. And, Type 2 errors can be corrected through the self-correcting administrative mechanisms already in place in the disability system, while Type 1 errors cannot be corrected except through the initiative of the individual applicants. On this latter point, it may be relevant that, by comparison with the general labor force, the sample population of disability recipients was discovered to be considerably older, more than twice as likely to have only an elementary school education (or less), and almost twice as likely to have jobs in the manual labor or service areas (rather than professional, management, technical or clerical areas).[61]

Overall, in about 30% of the sample cases, the clinical team assessment differed from that of the state agency assessment. However, the types of errors were not evenly distributed. The clinical team concluded that the claimant could do at least some work in about 19% of cases where the agency had allowed benefits, but found the claimant unable to work competitively in nearly 48% of cases in which the agency had denied benefits.

Robert Dixon—Consultant for the Administrative Office[62]

No study of the multi-stage disability decisional process—with its high internal and judicial reversal rates—will be meaningful or productive without emphasizing the problem with the statutory standard: Neither the initial legislative definition of disability nor the redefinition in 1967 seems to be administratively manageable. The variables of age, education and previous work experience, when coupled with often-conflicting medical data and uncertainty about the claimant's theoretical ability to downshift to some other line of work theoretically available somewhere in the national economy, simply leave too much room for difference of opinion in similar cases.

---

61. For a sophisticated discussion about error type and its relationship to easy and close cases, see BUREAUCRATIC JUSTICE, supra note 12, at 84–85.

62. DIXON, supra note 17, at 51, 53.

Jerry Mashaw—Distinguished Scholar of the Administrative Process, and SSA in Particular[63]

Establishing an instrumentally rational administrative process for resolving disability claims is rendered extremely difficult by two characteristics of the program. First, the line that Congress drew between the ability-disability continuum when establishing the eligibility standard cannot be precisely located. Hence, it is hard to say with confidence that any particular decision is a correct application of the statute. Second, the factual contexts presented to decisionmakers for resolution are inherently uncertain. The needed medical evidence is often fragmentary, it frequently involves highly subjective judgment, it always calls for predicting the future on the basis of the past, and it typically depends substantially on abstractions such as motivation, tolerance for pain and energy levels.

Even though the program's performance has been repeatedly studied since 1060 and repeatedly criticized for inconsistent treatment of like cases by different state agencies, for high reversal rates at hearing and on judicial review, and for decisional delay—remedies haven't been found because there is still not a workable definition of accuracy in this context. If state agencies in Arkansas and New York produce different results in analogous cases, SSA can't simply tell them to be consistent without first determining who is right (if anybody is). Without a similar determination, it cannot assess the significance of the high rate at which ALJs reverse at hearing. Finally, without a reasonably objective definition of accuracy, it cannot convincingly answer those critics who assert that the current decisional process disadvantages women, minorities and claimants of modest intelligence and education.

"... And The Probable Value, If Any, of Additional or Substitute Procedural Safeguards"[64]

Robert Dixon—Consultant for the Administrative Office[65]

The disability program is a high-volume decisional program in which the policies being administered and the decisional standards that can be articulated are sufficiently amorphous in relation to the myriad fact situations presented that borderline determinations and reasonable differences of opinion will be frequent. Because of this, it is important to

---

63. BUREAUCRATIC JUSTICE, supra note 12, at 52, 61–63, 195.

64. Although the Court's opinion presents this as another aspect of the second factor in the calculus, the parties treated it as distinct from their accounts of the risk of error in current procedures.

65. DIXON, supra note 17, at 30, 37, 135, 141.

reach finality of decision at as low a level in the claim processing procedure as possible.

Face-to-face contact should be a precondition to reaching such finality. Until the claimant actually appears in person, there is likely to be no single, connected account of the claimant's difficulties in the file. The record will contain much discrete information, but no written narrative account from the claimant's point of view, of his or her situation—for claimants normally do not avail themselves of their right to file written statements. Face-to-face contact with the decisionmaker enriches the record, particular in borderline cases (of which there are many). In such cases, psychological problems are often intertwined with physical problems, and personal contact is helpful in identifying this, and in suggesting the need for psychiatric examination. Also, face-to-face contact enhances the claimant's feeling that he has been dealt with fairly.[66]

Eldridge's Lawyer[67]

An evidentiary hearing where the claimant makes an appearance gives the decisionmaker the opportunity to actually view the claimant and witness his condition, whether it be physical or mental, and allow the claimant an opportunity to present his side of the case. George Eldridge is proof that written doctors' reports and other evidence in a "cold record" do not inevitably suffice to reveal the disabilities of a claimant.

The Government[68]

Decisions that disability has terminated rely heavily on what the Supreme Court has recognized as "routine, standard and unbiased medical reports by physical specialists concerning a subject whom they have examined."[69] We don't say that credibility and veracity of doctors

---

66. In the Supreme Court, the Government argued that beneficiaries could appear before the state agency responsible for the initial recommendation of non-disability. E.g., Brief at 28. This was, at a minimum, misleading. All the contemporary studies of the disability decisional system—including an experimental program SSA itself conducted with 5 state agencies in 1971—focused on the value and feasibility of inserting face-to-face interviews into the process earlier than the BHA hearing. See Cong. Staff Report, supra note 13, at 240. Obviously, the focus of concern would have been quite different if a robust practice of face-to-face interviews at the state agency level already existed. A more accurate statement was buried in a footnote in the appendix to the Government's brief: "The state agencies generally do not interview the worker. They are not barred from doing so, however, if the worker were to so request and to go to the state agency office."

67. See Respondent's Brief at 8–9.

68. This account is taken from the Government's Brief at 40–41, the Supplemental/Reply Brief at 13 and the Solicitor General's oral argument, see Tr. at 18.

69. Government's Brief at 40–41, citing Richardson v. Perales, 402 U.S. 389, 404 (1971).

can never be in issue, but procedural rules are designed for the average case, not the rare exception.

Mr. Eldridge's principal objection is that he is not entitled to appear personally before the person responsible for deciding whether he is still disabled before his benefits are provisionally terminated. However, the "subjective" evidence that a personal appearance would principally serve to provide cannot by itself be the basis of a determination of disability. 42 U.S. C § 423(d)(2)(A) requires a finding of disability to be supported by "medically acceptable" evidence. A beneficiary's descriptions of his ailments may have probative value, but if there is no medically acceptable evidence of disability, an oral presentation serves no purpose whatsoever. Medical condition is not an issue that an ALJ gets a great deal of information about by looking at a man in a room. Indeed, the decision *cannot* rest on the ALJ's "look" at the man and "feeling" about his condition; it has to rest on medical evidence.

Jerry Mashaw—Distinguished Scholar of the Administrative Process, and SSA in Particular[70]

The current disability decisional process tends toward underdevelopment of subjective evidence in favor of objective evidence. But this risks confusing objectivity with reality. A fetish for objectivity may have unfortunate effects on the quality of outcomes.

Medical diagnostic evidence consists of more than just "objective" scientific data such as EKG charts and blood chemistry analyses; it consists as well of interpretations of these data. Much clinical evidence consists only of visual, verbal and/or manual observations. Evaluation of these medical indicators involves professional judgment and is often heavily influenced by numerous subjective factors that are both implicit and difficult to evaluate. Similarly, the crucial evidence in disability cases is usually functional capacity—i.e., not what the claimant has, but rather how well he can function given what he has. Direct evidence on the point—if there is any—usually comes from the claimant himself, from friend or relatives, or from the claimant's treating physician. Or it may be supplied by the SSA staff physician based on evaluation of the medical evidence in the record (i.e., without seeing the claimant) or, less frequently, actual examination of the claimant. Again, this "evidence" is merely a judgment and is highly colored by subjective factors.

One of the most important strategies for countering this tendency to ignore subjective evidence is to make the claimants real to decisionmakers by forcing them to talk to the claimants and to treat them as important sources of information. If seeing the claimant tends to increase the number of claims granted, this does not necessarily imply a

---

70. See BUREAUCRATIC JUSTICE, supra note 12, at 128–32, 62, 198–9.

loss of appropriate objectivity. The result could occur in part from a change in the perspective the decisionmaker brings to interpreting the written material in the file. In part, it could occur from the decisionmaker's decision to order additional examinations and similar objective evidence in cases that seemed stronger than the current state of the file suggested.

Finally, the Government's Interest, Including the Function Involved and the Fiscal and Administrative Burdens That the Additional or Substitute Procedural Requisites Would Entail.

Social Security Administration[71]

We estimate a cost of roughly $25 million to provide pre-termination hearings, an estimate comprised of unrecoupable benefit overpayments plus costs of providing the hearings themselves. Here are the calculations:

For 1976, we expect to make 44,000 initial determinations that disability has terminated. Under current procedures, reconsideration is requested in 25% of cases. Therefore, assume 11,000 requests for pre-termination hearings. Apply to those 11,000 requests the historical rates of reversal at both reconsideration, and then (of a much smaller number of cases) at BHA hearing. The cases that are left represent cases in which continued payment of benefits will ultimately be determined to be unjustified. Based on our experience that the 2-month statutory grace period has already expired in half of all cases by the time of the initial determination, 50% of these cases will represent overpayments for every month following the initial determination, while the remaining 50% will represent overpayments beginning the second month after the initial determination.

To calculate the total cost of these overpayments, we have to make assumptions about recoupment. This is necessarily somewhat speculative, based both on the statutory defense of good faith and practical concerns of judgment-proofness. However, from past experience we believe that assuming a recoupment rate exceeding 33% would be unrealistic. Applying all these figures to the current average monthly benefit of $335 produces a cost of about $10 million for the first month following initial determination and $1.5 million for each subsequent month. Because the current delay from request for hearing to decision after hearing is 10 months, the cost of overpayments alone could amount to $23.5 million annually. This does not take into account any increase in the percentage of requests for hearing that might be produced by claimants knowing that benefits will continue while their request is pending.

---

71. This story is detailed in Appendix C of the Government's Brief.

The additional costs of providing the hearings themselves depends on a number of factors. If provided at BHA, the average cost of an ALJ hearing is currently $536. Thus 11,000 hearings would cost $6 million annually. If provided at the state level, the cost is estimated at $150–$200 per hearing, although this does not include the costs of training personnel to a totally new system. If all current post-termination hearings (i.e. 1900) and requests for reconsideration were eliminated and these costs are deducted, the net cost would be $1.3 million (using the $200 state cost) to $4 million (using the $500 ALJ cost).

Jerry Mashaw, Distinguished Scholar of the Administrative Process, and SSA in Particular[72]

Administrative costs seem the least problematic because they are measurable and can be expressed in monetary terms. But they can cause serious problems because they can so readily be shifted and traded against costs that are not readily monetizable. For example, costs are shifted to private parties when they (or their representatives) are forced to substitute their efforts for those of the agency in obtaining, organizing or presenting evidence. Or, costs may be shifted from the agency to society through a reduction in the accuracy, fairness or speed of the administrative decision process. These shifts may be efficient or inefficient—but the problem is that the shift is likely to avoid appraisal. The transferred administrative costs will not appear in the public expenditure budget. Moreover, some of the trade-offs (as, for example, increased delay costs to claimants, or the value of a process perceived as fair) are hard fully to monetize.

The Solicitor General[73]

In 1973, 1100 workers won reversal at the hearing which—given my previous calculation of loss of the use of the money at $147 per worker[74] —works out to a total loss of $162,000. Now, you have to measure that against the cost to the government, because we are, in effect, dealing here with a cost-benefit judgment. A conservative estimate of that loss is $20 million. That's a trade-off in costs, from government to individual, of 122 to 1.

Due process terms is an intensely practical subject and it doesn't make a great deal of sense to spend $122 which could have gone to other recipients to save $1.00 to the occasional deserving beneficiary.

---

72. See BUREAUCRATIC JUSTICE, supra note 12, at 98–99.

73. Once again, what follows comes, almost verbatim, from the oral argument. See Tr. at 22–23.

74. See text at note 47 supra.

The Supreme Court in *Bell v. Burson*[75]

"A prior hearing always imposes some costs in time, effort, and expense, and it is often more efficient to dispense with the opportunity for such a hearing. ... But the Constitution recognizes higher values than speed and efficiency. Indeed, one might fairly say of the Bill of Rights in general, and the Due Process Clause in particular, that they were designed to protect the fragile values of a vulnerable citizenry from the overbearing concern for efficiency and efficacy that may characterize praiseworthy government officials no less, and perhaps more, than mediocre ones."

* * * * *

In *Rashomon*, a samurai, his wife, a bandit, and a poor woodcutter go into the woods. Ultimately, the samurai is dead, the wife is traumatized, the bandit is tried for murder, and the woodcutter, sheltering from a downpour in the ruins of Rashomon gate with a Buddist priest and a cynical peasant, sets the film in motion when he mutters, "I just don't understand."

The viewer soon shares the woodcutter's perplexment. The bandit's tale is that he cunningly tricked the couple, seduced the wife with his machismo, and killed the samurai in a magnificent duel. The wife's tale is that she was perfidiously raped and abandoned by the bandit, callously rejected by her husband as dishonored, and ultimately responsible for killing him while distraught and disoriented. The samurai's tale—told by his spirit through a medium—is that the bandit fell in love with his wife after raping her but repudiated her when she demanded that the bandit kill him before they could leave together; after being freed by the unexpectedly sympathetic bandit, his only honorable option was suicide. Finally, the woodcutter discloses that he was a witness to the entire incident. As he tells it, the bandit, after raping the wife, proposes to her. She frees her husband, insisting that the men fight over her. The samurai reveals himself to be a coward who refuses to put his life in danger, and offers to give the bandit his wife; the bandit in turn decides he doesn't really want her. Accusing them both of unmanliness, the wife succeeds in provoking a swordfight, but it is a travesty of craven incompetence in which the samurai is finally, clumsily slain by the bandit, who stumbles off into the forest. This, however, is not the story the woodcutter had told at the bandit's trial, and when the cynical commoner finally forces the woodcutter to admit that he stole the wife's dagger from the scene, a further layer of ambiguity is introduced.

---

75. 402 U.S. at 542.

For American director Robert Altman, the multiple stories of *Rashomon* reveal that "it is all true and none of it is true."[76] And indeed, the classic interpretation of the film is that Kurosawa presents a allegory about the nature of reality. As critic James Berardinelli explains:

> All of the narrators in *Rashomon* tell compelling and believable stories, but, for a variety of reasons, each of them must be deemed unreliable. It's impossible to determine to what degree their versions are fabrications, and how many discrepancies are the result of legitimate differences in points-of-view. It's said that four witnesses to an accident will all offer different accounts of the same event, but there are things in *Rashomon* (namely, that each of the three participants names himself or herself as the murderer) that cannot be explained away on this basis. And the impressions of the "impartial" observer [i.e., the woodcutter] further muddy the waters, because, despite his protestations that he doesn't lie, we trust his tale the least.
>
> In the end, we are left recognizing only one thing: that there is no such thing as an objective truth. It is a grail to be sought after, but which will never be found, only approximated.[77]

There is a sense in which the lesson Altman took from *Rashomon* is also the revelation of the many stories of *Mathews v. Eldridge*:

- A system that continued to question George Eldrige's disability was humiliating and alienating; denying him the pre-termination hearing that had always, in his own experience, confirmed his right to the benefits for which he had paid during years of low-wage, physical employment was irrational and cruel.

- The disability program was already strained to the limit from too many claims and too few resources; giving all the George Eldridges in the system evidentiary hearings before benefit suspension would have destroyed it.

- SSA was a responsible agency, carefully studying the problem and creatively experimenting with ways to make the system more efficient and responsive to its client population.

- The Government's factual assertions in the Supreme Court were uninformed and contradictory, and its arguments were extraordinarily callous towards program beneficiaries.

---

76. Catherine Russell, *Men with Swords and Men with Suits: The Cinema of Akira Kurosawa*, 28 CINEASTE 4, 8 (2002).

77. *"Rashomon: A Film Review by James Berardinelli"* in Top All-Time 100, http://movie-reviews.colossus.net/movies/r/rashomon.html (visited Apr. 30, 2005).

- The public expected a compassionate federal disability program that really protected people who could no longer perform their prior jobs because of injury or illness.

- The public would not pay what such a system would cost, especially in a time of rising inflation and unemployment.

- An oral evidentiary hearing would have sorted out whether George Eldridge's benefits ought to continue uninterrupted far more accurately than decision on a written file.

- The statutory condition "disabled" is an amalgam of physical, psychological, educational, occupational, sociological and economic factors so complex that no single type of decisional paradigm can manage it, so the best the system can hope for is consistent (rather than "right") decisions.

- George Eldrige's claim presented an easy case under existing precedent.

- George Eldridge's claim presented an impossible case under existing precedent.

It was all true, and none of it was true.

But the *Mathews* Court did not have the luxury of taking a postmodern stance towards the concept of truth, or engaging in allegorical exploration of the nature of reality. Unless it was prepared to repudiate completely the post-*Goldberg* "new" due process jurisprudence—either by excluding social welfare benefits like disability from the interests protected by the due process clauses, or by considering any process provided by the legislature (or the agency acting as rulemaker) to be the process "due"[78]—it had to make a choice. It had to cast its lot with one, and only one, approximation of "whether the administrative procedures provided here are constitutionally sufficient [in light] of the governmental and private interests that are affected."[79]

The utilitarian calculus it adopted has been condemned from all sides. The traditional due process understanding—that a *pre-deprivation* hearing is required, absent compelling exigent circumstances—embodied the "precept that one should be able to continue living in quiet enjoyment of liberty or property unless and until there had been a fair determination that the state is entitled to intrude upon that situation of repose."[80] Now, "[n]o man's liberty or property are safe when the court simply asks case by case what procedures seem worthwhile and not too

---

78. See, e.g., Frank H. Easterbrook, *Substance and Due Process*, 1982 SUP. C. REV. 85, 112–13.

79. Mathews, 424 U.S. at 334.

80. LAURENCE H. TRIBE, AMERICAN CONSTITUTIONAL LAW 673–74 (2d ed. 1988).

costly."[81] Moreover, the calculus tends, "as cost-benefit analysis often does," to disregard ambiguity and complexity and to undervalue "soft" variables such as the dignitary and legitimation benefits of citizen participation in oral proceedings, and the demoralization costs of the grant-withdrawal cycle George Eldridge experienced.[82] In any event, no matter how broadly formulated, the calculus seems to pose questions (such as the social value and social costs of government income transfers) that are effectively unanswerable.[83] And if anyone were to undertake this sort of social welfare accounting, it certainly oughtn't be the courts. What is the judiciary doing second-guessing the political branches' judgment on such questions? "[P]rocedural rules usually are just a measure of how much the substantive entitlements are worth, of what we are willing to sacrifice to see a given goal attained. [T]herefore, t]he body that creates the substantive rule is the logical judge of how much should be spent to avoid errors in the process of disposing of claims to that right."[84] It's not just a matter of relative institutional competence, although this is a significant objection, but even more fundamentally an issue of institutional usurpation—and, because the 14th as well as the 5th amendment is at stake, of federalism.

The critical chorus is a bit like what might you might hear if you were forced to choose one of the *Rashomon* stories as what *really* happened that day in the woods. When the whole point is that "the truth" doesn't exist, any attempt to insist upon one version will inevitably array all sides against you.

There is, however, another—although decidedly nontraditional—interpretation of *Rashomon*.[85] As the priest, the cynical commoner, and the woodcutter huddle in the rain and ruin, contemplating the ignobility of human nature displayed in each of the stories, they hear the cry of an infant abandoned somewhere near the gate. This is just one more indication of a world dissolving into turmoil and darkness. (An opening text sets the time as "when famines and civil wars had devastated the ancient capital" of Kyoto, and the priest had bemoaned, "Wars earthquakes, great winds, fires, famines, plagues—each new year is full of

---

81. Todd D. Rakoff, Brock v. Roadway Express, Inc., *and the New Law of Regulatory Due Process*, 1987 Sup. Ct. Rev. 157, 162 (hypothesizing the reaction of the "typical American lawyer" to *Mathews*).

82. Jerry L. Mashaw, *The Supreme Court's Due Process Calculus for Administrative Adjudication in* Mathews v. Eldrige: *Three Factors in Search of a Theory of Value*, 44 U.Chi.L.Rev. 28, 48–49 (1976).

83. Id.

84. Easterbrook, supra note 78, at 112–13.

85. See, e.g., Stanley J. Solomon, The Film Idea, http://filmsociety.wellington.net.nz/FilmIdea.html (visited 9/4/2004)(reprinted from program notes issued by the Toronto Film Society).

disaster.'') The commoner rushes off to find the child but only, we discover, to steal the clothes in which the infant is wrapped. (It is when the woodcutter condemns him for this act of barbarism that we learn, in the commoner's sly rejoinder, that the woodcutter is also a thief, having succumbed in his poverty to the temptation of the valuable dagger.) The priest takes the infant and begins to move away, but the woodcutter follows him and offers to take the child. The priest, accepting the commoner's judgment of the woodcutter as equally corrupt, berates him for wanting to steal what little the infant has left. The woodcutter quietly explains, "I have six children of my own; another won't be any more difficult." After a moment, the priest hands over the infant. As the woodcutter walks away with his new child, the sun breaks out, highlighting him and the gate.

Many critics find this "happy ending" at best a problematic non-sequitur and, at worst, a pollyannish sell-out.[86] Another interpretation, however, finds it Kurosawa's answer to the confusion, and the despair in human nature, induced by the stories told by the bandit, the samurai, his wife, and the woodcutter. The final words spoken in the film are the priest's as he hands over the infant to the woodcutter: "I think I will be able to keep my faith in men." Saving a single foundling *seems* pitifully little in the chaos of natural disasters, societal collapse, and individual moral degeneration in which the two men find themselves. Indeed, the act may fail even on its own terms for, despite what woodcutter says, adding another mouth to his brood might spell disaster for all. Yet, this is an act of redemption. The woodcutter lives in an anarchic world, in which the commoner's amoral opportunism is the most rational way to behave; nonetheless, he rises above his own past weakness and does what he can—given what he has, and where he finds himself. This willingness to continue to strive to do what it is possible to do, acknowledging imperfection and despite imperfect understanding, has significance beyond the single act that might, or might not, succeed—a significance registered in the human world by the priest's declaration of renewed faith, and in the larger universe by sunlight breaking through darkness.

Just so, in a concededly nontraditional interpretation of *Mathews*, might we think of the Court's solution. Being forced to specify how the new procedural due process would apply to the gargantuan, and increasingly destabilized, Social Security benefit system must have seemed inevitable jurisprudential disaster. The Court's first reaction was abject, unprincipled retreat.[87] Ultimately, though, it grapples with the immense

---

86. See, e.g., Film Classic: *Rashomon*, http://www.thecityreview.com/rashomon.jhtml (visited Apr.30, 2005).

87. See note 11 supra and accompanying text. *Richardson* was decided by a three-judge court, appeals from which ran directly to the Supreme Court and were not discretionary under the statutes in effect at the time.

problems of the case, and it emerges—not with a legally sophisticated solution (notice the absence, in the analysis section, of any pretense of adequately distinguishing the line of precedent that augured so favorably for Mr. Eldridge's claim to predeprivation oral process), or an analytically powerful solution (notice the inconclusive treatment of individual need and rate of error data in an opinion that had seemed to require each to be decisively determined), but with a solution that has worked for nearly 30 years.

To be sure, "worked" is used here in a very modest sense. This doctrine has not been the constitutional catalyst radically to reform the relationship between the citizen and modern regulatory government. But neither has it brought regulatory government to its knees—and so triggered a political backlash in which social welfare programs were defunded and entitlements dismantled.[88] At a crucial moment, when the emergent new procedural due process jurisprudence was highly vulnerable, the Court chose a restrained, pragmatic solidification. It did what it could—given what it had, and where it found itself.

Easy for us to say that what it did, wasn't much. Hard for us to argue—almost three decades later—that what it did, wasn't enough. With the *Mathews* solution, the government often wins, as it did in the case itself. But the government doesn't *always* win.[89] *Mathews* has given lawyers a structure for telling the story of their clients (and the people like them) in a way that judges can locate, and assess, within the constitutional framework. And so we continue to experience procedural due process as a "real" right: a claim that can be made, with meaning, by a single citizen against even the most powerful agencies. As we enter the 21st century, and all momentum is towards transnationally integrated regulatory policy, and government structures that transcend conventional national boundaries, we start out with at least this.

Perhaps that is not, after all, such a modest accomplishment.

---

88. Even the one, most conspicuous political attempt to do so—the welfare "reform" legislation enacted 20 years after *Mathews*—in the end does not defeat due process protection. See Cynthia R. Farina, *On Misusing "Revolution" and "Reform": Procedural Due Process and the New Welfare Act*, 50 ADMIN. L. REV. 591, 619–23 (1998).

89. See, e.g., Brock v. Roadway Express Inc., 481 U.S. 252 (1987); Cleveland Bd. of Educ. v. Loudermill, 470 U.S. 532 (1985); Santosky v. Kramer, 455 U.S. 745 (1982).

258

Like a number of other essayists in this series, Professor Strauss attempts to see how the course of events leading to decision in Citizens to Preserve Overton Park v. Volpe might have appeared through a number of eyes. The decision in *Overton Park* helped to effect a transition from political to judicial controls over decisions broadly affecting a wide range of community interests. The late sixties and early seventies, as the controversy brewed, saw an explosion of new national legislation on social and environmental issues, that often provided explicitly or implicitly for citizen remedies. In many respects, the case marked the turn to judicial rather than political remedies. It was an example, as well, of the success of highly motivated recent law school graduates in contributing to major developments in national law. If for that reason alone, it is a fitting subject for a collection of essays intended to give students a more concrete sense of their subject.

8

Peter L. Strauss*

Citizens to Preserve Overton Park v. Volpe—Of Politics and Law, Young Lawyers and the Highway Goliath

* Betts Professor of Law, Columbia University. The original version of this essay, which appeared as Peter L. Strauss, *Revisiting Overton Park: Political and Judicial Controls Over Administrative Actions Affecting the Community*, 39 UCLA L. Rev. 1251 (1992), began with this:

> More people provided helpful support than one could normally list here—Memphians such as James Jalenak and Charles Newman, opposing counsel in the Overton Park litigation; Dean Fred Davis and his colleagues at the Cecil B. Humphreys School of Law of Memphis State University; participants in faculty colloquia at Columbia and the University of Minnesota Law Schools; the participants in this Symposium; and individual colleagues and friends like Bernie Black, Cynthia Farina, and Daniel Gifford. Iqbal Ishar, Columbia, LL.M. '87, William Bruce, Memphis State University '94, and the staff of the Memphis and Shelby County and the Memphis State University Libraries provided valuable research support, and the Frank A. Sprole Fund and Columbia Law School Alumni provided welcome financial assistance.

> Responsibility for any errors is, of course, mine. In this essay, in particular, I write with limited access to my research materials. Able to spend only a week in Memphis, I relied on the extensive clippings file and paper collections at the Memphis and Shelby County Library and the Memphis State University Library. Mr. Bruce subsequently went to the microfilm records of the Memphis Commercial Appeal and the Memphis Press-Scimitar to check what was in my notes and provide full citation forms. He was unable to find a few of these citations, as will be evident from the form of citation in some of the footnotes. This may be the result of my error in transcribing or a librarian's error in preparing a clipping for the file. While I am confident of the physical reality of the articles cited, I deeply regret that time has not permitted confirming the precise date and place of their publication.

I have not been able to return to the Memphis materials in revising this essay, but now have also to thank new colleagues Gillian Metzger and John Fabian Witt for their thoughtful readings and suggestions, CPOP attorney John Vardaman for hours of enlightening conversation and permission to cast my eye over his litigation files, and the faculty of the James Rogers School of Law at Arizona University.

Many years later, tired at last
I headed for home to look for my past
I looked for the meadows, there wasn't a trace
six lanes of highway had taken their place
where were the lilacs and all that they meant
nothing but acres of tar and cement . . . .[1]

Citizens to Preserve Overton Park v. Volpe is easily one of the most important cases in the administrative law repertoire, with 4,640 citing opinions listed by Sheppards as of the end of 2004. The great bulk of those citations draw on its elaboration of the scope of review appropriate for agency exercises of judgment. In the instance, as you know, what was at issue was the Secretary of Transportation's judgment that federal funds could be expended to build Interstate 40 through Overton Park, in Memphis, Tennessee, in the face of a pair of federal statutes that seemed severely to burden that judgment in order to protect parkland values. What may not be so readily apparent to you is that the case helps mark a turning point in American administrative law, brought about by a relatively small number of recent law school graduates. Its legal innovations occurred at the hands of lawyers just a few years out of law school, who successfully entered largely uncharted territory *pro bono publico*. It seems at least possible that you would be inspired by such a story.

The burgeoning Interstate Highway system had spawned heartache and controversy across the country, as the lyrics of a 1966 pop song attest. But until the litigation of *Overton Park* and a few other cases that accompanied it, citizens voiced their protests not in the courts but through politics. The beginning of public interest litigation on issues like highway construction or other environmental matters dates from its time. Lexis reveals that during the decade of the 60s, the two long-established national environmental organizations who were among the several named plaintiffs in *Overton Park*, the Sierra Club and the National Audubon Society, were plaintiffs in only one reported decision;[2] that decision was reported in 1969 (the year in which the *Overton Park* complaint was filed) and, as it happens, also concerned an element of the interstate highway system. For the 1970s, a search for these two names returns 149 hits; for the 1980s, 337; for the 1990s, 499; and for the period January 1, 2000 to mid-2004, 297.[3] Something happened.

Overton Park represents a transition from political to judicial controls over decisions broadly affecting a wide range of community inter-

---

1. Verdelle Smith's "Tar and Cement" (1966) climbed as high as 38 in Billboard's ratings, according to http://www.top40db.net/; for one week it was the most popular song in Australia.

2. Citizens Committee for the Hudson Valley v. Volpe, 302 F.Supp. 1083 (S.D.N.Y. 1969); *id.*, 297 F.Supp. 804 and 809.

3. Lexis search of combined federal and state cases for "Name(Sierra Club) or Name(National Audubon Society)" with appropriate date ranges, conducted July 28, 2004.

ests. Unmistakable and dramatic as it is, that transition is not universally applauded. One can easily find in decisions and legal literature today continuing hesitation over how deeply the courts should be engaged in controlling matters susceptible of political resolution—whether the gains in legality are not overmatched by losses to gridlock and inertia, whether the resulting system is not too open to the tactics of obstreperousness and delay. But the transition was striking and quick. The late sixties and early seventies saw an explosion of new national legislation on social and environmental issues, that often provided explicitly or implicitly for citizen remedies. Four scientists founded the Environmental Defense Fund in 1967, as part of their effort to halt the use of the pesticide DDT that devastated raptor populations by weakening their egg shells. In 1968, recent law school graduates founded Washington's Center for Law and Social Policy, a pioneering effort. Law Reports devoted to environmental law began to emerge in 1969,[4] the year the National Environmental Policy Act was enacted. Newly minted lawyers established the Natural Resources Defense Council in 1970. In that year, too, as clinical legal education began, young lawyer-teachers at a Columbia Law School program on law and welfare brought to the Supreme Court—and won—*Goldberg v. Kelly*[5] and *Barlow v. Collins*[6] (one of a pair of cases significantly extending standing doctrine that year). The Sierra Club established its Legal Defense Fund, and Ralph Nader his Public Citizen, in 1971. In many respects, *Overton Park* marked the turn.

Stories are uniquely the product of a narrator's vision. For a case, like this one, that has appeared to different participants in remarkably different ways, what seems appropriate is to attempt to see how the course of events leading to decision in *Overton Park* might have appeared through a number of eyes. After a brief *mis en scene* to set the framework, that is what these pages will do. Of course, you the reader have only one narrator; but he has attempted to people these pages and evoke their varying perspectives as faithfully as his research and capacity for empathetic understanding permit. Much of what follows draws on his earlier essay, *Revisiting Overton Park*, which appeared in the pages of the UCLA Law Review in 1992, and on the sensitive story-setting "reply" contributed by Prof. Lucie White.[7] The release of the papers of

---

4. The *Citizen's Committee* case, n. 2 above, appears in Volume 1 of both the Environmental Law Reports (1 ELR 20001) and BNA's Environment Reporter (1 ERC (BNA) 1096).

5. 397 U.S. 254 (1970).

6. 397 U.S. 159 (1970).

7. Peter L. Strauss, *Revisiting Overton Park: Political and Judicial Controls Over Administrative Actions Affecting the Community*, 39 UCLA L. Rev. 1251 (1992); Lucie E. White, *Revaluing Politics: a Reply to Professor Strauss*, 39 UCLA L. Rev. 1331(1992). The reader is entitled to know that I was an attorney in the Office of the Solicitor General, but

Justices Blackmun, Brennan and Marshall for public view, the availability of transcripts of oral argument in the United States Supreme Court library, and litigation files in the possession of CPOP Attorney John Vardaman, have permitted supplementing the 1992 account.

Overton Park and Interstate 40

In the 1950s, Memphis, Tennessee was a southern city of 450,000 or so, about sixty percent white and forty percent black. Long the center of the cotton trade, it was the largest commercial center on the Mississippi between New Orleans to the south and St. Louis to the north. Its civic leaders supposed it to be in competition with each. If one imagines a boll of cotton oriented east from a Mississippi River stem, the commercial center of town was where the boll joins the stem; the black population lived in the dark casing of the boll, north and south and bending eastward; and the white population lived in the cotton itself.[8] There was no circumferential road system—indeed, no highway system at all—and a single bridge across the Mississippi, a bit to the south of the city center, brought long distance travellers through.

Overton Park is the Central Park of Memphis, a 342-acre city park long considered the city's principal greenspace asset. It is roughly rectangular in shape, approximately a mile long by half a mile wide, with its longer sides pointing east and west. Surrounded by campuses and gracious homes, it lies in the center of the cotton, embedded in a predominantly white residential area. Its eastern boundary is a major north-south connector. At a time when the city was reasonably compact, the two wide boulevards marking the park's northern and southern boundaries were the principal streets carrying traffic between eastern suburbs and downtown. A zoo lies in the western half of the park's northernmost part; the zoo's fenced southern boundary is a long-established, two lane road whose use was restricted to municipal buses. South of the bus road and zoo are a nine-hole golf course, a theater, an art museum, and landscaped open areas. To the east, Lick Creek, a rivulet occasionally swollen by storm run-off, runs north to south. The eastern half of the park contains picnic areas and 170 acres (about a quarter of a square mile) of virgin forest; riding and walking trails integrate the ensemble.

The planners who created the interstate highway system in the 1950s mapped out Interstate 40 as a transcontinental route that would cross the Mississippi at Memphis on a new bridge, somewhat north of

---

not the attorney responsible for *Overton Park*, during this period. That professional relationship has, I hope understandably, limited my ability and willingness to write about the history of the case in that office.

   8. See D. TUCKER, MEMPHIS SINCE CRUMP: BOSSISM, BLACKS AND CIVIC REFORMERS, 1948–1968 104 (1980).

the existing one. It would connect Memphis with Nashville to the northeast and Little Rock, Arkansas to the southwest. As usual, the plans combined inter-city expressway with enhanced local commuter access, locating the bridge and route to provide a high-speed east-west corridor through the city's heart. A circumferential beltway was also planned, but the tight character of its interchanges (together with the economies of driving fewer miles) made clear the expectation that through traffic would stay on I–40 itself. From the outset, the plans called for the intra-city corridor to bisect Overton Park. Although the park might have been avoided without giving up that corridor, its central location, the established commutation routes, and the expected impacts of the alternatives all made this the "obvious" choice. Initially, I–40's footprint on the park was going to be quite large. Eventually, however— part of the following story—its imposition shrank to only 26 acres.[9]

The issues of *location* and *design* were treated separately both statutorily and administratively, and it will be useful to keep them separate. Although many locations were studied, two emerged as the park's chief competitors. One, following the northern edge of the park, would have cut off the park from the north, and disrupted university, school, church and other facilities that existed there.[10] The second followed creekbeds and a railroad right of way somewhat to the north; among its other disadvantages, it would severely have impacted one of the few racially mixed residential areas in the city. Location *within* the park was a more fluid issue: an early accommodation to the resistance was to superimpose the route through the park on the existing bus road rather than have it cut a new path; and moving a planned interchange outside the park boundaries significantly reduced the park acreage required.

Four principal design alternatives were debated throughout the long history of the controversy: building the road on the surface; building it below grade to the extent the water table and natural drainage constraints permitted; building it below surface throughout its length, overcoming water table and drainage problems; and constructing a tunnel in some fashion, hiding the road completely throughout its traverse of the park. Prior to the Court's decision, Tennessee highway officials consistently sought the first alternative—the cheapest, least

---

9. As described by the 6th Circuit,

[A]pproximately 4,800 feet in length[, t]he existing highway is 40 to 50 feet wide. The proposed interstate will consist of six lanes—three running in each direction, separated by a median strip approximately 40 feet wide. The interstate right-of-way will vary from approximately 250 feet in width to approximately 450 feet in width, and will require the use of approximately 26 acres of the Park. Citizens to Preserve Overton Park v. Volpe, 432 F.2d 1307, 1309–10 (1970).

10. Id. at 1311.

complicated, and most familiar form of construction—relying on land-scaping to reduce the impact of the road and its traffic on the park. City officials were more open to building below grade, but consistently expressed concerns about both the costs and the possible results of ignoring water table and drainage constraints: they feared that building the road below water table and creek levels would risk flooding if power outages in storms stopped the electric pumps that would then be required; and in any event they believed it would create bodies of still water in which malarial mosquitoes could breed at each end of the inverted syphon that would be used to conduct the creek under the roadway. Thus, for the city, the high local water table meant that I–40 should never be more than ten feet or so lower than the surrounding park, and that it should rise above grade to cross Lick Creek. Federal officials consistently pursued the more dramatic and far more expensive possibilities of building the road in a trench below the water table, of syphoning Lick Creek's flow under the entrenched roadway, or indeed of tunneling the whole length of the park. When in 1969 the Bureau of Public Roads approved the second design—below grade to the maximum extent drainage and the water table permitted—the parties to the litigation may well have thought that the principal statutory issue the courts would be called upon to decide would be whether this choice reflected "all possible planning to minimize harm to [the] park"; this was the *design* issue under the two federal statutes enacted late in the planning process. In the wake of the Court's decision, the Secretary never identified another feasible route; design remained the principal administrative issue for as long as Tennessee pursued its hopes of completing I–40 by constructing its inner-city Memphis leg, with federal officials offering a tunnel, and state and local officials proposing a ditch.

A Chronology

1944   Federal-Aid Highway Act of 1944 initiates federal role in planning a national system of highways.

1950   Congress requires state highway officials to provide an opportunity for public meetings if they plan for a federally supported highway to "bypass" a center of population.

1953   Memphis undertakes its first study of limited access freeway possibilities.

1955   Memphis's new "civic reform" government receives and preliminarily approves the study, proposing a circumferential ring highway, a new Mississippi River Bridge, a north-south expressway east of the commercial center, and an east-west expressway through the park.

1956   The Interstate highway system and Highway Trust Fund are launched; Congress amends the existing requirement that states hold a local hearing if a federally funded road will "bypass" a population center, by adding "or going through" such a center. I–40's siting in Overton Park is federally approved for the first time.

1957   Surveys for I–40 begin, giving prominence to the plan to use Overton Park; Citizens to Preserve Overton Park [CPOP] is founded; in November, the City Commission holds well-attended public hearings, resulting in an extensive restudy of alternative routes.

1958   Federal-Aid Highway Act extends the state hearing requirements to encompass *rural* routing of limited access highways, which might bisect farms or cut them off from town.

1961   Tennessee holds the federally required hearing for the Overton Park segment in Memphis, with the State Highway Commissioner presiding and much opposition voiced. Recordings are incomplete. The city's Engineer later promises to build it last, and only if needed. The first five miles of the southern circumferential highway are built.

1962   Federal-Aid Highway Acts further amended; state officials must now cooperate with the officials of cities larger than 50,000 in a "continuing, comprehensive transportation planning process" to resolve routing issues.

1964   The circumferential highways are substantially completed, and political pressure concerning the east-west highway mounts, reaching the governor (in an election year) and the head of the Federal Bureau of Public Roads [BPR]. BPR officials negotiate a reduced park footprint.

1965   The City Commission votes to approve the route 4–1, assuring the State Highway Commissioner of its support. He adopts further measures ameliorating its impact and, under gubernatorial pressure, again studies alternative routes. The north-south legs of the expressway are built. In December, the federal BPR head visits Memphis to consult.

1966   In January, "reaffirm[ing] our previous approval," the BPR head wrote the Tennessee Highway Commissioner that "the most exacting efforts to assure a finished product which is in keeping with the area and future park usage [are a] condition to our action." Congress later enacted the Federal-Aid Highway Act of 1966; effective July 1, 1968, states must assure "all possible planning, including consideration of alternatives . . . to minimize any harm to . . . [any] park" that might be affected by interstate highway construction. Within weeks, it also enacted the Department of Transportation Act creating the Department of Transportation [DOT] and giving new attention to environmental and "beautification" issues. Section § 4(f) of *this* statute, effective April 1967, directed the Secretary not to approve the use of important parklands for highways "unless (1) there is no feasible or prudent alternative to the use of such land, and (2) such program includes all possible planning to minimize harm to such park." In November, Tennessee voters elected a new Governor, and Memphis voters approved a new form of city government.

1967 Tennessee's new Governor and Highway Commissioner characterized the route through the park as "the most direct and the most economically feasible." On March 15, before § 4(f) became effective, the BPR gave preliminary approval to the *design* for I–40 in the park. On May 2, the City Commission again voted 4–1 to accept the route. Also that month, BPR authorized acquisition of approaches, and the state began preparing the ground for the east-west road. In November, the new city government was elected; the road was not a significant election issue. The Senate Public Roads Committee held hearings into urban highways, treating Overton Park as a trouble spot. In December, DOT promised a visit by top officials to help Memphis make a decision it "should make . . . because you are best equipped to make it— because you will know what will make your commerce thrive and what will make the lives of your people more meaningful."

1968 **January:** A number of political meetings in Memphis, including several with CPOP.

February: FHA Administrator Bridwell visits Memphis to talk with the new City Council and CPOP. After a public hearing, he says I–40 will be built through Overton Park unless the City Council changes its view. The racially charged garbagemen's strike begins.

March: On March 5, the Council unanimously adopted a resolution stating its preference that I–40 be routed elsewhere—if need be, along the park's northern boundary. Much political lobbying ensued, with Administrator Bridwell seeking a specific, reasonably well developed routing proposal. Equivocating, the Council asked to meet with Bridwell again. The garbagemen's strike escalated, leading to riots and the visit of Martin Luther King. On March 31, reflecting turmoil over Vietnam, Lyndon Baines Johnson announced that he would not be seeking reelection to the presidency.

April: On April 3, Administrator Bridwell met with City Council at the Memphis Airport. CPOP was excluded and recording instruments proved to have been inoperative. On April 4, the City Council voted 8–2 to approve both "the route presently designated" and its design. Moments later, Martin Luther King was assassinated at the Lorraine Motel, and the country erupted in flames. On April 19, Administrator Bridwell reaffirmed the earlier route approvals and called for further attention to design. Tennessee's governor and the congressman from Memphis announced their support of this decision.

May: Transportation Secretary Boyd and Administrator Bridwell testified at length in congressional hearings about their administration of § 4(f) in general and the Overton Park controversy in particular. The Committee appeared to receive his testimony sympathetically, and to reflect that in its subsequent report supporting what became the Federal-Aid Highway Act of 1968. That Act, effective August 23, 1968, changed the statutory formula of the FAHA to match § 4(f) of Department of Transportation Act.

June: Robert Kennedy was assassinated. Administrator Bridwell required the Tennessee Highway Department to considering deepening the trench in which I–40 would be placed or a tunnel, previously excluded for expense and engineering reasons.

November: A new federal President, Richard Nixon, was elected. His Secretary of Transportation would be John Volpe, former principal of a major construction company.

1969   After further discussions with federal officials about deepening the trench, the Tennessee Highway Department held a design hearing in Memphis May 19. Recording equipment again failed. Pressure for a tunnel continued, with a reported intervention by the Secretary of the Interior. In September, Tennessee paid Memphis over $2 million for 26 acres of Overton Park; by ordinance, the city committed those funds to purchasing 405 acres of additional park lands. On November 5 Secretary Volpe granted design approval after the state and city had accepted further deepening of the trench (but no tunnel). In December, CPOP filed suit to block construction of I–40 through Overton Park.

1970   CPOP lost in both the District Court and the 6th Circuit. Construction preceded on the approaches to the park, clearing all property up to its borders. CPOP filed in the US Supreme Court an emergency motion for stay pending the filing of a petition for certiorari; opposed by the government, it was argued December 7.

Certiorari was immediately granted, with CPOP's brief on the merits due December 21 and the government's January 4, 1971; argument was set for January 11. The government then filed a motion to remand (to permit departmental officials to file statements of reasons), which was denied December 18.

1971 At oral argument, the Solicitor General presented statements by the Secretary and the Administrator purporting to explain their reasoning. The opinions remanding the case were handed down seven weeks later, on March 2. The district court then held a 27-day hearing.

1972 On Jan. 5, 1972, the district court remanded the case to the Secretary with instructions to reconsider the case under a correct understanding of the statute. The Secretary held hearings in Memphis in the fall.

1973 Without specifying what it was, Secretary Volpe found that there was at least one "feasible and prudent alternative" to the route through Overton Park.

1974 The 6th Circuit upheld the Secretary's judgment, declining to require him to say what the "feasible and prudent alternative" was. President Nixon resigned and was replaced by President Ford. Tennessee submitted a new proposal to use an open cut in the park.

1975 William Coleman became Secretary of Transportation and announced a provisional decision favoring tunneling under the Park.

1976 In August, Tennessee held hearings on tunnel design in Memphis; when Jimmy Carter was elected President, federal officials cancelled a mid-November hearing at the state's request.

1977 Tennessee twice submitted designs for partial tunneling; the Department rejected both.

1978 The U.S. Senate held hearings on the tunnel/trench controversy.

1981 Three days before the inauguration of Ronald Reagan, Tennessee asked that the segment of I–40 through Memphis be dropped from the Interstate system and that $300 million in federal funds committed to the project be released to the city for other transportation purposes.

1987 Tennessee deeded the 26 acres of Overton Park back to Memphis.

BUILDING THE INTERSTATES NATIONALLY

The United States Congress

As the preceding timeline reveals, highway planning legislation developed step by step over the quarter century preceding *Overton Park*.

It began with straightforward economic concerns and gradually incorporated a wider range of issues and an expanding federal bureaucracy.
Congress reached the environmental and amenity issues of parkland use
ambiguously and late, and before the courts had been invoked. As is
hardly surprising in the absence of highway planning litigation, the
congressional documents and debates address neither the place of the
courts nor the utility of judicial processes. In this story the issues are
largely political ones. To the extent politics was distrusted—as, for
example, productive of corruption at the hands of those who stood to
profit from routing decisions[11]—the proper response was to put planning
into the hands of professional technocrats—first, the highway engineers,
and then the city planners.

Until the second half of the 20th century, roads were the business of
local communities if they were in-town; states if they connected towns;
and the federal government hardly at all. Federal aid to the states for
highway construction began in 1916,[12] but a federal role in planning did
not emerge until definition of the National Interstate and Defense
Highway system in mid-century. By the time Congress began to focus on
road-building as a setting for possible federal standards and/or procedures, states and localities had settled into a general pattern: outside
incorporated areas, states generally controlled which roads would be
built and where. If Highway 12 passed through Elmtown, the state
would bring the road to the town limits on either side, leaving the town
to plot and pay for its transit. It was the state that made the judgment
whether to go through Elmtown at all, or rather to bypass it in favor of a
straighter, cheaper, or faster route elsewhere.

These allocations of responsibility, and the tensions and political
temptations they produced, were reflected in the arrangements made for
decision. Highway planning at the state level became the domain of the
professionalized highway engineer. Limited funds were available for
building the connective road tissue of the state, and every community
had a stake in how those judgments were made; judgments had to be
made about construction, safety and carrying capacity as well as route. It
was obvious in the circumstances that responsibility should be placed in
the hands of a technocratic office removed from the distortions of politics
and informed by the science of road-building, that could translate traffic
patterns, geography and engineering parameters into an efficient network.[13]

---

11. See Tippy, *Review of Route Selections for the Federal-Aid Highway Systems,* 27
Mont. L. Rev. 131, 137 (1966).

12. Federal-Aid Road Act, ch. 291, 39 Stat. 355 (1916).

13. As the President of the American Association of State Highway Officials told
Congress in 1968,

Within the cities, roads were in the domain of the urban planner. People more easily saw that roads were only one element of infrastructure and of future growth, in relation to others. And the professional interests of city planners are correspondingly more embracive than those of highway engineers; whether to use roads or subways to transport urban workers, or what balance to strike between transportation and the need for urban green spaces, were questions much more likely to appeal to, and to be relevant to the professional judgments of, the one than of the other. State and urban political tensions were mirrored in the resulting professional juxtapositions.[14]

Thus we see in 1950, as the first effect of the post-war explosion of suburban growth and road-haul commerce, Congress requiring states to hold public meetings to air the possible economic effects of bypassing a center of population before it could route a federally supported highway around town. The state must certify that the state official making a bypass judgment has considered the question of economic impact. Evident in the limited legislative history of the provision is both an awareness of the professionalization of state judgments on such questions, and skepticism about their soundness.[15] Providing a forum for the small businessmen of a community to express their views on the proposal (there can have been little doubt what those views would be) would arm political processes that might avoid the worst excesses of cold technocratic judgment.

Congress soon heard from other voices wanting a seat at the state planning table. In 1956 it amended the statute to require a hearing on the question of economic effects (and a certification by the state department that these issues had been considered) for every routing decision made in the vicinity of a concentration of population—whether it would "bypass" a city, town or village, or go through it. And 1958, with

---

State highway administrators by and large dislike the philosophy that local lay people [should] have a more prominent role in highway location and design. ... To allow local people to have a greater voice ... for which they are not trained would negate the experience of trained highway professionals.

Quoted in BEN KELLEY, THE PAVERS AND THE PAVED 128–29 (1971). Kelley directed the press office in the Department of Transportation from its founding in the Johnson administration. While his book has some of the flavor of the several "highway exposes" published in the late 1960s and early 1970s (e.g., A. Q. MOWBRAY, ROAD TO RUIN (1968); H. LEAVITT, SUPERHIGHWAYS—SUPERHOAX (1970)), his position gives his account particular interest. The account of general change in these paragraphs draws significantly on it.

14. *See* M. LEVIN & N. ABEND, BUREAUCRATS IN COLLISION: CASE STUDIES IN AREA TRANSPORTATION PLANNING 236–42 (1971).

15. Little towns and villages are being ruined because ... an engineer has an idea that automobiles going to the next town should be able to reach it five minutes sooner. 96 Cong. Rec. 13,006 (1950) (statement of Sen. Chavez, chairman of the Senate Public Works Committee).

limited-access interstate highways now in prospect, it acted again—to extend the hearing process to persons in rural areas through or contiguous to whose property a highway would pass; the engineers were making their decisions without much regard for the impact on Farmer Jones' acres or his ability to get to town.[16]

The political character of the remedies thus created is clear when one sees that Congress attached no substantive requirement to its hearing demands. It did not ask the hearer to opine or to judge, or to articulate a reasoned conclusion; it does not seem to have imagined that judicial review could ensue. Within the structure of the highway grant program, as it was understood, the federal government had little if any enforcement role. Congress put such federal responsibility as there was in the Bureau of Public Roads, a unit of the Department of Commerce. The BPR served largely as a conduit for grant program funds, and did not actively supervise state highway commissions. Refusing funds because a state made the wrong choice, or imperfectly implemented procedures, does not seem to have been part of its repertoire.[17] Without flatly banning any routing choice, these provisions provided a focus for arousing opposition. Such congressional discussion of the provisions as there was—and there was very little—focused on the immediate political benefits of having an opportunity to be heard. It expressed the hope, perhaps even sentimentally, of having some impact within state processes; there was no plan for enhancing federal bureaucratic, much less federal judicial, controls.[18] The evident expectation was that having to discuss plans in public before they were made final would tend both to

---

16. The resulting statute may now be found in 23 U.S.C. § 128, an element of the 1958 codification of the Federal-Aid Highway Acts.

17. As the Federal Highway Administrator informed his senatorial oversight committee:

Under Bureau procedures, the States first propose the general location of a designated route or section thereof, which, if found satisfactory, is tentatively agreed upon by the Bureau. Following this, the States proceed with the development of preliminary plans for the route proposed by the State to the degree adequate for presentation at a public hearing. They also collect appropriate data concerning alternate locations. This material is presented and fully discussed at the public hearing. The States then weigh the evidence presented at the hearing, determine a final location, and request Bureau approval for further advancement of the project.

Hearings before a Subcommittee of the Senate Committee on Public Works on Bills Relating to the Federal-Aid Highway Act of 1958, 85th Cong. 2d Sess. 98–99 (1958).

18. The decision to honor local interests in this way, it may be noted, had overtones contrary to the usual federal interest in interstate commerce. It was *bypassing* a town that would facilitate the interstate carriage of goods; there would be no traffic light at the intersection of Main and Oak, no slowing for a school crossing or reduced speed limit. To insist that towns about to be by-passed have notice and an opportunity to speak—roughly translated, to gather whatever political force they could in opposition to the plan—was to acknowledge the local character of the decision in an unusually forceful way.

assure attention to the issues and to arm the informal processes by which various interests might be expected to make their wishes known. The legal literature of the time, two decades before "The Reformation of American Administrative Law,"[19] is virtually empty of discussion[20] and the caselaw, undeveloped.

To cast the provisions in this light is not to suggest that they were thought inconsequential. Members of Congress are practical politicians, and need not have acted with either judicial or bureaucratic controls foremost in their thoughts. They would have understood that road-building decisions were matters of tremendous consequence to states and localities, and that the states would have decision mechanisms roughly responsive to political realities. Leaving the judgment to politics, in this sense, was a natural instinct; forcing the issue onto the table, thus giving access to local politics, was a significant federal intrusion—yet one that respected the local character of the ultimate decision.

By 1962, Congress was directly responding to tensions between highway engineers and urban planners over roadbuilding issues. Now the Federal–Aid Highway Acts conditioned approval of federal-aid highway projects in an urban area of more than 50,000 population on the use of a "continuing, comprehensive transportation planning process carried on cooperatively by states and local communities." The states *must* talk to the cities; and they must talk to them in the professional terms that most concerned the cities—city planning, not simply highway engineering. This change was not connected with the hearing processes, as such; indeed, explanations of it tended to stress (however unrealistically) that city planning, like highway engineering, was a technocratic process removed from "the vagaries of the political system."[21] The apparent impulse was to provide for inputs that, within state processes, would inform and perhaps divert the highway juggernaut from concerns only about speed, directness, safety and cost.

Parklands entered the picture in the mid-1960s. The publication of Rachel Carson's **Silent Spring** in 1962 catalyzed environmentalism as a public movement. People began to see the Interstate Highway System as a threat to beloved parks and historic areas—not just Overton Park, but the French Quarter in New Orleans and, notably, Breckinridge Park in San Antonio, Texas. Although the BPR was already requiring adminis-

---

19. Richard Stewart, *The Reformation of American Administrative Law,* 88 Harv. L. Rev. 1667, 1760–90 (1975).

20. See Schwartz, *Urban Freeways and the Interstate System,* 49 S. Cal. L. Rev. 406, 480–82 & n.455 (1976).

21. Hearings Before the Subcomm. on Roads of the Senate Committee on Public Works, 90th Cong., 2d. Sess., 509 (1968) [hereinafter *Hearings*] (testimony of FHWA Administrator Bridwell).

tratively that state processes include consultation with public agencies having jurisdiction over parks and other outdoor amenities that might be affected by highway construction, the political uproar—and perhaps the convenience of a beautification diversion from the horrors of the war in Vietnam[22]—persuaded Congress that this was an issue it had to address.

Texas Senator Ralph Yarborough's concern over Breckinridge Park spurred enactment in 1966 of the park-protective provisions in both the Federal-Aid Highway Act of 1966 and the Department of Transportation Act. The two provisions differed in their requirements for consideration of park values. The Federal-Aid Highway Act, passed in September and effective July 1, 1968, required federal highway administrators to engage in "all possible planning, including consideration of alternatives ... to minimize any harm to ... [any] park" that might be affected by interstate highway construction.[23] Section 4(f) of the Department of Transportation Act, passed one month later but effective upon the Department's formation in April, 1967, directed the Secretary not to

> approve any program or project which requires the use of any publicly owned land from a public park ... of national, State, or local significance as determined by the Federal, State, or local officials having jurisdiction thereof ... unless (1) there is no feasible or prudent alternative to the use of such land, and (2) such program includes all possible planning to minimize harm to such park ... resulting from such use.[24]

The meaning of § 4(f) proved central to decision in *Overton Park*.

While one could go on at length about the specific legislative histories of these two provisions and their differences,[25] perhaps the most

---

22. LadyBird Johnson's role in promoting highway beautification was perhaps her most visible activity as First Lady.

23. Federal Highway Act of 1966, Pub. L. No. 89-574, 80 Stat. 766, 771.

24. Department of Transportation Act of 1966, § 4(f), Pub. L. No. 89-670, 80 Stat. 931, 934.

25. Both provisions originated in the Senate. The Federal-Aid Highway Act originated in the Senate Public Works Committee, the Department of Transportation Act, concerned overall with government organization, in the Senate Committee on Governmental Operations. In each case, the Senate language concerning park values was more restrictive than ultimately enacted, reflecting the Senate's (and, particularly, Senator Yarborough's) consistently greater enthusiasm for elevating park protection than the House felt. In the House, these measures were explained in the House as reflecting concern for human values ("if there were a choice between using public parkland or displacing hundreds of families ... I would want the Secretary to weigh his decision carefully and not feel he was forced by the provision of the bill to disrupt the lives of hundreds of human beings," Rep. Rowstenkowski, 112 Cong. Rec. 25,591-92 (daily ed. 10/13/66)), although it was associated in some other minds with greater House attachment to pork barrel politics and the highway lobby. See, e.g., Mowbray, n.13 above, p. 220 ff. In considering the Federal-Aid Highway Act of 1966, the conference committee substituted the language

important point—and one that helps explain the apparent casualness of
the difference between two provisions on the same subject enacted
within weeks of one another—is that they were small elements of larger
packages, elements respecting which close congressional attention was
not to be expected. In framing the larger context, the change of importance was the creation of a national Department of Transportation,
which assumed the prior responsibility of the Department of Commerce
for highway construction, but now as an element of national transportation planning generally. Embedding the Bureau of Public Roads (now the
Federal Highway Administration) in a new structure with responsibilities for mass transportation and other like issues changed the dynamics
from promotion to balance, made it more likely as a political and
bureaucratic matter that highway decisions would be taken with more in
view than the professional concerns of highway engineers. To take only
one example—itself a product of increasing environmental awareness—
the engineers would now have to deal with an office within the Department specifically responsible for promoting environmental awareness
and responsiveness.[26]

For the first time, Congress had unambiguously made federal highway officials the source of approval, not merely guidance, respecting
highway location issues. Yet the legislation and its supporting materials
suggest an expectation that these requirements would be enforced politically, not judicially. Section § 4(f), like other aspects of the Department
of Transportation Act, required consultation with other parts of the
federal government—the Departments of Agriculture, Housing and Urban Development, and the Interior—that could be counted upon to bring
other values to bear in controversial situations. The legislative materials
suggest no recognition, much less expectation, that judicial enforcement
might be in the offing. Congress's surprising experience with judicial
enforcement of the National Environmental Protection Act still lay in
the future. "Public interest representation" rationales had, as yet, no
prominent voice. It is difficult to ascribe to the approval requirement any
expectation that highway decisions would be controlled by other than
bureaucratic and associated political means.

---

enacted for a Senate-passed provision that would have prohibited approval unless there
were "no feasible alternative to the use of [park] land," 112 Cong.Rec. 14074 (1966); in
considering the Department of Transportation Act, it inserted the additional qualifier "and
prudent." 112 Cong.Rec. 19530 (1966); see also Gray, *Environmental Requirements of
Highway and Historic Preservation Legislation*, 20 Cath.U.L.Rev. 45 (1970). Neither
provision was much discussed at the time; the difference in effective date was ascribed, in
the House, to simple oversight on the part of the conference committee. 112 Cong.Rec.
25592 (Rep. Holifield, Daily ed. 10/13/66).

    26.   Gray, n. 25 above.

Two years later, Congress was asked to reconcile the competing statutory formulations; in the Federal-Aid Highway Act of 1968[27] it chose the formulation of § 4(f). Litigation was in the air by now, but had not yet emerged as a significant source of control over highway administrators. In May of 1968, both Secretary Boyd and Federal Highway Administrator Bridwell testified as months of hearings on urban planning, location and design before the Subcommittee on Roads of the Senate's Committee on Public Work drew to a close. Their testimony continued to envision highway decisionmaking in essentially political terms. It strongly supported wide consultation and the involvement of local politics to determine community interests and engage planning across a wide range of issues, rather than simple reliance on the professional expertise of highway engineers. "We have no choice," the Secretary argued, "but to follow planning procedures which are sensitive to the needs of individual communities and elicit community involvement in the development of the plans."[28]

What transpired about Overton Park in particular is best left to later discussion,[29] but one can say summarily that the committee heard the administrators sympathetically, and then turned immediately to the Federal-Aid Highway Act of 1968. This bill would resolve the linguistic inconsistency between section 138 of the Federal-Aid Highway Act of 1966 and § 4(f) by choosing the § 4(f) formulation.[30] The bill's focus,

---

27. Pub. L. No. 90–495, 82 Stat. 815 (1968).

28. *Hearings, supra* note 21, at 455 (testimony of Alan S. Boyd, Secretary of Transportation). In contrast, consider the May 6 testimony of Governor John Volpe of Massachusetts, the former contractor who would shortly become President Nixon's first Secretary of Transportation, who spoke on behalf of the Governor's Conference. Perhaps state highway departments should expand the range of disciplines they incorporated, he conceded, but to provide for an urban design team or for consultation with local politics in competition with these professionals would be to invite chaos. *Id.* at 248–49 (testimony of John A. Volpe, Governor of Massachusetts and Chairman of the Governor's Conference).

To the same effect, again promoting professionalization centered in the highway department over politics or authority shared with municipal planners, see the testimony of the President of the American Association of State Highway Officials before the same subcommittee at its June 4, 1968 hearings specifically on S. 3418, which became the Federal-Aid Highway Act of 1968: "[T]he manner in which section 4(f) of the Transportation Act of 1966 is being administered is working as a delaying factor in getting the program completed and some of the material being drafted relative to double public hearings would allow dissidents, through legal procedures, to tie highway projects up almost indefinitely"; the Department was guilty of "over-emphasis and over-enthusiasm in administering Section 4(f)"; and Section 4(f) was "being used to reopen decisions previously made or to slow down the program." Highway Safety, Design and Operations; Freeway Signing, and Related Geometrics: Hearings Before a Special Subcomm. on the Federal Aid Highway Program of the House Comm. on Public Works, 90th Cong., 2d Sess. 74, 76, 108–09 (1968).

29. See text at note 116 below.

30. See text following note 23 above.

however, was not on this detail but on the general problem of urban disruption occasioned by expressway construction. In that context, the legislation moved unmistakably toward balance, and larger participation of local political processes as against the state highway technocracies. Thus, much of the Committee effort, led by Senator Baker of Tennessee, was to develop a more effective and equitable program for relocation of displaced individuals, an effort which matured as Title II of the 1968 Highway Act. Section 128 of Title 23, which previously required State highway departments to provide public hearings only to consider the *economic* effects of urban highway projects, was amended to require that these hearings also consider the "social effects of such a location, its impact on the environment, and its consistency with the goals and objectives of such urban planning as has been promulgated by the community."[31] Having heard both departmental plans for enlarging political participation in highway planning, and highway officials' objections that the Department's political approach to § 4(f) would slow and deprofessionalize the process,[32] the Committee knew that adding these factors would require greater involvement by local government officials and agencies and by private individuals and groups.[33] It followed the Secretary's suggestion and endorsed the § 4(f) formulation. There was no discussion of the possibility or effects of judicial enforcement.

The Senate Committee's actions overall seem strongly to endorse the general approach to that section the Department had described in its testimony. The Committee remarked in its report,

> The Committee is firmly committed to the protection of vital park lands, parks, historic sites, and the like. We would emphasize that every thing possible should be done to insure their being kept free of damage or destruction by reason of highway construction. The Committee would, however, put equal emphasis on the statutory language which provides that in the event no feasible and prudent alternative exists, that efforts be made to minimize damage. . . .

---

31. Section 128 of Title 23 was amended again in December 1970, effective immediately, to add the requirement that the certification by the State Highway Department regarding public hearings and the consideration of economic, social, and environmental effects "shall be accompanied by a report which indicates the consideration given to the economic, social, environmental, and other effects of the plan or highway location or design and various alternatives which were raised during the hearing or which were otherwise considered." Federal-Aid Highway Act of 1970, Pub. L. No. 91–605, § 135, 84 Stat. 1713, 1734.

32. See n. 13 above.

33. S. Rep. No. 1340, 90th Cong., 2d Sess. 11, *reprinted in* 1968 U.S. Code Cong. & Admin. News 3482, 3492. Based on the information received during the hearings, the Committee was of the view that many controversies now facing the highway projects would be ameliorated, if not eliminated, had local officials been brought into discussions at a sufficiently early stage in the hearing process. *Id.*

> The committee would further emphasize that while the areas sought to be protected by section 4(f) . . . and section 138 . . . are important, there are other high priority items which must also be weighed in the balance. The committee is extremely concerned that the highway program be carried out in such a manner as to reduce in all instances the harsh impact on people which results from the dislocation and displacement by reason of highway construction. Therefore, the use of the park lands properly protected and with damage minimized by the most sophisticated construction techniques is to be preferred to the movement of large numbers of people.[34]

The Committee leadership reiterated this understanding on the Senate floor.[35]

Transportation Secretary Boyd also argued for the § 4(f) formulation on the House side:

> The [House] report indicates the Committee's belief that the perspective in decision-making should be broadened, not narrowed, and that preservation for use is sound conservation philosophy. . . . It is in this spirit that the [Department of Transportation] proposes to administer the Act. . . . The department is aware of no problems which have arisen in the course of administering the present language, nor does the Committee report refer to any. We think the present language of 4(f) is a clear statement of Congressional purpose.[36]

The House nonetheless chose the words of § 138 over those of § 4(f). While the Senate prevailed on this issue in the ensuing conference, choosing the § 4(f) formulation, it would be hard to take its victory as a repudiation of what the Administration had advised Congress it was doing. This was the course the Administration had urged on both houses.

The Managers on behalf of the House included the following statement in their conference report to their colleagues:

> This amendment of both relevant sections of law is intended to make it unmistakably clear that *neither* section constitutes a mandatory prohibition against the use of the enumerated lands, but rather, is a discretionary authority which must be used with both wisdom and reason. The Congress does not believe, for example, that sub-

---

34. Id. at 18–19, reprinted in 1968 U.S. Code Cong. & Admin. News 3482, 3500.

35. 114 Cong. Rec. 19,530 (1968). When Senator Jackson sought assurance from Senator Randolph, Chairman of the Public Works Committee, that his Committee had determined not to modify Section 4(f) and to uphold the previously expressed intent of the Congress on the question of protection of parks, Senator Randolph gave that assurance by quoting from the Senate Public Works Committee Report the second of the two passages in the text as evidence of what the Committee had decided.

36. Id.

stantial numbers of people should be required to move in order to preserve these lands, or that clearly enunciated local preferences should be overruled on the basis of this authority.[37]

In the Senate, discussion of this aspect of the conference report focused on preserving the Secretary's *discretion* to disapprove local choices that ran counter to the statute, not the possibility that external enforcement might ensue.[38] As would be surprising if it expected the latter, Congress did not explore the consequences of its choice either for ongoing projects or for other strongly held values at stake in highway construction—in particular, for the urban relocation of residents of poor and/or minority neighborhoods that was the principal focus of the legislation at hand. Significantly, President Johnson felt that the statute, as a whole, represented a defeat at the hands of highway interests of his campaign for highway beautification and amenity.[39] The Federal-Aid Highway Act of 1968 became effective August 24, 1968.

PLANNING I–40 FOR MEMPHIS

The Memphis Chamber of Commerce

The business community of Memphis had high stakes in I–40 and the progressive change it represented. When thoughts about that highway first emerged in the 1950s, their city lacked any circumferential road system—indeed, any highway system at all. For decades, Memphis had been administered under the watchful eye of E. H. Crump, an unusually effective machine politician whose taste for low taxes led him to ignore infrastructure and planning.[40] His hand-picked Mayor from 1949 to 1953, Watkins Overton, for whose distant relative Overton Park had been named, was also a bitter opponent of planning and reform. It was not until 1953, when Overton was succeeded by Frank Tobey and Crump's grip on the city was beginning to fail, that the city began to think about the limited access freeways other southern cities had already begun to construct. In the effort to catch up, the city commissioned a thorough planning study by Harlan Bartholomew & Associates, a St. Louis firm, in 1953. With Crump's death the following fall, a civic reform group that had been working with progressive business leaders to

---

37. H.R. Conf. Rep. No. 1799, 90th Cong., 2d Sess. 32 (1968) (statement of House managers) (emphasis in original).

38. 114 Cong. Rec. 24,033, 24,036–37 (1968) (statements of Sens. Jackson, Yarborough, Randolph, and Cooper).

39. Statement of President upon signing bill into law, 4 Weekly Comp. Pres. Doc. 1277 (Sept. 23, 1968); J. Robinson, Highways and Our Environment 296–99 (1971); Callison, *National Outlook,* Audubon, Sept.-Oct. 1968, at 94–95.

40. The narrative in this paragraph draws largely on the accounts given by Tucker, n. 8 above at 67–72.

develop support for planning and urban development emerged as the most important political force among the white voters of the city. In 1955, shortly after submission of the multivolume comprehensive plan, they would elect their leader, Edmund Orgill, as mayor.

For the limited access roads that were among its recommendations, the Harlan Bartholomew plan proposed the familiar pattern of a circumferential ring, with north-south and east-west expressway components to carry traffic to and through the commercial center (and Overton Park). Although the Chamber of Commerce was not particularly concerned with the displacements these projects would cause, one could note that they mostly passed through relatively undeveloped or African-American population areas, including a park used by the African-American community; the east-west expressway was the one element of the proposed system that crossed the white residential area of Memphis (as well as Overton Park). For the business community, having the new Mississippi River bridge and the central artery were the central concerns—even before the city's effective center had moved away from the river and competing shopping and commercial areas had sprung up along the circumferential. Over the years, as threats to the proposal rose and fell—at one point, for example, a major hospital threatened to move out of concern for the impact of vibrations, noise and fumes[41]—they were among its most consistent and vociferous supporters. Overton Park, as such, figured little in their support; perhaps some valued the marginally shorter commute they might expect from homes in the eastern suburbs, but this does not surface in the materials. Their central concern was the health of the downtown financial and commercial community, as well as containing the costs of the enterprise as they understood them.

The business community remained, as well, a force for "modern government" for Memphis. It supported a number of civic reform initiatives, beginning with the ouster of the Crump regime and ending for our purposes in 1966. On the eve of the Overton Park controversy, Memphians voted to replace the existing five-member City Commission with a Mayor and a thirteen-member City Council, whose members would be elected by representative districts to strictly legislative capacities rather than by the city as a whole to executive responsibilities (as the commissioners had been). In 1966, too, the flight of conservative southern white voters from the Democrats to the Republicans led to the election of Memphis's first Republican Member of Congress, Dan Kuykendall. The subsequent municipal elections, in 1967, elected a collection of political tyros—"a business oriented group ... moderately wealthy and middle class," only one of whose members had previously held elective office—as

---

41. Williams, *Expressway Project Voted a Green Light Despite Ingram's "No,"* Com. Appeal, Apr. 14, 1965, at 1; *Ingram Loses X-Way Vote by 4 to 1*, Memphis Press-Scimitar, Apr. 14, 1965, at 1.

the first City Council.[42] Racial polarization in the mayoral elections that year, however, had also resulted in the election of former Mayor Henry Loeb, a well-established opponent of civil rights; this set the stage for the 1968 Memphis garbagemen's strike that tragically culminated in the assassination of the Reverend Martin Luther King. The proposal to build an expressway through Overton Park received its final municipal imprimatur, for our purposes, when this new City Council took time from its consideration of that agonizing and racially charged strike to meet twice with Federal Highway Administrator Lowell Bridwell and, after vacillating, to assure him that the proposal had the city's support.

The African-American Community of Memphis

The feelings of Memphis's sizeable African-American community about Overton Park do not often emerge from the available materials, but they can be imagined. Before segregation was disestablished—that is, during much of the run-up to the dispute—the park was generally available to whites only; black citizens could visit its Zoo on Tuesdays. Professor Lucie White sensitively imagined the feelings of a

> Memphis school girl ... of African descent. If this girl were visiting Overton Park, it would be a Tuesday.... This girl's school bus would drive from a segregated school on the black fringes of the city—fringes that were already crossed by a freeway. It would pass the elegant homes where her own people, forty percent of the city's population, worked as maids and yardmen, until finally, in the center of this area, it would enter Overton Park. As I imagined this ... girl taking that journey, I imagined mixed-up feelings of bitterness and awe. Although she loved the park, she also hated what its *preservation* would represent. Therefore, I imagined her spitefully, if also silently, allying with the bulldozers to fight those privileged groups who would suffer neither highways nor Negroes anywhere near their neighborhoods, and who knew how to work the system to get their way. I imagined her concluding that unless some of the freeways were built in the Overton Parks of the world—at least as a precedent—all of them would end up in her own back yard.[43]

Indeed, the other Memphis elements of the Interstate system *were* in her back yard, and a park she might have used had been taken without evident concern for park or community values. The principal alternative to Overton Park investigated, the one using railroad rights of way and old creek beds north of the park, would have had a major impact on a stable mixed residential area in Memphis, one of the few places where its

---

42.   J. BEIFUSS, AT THE RIVER I STAND: MEMPHIS, THE 1968 STRIKE, AND MARTIN LUTHER KING 145 (2d ed. 1989).

43.   See n. 7 above, 39 UCLA L.Rev. at p. 1336.

two communities lived together. Unmentioned by the planners, this characteristic of the area became, for some, an important reason to resist moving I–40 away from the park.

By the time the Overton Park issue emerged sharply, black Memphians would have learned of problems associated with the routing of I–40 through Nashville—an episode that reached the Sixth Circuit in 1967.[44] There, the proposed route would have separated the campuses of two traditionally African-American faculties, Fisk University and Meharry Medical College, from the nearby black community of North Nashville. In addition to disrupting their classes with its noise and diverted traffic, it would have destroyed a public park used largely by blacks. Accompanying street changes the city proposed would have closed a substantial segment of Jefferson Street, site of Nashville's most successful black merchant community. According to the plaintiffs in litigation challenging these plans, preliminary indications of I–40's route had not revealed these dramatic impacts. As originally proposed in 1956, the route had been a direct east-west road traversing railroad tracks, rail yards, and a few white-owned retail businesses. This was the only portion of the initial plan not finally approved in preliminary meetings among state and local officials; by the time the proposal was made public for the federally required hearing in 1957, it had been mysteriously rerouted to swing north through the black community.[45] As would not be the case in Memphis, the required public hearing was—perhaps intentionally—obscure; notices were sent only to the County Judge, to the Mayor, and to a few post offices located in white neighborhoods. The notices were unspecific about the route, and they gave as the date for the hearing May 14, 1957; in fact, the hearing occurred May 15.[46] While the *Ellington* court concluded that the location issue had in fact been prominent in Nashville politics for over a decade,[47] it also agreed with the district court's conclusion that "the consideration given to the total impact of the link of I–40 on the North Nashville community was inadequate."[48] And while

44. Nashville I–40 Steering Committee v. Ellington, 387 F.2d 179 (6th Cir. 1967), *cert. denied,* 390 U.S. 921 (1968).

45. See B. Kelley, n. 13 above, at 98–99; A. Mowbray, n. 13 above, at 178–79, 181.

46. As *would* often be repeated for important meetings in Memphis, the hearing was imperfectly transcribed—only remarks from the podium were recorded, not those from the audience—and the only formal reference to its use appeared in the following statement of the attorney for the state highway department, responsible for route selection:

> I certify that I am an official of the Department of Highways and Public Works of the State of Tennessee and that the above transcript of the public hearing heretofore conducted regarding the location of the above mentioned project has been read by me. I further certify that said Department has considered the economic effects of the location of said project and that it is of the opinion that said project is properly located and should be constructed as located.

Ellington, 387 F.2d at 184.

47. Id. at 183.

48. Ibid.

the *Ellington* court found on the merits that claims of racial discrimination had not been well enough proved to require reversing the lower court's denial of preliminary relief,[49] it would not have been hard for a black Memphian to believe that the state highway department had been a party to manipulations producing an outcome improperly favoring dominant white interests over black interests; another contemporary account, this in one of the several "superhighway exposé" books of the time, presented Nashville officials as having refused to specify the exact route until construction bids were sought in 1967.[50]

---

49. *Ellington,* 387 F.2d at 185.

> Acting on such claims would have carried its own risks to a setting complicated by the existence of many conflicting and important interests. Not only would "alternative routes undoubtedly . . . impose hardships upon others"; the more public precise route selection is required to be, the greater the chance for real estate manipulations increasing public costs for private profit. Moreover, delay in effecting a project that will serve the public good also creates public expense; at some point, one must be able to act.

Id. The *Ellington* court drew on the preliminary character of the proceedings it was being asked to review, and the corresponding prospect that the asserted harms might still be avoided.

> In oral argument, the United States Department of Transportation has announced that it will not approve the letting of the contract for this project pending further study, it would appear that final approval of this segment of highway may not yet have been given by that Department. We cannot presume that the Department of Transportation will fail to give consideration to possible revisions in the plans and specifications so as to alleviate as much as feasible the grave consequences which this record shows will be imposed under the present plans upon the North Nashville community.

Ellington, 387 F.2d at 186. Similar awareness of the place of politics may be reflected in the court's reasons for reversing the district court's dismissal of one defendant, the Metropolitan Mayor of Nashville and Davidson County, on the ground that this official lacked jurisdiction over the locating of an interstate highway and could not participate in any decision with respect thereto.

> Although the District Court is correct in its conclusion that the Mayor has no legal power to decide the location of an interstate highway, it cannot be doubted that he possesses considerable powers of persuasion and cooperation. We cannot predict the ultimate disposition of this case in the District Court on its merits. It is conceivable that the final solution could require the closing, opening, or rerouting of city streets, rezoning or other municipal action. A correction of these problems could require cooperation among Federal, State and local governments. We consider it proper to retain a representative of the Metropolitan Government as a party defendant.

Id.

FHWA Administrator Bridwell eventually reaffirmed approval of the route, but with some changes to reduce the barrier effect of the highway and recommendations to the city for action that would ease the relocation of black businesses. A. Mowbray, *supra* note 13, at 183. His explanation for the approval, that by this point the location issue was fait accompli, and his specification of desirable changes are part of the record of the 1968 hearings on Urban Highway Planning, Location and Design that also figured significantly in the Overton Park controversy. *See Hearings, supra* note 21, at 509–16, 560–64.

50. See A. Mowbray, n. 13 above, at 179–80.

In any event, as the Overton Park controversy reached its climax in local politics, the dominating concern of the Memphis black community was not how the city, state and federal government would accommodate transportation needs with an unfamiliar urban amenity. It was how the new city government would deal with a racially polarizing garbagemen's strike, a strike that would end in tragedy and outrage when the Reverend Martin Luther King was assassinated in Memphis, just as the City Council took its final vote to accept the routing of I–40 through the park.

Martin Luther King's Last Testimony

"Well, I don't know what will happen now. We've got some difficult days ahead. But it doesn't matter with me now. Because I've been to the mountaintop. And I don't mind. Like anybody, I would like to live a long life. Longevity has its place. But I'm not concerned about that now. I just want to do God's will. And He's allowed me to go up to the mountain. And I've looked over. And I've seen the promised land. I may not get there with you. But I want you to know tonight, that we, as a people, will get to the promised land. And I'm happy, tonight. I'm not worried about anything. I'm not fearing any man. Mine eyes have seen the glory of the coming of the Lord."

— The final words from Martin Luther King's last speech, given in Memphis Tennessee the night before he was assasinated on April 4, 1968

Citizens to Preserve Overton Park

Professor White imagined, alongside the young African American woman evoked above, a young white girl who

> had grown up in the elegant residential enclave bordering Overton Park. This young girl had many wonderful memories of the park—of hikes through the acres of virgin woodland, family picnics, visits to the zoo. I could imagine her feeling not just saddened, but threatened by the prospect of a freeway cutting through her park, even a freeway unobtrusively depressed below street level for most of its length. It would not just be a question of noise and pollution. Rather, a freeway invading Overton Park would rupture her entire social world. As the 1950s became the 1960s, the tranquility of that world was beginning to unravel—first with the desegregation of the park itself; then with the civil rights movement and the urban riots; and finally with the assassination of Martin Luther King in Memphis; and the enactment, a week later, of a sweeping federal Fair Housing Act. To this young girl, the prospect of a freeway through Overton Park was not just a tradeoff of trees for asphalt; it signified the threat that she felt all around her . . . , a threat to her very way of life.[51]

Although planning began earlier (the first federal route approval came as early as November 1956),[52] that threat became manifest in April 1957, when Memphis newspapers first printed maps that clearly showed the proposed routes I–40 would take through the city, including the park, and indicated that the public would get its chance to speak out on routing issues. There followed a well-attended meeting of the City Commissioners to hear citizen questions and views (Overton Park was only one of the subjects), and the formation of Citizens to Preserve Overton Park (CPOP).[53]

Citizens to Preserve Overton Park was a citizen's action group in familiar form, created in outrage and enduring for the time it took

---

51. White, n. 7 above, 39 UCLA L.Rev. at 1335–36.

52. *City Looks to Future on Expressway Plan,* Com. Appeal, Sept. 17, 1955, at 3; *Expressway Is OK-ed by City Commission,* Com. Appeal, Sept. 21, 1955, at 16; *see also* Richard H. Ginn, Interstate 40 Through Overton Park: A Case Study of Location Decision-making 26 (1970) (unpublished M. Sci. thesis, University of Tennessee) (citing correspondence between engineers of the Tennessee Highway Department and the federal Bureau of Public Roads to place the first federal approval on November 8, 1956).

53. Gray, *Public Gets Chance Thursday to Speak Out on Expressway,* Com. Appeal, Apr. 16, 1957, at 17; Gunter, *Residents Confused at State's Hearing on City Expressway,* Com. Appeal, Apr. 19, 1957, at 1.

finally to defeat the project. Its papers, preserved in the Shelby County Library in Memphis, reveal an organization that was never very large, and had dwindled considerably by the late '60s. John Vardaman, the Washington D.C. lawyer who became CPOP's attorney in 1969 shortly after it had decided to litigate over the Park, doubts there were more than ten members during the time he was dealing with it; he recalls that Anona Stoner, its tireless secretary, would type copies of documents for him, rather than incur the then considerably greater costs of Xeroxing.[54] For Charles Newman, whom he brought on as local counsel at the suggestion of a mutual friend when the suit moved to Memphis

> CPOP's motives were about as free of self-interest as I can imagine. They were a tiny, idealistic group, who had no financial or other tangible interest in the outcome of matter and withstood a lot of abuse over a lengthy period of time. Most of them did not live in the surrounding neighborhood and did not use the park. A couple of them did live in nearby neighborhoods. One or two were on the faculty at the nearby college (then Southwestern, now Rhodes). Some of the most important and determined ones lived well South or East of the park. It's clear that even those few who lived or worked in nearby neighborhoods were driven by motives more abstract than their proximity to the park, and virtually none of them "used" the park in any meaningful way.[55]

Certainly some of the initial support for Citizens to Preserve Overton Park (CPOP)—remnants of the old, anti-planning Crump machine, for example—seemed to be in the defensive mode Professor White's narrative suggests; former mayor Overton was among its more active early members. As the following narrative suggests, its leaders were resourceful and imaginative in their efforts to marshal political support against I–40; they did not turn to litigation for over a decade. Neither, however, were they willing to accept the compromises and modifications that their political efforts in fact produced. CPOP's core membership was unmistakably animated by a passion for the park; little else could explain their energy and perseverance in the face of an establishment—local, state, and federal—that was willing to bend, but not to abandon its path.

In its initial efforts, CPOP enjoyed partial success. By mid-May, the city was urging the state to change the expressway's route through the park to reduce its impact by aligning it with the existing bus road.[56] In

54. Telephone conversation of August 6, 2004. Vardaman's correspondence files hold several boxes of this material; Ms. Stoner and a few other members of CPOP were passionate correspondents.

55. Email of January 26, 2005.

56. Gray, *Altered Expressway Route Suggested in Overton Park,* Com. Appeal, May 9, 1957, at 1.

September, William Pollard, Harlan Bartholomew's chief engineer in Memphis, appeared before a hearing of the City Commission to present a design that he hoped would accommodate the Commissioners' concerns. It proposed a roadway depressed below the surface, fenced, with provision for pedestrian crossings, and landscaped to reduce its impact. He was met by more than 300 protesting citizens, unwilling to hear him speak or to entertain any plan that would use the park; they had gathered more than 10,000 signatures on petitions opposed to use of the park—the apparent highwater mark in numerical support for the opposition. Fred Ragsdale, head of the city's traffic advisory commission, strongly urged limiting the expressways to the circumferential highway.[57]

On the surface, accommodation was all that those favoring the park route seemed willing to offer. Mayor Orgill, presiding, expressed annoyance: "[A]ny group of people who will sit down and listen to how the expressways were planned, the reasons they were placed where they are, will be just as convinced as I am."[58] Perhaps he experienced the meeting as an echo of his earlier struggles with then-Mayor Overton and the Crump machine whether to have such planning at all. Nonetheless, the Commission asked Harlan Bartholomew to restudy the railway/creekbed route; it reported back a continued preference for the park route— although not for the reasons that later generated the greatest resistance from the local black community, its neighborhood impacts.[59]

The Overton Park controversy then receded from public prominence[60] until the federally prescribed hearing for the segment of the east-

---

57. Gray, *Foes of Expressway Clamor: Keep Overton Park Intact*, Com. Appeal, Sept. 18, 1957, at 1; Johnson, *Protesters Plead "Don't Take an Inch of Overton Park"*, Memphis Press-Scimitar, Sept. 18, 1957, at 1; Johnson, *A Young Man Learns About Democracy's "Noisy Side,"* Memphis Press-Scimitar, Oct. 25, 1957, at 31.

58. Johnson, *A Young Man, supra.*

59. All in all, Harlan Bartholomew would undertake preliminary studies of twenty-five distinct routes using the railway/creekbed alternative, with more detailed studies of six; it considered as factors present development, neighborhood boundaries, traffic needs, relation to the current road system (including crossings of major thoroughfares and the ease of locating desired interchanges), maximizing use of the railroad right-of-way, extent of taking required, and relationship to routes to public schools. It chose the park as much more direct (saving time and energy resources), more readily accommodated to existing roads and useful spacing of interchanges, and as offering less disruption to industry. *See* Ginn, n. 52 above, at 31 (citing 1970 correspondence within the Bureau of Public Roads). At the height of the Overton Park dispute in 1968, the *Press-Scimitar* published excerpts from what was apparently this report, taken from the Federal Highway Commissioner's files. Ray, *Federal Highway Commission Says City Council Must Act on Overton Cross—Way*, Memphis Press-Scimitar, Mar. 26, 1968, at 1.

60. Clippings files are dominated by general debate about the Ragsdale proposal to limit the expressway system to a circumferential highway, and stories about the construction that had begun on the southern part of the circumferential. It appears that one candidate for Public Works Commissioner ran on a platform of opposition to the east-west

west route, including Overton Park, in 1961. The Commissioner himself conducted that hearing in light of the controversy, with Harlan Bartholomew's engineer Pollard presenting a strictly economic analysis of the route. Several hundred crowded the auditorium. Downtown Association speakers were supportive, but on the whole the largely white and well-dressed audience wanted to ask "what we can do to stop you from going through the park?"[61] Within two weeks, Mayor Loeb had met with CPOP and endorsed the east-west expressway as the route that "will help Memphis more than any other expressway segment."[62] A month later, the City Engineer is reported to have said that the controversial route would be built last, to see if it was in fact required; "We've tried to get every other possible route approved by the engineers, and they have made at least 32 studies to avoid going through Overton Park, and they found it impossible."[63]

Controversy subsided until 1964, while construction of other parts of the expressway pushed forward steadily. In that year, as their completion neared the half-way point, the east-west expressway issues resurfaced, now in the administration of Mayor William Ingram. The Tennessee Highway Department hired Buchart-Horn, an engineering firm, to design this segment; this was the *only* segment for which the original planners, Harlan Bartholomew, were not hired.[64] By late spring, CPOP had promised an eleventh hour blitz,[65] and it seems to have been

---

route in 1959; he lost the election—but then, he had not been selected as a member of the "white unity" ticket that swept all results that fall. D. Tucker, n.8 above, at 102–03.

61. Allen, *State Officials Get Earful at Hearing on Expressway,* Com. Appeal, Mar. 15, 1961, at 1.

The report given to Federal Highway Commissioner Bridwell characterized the hearing this way:

> At a public hearing ... there was some opposition to the location that goes through the park. The opposition came from private citizens whereas approval for the route came from city and county authorities, various planning groups and civic groups as well as individuals and businesses. Because of opposition at the hearing and by letters received after the hearing, the State Highway Department had further alternate studies made in 1964.

Gray, n. 57 above. The report characterized in some detail the comparative merits of the routes studied.

62. *Loeb Opposed to Rerouting Expressway,* Memphis Press-Scimitar, Mar. 29, 1961, at 8.

63. *East and West Crossway Will be Built Last,* Memphis Press-Scimitar, Apr. 26, 1961.

64. See Record at 134, Citizens to Preserve Overton Park, Inc. v. Volpe, 401 U.S. 402 (1971) (No. 70–1066) (Keeler affidavit).

65. *Should the New Expressway Go Through Overton Park?,* Memphis Press-Scimitar, June 3, 1964, at 6; *Bridge Meet Set June 9,* Memphis Press-Scimitar, May 27, 1964, at

successful in gaining the attention of relevant figures: although the City Beautiful Commission ("CBC")[66] and local newspapers[67] supported the expressway, others voiced shared concern. The Park Commission, the Shelby Forest Council, a number of City Commissioners, and Mayor Ingram all said they'd prefer that Overton Park not be used—although doubtful that change was now possible, and in some cases satisfied that "every effort" had already been made to find another feasible location.[68]

CPOP extended its political efforts well past city government. State Highway Commissioner David Pack (later, Tennessee's Attorney General) first announced that the state planned "to push right ahead,"[69] but then (apparently under instructions from Tennessee Governor Frank Clement, who was seeking the Democratic nomination for U.S. Senator) wrote CPOP that his office would study all possible alternatives before going ahead. He did this in the face of pressure from the Memphis Chamber of Commerce and the Downtown Association for an immediate start on what was already a considerably delayed project.[70] His public vacillation continued through the campaign season;[71] newpaper reports asserted that, in an early fall meeting with Governor Clement and CPOP, the Governor had said that he "didn't mind saying . . . in front of the engineers [that he] would prefer to keep the expressway out of the

1; *Overton Park Group Renews Fight to Block Expressway,* Memphis Press-Scimitar, May 27, 1964, at 5; Edmundson, *Push Is Given to Expressway,* Com. Appeal, May 4, 1964, at 1.

66.   *Overton Park Group Renews Fight to Block Expressway,* Memphis Press-Scimitar, May 27, 1964, at 5. Formed in the Crump days as an official women's organization to monitor the neatness of Memphis neighborhoods in each of the city's wards, the CBC had survived as a voluntary group since Mayor Orgill's election. D. Tucker, n.8 above, at 27, 80.

67.   *Through the City,* Com. Appeal, May 5, 1964, at 6 (editorial). Newspaper support for the roads presented the route choices as the product of balanced judgment ("If we saw another way, we would oppose the Overton Park route," response to Skinner, Letter to the Editor, Memphis Press-Scimitar, Mar. 8, 1961). This was a constant irritant to the supporters of CPOP, who believed their viewpoint had no fair hearing in the press.

68.   Brown, *Commissioners Think Park Route Is Certain,* Memphis Press-Scimitar, June 22, 1964, at 1; White, *Moore Is Opposed to Overton Park Route,* Memphis Press-Scimitar, June 18, 1964, at 25; Porteous, *Forest Council, Park Board Oppose Overton Expressway,* Memphis Press-Scimitar, June 5, 1964, at 17.

69.   "We have studied and restudied this question and decided some time ago that the Overton Park route is the most realistic. To change now would mean a loss of considerable money and time. . . . We're definitely going through Overton Park . . . barring intervention by Washington." Vanderwood, *X-Way Will Go Through Park,* Memphis Press-Scimitar, June 24, 1964, at 1.

70.   Vanderwood, *Park X-Way Studied Again,* Memphis Press-Scimitar, July 30, 1964, at 1.

71.   Compare Topp, *Overton Park Route Seems All Settled,* Memphis Press-Scimitar, Sept. 24, 1964, at 1 Whisenhunt, *X-Way Opponents Win New Delay,* Memphis Press-Scimitar, Oct. 10, 1964, at 7, reporting the meeting next described in text.

park."[72] The same story indicates that the controversy had reached the head of the Federal Bureau of Public Roads ("BPR"), Rex Whitton, who had said that the necessary studies had not yet been finalized, and that no effort would be spared to see that all considerations were properly balanced. Within a few weeks, CPOP was meeting with mid-level BPR officials and the engineers from Buchart-Horn to discuss possible changes—albeit changes to reduce the road's impact rather than reroute it altogether. By mid-winter, CPOP had approached Tennessee Senator Albert Gore, Sr., prompting him to ask Mr. Whitton for a status report after the BPR visit. The response, which he forwarded to CPOP, ascribed support for the Overton Park routing to city officials, but indicated the matter had not yet been resolved at the state level.

CPOP's engagement with city politics reappeared after Memphians had agreed to replace their City Commission with Mayor and City Council.[73] It attempted without *apparent* success to make the expressway an overt issue in the 1967 Council elections, sending each of the more than one hundred candidates a questionnaire about his or her attitude. Only a third responded;[74] the one candidate for the Council who made opposition to the road a centerpiece of his campaign lost. Nonetheless, once the elections were over CPOP quickly sought meetings with the new Council to explore the possibility of change.[75]

At the same time, CPOP had been actively seeking intervention in Washington. By this time, § 4(f) was in force, and the Johnson administration had given prominence to highway beautification—a diversion from Vietnam, perhaps, but from CPOP's perspective certainly a welcome one. The Senate Public Roads Committee opened hearings into urban highways in November 1967, with Overton Park identified as a trouble spot from the outset. In early December, Representative Kuykendall announced that Highway Administrator Bridwell would be visiting Memphis, and asked for reexamination of the route.[76] CPOP's indefatigable secretary Anona Stoner—older than Prof. White's young schoolgirl but surely just as passionate about the park—repeatedly wrote Secretary

---

72. Ibid.

73. See text at note 42 above.

74. That third, not surprisingly, said they preferred alternatives over the park route by a substantial margin. Correspondence in Box 6, CPOP collection, Memphis & Shelby County Library.

75. Ibid.

76. *The Overton Park Issue Again,* Memphis Press-Scimitar, Dec. 7, 1967, at 8 (editorial). The Representative hedged his bets—he was not seeking "economic suicide"— but still encountered predictable editorial criticism. "Instead of rising at this late hour in support of die-hard opposition to the project," wrote the *Press-Scimitar,* "Kuykendall should be exerting his efforts toward speeding completion of the expressway as planned and approved."

of Transportation Boyd and Administrator Bridwell. Bridwell now responded that "I have spent some time looking into the issues ... and
reviewing the files ... [and] plan to visit Memphis to take a first-hand
look at the situation and discuss the problem with interested citizens
and State and city officials."[77]

Bridwell's first visit (overall, at least the third visit that a ranking
federal highway official had made) would eventually occur in mid-
February; in the two months intervening, proponents and opponents
jockeyed for position. In January, CPOP and other interested opponents
had the first of two meetings with the new Council to express their
views, and CPOP's Chair, Arlo Smith, wrote Bridwell that it hoped for a
private audience with him, at which CPOP, rather than Mayor Loeb,
would control the presentation made:

> The new Mayor Henry Loeb is one of the most obstinate proponents
> ... although this was not a campaign issue of his.... The new
> council members are strongly influenced by the mayor, and anxious
> to get along with him, and they are unaware of the factual informa-
> tion as we have long been in a news blackout, in all media, relative
> to such information.[78] ... Previous "hearings" ... have been
> chaired and controlled by persons refusing to hear or "have time
> for" further consideration.... [Attending a meeting between you
> and the Council] will not enable us to fairly present to you our well
> documented factual information. We will still need a minimum of an
> hour with you, privately, for our case to be presented. If you wish a
> joint meeting with the council and the mayor, it should follow our
> private meeting with you.... We are anxious to have you visit
> Memphis as soon as possible, because frantic efforts are being made
> to ... skip-buy property to show "it is too late to change" now.[79]

On February 13—the day on which the Memphis garbagemen's
strike began—CPOP spent half an hour with the Council presenting its
case. The next day it was among seventy-five persons both opposing and
favoring the road who participated in a four-hour hearing with federal

---

77. CPOP collection, n. 74 above.

78. While the letter is not explicit just what this information was, it probably
concerned the projected costs of alternative routes. State officials regularly presented these
costs as millions higher than the costs of the park route, and newspaper stories tended to
repeat these figures. Opponents of the park route had a different set of figures, which
showed less community disruption and lower costs for some alternatives. Repeatedly
presented to various official bodies, including Administrator Bridwell in this instance, these
competing figures were never accepted.

79. Letter from Arlo Smith to Lowell Bridwell (Jan. 19, 1968), CPOP Collection, n.
73 above. Preparation and even construction at the outer ends of the ten-mile east-west
highway had, of course, been going on for some time. An account of progress appearing in
the *Press-Scimitar* on March 26, 1968 gives a break-down tending to confirm the skip-
buying complaint.

Administrator Bridwell. On March 5, it seemed finally to have won its case; the City Council unanimously adopted a resolution expressing its preference that another route be used—if necessary the northern boundary of the park. But CPOP feared, with reason as matters eventuated, that the Council might not hold its ground.[80] During the weeks following, CPOP and the proponents of the road contended for the attention of the Council and Administrator Bridwell. For its part, CPOP kept up a steady stream of letters, keeping Bridwell informed of local machinations such as the Highway Department's efforts (as CPOP saw them) to force the issue by removing tenants from housing on the approaches to either side of the park.[81] Similarly, it wrote privately to the chair of the Council to be sure he was aware of Bridwell's eagerness, as it averred it had learned, to have the Council's help in "reaffirming its stand against the Expressway."[82] On April 4, a few days after the strikers' riots and minutes before Martin Luther King, Jr. would be assassinated at the Lorraine Motel, the City Council reversed its course and approved the route through the park.

This resolution resulted from an April 3 meeting between the Council and Administrator Bridwell. CPOP was excluded from this meeting, although the press, state and city representatives, and a representative of Harlan Bartholomew & Associates were present. CPOP knew that in the 1961 state hearing, audience comments, largely opposing the route, somehow had not been recorded; a similar mishap had befallen the Nashville I–40 process. It got Bridwell to promise that the April 3 meeting would be recorded; but no sooner had the meeting concluded than he called CPOP Chair Smith to report that the City Council's recording equipment had been, embarrassingly, inoperative.[83]

---

80. Thus, barely a week after the Council's vote, Councilwoman Gwen Awsumb had written Anona Stoner of CPOP that "The Council does not wish to be responsible for further delay on a needed section of the Expressway, nor for added unnecessary expense. The response to the resolution seems to indicate that no doubt the original route will more than likely prevail. But we felt we had to try to do what we could. It was worth a try but probably an effort made at too late a date." Letter from Gwen Awsumb to Anona Stoner (Mar. 11, 1968).

81. E.g., Letter from Arlo Smith to Lowell Bridwell (Mar. 8, 1968), CPOP Collection, n. 73 above (also questioning the good faith of one council member's reported second thoughts about the March 5 resolution); Letter from Arlo Smith to Lowell Bridwell (Mar. 18, 1968), id., (also asking whether, and if so why, federal funds were being used to finance the acquisitions, if the Department had reopened the park issue); cf. Lentz, *Homeowners Stew over I–40 Path Uncertainties,* Com. Appeal, Mar. 17, 1968, at 12.

82. "So much pressure has been brought to bear on Mr. Bridwell and his supporter, Secretary Boyd, by conservation and recreation organizations throughout the country that they are ready to favorably negotiate alternate routes." Letter from Anona Stoner to Charles Pryor (Mar. 30, 1968), CPOP Collection, n. 74 above.

83. A year later, at the hearing on design, recording equipment would again fail as those challenging the proposal came forward to present their views.

An anguished letter of April 6 from Smith to Bridwell refers to television clips he had seen of Bridwell explaining the diversion costs of the outside-the-park alternatives and to reports he had received from a councilman about Bridwell's "very fair ... magnificent presentation." What, Smith wanted to know, were the alternatives discussed? Did Bridwell realize with how much regret Council members had now cast their votes favoring the park route? Wasn't this all the product of permitting the state to continue purchases that basically forced the city's hand?[84] At about the same time, CPOP's energetic secretary, Anona Stoner, was writing Secretary Udall of the Department of the Interior, seeking to enlist his aid.[85]

CPOP would continue its fight, as indeed the litigation amply demonstrates; but it may be best at this point to turn to the engagement of other participants.

State Highway Officials

State highway officials (and perhaps, as well, other members of Tennessee government) were the most persistent advocates of putting I–40 through Overton Park, and doing so for the professional reasons of highway engineers—it would be the cheapest route, the most direct route, and the route that served the most traffic.[86] It is worth emphasizing that, as a legal matter, state offices and state officials were the persons primarily responsible for the routing decisions made, and for conducting any public hearings that concerned those decisions. Their relationship with the federal government was as a supplicant for funds; federal financial support would cover 90% of the expense of the roadway if federal approvals could be won. What the federal government might or might not be approving, however, were decisions made by the state of Tennessee and its Highway Commission.

The year 1965 saw a series of events involving state officials and politicians that suggest both the consistent pressure from its highway establishment for resolution, and the political pressures being brought to

---

84. CPOP Collection, n. 74 above. Newspaper accounts confirmed the regret with which the vote had been cast and the members' stated sense that it was virtually forced by decisions made a decade earlier. Kellett, *Overton Parkway Route Cleared by City Council,* Com. Appeal, Apr. 5, 1968, at 25.

85. Letter from Mackey to Anona Stoner (June 11, 1968) CPOP collection n. 74 above, (referring to letter of Apr. 15, 1968, *ibid.*).

86. Whatever may have been the racial element in Nashville, and however black Memphians may have viewed their state government generally during the period we are discussing, it is hard to find any element of racial exploitation in the state establishment's support for the routing through Overton Park. The route it preferred for *this* segment of the Memphis limited-access highway system did not significantly impinge African-American interests.

bear in Nashville. Perhaps, Commissioner Pack intimated, the new bridge over the Mississippi would not be built in Memphis if the east-west leg were not constructed, and the funds would be used to speed construction of another bridge further to the north. But perhaps, also, building the expressway would lead a major Memphis facility, St. Jude's Hospital, to move out of the city, as its leadership began to express fears that vibrations and fumes from the highway would interfere with medical care.[87] Aware that this dispute was becoming a national symbol of a viewpoint with which Pack claimed some sympathy,[88] and with the results of a new alternative route study again demonstrating the economic advantages of the park route in hand,[89] Commissioner Pack announced two modifications at the end of July: construction measures would be taken to protect the hospital, and the design of the projected interchange on the eastern edge of Overton Park would be altered to remove most of it from the park. There would, however, be no departure from the route as a whole.[90]

Commissioner Pack's correspondence with Administrator Whitton makes plain that his purpose was to recognize the opposition to the road, to go a substantial distance toward meeting it, but to keep the road in Overton Park.[91] He led the resistance to design changes in the park that would add to I-40's expense. In January 1966, after personally inspecting the route and possible alternates, Administrator Whitton wrote him to "reaffirm our previous approval" of the Overton Park route, subject however to "the most exacting efforts to assure a finished product which is in keeping with the area and future Park usage" as "a condition to our action. We ask that the design be subjected to continuous evaluation by qualified architectural landscape personnel . . . fully coordinated with the appropriate city park officials."[92] Pack's reported and peculiarly ungracious reaction was to respond that "the route through the park probably will not be depressed, as was earlier considered. Rather, the

---

87. Williams, *Expressway Project Voted a Green Light Despite Ingram's "No,"* Com. Appeal, Apr. 14, 1965, at 1; *Ingram Loses X-Way Vote by 4 to 1,* Memphis Press-Scimitar, Apr. 14, 1965, at 1.

88. *Park v. X-Way—A "National Symbol,"* Memphis Press-Scimitar, June 1, 1965, at 4.

89. See Ginn, n. 52 above, at 49.

90. Brown, *Green Light Flashes for E-W X-Way,* Memphis Press-Scimitar, July 31, 1965, at 11.

91. See Letter from David M. Pack to Rex M. Whitton (Aug. 23, 1965), *reprinted in* Record at 143–48, Citizens to Preserve Overton Park, Inc. v. Volpe, 401 U.S. 402 (1971) (No. 70–1066).

92. Letter from Rex M. Whitton to David M. Pack (Jan. 17, 1966), *reprinted in* Record at 149, Citizens to Preserve Overton Park, Inc. v. Volpe, 401 U.S. 402 (1971) (No. 70–1066).

plan is to have the route on grade and to make full use of landscaping.''[93] This reaction must have suggested to those Memphians who wanted to have the road, but protect the park, that the engineers in Nashville could not be fully trusted.

Nineteen sixty-seven brought a new governor and a new highway commissioner, who soon indicated that after reconsidering the route and its alternatives they were convinced that "the route through the park is the most direct and the most economically feasible."[94] Not long after, D. Jack Smith, the member of the Tennessee House of Representative serving the Overton Park district, introduced in the House a bill to prohibit the spending state funds to build a road through any public park in Shelby County—i.e., to block I–40's routing through Overton Park.[95] To the Press-Scimitar, the bill illustrated the evils of the small election districts against which it had recently inveighed, by putting "a legislator under pressure to put the wishes of his particular district ahead of the welfare of the whole community."[96] Representative Smith's proposed statute appears to have sunk into oblivion.

In the wake of the *Overton Park* decision, consistent with their previous efforts, state highway officials continued to push not only for the route through the park, but for the least expensive design elements.

Federal Highway Officials

Although this might not be the impression readers would get from the *Overton Park* opinion, federal highway officials were at the other end of the spectrum from their state counterparts. We have seen already how often instructions to attend to amenities like parks came, first, from the Bureau of Public Roads and then, after its creation in 1966, from the Department of Transportation. Of course, as prior pages will also have suggested, there was an evolution, as the fact and impacts of the interstate system became more evident. But whether as a result of their dealings with Congress—which as we have seen was almost yearly

---

93. Bennett, *U.S. Endorses Freeway Link Through Park,* Com. Appeal, Jan. 19, 1966, at 1.

94. Bennett, *Interstate 40 Route Through Park Called "Final" by Ellington,* Com. Appeal, Feb. 4, 1967.

95. *Park, I–40 Bill Rekindles Friction,* Com. Appeal, Mar. 11, 1967, at 1. Ginn cites a March 9 meeting of the Shelby County caucus with a CPOP representative as the genesis of this measure. Ginn, n. 52 above, at 63.

96. *The Expressway, and Log-Rolling,* Memphis Press-Scimitar, Mar. 13, 1967, at 6 (editorial). In a southern city, so soon after the Voting Rights Act had been passed, the virtues (or vices) of election district size included the greater tendency of small districts to return an ethnically diverse body of representatives. The recent agreement of Memphians to adopt a city council form of government, in which district representation would for the first time play a role, promised to inject African-Americans into municipal government.

sending signals of increasing complexity and responsibility about the road-planning enterprise—or simply as the product of a somewhat different kind of professionalization of their bureaucratic function, federal highway officials were more likely to see the larger picture, the contending interests, the need for accommodation and compromise.

Rex Whitton, for example, one of earlier federal administrators to deal with the Overton Park issue, was no enemy of parks. Within six months of his flurry of correspondence in the fall of 1964 and subsequent visit to Memphis,[97] the BPR had issued a circular promoting the protection and improvement of public recreational resources in the road-building process. Not long after (following a BPR conference calling on highway planners to relate transportation plans and programs to social and community values[98] and before legislation on the subject), Administrator Whitton wrote that the Bureau now required states to give "full consideration to the preservation" of parklands and to demonstrate their responsiveness to suggestions made.[99] Although doubtless other pressures sometimes contributed to rather quick and dirty decision-making by the federal bureaucracy, it was sending clear signals that these considerations were valid and valued. Recall in this respect Administrator Whitton's 1966 direction to State Highway Commissioner Pack to make "the most exacting efforts to assure a finished product which is in keeping with the area and future Park usage" as "a condition to our action."[100]

Lowell Bridwell, Whitton's successor (and the first administrator of highway programs for the new Department of Transportation), was also attentive to park issues.[101] Indeed, this was true of DOT officials generally—albeit in the context of a general and continuing effort to hear, not from state highway bureaucrats but from city politicians. The creation of the Department of Transportation had produced typically complex, not

---

97. See text at note 71 above.

98. See Holmes, *The State-of-the-Art in Urban Transportation Planning or How We Got Here,* 1 TRANSP. 379, 391–93 (1973).

99. Whitton, *Highway Location: A Socio-Economic Problem,* 1 PARKS & RECREATION 24, 26 (1966) (emphasis omitted).

100. See text at note 92 above.

101. Bridwell's personal commitment to environmental values is suggested, inter alia, by a talk given during this period to a Pennsylvania Department of Highways seminar. 1968 Highway Research Record, Highway Research Board (1968). Addressing the problems his office faced in quantifying many values, Bridwell spoke about the importance of considering and integrating them; highways are not everything, he acknowledged, and must coexist with the rest of the communities they serve. He used as his example in this talk a recent effort in Baltimore, where he had undertaken a series of meetings, contacts, etc., seeking to develop consensus and understanding. Without these efforts, he warned, likely results included poor design, loss of community values, placards and lawsuits. See also n. 21 above.

dichotomous, change. Certainly, in creating the new Department with its multiple responsibilities, Congress had repudiated the almost mechanical "cost-benefit" calculations of economic advantage that had marked early highway planning. Planners must now consider more than the quantifiable issues of time, cost, anticipated traffic burden, and miles. To demand that the not-readily-quantified be considered, however, is not to choose *which* such value is to be favored; the political history gave the Department little reason to think that Congress and the President had required more than that they require local processes to consider these questions in the first instance, under some supervision to see that park values were seriously weighed. Neighborhood disruption, the requirement of resettling, the erection of racial barriers and interference with racial integration entailed values as ineffable as the use of parks, and the new statutes (like the political temper of the times) were emphatic about these values too. Intuitively, one would believe that the first Secretary of Transportation and his associates would have a reasonable understanding of the political play.

What one sees in the relevant federal materials, then, is sensitivity, but *not* an understanding that any one of these ineffable values—park values in particular—must be controlling. Many elements of the then developing Interstate Highway network were in contentious play, often in the context of local politics and city planning issues generally.[102] Internally, the issues of § 4(f) and its initial seeming inconsistency with the Federal-Aid Highway Act of 1966 were debated. Yet no one, not even those responsible for its environmentalist bureaucracy, imagined that in problematic contexts the park value would be regarded as absolute or presumptively controlling.[103] And one can see that this is the course the Department followed, without resistance from the Congress.

Certainly this was how the new Department and Administrator saw the issues concerning the use of Overton Park. Thus, in connection with his visits in the winter of 1967–68, a DOT Assistant Secretary, referring specifically to the Overton Park controversy and Bridwell's coming visit, told Memphis Kiwanis that Memphians would have a "much greater

---

102. New Yorkers well remember the long battles over the proposed West Side Expressway; as in San Antonio the brouhaha over Breckinridge Park, in New Orleans that over the French Quarter and in Washington, D.C. the Three Sisters Bridge—probably every major metropolitan area had at least one such battle royale.

103. See Gray, *Section 4(f) of the Department of Transportation Act*, 32 Md.L.Rev. 327, 371–72 (1973). Oscar Gray, director of the Department of Transportation's environmental programs during the Overton Park controversy and a strong supporter of an aggressive approach to the requirements of § 4(f), acknowledges that the Court's interpretation was beyond what even the "stau[n]chest environmentalists in the Office of the Secretary" had urged during the internal considerations; they had argued that the statute prohibited regarding parkland values as on a par with non-environmental considerations, but did not exclude the possibility of a balancing approach within that framework.

voice" in making the transportation decisions that affect their lives. "We
[DOT] feel you should make this decision because you are best equipped
to make it—because you will know what will make your commerce thrive
and what will make the lives of your people more meaningful."[104]

Administrator Bridwell must have been aware that the course of
action he took that winter reopened the siting issue and thus permitted
the new standards of § 4(f) to apply. He was under no apparent *legal*
obligation to do this. On his first visit, the day after CPOP had spent
half an hour presenting its case to the new Council,[105] he briefly met the
Mayor, the Chairman of the Council and representatives of the Downtown Association together with the press. He then made a tour of the
park and the expressway route, and returned to the federal building for
a four-hour hearing at which CPOP and others both opposing and
favoring the road made presentations; about seventy-five were in attend-
ance. He left the city indicating that he had a decision to make in
"several days"; that "we have had all the studies on this that we need";
that if he didn't act, the expressway would be built; and that "as of right
now, the city of Memphis' official position is in favor of I-40 and going
through Overton Park."[106]

The City Council changed that position with its March 5 resolution
seeking rerouting.[107] In response, he let it be known that he needed a
specific, reasonably well-developed alternative routing proposal; the
newspapers presented this in a manner that made him appear impa-
tient—possibly threatening the east-west expressway project and the
Mississippi River bridge.[108] Yet underlying the stories was not only
Bridwell's clear understanding that the requirements of § 4(f) would
now have to be met if the route were to go through Overton Park, but
also his acknowledgment of an enforcement device within the Executive
branch that would serve to keep the Department honest in its approach
to the provision. Secretary of the Interior Udall had been charged by a
President notably committed to highway beautification with assuring the
enforcement of the new law, and would not likely be satisfied unless the
Council were to take a positive position.[109]

Annoyed that the Administrator would air the controversy in the
pages of newspapers already full of criticism over the garbagemen's

---

104. *Federal Aide Cites Independent Ideas,* Com. Appeal, Dec. 14, 1967, at 7.

105. See text at note 80 above.

106. Riker, *Expressway Case Gets Last "Ride",* Com. Appeal, Feb. 15, 1968, at 55;
McKee, *X-Way Man Tells City: Decide,* Memphis Press-Scimitar, Feb. 14, 1968, at 1.

107. See text at note 80 above.

108. *City Sticks to X-Way Alternate,* Memphis Press-Scimitar, Mar. 12, 1968, at 1.

109. Id. By 1968, Bridwell appeared also to be aware that a lawsuit might be brought
to challenge any final decision to route I-40 through the park.

strike,[110] the Council first discussed the matter with him in a conference call, and then persuaded him to meet them at Memphis airport on April 3. He remarked on the eve of that meeting—which, as we have seen, produced Council approval of the route[111]—that

> the Overton Park route and a similar park crossing in San Antonio are two "hot spots" being eyed closely by the conservation interests for compliance with a 1966 federal law limiting the use of park property for expressways. What we have in Memphis is a question of conflicting values.... It is preferable for the City of Memphis, through the mayor and council, to decide what values are to be applied. If city officials don't do this, then I have the obligation of doing it. But I would much rather be guided by local officials. This doesn't mean of course, that I will accept any kind of guidance from them. It must be reasonable, rational and prudent.[112]

Later arguments would question how open Bridwell was to reconsideration, whether he had not extorted the Council's agreement by monetary threats or perhaps misrepresentation. Yet although contemporary newspaper accounts and correspondence give some support to this view, it is hard to square with the general course of action he took toward Overton Park in particular, and toward his responsibilities in the new Department in general. His DOT administration repeatedly emphasized its openness to the consideration of multiple values, and took a variety of steps (including the legally unnecessary step of reopening the Overton Park controversy) to implement that attitude. It knew it was acting under close political oversight. For the Administrator to make two trips in a two-month period personally to review a three-mile segment of public road was an extraordinary commitment of effort, one not readily made simply for show. More than a decade had transpired since the route had been fixed; it had been reconsidered again and again under political impetus not readily discredited as a comprehensive and continuing sham. And life *had* continued. The issues *were* close; as the remainder of Memphis expressway system grew and as citizens and businesses began to appreciate and accommodate themselves to its changes, commitments *had* been made that over time narrowed options and hardened attitudes.

On April 19, Administrator Bridwell announced his decision to reaffirm the earlier federal approvals to direct I–40 through Overton Park. As with earlier federal approvals, this one came with instructions—now undergirded by federal statutory requirements—that "in the

---

110. Porteous, *Council Delays Action on Overton Park X-Way, Will Reconsider Next Week,* Memphis Press-Scimitar, Mar. 27, 1968, at 16.

111. See text preceding note 83 above.

112. *Expressway Route Decision Urged by US Road Official,* Com. Appeal, Apr. 3, 1968, at 21.

actual design stages we will try to minimize as much as possible the
impact of the highway on the park facilities."[113] And it came with
evidence of political blessing; simultaneously, Governor Ellington and
Representative Kuykendall announced their acceptance of the decision.[114]
Secretary Boyd wrote to CPOP Chairman Arlo Smith in explanation of
the decision, saying "Now that the decision has been made on the
specific alignment of the route, I have asked Mr. Bridwell . . . to develop
a number of specific design alternatives to minimize damage to the park
and its facilities."[115] As would be lost on neither CPOP nor, eventually,
the Justices of the Supreme Court, this letter neither used the statutory
"feasible and prudent alternative" formula nor asserted that Secretary
Boyd had himself made the decision he was purporting to explain.

Within a month, Administrator Bridwell and Transportation Secretary Boyd would be testifying in the congressional hearings that led to
enactment of the Federal-Aid Highway Act of 1968. As we have seen,
with the Department's encouragement, this Act reiterated the § 4(f)
formulation.[116] In his testimony, Administrator Bridwell had detailed
both the Department's understanding of and support for § 4(f), and the
course of action it had followed in a number of controversial highway
decisions, specifically including Overton Park. "Unfortunately," he told
them, "there is no legislative history on [§ 4(f),] so there is no real
guidance from the Congress in interpreting the act. Therefore, we are
faced with the bare words, 'if prudent and feasible,' and if it is not
prudent and feasible, to minimize the damage."[117] The Department had
been experimenting with a variety of approaches to section 4(f) in a
number of urban settings where conflict had arisen over conflicting
values: redevelopment, community displacement, racial justice, "white
flight," business district reorganization, environmental and historic
preservation, and so forth.

He described an approach that relied heavily on the injection of park
values into local hearing processes where issues such as neighborhood
integrity and dislocations would also be considered. Rather than treat
route decisions as primarily for the Washington bureaucracy, it accorded
substantial decisional responsibility to properly instructed and supported
local officials. The statutory recognition that there might be no "prudent" alternative route permitted a balancing of competing interests—

---

113. Adams, *Park X-Way Route Gets Final O.K.,* Memphis Press-Scimitar, Apr. 19,
1968, at 1.

114. Ibid.

115. Transcript of Oral Argument on a Motion for Stay before the United States
Supreme Court in Citizens to Preserve Overton Park v. Volpe, OT 1970–1076, 25 (Dec. 7,
1970).

116. See text at note 27 above.

117. *Hearings* n. 21 above, at 473.

safety, neighborhood integrity, and the avoidance of large-scale urban relocations. Although "a few years ago" federal officials had emphasized both "developing local planning competence . . . and . . . removing it from the vagaries of the political system," he now acknowledged that the professionals had proved insufficiently responsive to community values;[118] hence the Department was seeking to promote greater community involvement in the development of the transportation plans, to make professional planners and engineers more responsive to community needs and goals.[119] Bridwell told the Subcommittee that approximately twenty-five cases pending in the Department raised "fundamentally . . . the same problem, namely, the conflict of community values."[120]

> I reject the idea that we have an either/or situation before us, either/or in the sense that you must choose one as distinct from the other and that you cannot have both. In other words, either you can't have highway or you can't have housing or you can't have a highway and you can't have a park, because in my opinion if we do

---

118. Id. at 533. The point was well expressed in M. Levin & N. Abend, n. 14 above, at 245:

> Area transportation planning, like other subjects that most people find both complex and boring, is relegated to professionals. Decisions are frequently made in back rooms on the basis of narrow technical criteria far removed from public discussion. Public hearings, until recently at any rate, have tended to be perfunctory pro forma affairs in which the participants are overwhelmed by masses of expensive maps and data. Accordingly, most significant development decisions are made by members of narrow professional guilds. Alan Altshuler has called this "creeping fait accompliism," in which agency professionals adopt a series of decisions under the guise of technical necessity until those decisions eventually, and sometimes unwittingly, accumulate into a major policy.

The colliding bureaucrats, in Levin and Abend's account, are highway planners and general purpose city planners—the one group focused in the Department of Transportation (at the federal level), the other at the Department of Housing and Urban Development. Their case studies, they thought,

> helped to bring into focus the long-standing suspicion, current among [city] planners, that highway engineers are narrow, callous technicians, heedless of the social impact of their efforts. Highway engineers were confirmed in their belief that planners are woolly-headed theoreticians lacking the practical sense to build a birdhouse, let alone to exert a useful influence on the routing of major expressways. The planning agencies were firmly committed to the concept of citizen participation, the highway agencies to the limited involvement of affected individuals and groups through statute-satisfying public hearings.

Id. at 244.

119. We are trying to accommodate it by much more deeply involving the public in discussion, in the presentation of facts, and hearing of their points of view, and instead of letting the professional planners make the decision saying to the elected representatives of these people, "this is your decision to make."

Hearings, n. 21 above, at 533–34.

120. Id. at 486.

our job, do it thoroughly, do it right, and you give us the tools to work with there isn't a reason in the world why we can't accomplish both.[121]

Bridwell told the committee that in Memphis the controversy involved a park that was "extremely attractive and highly used," and that the long-standing plans to build the highway through it had culminated "recently in considerable controversy over whether the park could or should be used" for the highway.[122]

> Once again this 4(f) portion of the Department of Transportation Act came into play. In effect it required us to do the same type of thing that we did in New Orleans,[123] go back and look at, is there another feasible and prudent location.

> Again experimenting we handled this one a little bit differently. We went to the city council of Memphis and we said, "Yes, there are alternatives.... " We told them that a highway could be built through the area on almost any conceivable line that they could pick, that engineeringly [sic] it was feasible ... We went through this for approximately [three and a half] hours in which we left it completely in the hands of the city council to choose anything they wanted to choose, and after several days the city council voted to stick with the original line through the park.[124]

Bridwell said he and the City Council had discussed four alternatives and the disruptions each would cause, and that he had put to them the issue

---

121. Ibid.

122. Id. at 479.

123. Bridwell explained, *id*. at 471–73, that the New Orleans project, like the Memphis project, illustrated the Department's effort to form "joint concept teams" to bring "a multiple professional discipline effort" to bear on the problems of highway location and design. The issue in New Orleans had been the city's historic French Quarter, which both state and city planned to use. The FHWA understood § 4(f) to entail two issues—first, whether there was "another reasonable, feasible location for this highway"; and second, whether all possible measures had been taken to make the road in its projected location consistent with "preserving and enhancing the historical features of the city of New Orleans and the French Quarter."

Regarding location, the Department had found that

alternative locations would have been more disruptive to the community than the originally chosen; or that the alternative locations, did not serve the same corridor of traffic or; third, that alternatives were so much different that those originally planned that they couldn't be accomplished for other reasons, for example, limitation upon the number of interstate miles available.

Design thus became a central issue. "From my standpoint, we have made the determination that there is no feasible and prudent alternative so the problem then becomes one of minimizing damage." Bridwell used photographs to show how the design had been altered to minimize the damage.

124. Id. at 479–80.

of priorities. Many sociological factors, that are not particularly susceptible to quantification "in our ordinary use of the word 'quantification'
have been and are being taken into account and without any question
increasingly so now and in the recent past."[125] Although some of the
contending community values in Memphis could be measured, some
could not be, and none could be measured in a "completely satisfactory
sense." Nor could hearings be relied upon to supply a resolution.
Witnesses who appeared in Memphis hearings, as elsewhere, had been
critical of the decision to go through the Park; but those witnesses were
understandably expressing a preference for "their own personal set of
values" in a situation of inevitable conflict.

> There is no nice, easy answer to this and there never will be. . . .
> Anytime there is disruption to an established pattern in the urban
> environment there necessarily must be conflicting sets of values
> brought into play and some one has to make the decision about
> which set of values prevails. The Secretary testified yesterday that
> except for very unusual circumstances the decision of the local
> people would prevail, in the form of the action of the elected
> representatives, their mayor, their city council, their appropriate
> local officials.
>
> That was precisely the reason that we went to the Memphis city
> council and in effect said, "Take your choice. You can have anything
> you want and we won't even as much as tell you how many dollars it
> costs because we don't want to influence your decision. You have to
> decide on the basis of contending unquantifiable community val-
> ues."[126]

His lively dialogue with the Subcommittee sympathetically explored, and
did not condemn, the approach he described. And once these hearings
were concluded, the Subcommittee moved immediately to consider the
Federal-Aid Highway Act of 1968.

It may suffice merely to sketch the events leading to Secretary
Volpe's refusal to revisit the location issue, and his approval of a design
sunk more deeply into the ground than the state wanted, albeit not deep
enough to avoid the impacts the road's opponents feared. As the preceding narratives show, issues of design to protect the park had been
important from at least the hiring of Buchart-Horn to design the park

---

125. Ibid.

126. Ibid. As part of his deposition on the 1971 remand in *Overton Park,* Mr.
Bridwell's then deputy, Edgar Swick, would testify that Bridwell had been concerned
throughout the process with the overall attitude of Memphians to the controversy. "He had
a real desire to know if the people wanted it, if it was just a splinter group opposed to it
and if there was any real concern in the city as a whole about the route. It was an attitude
he took in regard to all urban controversies of this nature. . . . " Black & Jones, *Appeal
Court Denies Pleas by X-City Route Protesters,* Memphis Press-Scimitar, Sept. 29, 1971.

segment in 1964, and "the most exacting efforts" to protect the park had been a stated condition of the federal route approval in January 1966, months before the appearance of a statutory command. The effect of § 4(f), however, was to permit the Secretary to force the Tennessee Highway Department's hand on the question of design; and the effect of section 128, as the Secretary understood it,[127] was to increase the political pressures on this issue. Thus, when in early June of 1968 the Highway Department sought federal approval of its design for the road, which the City Council had already approved, Bridwell promptly responded with a request that it study a lowered grade line.[128] A September story in the *Commercial Appeal* made it clear that East-West expressway construction had been slowed on instructions from Washington to take all possible steps to minimize damage to the park.[129]

With the pendency of a presidential election and then the election of Richard Nixon, construction slowed still further—now, at the initiative of state and city officials who may have understood that Secretary Boyd was likely to require some form of tunnel[130] and hoped a Republican Secretary of Transportation and Highway Administrator would permit the road to be built at or near ground level.[131] President Nixon had appointed as his first Secretary of Transportation the former head of a large construction company, John Volpe. Revised plans for a lowered grade line traveled from the DOT to the Tennessee Highway Department and back again in February and March of 1969. On May 19, the THD held the required design hearing in Memphis before an audience of about 100. The principal issue discussed was whether the road should be tunneled under the park; the Department of the Interior's Bureau of Outdoor Recreation and the National Park and Recreation Association, among others, strongly supported that option.[132] The state's recording of

---

127. See text at note 36 above.

128. Record at 134, Citizens to Preserve Overton Park, Inc. v. Volpe, 401 U.S. 402 (1971) (No. 70–1066) (Keeler affidavit).

129. See *Brakes Put to Expressways*, Com. Appeal, Sept. 15, 1968, at 2.

130. He would so testify at the hearing on remand. Lollor, *Planning Expert Offers Alternate Park Routes*, Com. Appeal, Oct. 1, 1971; Lollar, *Nixon Officials Cut Plan to Depress Park Route, Says Johnson-Era Chief*, Com. Appeal, Oct. 13, 1971; *see also supra* note 187.

131. See Means, *Freeway Route Bisecting Park Delayed Again*, Com. Appeal, Jan. 30, 1969, at 1; *Park Route's Up-or-Down Issue: Whose Decision?*, Com. Appeal, Feb. 11, 1969, at 15 ("[Tennessee Highway Commissioner] Speight decided two weeks ago to stop expressway work and see what the Nixon Administration's view would be. 'Any engineers that would recommend that we build that monstrosity [a depressed freeway across the park] ought to have his head examined,' he said.")

132. Chisum, *Expressway Through Park Is Likely to Start in Fall*, Com. Appeal, May 20, 1969, at 1; Porteous, *Foes Attack X-way Route Once Again*, Memphis Press-Scimitar, May 19, 1969, at 1.

the proceedings once again failed, although at DOT's insistence written submissions were obtained.

While design approval was pending, state and city officials took an action that seems strongly to reflect an understanding that they were obliged to protect park values. Tennessee had permission to secure the necessary rights of way, and in September it completed that process by purchasing from the city the 26 acres of Overton Park land it required, for a negotiated price in excess of $2,000,000. The city had undertaken by ordinance to spend all the funds thus received for the acquisition of new park lands; half the purchase price was immediately committed to purchase a 160-acre golf course that had long been on the city's list of possible park acquisitions.[133] Although the materials consulted for this study are not explicit that the ordinance was prompted by the requirements of § 4(f), one readily understands the undertaking as a direct means by which park values were protected in the transaction as a whole.

In the meantime, the opposition to the road once again had reached the Secretary of Transportation. In July, the Secretary of the Interior wrote to urge the use of a tunnel "to minimize harm to the park";[134] a late September story in the *Press-Scimitar* remarked that Department officials had ordered a halt to development of I–40, pending Secretary Volpe's return from a European trip;[135] and the Commercial Appeal reported first a telephone interview on October 1 indicating that he was having a "second look [at the *route*] to see that it is the most feasible location" and then a telegram that "there is no feasible alternate route" and "therefore my decision, which will be made as soon after my return as possible, will be related to design considerations in preserving the environmental quality of the park."[136] Those considerations, the story

---

133. Eventually, 405 acres of new park land would be acquired to "replace" the 26 acres to be removed from Overton Park. Memphians had recently been told that the city had only about half the acreage national standards suggested for a city of its size, *Land Purchases from Overton Park Account*, Com. Appeal, Oct. 7, 1977, at 29, and the new acreage represented only a very small proportion of the new park facilities a city planning document had suggested were required (Vol. 5, Community Facilities Study for the Memphis City Council, June 1968, in CPOP Box 1, recommended that city parks be expanded from 10,334 acres to 42,719 by 1990, at a cost in excess of $100,000,000). Yet the transaction produced a 16:1 improvement in committed "green space." A map of land purchased from the Overton Park land account, published in the *Commercial Appeal* for October 7, 1977, shows the bulk of the new acreage falling outside the city center and, as with Overton Park, in areas of predominantly white population.

134. *Numerous Expressway Memos Revealed,* Memphis Press-Scimitar, Oct. 2, 1971, at 6.

135. *U.S. Official Blocks Park X-Way, Loeb Says,* Memphis Press-Scimitar, Sept. 30, 1969, at 1.

136. Covington, *Volpe Now Says Design Only in Overton Park Route Case,* Com. Appeal, Oct. 4, 1969, at 1.

related, included a tunnel in at least some portions of the park; and documents at the hearing on remand showed that there had been a strong internal recommendation to that effect from the Department's Assistant Secretary for Urban Systems and Environment.[137]

Secretary Volpe issued his approval of I–40's design November 5, 1969, after the state and city had agreed to depress most of the roadway by an additional one or two feet, so that even the tops of trucks would be below ground level at most locations. Whether for reasons of expense or genuine fear of the consequences of floods and of still water as a breeding ground for mosquitoes, however, the city remained adamant that the road could not interfere with the natural drainage of Lick Creek, and so the design provided for the road to rise above grade level to cross the creek.[138] One month later, CPOP filed its lawsuit. Preparation moved fitfully as the case made its way from district court to Sixth Circuit to the Supreme Court, with the Department prevailing in each venue but the last; the park itself was untouched, but the approaches could be—and were—prepared.

City Officials

Cities have bureaucracies, too, and it would be a mistake to see the city issues as if they were solely for the Mayor and Commissioners or, after 1967, the Mayor and City Council. As we have already seen, the City Engineer was constantly heard from concerning design issues, and a variety of boards and commissions were consulted or voiced opinions from time to time. Memphis politicians might easily see the use of Overton Park as a decisive political issue.[139] One might even characterize the course of development leading up to the Council decision of April 5, 1968 as one that increasingly placed responsibility for this decision on elected City's officials. As late as 1964, the Mayor and Commissioners had tended to discuss decisions as ones to be made by state and federal officials, not them. In 1965, Mayor Ingram could remember no Commission vote on the subject,[140] and in an April vote only he opposed the route.[141] On May 2, 1967 (after Representative Smith's abortive bill in

---

137. *Numerous Expressway Memos Revealed,* Memphis Press-Scimitar, Oct. 2, 1971, at 6; Black, *Witness Says U.S. Rejected X-Way Tunnel on Cost Basis,* Memphis Press-Scimitar, Oct. 9, 1971, at 11 (testimony of Oscar Gray, Director of DOT's Office of Environmental Impact).

138. *Expressway Improved and OK'ed,* Memphis Press-Scimitar, Nov. 5, 1969, at 8 (editorial).

139. The voters of Memphis never clearly treated it as such; CPOP and others tried to make I–40 an issue in local elections, but no declared opponent of the road ever won election.

140. Whisenhunt, *Mayor Bucks Overton Park Expressway,* Memphis Press-Scimitar, Jan. 4, 1965, at 18.

141. See D. Tucker, n. 8 above,, at 111–12. Ingram, it may be remarked, was something of a maverick in Memphis politics; his election had been an unpleasant surprise

the Tennessee House of Representatives *and* BPR's preliminary approval of the road design), the City Commission again voted to accept the park route, with Mayor Ingram again in dissent.[142]

Then came the new form of city government, and Administrator Bridwell's willingness to reopen the routing issue in a context to which § 4(f) would clearly apply, all the while insisting that what he wanted to do was to make this a decision for Memphians. As late as January, 1968, the *Commercial Appeal* reported that Mayor Loeb (Memphis' Commissioner of Public Works and a supporter of the road when the plan was first received in the mid-'50s) had assured Tennessee Highway Commissioner Speight that the city stood behind use of the park and urged its construction.[143] Then came the February meetings already recounted, and the same paper was able to count at least three City Council members as "obviously support[ing] relocation, [one, the immediate past president of the Downtown Association,] to the point of presenting his own alternative route swinging north."[144] Perhaps distracted by the garbagemen's strike, the Council did not act until its March 5 meeting, when it unanimously adopted the following resolution:

> The Council of the City of Memphis prefers that the Expressway through Overton Park not be routed in its present proposed location but that the said proper authorities select another feasible route, with the provision that if no better route can be obtained, the route using the northern perimeter of Overton Park and the southern part of Northern Parkway be chosen.[145]

One month later, following Administrator Bridwell's interventions and their meeting at the Memphis airport, and in the face of CPOP's continuing effort to hold on to its seeming victory, the City Council adopted the following resolution by a vote of 8–2 (three members not participating):

> Whereas ... representatives of the Federal Government and the Department of Highways of the state of Tennessee have furnished the Council with considerable information and data to the effect that no other feasible and prudent route is available through Overton Park for Expressway I–40; and
>
> Whereas the Council has likewise been informed ... that its action to date has caused no delay in the building of this part of the

---

to the city establishment, and four-to-one face-offs between him and his commissioners seem to have been commonplace.

142. *Park Freeway Gets City's OK,* Com. Appeal, May 3, 1967, at 25.

143. *Mayor Reaffirms Park Route Stand,* Com. Appeal, Jan. 23, 1968, at 13.

144. Riker, *Plan for Rerouting Gains Support,* Com. Appeal, Feb. 14, 1968, at 19.

145. 49 Minutes of the Memphis City Council 410 (1968).

expressway, but that further study and hearings could materially affect the beginning of construction;

Whereas the Council realizes that the construction is very essential for the growth and progress of the City of Memphis;

Now Therefore be it resolved ... that the Council finds the route presently designated ... is the feasible and prudent location for said route and that the design as presently made is acceptable to the Council.[146]

FROM POLITICAL TO JUDICIAL OVERSIGHT

The story of Overton Park to this point—specifically, from 1955 to late in 1969 when Secretary Volpe finally approved the proposed design of I–40 and CPOP sought a lawyer to take its case to the courts—has been a political story. In this respect, it mirrored the growth of controversies throughout the country; and so also, one may say, in the turn now from the world of politics to the courts. While in a sense judicial review (looking backwards) is always a late entrant, litigation did not emerge as an important control strategy for routing decisions until late in this story. Like the Nashville dispute earlier recounted,[147] lawsuits over routing issues blossomed in the late 60s.

When it began, anti-highway litigation tended to raise straightforward legal issues, rather than challenges to the exercise of discretion and judgment. Thus, the Nashville case turned on assertions of racial motivations, a familiar litigation subject at the time. A challenge to the Three Sisters' Bridge in Washington, D.C., ultimately successful on political grounds that would help shape the argument in *Overton Park*, began with contentions that municipal officials had simply ignored obligations long in place in city legislation;[148] another lawsuit, challenging construction of an expressway that would have been constructed on fill placed in the Hudson River alongside Westchester county, alleged simple noncompliance with statutes requiring permits from the Army Corps of Engineers, that had never been applied for.[149] *Overton Park* was initially framed in a similar way—whether the Secretary of Transportation had complied with his statutory obligations, not whether his judgment in exercising statutorily conferred discretion was "arbitrary, capricious, or an abuse of discretion." CPOP's attorney's first brief in the Supreme Court, although also expressing concern how a court could know what

---

146. Id. at 515.

147. See text at note 44 above.

148. See n. 158 below.

149. Citizens Committee for the Hudson Valley v. Volpe, 297 F. Supp. 804 and 809, 302 F. Supp. 1083 (S.D.N.Y. 1969).

decisions had been taken in the absence of a formal administrative record and opinion, would assure the Court that

> The question here is not, as [respondents] would pose it, the vague and limitless one of whether the officials have correctly balanced the need to preserve the parks against all other governmental projects such as health care and welfare. Instead the question is whether those officials have complied with specific laws governing expenditure of federal monies from the Highway Trust Fund.[150]

The Supreme Court's decision in *Overton Park* marks the expansion of lawyers' targets from claims of *ultra vires* action to assertions that a discretion decisionmakers possessed had not been reasonably exercised. The remainder of these pages explore that change.

Lawyers today may find it hard to understand quite how unusual and challenging litigation like *Overton Park* was—although, fair to say, the distress created by developments imperiling beautiful, wealthy neighborhoods as well as their parks helped to animate its development. The ground was prepared in the latter part of the 1960s, when important decisions opened doors to "public interest" participation before agencies,[151] judicial review,[152] and the standing to seek it[153] that previously had seemed closed; one section of the new Department of Transportation Act explicitly subjected DOT's decisions to the Administrative Procedure Act, and the APA at least for a time was seen to have conferred federal subject matter jurisdiction over challenges invoking its review standards.[154] Still, large questions remained unanswered. Were volunteers, only indirectly affected by highway development, proper persons to invoke the jurisdiction of the federal courts, when the effects even of

150. Brief in Support of Petitioner's Application for a Stay Pending Petition for a Writ of Certiorari to the United States Court of Appeals for the Sixth Circuit 15 (filed Dec. 3, 1970).

151. Office of Communication, United Church of Christ v. FCC, 359 F.2d 994 (D.C. Cir. 1966).

152. Abbott Laboratories, Inc. v. Gardner, 387 U.S. 136 (1967).

153. Scenic Hudson Preservation Conference v. FPC, 354 F.2d 608 (2d Cir. 1965)(protection of scenic amenity an important motivator). It would be five years before the Supreme Court would confirm the expanded concept of standing *Scenic Hudson* had embraced; it handed down Association of Data Processing Service Organizations, Inc. v. Camp., 397 U.S. 150 (1970) just a year prior to its decision in *Overton Park,* and in doing so virtually leveled the "standing" obstacle. See Allan Butzel, *Intervention and Class Actions Before the Agencies and the Courts,* 25 Ad.L.Rev. 135, 136 (1973).

154. 49 U.S.C. § 1655(h); see Road Review League v. Boyd, 270 F.Supp. 650, 659–60 (S.D.N.Y. 1967). In 1977, the Supreme Court would hold that the APA did not grant subject-matter jurisdiction, Califano v. Sanders, 430 U.S. 99, a problem easily cured by pleading the general federal-question statute, 28 U.S.C. § 1331. In the interim, placing the DOT under the APA had been taken as an affirmative decision, as well, to place its decisions under court review.

delay might be substantially to increase public costs? Could they be required to post a bond to cover those additional expenses, should their actions prove unavailing? Were the judgments entrusted to departmental officials susceptible of judicial review, or rather matters to be treated as having been committed to their executive discretion—matters citizens could hope to control as they controlled legislation or executive functioning generally, "in the only way they can be in a complex society, by their [political] power, immediate or remote, over those who make the rul[ing]."[155]

The place of politics and political power raised the most delicate questions. One way to understand these questions is to consider that political influences are often felt outside the usual formalities of a hearing process, even a process as informal and legislative as accompanied highway decision-making. If in fact these administrative judgments were subject to the controls of judicial review, what was the "record" against which they should be measured? How could that record be prepared and authenticated for judicial use? The processes we have been describing were fundamentally bureaucratic and political ones. Certainly at that time, no one was thinking about creating internal records of decision, like those that attend trials. We have been viewing the development of I-40 as one almost necessarily would, through newspaper accounts, congressional records, correspondence and other informal means. How could one establish what actually had happened inside the government, as questions went from desk to desk to their ultimate resolution there? By, for example, pretrial discovery directed to the myriad government officials who may have been involved in its creation over the years that a decision moved back and forth within the bureaucracy?[156] And if politics had played a role in the decisions—as, indeed, in highway routing and design it inevitably did—in what if any circumstances was that an improper element? Could a reviewing court inquire into political influences as well as the bureaucratic decision path? Must a

---

155. Bi-Metallic Investment Co. v. State Board of Equalization, 239 U.S. 441, 445 (1915). This decision, of course, directly concerned only a constitutional claim to procedural rights—an issue not presented here. Yet plaintiffs in cases like *Overton Park* did not fit the Hohfeldian mode of persons whose individual legal rights had been directly affected by government action; they were, rather, like the citizens of Holmes's famous distinction, persons holding only one of many possible political stakes in the outcome of the many-sided disputes they were attempting to control. One recalls as well Chief Justice Marshall's famous assurance, in Marbury v. Madison, 5 U.S. (1 Cranch) 137, 166 (1803) that "where the heads of the department are the political . . . agents of the executive . . . to act in cases in which the executive possesses a constitutional or legal discretion, nothing can be more perfectly clear than that their acts are only politically examinable. But where a specific duty is assigned by law, *and individual rights depend upon the performance of that duty,* it seems equally clear that the individual who considers himself injured has a right to resort to the laws of his country for a remedy." (Emphasis added.)

156. Cf. the Morgan cases, n. 159 below.

decision communicating to a state the DOT's decision to approve a given route (or design) for 90% federal funding take the form of an opinion, communicating findings and conclusions? If such decisions were reviewable, what was the standard of review to be applied, and how should it be understood?

Although efforts to explore the Department's decision processes generally failed,[157] they had succeeded in one protracted and bitter lawsuit well known to the Justices and also closely coordinated with the litigation of *Overton Park*. This lawsuit concerned the Three Sisters' Bridge proposed to carry I–66 over the Potomac River from the Virginia suburbs into their hometown, Washington, D.C.; its later stages turned on a public and highly coercive congressional campaign to force the construction issue.[158] As it would later do in *Overton Park*, the govern-

---

157.   See, e.g., Road Review League, Town of Bedford v. Boyd, n. 154 above. This case involved the routing of I–87 through Bedford, N.Y., a wealthy and bucolic New York City suburb, and the opinion chronicles a political, bureaucratic struggle just like CPOP's; although the developments of the mid-'60s permitted a lawsuit, the Bedford plaintiffs failed to persuade the presiding judge that the political contacts were questionable or that DOT's officials had acted unlawfully.

158.   Initially, the District Government had lost a suit brought to block the project, because it had failed to observe statutorily required procedures. D.C. Federation of Civic Associations v. Airis, 391 F.2d 478 (D.C. Cir.1968), reversing 275 F. Supp. 540 (D.D.C. 1967). The District government then decided to abandon the bridge proposal, and sought to remove that aspect of I–66 from the map. Perhaps more concerned with the ease of commuting from Virginia homes than local amenities, Congress in 1968 passed a statute seeming to command the project immediately go forward; when the municipal government did not resume construction , influential members of Congress reacted with unusual force. In the words of Judge Siraca, who conducted a subsequent hearing *after* permitting the deposition of Secretary Volpe,

> . . . Congressman Natcher [chair of the House committee responsible for D.C. appropriations] stated publicly and made no secret of the fact that he would do everything that he could to withhold Congressional appropriations for the District of Columbia rapid transit system, the need for which is universally recognized in the Washington metropolitan area, until the District complied with the 1968 Act [seeming to require construction of the bridge]. On July 9, 1969, the House of Representatives passed the conference version of the supplemental appropriations bill for the District of Columbia which did not include the rapid transit funds.[115 Cong. Rec. H 5743 (daily ed. July 9, 1969).] Congressman Natcher at that time made his position perfectly clear, stating that "as soon as the freeway program gets under way beyond recall then we will come back to the House and recommend that construction funds for rapid transit be approved."[*Id.* at p. 5737.] Congressman Broyhill also threatened at that time to withhold other appropriations for the District unless the freeway program went forward. [*Id.* at p. 5738.] Subsequently, on August 8, 1969, the District of Columbia revenue bill was reported to the House with an amendment which would " 'freeze' the appropriation of any part of the authorized Federal payment to the District of Columbia, until the President has reported to the Congress that the city had committed itself irrevocably" to the construction of the freeway system. [H.R. Rep. No. 91–463, 91st Cong., 1st Sess. 21 (1969)].

ment had sought to establish the regularity of its decision in the I–66 litigation by submitting an affidavit attested to by Edgar Swick. As Deputy Director of Public Roads, Swick could credibly assert familiarity with the bureaucratic processes before and after the Department's creation. Ordinarily, government attorneys could be confident that private parties would be unsuccessful in efforts to peer behind such an affidavit; the *Morgan* cases of the early 1940s[159] stood as a nearly impervious barrier. But the public and extraordinary character of the congressional pressures on the I–66 process opened a door to further inquiry, and that inquiry produced an account that shadowed the dispute over I–40 in Memphis as well. The BPR official responsible for preparing Swick's affidavit "admitted that although the document purported to explain what the Secretary had done . . . it was prepared some two months after the purported decision and that in fact [the official] had no personal knowledge on which to base the memorandum." The court, somewhat incredulous at this procedure, asked [the official]:

> "THE COURT: Is this the only time that you can recall that it was followed, in this case?
>
> "THE WITNESS: Well, there is something similar to this in I–40 in Memphis, but I am not just sure of the sequence of events."[160]

D.C. Federation of Civic Associations v. Volpe, 316 F.Supp. 754, 762–63 (D.D.C.1970). The District folded, and Secretary Volpe then permitted construction to go forward, but *after* the park-protective statutes involved in *Overton Park* had taken effect; this stage of the litigation thus concerned his compliance with their requirements. Permitting deposition of the Secretary (a deposition Judge Siraca found reassuring about his integrity) was unusual, see n 159 below, but the necessary threshold had been crossed. In addition to the congressional action, the evidence included a letter from President Nixon to Congressman Natcher leading inescapably to the conclusion that Congressman Natcher's pressure had influenced not only the District government's but also Secretary Volpe's decision to go forward with the bridge project. Nonetheless, Judge Siraca found sufficient to sustain that decision

> the Secretary's testimony that his decision was based on the merits of the project and not solely on extraneous political pressures. It is true that Mr. Volpe was also interested in securing the release of the rapid transit appropriations, and that the approval of the bridge led to the release of those funds. But the Court finds that the mere fact that the Secretary was aware of this pressure does not invalidate his decision that the Three Sisters Bridge is an important and necessary part of the Interstate Highway System.

at 765–66. The political influence issue would lead the D.C. Circuit to reverse Judge Siraca's decision six months after the Court had decided *Overton Park*, 459 F.2d 1231 (D.C. Cir. 1971), cert. den. 405 U.S. 1030. But the issue was in the air, and references to the I 66 dispute and, especially, to the record irregularities it revealed, recurred often in petitioner's *Overton Park* papers.

159. Morgan v. United States, 304 U.S. 1 (1938) and 313 U.S. 409 (1941).

160. Brief in Support of Petitioner's Application for a Stay Pending Petition for a Writ of Certiorari to the United States Court of Appeals for the Sixth Circuit 26 n. 17 (filed Dec. 3, 1970).

The Attorneys for CPOP

Because the I–66 and I–40 disputes were attorney-linked as well as issue-linked, we should turn now to the young attorneys involved in them. It may be as hard to appreciate the changes in legal practice occurring in the late 1960s and early 1970s as it is to appreciate the changes in doctrine. As remarked at the beginning of this essay, the "public interest law" movement's litigation over environmental and social issues took shape only in the late 60s and early 70s.[161] In 1969, as CPOP finally contemplated the necessity to go to court, no organized group yet coordinated highway actions; people found each other by reading the reports. Thus it was not surprising to the attorney in the Three Sisters' Bridge litigation, Gerald Norton,[162] when CPOP called him to ask if he would represent them; Charles Newman of Memphis, a 1963 graduate of Yale Law School (who had spent the following year as law clerk to U.S. District Judge Bailey Brown of Memphis) and a future President of the Memphis Bar Association, served as local counsel.[163] But at the time Norton was a young associate in the Washington, D.C. firm of Covington & Burling, barely five years out of law school, and his partners thought the bridge litigation he was handling *pro bono publico* was distracting enough. Norton thus recommended a friend, John Vardaman, Jr. Vardaman would remain lead counsel for CPOP throughout the litigation. Like Norton, Vardaman was a young associate at a leading Washington firm, in his case Wilmer, Cutler & Pickering.[164] A native Alabaman, he had been law clerk to Justice Hugo Black in 1965–66 immediately following his graduation from Harvard Law School, and this experience would stand him in good stead. Since he and Norton coordinated their work closely (as indeed did many of the young lawyers who were spearheading the growing number of highway cases), he knew all about the facts emerging in the I–66 litigation.

Vardaman filed CPOP's action in Washington, D.C., where he and Secretary Volpe had their offices; but on government motion the case

161.   See text at note 2 above.

162.   Telephone conversation with Gerald Norton, July 30, 2004. Mr. Norton graduated from Columbia Law School in 1964 and clerked on the Second Circuit before joining Covington & Burling; he subsequently worked in the Solicitor General's Office and at the FTC, and is now a senior partner at the Washington firm of Harkins Cunningham LLP.

163.   Mr. Newman is now a senior partner in the Memphis law Firm, Burch, Porter & Johnson.

164.   Vardaman is now senior partner at Williams & Connolly, another prominent Washington law firm. In August 1970, with decision in *Overton Park* still pending in the Sixth Circuit, he moved from Wilmer Cutler to the law office of the noted litigator Edward Bennett Williams as a contract employee; the firm would not become a partnership for several years, when he would be one of the initial partnership group. It was a considerably smaller office than Wilmer Cutler, and offered a young lawyer more opportunities for litigation and responsibility than he had enjoyed there. See n. 54 above.

was soon transferred to the Western District of Tennessee, where
Charles Speight, Commissioner of the Tennessee Department of Highways, was added as a defendant. Two local residents and two national
organizations asserting an interest in the park values threatened by I–
40, joined CPOP as plaintiffs. Appearing before the Honorable Bailey
Brown in District Court, the judge for whom Charles Newman had
clerked five years previous, CPOP pressed arguments of the kind that
had already proved successful elsewhere—that the Secretary had failed
to honor straightforward legal obligations. It claimed a variety of alleged
procedural defects, including but not limited to the Secretary's failure to
make formal findings (in effect, his failure to write an opinion). It
characterized §§ 4(f) and 138 as provisions imposing binding legal requirements that the Secretary had ignored, rather than as provisions
giving him significant discretion whose abuse should be judicially measured. Under the caselaw of the time, attorney Vardaman could not have
expected any examination of discretion, even if permitted, to be very
demanding.

Perhaps the one chance he had of exploring the decision process
arose out of the question of political influence. It appears from a dissent
to the subsequent court of appeals decision that during the discovery
period plaintiffs had unsuccessfully moved to depose departmental officials about their decision process.[165] Attorney Norton had by now been
successful in deposing the Secretary in the Three Sisters Bridge case,
still in process as *Overton Park* wound its way through the courts. The
evidence of political coercion to force the building of that bridge was
public and unmistakable.[166] But CPOP's attorneys had no such smoking
guns. They failed to persuade Judge Brown that they had overcome the
presumption of regularity that ordinarily protects public officials against
such inquiries,[167] and so the motions for summary judgment were decided
on the basis of dueling affidavits. The government filed an extensive
account by Edgar Swick, who as Deputy Director of Public Roads could
credibly assert familiarity with the bureaucratic processes, before and
after the Department's creation.[168] Unable to use discovery to build a
record in court and lacking any kind of findings document from the
department, plaintiffs were limited to such public accounts of the process
as had appeared in newspapers, to Administrator Bridwell's testimony in
the 1968 Senate Hearings,[169] and to an affidavit submitted by CPOP's

---

165. Citizens to Preserve Overton Park v. Volpe, 432 F.2d 1307, 1315 n.1 (Celebrezze, J., dissenting).

166. See n. 158 above.

167. As established by the *Morgan* cases, n. 159 above.

168. It is lengthily described in the 6th Circuit opinion, n. 165 above, 432 F. 2d at
1311–12. See text at note 159 above.

169. See text at note 122 above, 432 F.2d at 1313.

long-time leader, Arlo Smith, asserting on "information and belief" that the Secretary had "made no finding that there is no feasible and prudent alternative to the use of [Overton Park]."[170]

On February 26, 1970, Judge Brown denied CPOP's motion for a preliminary injunction and granted the government's motion for summary judgment; he dismissed the complaint.[171] Already, the court noted, "All of the property along the proposed corridor has been condemned, most of the buildings within the expressway path have been destroyed, and the persons and businesses affected have been relocated."[172] The bulk of Judge Brown's opinion dealt with and dismissed the claims of procedural violation.[173] Turning then to the provisions of §§ 138 and 4(f), he concluded that their

> legislative history ... makes it clear that it was not the intent of Congress to prohibit the building of an expressway through a park if there was *any* alternative; rather, by providing that such should not be done if there is any feasible and prudent alternative, it was the intent of Congress to avoid the park if, after considering all relevant factors, it is preferable to do so. In short, it appears to have been the intent of Congress to point up the wisdom of conserving park lands and the lack of wisdom in routing an expressway through a park because the land is cheaper and the construction is easier.[174]

Having once concluded that the statutes gave the Secretary a rather large discretion, he easily found its exercise not even arguably "arbitrary and capricious."

> We recognize that normally a motion for summary judgment should not be granted if it is made properly to appear that a determinative fact is in dispute. Here, however, we would not, at a plenary hearing, have for determination whether there is a feasible and prudent alternative to the corridor or whether there is a reasonable alternative to the design that would protect the park more. These are determinations to be made by the Secretary of Transportation, and he has decided that no such alternatives exist. We could be concerned with the question and only the question of whether or not

---

170. Cf. n. 115 above; Secretary Boyd's letter was an attachment to Smith's affidavit.

171. Citizens to Preserve Overton Park v. Volpe, 309 F.Supp. 1189 (W.D Tenn. 1970).

172. Id. at 1195.

173. For example, plaintiffs had complained of the Department's failure to honor an internal Policy and Procedure Memorandum defining the contents of the notices and of the hearing transcripts that states were to provide the public and the Department, respectively. While doubting whether the Memorandum was legally binding, the court found that in any event any errors were neither substantial nor prejudicial. 309 F.Supp. at 1191–94.

174. Id. at 1194.

the determinations as made were arbitrary and capricious. Our study of the affidavits and exhibits on file convince us that, from the undisputed facts, we could never find in this case that, as contended by plaintiffs, such determinations are so wrong as to be arbitrary and capricious. This being so, we conclude that defendants are entitled to summary judgment on this issue as well as the other issues in the case.[175]

This conclusion framed the *only* issue the Sixth Circuit considered on appeal, "whether there remains a genuine issue over any material fact in dispute."[176] CPOP's attorneys would have to have been "able to show by affidavit, or other evidence, that there is at least a possibility that [they] will be able to overcome the presumption of regularity."[177] For a majority of the panel, Judge Weick of the Sixth Circuit writing for himself and Judge Peck, they had been unable to accomplish this. But CPOP's attorneys had succeeded, in the Sixth Circuit, in winning their first judicial vote. For Judge Celebrezze, dissenting, the Secretary's failure to explain his decision had precluded effective review or enforcement of his statutory obligations to respect park values. The contending affidavits that took the place of such an explanation (an explanation Judge Celebrezze would have required) raised genuine issues of fact respecting which plaintiffs were entitled to both discovery and a trial.

Attorney Vardaman had succeeded in linking the I–40 problem to the ongoing dispute about the Three Sisters Bridge in one judicial mind; and the result would have been to open the bureaucratic decision process to examination at trial. Now he filed a petition for rehearing. In denying it, October 30, 1970, the panel majority made the stakes clear: the contending affidavits had raised triable no issue of fact, it concluded, because Arlo Smith's "information and belief" that no finding had been made could not create a triable issue when counterposed to the contrary affidavit of a participant-official.[178] And the link to the Three Sisters Bridge litigation was unavailing; here there were no such political pressures as had been alleged in that case, and the barrier to probing the mental processes of the Secretary set by such decisions as Morgan v. United States[179] had not been overcome.

In ordinary course, CPOP's attorneys would now have had ninety days to compose and file a petition for certiorari with the United States Supreme Court. But bulldozers and wrecking cranes were roaring on the verge of the park, clearing the land on both sides right up to its edge. In

---

175.   Id. at 1195.

176.   432 F.2d at 1310 (1970).

177.   Ibid.

178.   432 F.2d at 1318–19 (Per Curiam on petition for rehearing).

179.   See n. 159 above.

denying rehearing, the Sixth Circuit had also denied an application for stay pending a petition for certiorari, and Tennessee made abundantly clear that it was prepared to begin construction inside the park at once. The Highway Department opened bids for the contract October 30 and awarded it November 2, the next working day. Vardaman sought a stay from Justice Stewart, the Circuit Justice for the Sixth Circuit, November 5; Tennessee informed him that it would not await the Justice's ruling, but begin work unless affirmatively restrained. On November 6, Justice Stewart issued an order inviting replies to the stay petition and restraining Tennessee from construction activity in the meantime. Two weeks later the Court requested briefs on the stay issue, and set the matter for oral argument December 7.

In many ways, the arguments over the stay seemed to set a tone for the merits. One could begin with Tennessee's decision to press forward urgently for construction, when the matter had been pending in one form or another since 1955. Its exasperation with delay is understandable; yet in acting on it Tennessee officials risked the impression that would create. Attorney Vardaman would represent to the Court that as recently as filing of its petition for rehearing in the Sixth Circuit, Tennessee's attorneys had assured that court that no contract would be let nor work begin until the Supreme Court's processes had been exhausted.[180] The State's rush to moot the issue opened the door to suggestions that it (and the Secretary) might have something to hide. Vardaman filled his brief in support of CPOP's stay application with questions about the non-existent record, and asserted parallels to the problems in the Three Sisters' Bridge litigation.[181] Thus could questions about the record and the actual basis for the Secretary's decision be planted in the minds of Justices who were living daily, please recall, with press accounts of the I–66 imbroglio and their own possible interests in how they would be able to drive from home to work. Even as he expressed surprise that a project so long in the works needed now to be so urgently pursued, attorney Vardaman acted to meet the criticism that CPOP was seeking delay for its own sake and imposing significant costs on the state. The petition for stay, he wrote, could be treated as his petition for certiorari.[182]

When the Court set the motion for stay for oral argument Monday, December 7, it not only marked Jack Vardaman's first return to the

---

180. Brief in Support of Petitioner's Application for a Stay Pending Petition for a Writ of Certiorari to the United States Court of Appeals for the Sixth Circuit 17 (filed Dec. 3, 1970).

181. Perhaps the most remarkable was a footnote quoting testimony in that case by the BPR official responsible for preparing the affidavit Edgar Swick had filed in *that* case. See n. 160 above.

182. Id. at 14 n. 12.

Supreme Court since his days as Justice Black's law clerk; his boss, Edward Bennett Williams, had been scheduled for the first argument that day,[183] and now—awaiting his own argument—he would be present in that imposing courtroom as a witness to his new employee's efforts. The attorney appearing for the Solicitor General's office at that argument was even greener than Vardaman; William Bradford Reynolds had graduated Vanderbilt Law School just three years earlier, in 1967, and was making his first appearance at the Court[184]—a fact that suggests, as your editor can attest from his own experience, that the office did not see this assignment as a very important or demanding one. Very likely, given his habitual practice with the young attorneys in his office, Solicitor General Erwin Griswold—Dean at Harvard Law School when Vardaman was a student there—was also in the Court that day, watching *his* young attorney's first argument. Once the importance of the case became apparent, Griswold would take the leading role, and argue on the merits.

In the Supreme Court

Among the scholarly delights of Capitol Hill are the papers of several Supreme Court Justices kept in the Library of Congress's manuscript collections, and the complete files of briefs and oral argument transcripts maintained in the Supreme Court Library. They permit a fuller account of *Overton Park* in the Supreme Court than could otherwise be imagined.

Three attorneys appeared at oral argument on the stay; in addition to Mr. Vardaman and Mr. Reynolds, J. Alan Hanover appeared for the state of Tennessee. In opening his argument, Vardaman quickly exploited the "rush to judgment" tone Tennessee's behavior had suggested:

> If the respondents are permitted to proceed with this construction they may likely moot this case. If they do, they will have been successful without ever having filed an answer to the Petitioners' complaint, without putting one witness on the witness stand, without having one other official subject to examination by deposition, but instead rely [sic] on a basis of out of court litigation affidavits filed in support of a motion for summary judgment.[185]

Much of the argument, on all sides, was consumed by questions about the timing and extent of Tennessee's preparation of the approaches to

---

183. Ramsey v. United Mine Workers, 401 U.S. 302 (1971).

184. Like Mr. Vardaman, Mr. Reynolds has become a prominent Washington attorney. Assistant Attorney General for the Justice Department's Civil Rights Division during Ronald Reagan's presidency and long an important figure in the Federalist Society, he is now a litigation partner in the Washington office of Howrey Simon Arnold & White.

185. Transcript of oral argument on the motion for stay 5 (Dec. 7, 1970, on file in the US Supreme Court library).

the park—whether the Court was being asked to "unring the bell"—about DOT's actions in relation to its statutory responsibility, and about what the record was. It reflected awareness about the transitional character of the I-40 issues, in relation to changing statutory instructions, and some confusion about the timing of departmental decisions in relation to the effective dates of the new legislative instructions.[186] One interchange with Mr. Vardaman presumably contributed to later developments that would put the government in an unflattering light:

Q Well, would your first point be mooted if [the Secretary] presented in this Court a piece of paper that made the findings that you say are missing?

A I think that first point would be mooted. We would then proceed to whether or not the determination was infirm. . . .

The second point which could possibly also be mooted if he gave a satisfactory written determination, although I wouldn't concede that it would be mooted, is that the Court below [found], even though the Secretary made no documentation of his finding[,] that this Court's decision in United States against Morgan prohibited any inquiry of the Secretary as to whether he did make the finding.[187] And the difficulty which is presented to anyone seeking review under the statute . . . is that first the secretary is not required to record the fact that he made the determination . . . and [second] those seeking review aren't entitled to ask him whether he made it.[188]

Tennessee's argument, in any event, could hardly have helped respondents; the state took the position that all that was involved was the possibility of 90% federal subvention of the $2 million section through the park proper, and that it could and would proceed on its own if that support was not available. Where Mr. Reynolds' argument addressed the merits, the importance of the case for grant or not of the writ of certiorari, Tennessee could have been seen to have thumbed its nose at the Court.

---

186. Thus, Mr. Vardaman argued consistently as if both the route and the design decisions had been made in November of 1969; Tennessee, as if the route had been established before 1968; Mr. Reynolds clearly distinguished between the April 1968 route approval, reading a letter Secretary Boyd had written CPOP at the time explaining the decision and his instructions to design the road to minimize damage to the park, and the later design approval. Id. at 25. This was followed by extended discussion of the documentation of the 1968 decision for the Court; the Justices asking questions appear to have been both aware of and unhappy with the limited state of the "record" before them.

187. [Ed.] See n. 159 above.

188. Transcript, n. 185 above, 14–15; this last remark resonates strongly with what had emerged in the *Three Sisters' Bridge* litigation, see text at note 158 above, related to the Court in Petitioners' brief in support of their motion for stay.

The Court met in conference immediately following the day's arguments; Justice Blackmun's notes of its discussion[189] and the Court's subsequent order granting a stay and providing for expedited briefing and argument are both also dated December 7, 1970. This was an unusual step for a Court usually conferring on Fridays, doubtless reflecting the waiting bulldozers. Justice Blackmun's notes reveal a Court closely divided whether the motion for stay and petition for certiorari (as it was agreed the Justices would treat the motion) should be granted. The Justices do not seem to have doubted that the Secretary had made a decision, and the Government's opposition to the motion for stay had informed them that he had instructed his staff to develop findings in all future such cases.[190] Seeing a statutory regime in transition, a commitment to future regularity, and the likelihood that future proceedings would produce no change in outcome, the Chief Justice and Justices White, Stewart and Blackmun were opposed taking up the case; impressed by the forcefulness of Congress's instructions and the sloppiness with which the case had apparently been handled in the Department, Justices Black, Brennan and Harlan supported the motion. Justice Douglas had withdrawn from the case. Justice Blackmun's notes show that Justice Marshall (ultimately the opinion writer) first voted for, then against, and finally for grant; he predicted that "if we remand, all we get is a sno job."[sic] Justice Marshall's files say nothing that directly explains his ultimate decision in petitioners' favor. Possibly, however, he was influenced by the simultaneous pendency of a motion for stay in litigation involving Breckinridge Park in San Antonio, the very dispute that had catalyzed enactment of the statutes in question. That stay would also be granted December 7, although in this case with an invitation to petition for certiorari on an accelerated basis, and he would (unsuccessfully) support its continuance.[191] Among Breckinridge Park, I–66 in Washington, D.C., and now Memphis, it would have been apparent that large issues were involved.

---

189. These and all subsequent materials drawing on Justice Blackmun's papers are drawn from the file for *Overton Park*, OT 1970–1066, in the manuscript collection at the Library of Congress.

190. United States Opposition to the Motion for Stay 9 (1970).

191. San Antonio Conservation Soc. v. Texas Highway Comm'n, 400 U.S. 939 (1970). This case was compromised in a number of respects: certiorari was being sought in advance of judgment in the Fifth Circuit; party status was unclear; the litigation concerned decisions respecting the approaches to the park, and not the use of parkland itself. Whatever its weaknesses, it could hardly have been lost on Mr. Vardaman, who subsequently became associated with that litigation, how useful it would be for the Justices to have this second highway-and-parkland dispute under their gaze at this important juncture. The stay was vacated December 20, 1970 with Justices Douglas, Black, Brennan and Marshall dissenting, 400 U.S. 961, and certiorari was denied the following Monday (December 21, 1970), Justices Douglas, Black and Brennan dissenting. 400 U.S. 968.

The Court's December 7 order accommodated Tennesse's impatience by placing the attorneys under unusual time pressures. Customarily, petitioners have 90 and respondents then 60 days to brief their cases in the Court once certiorari has been granted, with argument following within a few weeks. The Court's order provided two weeks briefing time to each side followed one week later by argument. Petitioners' brief, then, was due December 21. For the respondent state and federal governments, the two weeks in question, were Monday, December 21, 1970 to Monday, January 4, 1971—the winter holiday season.

On the heels of the December 7 order, the Solicitor General complicated matters for attorney Vardaman (and also ultimately for the government). He filed a motion suggesting remand to the district court to permit the Secretary to introduce "the entire administrative record on which his decisions were based." In the world of hardball litigation tactics, you might be tempted to understand such a motion as a questionable device to bleed time from what was already a pressured preparation. Yet the motion can as readily be understood as responsive to by-play with Mr. Vardaman in oral argument on the stay,[192] as well as to the general concerns the Justices evidenced then about the state of the record. Nor was it unambiguously advantageous to its maker; it both seemed to acknowledge weakness in the case, and infuriated Memphians favoring construction of the road by conceding the appropriateness of a further, indefinite stay during the requested remand. Petitioners as well as Tennessee opposed the motion, on the ground that much remained for the Court to decide[193] and that the result could be unnecessary time and expense. At the same December 17 conference as the Court decided to vacate its stay of construction in Breckinridge Park and to deny certiorari in that litigation, the Court denied the motion.[194] Little appears in the available papers to suggest why.

As the remand would eventually show, the suggestion instinct in the Solicitor General's motion, that there *was* a record in the case, was itself mischievous. Note how the compression of time to develop argument in the Court may have compromised the SG's ability to inform himself on this question. An informal and largely bureaucratic action such as this continuing course of route and design negotiation and approval generates no record in the judicial sense—indeed, at one point in its opinion the Court recognizes that the agency process "is not designed to produce a record that is to be the basis of agency action—the basic requirement

---

192.   See n. 188 above.

193.   Whether the statute required contemporaneous written findings, conceded not to have been made; whether petitioners were entitled to depose the Secretary and FHA Administrator (the Three Sisters' Bridge connection); and what was the proper standard of review.

194.   See n. 191 above.

for substantial evidence review." Nonetheless, the Court was persuaded that "there is an administrative record that allows the full, prompt review of the Secretary's action that is sought without the additional delay which would result from having a remand to the Secretary." Unsurprisingly, the remand proved that no such record existed. Time to develop the appeal would have avoided the error indeed, by focusing the Court's attention on the difficulties of reviewing the factual and judgmental bases of informal agency action, it might have led to a rather different result.

The briefs were timely filed on all sides. Influenced by what had gone before, as well as by the strategic sense that arose from the Three Sisters' Bridge controversies, petitioner's brief tended to emphasize two arguments—first, that the new statutes imposed an obligation that could be satisfied only by written findings, and that at the least, in the absence of written findings, *Morgan* should be understood to permit an inquiry into *whether* the Secretary had made the statutorily required decisions (as distinct from how they were made, which petitioners conceded to be an improper inquiry); second, that any review should use the substantial evidence test, under which one would find questions of fact precluding summary judgment. Implicit in the first argument was a relatively absolutist take on the requirements imposed by § 138 and § 4(f); petitioners also argued that the findings policy the Secretary had subsequently adopted should be applied in this case; and that the SG's motion to remand implicitly conceded the need for submission of the administrative record, rather than Swicker's litigation affidavit. The Three Sisters' Bridge litigation was extensively invoked to suggest a rotten smell from the Department.[195] Implicit in the second was a concession that "arbitrary and capricious" review would not amount to much; petitioners did *not* significantly address its meaning. The SG's brief was responsive. Agreeing that the Secretary must address parkland values and protect them, it argued that this had to occur in the context of a "delicate task of balancing," inter alia, the possibly harsh impact of alternatives on other values.[196] This of course suggested that it would be useful to know whether such balancing had in fact occurred, but the SG argued that here there was no indication of the bad faith claimed in *Morgan* and shown in the Three Sisters' Bridge litigation. The statute imposed no findings requirement, the Secretary's new policy was discretionary (i.e., not an action recognizing legally binding requirements) and should not be applied to processes that had reached administrative finality before its announcement; inquiry into the Secretary's decision process would be improper. He argued, as well, that under the APA the only available standard of review was to determine whether the Secretary's judgment

---

195. E.g., Brief for Petitioners, pp. 24–26.

196. Brief for the Secretary Volpe, pp. 19–22.

had been "arbitrary and capricious." Again, there was *no* argument about the meaning of that standard; both sides seem to have assumed that (as any lawyer would have advised before the decision in *Overton Park*) "arbitrary and capricious" review would prove highly deferential. But, consistent with the motion to remand the SG had filed, the government's brief conceded that if the Court concluded either that the statutes required findings or that petitioners had successfully raised genuine questions of fact about whether the Secretary's judgment had been "arbitrary and capricious," then a remand to permit introduction of the entire administrative record would be appropriate.[197]

What had actually happened? How could a court know this? Had the Secretary correctly understood the new requirements imposed by the statutes under which he was acting? These had emerged as central questions in the litigation, and the SG's course of conduct tended to underscore them. Now, minutes before oral argument was to begin, he took a step that drove this perspective home. Attorney Vardaman wrote a friend a few weeks after the argument,

> As I was sitting at counsel table at 9:55 a.m. . . . my former Dean, now Solicitor General, decked out in full regalia [came] over tome and handed me two pieces of paper. He said they were affidavits of Secretary Volpe and former Secretary Boyd in which they swore that they had made the decisions required by statute. Conjuring up my best expression of disbelief, I inquired as to whether I correctly understood that he was attempting to file those as evidence in the case about to be argued. He replied that he was filing them for whatever they were worth.[198]

The two certificates were each two pages long. Secretary Boyd:

> . . . In view of the mandate of section 4(f) . . . and protests received concerning the routing of Interstate Highway 40 through Memphis, Tennessee, I decided to have this routing studied to see that it conformed to that provision of law. Alternative routes were examined, and local government officials and local groups, such as Citizens to Preserve OVerton Park, were consulted on this matter. . . . I determined and found as a fact that there was no feasible and prudent alternative to routing this highway generally along the bus roadway through Overton Park . . . Because section 4(f) required that the project must include all possible planning to minimize harm to the park, I insisted upon a rigorous investigation of measures which might be taken to minimize adverse impact. . . .

---

197. Tennessee also filed a brief, of course, but it is of limited significance for this discussion.

198. CPOP correspondence files, letter dated March18, 1971.

And Secretary Volpe:

> ... At the time I took office, my predecessor had made his determination that there was no feasible and prudent alternative to the route location of I–40 in Memphis Tennessee. During the [subsequent months] ... work proceeded on those sections of I–40 leading to the park. I therefore made a determination that there was no feasible and prudent alternative to the location ... it was my responsibility to decide whether the project included all possible planning to minimize harm to the park. ... After personally reviewing the results of studies of suggested design alternatives in October and November, 1969, I determined and found as a fact that the "depressed" highway design is the one which would include all possible planning to minimize harm to the park if certain modifications were adopted. I therefore granted my approval subject to the acceptance by the Tennessee Highway Department of certain conditions ... subject to my continuing review.

As with the motion to remand, one might fear that submitting these certificates on the very day of argument was a litigation tactic calculated to distract a young and relatively inexperienced adversary. Yet one might also understand it more innocently, as directly responsive to the invitation implicit in the Q & A with Vardaman at the argument over the stay.[199] If one took that byplay seriously, the government—after giving the Court an opportunity to send the case back—had now supplied what the record lacked: personal attestations by the responsible Secretaries that they had made the relevant decisions in awareness of the governing law. Given how one might reasonably have understood the meaning of "arbitrary and capricious" at the time—and if *Morgan* had successfully been invoked and the Three Sisters Bridge imbroglio distinguished—the government might be home free.

Still, on the very cusp of argument? Perhaps the lateness of this filing was the product not of scheming for litigation advantage, but of the holiday season, and resulting difficulty in finding Secretaries Boyd and Volpe and creating the necessary papers.[200] The Solicitor General is

---

199. Recall the question asked of Vardaman, "Well, would your first point be mooted if [the Secretary] presented in this Court a piece of paper that made the findings that you say are missing?" See text following note 186 above. When his turn came at oral argument on the merits, the Solicitor General would twice refer to the submissions as stemming from the "suggestion" made in the "previous oral argument." Tr. of oral argument, No. 1066, OT 1970, Jan. 11, at p. 25. The two certificates supplied, over secretarial oath, the missing findings. Note, however, that while they invoked the language of the statute, "feasible and prudent" and "all possible planning," they gave *no* indication what the Secretary had understood that language to mean. The certificates averred conclusions; they did not provide explanations.

200. This was the explanation Solicitor General Griswold offered the Court. "We recognize that the presentation of these documents is unusual. We submit them for what

an institutional litigator, appearing before the Court dozens of times each Term. This was no longer a fledgling attorney; the Solicitor General himself was acting. While the familiarity of the SG and the Court might breed a certain insouciance about referring to supplementary materials,[201] it also creates a certain sensitivity to signals like the one apparently given at the oral argument on the stay. And it entails an institutional reputation quite transcending issues of victory and loss in any individual case, an institutional reputation that any Solicitor General would be assiduous to protect. It seems unlikely that any SG would act to secure an immediate litigating "advantage," if indeed he could think that apparent unfairness to an adversary would benefit his argument, at cost to that reputation. Nor did any of the Justices abrade him about the filing.

Still, you might put yourself in the shoes of attorney Vardaman, surprised in this way just as he was composing himself for his thirty minutes of oral argument about to begin. How would you respond?

> Shortly into my oral argument I called attention to the fact approximately five minutes before argument had begun I had seen these "too-late formulations"[202] for the first time and suggested that if the Solicitor General wished to supplement his record with the testimony of additional witnesses, the proper place to do that was in district court where the plaintiffs would have the full right of cross-examination.[203]

Vardaman's basic approach was to seek to persuade the Court that it was in no position to know what had happened in the Department; that the Solicitor General's intervention—both the motion to remand and now these certificates—essentially conceded as much; and that given the chance, he could prove that the averments of at least Secretary Boyd's certificate, that he had made a decision in April 1968, were false. No prior document had connected the Secretary, rather than Administrator Bridwell, to the April decision; and Administrator Bridwell had testified to Congress and would state on the record if permitted to that he had made no *independent* findings himself, but had left matters in the hands

---

effect they can properly be given. ... We had them nicely printed up, but Secretary Volpe has been out of town. His affidavit [sic] was cleared with him by telephone; it was to be signed this morning and when he came to sign it he wanted to change it and of course it's his certificate, and so he changed it and the result is that we have withdrawn the printed copies which we had prepared in advance and have submitted the original of the certificates to the Clerk and have provided these Xerox copies to our counsel and to the Court." Id. at 25–26.

201. A temptation to which your editor occasionally fell prey when preparing himself for argument.

202. The quoted phrase is from Justice Black's separate opinion.

203. See n. 54 above.

of the Memphis City Council. The certificates essentially made Vardaman's point about the one-sidedness of the materials before the Court:

> I think that this is an extraordinary effort in which to, manner in
> which to present evidence in a case; particularly since we were not
> permitted—in fact the Court of Appeals held that we were barred by
> this Court's decision in *Morgan,* from taking a deposition [of Admin-
> istrator Bridwell] which we specifically offer would dispute one of
> these affidavits.[204]

The bulk of his oral argument (and rebuttal) then explored just what
propositions of fact he thought he should be entitled to inquire into.
Vardaman knew that he would not get past *Morgan*; he denied again and
again that he was interested in exploring the details of the Secretary's
(or Bridwell's) decision process if in fact the Secretary (or Bridwell) had
made a decision; but that what he thought he could show was that these
individuals had not in fact decided matters, but had in effect unlawfully
delegated decision to the Memphis City Council.

> [T]hose attacking decisions must be able to ascertain what decisions
> were made and what the basis, that is what the documents before
> the person would have been in order that they can seek a review . . .
> of what he did on the basis of what he purportedly acted upon.[205]

Whether the statute required formal findings, an important element of
petitioner's brief, hardly figured in the oral argument; whether review
should be under a "substantial evidence" or "arbitrary and capricious"
standard was mentioned only in the last fifteen or so seconds of the
argument; what the content of the "arbitrary and capricious" standard
might be—that is, what you have probably read the case to learn—was
not discussed at all.

The Solicitor General's argument was a good deal calmer than Mr.
Vardaman's. The first half of it dealt essentially with the geography of
the park and the highway through it—how little land would be taken
(and how considerately, given the existing bus road configuration), and
that Memphis had now used the funds it had received for the 26 acres to
acquire more than twelve times as many acres of new parklands to
replace them. Then turning to the question whether findings were
required, he explained the submissions he had made[206] and reasserted
the government's reading of the statute, that—as the legislative history
established—it entailed delicate secretarial balancing of competing considerations. Review, he asserted, should be under the "arbitrary or
capricious" standard—but he, too, did not explore what that might be,

---

204. Tr. at 6. See also id. at 16.

205. Id. at 9.

206. Id. at 25. See text at note 3198 above.

nor did any Justice seem to be interested in that question. But, in a way confirming Vardaman's reading of the government's behavior as a soft confession of error, he argued

> If the Court feels that the question of arbitrary and capricious cannot be determined on this record, and we felt that there was some indication of that in the previous argument, then we rely on our motion to remand for the purpose of allowing the admission of the administrative record in the District Court.
>
> We do not think there should be a remand for a full trial unless the District Court finds after examining the administrative record that it cannot decide the issue of arbitrary and capricious action without a further trial. We filed the motion of remand not for the purpose of conceding error, as Mr. Vardaman says, but for the purpose of narrowing the scope of any remand....[207]

Then echoing Justice Marshall's remarks in the first conference,[208] he suggested that a remand would prove

> a triumph of formalism. With the benefit of hindsight, this record is not all that I might like to have. ... It would be better if we didn't have to piece out the essence of their determinations from other actions which they took like press releases and resolutions and letters and affidavits ... [but] remand for further proceedings would, I think, be a kind of mechanical jurisprudence more fitting for a Baron Park than for the final third of the 20th century.[209]

These words evoked some rather querulous questioning by at least one Justice. Do you think the SG's peroration, following, any more likely to have been successful—however well it may have invoked what ultimately proved to be the stakes?

> The fundamental question here [is] one of the separation of powers, of the proper allocation of function to courts, legislatures and the executive branch, in the important and complex task of carrying on government. Two things are clear: one is that Congress has legislated certain specific requirements with respect to the use of parklands and the other is that it has allocated the administration of that provision to the executive branch, specifically to the Secretary of Transportation.
>
> This does not mean that there is no role for the courts, for the Secretary should be held in check if he ignores the legislative requirements. But it does mean that the proper role of the courts is

---

207. Id. at 29.

208. See text following note 190 above.

209. Tr. at 30–31.

a narrow and limited one and it is important, I submit, both for the administration of the government and for the court that the limited nature of that role be recognized and observed. It is not good government to have all governmental decisions decided by courts, or even to have a situation where, as a matter of routine, all questions arising in the administration of the government are habitually referred to courts.

In recent years more and more governmental decisions are being made by courts. The recent broadening or near elimination of concepts of standing and the limitations on sovereign immunity as a defense have contributed to this result.

Of course, courts should see that the Constitution is complied with when the statutory rules are followed, but is it wise that the substance of all administrative action should be subject to reevaluation in the courts?

What the two Secretaries have done here, they have acted; what they have done is rational; and it complies with the directive given to them by Congress; the decision was for them. It should be upheld and the judgment below should be affirmed.[210]

Mr. Vardaman's final words would invoke "the battle to preserve this nation's environment against projects such as that involved here."[211]

Justice Blackmun wrote a memo to himself, reflecting again a view that "this is a great tempest without much outrageous substance." *Morgan* should preclude inquiry into the Secretaries' thinking, but the record is "fuzzy," and "what we may get down to is whether the case should be remanded for adherence to some of the formalities. The ultimate result is perfectly clear ... As Justice Marshall pointed out in conference, if we remand we will get only a snow job and nothing more. The practicalities of the situation argue against the remand. On the other side is the fact that this is good discipline for the agency and it may well satisfy the objectors." His notes of the ensuing conference suggest that the dividing line between majority and dissent reflected feelings about the importance of the case. The remand to the district court was to a significant degree the product of what was understood as the SG's acceptance (if not urging) of that outcome, and was not expected to produce change; Justices Black and Brennan, initially joined by Justice Harlan, felt much more strongly that substance was at stake.

The Chief Justice assigned Justice Marshall the opinion, asking him to give it priority;[212] it would be issued a mere six weeks after argument.

210. Id. at 32–33.

211. Id. at 44.

212. The opinion assignment to Justice Marshall, contained in his papers in the Library of Congress, OT 1970 1066, stated

He would, as you know, write extensively and influentially about the meaning of "arbitrary and capricious" review—a question that although essentially unbriefed would be the enduring contribution of the case. The records at the Library of Congress suggest little appreciation that this would be the case's future import, or difficulty among the Justices with what he had written.

Epilogue

Victory came both as vindication and as challenge. The young lawyers who had been pursuing and coordinating the growing body of highway litigation—not just Vardaman, Norton, and Newman, but Anthony Kline in California, Al Butzel in New York—were having a remarkable impact.

> "We were the masters of this subject; to be only thirty and know you know more about an important set of issues than anyone else, that is a remarkable place to be at the beginning of a professional career."[213]

Yet, promising further proceedings, victory also underscored significant personal and professional issues. Although settings in which a young lawyer could take responsibilities unusual for his newness to the profession and grow considerably in skill and reputation, these lawsuits were not valuable business opportunities for the lawyer or, particularly, his firm. Vardaman was fortunate as a young lawyer developing a career to have an employer who understood the long-term benefits for his firm of the experience he was getting; Edward Bennett Williams, who had started his own career in not dissimilar ways, continued to pay his salary and provide a year-end bonus, But it hardly had to be that way. Vardaman's correspondence files show continuing struggles to have even out-of-pocket expenses paid; one letter written shortly after victory in the Supreme Court remarked that he and Charles Newman had been paid a fee of $4000—$4/hour—for an estimated 1000 "billable hours"

Dear Thurgood:

   I have not completed assignment on last week's argued cases, but the *Overton* case should have a priority.

   Since you were one of five voting for remand to the District Court to decide whether the statutory determination was in fact made as claimed, will you undertake an opinion?

   The five voting to remand to the District Court also voted that the standard of "arbitrary and capricious" was the appropriate yardstick.

Regards,

WEB

213. Conversation with John Vardaman, December 16, 2004.

through the Supreme Court decision.[214] Now he would have to prepare for an extended trial, with depositions, transcripts and other expenses as well as his own commitments of time. Shortly after the Supreme Court's decision, Vardaman's correspondence estimated the post-decision trial expenses at $17,000; he asked as well for some compensation—but he was clear from the outset that he would not insist on the latter, and that he had set that request "considerably below our normal hourly rates."[215] Much of his correspondence files in the wake of victory are taken up with efforts to get reimbursement, including CPOP's reports of appeals both to foundations and national organizations that might prove willing to help and to their neighbors. A momentous victory had to be nailed down, and that would not come cheap. CPOP was struggling with a treasury balance under $1500;[216] a few weeks later, one of its members reported to Vardaman that she had "contributed a bronze vase which brought us $75 ... placed contribution cans and collected funds at neighboring store."[217] It is unlikely these sums compensated the firms even for secretarial time; and then there was always the chance that other firm clients would fail to appreciate what the law suits were accomplishing.

The events following Vardaman's estimates—25 days of trial before Judge Brown and a 6500-page record seeking to reconstruct what the administration knew or should have known on the questions of prudence and feasibility, numerous administrative proceedings and appeals—would make them risibly low.[218] On January 5, 1972, Judge Brown ordered the case remanded to the Secretary to decide the matter in accordance with the statute as the Supreme Court had interpreted it. The Department's prior action had not been based on a correct understanding of the statute, he found; but Judge Brown's opinion also strongly signalled a substantial willingness to uphold whatever decision the Secretary might reach.[219] Now, however, Secretary Volpe found himself obliged to apply the National Environmental Policy Act of

---

214. Id., letter of March 18, 1971.

215. Id., letter of March 16, 1971.

216. CPOP correspondence files, letter of March 20, 1971.

217. Id., letter of June 17, 1971. CPOP's members support included the use of a room over a garage for living, the loan of a car for transportation, and home-cooked meals. Conversation with John Vardaman, Dec. 16, 2004.

218. Vardaman would tell the Supreme Court in his petition for certiorari, n. 223 below, that "counsel for the petitioners had spent approximately 2700 hours on this litigation between the filing of the complaint and the notice of appeal."

219. Citizens to Preserve Overton Park, Inc. v. Volpe, 335 F.Supp. 873 (W.D. Tenn. 1972). In particular, the trial judge indicated his skepticism about the principal alternative route that had been argued for on remand, following creekbeds and railroad tracks north of the park—a route that threatened racially integrated neighborhoods, water supplies, and several small parks. Id.; see also Memphis Press-Scimitar, Oct. 7, 1971, at 1.

1969;[220] in January of 1973, after further hearings in Memphis, he found—without specifying what it would be—that there was at least one "feasible and prudent alternative" to the route through the park.[221] Judge Brown would have required him to specify that alternative, but in April 1974, the Sixth Circuit upheld the Secretary's judgment; the statute required him only to find that at least one such alternative existed, and he need not specify what it was.[222]

This stage of the litigation held out some possibility of financial relief. If attorney Vardaman was able to persuade the courts both that his services fell within the "private attorney general" rationale that had recently acquired substantial currency in the courts, and that the Eleventh Amendment did not preclude applying that line of cases to a state, he might be able to recover compensation for his services that CPOP had proved unable to provide. The Sixth Circuit had found the Eleventh Amendment precluded recovery, and on this issue alone Vardaman once again filed a petition for certiorari in the Supreme Court.[223] The Court had already granted certiorari in Alyeska Pipeline Service Co. v. The Wilderness Society, and with its decision in that case repudiating the private attorney general rationale,[224] any such possibility disappeared. Whatever the rewards of this representation, they were not going to be financial.

Vardaman continued to hear about Overton Park from time to time, as DOT officials would seek to include him in the ongoing discussions. As CPOP's Memphis attorney Charles Newman recalls it, throughout this time

> the Memphis establishment believed that their interests and the interests of the State DOT were the same, and therefore made the mistake of delegating virtually all decisions to the State DOT.... The City leadership's main objective was to get a midtown express-way and to solve what they saw as a transportation problem. The State DOT exhibited the usual bureaucratic recalcitrance, being determined to vindicate their original decision about the route and fearing that any good faith study of alternate routes would demon-

---

220. 3 Env.L.Rep. 20423.

221. He reached this judgment despite a finding from the FHWA that no feasible and prudent alternative to the park route did exist. Highway proponents, recalling that at the time his nomination to be Ambassador to the Vatican was pending, are as willing to speculate about the politics of *this* judgments as highway opponents had been about earlier federal judgments.

222. Citizens to Preserve Overton Park, Inc. v. Brinegar, 494 F.2d 1212 (6th Cir. 1974), rev'g, 357 F. Supp. 846 (W.D. Tenn. 1973), cert. denied sub nom. Citizens to Preserve Overton Park v. Smith, 421 U.S. 991 (1975).

223. October Term 1974, No. 74–757, filed December 1974.

224. 421 U.S. 240 (1975).

strate the existence of feasible and prudent alternates ... If the City had fully understood what was happening, they might have been able to get approval for a route around the park....[225]

Instead, under continuing pressure from the state, the Department kept studying how I–40 might be completed through the park. In September 1974, Tennessee submitted a new proposal opting for an open cut design through the park. Secretary Brinegar instructed the FHWA in January of the following year that an open cut design could not be approved under § 4(f) and asked for an evaluation of tunneling alternatives. In April 1975, President Ford's then Secretary of Transportation, William Coleman, announced his provisional judgment that the road should be built as a two-tier tunnel under the Park;[226] even apart from the initial outlay, the expense of maintaining such a tunnel—not then payable from the federal Highway Trust Fund—made that alternative unacceptable to the state. A study of a single level tunnel was completed in March 1976, and Tennessee held further hearings in Memphis in August. The Deputy Secretary of Transportation scheduled a hearing in Memphis for November 1976, but canceled it once Jimmy Carter had been elected, in response to a request from Tennessee officials who evidently expected to find the new administration more cooperative.[227] The state then proposed a design that would be partially tunneled, partly depressed, and in October 1977 the Department rejected it;[228] within weeks a new design for more, but still not complete, tunneling had been presented and, again, rejected.[229]

The State threw in the towel in the waning moments of the Carter administration and asked that the segment through Memphis be dropped from the interstate system, under a generous exchange program they must have feared the incoming Reagan administration might alter.[230]

---

225. Email of January 27, 2005.

226. *Coleman's Park X-Way Ruling Received Coldly By Both Sides*, Memphis Press-Scimitar, Apr. 22, 1975.

227. *Ford Staff Passes Problem of Park Route to Democrats*, Com. Appeal, Nov. 19, 1976, at 3.

228. Cunningham, *"We Are Through With Overton Park,"* Officials Say, Ending Decades of Delay, Com. Appeal, Oct. 1, 1977, at 1, 3.

229. Cunningham, *It's a Tunnel or Nothing, State Told*, Com. Appeal, Nov. 18, 1977, at 1.

230. *"Windfall Needs Vision,"* The Commercial Appeal, Monday, Jan. 19, 1981, p. 4 remarked

Opponents of the route were sometimes criticized as busybodies and obstructionists. Events have proved, however, that they were the ones with vision. Protection of the park became, in their lengthy battle through the courts, a symbol not only of environmental quality but also of larger concerns about what kind of a city Memphis should try to become ...

About $300 million in federal funds committed to building the road then began to be released to Memphis for other transportation purposes.[231] In 1987, Tennessee returned the parkland to the city. The approaches nearest the park, that for years had remained greensward, have now begun to fill in with new houses.

Perhaps the possibility of an east-west expressway lives yet in the minds of some Memphians. Its eastern elements were built, and feed into a near-expressway pointed downtown. For others, the iconic values CPOP saw have been magnified. Whatever impact the racial issues of its time may have had (and Attorney Newman doubts the controversy was ever viewed by anyone as much of a racial issue)

> the park became something of a symbol of what a small group of determined people can do, for people in both communities, especially the younger generation. . . . [F]or a significant period of time during the 1960s, 1970s and 1980s the park was a very visible meeting ground for young people of both races. . . . [T]o the extent the park was or is a meeting place for the races, this is not because very many people of either race have viewed the proposed highway as having racial motivation or consequences (though, if built, it might well have become a racial and socio-economic dividing line). It is instead because of the kind of place it is, centrally located, attractive, open to all, plus perhaps because of the symbol it has become.[232]

In saving Overton Park for the city, against its wishes at the time, CPOP may have saved Memphis from itself.

Newman recalls that "It took the City leaders quite a while to recognize the merits of doing this and, when they did, they had a very hard time convincing the State DOT and the Governor, but finally it happened." Email of January 27, 2005.

231. In 1990 the Memphis Business Journal reported that $100,000,000 of these funds remained unexpended. *"$17 Million Raleigh-Millington Project Moving Forward,"* Vol. 12, No. 17, Sec. 1 p. 3. Projected cost of the roadway portion through the park, in the 1960s, was variously estimated between $2,000,000 and $16,000,000, with still higher estimates if a tunnel design was to be used.

232. Email of January 26, 2005.

Professor Mashaw's story of the *State Farm* case uncovers the messy world of regulatory politics barely visible in the rational-analytic pages of judicial decisions. In that world opportunistic congresses routinely over-promise in regulatory legislation and under-fund regulatory bureaucracies, powerful economic interests use and abuse legal and political processes for financial advantage, presidents attempt to bend regulatory mandates to suit their own ideological predispositions, fickle publics simultaneously demand perfect security and total freedom, and courts intervene in ways that preserve valued constitutional symbols while wreaking havoc on the development of sensible regulatory policy.

9

Jerry L. Mashaw*

The Story of *Motor Vehicle Manufacturers Association of the U.S. v. State Farm Mutual Automobile Insurance Co.*: Law, Science and Politics in The Administrative State

What are we to make of the Supreme Court's iconic decision in the *State Farm*[1] case? At one level *State Farm* represents a triumphant vindication of reason as administrative law's core value and of independent judicial review of administrative action as the keystone of the rule of law in the administrative state. In *State Farm* a unanimous Supreme Court blocked the Reagan administration's attempt to rescind the centerpiece of the federal government's ambitious program to make American automobiles safer for their occupants—Federal Motor Vehicle Safety Standard 208, the so-called "airbags" or "passive restraints" rule. Although ideologically committed to deregulation, and elected in part on the basis of its promise to provide economic relief for the American automobile industry, the Reagan team at the Department of Transportation (DOT) was instructed by the Supreme Court that politics was not enough. The administration had presented no "adequate basis and explanation for rescinding the passive restraint requirement."[2] DOT was sent back to think again. Through the force of independent judicial review politics and ideology were required to take a backseat to administrative law's demand for reasoned policy judgment. In the great Weberi-

---

* Sterling Professor of Law and Management, Yale University.

1. Motor Vehicle Manufacturers Ass'n v. State Farm Mut. Ins. Co., 463 U.S. 29 (1983).

2. 463 U.S. at 33.

an bureaucratic tradition, the *State Farm* decision demanded that administrative legitimacy be premised on the transparent demonstration that power is being exercised on the basis of knowledge.

Of such interpretations are legal icons made. But this triumphalist account of *State Farm* may miss much of the action. What if the Reagan administration's rescission efforts were feasible only because earlier, and obtuse, rounds of judicial review had delayed promulgation of the passive restraints standard for over a decade? What if the scientific underpinning for the passive restraints rule was uncertain, even problematic? What if the Reagan team's actions were a better approximation of the contemporary preferences of voters for policymaking under the Motor Vehicle Safety Act of 1966's vague statutory mandate than was the imposition of unproven, new, and costly safety requirements on the production of motor vehicles? What if the *State Farm* decision itself produced, not a new and better rationalization for administrative action, but a creative political compromise that shifted the locus of decisionmaking from the domain of NHTSA's traffic safety engineers to something like a national referendum conducted in the oblique form of state legislation? What would we think of *State Farm* then?

To get some perspective on these questions we must become time travelers. We must traverse the extraordinary history of motor vehicle safety regulation both before and after the *State Farm* decision.[3] For *State Farm* was but a high-visibility legal event in an administrative, political, and legal donnybrook spanning now nearly four decades. Examining that story will take us from the heyday of public support for energetic federal regulation to the increasingly common vision of government as a problem rather than a solution; from the 1960s and early 1970s reformation of administrative law to its counterreformation in the 1980s and beyond. It is a story of high drama and low comedy; of high-visibility actors—figures such as Ralph Nader, Richard Nixon, and Lee Iacocca—and of subterranean bureaucratic warfare; and, as the *State Farm* decision itself suggests, of constant competition between scientific understandings and political and legal imperatives. The *State Farm* story thus provides a microcosmic glimpse of the development of the administrative state, and of the shifting visions of administrative law, in late 20th century America.

The Revolution of 1966

The National Traffic and Motor Vehicle Safety Act of 1966[4] was a dramatic attempt at legal transformation. Indeed, it represented the

---

3. Much of the material in this story is taken from JERRY L. MASHAW AND DAVID L. HARFST, THE STRUGGLE FOR AUTO SAFETY (1990) (hereafter "STRUGGLE"), and Jerry L. Mashaw, *"Law and Engineering: In Search of the Law-Science Problem,"* 66 L. & Contemp. Prob. 135 (2003).

4. Pub. L. No. 89–563, 80 Stat. 718.

convergence of two revolutionary movements: The first was a decisive shift in the intellectual conception of motor vehicle safety law; the second was a broad-based campaign to reform federal administrative regulation.

The New Science of Accidents. The use of law to regulate automobile safety was hardly novel in 1966. Traffic rules backed by legal sanctions were not just traditional; they were, and are, probably the most often encountered, and most often violated, legal norms ever enacted. Our streets and highways are alive with legal communication. Stripes and arrows, broken and solid lines adorn the pavements. Signs and flashing lights provide constant reminders of required speeds, required stopping places, areas of caution, required and prohibited turns, and so on, and on. The law encouraged good driving behavior in other ways as well. All states licensed drivers; many required or strongly encouraged driver education courses. These routine forms of vehicle safety regulation were punctuated by episodic, high-visibility enforcement campaigns, often on holidays, during which police cracked down on speeders, drunk drivers, and other vehicular malefactors. Much of this activity was given heavy play on television and in the press.

Yet, decades after the private motor vehicle had become the dominant mode of personal transportation, this gargantuan effort at legal control and motor vehicle safety had had limited success. In 1965 the number of vehicular deaths per year on American highways topped 50,000—an awesome figure that was expected to double within the next decade.

In 1966 Daniel Patrick Moynihan, then Assistant Secretary of Labor, described the traditional and generally accepted law enforcement approach to traffic safety with a disdain bordering on contempt:

> The entire pattern of state police management of the automobile complex is derived directly from the model of the prevention detection, and punishment of crime. From the cowboy hats, to the six guns, to the chase scene, the entire phenomenon is a paradigm of the imposition of law on an unruly and rebellious population.... There is not much evidence that this works. More to the point, the police have almost no tradition of controlled inquiry that would find out.... Their response to the gentlest criticism is simply wholesome Hibernian apoplexy.[5]

As Moynihan (but few others) understood, two sets of professionals had begun to take a dramatically different approach to automobile safety—an approach that downplayed the importance of controlling

---

5. National Traffic and Motor Vehicle Safety Act: Hearings on H.R. 13,228 Before the House Comm. on Interstate and Foreign Commerce, 89th Cong. 1319 (1966).

driver behavior in favor of other, engineering-based strategies. One group was the highway engineers who were deeply involved in the construction of President Eisenhower's cherished, post-war interstate highway system. It was clear by the early 1960s that their conscious efforts to design highways for safety had produced results: interstates were three times safer than other highways.

But for purposes of the *State Farm* story a second group was more important. Its leaders were the medical profession,[6] especially the members of that profession concerned with epidemiology and public health.[7] From a medical standpoint, the mayhem on American highways looked statistically like an epidemic. Automobiles were not only the leading cause of accidental death; they were, for the population below age 44, the leading cause of death, period. The efforts of these individuals to understand and control the epidemic of motor vehicle injuries and fatalities produced an entirely new way of thinking about automobile safety.

Epidemiologists analyze problems of injury or illness in terms of a conceptual triad that includes the *host* (the person who becomes injured or ill) the *agent* (the cause of the injury or illness), and the *environment* (the setting within which the host and agent interact). In an automobile accident, epidemiologists see a host—the occupant of a motor vehicle—coming into contact with an agent—rapid energy transfer—caused by the occupant's collision with a particular environment—the interior of the automobile. The epidemiologist thus sees an injury or death in an automobile accident as caused not by the accident itself, but by the occupant's collision with the various features of the interior of the vehicle. From this perspective, preventing accidents is only one of many strategies for preventing deaths or ameliorating injuries. An alternative route would be to interdict the energy transfer from the vehicle's interior to the occupant after an accident has occurred—the so-called "second collision" approach to automobile safety.

William Haddon, who became the Motor Vehicle Safety Act's first administrator, was a part of this epidemiological fraternity. He had written extensively on the etiology of accidental injury and had become increasingly active in the field of automobile accidents.[8] Like all epidemiologists, Haddon had a professional bias in favor of interventions that did not rely on changing human behavior. In a 1962 paper Haddon

---

6. See description in J. EASTMAN, STYLING VS. SAFETY: THE AMERICAN AUTOMOBILE INDUSTRY AND THE DEVELOPMENT OF AUTOMOBILE SAFETY, 1900–1966, at 177–208 (1984).

7. For early pronouncements of the new perspective, see ACCIDENT RESEARCH: METHODS AND APPROACHES (W. Haddon, E. Suchman, and D. Klein eds., 1964); Gordon, *"The Epidemiology of Accidents,"* 39 Am. J. Pub. Health 504 (1949) (accidents conform to same biological laws as disease).

8. W. HADDON, SELECTED WORKS OF WILLIAM HADDON, JR., Vols. 1–2 (Insurance Institute of Highway Safety comp. 1987).

wrote, "It has been the consistent experience of public health agencies concerned with the reduction of other causes of morbidity and mortality that measures which do not require the continued active cooperation of the public are much more efficacious than those which do."[9]

By "proven measures" Haddon was referring to more than the increasing evidence of the efficacy of highway safety design. Building on Hugh DeHaven's pioneering research at the Cornell Medical School,[10] and borrowing engineering techniques from aeronautical engineers, teams of doctors and safety engineers had by 1962 designed or redesigned the interior of experimental automobiles to make them much more forgiving of their human occupants in the event of a crash. This research was widely known within the automotive engineering fraternity and by some state and federal officials, like Moynihan, who were particularly interested in automobile safety. (Moynihan had cut his teeth on automobile safety issues while an aide to Governor Averell Harriman of New York.) These ideas were also coming to be understood by the insurance industry, by medical professionals who dealt with automobile trauma, and by the American Trial Lawyers' Association.

For reformers the epidemiological approach suggested a radically new role for automobile safety law. Rather than attempting to modify the driver, the law should attempt to modify the motor vehicle. Yet nothing much seemed to be changing in the design of automobiles—at least not in their safety design. In the 1950s and early 1960s automobile "design" still meant automobile "styling." The urgent design questions seemed to be concerned with tail fin height and the shape of the grill, not with occupant safety.

Regulatory Reform. When the revolution in the substantive conceptualization of motor safety came to be translated into law, it converged with a concurrent revolution in the form of legal regulation.[11] The 1966

---

9. Goddard & Haddon, "An Introduction to the Discussion of the Vehicle in Relation to Highway Safety," in PASSENGER CAR DESIGN AND HIGHWAY SAFETY: PROCEEDINGS OF A CONFERENCE ON RESEARCH 1, 5 (1962).

10. See, for example, DE HAVEN, MECHANICAL ANALYSIS OF SURVIVAL IN FALLS FROM FIFTY TO ONE HUNDRED FIFTY FEET, 2 War Medicine 586 (1942). See also Hasbrook, *The Historical Development of the Crash-Impact Engineering Point of View*, 8 Clinical Orthopaedics 268 (1956).

11. For a contemporary argument in favor of broader administrative rulemaking authority, see David Shapiro, *The Choice of Rulemaking or Adjudication in the Development of Administrative Policy*, 78 Harv. L. Rev. 921 (1965) (suggesting that greater rulemaking authority would allow agencies to develop policy in a more coherent and forthright fashion). See also Richard J. Pierce, Jr., *Rulemaking and the Administrative Procedure Act*, 32 Tulsa L.J. 185 (1996) (tracing the history of the development of rulemaking); Mark H. Grunewald, *The NLRB's First Rulemaking: An Exercise in Pragmatism*, 41 Duke L.J. 274 (1991) (explaining how the National Labor Relations Board traditional insistence on regulation through adjudication gave way to rulemaking); R.

Motor Vehicle Safety Act created the first of a new breed of federal regulatory agencies, the National Highway Traffic Safety Administration (NHTSA). Like other familiar regulatory actors, such as the Occupational Safety and Health Administration (OSHA), and the Environmental Protection Agency (EPA), NHTSA was the institutional offspring of a distinctive political-intellectual union. The first parent of regulatory reform was the "liberal" political activism of the 1960s and early 1970s. Its central political heuristic was the development of civil rights law from *Brown v. Board of Education* to the Civil Rights Act of 1964. This was an activism that viewed most social issues, whether civil rights, poverty, pollution, or product safety, as problems to be solved by the application of federal governmental power. The second parent of reform was an intellectual climate created by critiques of government from both the left and the right. These mostly academic, analysts described some of the existing venerable federal agencies—such as the Interstate Commerce Commission (ICC), Federal Power Commission (FPC), and Federal Trade Commission (FTC)—as "captured" bureaucracies, institutions that had failed to make effective public policy because they had been too busy serving the economic interests of their regulatory clientele.[12] The reform agenda generated at the intersection of liberal political activism and skeptical intellectual criticism of federal bureaucratic performance included, therefore, two elements: The need to move the federal government forcefully into new areas of activity to solve pressing social problems; and the need to provide this federal action in a new organizational form that would avoid the administrative lethargy of the past.

There were many diagnoses of the structural problems of the old agencies. The vagueness of their statutory mandates, their collegiate form, their broad prosecutorial discretion, their imperviousness to the interests that they were designed to protect, their independence from executive direction, and their ponderous and inefficient adjudicatory techniques, were all indicted as contributing to their ineffectiveness.[13] Most of the new regulatory agencies created in the 1960s and early 1970s were to be different: Their mandates were to be more specific; their

MELNICK, REGULATION AND THE COURTS: THE CASE OF THE CLEAN AIR ACT 5–9 (1983) (describing "new regulation" in general terms); Stewart, Vermont Yankee *and the Evolution of Administrative Procedure*, 91 Harv. L. Rev. 1804, 1811 (1978) (noting that "burdens of trial-type hearings ... led ... federal agencies to turn from case-by-case adjudication to general rulemaking proceedings in order to develop administrative policy").

12. Two early and influential works were M. BERNSTEIN, REGULATION BY INDEPENDENT COMMISSION (1955), and G. KOLKO, THE TRIUMPH OF CONSERVATISM (1963).

13. See, for example, SENATE COMM. ON THE JUDICIARY, 86TH CONG., 2D SESS., REPORT ON THE REGULATORY AGENCIES TO THE PRESIDENT-ELECT (JAMES M. LANDIS) (1960); Louis L. Jaffe, *The Effective Limits of the Administrative Process: A Reevaluation*, 67 Harv. L. Rev. 1105 (1954) (listing critiques of the contemporary administrative state, including agency capture, a presumption in favor of regulation, and overly conservative policies).

powers more concentrated in a single administrator; their enforcement discretion more circumscribed; their processes more open to the participation of putative beneficiaries; and their powers more focused on the establishment of mandatory policy by general rule.

This last change was the most significant legal innovation of the new era of regulation. From the perspective of the legal reformers of this period, rulemaking was vastly superior to adjudication as a regulatory technique.[14] General rules could be made through informal, and presumably more expeditious, procedures. Policy would thus apply immediately to whole areas of regulated activity. Any person or organization, not just the "regulated interests," was entitled to participate in informal rulemaking proceedings under the federal Administrative Procedure Act (APA). General rulemaking would, therefore, also foster broadly informed policy making rather than ad hoc decisions in the context of particular adjudications. Agency initiative, or lack of initiative, would be transparent and subject to political debate and direction.

Hopefully judicial review would afford regulators wide latitude in shaping policies while avoiding the courts' prior preoccupations with adjudicatory formalities—formalities that had often paralyzed individualized enforcement and licensing proceedings. Judicial review of rules might also be structured to include review of agency failures to act. Hence, potential beneficiaries would be able to back their demands for action with credible threats of legal recourse, a reform promise that *State Farm*, in part, redeems. The virtues of regulation by rulemaking seemed endless.

Operating at the forefront of this public health and regulatory reform movement, the Motor Vehicle Safety Act of 1966 defined the regulators' central task quite simply. The National Highway Traffic Safety Administration was to promulgate rules that would force manufacturers to build vehicles that better protected their occupants in case of a crash. The agency's mandate also included rulemaking authority to promote crash avoidance and adjudicatory authority to force manufacturers to recall and repair defective automobiles. The National Highway Safety Act, passed in the same year, gave the new agency authority to attempt to coordinate and improve state programs aimed largely at driver behavior. But the big safety payoff was thought to lie in the agency's central mission of forcing the development of technology that protected vehicle occupants.

Activists who supported the MVSA foresaw public health benefits from redesigning the automobile that rivaled the most significant public health breakthroughs of the past, including such staggering successes as

---

14. See, e.g., KENNETH CULP DAVIS, DISCRETIONARY JUSTICE: A PRELIMINARY INQUIRY 65–66 (1969) (describing rulemaking as "one of the greatest inventions of modern government").

the protection and treatment of water supplies. Proponents of the new science of accidents also often drew their supporting political images from the technological and managerial accomplishments of the space program.[15] With a NASA-like combination of political will and technical sophistication, success in the battle against vehicle injury and death seemed inevitable. The Motor Vehicle Safety Act was grounded in these beliefs, law and science would combine to produce major improvements in American life.

These political symbols proved politically powerful. Safety proponents characterized the vehicle safety problem as a problem of social irresponsibility. Fixated on styling and power, the manufacturers of automobiles were said to have failed to provide the public with safer vehicles to which they were entitled. Regulation was essential to shift the industry's design priorities from tail fins to passenger protection. Acting out an apparent consensus that rarely attends legislative programs more controversial than the declaration of National Crocus Week, Congress passed the National Traffic and Motor Vehicle Safety Act[16]—for the first time directly regulating at the federal level the largest industry in the United States—without a single dissenting vote in either house.

The Dance of Legislation

Congress seemed to back its voting enthusiasm with substantive powers. Epitomizing the new regulatory reform paradigm, the Motor Vehicle Safety Act provided for administration by a single chief administrator, who was not merely empowered, but required, to establish "appropriate federal motor vehicle safety standards" that would "meet the need for motor vehicle safety." The legislation demanded that initial standards be in place by January 31, 1967, and new and revised standards by the same date the next year. These standards were to be

---

15.   See, for example, Traffic Safety: Hearings on S. 3005 Before the Senate Comm. on Commerce, 89th Cong. 208 (1966) (remarks of Robert F. Kennedy) (urging application of "same imaginative techniques that we are using to win the race to the moon to eliminate the most deadly features of today's cars"); National Traffic and Motor Vehicle Safety Act: Hearings on H.R. 13,228 Before the House Comm. on Interstate and Foreign Commerce, 89th Cong. 450 (1966) (remarks of N.Y. State Rep. Edward Speno) ("[I]f we can send a man to the moon and back, why can't we design a safe automobile here on earth?"); id. at 781 (remarks of Col. John P. Stapp) (urging that "most completely regulated form of transportation by the federal government is space flight" and that "the international record in space flight today" is "17 flights, 733 orbits, 1,163 hours, 31 minutes, 28 seconds" and "19,033,250 miles covered without a single injury or fatality"). Amazement over the nation's progress toward reaching the moon subdued concern over the costs of auto safety regulation. See Traffic Safety: Hearings on S. 3005 Before the Senate Comm. on Commerce, 89th Cong. 211 (1966) (remarks of Robert F. Kennedy) (arguing that the country could afford to spend $150 million on auto safety, if NASA was spending several billion dollars to ensure astronauts' safety).

16.   15 U.S.C. §§ 1381 et seq.

performance, not design standards,[17] but the agency was given wide latitude. When prescribing "objective" performance standards, regulators were required to consider relevant data, to consult to the extent "appropriate" with state officials, and to consider whether their proposed standards were "reasonable, practicable and appropriate" for the particular type of motor vehicle or equipment for which they were prescribed. This statutory language seemed redolent with discretion. Discretion to be wielded by an activist administrator in pursuit of motor vehicle safety. The statute made it a civil offense for manufacturers to offer for sale or introduce into interstate commerce any automobile or automobile equipment not conforming to the new agency's standards. Violations were subject to a civil penalty of $1,000.00, with each vehicle or item of equipment constituting a separate offense. In addition, the agency could seek injunctions prohibiting the sale of any non-complying products.

Yet, notwithstanding unanimous legislative consent and the statute's broad powers, the depth of the political will behind the Motor Vehicle Safety Act of 1966 was always questionable. Like any "revolution" worthy of the name, it was strongly against the grain of history. Ever since the development and mass marketing of the private automobile, motor vehicle law had promoted three paramount values: mobility, choice, and freedom.[18] Although the ubiquity of traffic rules and the prominence given to their enforcement may have suggested a nation fixated on safety, those rules actually mostly promoted mobility. Without traffic rules to coordinate driver behavior, the progress of automobiles on the roads would probably be so lethargic that collisions between them, or anything else, would produce little damage to either automobile or occupant. And, the common law of liability had always acted on the common sense notion that "accidents" were either just that, or the fault of one or another motorist. To be sure, manufacturers had been held liable for defective products, but liability for design defects—particularly designs which failed to protect the occupant of the vehicle—had been firmly rejected.

Indeed, the notion that manufacturers should be liable for failing to protect occupants in collisions was almost laughed out of court. As one judge put it, "automobiles might be driven into lakes or rivers, but that did not impose any responsibility on manufacturers to equip them with

---

17. As the First Circuit has explained: "A performance standard establishes a test for a certain aspect of a vehicle's performance, without mandating how the vehicle should be designed to comply with the test.... In contrast, a design standard mandates how a vehicle or item of vehicle equipment should be designed, and does not dictate how the product should perform in response to certain tests." Wood v. General Motors Corp., 865 F.2d 395, 416 (1st Cir. 1988).

18. See STRUGGLE, supra note 3, at 27–46.

pontoons."[19] The job of manufacturers was to produce more and better cars so that more Americans could enjoy the freedom of the open road. Had a population that viewed motor vehicles as expressions of their own personalities,[20] and that viewed the injury and deaths from automobile accidents as primarily the fault of bad drivers, really come to see their "freedom machines" as a public health hazard? The peculiar series of events that led to the adoption of the Motor Vehicle Safety Act certainly were not themselves evidence of any broad-based change in the popular culture.

Competition for the Limelight. When Senator Abraham Ribicoff tried to generate interest in the new second collision approach to automobile safety regulation just a year before the Motor Vehicle Safety Act was passed, he could hardly get anyone's attention. Like most ambitious and effective politicians, Ribicoff had achieved some of his electoral success by becoming identified with a popular issue. For him the issue was traffic safety. Indeed, it was Governor Ribicoff of Connecticut's 1950s crack down on unsafe driving that was the subject of Moynihan's scathing critique of the crime and punishment model of automobile safety regulation.

But since moving to the Senate, Ribicoff had become aware of the new epidemiological approach to automobile injury and death. He was determined to reframe the automobile safety debate, and to take credit for doing so.[21] But with automobile safety ranking behind crime, disease, unemployment, poverty, environmental degradation, racial discrimination, and a host of other issues as problems in the public mind,[22] he could gain little traction.

Political help appeared in an unexpected form. In November, 1965, Ralph Nader, then a recent graduate of the Harvard Law School, released his book, **Unsafe at Any Speed**. Nader's research seemed thorough, his story was well-written and his message was compelling— cars could and should be made safer. This was, of course, the same story that the epidemiologists and safety engineers had been telling for years, to no effect. But Nader had made a discovery of momentous political

---

19. Evans v. General Motors, 359 F.2d 822, 825 (7th Cir. 1966). Ironically, perhaps one should say perversely, manufacturers had been held liable for safety improvements that were advertised to consumers but failed to work perfectly. See Baxter v. Ford Motor Co., 168 Wash. 456 (1932).

20. See, e.g., Bill Geist, "A Nation on Wheels: Car Culture," in DEFINING A NATION: OUR AMERICA AND THE SOURCES OF ITS STRENGTH (David Halberstam ed., 2003).

21. Examination of Public and Private Agencies' Activities and Role of the Federal Government: Hearings Before the Subcomm. on Traffic Safety of the Senate Comm. on Governmental Operations, 89th Cong. (1965).

22. G. Bloomquist, Traffic Safety Regulation by NHTSA IV–14 (A.E.I. Working Paper 1981) (citing Gallup data).

significance. He had found a villain. Nader claimed that General Motors was marketing Corvair automobiles although the company knew that they had a propensity to go out of control on turns. The New York Times gave Nader's book front page coverage, and reviewers around the country embraced it.[23] Nader's stock soared, and so did automobile safety as a political issue.

Sensing that a political groundswell was in the making, politicians began to compete to stake out the territory. Ribicoff had been running his safety campaign from his perch as chair of the relatively obscure Subcommittee on Executive Reorganization of the Senate Government Operations Committee. But federal regulation of interstate commerce was the traditional jurisdiction of the Commerce Committee. Senator Warren Magnuson of Washington state, whose staff had warned him that he was suffering from a "visibility" problem back home, quickly opened hearings on automobile safety before the Senate Commerce Committee.[24] The Committee had before it a transportation package introduced by President Johnson, which included giving federal regulators authority to set vehicle safety performance standards. Seldom slow off the political mark, Johnson's presidential message in support of his bill declared that the time had come to "replace suicide with sanity and anarchy with safety."

Still the Johnson proposal was for a weak bill by comparison with the one that ultimately emerged from the legislative process. That proposal (or an even weaker version) would have been compromised to overcome industry objections, and might have been the legislative outcome—had not Nader's villain turned villainous.

Ribicoff reclaimed the automobile safety issue by generating another scandal. Acting on reports that General Motors had placed Ralph Nader under surveillance, he called a special hearing before his subcommittee.[25] At the hearing, General Motors President, James Roche, had to admit that his company had hired a law firm to conduct a "routine investigation" of Nader. But further committee prodding revealed that more had taken place. As Ribicoff described it, the investigation "had to do with trying to smear a man, the question of his sex life, whether he belonged to left wing organizations, whether he was anti-Semitic, whether he was

---

23. See, e.g., Norman C. Miller, *Pleasure—and Danger—on Wheels*, Wall St. J., Dec. 3, 1965, at 16 ("Ralph Nader presents a powerful and persuasive case that Detroit has indeed slighted safety considerations in a headlong pursuit of pleasurable styling.").

24. Bills to Establish a Department of Transportation: Hearings on S. 3010, S. 1122, and H.R. 13,228 Before the Subcomm. on Traffic Safety of the Senate Comm. on Commerce, 89th Cong. (1966).

25. Federal Role in Traffic Safety: Hearings before the Subcomm. on Executive Reorganization of the Senate Comm. on Government Operations, 89th Cong. (1966).

an odd ball, whether he liked boys instead of girls. The whole investigation was to smear an individual."

An issue that had been slowly heating up boiled over. Representatives and Senators tripped over each other in the stampede to express their outrage. The press' response was equally powerful. The story of General Motors versus Ralph Nader provided a perfect media melodrama—a spry David against an oafish Goliath. A pro-Nader, pro-safety, pro-federal-intervention mood swept the country. On April 1, *Time* ran one of its periodic editorial essays, entitled "Why Cars Must—And Can—Be Made Safer." The magazine continued its campaign for auto safety with articles in each of its next three issues.

The remainder of the legislative action on the 1966 Act proceeded in accordance with this revised script. Nader's expertise and credibility seemed to be viewed as limitless. Every Senator or Representative with plausible jurisdiction over the issue called a hearing. And they competed with each other to strengthen the provisions of the Johnson proposals. Apparently hoping to limit their reputational damage, the Automobile Manufacturers' Association went in the space of three weeks from demanding voluntary, industry-established vehicle standards, to embracing federally mandated safety requirements.[26] An industry that had never been regulated at the federal level, and that had paid little attention to Washington politics, capitulated to the combined forces of political entrepreneurs and the Nader phenomenon.

Was the Motor Vehicle Safety Act a Fluke? Although peculiar events gave life to the Motor Vehicle Safety Act of 1966, the Act was not an anomaly. The zeitgeist of the mid-1960s—a combination of egalitarian ethical judgment, scientific enthusiasm and activist national politics—produced a prodigious outpouring of additional legislation.[27] From 1964 to 1966 Congress not only generated 1,000 bills, it enacted 650 of them. The "Great Society" congresses—the second session of the 88th and both sessions of the 89th—produced law at a volume and at a rate matched only in the early years of the New Deal and the first half of the Wilson administration. The Motor Vehicle Safety Act, while contradicting decades of automobile law, was clearly not flying in the face of the contemporary national mood.

---

26. An account in Fortune Magazine ascribed the automobile industry's weakness in the political process to the insularity of top management, a group described as utterly confounded by problems whose nature was sociological or political rather than technological or economic. Cordtz, "The Face in the Mirror at General Motors," 74 Fortune 117 (1966).

27. This account of the legislative milieu is drawn largely from the weekly reports of the Congressional Quarterly Almanac for the years 1964–1966.

It remained to be seen, however, whether this outpouring of reformists legislation could sustain itself as it moved from legislative exhortation to administrative action. Over time, interest and resources matter. The automobile industry may have been, as Elizabeth Drew proclaimed,[28] a "paper hippopotamus" in 1966, but it was nevertheless a very big animal with at least the usual instincts for self-preservation. If that animal was to be bent to the collective will, its keepers would have to be both vigilant and powerful. Such a posture is particularly difficult to maintain, however, in a democratic polity committed to limited government. As the president and committee chairs competed to strengthen the 1966 Act, the system of checks and balances may well have looked more like a system of ratchets and amplifiers. But American institutions do not routinely operate that way. In designing our particular zoological garden, the architects seem to have been more intent on avoiding the criticisms of the SPCA than on allowing the zoo keepers to keep the animals restrained. The preference for private or decentralized state and local control of most social decisionmaking is a structural feature of the American polity generally, not just a peculiarity of preexisting automobile law.

The Realities of Regulation

The 1966 Motor Vehicle Safety Act was an exercise in energy and idealism, fueled by outrage and scientific discovery. But transforming its legislative mandate into operational requirements turned out to be a much more complicated process than any one had imagined.

The statute demanded that NHTSA issue its first set of rules, based on the existing public and private standards, by January 31, 1967. That deadline, a hallmark of the new "action-forcing" forms of federal regulation, was wildly ambitious. William Haddon was appointed head of the agency less than 4 months before the deadline, and NHTSA did not receive an appropriation to begin work until November 15, 1966.

Even so, working with a borrowed staff and temporary offices in the Department of Commerce, Haddon issued an Advance Notice of Proposed Rulemaking (ANPRM) on October 8, 1966, informing the public of his agency's intent to issue standards and inviting proposals and suggestions. The response was a blizzard of paper, mostly from the automobile industry. By December 3, 1966, the agency had digested this material and formalized its proposal into a Notice of Proposed Rulemaking (NPRM) setting forth 23 separate standards for possible adoption. These rules, as the Act commanded, were based on existing standards that had already been established by the General Service Administration for the purchase of government vehicles, the Society of Automobile Engineers,

---

28. Drew, "The Politics of Auto Safety," Atlantic Monthly, Oct. 1966, at 96.

as well as some requirements drawn from the Post Office, the National Bureau of Standards, the Uniform Vehicle Code, and the Swedish National Road Board. Another blizzard of comments descended on the Agency, but it met the January 31, 1967, deadline.

This flurry of activity seemed to redeem the reformers' hopes, but hyperactivity is not necessarily progress. To be sure, many members of the automobile industry thought the new standards outrageous. Henry Ford II complained that many of their requirements were unreasonable, arbitrary, and technically infeasible. Volkswagen predicted that it would no longer import vehicles into the United States. Checker Motors Corporation declared that compliance was absolutely impossible.[29]

Yet, of the 20 standards issued, eight had been significantly modified in response to these criticisms and three had been withdrawn altogether. Ralph Nader and other safety advocates were apoplectic—in their view the regulators had caved in the face of pressure from the manufacturers. According to Nader, who complained about the administration in some forum almost weekly, Haddon was a timid administrator who operated under a host of self-imposed restraints because he was "petrified of a court test." At one point Nader described Haddon as so sensitive to criticism that he could be "blistered by moonbeams."[30]

There was something to Nader's complaint, but the world of standard setting looked quite different from the regulators' perspective than it had from the halls of Congress. The action-forcing provision of the legislation that required that standards be applied uniformly to all manufacturers turned out to be a major liability. For the automotive world was not just made up of the big three, but of dozens of other small producers for whom compliance with proposed standards, particularly the cost of destructive testing and sophisticated test instrumentation, posed insuperable burdens. Many of the proposed standards would not be "practicable" or "reasonable" given these manufacturers' situations. And Congress' injunction that "vigorous competition in the development and marketing of safety improvements must be maintained" could hardly mean that the agency should drive all small manufacturers out of business.

Uniformity plus practicability plus firm deadlines thus led to a lowest common denominator approach that massively weakened the standards adopted. Moreover, the agency discovered that many existing governmental or "consensus" standards were not based on significant scientific investigation. And the statute's demand that the agency's standards be "objective" reinforced the feeling among Haddon's research

---

29. Motor Vehicle Safety Standards Hearings Before the Senate Comm. on Commerce, 90th Cong. 141 (1967).

30. Id. at 235.

scientists that anything the agency put out should be based on unim-
peachable data.

Standard 101, for example, which originally required that controls in
passenger cars be located within comfortable reach of a "fifth percentile
adult female restrained by a lap and upper torso restraint seat belt," was
modified to simply require that instrument controls be within the reach
of "a person." The change was based not only on the vituperative
objections of the automobile industry, but also on Haddon's discovery
that the underlying science defining the size of a "fifth percentile adult
female" had been based on an unrepresentative sample of the female
population. But, of course, the standard as issued was utterly meaning-
less from the standpoint of providing safety.[31] Shaquille O'Neal, after all,
is "a person."

Proposed Standard 105 met a similar fate. Prepared originally under
the supervision of William Stieglitz, an MIT trained aeronautical engineer and a fierce partisan of automobile safety, Standard 105 required
that every motor vehicle have a dual braking system and that the backup
brakes be capable of stopping the vehicle within 160 feet at an initial
speed of 60 mph. Over Stieglitz's objections, the proposal was modified to
call for a stopping distance of 194 feet, a distance that was greater than
the stopping distance of most existing production automobiles.

Even so, manufacturers complained that the standard was an engineering "impossibility," and that the dual braking system would make
the automobile less safe under normal operating conditions. They further objected that the standard was not "objective": What exactly was
the surface on which this car was to be stopped, and under what
conditions? After further revision, the standard demanded only that
residual brakes "stop a car on a clean, dry, Portland cement, concrete
pavement." After resigning from the agency in disgust, Stieglitz testified
to the Congress that no car could fail this test. In neutral it would
eventually stop, and even in gear, it would stop when it ran out of gas.
The standard could be met by a car with no brakes at all.

And so it went with standard after standard. The agency proposed,
the industry objected, and in the absence of clear scientific evidence, the
agency downgraded the standards. If making sure that automobile safety
standards were reasonable, practicable, and objective involved a high
degree of scientific certainty concerning both safety benefits and production feasibility, rulemaking was going to be a very laborious process—
even though these standards were based on existing requirements and,
often, even on widespread industry practice. What would happen when
regulation moved on to topics not embodied in existing standards?

31.   Id. at 175.

The answer seemed to be more of the same. The agency's second generation of safety standards, issued between November 1967 and December 1970, was no more innovative than its first generation had been. A study by the National Commission on Product Safety (NCPS)[32] found that virtually all the rules issued during this period were of little or no significance. Most simply incorporated criteria that were already in widespread use in the industry.

A substantial part of NHTSA's problem may have been its particular approach to standard setting. Rather than articulating broad performance criteria, such as that automobiles be constructed so that their occupants could survive a crash into a fixed barrier at 30 mph, the agency adopted the preexisting General Services administration technique of equipment-specific regulations. These quasi-design standards were much more time consuming to develop and specify in performance terms. But NHTSA seemed to believe that only by taking this piecemeal approach could it justify its rules against the manufacturers' consistent assertions that they were "infeasible," "impracticable," "unreasonable," and "non-objective."

The practical difficulties of regulating the automobile piece by piece might have been solved with a generous dollop of additional manpower and money. But instead of acquiring more rulemaking resources, NHTSA during the late 1960s and early 1970s ended up with substantially less than had been envisioned when the Motor Vehicle Safety Act was passed. The Johnson Administration's resistance to a guns-and-butter trade-off had given way to the Nixon Administration's determination to stay the course in Vietnam, while cutting back on domestic programs enacted by prior Democratic congresses. Nixon imposed a series of personnel freezes that brought Haddon's recruiting efforts to a standstill. Many agency sections were staffed by only one or two employees; others were empty.

The Congress that unanimously passed the Motor Vehicle Safety Act in 1966 suddenly turned fiscally cautious. Its Expenditure Control Act of 1968 required that federal employment be reduced to levels in effect on June 30, 1966.[33] And, although the 1966 Act envisioned a major research facility to support NHTSA's rulemaking, Congress appropriated no funds for even a test facility until 1972. Nor was Haddon able to garner much support from his colleagues in the Department of Transportation. NHTSA was located in the gargantuan Federal Highway Administration (FHWA), where it was both a pigmy and an orphan. The FHWA was dominated by the old style "three Es" safety philosophy—engineering

---

32. NATIONAL COMMISSION ON PRODUCT SAFETY, FEDERAL CONSUMER SAFETY LEGISLATION (January 1970).

33. Expenditure Control Act, Pub. L. No. 90–364, § 201, 82 Stat. 270–71 (1968).

(meaning "highway engineering"), enforcement, and education. FHWA focused on highways and drivers. It had little interest in NHTSA's "second collision" regulatory mission to reengineer the automobile. Indeed, Haddon reported that personnel in FHWA were more interested in "sabotaging" NHTSA than giving it assistance.[34]

The Promise of Passivity

Mired in regulatory trench warfare with the industry; starved for revenues, personnel, and facilities; under constant attack by its putative public interest friends; flanked by protean bureaucratic bedfellows; and trapped in part by its own sense of professionalism, in a staggeringly laborious regulatory approach, NHTSA faced the decade of the 1970s desperately in need of some new ideas and allies. Federal Motor Vehicle Standard 208, the rule reviewed in the *State Farm* case, was the embodiment of NHTSA's third generation approach to regulation. It promised to make good on the epidemiological underpinnings of the 1966 statute, to break the agency out of its regulatory lethargy, and finally to provide some significant safety benefits to the motoring population.

Amid the many ideas for protecting vehicle passengers from the effects of the "second collision," one general approach stood out— keeping occupants in place during those crucial fractions of a second when the energy from a crash was absorbed and dissipated by the vehicle surrounding them. This was the basic logic behind seatbelts and shoulder harnesses, equipment that by 1970 was available on 75–80% of American motor vehicles. But availability was not enough. Agency studies showed that only 25–30% of motorists wore their seatbelts, and that figure was probably inflated. A much smaller proportion wore the more protective shoulder belt. As the epidemiologists knew, when public health measures require continuous active cooperation of the populace they are likely to fail. NHTSA, therefore, proposed in July 1969 that Standard 208 (which required lap and shoulder belts) be amended to switch from an active to a passive technology.[35] The technology it had in mind was the airbag.

The airbag is now a commonplace piece of equipment in American automobiles, but in 1969 the technology was viewed as at once simple and exotic. In truth, it was hardly novel. The first U.S. patent on a "safety cushion for automotive vehicles" was granted in 1953.[36] Major domestic manufacturers—particularly General Motors, which held several air cushion patents—had already conducted extensive research and development testing of the airbag. Component suppliers such as Eaton

---

34. C. McCarry, Citizen Nader 95 (1972).

35. Inflatable Occupant Restraint Systems, 34 Fed. Reg. 11,148 (1969).

36. U.S. Patent No. 2,649,311 (issued Aug. 18, 1953).

Yale & Towne had also done significant research and development. Airbags were not an idea cooked up by wild-eyed safety engineers in the basement of the Department of Transportation. NHTSA's July 1969 Advanced Notice of Proposed Rulemaking (ANPRM) predicted that air-bag technology was nearing production readiness. More importantly, it predicted that the switch to passive restraints would save ten to twelve thousand lives a year—thousands more than all of the agency's prior 49 rules combined.

The airbag proposal was not only epidemiologically sound and scien-tifically innovative, it contained a legal novelty as well. The proposed amendments to Standard 208 presumed the existence of a particular type of equipment, the airbag, but did not mandate its use. Instead it permitted the use of any "passive" technology that would meet the standard's performance criteria. "Automatic" belts, for instance, were an alternative that might comply with Standard 208. So might "passive interiors." Moreover, the revised Standard 208 did not specify perform-ance criteria in terms of equipment characteristics. Rather than speak-ing of airbag inflation times, belt anchor strengths, or the like, the proposal was framed in terms of the effects produced on an anthropo-morphic dummy in frontal barrier crashes at 30 mph. Here, at last, was a true performance standard. The industry was told what to accomplish, not how to accomplish it. The choice and design of specific equipment would be the industry's responsibility.

The usual trench warfare ensued, although with one notable excep-tion. The General Motors Corporation decided not to fight the agency on the passive restraints rule. It held many of the basic patents on airbag technology and believed that the airbag would actually give it a signifi-cant advantage over its competitors. Even so, the usual objections to cost, lead times, and production feasibility battered the rulemaking process through three years and 24 separate rulemaking notices. In the process the deadline for compliance was pushed back three years as well, from January 1, 1972 to August 15, 1975. Having provided that generous grant of leadtime, the agency stood fast in its conviction that manufac-turers should bear the remainder of the research and development burdens necessary to implement the standard. But before Standard 208 could be implemented, both law and politics intervened.

Engineering Science in Court

On December 2, 1972, the U.S. Court of Appeals for the Sixth Circuit enjoined the implementation of Standard 208 in *Chrysler Corp. v. DOT*.[37] The *Chrysler* decision would not be the agency's last loss in court, nor was the opinion as broadly critical of NHTSA's rulemaking

---

37. 472 F.2d 659 (6th Cir. 1972).

efforts as some future decisions would be. Yet its effects on NHTSA's new regulatory strategy were devastating. It was this case, more than any other, that taught the agency how precarious its legal position in rulemaking really was—a lesson that surely was not lost on its perennial antagonists, the vehicle manufacturers, who had had the good sense to initiate their challenge in a judicial circuit that might be described as their "home court."

The plaintiffs' briefs in *Chrysler* threw the book at Standard 208. They urged that NHTSA lacked statutory authority to force technology and that the agency was limited to issuing requirements based on available equipment; that the standard was neither "practicable" nor "reasonably related to the need for motor vehicle safety," in part because seat belts (when worn) were more effective than airbags in some crash modes; that the standard's test procedures were flawed; that dummies meeting the standard's specifications were not readily available; that various procedural errors had been committed; and that many logical, judgmental, and evidentiary failings rendered the standard "arbitrary and capricious."

In peppering the court with reasons for invalidating the standard, Chrysler and the other plaintiffs were behaving like any other litigant seeking to overturn an agency's discretionary exercise of broad statutory authority. It was thought to be an uphill fight, and one never knew what line of reasoning a court might find persuasive. The comprehensive, scattershot attack also reflected the automobile manufacturers' customary strategy in attacking NHTSA's rulemaking efforts: to defend the status quo at every point with every available stratagem, and to keep up a relentless pressure via petitions, objections, comments, and criticisms.

The agency, for its part, played the familiar role of passive defendant, meeting the plaintiffs' claims and letting the latter's arguments provide the organizing principle for its brief. Thus were the issues in the *Chrysler* litigation framed. No mention was made of the agency's new systems approach to rulemaking, the strategic impossibility of equipment-specific rules, the research and development and other informational burdens that the agency had shouldered in prior rulemaking efforts, or any of the other considerations that had led NHTSA to reform its rulemaking approach. The *Chrysler* court addressed the objections to a specific rule, Standard 208, not the broader issue of how technology-forcing regulation could be made both reasonable and effective.

After considering the appropriate standard of judicial review, the court turned to the principle issue in the case. Was NHTSA legally empowered to force automotive technology? Unequivocally (or so it seemed) the court resolved the issue in NHTSA's favor. In sweeping language, Judge Peck wrote:

The explicit purpose of the Act, as amplified in its legislative history, is to enable the federal government to impel automobile manufacturers to develop and apply new technology to the task of improving the safety design of automobiles as rapidly as possible ... [T]he agency is empowered to issue safety standards which require improvements in existing technology or which require the development of new technology, and it is not limited to issuing standards based solely on devices already fully developed. This is in accord with the Congressional mandate that "safety shall be the overriding consideration in the issuance of standards."[38]

One by one, the court rejected the plaintiffs' other arguments. Standard 208 was "practicable," reasonably related to the need for motor vehicle safety, procedurally irreproachable, and in all other respects legal—save one.

The court believed the testing procedures by which the crashworthiness of vehicles was to be judged were inadequate. Specifically, Judge Peck found that the test dummy specified by Standard 208 did not provide an "objective" standard, as required by the Motor Vehicle Safety Act. The dummy criteria were deficient in at least three respects: the flexibility criteria for the dummy's neck, the "dynamic spring rate" for the dummy's thorax region, and the construction criteria for the dummy's head were all said to be incompletely specified. Differently constructed dummies, which met the literal requirements of Standard 208, might thus yield substantially different results in performance tests measuring the forces applied to the dummy in a crash. The court concluded that these possible variations offended the statute: "Objective, in the context of this case, means that tests to determine compliance must be capable of producing *identical* results when test conditions are *exactly* duplicated, that they be *decisively* demonstrable by performing a rational test procedure and that compliance is based upon the readings obtained from measuring instruments as opposed to the subjective opinions of human beings."[39]

The Sixth Circuit's demands for "objectivity" were carefully articulated in its opinion. Where the court had found the requirement of identical results as an element of objectivity, however, was much less clear. The Senate Report on the 1966 Act did not elaborate on the statute's requirement that standards be framed in "objective terms," and the House Report merely stated that "in order to ensure that the question of whether there is compliance with the standard can be answered by objective measurement ... every standard must be stated

---

38. 472 F.2d at 671–673.

39. 472 F. 2d at 676 (emphasis added).

in objective terms."[40] The performance criteria of Standard 208 plainly were "objective" in this sense. The court's demand for "repeatability," meaning "identical results," in "exactly duplicated" tests that "decisively demonstrated" their conclusions without the necessity for human judgment was a heavy gloss on the statute.

The court's analysis and its order both took NHTSA almost completely by surprise. The agency had not anticipated that the suit would turn on "objectivity"; it had devoted a scant three pages of its 123-page brief to the issue. This position was understandable. General Motors had expressed no serious reservations about the standard's objectivity and had publicly announced that it could meet the compliance deadline with little difficulty. Airbag suppliers, who arguably had the most to lose if their products did not comply, had also indicated that they could provide airbag systems satisfying Standard 208 by August 1973, as long as purchasing commitments were received by July 1971. Those involved also knew that, at the time the suit was filed, three years remained before passive restraints were required. If the dummy were indeed inadequately specified, there was adequate time to iron out the details, without upsetting the implementation schedule.

The delay and disruption of agency rulemaking caused by the holding seemed wholly unnecessary for several additional reasons. At the heart of the court's analysis was a fairness-of-expectations test: manufacturers could not fairly be subjected to the uncertainty (financial risk and legal liability) that variable test results would create. But in fact the standard would not expose manufacturers to such risks. The requirements for the test dummy were set out in specification SAEJ963 and had been developed by engineering committees composed of the automobile industry's own technical personnel. As the agency explained in its brief, "So long as a manufacturer's dummy complies with the specifications of SAEJ963, it can use any form of dummy it pleases, and if its cars meet the requisite injury criteria, they will not be determined to be out of compliance with Standard 208."[41] It was possible, of course, that manufacturers might exploit the looseness of the dummy's specifications in order to take engineering short cuts, if doing so would cut costs. That might be a questionable regulatory policy, but it was not unfair to the manufacturers. Underspecification actually worked to their advantage. NHTSA's assurance that it would not take enforcement action where variation could be tied to the dummies should have quieted any residual concern. The agency's position could be taken as a binding statement of policy that the court itself could enforce.

---

40. H.R. Rep. No. 89–1776, at 16 (1966).

41. Brief for Respondent at 105–106, Chrysler Corp. v. DOT, 472 F.2d 659 (6th Cir. 1972) (Nos. 71–1339, 71–1348–1897, 71–1349–1896, 71–1350–1826, and 71–1546).

Similarly, the plaintiffs' own treatment of the "objectivity" issue should have alerted the court that it was not a serious problem. The manufacturers seemed to concede that airbags would save thousands of lives, and the court in *Chrysler* flatly stated that the agency's predictions of airbag effectiveness were supported by "substantial evidence." If variations in test procedures were in fact material, how had the agency come to make and support these predictions? If based on subjective, nonreproducible tests, the agency's predicted benefits should have been attacked as premised on insubstantial evidence. But the life-saving potential of airbags was challenged by no one.

The court's conclusion that variable test results would make compliance turn on "subjective determinations" seemed to reflect its own technical illiteracy. The court was confusing "objectivity" with mechanical measurement. Qualified engineering personnel reviewing test results could in fact come to a principled ("objective") determination of whether variable results were attributable to dummy differences rather than to the airbag itself. Indeed, a performance test that requires no engineering judgment is an impossibility.

Nor was the Sixth Circuit's attachment to an unachievable level of scientific certainty its only display of technological naiveté. The court also treated it as "axiomatic" that "a manufacturer cannot be required to develop an effective restraint device in the absence of an effective testing device which will assure uniform, repeatable and consistent test results."[42] The realities of automotive manufacturing were just the opposite. Manufacturers routinely proceeded along several parallel paths in developing new technologies. Standard 208 required no different development process. Much of the critical work on installing airbags— such as redesign of the dashboard, retooling, perfection of the sensor, quality-control measures to ensure against inadvertent deployment, and a host of other technical issues—could proceed in tandem with refinement of the dummy—provided manufacturers had the incentive to do so. And yet, without discussion of schedule or other intricacies of production planning, the court simply declared that "implementation of passive restraints be delayed until a reasonable time after such test specifications are issued."[43]

In practical effect, *Chrysler* cast NHTSA's technology-forcing mission in procedural terms that made it extraordinarily difficult to complete. As the dissenting judge in *Chrysler* stated:

> If the statutory concepts of motor vehicle safety standards and compliance testing are not separated, the effect is substantially to undermine the legislative scheme.... New testing procedures prog-

---

42.   472 F.2d at 678.

43.   472 F.2d at 681.

ress only as they are needed by advancing technology.... [I]f the rationale of the majority is adopted, industry is in effect relieved from the responsibility of developing a concomitant part of new automotive safety technology since without a previously developed testing device and procedure the agency is powerless to press industry toward this end.[44]

The *Chrysler* ruling was thus an automobile manufacturer's dream. The decision articulated no limits on how objective the test device had to be, but demanded that the agency withhold regulatory action until every detail had been worked out. Given the nature of the technical task at hand, regulation under these conditions was ideally suited for the manufacturers' full-court press. There were an almost infinite number of characteristics that might come into play in the biomechanics of injury. Regulators could not reasonably be expected to specify them all.[45]

It is important, nevertheless, not to overstate the specific problem that *Chrysler* created. The agency was able to reissue dummy specifications nine months later because General Motors had a competitive incentive to come to its rescue. General Motors was ready to produce airbag-equipped cars, while its competitors were not. The delay in Standard 208's compliance deadline directly attributable to the court's decision was little more than a year. The major significance of the decision was the way that it interacted with political events that were beyond the agency's control.

The New Politics of Automobile Safety

NHTSA's trouble in court was being simultaneously compounded by trouble from the White House. That trouble ultimately produced a fateful decision that virtually destroyed the agency's political base in Congress and derailed passive restraints regulation for an additional decade.

Nixon Intervenes. In the extensive rulemaking proceeding leading up to the rule that was invalidated in *Chrysler*, NHTSA had rejected a Ford petition for a declaration that the passive restraints requirement could be satisfied by forcing seat-belt use through an ignition interlock, a device that disabled the vehicle unless the passengers were buckled up. The agency argued that "forced action" was not the "no action" required for a truly passive system. The industry would not be permitted

---

44. 472 F.2d at 691–92 (Miller, J., concurring in part and dissenting in part).

45. Ralph Nader reported to the Congress that the effects of judicial review had so demoralized the NHTSA staff that people were predicting that there would be no significant new standards imposed on motor vehicles until well into the 1980s. Amendments to the National Traffic and Motor Vehicle Safety Act of 1966: Hearings on H.R. 7605, H.R. 5529, and S. 355 before the House Subcomm. on Commerce and Finance of the Comm. on Interstate and Foreign Commerce, 93d Cong. 196 (1973).

to substitute $40 interlocks for $400 airbags. NHTSA, however, soon reversed its position.

On April 27, 1971, Henry Ford II and Lee Iacocca met in the Oval Office with President Richard Nixon and Domestic Affairs Advisor John Ehrlichman. Although Nixon promised that the auto executives' remarks would be held in complete confidence, his secret office taping system, excerpts from which would later drive him from office, was running.[46]

The conversation was in fact pretty tame. In typically garbled fashion Nixon made it "perfectly clear" at the outset that he was one of the boys: "[Our] views are, are, are frankly, uh, whether it's the environment or pollution or Naderism or Consumerism, we are extremely probusiness." That was certainly encouraging to Ford and Iacocca, who had come to ask for help. Their pitch was essentially the same as the industry's testimony would be before Senator Vance Hartke's oversight committee in 1973. Uncoordinated regulatory burdens were adding frightful costs to car prices. The regulators threatened to cripple the domestic auto industry. Ford and Iacocca claimed that compliance with some of the proposed regulatory requirements, particularly the airbag, was simply beyond the industry's technical capacity within the deadlines specified. They needed time to phase in new technology in an orderly fashion. If they didn't get it, they were in trouble.

At times the president and chairman of one of the world's largest corporations sounded pathetic. "We're not only frustrated," said Iacocca, "but, uh, we've reached the despair point. We don't know what to do anymore." And again, "[W]e are on a downhill slide, the likes of which we have never seen in our business. And the Japs are in the wings ready to eat us up alive." Nixon's intervention with the Department of Transportation was apparently their only hope. They wanted relief from environmental requirements too (fuel economy regulation was yet to come), but they knew that was impossible. They had already talked to William Ruckelshaus at the Environmental Protection Agency (EPA) and had been given a lesson in statutorily mandated regulation. The Congress had put EPA emission control criteria under a strict statutory timetable that neither the agency nor industry could evade for long. Under that statute manufacturers might get a year's relief, but only if they could demonstrate their own failure in a good faith effort at compliance.

Nixon was ideologically sympathetic. "It's true in, in the environmentalists and it's true of the consumerism people. They're ... [not] one really damn bit interested in safety or clean air. What they're interested

---

46. Transcript of a conversation among President Nixon, Lide Anthony Iacocca, Henry Ford II, and John D. Ehrlichman in the Oval Office on April 27, 1971, between 11:08 and 11:43 a.m., Nixon Presidential Papers, National Archives, Washington, D.C.

in is destroying the system. They're enemies of the system." But he was also ignorant of the issues and cautious in his promises. At the very end of the meeting, after apparently agreeing with everything Ford and Iacocca had said, Nixon warned them not to expect too much—or perhaps anything. "[U]h, particularly with regard to this, uh, this airbag thing. I, I don't know, I, I, may be wrong. I will not judge it until I hear the other side."

What transpired at the White House and the Transportation Department after this exchange is not known in detail by anyone who is willing to talk for the record. In a Los Angeles television interview,[47] Ehrlichman stated that he and Peter Flanagan ordered the Department to go along with the ignition interlock. Indeed, Ralph Nader later charged that Nixon, Ehrlichman, Iacocca, and Ford, and perhaps Flanagan as well, had concocted a devilishly clever plan to defeat passive restraints by requiring a mechanism (the interlock) so obnoxious to the American people that Congress would rise up and rescind the rule entirely.

If so, the strategy was not developed on April 27, 1971: no one at the meeting in the Oval Office mentioned the interlock. But that a memorandum subsequently went to the Transportation Department is not seriously disputed. Authors of a Senate Commerce Committee investigative report in 1976 describe John Volpe, then Secretary of Transportation, returning dejectedly from White House meetings at which he had failed to save the airbag. The Commerce Committee staff further reported that the "notorious [but never revealed] memorandum" demanded delay on passive restraints *and* adoption of the interlock.[48]

In any event, the Department complied. In October 1971 it issued a notice delaying passive protection until August 15, 1975.[49] In the interim, compliance with Standard 208 could be achieved with an ignition interlock system. That choice then became the single option available when the *Chrysler* decision enjoined enforcement of Standard 208's passive restraints timetable on December 5, 1972. Because the interlock system was attached to normal belts, interlocks were not subject to the dummy-testing criteria in Standard 208 that were invalidated in *Chrysler*. Interlocks were an enforceable technology even though all other passive techniques had to be delayed. It was thus the interlock that found its way into new cars for model year 1974.

The Public Speaks and Congress Listens. Although with the interlock NHTSA had an enforceable rule, evidence quickly mounted that the public's opinion of it was at least as low as NHTSA's. In reissuing

---

47. Transcript of interview by Byron Block, KABC–TV, Los Angeles, with John Ehrlichman, President Nixon's Domestic Affairs Advisor, November 9, 1982.

48. H.R. Rep. No. 94–781, at 188 (1976).

49. 36 Fed. Reg. 19,266 (1971).

Standard 208 in March 1974, with the dummy now "fully" specified, the agency noted that the interlock had improved belt usage enormously in model year 1974.[50] But storm clouds were on the horizon. NHTSA's investigations found that usage rates of lap and shoulder belts in 1974 models equipped with the interlock were below 60 percent.[51] In other words, over 40 percent of those who had bought 1974 cars presumably had disabled the interlock equipment.

Motorists interested in defeating the interlock were about to get some help. If the 1966 Act marked a legislative revolution in legal control of automobile safety, the counterrevolution might be said to have erupted on the floor of the House on August 12, 1974. During the course of a one-hour open debate on H. R. 5529, the House's version of the recall and school bus safety amendments, Congressman Louis Wyman rose to introduce his "citizens' rights amendment," which would repeal the interlock, outlaw any continuous light and buzzer system to "remind" motorists to buckle up, and make any subsequent passive restraints system only an "option." Wyman explained: "All this amendment does is to provide that in the future automobiles can have seat belts and harnesses, but they are not going to be tied to any sequential warning system with lights and buzzers. They can have a red warning light on the dash which says, 'seat belts are not fastened,' but that is all they can have. Anyone who wants to buy a car in America can have a car with seat belts and harnesses. That is his privilege. He will not have to buy the interlock."[52]

Wyman, it seemed, spoke for many. NHTSA's ignition interlock was "universally despised," as one press account put it, and thousands of letters from constituents attested to the fact. As representatives skimmed their mail, it was obvious something was up. This was no orchestrated letter-writing campaign by a trade association or other pressure groups. It looked more like the firestorm that had followed Nixon's dismissal of Archibald Cox as Special Prosecutor a few months before. One congressman reported that 85 percent of those responding to a questionnaire circulated in his district opposed "compulsory" seat belts.[53] The Wyman amendment caught safety activists by surprise. Some hurriedly returned from long-planned August vacations to heed the call to arms; all were perhaps still bleary-eyed from the long television vigil that had culminated only three days earlier in the President's resignation. But there was reason to believe that the skirmish would be

50.   39 Fed. Reg. 10,271 (1974).

51.   Occupant Crash Protection, 39 Fed. Reg. 10,272 (1974) (codified at 49 C.F.R. § 571.208).

52.   120 Cong. Rec. H. 27815 (daily ed. Aug. 12, 1974) (statement of Rep. Wyman).

53.   Id. at H. 27817.

shortlived. A compromise amendment requiring that motorists have the option of purchasing a seat-belt ignition interlock system or a combination light and buzzer "reminder" had already been hammered out by Congressman John Dingell and safety partisans on the House Commerce Committee when it reported H. R. 5529 on July 11. Perhaps Congressman Wyman, who was a newcomer to vehicle safety matters, had failed to recognize that he had already received satisfaction on the interlock, light, and buzzer issues.

The committee's concession in the Dingell amendment, however, was not responsive to Wyman's core concerns. Wyman was not interested in the "option" to buy one of two obnoxious systems. He was in favor of motorists' freedom to buy exactly as much safety equipment as they wanted. As floor debate raged on, the safety activists steadily lost ground to Wyman's liberation army. The rhetoric of prudent paternalism was no match for visions of technology and "big brotherism" gone mad.

Although the safety coalition that had mounted the 1966 revolution fought back gamely, and from institutional positions that usually confer overwhelming power, the 1974 legislative process was far from business as usual. Committee discipline evaporated in the heat of a grassroots rebellion.

On Liberty. Although the proposals surrounding the interlock, buzzer, and other passive restraints were technologically and procedurally complex, the rhetoric was sweeping and impassioned, as can be seen in the statements of various participants:

> Senator Buckley, on the rationale for his amendment: "I view such coercive measures as the interlock as an intolerable usurpation by Government of an individual's rights in the guise of self-protection."[54]

> Congressman Wyman expostulated: "This is a most extraordinary, most unfounded, most unreasonable, and most irrational position. Actually it is un-American."[55]

And so it went as legislator after legislator rose to defend Americans' freedom of choice.

The safety coalition leadership defended the interlock as best it could. They noted that it had "brought about a dramatic increase in the usage of current belt systems," and that 50 percent of occupants in 1974 models were using their seat belts.[56] Increased usage meant lives saved. Was it not ironic that the interlock should be prohibited under these

---

54.   120 Cong. Rec. S. 30837 (daily ed. Sept. 11, 1974).

55.   120 Cong. Rec. H. 27817 (daily ed. Aug. 12, 1974).

56.   120 Cong. Rec. H. 27820 (daily ed. Aug. 12, 1974).

circumstances. The Department of Transportation estimated that the interlock system alone would save 7,000 lives per year and prevent 340,000 injuries.[57]

But this sober and "socially responsible" position crumbled before the freedom fighters' fusillades, which combined ideological defense of liberty with horror stories and broad farce. Malfunction stories became the order of the day. Ignition interlocks had stranded (or could strand) a motorist in the path of an oncoming train. Women were unable to flee rapists. Parking attendants, who had to buckle up no matter how short the trip, were going nuts. Housewives were buckling in their groceries. Hertz could not obtain sufficient towing services to retrieve malfunctioning vehicles. And in account after account, the family pet, usually a dog, set lights blinking, buzzers buzzing, and interlocks locking.[58]

> Senator Cotten: The other day, I spent a half hour trying to get my car started simply because I had laid a pound of cheese and a loaf of bread on the seat next to me. [Laughter.][59]

> Senator Eagleton: The cases are legion, Mr. President, of how nonsensical this system is. The distinguished Senator from Vermont (Mr. Stafford) and I exchanged some experiences on this subject on the Senate floor a few weeks ago. He told me of a personal experience of a rental car in his home state on a weekend visit. When he put his hand on the seat next to the driver's seat, the thing went berserk, and he had difficulty stopping it.

> I responded by telling him about my hapless constituent who, on instructions of his wife, was sent to the supermarket to buy a turkey. He then had to strap in the turkey to drive home. As the poor constituent observed, it was the safest ride a turkey ever had on the way to the oven.

> Then the distinguished Senator from Texas (Mr. Tower) happened into the Chamber. He has a dachshund. He puts his dachshund on the seat. It is hard to strap in a human being, Mr. President, but a dachshund is damnably hard to strap into one of those seat belts.[60]

There was merriment in the chambers. The members rocked with laughter. The United States Congress was about to enact legislation that experts told them would send seven thousand citizens each year to an early grave. Senator Hartke, who had become one of the safety act's staunchest defenders, was both indignant and bewildered:

---

57.   120 Cong. Rec. S. 30587 (daily ed. Sept. 10, 1974).

58.   120 Cong. Rec. H. 27816 and 120 Cong. Rec. S. 3842 (daily ed. Sept. 11, 1974).

59.   120 Cong. Rec. S. 30841 (daily ed. Sept. 11, 1974).

60.   Id. at S. 30840.

All the gaiety that we have heard on this floor about people who have had annoyance disappears very rapidly when you consider what we are talking about.... Truthfully, you can talk about "big brotherism." But "big brotherism," as this is called, is not unique to this situation. Look at any type of effective disease immunization program. Whether we are right or wrong and whether human nature should be that way, we have to make it mandatory.

That is what we did about smallpox. That is what we did about the various childhood diseases, such as diphtheria. And that is also what we do in a manufacturing plant ...

In other words, in the whole field of safety human nature seems to require something to force us to do what is safe.

What everyone is saying here is that seat belts are a good idea, but we ought not have them. It is a paradox.[61]

The paradox could be explained, perhaps, by attention to context. Safety was important, but it did not always trump liberty. And in Hartke's examples the freedom fighters saw precisely the dangerous, progressive logic of regulation that they abhorred. The private passenger car was not a disease or a workplace, nor was it a common carrier. Those were images from 1966. For Congress in 1974, the passenger car was a private space. The automobile was still a freedom machine.

Liberty was not the only value instinct in the 1974 Amendments to the MVSA. Indeed, other parts of that statute suggest that the real lessons may have been lessons about the difference between technocratic and political cost-benefit analysis. The 1974 Amendments related to school bus safety played this tune in a decidedly different key, demanding security for children in school buses however small the problem and whatever the costs.

NHTSA had studied the issue of school bus safety very carefully, and from a dispassionate view of the data it seemed relatively clear that the proposed amendments made no sense. Motor vehicle accidents had reached an all-time high in 1972 and 1973; accidents in those years claimed 54,589 and 54,052 lives, respectively. But of these, only 150 fatalities (and 4,600 injuries) resulted from school bus accidents. And 60 of the 150 fatalities, plus a more indeterminate number of injuries, were adults who had the misfortune of finding themselves, as pedestrians or motor vehicle occupants, in the path of an oncoming bus. Of the remaining 90 fatalities, moreover, 60 were children who perished *after* they had disembarked. The children were run over either by the bus itself or by another vehicle. Yet the school bus amendments, ignoring 80 percent of the fatalities, did not mention pedestrian protection as one of

---

61. Id. at S. 30846–47.

the eight areas for mandatory rulemaking. The rules that Congress wanted NHTSA to promulgate would, therefore, only address the remaining 30 fatalities, plus some fraction of associated injuries.

The cost side of the equation reinforced regulatory caution. The average purchase price of a school bus was then $8,000. The vehicles' useful life was nine to ten years. The manufacturers' data indicated that improvements in seats, body structure, and frontal barriers would add approximately 2,000 pounds in weight and $1,500 in cost. The added weight, in turn, would require other improvements—a larger chassis, heavier front and rear axles, and larger tires—that would further magnify weight and cost increases. The total tab could come to 2,430 pounds in increased weight and $2,070 in added costs, roughly 25 percent of the vehicle's base price, not including extras. Work on emergency exits, windows, and windshields, for example, would cost an additional $112. And the economics of retrofitting buses were even more unappealing. Vehicles depreciated 15 percent the first year, and 10 percent annually thereafter. The resale value of a nine-year-old bus was $600. Retrofit costs would probably exceed $4,000, more than twice the amount required to incorporate safety features in new buses.

Some legislators seemed to think that the price tag might be less, about $1,000, and the president of Ward Manufacturing testified that "the cost will not be as great as many suggest."[62] But whatever figures were used, it was obvious the costs were so substantial that the regulations Congress was demanding might actually reduce school bus safety. At the Senate oversight hearings in 1974, before the provisions were enacted, the agency's chief rulemaking engineer conceded that regulators could "make a schoolbus as safe as a Greyhound bus" but that doing so would drive up procurement costs by 41 percent. "If you increase the cost by 40 percent, these people will have to drive the buses at least 10 to 12 years," he cautioned. "If we are not careful," the engineer continued, "if we try to put too much safety into a new bus, we will be counterproductive in that older, unsafe buses will be on the road for a much greater period of time."[63]

This sort of careful attention to costs, benefits, and priorities was, of course, exactly what the courts, the executive branch, and Congress itself had been urging on the agency. Yet on the school bus issue, Representative Les Aspin apparently spoke for a majority in both houses when he complained that "Given the comparatively low accident rates on school-

---

62. Amendments to the National Traffic and Motor Vehicle Safety Act of 1966: Hearings on H.R. 7505, H.R. 5529, and S. 355 Before the Subcomm. on Commerce and Finance of the House Comm. on Interstate and Foreign Relations, 934 Cong., 1st Sess. 84–85 (1973).

63. Motor Vehicle Safety Oversight: Hearings Before the Senate Comm. on Commerce, 93d Cong., 2d Sess. 84–85 (1974).

buses, the Department of Transportation—DOT—argues that the school-bus safety regulation is an extremely low priority item. DOT maintains that in terms of a cost-benefit analysis, it is worth neither the time nor the effort of DOT to protect our school children from shoddily construct-ed schoolbuses. DOT is misusing the concept of cost-benefit analysis."[64] Other members were far less charitable. As Congress lurched toward adoption of the amendments, it was obvious that regulatory officials had badly botched their assessment of the costs and benefits of school bus safety. They had confused economics with politics. In the political process and in the media, sober cost-benefit calculations are about as popular as rich, absentee slumlords.

The media weighed in as well. ABC News calculated that the added cost per pupil per day of a far safer schoolbus would be 1/2 cent.[65] An "investigative" report by Metromedia News produced similar provoca-tive (and misleading) revelations of NHTSA's "cavalier attitude." Only one of the Department of Transportation's 72,000 employees, it reported, worked full time on school bus safety matters

The space program metaphor that had figured in the original passage of the MVSA returned, but in a new guise. The mayor of Lomita, California, testified: "[Senator Percy] mentioned the millions of dollars that were rightfully spent to create a better safety situation for the astronauts—many millions of dollars. I know it's pretty far up there. As he said, don't we owe our children the same protection as we owe these astronauts? They are all American lives, human lives, and we do owe them the same protection."[66]

Heated political and media rhetoric notwithstanding, the demand for regulation might have sputtered out. After all, exhortation of this general sort was a daily staple of political life and there was no end to the domestic programs that might be justified by reference to the costs of going to the moon. As the school bus safety amendments leapfrogged over thousands of other legislative proposals on Congress's crowded agenda, however, it was obvious that some deep resource of political will was being tapped.

In some sense, the demand for more protection in school buses appears to have been tied to the national furor surrounding "forced"

---

64. Amendments to the National Traffic and Motor Vehicle Safety Act of 1966: Hearing and Finance of the House Comm. on Interstate and Foreign Relations, 93d Cong., 1st Sess. 547 (1973).

65. Amendments to the National Traffic and Motor Vehicle Safety Act of 1966: Hearings on H.R. 7505, H.R. 5529, and S. 355 before the Subcomm. on Commerce and Finance of the House Comm. on Interstate and Foreign Relations, 93d Cong., 1 Sess. 814 (1973).

66. Id. At 864.

busing to achieve school integration. In an article in the *Washington Post* on April 14, 1972, entitled "The Other Schoolbus Problem," the reporter Coleman McCarthy alluded to the connection: "As if schoolbuses weren't getting enough national attention already—on school integration—the recent crash in Valley Cottage, New York, suggests there is another kind of attention schoolbuses ought to be getting, on safety." Busing was not upheld definitively as a means of school desegregation until the Supreme Court's decision in *Swann v. Charlotte-Mecklenburg Board of Education*[67] in 1971. The decision was not popular. A 1971 poll found that 77 percent of the nation opposed busing.[68] Antibusing pressures peaked in Congress in 1972, when they reached the proportions of a "national uproar," as the Congressional Quarterly put it.[69]

But in the Congress, majorities do not always prevail. On August 18, 1972, the House, by a vote of 283 to 102, adopted H.R. 13915, which would have banned busing except to the school closest or next-closest to the students' homes. In the Senate, however, pro-busing forces filibustered the measure and withstood three votes to invoke cloture. The bill died on the Senate floor. Looking back, the Congressional Quarterly called busing "one of the most bitterly fought congressional battles in 1972."[70] And although the controversy quieted in 1973, the politicians' torment continued. The Senate held hearings on a proposed constitutional amendment to prohibit busing, but took no action.

The "involuntariness" of school bus ridership may explain, in part, the distinctive perspective on costs and benefits that the school bus amendments generated. School bus safety could tap reservoirs of concern about equality and freedom simultaneously. If the state was responsible for children being in buses, it surely had the responsibility to compensate their loss of freedom by providing the safest possible involuntary trip. It was essential to "fairness" that these involuntary riders be as safe as those who freely chose to ride commercial buses. A Congress that had participated vigorously in civil rights lawmaking, which in turn had led to a vast increase in involuntary school bus ridership, and that had refused to deny the courts busing as a remedy, could at least try to make the ride safe. It could do something about "busing," even if "safe busing" was at best a distant second on the busing agenda of angry parents around the nation.

It is also true that the vision of protection children gives any measure that can be so characterized a considerable degree of political appeal. But the overall motor vehicle safety problem would very nearly

---

67. 402 U.S. 1 (1971).

68. "Congressional Anti-busing Sentiment Mounts in 1972", 28 Cong. Q. 119 (1972).

69. "Opponents to Major Legislation Score Success," 28 Cong. Q. 119 (1972).

70. Id. At 1075.

bear that characterization. The epidemic that Haddon and his colleagues had described was largely a health problem of children and youth. If Congress wanted to protect the lives of children, it would have done better to reenergize NHTSA's lagging standard-setting enterprise as it applied to the passenger car. Even modest safety enhancement there would decrease the risk of death or serious injury for tens of thousands of children who were involved in motor vehicle accidents each year.

But that sort of analysis of the problem is more reminiscent of the legislative agenda of 1966. The 1974 amendments gave a new and highly "political" twist to the concept of federal motor vehicle safety regulation. Henceforth, it seemed, NHTSA's information needs would run at least as much to political intelligence as to scientific data and analysis. If NHTSA was to understand its own regulatory mandate, it would have to understand the political mood of the country.

The Stage is Set for *State Farm*

As the Nixon Administration gave way to the Ford presidency, NHTSA's Administrator, James Gregory, told Congress that he was anxiously searching for some "publicly acceptable" way to reissue Standard 208. But, after Gregory's rapid exit from the scene, Department of Transportation Secretary William Coleman took charge of the proceeding. In fairly short order he decided not to issue any rule, even though he was convinced that airbags were both technically feasible and effective. Coleman's approach instead was to negotiate a deal with the auto companies. He would not issue the rule if they would build a substantial fleet of airbag-equipped cars.[71] The point of this exercise was to permit on-the-road experience to either confirm or overcome public and congressional doubts concerning the effectiveness and costliness of the technology. Those doubts clearly were Coleman's, as they had been Gregory's, preoccupation. The time had come for political prudence. References to the interlock episode run like a *leitmotif* through the order announcing Coleman's decision.[72]

But Jerry Ford and Bill Coleman were not long for their respective offices either. Brock Adams, the new Secretary of Transportation under Jimmy Carter, reopened the passive restraints rulemaking docket almost immediately upon entering the DOT building. Adams's notice of proposed rulemaking disagreed sharply with the Coleman decision.[73] He believed that a demonstration program was inconsistent with NHTSA's

---

71. Occupant Crash Protection, 42 Fed. Reg. 5071 (1977).

72. Occupant Crash Protection: Highway Safety Programs Standards, 41 Fed. Reg. 24,070 (1976).

73. Occupant Crash Protection: Alternatives for Passenger Cars, 42 Fed. Reg. 15,935 (1977).

statutory responsibility to reduce highway deaths and injuries. He also disagreed with Coleman's use of public resistance as a ground for decision. In his view, the airbag (and other passive restraints) was a vastly different technique from the interlock. The interlock had involved constant interference with automobile operation; by contrast, airbags were not even visible to automobile passengers, and automatic belts were supposed to operate without interfering with the operation of the automobile. Hence there was no reason to imagine that automobile owners would disable passive restraint equipment with anything approaching the frequency that they disabled the interlock device.

Secretary Adams decided quickly, on July 5, 1977, to require passive restraints—encompassing airbags, automatic belts, and other technologies—in all passenger vehicles.[74] He thus demonstrated the Carter Administration's political will. But the rule's lead times left implementation to the early years of a second term that was not to be. And as it turned out, subsequent tinkering with the rule provided the rationale for the Reagan Administration's abandonment of passive restraints.

Muddling in a Circle. NHTSA initially had required that passive belt systems be detachable by means of a push-button release mechanism.[75] This requirement was adopted to quell consumer fears of being trapped in burning vehicles after a crash. Indeed, the rulemaking record on emergency exit technologies is replete with speculations about consumer preferences and consumer fears. The agency debates resolved themselves into a simple trade-off between acceptability and defeatability. The push-button system was likely to be acceptable to the public because it replicated the devices currently on manual belts. But, by the same token, it could be used to make passive belts *into* manual belts, thus defeating the basic purpose of passive restraints. Technologies such as the continuous spool, however, which did not reassure consumers that they would be able to exit from their belts on demand, might produce an even greater public reaction and a greater tendency to disable the belt entirely. Unless attached to an interlock, a passive belt system could, after all, be defeated with a pair of scissors. In the end the agency yielded to the imponderables and permitted manufacturers to choose their own emergency exit technology. This seemingly innocuous decision set the stage for the Reagan Administration's rescission of the rule in 1981.

Connoisseurs of political irony might like to note that on February 2, 1981, NHTSA granted[76] Ralph Nader's petition for the initiation of rulemaking to raise the barrier-crash test speed in Standard 208 from 30

---

74. Occupant Restraint Systems, 42 Fed. Reg. 34,289 (1977).

75. Passive Belt Requirements, 39 Fed. Reg. 14,593 (1974).

76. Grant of Petition for Rulemaking, 46 Fed. Reg. 10,428 (1981).

miles an hour to 40 miles an hour in model year 1984 and 50 miles an hour in model year 1986. Nader's petition pointed out the expected increase in fatalities accompanying the shift to smaller cars and recent technical studies indicating that airbags could be constructed that would meet the injury criteria of Standard 208 at a barrier impact speed of 50 miles per hour. In granting Nader's petition that the agency pursue the matter, NHTSA agreed with his basic position, but stated that it was in the process of analyzing accident data files to evaluate injury modes and injury distributions as a function of crash mode and crash speed. Only after it finished this analysis would the agency be in a position to reconsider the Standard 208's injury criteria in a systematic way.

While this polite exchange was going on in the *Federal Register*, the *Washington Post*[77] was reporting the deregulatory proposals and initiatives of the incoming Reagan administration. High on Reagan's list of immediate targets were regulatory requirements affecting the automobile industry. The stagflation of the 1970s had been devastating for American automobile manufacturers and auto workers. It was actually not at all clear that regulatory relief would help reverse these trends. But candidate Reagan had promised that if he were elected, regulatory relief would be forthcoming. The Federal Register began to reflect the new political world reported in the *Washington Post* only ten days after the grant of Nader's petition. On February 12, 1981, NHTSA proposed[78] a one-year delay in the effective dates of its passive restraints requirements.

The stated reason for this proposal was to allow the agency to reconsider Standard 208 in the light of the major changes that had occurred since its adoption in 1977. The agency was particularly concerned that the current phase-in schedule, which began with large cars in 1981 and proceeded through mid-size to small cars in 1983, might exacerbate the economic troubles of the domestic automobile industry. In addition, the automakers' plans for compliance with Standard 208's demand for passive restraint systems had altered radically in the intervening years. Whereas airbags were the passive restraint of choice when Adams acted in 1977, it seemed clear that most manufacturers in 1981 would attempt to comply through the use of passive belts.

As usual, the commentary flooded in. The most comprehensive comments opposing the proposed suspension came from the insurance

---

77. See, e.g., Peter Behr & John M. Berry, "Reagan Decontrols Gasoline, Crude in Deregulation Debut," Wash. Post, Jan. 29, 1981, at A1; Joanne Omang & Peter Behr, "Rules Freeze: Everybody Is Scrambling; President's Rules Freeze Sets Off a Scramble," Wash. Post, Jan. 31, 1981, at A1; Peter Behr, "Orders Pending to Cut Impact on Regulations," Wash. Post, Feb. 4, 1981, at E1; Peter Behr, "Reagan Team Takes Stock of Prospects for Reshaping Regulations," Wash. Post, Feb. 6, 1981, at A2.

78. 46 Fed. Reg. 12,033 (1981).

industry. Capitalizing on the government's increasing enthusiasm for cost-benefit analysis, State Farm Insurance Company sponsored a cost-benefit analysis by William Nordhaus of Yale University. According to the Nordhaus analysis, the economic costs of delay were five times greater than the benefits.

The automobile manufacturers' most telling argument in favor of the suspension was that the passive restraints standard might well be ineffective. The extremely high price of airbags per vehicle dictated that, under current economic conditions, the manufacturers would use passive belts. But passive belts were, in the manufacturers' view, unacceptable to the public unless they were easily detachable. If they were easily detachable, then they would probably function essentially like manual belts. And if they functioned like manual belts, the industry and consumers were being asked to spend millions of dollars for no increase in safety. NHTSA's earlier "flexibility" on the issue of detachment technology was thus turned against the passive restraints rule itself.

Predictably, the agency concluded that it should delay implementation for one year in order to reevaluate the passive restraints standard.[79] In October 1981, having completed its reevaluation, the agency published a notice rescinding the passive restraints requirement entirely.[80] The rescission order, essentially adopting the manufacturers' assertions, explained that the agency could no longer conclude that passive restraints were reasonable and practicable. Because of uncertainty about public acceptability and usage rates for detachable passive belts, the passive restraints requirement might be adding substantial costs to motor vehicles without any attendant benefits. Events since 1977 that had changed the economic and political context of rulemaking were also significantly influencing the agency's decision. There were less costly alternatives, such as public information campaigns and the Coleman demonstration project, which the agency had never seriously undertaken. NHTSA now believed that these efforts, combined with the possibility of manufacturers' installation of passive belts as optional equipment, might better meet the need for automobile safety.

State Farm Insurance Company immediately sought judicial review of the rescission order in the D.C. Circuit Court of Appeals. The order was held invalid by a panel of the D.C. Circuit in a long, somewhat confusing, occasionally bizarre, opinion.[81] The government immediately

---

79. Id.

80. 46 Fed. Reg. 53,419 (1981).

81. State Farm Mut. Automobile Ins. Co. v. DOT, 680 F.2d 206 (D.C. Cir. 1982). For a discussion of that decision see, Peter Lehner, *Judicial Review of Agency Inaction*, 83 COLUM. L. REV. 627, 663 et seq. (1983).

appealed to the Supreme Court, which sustained the D.C. Circuit's determination, but on quite different grounds.

The Supreme Court Speaks

In its decision in *State Farm,* the Supreme Court found two major faults with NHTSA's rescission of Standard 208. First, it could not understand why NHTSA believed that passive belts with an easy means for detachment would function like manual belts. After all, as long as the belts were not detached, they required no effort by motorists to provide passive protection. Hence, by contrast with manual belts, inertia favored use rather than nonuse. Given this inertial factor, how could NHTSA conclude that no increase in belt usage should be predicted? If "detachability" was a problem, why not use General Motors's preferred continuous-spool technology?

Second, the Court was baffled by NHTSA's apparent but unexplained abandonment of airbags. The agency might ultimately conclude that it could not require a passive belt technology that was both acceptable to the public and likely to increase belt usage. But that said nothing about airbags, devices that the agency had maintained for over a decade were technologically available and cost-beneficial. Why had the agency not simply eliminated passive belt systems as a means of satisfying Standard 208, leaving airbags as the only feasible means for compliance? Finding no answer to that question in the agency's rationale for its decision or in the immediate rulemaking record, the Court remanded the question to the agency for redetermination.

In many respects the *State Farm* opinion broke no new ground. By the time it was decided the lower federal courts had ruled on the legality of a host of rules promulgated by the new social regulatory agencies—principally NHTSA, OSHA and EPA. Although many of those judicial decisions might be criticized, like the *Chrysler* decision, as technically incompetent, they followed the broad outlines laid down in the first review proceeding concerning a NHTSA crashworthiness standard.

The basic framework for judicial scrutiny of NHTSA's efforts had been established in 1968 in a careful and scholarly opinion by Judge Carl McGowan of the D. C. Circuit Court of Appeals in *Automobile Parts and Accessories Association v. Boyd.*[82] Two aspects of that opinion are of particular interest; both in some sense "proceduralize" the reviewing court's investigation of the reasonableness of the agency's standard setting. Although designed to protect agency substantive choice from uninformed judicial meddling, Judge McGowan's "restrained" approach to judicial review may actually render judicial review more disabling. Given the dynamics of notice and comment rulemaking, proceduraliza-

---

82. 407 F.2d 330 (D.C. Cir. 1968).

tion reinforces the agency's caution when dealing with an aggressive opposition.

Judge McGowan set forth what he perceived to be the basic scope of review under the "arbitrary and capricious" standard of the Administrative Procedure Act. In his words, "The paramount objective is to see whether the agency, given an essentially legislative task to perform, has carried it out in a manner calculated to negate the dangers of arbitrariness and irrationality in the formulation of rules for general application in the future."[83] So stated, whether an agency's rule is deemed arbitrary or capricious may turn as much on the agency's apparent reasoning process as on the good sense of the final judgment under review. This was precisely the Supreme Court's position in *State Farm*. NHTSA may have had good reasons for its rescission order, but it had not cogently explained them.

In a similar vein, Judge McGowan addressed the question of whether NHTSA's "concise general statement of basis and purpose," which accompanied the challenged regulation, was sufficient to pass muster under Section 553 of the Administrative Procedure Act. The pertinent NHTSA statement was certainly concise and general. It stated in full: "This standard specifies requirements for head restraints to reduce the frequency and severity of neck injury in rear-end and other collisions."[84] The court viewed this statement as unnecessarily terse:

> [O]n the occasion of this first challenge to the implementation of the new statute it is appropriate for us to remind the Administrator of the ever present possibility of judicial review, and to caution against an overly literal reading of the statutory terms "concise" and "general." These adjectives must be accommodated to the realities of judicial scrutiny, which do not contemplate that the court itself will, by a laborious examination of the record, formulate in the first instances the significant issues faced by the agency and articulate the rationale of their resolution. We do not expect the agency to discuss every item . . . in informal rulemaking. We do expect that, if the judicial review which Congress has thought it important to provide is to be meaningful, the "concise general statement of . . . basis and purpose" mandated by Section 4 *will* enable us to see what major issues of policy were ventilated by the informal proceedings and why the agency reacted to them as it did.[85]

Although Judge McGowan articulated this requirement in his *Auto Parts* opinion as a necessity of judicial review, the demand for more

---

83. 407 F.2d at 338.

84. 33 Fed. Reg. 2916 (1968).

85. 407 F.2d at 338.

elaborate discussion of the major issues thrown up by the rulemaking proceeding has the equally important effect of reinforcing the participation of outside parties in an agency's deliberations. The agency's failure to respond to significant issues raised by participants can hardly satisfy the basic standard of reasonableness that the court had set forth: to perform its task in a manner "[c]alculated to negate the dangers of arbitrariness and irrationality."[86]

Judge McGowan's approach highlights two consistent features of judicial review of agency rulemaking. First, the courts are there to see that administrators do their jobs. The teaching of our constitutional culture is that delegation of policy choice to administrators is constitutionally permissible, but it is a reluctant necessity. Delegation is justified primarily by the complexity of the regulatory tasks assigned and the need for a high level of expertise. It is hardly remarkable, then, that reviewing courts are on the lookout for agencies operating on the basis of hunches or bromides. NHTSA cannot respond to a judicial demand that it demonstrate the practicability of a rule by intoning, "Necessity is the mother of invention." Such "experts" are viewed as having failed to execute their legitimate statutory mandate.

Second, our constitutional culture also teaches that keeping administrators within their delegated authority is an essential element of maintaining the rule of law, the separation of powers, and ultimately our liberal, democratic polity.[87] Fears of arbitrary and undemocratic exercises of power make delegations of administrative authority reluctant in the first instance. From this perspective, any loss of effectiveness in substantive policy caused by judicial review is but a necessary cost to pay in the crucial project of maintaining the constitutional structure. These very general institutional considerations help explain why courts have taken rulemaking review seriously and why, far from relaxing the criteria for judicial review, congressional interest in the matter focuses almost exclusively on proposals to increase the judicial role in overseeing agency

---

86. 407 F.2d at 338.

87. For two of many developments of this theme, see JAMES FREEDMAN, CRISIS AND LEGITIMACY IN THE ADMINISTRATIVE STATE (1978) (arguing that fair administrative procedure will supply legitimacy that agencies need to function efficiently); Richard B. Stewart, *The Reformation of American Administrative Law*, 88 Harv. L. Rev. 1667 (1975) (suggesting that current administrative process inadequately represents various interests). See also Richard B. Stewart, *Administrative Law in the Twenty-First Century*, 78 N.Y.U. L. Rev. 437, 438 (2003) ("The traditional core of administrative law has focused on securing the rule of law and protecting liberty by ensuring that agencies follow fair and impartial decisional procedures, act within the bounds of the statutory authority delegated by the legislature, and respect private rights."); Thomas O. Sargentich, *Reform of the American Administrative Process: The Contemporary Debate,* 1984 Wis. L. Rev. 385, 397 (describing the "rule of law ideal" of administrative law).

rulemaking.[88]

Yet there is still a puzzle concerning the preferred judicial technique for policing NHTSA's rulemaking efforts. That our most general constitutional presuppositions promote serious review of agency rules does not tell us why we find courts reshaping the issue of regulatory reasonableness into an issue of procedural rationality, or why courts have jealously guarded rights of notice and participation by insisting on responsiveness to issues raised during the rulemaking proceeding. It is, after all, this "proceduralized" form of judicial review that is particularly debilitating from an agency's perspective. It is "proceduralism" that legitimates and empowers the full-court press that was employed so effectively by the automobile industry in the *Chrysler* case. What cultural imperative has driven the courts in this direction?

The demand for a rational decision *process* is the judiciary's response to a dislocation in the legal culture. The Motor Vehicle Safety Act, like most regulatory statutes adopted after 1966, permits immediate review of an agency rule, or of the withdrawal or amendment of a rule, by any party who may be adversely affected. Superficially this is only a change in the usual timing of review: without such a provision, an adversely affected party could nevertheless challenge a rule's validity when the agency attempted to enforce it.[89] The consequences of the legislative shift to pre-enforcement review, nevertheless, are profound. It allows affected parties to go to court without attempting to comply with the rule and, in the absence of any attempt to enforce it against them, to

---

88. See, for example, William Funk, *Report Card on Regulatory Reform,* Admin. & Reg. L. News, Summer 1995, at 9 (describing "discussion draft" bill by Senate to "add[] a new ground for holding unlawful and setting aside agency action"); James O'Reilly, *Deference Makes a Difference: A Study of Impacts of the Bumpers Judicial Review Amendments,* 49 U. Cinn. L. Rev. 739 (1980); Woodward and Levin, *In Defense of Deference: Judicial Review of Agency Action,* 31 Admin. L. Rev. 329 (1979).

89. One year after the enactment of the Motor Vehicle Safety Act, the Supreme Court gave hesitant approval to the pre-enforcement review of agency regulations under the Administrative Procedure Act. But it is far from obvious that many of the lawsuits contesting NHTSA's rules would have been ripe for review without the specific statutory authorization provided by the National Traffic and Motor Vehicle Safety Act. Compare Abbott Laboratories v. Gardner, 387 U.S. 136 (1967) (holding pre-enforcement review of FDA drug-labeling requirements justified given substantial impact of regulations on petitioners), with Toilet Goods Ass'n. v. Gardner, 387 U.S. 158 (1967) (holding pre-enforcement review of FDA inspection procedures unnecessary, since injury to petitioners was speculative). As a reading of *Auto Parts* reveals, the parties to the case recognized the novelty of the issues and put a wide variety of claims before the court. Judge McGowan was particularly troubled by the fact that the plaintiffs were attempting to have the rule overturned on the basis of arguments that directly contradicted the positions that they had taken in the rulemaking proceeding itself. Although unhappy with the plaintiff's "effort to analogize themselves to private attorneys general with unlimited right to expose all danger to the public interest," the court seemed to believe that the judicial review provisions of the Motor Vehicle Safety Act demanded a judicial answer on the merits. Id.

obtain a declaration whether it is valid. Review in this form, like an attack on the facial validity of a statute, addresses not the particular circumstances of a rule's application but the abstract legality of its commands.

Put in this way, the traditional legal view is that such abstract issues are usually nonjusticiable. The American legal culture has historically maintained that courts declare the law only as a by-product of the adjudication of concrete controversies about the legal rights of particular parties.[90] This understanding is given constitutional status by Article III of the Constitution, which limits the federal judiciary to the adjudication of "cases or controversies." An enforcement action against Chrysler for violating the passive restraints rule, in which Chrysler argues that it could not comply because the dummy specifications were inadequate, is a conventional case or controversy. The adjudication is about individual rights and responsibilities on the basis of particular facts. The need to address the validity of the rule is a mere by-product of the need to determine individual rights. A suit by Chrysler to invalidate a rule on any of a score of grounds before the rule's effective date, and preceding any attempt at compliance or threat of enforcement, is obviously not a case cast in this same mold.

Without going further into the dense thicket of the federal jurisprudence of justiciability, we need only note here that this jurisprudence renders the type of review contemplated by the Motor Vehicle Safety Act, and pursued in the *Chrysler* case itself, problematic, if not downright suspect. It makes a case like *State Farm* seem almost aberrational. The insurance industry was neither the target nor the intended beneficiary of Standard 208. Its only interest was in saving money—or more accurately put, enhancing profits—during the period when passive restraints reduce the costs of injuries and deaths, but before new actuarial data begin to drive down insurance premiums. In order to square the congressional command to decide cases in the abstract with the conventional and constitutionally required judicial role of deciding concrete cases, courts have been forced to identify some individual legal right that the Congress has called upon the courts to protect. What could it be?

This was the question that Judge McGowan was required to answer in the *Auto Parts* case. Repairing to the Administrative Procedure Act, he found that the plaintiffs' entitlement was to be free from "arbitrary" exercises of administrative power. This again is, superficially, an unremarkable legal move. Reviewing courts have traditionally employed the arbitrariness standard, and it has caused little difficulty when applied to

---

90. See Marbury v. Madison, 5 U.S. (1 Cranch) 137, 177 (1803) ("It is emphatically the province and duty of the judicial department to say what the law is. Those who apply the rule to particular cases, must of necessity expound and interpret the rule").

376 MOTOR VEHICLE MFRS ASS'N v. STATE FARM

the traditional forms of agency decision making—specific agency decisions to grant or deny a benefit or to impose a sanction. Adjudicatory decisions that are either against the preponderance of the evidence or contrary to customary policies are "arbitrary" in the straightforward sense of "not according to law." For an appellate court to say so is only to treat an agency like a lower court which is, of course, the way in which an agency acts when adjudicating specific controversies. But the legally innovative aspect of the Motor Vehicle Safety Act and the revolution of 1966 was to abandon traditional adjudicatory forms. How should the arbitrariness criterion be applied to general policies embodied in rules that had never been applied?

The task of translation is rhetorically simple but, given the legal culture, profoundly transformative. By analogy to adjudicatory decision making, rules are said to be arbitrary in two situations: (1) if they have no adequate factual predicate, an evidentiary interpretation of "arbitrary"; or (2) if they violate existing legal norms, in particular the statute pursuant to which they were promulgated. So far so good; but let us now examine the application of these two grounds of arbitrariness in the context of rulemaking review.

First, conformity with the statute. The Motor Vehicle Safety Act requires that rules "meet the need for motor vehicle safety," protect against "unreasonable risk," be "practicable" and "appropriate," and be stated in "objective" terms. All the quoted terms demand policy choices, not the application of legal rules. Is the court really to judge these questions? And, if so, how can it judge them without appearing to be merely substituting its policy preferences for those of the agency? For surely neither the Motor Vehicle Safety Act, the Administrative Procedure Act, nor the Constitution gives anyone the "right" to have motor vehicle safety policy set by federal courts.

In order to appreciate the judiciary's dilemma more fully, focus for a moment on the statutory requirement that the agency's rules eliminate "unreasonable risks." Remember that the passive restraints rule was premised not on the superiority of passive restraints technology over manual lap and shoulder belts, when used, but on the agency's despair that any significant number of Americans could ever be convinced to buckle up. Now suppose some litigant. makes the following claim: to be "reasonable" in most common law contexts means to behave as an ordinarily prudent person would behave in similar circumstances. Ordinary Americans overwhelmingly decline to use restraint systems that they already own. Put another way, we know that most Americans elect to run the risk of being in an auto accident without the protection of a universally available and highly effective restraint system. In short, the risk that the passive restraints rule is designed to avoid has been demonstrated, by the very behavior upon which the rule is premised, to be a reasonable one. It is, therefore, outside NHTSA's statutory authority to regulate.

This straightforward claim of statutory violation presents all sorts of questions. The fundamental issue is one of determining how the Congress intended "reasonableness" to be judged. But there are many candidates for an appropriate methodology. Does the statute demand that the agency analyze its rulemaking proposals on the basis of common law standards of "reasonableness"? On the basis of the public health consequences of maintaining the status quo? On the basis of current social perceptions of the acceptability of particular risks? On the basis of predictions of what those perceptions might be after technology forcing has altered existing cultural presuppositions?

These questions and many similar ones are answered neither by the language of the statute nor by its legislative history. Yet choosing among them will have profound consequences for the policies actually chosen by NHTSA. And it is this prospect that poses the judicial dilemma. If the court chooses a particular construction of "unreasonable risk," it has in a very substantial sense chosen the agency's regulatory program. Nothing in our constitutional arrangements suggests that courts should play such a political role. Precisely this concern underlies the Supreme Court's famous *Chevron* decision,[91] whose story is told elsewhere in this volume.

Yet if the court permits the agency to choose any approach to unreasonableness that is reasonable, it knows that any of the candidates just mentioned, plus perhaps a host of others, will pass muster. If that is the breadth of discretion provided the agency by the statute, then the notion that NHTSA operates under law and is subject to judicial review becomes the skimpiest of fig leaves over a naked reality that is itself constitutionally unacceptable: the complete delegation of legislative policy choice to administrators.[92]

The twin shoals of judicial policymaking on the one hand and unconstrained administrative discretion on the other are hardly novel landmarks when steering for the safe harbor of judicial legitimacy. They are traversed routinely by judicial navigators. But in the context of judging the abstract legality of rules under vague statutory criteria, the

---

91. Chevron U.S.A., Inc. v. Natural Res. Def. Council, Inc., 467 U.S. 837 (1984). For an insightful harmonization of the Supreme Court's *State Farm* and *Chevron* cases in terms of the Court's capacity to give direction to the lower federal judiciary, see Peter L. Strauss, *One Hundred Fifty Cases Per Year: Some Implications of the Supreme Court's Limited Resources for Judicial Review of Agency Action,* 87 Colum. L. Rev. 1093 (1987).

92. For an appreciation of the Supreme Court's difficulties in mediating these contradictory impulses, compare Chevron U.S.A., Inc. v. Natural Res. Def. Council, 467 U.S. 837 (1984), with NLRB v. United Food and Commercial Workers' Union, 484 U.S. 112 (1987).

task of maintaining the confidence of passengers and crew is made more difficult by the absence of some important aids to navigation. The conventional lawyerly moves for separating law and policy or for camouflaging their inseparability are largely unavailable when reviewing agency regulations. When reviewing the abstract legality of rules it is simply preposterous to claim (1) that the court is addressing not these broad issues of policy but only the agency's application of law to fact in an adjudication of narrowly focused claims of right, or (2) that these interpretive issues are routinely decided in agency enforcement proceedings and, therefore, have long legal histories that constrain both the agency's and the judiciary's roles.

Other obvious features of rulemaking review proceedings under the Motor Vehicle Safety Act belie the claim that the courts are here merely engaged in reviewing run-of-the-mill administrative dispute settlements. The parties look more like legislative claimants than ordinary litigants. As in *State Farm*, they often are tangentially affected business interests, such as the insurance industry, or ideological champions of the left or right, such as the Center for Auto Safety or the Pacific Legal Foundation. Even the directly affected manufacturers may be litigating for strategic competitive advantage (remember General Motors's absence from the *Chrysler* litigation) rather than to protect any conventional form of property interest. And no matter who is litigating, the judgment usually will bind everyone. The question is the validity of the rule, not the propriety of its application. The litigant's "rights" and the "rights" of the public are indistinguishable.

The line between law and policy can also disappear in judicial review of agency adjudication. The pre-enforcement review of rules facilitated by the Motor Vehicle Safety Act is but a recognition of the changing structure of federal administrative regulation. Yet no amount of scholarly celebration of this so-called public law litigation[93] is likely to eliminate judicial anxiety in the face of a task that calls for repeated, transparent, and general policy choices.[94] The task must be redefined to integrate it

---

93.   See, for example, Charles F. Sabel & William H. Simon, *Destabilization Rights: How Public Law Litigation Succeeds*, 117 Harv. L. Rev. 1015 (2004); Abram Chayes, *Foreword: Public Law Litigation and the Burger Court*, 96 Harv. L. Rev. 4 (1982); Carl Tobias, *Public Law Litigation and the Federal Rules of Civil Procedure*, 74 Cornell L. Rev. 270 (1989); Owen Fiss, *Foreword: The Forms of Justice*, 93 Harv. L. Rev. 1 (1979); Abraham Chayes, *The Role of the Judge in Public Law Litigation*, 89 Harv. L. Rev. 1281 (1976); cf. Harold Hongju Koh, *Transnational Public Law Litigation*, 100 Yale L.J. 2347 (1991).

94.   Critics of such efforts are quick to point out the errors of the courts' ways. See, for example, Richard E. Levy & Robert L. Glicksman, *Judicial Activism and Restraint in the Supreme Court's Environmental Law Decisions*, 42 Vand. L. Rev. 343 (1989); Richard Pierce & Sydney Shapiro, *Political and Judicial Review of Agency Action*, 59 Tex. L. Rev.

with a more conventional conception of judicial competence. For it is on that convention that the judiciary's political legitimacy depends.

From this strategic perspective the other, "evidentiary," interpretation of arbitrariness has much to recommend it. Yet here again the courts encounter an awkward gap between their traditional reviewing functions and the pre-enforcement review of rules. Judicial review of agency adjudication, like appellate court review of trial court proceedings, focuses on whether the trial record contains appropriate proofs to sustain the initial adjudicator's findings of fact. If not, the trier of fact has behaved arbitrarily. Rulemaking processes, however, are vastly different from trials. There are no obvious boundaries on the rulemaking record, no accepted standards of "proof" for policy judgments, and no procedural vehicles that sharply delineate the "issues" in a rulemaking proceeding. As Judge McGowan noted in *Auto Parts*, the agency is engaged essentially in a legislative activity. In our legal system legislatures may operate on the basis of any evidence that a majority is willing to credit-or even on no evidence at all.

Notwithstanding these difficulties, *evidentiary* policing of agency rulemaking threatens judicial legitimacy much less than does outright policy revision. Agencies are not legislatures. Indeed, they are substituted for legislatures precisely in order that policy may be based on a more expert understanding of the problems addressed. Agencies are supposed to get the facts right. Hence, from *Auto Parts* on, courts have experimented with a series of techniques designed to sharpen issues, reveal factual assumptions, and thereby shape a record within which judicial review of rules for factual adequacy makes sense. This story of procedural innovation has been told elsewhere and need not be rehearsed in detail.[95] The point here is only that the need to integrate a novel judicial role into the accepted legal culture helps explain the use of the particular techniques that the *State Farm* court viewed as the conventional approach to the review of NHTSA's rules.

Auto Parts creatively transformed the requirement of a "concise statement of basis and purpose" into a demand for the presentation of a rule's factual support and policy rationale. These materials constituted a "record" from which the court could judge means-ends rationality and thereby police for arbitrariness in its traditional forms: the inadequacy of the record[96] and inconsistent[97] or incoherent[98] decision making. Of

---

1175 (1981); DONALD HOROWITZ, THE COURTS AND SOCIAL POLICY (1977); Nathan Glazer, *Should Judges Administer Social Services?* 50 Pub. Interest 64 (1978).

95. See, e.g., DeLong, *Informal Rulemaking and the Integration of Law and Policy*, 65 Va. L. Rev. 257 (1979) (examining criticisms of informal and "hybrid" rulemaking and suggesting alternative approaches for judicial review).

96. National Tire Dealers & Retreaders Ass'n v. Brinegar, 491 F.2d 31 (D.C. Cir. 1974).

97. Public Citizen v. Steed, 733 F.2d 93 (D.C. Cir. 1984).

98. Motor Vehicle Mfrs. Ass'n v. State Farm Mut. Ins. Co., 463 U.S. 29 (1983).

course, the agency's presentation of factual material might be incomplete. The "record" therefore had to be expanded to include submissions of outsiders and the agency's responses to those submissions. As the record grew in importance, so did meaningful opportunities to participate in its formulation.

So structured, judicial review necessarily transforms the image of rulemaking from a legislative-political (which would be reviewed on the stunningly undemanding "rational basis" standard) endeavor into an analytic-policymaking enterprise (to be reviewed for the adequacy of the record and the cogency of explanation)[99]—Judge McGowan's language about "essentially legislative" tasks to the contrary notwithstanding. Given this transformation, the judicial role is not to remake political choices, but instead to examine agency reasons and agency choices in the light of an appropriate factual record. This is, then, only a familiar role in a new context, or so it can be made to appear. As the conventional reviewing court remands for new trial upon discovering evidentiary gaps in the trial-court record, so the court reviewing administrative rules remands to the agency for reconsideration when the record seems inadequate to support the agency's policy choice. If this approach strongly reinforces the opposition tactic we have called the full-court press and severely burdens and delays the rulemaking process, that is perhaps unfortunate. But it is surely consistent with an adversary legal culture whose libertarian values have always given the advantage to the defendant and the status quo.[100]

The translation of legislative-political questions into analytic policymaking issues through proceduralized judicial review, of course, never really fools the sophisticated regulatory players. Judicial review for process regularity was the opposition technique both of "conservatives" confronting the New Deal and "liberals" confronting the Reagan Administration's desire to deregulate.[101] Yet notwithstanding proceduralism's penchant for the status quo, such political shifts in some sense signal the legal culture's success in pursuing its aspiration to political neutrality. Judicial review in a proceduralist form, like lead ballast, tends to

99. See generally Diver, *Policymaking Paradigms in Administrative Law,* 95 Harv. L. Rev. 393 (1981) (arguing that incremental decision making should be the norm except where irreparable harm will ensue).

100. See generally Galanter, *Why the 'Haves' Come Out Ahead: Speculations on the Limits of Legal Change,* 9 L. & Soc'y Rev. 95 (1974) (arguing that nature of legal system limits possibility of redistribution).

101. See, for example, Shapiro, *APA: Past, Present and Future,* 72 Va. L. Rev. 447 (1986) (arguing that courts' demand of synoptic rationality in administrative decision making reflects judicial preference for status quo).

stabilize the ship of state whether the political winds blow from left or right. And as the history of FMVSS 208 amply illustrates, those winds can blow across administrative jurisdictions with tornadic intensity.

What was not entirely clear before *State Farm* was whether the Supreme Court would take this neutral, proceduralist approach in a situation in which an agency was deregulating rather than regulating. Indeed, the government argued that review in the *State Farm* case should be analogized to an agency's decision to begin either an enforcement proceeding or a rulemaking process. These are matters about which an agency has almost complete discretion. But, the *State Farm* court saw the matter quite differently. There was a rule on the books. Rescinding the rule required the same procedures and actions as adopting it in the first place. Hence, if commentators made sensible objections to the agency's decision, and the agency supplied no reasonable response, its actions were arbitrary and could not be upheld.

In a concurring (and partially dissenting) opinion, several members of the Court were at pains to point out, nevertheless, the limits of the judicial function. They made clear that the Court was not saying that new administrations must pursue and maintain the policies of old ones. Under uncertainty political values could be trump cards. The Reagan administration could act on a motto of "If in doubt, don't regulate." But its rulemaking agencies would have to demonstrate, in a rational-analytic fashion that was responsive to the complaining parties' arguments, that those doubts were real, not trumped up excuses for promised regulatory relief. The line between law and politics would be maintained, at least in principle.

But principled judicial review has limited power to control events post-remand. The Reagan Administration's response to the *State Farm* decision rapidly demonstrated the limits of the law in constraining political choice.

Passive Restraints After *State Farm*

The Dole Finesse. Responding to the remand order, in October 1983, NHTSA returned to the passive restraints rule. Elizabeth Dole, the new Secretary of Transportation, issued an NPRM requesting comment on various alternatives for amending Standard 208. After a lengthy discussion of the regulatory history leading to the Court's decision in *State Farm*, Dole presented some of the data the department had gathered.[102] That presentation demonstrated both how much and how little the agency had learned since 1969.

---

102.   48 Fed. Reg. 48,622 (1983).

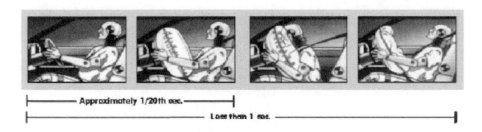

Secretary Dole's notice revealed an agency awash in data. Yet the critical uncertainties identified in *State Farm* remained. There was still no on-the-road experience with sufficient numbers of airbags or passive belt systems to determine their effectiveness when used and, more critically, their probable utilization rates. Nor was the agency any closer to answering the Supreme Court's apparently sensible questions: If detachable automatic belts might merely replicate the utilization rates of manual belts, why not make the belts nondetachable? What are the effects of *inertia* on the utilization rates of detachable passive belts? Why not use airbags?

There was, of course, an answer to some of these questions. Technologically there was no good reason to make belts detachable. The continuous-spool belt systems were thought to be reliable and to provide easy exit from the automobile after a crash. And airbags were considered both reliable and effective. The problem was not *technology*. The problem was predicting consumer behavior, or, as the issue had come to be phrased, "public acceptability." Continuous-spool belts were removable with a pair of scissors, and a significant public outcry might motivate Congress to excise the vastly more expensive airbag requirement. The agency had hardly forgotten its experience with the ignition interlock. As the Secretary awaited comments on her NPRM, public acceptability loomed as the core issue in choosing among the regulatory alternatives that the agency had identified.

Comments flooded in, 7,800 of them. But, as usual, the commentators raised as many new issues as they answered. After preliminary analysis of the comments the agency felt compelled to issue a supplemental notice of proposed rulemaking requesting further information on prior issues and identifying some additional issues for comment. With all this information in hand, a special task force prepared a 700-page Final Regulatory Impact Analysis analyzing the costs and benefits, and the imponderables, of the agency's alternative proposals. On July 17, 1984, a final rule was issued.[103] The statement of basis and purpose runs 50 pages in the Federal Register and incorporates the Final Regulatory Impact Analysis by reference. The core of the agency's decision, however, was captured in four paragraphs:

> Effectively enforced state mandatory seat belt use laws (MULs) will provide the greatest safety benefits most quickly of any of the alternatives, with almost no additional cost.

> Automatic occupant restraints provide demonstrable safety benefits, and, unless a sufficient number of MULs are enacted, they must be required for the most frequently used seats in passenger automobiles.

> Automatic occupant protection systems that do not totally rely upon belts, such as airbags or passive interiors, offer significant additional potential for preventing fatalities and injuries, at least in part because the American public is likely to find them less intrusive; their development and availability should be encouraged through appropriate incentives.

> As a result of these conclusions, the Department has decided to require automatic occupant protection in all passenger automobiles based on phased-in schedule beginning on September 1, 1986, with full implementation being required September 1, 1989, unless, before April 1, 1989, two-thirds of the population of the United States are covered by MULs meeting specified conditions.[104]

---

103.   49 Fed. Reg. 28,962 (1984).

104.   Id. at 28, 962–63.

How Could We Have Gotten Here from There? The July 17 decision was by any standard astonishing. Although the *State Farm* decision had been read by many as virtually assuring the requirement of airbags, the July 17 rule in effect left the question of whether any passive restraints would be required, and if so, what technology would be used, to the future decisions of state legislatures and automobile manufacturers. In addition, the preferred regulatory strategy now seemed to be the mandatory use law. Not only had such laws heretofore been unpopular with state legislatures and with the Congress, they were a return to the behavior modification strategies of the pre-1966 era. The agency was proposing to implement the 1966 Act by abandoning its animating intellectual vision.

Reaction to Secretary Dole's new rule ranged from the ambivalent to the apoplectic. As Ann Cooper of the National Journal noted in an article entitled "Who Won?", "even some insiders, who had reacted with passionate rhetoric to every twist in the 15-year air bag saga, seemed uncertain whether they should be celebrating [this] complicated plan or condemning it."[105] The Ford Motor Company lavishly praised Dole's endorsement of MULs, but said nothing about the portion of the rule that supported airbag installation.[106] Ralph Nader as usual was less circumspect: "It's a bloody snare and a mischievous delusion. I didn't believe [the government] could be so Machiavellian in giving the auto companies a chance to do in the airbag once and for all."[107]

The parties who historically had pressed passive restraints technology on the agency, the insurance companies in particular, found NHTSA's rule not only astonishing but irrational. They were shortly back in court seeking review of the rule on numerous grounds. They were told by the D.C. Circuit Court of Appeals, however, that their suit was not ripe for review.[108] After all, their basic complaint concerned the substitution of MULs for passive restraints. That had not happened yet, and it might never happen, although a remarkable number of states had enacted MULs pursuant to the agency's invitation and a massive lobbying effort by the automobile manufacturers. But, the court reasoned, these laws were quite diverse and the new rule left some discretion for NHTSA to determine how any of them might "count" toward the required minimum level of "effective" MUL coverage.

As we now know, the Court of Appeals was prescient. A major legislative campaign in the states by the automobile manufacturers, joined in many cases by safety advocates such as Mothers Against Drunk

---

105. Ann Cooper, *Who Won*, Nat'l J., July 28, 1984, at 1441.

106. Id.

107. *Middle Lane: Bags, Belts—And a Loophole,* Time, July 23, 1984, at 47.

108. State Farm Mut. Auto. Ins. Co. v. Dole, 802 F.2d 474 (D.C. Cir. 1986).

Driving (MADD), generated mandatory use laws in virtually every state. While the manufacturers and the safety partisans both wanted MULs, however, they wanted quite different ones. And legislature after legislature, responding to the safety advocates' preferences, adopted statutes that failed to satisfy the requirements of revised Standard 208, and that therefore did not count toward the regulation's two-thirds threshold for dropping the passive-restraints requirement.[109] As a consequence, the American public got both airbags and mandatory use laws.

The law's ultimate response, passive protection plus regulation of motorists' behavior, seems to have had stunning effects on consumer and driver preferences. Although MULs are mostly unenforced, seatbelt usage rose dramatically with the passage of state mandatory use laws and has remained high. And the same consumers who pelted their representatives with objections to the airbag, fearing that it would be both unreliable and dangerous, now seem so enamored of this safety device that manufacturers compete with each other to see how many of them they can cram into each automobile.[110]

Politics, Science and Regulation Under Law

In 1966 politics embraced science. It chartered a federal agency to force the technology of automobile safety, an agency populated by safety engineers and headed by a man who had pioneered the epidemiology of accidents. Recognizing its own technical incompetence, Congress left virtually all substantive regulation to the experts at the National Highway Traffic Safety Administration. Their regulations would define the performance characteristics of new generations of motor vehicles—vehicles that would better protect their occupants in the case of an accident. This was a legislative pattern to be repeated in the chartering of other health and safety regulators, such as, the Environmental Protection Agency, the Occupational Safety and Health Administration, and the Consumer Product Safety Administration.

These new and powerful forms of regulation would, nevertheless, be regulation subject to law. All of the social regulatory statutes of the 1960s and 1970s provided for immediate judicial review of final rules. In

---

109. See, *e.g.*, Joseph F. Sullivan, "Law Signed Making New Jersey 2d State with Seat-Belt Rule," N.Y. Times, Nov. 9, 1984, at B4 ("[T]he New Jersey Legislature amended its bill before final passage last month to insure that it would not meet the Federal guidelines. The lawmakers said the New Jersey statute could not be counted among the laws that might be used in place of requiring mandatory passive restraints.").

110. See, *e.g.*, Tom Matthews, "Honda Ad Campaign Takes Safety Seriously: Side Air Bags to Be Standard on Some Models," Columbus Dispatch (Ohio), July 27, 2004, at 01E ("Honda will only say it is publicizing plans to make side air bags and other features standard on many Acuras and Civics by the end of 2006."); cf. Art Chamberlain, "Sales Pitch a Smash with Drivers: Airbags, Anti-Lock Brakes Are Now Turning the Cranks of Buyers, Car Makers Find," Toronto Star, Feb. 23, 1995, at D1.

many ways this was an unfamiliar judicial task, and one that stretched the capacities of courts to maintain legality without invading the realms of administrative and legislative policy. The judiciary responded by proceduralizing rationality review in ways that vindicated the judicial role but that severely complicated the lives of the new social regulatory agencies. It was this vision of administrative, scientific policy making under law that the *State Farm* opinion crystalized. It is a vision that continues to structure the rhetoric of judicial review proceedings across the regulatory landscape.

Yet, the reality of this vision of the role of science and law in regulation was questionable in 1983, and is, perhaps, even more questionable today. As we have seen, the *State Farm* opinion can be read to overstate the capacity of judicial review to protect scientific regulation from political manipulation, while understating the contribution of judicial review to administrators' incapacity to make effective regulatory policy. Although the Reagan administration's particular attempt at rescission was rejected in *State Farm*, the pre-Reagan history of Standard 208 reveals a change of direction with virtually every administration that had a hand in that almost interminable rulemaking proceeding. And the rule that emerged after the *State Farm* remand has all the earmarks of a shrewd political compromise, wrapped in the rhetoric of reasoned policy analysis.

Congressional politics, of course, constantly played a role as well. Congress was initially guilty of imagining a scientific world in which answers were easy and discovered without cost. It then made clear, in its 1974 amendments forbidding the ignition interlock, that sound scientific approaches might be politically unacceptable, while politically necessary approaches were imperative even if scientifically silly. For in 1974 Congress not only repealed the passive restraints rule, it mandated a host of new safety features in school buses—features addressing such a minor safety problem at such great cost that the legislation arguably increased the risk that children would be killed or injured in a school bus accident. Meanwhile Congress kept NHTSA both understaffed and under-funded to play the techno-political game of standard setting envisioned by the revolution of 1966.

And while *State Farm* seems both pro-regulation and pro-science, the judicial demand for reasoned decisionmaking has not routinely functioned that way. Between *Auto Parts* and *State Farm*, most of NHTSA's even mildly innovative rules were challenged in court, and the agency lost half of those challenges.[111] The usual reason was that the

---

111. NHTSA lost in six of the twelve rulemaking cases that were decided on the merits. Jerry L. Mashaw & David L. Harfst, *Regulation and Legal Culture: The Case of*

agency could not demonstrate that its requirements were reasonable and practicable. Why? Because there was no significant "on-the-road" experience with the engineering requirements embodied in the rules. But, if that were the requirement for legality, then the agency was legally impotent to force the development of automotive safety technologies. A statute, apparently designed to put safety on a par with style in the engineering of automobiles, had morphed into a statute that only permitted NHTSA to demand the dissemination of off-the-shelf equipment. The automobile industry could be required to improve its engineering performance only to the extent that some firm had already paved the way by demonstrating reasonableness and practicability through inclusion of new safety features in its own cars. The judiciary implicitly reinterpreted the statute as a civil rights regime. All Americans would be entitled to equal protection, that is, to the same safety engineering pioneered by Cadillac, Mercedes, and Volvo.

Meanwhile, the courts took a radically different approach to the agency's demands that automakers recall a vehicle that contained some "defect related to automobile safety." Whether recalling torsion bars on nine-year-old Cadillacs[112] that could only break at speeds below three miles per hour, or protecting Ford drivers from windshield wipers that might fly off once every million miles traveled,[113] the agency's recall efforts were always blessed by the courts. And Congress happily funded the agency's recall efforts, a political posture strongly supported by the ever-potent trial lawyers lobby. Unhappily, for reasons too complicated to go into here, there is essentially no evidence that mandated recalls contribute anything to motor vehicle safety.

With its rulemaking activity bludgeoned both by lawmakers and judges, and its recall efforts applauded by everyone, by 1990 NHTSA had turned into an agency dominated by lawyers, and awash in the "investigate and punish" regulatory culture that the Motor Vehicle Safety Act of 1966 was designed to suppress. With one notable exception, the eventual promulgation of the passive restraints rule, NHTSA had by the late 1980s gone out of the technology-forcing business—the unique province of its engineering staff. Indeed, it had virtually gone out of the rulemaking business. The *State Farm* decision had a hand in preserving what has turned out to be NHTSA's most important safety rule. But its effect in preserving the vision of energetic, scientific, and politically independent health and safety regulation has been very modest.

Motor Vehicle Safety, 4 Yale J. Reg. 257, 273 n. 38 (1987) (listing the twelve rulemaking cases).

    112.   United States v. General Motors Corp., 518 F.2d 420 (D.C. Cir. 1975).

    113.   United States v. Ford Motor Co., 561 F.2d 923 (D.C. Cir. 1977).

This is hardly the place to write yet another monograph about automobile safety regulation. But a look at more contemporary answers to three questions that seem crucially related to NHTSA's potential for success as a safety regulatory agency can provide further perspective on the balance between law, science and politics as regulators feel their way into the 21st century.

First, has the judiciary become more accepting of the realities of engineering (and most scientific) methodology, the need to proceed incrementally without necessarily having complete answers to all possible questions of efficacy and reliability at the outset of real world experience? Second, has rulemaking at the National Highway Traffic Safety Administration moved forward in directions that attack major vehicle safety problems that might be susceptible to engineering solutions? Finally, has Congress been willing to supply critical funding for NHTSA's legal-scientific enterprise and to permit the agency's policies to be guided by scientific criteria rather than political expediency?

In some ways, litigation about NHTSA's rules over the past dozen years suggests judicial accommodation to the inherent uncertainties of the engineering-regulatory process. The Sixth Circuit Court of Appeals, for example, is the court that first derailed NHTSA's passive restraints rule in 1972,[114] and is an adherent to the so-called "hard look" approach to judicial review of agency rulemaking.[115] Yet, in 1995, that circuit upheld NHTSA's rejection of a petition to modify its rules on the safe transport of students in wheelchairs, rejecting a barrage of technical and legal arguments.[116] The court affirmed the agency's decision on the essentially prudential ground that the agency had behaved reasonably and was under no obligation to consider every conceivable alternative offered up by a litigant or rulemaking participant.

Similarly in the denouement of a rulemaking proceeding that had been on-going even longer than the passive restraints rule, the Court of Appeals for the Tenth Circuit upheld NHTSA's anti-lock brake system performance standards for vehicles with air brakes (meaning generally large trucks and buses) without even permitting oral argument.[117] The petitioner had claimed that because NHTSA's standard presumed the use of automatic braking system technology, it was in effect a "design standard" rather than a "performance" standard, and therefore not

---

114. Chrysler Corp. v. Department of Transp., 472 F.2d 659, 669 (6th Cir. 1972).

115. See Simms v. National Highway Traffic Safety Admin., 45 F.3d 999, 1004 (6th Cir. 1995); Neighbors Organized to Insure a Sound Env't. Inc. v. McArtor, 878 F.2d 174, 178 (6th Cir. 1989); Crounse Corp. v. Interstate Commerce Comm'n, 781 F.2d 1176, 1193 (6th Cir. 1986); MASHAW & HARFST, supra note 3, at 87–92.

116. Simms v. National Highway Traffic Safety Admin., 45 F.3d 999 (6th Cir.1995).

117. Washington v. Department of Transp., 84 F.3d 1222 (10th Cir. 1996).

authorized by the Motor Vehicle Safety Act. Recognizing that the distinction between performance and design is "much easier to state in the abstract than to apply,"[118] the Tenth Circuit concluded with an affirmation of pragmatic problem solving: "We would, accordingly, be hesitant to invalidate this carefully developed safety standard solely on the basis of its indefinite place on the conceptual spectrum between performance and design."[119] Theoretical purity seems to be retreating before the armies of engineering practicability.

But not so fast. The wheelchair litigation involved a host of claims that skated dangerously close to sanctionable frivolity under Rule 11 of the Federal Rules of Civil Procedure. And the anti-lock brake system performance criteria were being applied to technology now in widespread use throughout the trucking industry. The Sixth Circuit exhibited considerably greater skepticism, if not quite its 1970s antagonism, toward NHTSA's rulemaking in a 1990 case involving standards for the deflection of steering columns in front end collisions.[120] In a decision reminiscent of *Chrysler*, the court invalidated NHTSA's requirements applicable to a particular weight range of trucks because the agency had not provided any practicable testing procedure for manufacturers who built specialized vehicles on standard truck chassis supplied by major manufacturers. Crash testing of these limited production vehicles was obviously out of the question on economic grounds, and no simulation testing methodology had been developed. The agency's pleas that these specialty manufacturers could avoid compliance difficulties simply by requiring a certificate of compliance from the chassis manufacturer fell on unsympathetic judicial ears. NHTSA had not demonstrated that the manufacturers would be willing to supply the certificates.

Moreover, when NHTSA finally lost a recall case,[121] the court's rationale revealed that the case might as easily be understood as a rulemaking review proceeding. The ground for the court's refusal to allow the recall was its belief that the agency's rule had given inadequate notice to the manufacturer of the safety requirements that the agency claimed the manufacturer was violating. The recall was disallowed because the rule was incomplete.

Most other cases during the last decade involving NHTSA related to the non-safety aspects of its jurisdiction, particularly its power to adopt mileage standards for automobile fleets. The agency won all of these cases, but their posture is revealing. Almost all of them were suits

---

118. Id. at 1224.

119. Id.

120. National Truck Equip. Ass'n v. National Highway Traffic Safety Admin., 919 F.2d 1148 (6th Cir. 1990).

121. United States v. Chrysler Corp., 158 F.3d 1350 (D.C. Cir. 1998).

attempting to force the agency to exercise regulatory authority that it had declined to use.[122] In short, when subjected to substantive review, NHTSA still seems to do no better than chance in the courts of appeals—unless it doesn't do anything. Then it always wins.

Nor has NHTSA launched new rulemaking initiatives with anything like the scope of Standard 208. Most of the agency's recent rules merely extend requirements adopted in the late 1960s and early 1970s to new classes of vehicles, or update preexisting rules to deal with new technologies, such as electric braking systems. The few truly "new" standards seem unlikely to have major effects on the numbers of deaths and injuries in vehicle accidents. It may be important, for example, to have a fuel tank integrity standard for vehicles powered by compressed natural gas, but this is a pretty small fleet.

Moreover, even with the great majority of its resources devoted to updating its rule inventory, many of NHTSA's rules remain in the same form that they had in the late 1960s or early 1970s. When the Firestone tire controversy broke in the late 1990s, for example, NHTSA's 1969 standard did not even apply to the suspect equipment. Its rule covered only bias-ply tires—an outdated technology in an almost universally radial-tire world. Extension of passenger car rules to light trucks has made some progress, but is far from complete, even though that has been the fastest growing segment of the automobile industry for nearly 20 years.

To say that the agency has been engaged in updating old rules thus may not be to say much. Moreover, a review of both agency rulemaking issuances and the secondary literature suggests that a huge proportion of NHTSA's energy over the last decade or so has been spent on two controversies—the problem of deaths and injuries from air bag inflation and the response to tire safety and rollover problems involving sport utility vehicles.[123] In both cases the agency's agenda and approach have been dictated by congressional politics, not safety engineering.

---

122. In Competitive Enterprise Institute v. National Highway Traffic Safety Administration, 956 F.2d 321 (D.C. Cir. 1992), the court ordered NHTSA to reconsider its refusal to reduce the corporate average fuel economy (CAFÉ) standards for model years 1989 and 1990, but ultimately affirmed the agency's position in Competitive Enterprise Institute v. National Highway Traffic Safety Administration, 45 F.3d 481 (D.C. Cir. 1995). The same court similarly rejected petitions for changes in the CAFÉ standard in Competitive Enterprise Institute v. National Highway Traffic Safety Administration, 901 F.2d 107 (D.C. Cir. 1990) and in General Motors Corp. v. National Highway Traffic Safety Administration, 898 F.2d 165 (D.C. Cir. 1990).

123. On the air bag crisis, see, e.g., "New Push in Campaign on Air-Bag Threat," Chi. Trib., Feb. 24, 2000, at 3; David B. Ottaway & Warren Brown, "From Life Saver to Fatal Threat; How the U.S., Automakers and a Safety Device Failed," Wash. Post, June 1, 1997, at A1; Jim Mateja, "NHTSA Offers Ways to Make Air Bags Safer", Chi. Trib., Dec. 1, 1996, Transp., at 3; and Jayne O'Donnell & James R. Healey, "Deadly Delay: Agency Spins

Indeed, both the agency's modest rulemaking output and its choice of topics can be laid at the door of the Congress. NHTSA has continued to be understaffed and underfunded. The agency's budget and staff were cut nearly in half by the Reagan administration and have never recovered.[124] Adjusted for inflation, NHTSA's budget at the turn of the century was one-third less than its budget in 1980. Its staff peaked at just over 900 employees in the late 1970s, but was down to just over 600 in 1982, and has hovered there ever since. Equally importantly, Congress has been willing to fund public information and recall activity at much higher levels than the development of safety standards. In the fiscal year 2002 budget NHTSA was authorized to spend twice as much on the development of front and side impact test ratings for new vehicles than it was on the development of safety standards. The budget for recall investigation and enforcement was six times the figure authorized for standards development. Congress has in essence required the agency to direct its energies in directions—recalls and consumer information—which have little, if any, scientific support as effective safety strategies.

In addition, congressional intervention into the agency's rulemaking process has diverted its rulemaking energies, such as they are, to problems that are essentially of the Congress's own making. In 1991, for example, the Intermodal Surface Transportation Efficiency Act[125] required that all passenger cars manufactured on or after September 1997, and light trucks manufactured after September 1998, have both passenger and driver side air bags in addition to manual lap and shoulder belts. This legislation effectively took the agency's performance requirements embodied in Standard 208 and transformed them into design requirements. But the design had some difficulties.

Wheels As Air-bag Death Toll Rises", USA Today, Nov. 15, 1996, at 1B. For a brief glimpse into the problems with sport utility vehicles, see, e.g., Danny Hakim, "Safety Gap Grows Between S.U.V.'s and Cars," N.Y. Times, Aug. 17, 2004, at C1 ("People driving or riding in a sport utility vehicle in 2003 were nearly 11 percent more likely to die in an accident than people in cars, the figures show."); Danny Hakim, "Rollovers Led the Rise in Traffic Deaths Last Year," N.Y. Times, July 18, 2003, at C2; John O'Dell & Terril Yue Jones, "Tire Recall Has Brought Many Changes in the Name of Safety", L.A. Times, Aug. 9, 2001, Business, at 1; Judy Pasternak, "Safety Agency Takes Heat over Firestone Tire Recall", L.A. Times, Aug. 19, 2000, at A1; and Myron Lovin, "NHTSA Inaction on Rollover Issue Seen as Typical", L.A. Times, Sept. 18, 2000, at C1.

124. NHTSA budget and personnel data referred to here and elsewhere have been compiled from the supplements to the annual Budget of the United States government. *E.g.*, U.S. OFFICE MGMT. & BUDGET, BUDGET OF THE UNITED STATES GOVERNMENT (Supp. 1989). Some numbers have also been compiled from NHTSA budgets in brief, which are available at NHTSA, Budget in Brief, *at* http://www.nhtsa.dot.gov/nhtsa/whatis/bb (last visited Apr. 18, 2002).

125. Intermodal Surface Transportation Efficiency Act of 1991, Pub. L. No. 102–240, 105 Stat. 1914 (codified as amended in scattered sections of 23 U.S.C. and 49 U.S.C.).

By the mid-1990s it was becoming clear that, while air bags have substantial safety advantages, they also injure and kill passengers who would otherwise escape vehicle accidents with lesser injuries or no injuries at all. The problems have to do particularly with children and small adults.[126]

Congress responded, not by giving the agency back its discretion to trade off air bags against other technologies, but with the Transportation Equity Act for the 21st Century.[127] That statute specifically required the agency to improve vehicle restraint protection for all sizes of occupants; to minimize air bag risks to infants and children; to maintain protections for unbelted occupants; to require advanced air bag technology; and to do so with rules that would be completed no later than September 2003 and phased in no later than September 2006. Is this doable? Sensible? Who knows, and NHTSA is now legally prohibited from asking those questions.

It also seems fair to say that the agency's rulemaking activities since 1998 have largely been devoted to implementing this legislation and TREAD, the Transportation Recall Enhancement, Accountability and Documentation Act of 2000.[128] As its acronym suggests, this latter statute was Congress's response to the Ford-Firestone tempest of the late 1990s. As many readers will remember, evidence mounted during the late 1990s that Ford Explorer sport utility vehicles were involved in a substantial number of rollover accidents and that the failure of Firestone tires were implicated in many fatal Explorer rollovers. This episode took on the character of a morality play when it was discovered that Firestone had recalled these same tires in a number of other countries; that both Firestone and Ford had failed to keep NHTSA informed of the mounting evidence that the tires were unsafe, at least as used on Ford Explorers; and that NHTSA itself had received a number of warnings that had somehow gotten lost in its antiquated data processing system.[129] Congress responded once again by beefing up NHTSA's recall authority and by requiring that it adopt a number of rules, all related to defect investigations and notifications (i.e., recalls). Once again the statute had a mandatory time limit that would commandeer the agency's limited resources.

---

126. E.g., Ottaway & Brown, *supra* note 123.

127. Transportation Equity Act for the 21st Century, Pub. L. No. 105–178, 112 Stat. 107 (1998) (codified as amended in scattered sections of 23 U.S.C. and 49 U.S.C.).

128. Transportation Recall Enhancement, Accountability, and Documentation (TREAD) Act, Pub. L. No. 106–414, 114 Stat. 1900 (2000) (codified as amended in scattered sections of 49 U.S.C.).

129. E.g., Ricardo Alonso-Zaldivar, "Errors, Short Staffing Led to Missed Tire Warnings", L.A. Times, Nov. 10, 2000, at A1; Tom Incantalupo, "Agency in Hot Seat", Newsday, Sept. 13, 2000, at A7; Pasternak, supra note 123.

The dog that is not barking in this scenario is the propensity for sport utility vehicles of all types to experience an excessive number of rollover accidents when compared with the passenger car vehicle fleet as a whole. Both NHTSA and industry testing have documented this propensity for over a decade.[130] The regulatory response, one might have thought, would be a stability standard for passenger vehicles that would require some redesign of the sport utility vehicle fleet. Yet, at the behest of the motor vehicle industry and its allies in Congress, NHTSA has rejected this solution, maintaining that such requirements would be impracticable. By that it means that redesign would add substantial economic cost to the most profitable segment of the American motor vehicle industry.

Meanwhile, the agency has done some work on the development of dynamic rollover tests for purposes of beginning a consumer information program on rollovers. The TREAD legislation cements this approach by requiring NHTSA to develop dynamic tests for motor vehicle rollovers, carry out a set of tests, and initiate a rulemaking proceeding to determine how best to disseminate these test results to the public. Dissemination will not be easy. Like NHTSA's now-famous barrier crash tests for passenger restraint systems, the real world applicability of these test results will be problematic. Just as most cars do not crash into static barriers, stability measured on a single, well-specified slalom course is unlikely to mimic the behavior of automobiles maneuvering in highly diverse driving circumstances. In the end, the consumer information may be misleading, as the industry has long maintained concerning NHTSA's (and the insurance industry's) crash test results.[131] But Congress likes information regulation. It funds NHTSA's crash test information program alone at 200% of the agency's budget for rulemaking.

We have already observed the congressional actions embodied in the Intermodel Surface Transportation Efficiency Act of 1991—its instructions to NHTSA to solve the problem of airbags injuries and to mandate ever more advanced airbag technologies. For, whatever their risks, airbags have become enormously popular with the car-buying public. If the halting implementation of Standard 208 did nothing else, it changed the psychology of automobile consumers from deep skepticism about the airbag technology to the belief that airbags can and should protect them from all harm in virtually any conceivable crash. Congress has responded by demanding that the agency insist on more and better airbags, without pausing to ask whether this approach is the most cost-effective way to

---

130. See Levin, supra note 123.

131. For an early example, see Peter Behr, "U.S. Automakers Refusing to Use a Recent NHTSA Crash Test in Ads," Wash. Post, Aug. 24, 1980, at G4 ("GM told NHTSA in April that 'there is no justification for representing these tests results as realistic comparative crashworthiness measures.' ").

further reduce automobile injuries and deaths. On these rational-analytic grounds the seatbelt interlock was probably superior.

To be sure, administrative lawyers have long understood that the practice of administrative decisionmaking might be better described as "interest representation" or "micro-political accommodation" or just "muddling through," rather than as the embodiment of "instrumental rationality."[132] And recent regulatory reform efforts have emphasized the desirability of negotiation, collaborative rulemaking, and regulatory flexibility rather than expert judgment.[133] We seem capable of admitting that regulation is policy making and that policy is never apolitical.

Yet, in some fundamental ways we maintain our bedrock normative expectations of instrumentally rational administration.[134] Juries and legislatures (and courts who often avoid opinion writing) can decide without reasons. Administrative rules or orders without contemporaneous supporting reasons are generally illegal for that reason alone. Moreover, we mean by reason-giving a demand for instrumental explanation, how this policy or that decision implements a legislative norm given the current state of the world and the predictable impact of compliance with the administrative command. We thus demand causal explanation, the stuff of scientific inquiry, and reject the agency's determination as unlawful unless it can tell a factually and scientifically plausible story. Unreasoned decisions, silence, imagined states of the world are not allowed. We soften the hard edges of the demand for rationality with deference norms and occasional instances of non-reviewability. But candid political rationalization, assertions, for example, that this resolution of the matter was acceptable to most affected interests, was in line with administration policy, was dictated by resource constraints, or was demanded by powerful legislative factions, are ruled out of bounds.

In short, the normative demands of administrative law are at war with our understanding of the practical necessities of administration. We have failed to construct a normative model of administration that fits its realities, or more properly, a normative model that builds on best practices in an administrative world beset by inadequate budgets, legislative imperatives, public resistance, as well as real scientific uncertainties.

We are thus still inclined to ascribe the failure of regulatory policies to track the best scientific or technological understanding of a problem as a failure somehow to design a "good" administrative process, that is,

---

132. See, *e.g.*, Charles E. Lindblom, *The Science of 'Muddling Through,'* 19 Pub. Admin. Rev. 79 (1959).

133. Jodi Freedman, *Collaborative Governance and the Administrative State,* 45 UCLA Rev. 1 (1997).

134. Jerry L. Mashaw, *Small Things Like Reasons are Put in a Jar: Reason and Legitimacy in the Administrative State,* 70 Fordham L. Rev. 101 (2001).

one that is impervious to the forces—political, social and economic—that deflect administrators from the path of scientific virtue. But the truth of the matter may be that we do not always want the law to follow science—even law as made by administrators. Our practice belies our proclaimed rationalistic commitments. The problem from this perspective is not how to reform law to better accommodate science, but how to reframe our aspirational norms about administrative law to better accommodate what we really seem to demand of administration.

The *State Farm* case exemplifies the tensions among politics, science and law that continue to bedevil the regulatory process. Instructed by a vague and ambivalent Congress, agencies like NHTSA are bound by their statutes and judicial review proceedings, but may not be protected by them. And as *State Farm* makes clear, in the absence of congressional clarity, NHTSA cannot rely with the assurance either on executive political direction or on its own internal expertise.

The fundamental separation of powers ideas that prevent the courts from insisting on congressional clarity and specificity and that restrain presidential distortions of congressional directives also leave the regulators legally and politically exposed. They have a political job without a political mandate, and they are subject to judicial review for "legality." Regulation must proceed legally, therefore, under the cover of a fiction— that regulation is only the application of law to fact, the carrying out of statutory instructions. But the fictional quality of this posture becomes all too transparent in the glow of the political warfare that surrounds high-stakes rulemaking. Indeed, recognizing the legal limits on direct presidential direction of agency policymaking, all presidents since Jimmy Carter have sought to leverage the policy influence that they exercise through appointment, removal and budget controls, by even more elaborate structural and procedure devices designed to nudge administrators in the direction of the administration's overall views. The most conspicuous executive monitoring device since the 1980s has been OMB review of major proposed regulations through the medium of its "comments" on required regulatory-impact analyses. And both the Executive Office of the President and the Congress have added numerous further analytic requirements over the ensuing two decades.[135]

Our notions of separation of powers have thus produced not only a proceduralized rationality review of rules in the courts, but also a proceduralized executive oversight. The resulting multiple tiers of process have had dramatic affects on regulatory output. Not only must

---

135. See generally, JERRY L. MASHAW ET AL., ADMINISTRATIVE LAW: THE AMERICAN PUBLIC LAW SYSTEM, 268–311 (5TH ED. 2003), and Jerry L. Mashaw, *Reinventing Government and Regulatory Reform: Studies in the Neglect and Abuse of Administrative Law*, 57 U. Pitt. L. Rev. 405 (1996) and authorities therein cited.

administrators like the head of the National Highway Traffic Safety Administration satisfy executive branch overseers that they have faithfully done the required analyses, these analyses become a part of the rulemaking record, a treasure trove of facts and assertions that can be deployed to advantage by opponents in subsequent judicial review proceedings.

Some might argue that in *Chevron, U.S.A., Inc. v. Natural Resources Defense Council, Inc.*,[136] decided only a year after *State Farm*, the Supreme Court effectively rejected *State Farm's* vision of judicial review of administrative action. After *Chevron* courts should be more deferential to agency administrative interpretations and more willing to rely on the political accountability of administrators to an elected president. Post-*Chevron*, both supporters[137] and critics[138] of that decision have argued that we have entered a new age of presidential administration with a new paradigm of regulation as a political, rather than a scientific or rational-analytic activity. But that would be to overstate the impact of *Chevron* in the same way that it is easy to overstate the importance of *State Farm*. To the extent that the National Highway Traffic Safety Administration had trouble in court with respect to its rulemaking activities, and it had plenty, that trouble usually was not because of alleged misinterpretation of its statutes. Rationality review of NHTSA's rules has focused largely on the agency's application of law to fact and on its rationalization for its policy choices, as illuminated by the critical commentary of participants in its rulemaking processes.

It is possible, of course, that if *Chevron* had been decided before the promulgation of Standard 208, then NHTSA's lawyers might have been able to convince the Sixth Circuit that the real issue was an interpretive question about which the agency had behaved reasonably. But who knows? That court might easily have believed that "objective" necessarily meant "fully specified" and "repeatable," or that demanding testing without a completed procedure for carrying it out could not qualify as a reasonable construction of the agency's statutory obligations.

NHTSA's political troubles certainly did not come from misunderstanding its statute, but from misunderstanding the shifting politics of automobile safety regulation in a world of separated political power and

---

136.   467 U.S. 837 (1984).

137.   See, e.g., Richard J. Pierce, Jr., *The Role of Constitutional and Political Theory in Administrative Law,* 64 Tex. L. Rev. 469, 520–24 (1985).

138.   See, e.g., Elena Kagan, *Presidential Administration,* 114 Harv. L. Rev. 2245, 2372–82 (2001); Cynthia F. Farina, *The 'Chief Executive' and the Quiet Constitutional Revolution,* 49 Admin. L. Rev. 179, 179 (1997); Abner S. Greene, *Checks and Balances in an Era of Presidential Lawmaking,* 61 U. Chi. L. Rev. 123 (1994); Thomas W. Merrill, *Judicial Deference to Executive Precedent,* 101 Yale L.J. 969, 996 (1992).

fickle public preferences. And when the agency apparently relied too heavily on politics when rescinding the passive restraints rule, its actions were deemed illegal. *State Farm*'s demand for reasoned decisionmaking thus remains the legal system's vision of ideal administration, a poorly marked safe harbor for regulatory agencies attempting to navigate the treacherous currents where law, science and politics converge.

Chevron U.S.A. Inc. v. NRDC is one of the most famous cases in administrative law, but it was not regarded that way when it was decided. To the Justices who heard the case, *Chevron* was a controversy about the validity of the "bubble" concept under the Clean Air Act, not about the standard of review of agency interpretations of statutes. Drawing on Justice Blackmun's papers, Professor Merrill shows that the Court was initially closely divided, but Justice Stevens' opinion won them over, with no one paying much attention to his innovations in the formulation of the standard of review or his invocation of presidential oversight as a reason to regard agencies as more appropriate interpreters than courts. *Chevron* was almost instantly seized upon as a major decision by the D.C. Circuit, however, and after establishing itself as a leading case there, it migrated back to the Supreme Court, where it eventually came to be regarded as a landmark decision by the Court that rendered it. The story of *Chevron* raises interesting questions about the role of accidents and self-interested promotion in the making of great cases, as well as about how judicial mutations have shaped the development of administrative law.

10

Thomas W. Merrill*

The Story of *Chevron*: The Making of an Accidental Landmark

INTRODUCTION

Chevron U.S.A. Inc. v. National Resources Defense Council, Inc.[1] is the Supreme Court's leading statement about the division of authority between agencies and courts in interpreting statutes. The two-step framework announced by *Chevron* for resolving such questions has taken the judicial world by storm. In its relatively brief life span, the decision has been cited in over 7,000 cases, making it the most frequently cited case in administrative law.[2] Although *Chevron* cannot claim to be the overall citation champion in our legal system—that title may belong to *Erie R. Co. v. Tompkins*[3]—*Chevron* is catching up fast and may yet become number one.

---

* Charles Keller Beekman Professor of Law, Columbia University.

1. 467 U.S. 837 (1984). Although the West Reporter system, law reviews, and casebooks routinely get it wrong, the correct form of citation of the decision, following the official U.S. Reports, has no commas in the petitioner's name.

2. *Chevron* has been cited in 7,073 federal cases, which exceeds the citation count for other leading cases discussing aspects of the standard of review of agency action. For example, Universal Camera Corp. v. NLRB, 340 U.S. 474 (1951), the leading decision discussing the standard of review of questions of fact, has been cited in just over 4,700 cases (over a much longer span of time); Citizens to Preserve Overton Park v. Volpe, 401 U.S. 402 (1971), the leading decision discussing the arbitrary and capricious standard of review, has been cited in just over 4,000 cases; and Motor Vehicle Manufacturers Assn v. State Farm Mutual Automobile Ins. Co., 463 U.S. 29 (1983), the leading decision endorsing "hard look" review of agency policy choices, has been cited in just over 2,000 cases. (All counts in this and following footnotes are based on Lexis searches conducted in September, 2004.)

3. 304 U.S. 64 (1938). *Erie* has been cited in 10,127 federal cases. *Erie* of course is also a case directing that federal courts defer to another institution's interpretation of law—in this case, state courts' interpretations of state common law. This suggests that

Chevron is also a controversial decision. The opinion marks a significant shift in the justification for giving deference to agency interpretations of law. Before *Chevron*, deference was justified largely on pragmatic grounds; after *Chevron*, deference has been justified largely in terms of implied delegations of authority from Congress. This shift in the theoretical underpinnings of the deference doctrine has made *Chevron* a magnet for commentators, with the result that "the *Chevron* doctrine" has been debated, analyzed, and measured in countless articles.[4]

Legal revolutions are rare, and the general proposition for which *Chevron* stands—that courts should accept reasonable agency interpretations of statutes they are charged with administering—was not in and of itself revolutionary. The Court had said something similar in previous decisions.[5] What was new was the way Justice John Paul Stevens creatively packaged this proposition in his opinion for a unanimous but short-handed Court of six Justices. The *Chevron* opinion contains three significant innovations relative to previous judicial discussion.

First, the Court laid down a new two-step framework for reviewing agency statutory interpretations. At what was quickly dubbed "step one," courts, using "traditional tools of statutory construction," were to ask whether Congress had a "specific intention" with respect to the issue at hand.[6] "If the intent of Congress is clear, that is the end of the matter; for the court, as well as the agency, must give effect to the unambiguously expressed intent of Congress."[7] But if no clear congressional intent could be discerned, then the court, at "step two," was to ask whether the agency's interpretation was a "permissible construction of the statute."[8] The court should not ask whether the agency construction was the one "the court would have reached if the question initially had arisen in a judicial proceeding;" it was enough to show that "reasonable" interpreter might adopt the construction.[9]

This two-step framework seems innocuous enough, but in fact contained subtle but significant departures from prior law. That law had been something of a hodge-podge, but the conventional wisdom was that it required courts to assess agency interpretations against multiple factors, such as whether the agency interpretation was longstanding,

---

leading decisions about choice of law, broadly construed, may garner high citations counts because of their trans-substantive nature.

4. *Chevron* has been cited in over 3,600 articles available on Lexis.

5. See, e.g., NLRB v. Hearst Publications, 322 U.S. 111, 131 (1944).

6. *Chevron*, 467 U.S. at 843 n.9; 845.

7. Id. at 842–43.

8. Id. at 843.

9. Id. at 843 n. 11; 844.

consistently held, contemporaneous with the enactment of the statute, thoroughly considered, or involved a technical subject as to which the agency had expertise.[10] The two-step formula provided no logical place for courts to consider these traditional factors.[11]

The two-step formula also implied that deference to the agency interpretation was all-or-nothing. If the court decided the matter at step one, the agency would get no deference (although the court might uphold the agency if it agreed that its interpretation was the one intended by Congress); if the court decided the matter at step two, the agency would get maximal deference. In contrast, the prior approach had seemed to suggest that any particular agency interpretation would get more or less deference along a sliding-scale, depending on how it stacked up against the traditional factors.

Second, *Chevron* departed from previous law by suggesting that Congress has delegated authority to agencies to function as the primary interpreters of statutes they administer. Sometimes, the Court noted, Congress expressly delegates authority to agencies to define specific statutory provisions by regulation. In these circumstances, the Court observed, agency regulations are "given controlling weight unless they are arbitrary, capricious, or manifestly contrary to the statute."[12] The opinion then immediately noted that delegations can be implicit rather than explicit, and seemed to suggest that the same consequences would follow. By equating explicit and implicit delegations to agencies to fill in statutory gaps, the Court seemed to say that anytime Congress charges an agency with administration of a statute and leaves an ambiguity in the statute, it has impliedly delegated primary authority to the agency to the interpret the statute. This vastly expanded the sphere of delegated agency lawmaking.

Third, *Chevron* broke new ground by invoking democratic theory as a reason for deferring to agency interpretations of statutes. In an unusual passage near the end of the opinion, the Court explained that judges "are not part of either political branch" and hence "have no constituency."[13] Agencies, while "not directly accountable to the people," are subject to the general oversight and supervision of the President,

---

10. See generally, Thomas W. Merrill, *Judicial Deference to Executive Precedent*, 101 Yale L. J. 969, 972–75 (1992); Colin S. Diver, *Statutory Interpretation in the Administrative State*, 133 U. Pa. L. Rev. 549, 562 (1985).

11. Indeed, it appears *Chevron* has had a marked effect in reducing consideration of these factors by reviewing courts. See Orin S. Kerr, *Shedding Light on Chevron: An Empirical Study of the Chevron Doctrine in the U.S. Courts of Appeals*, 15 Yale J. on Reg. 1, 46 (1998) (reporting that in 1995 and 1996 only 5% of the courts of appeals decisions that applied *Chevron* considered the traditional factors).

12. Id. at 844.

13. Id. at 866.

who is elected by all the people. Hence, it is fitting that agencies, rather than courts, resolve "the competing interests which Congress itself either inadvertently did not resolve, or intentionally left to be resolved by the agency charged with the administration of the statute in light of everyday realities."[14] The new emphasis on democratic theory reinforced the presumption of delegated interpretational authority, and seemed to offer a universal reason to prefer agency interpretations to judicial ones.

Most landmark decisions are born great—they are understood to be of special significance from the moment they are decided. But *Chevron* was little noticed when it was decided, and came to be regarded as a landmark case only some years later. This may be the most interesting aspect of the *Chevron* story—how a decision that was considered routine by those who made it came to be regarded as one of potentially transformative significance. Before we get to that part of the story, however, we need to understand what *Chevron* did decide, and why.

I. THE BUBBLE CONTROVERSY

When it was briefed and argued, no one thought *Chevron* presented any question about the standard of review of questions of law. Instead, all understood the case to be about the "bubble concept," a catchy phrase for a particular way of interpreting the term "stationary source" under the Clean Air Act. One cannot understand how Justice Stevens was able to obtain unanimous support for his provocative opinion, or why that opinion came to have such compelling power for lower court judges, without some sense of the controversy over the bubble.

Three different programs established by the Clean Air Act require that stationary sources of air pollution, like power plants and smelters, adopt strict technology-based limitations on emissions. Each of these programs kicks in when firms either construct "new" stationary sources, or "modify" existing stationary sources. The programs impose much less demanding limitations on existing stationary sources. Yet each of the programs contains a critical ambiguity about the meaning of "source": it is unclear whether this word refers to each *apparatus* that emits pollution within a plant, or whether it refers to the *entire plant*.

Under the narrow apparatus definition, if a plant installs a new boiler with a smoke stack, this would either be new source (if the boiler was added to existing processes) or a modified source (if the boiler replaced an existing boiler and emitted more pollution than the original boiler). Hence the new boiler would have to comply with tough technology-based controls. The plant-wide definition of source, in contrast, in effect puts an imaginary bubble over an entire industrial complex and looks at changes in the amount of pollution coming out of a hole at the

---

14. Id. at 865–66.

top. Under this bubble definition, if a firm adds a new boiler with a smoke stack, but makes offsetting changes in other parts of the operation such that the net effect is to reduce or hold pollution levels unchanged, the addition of the new boiler would be neither a new source nor a modification of a source. Hence the change could be ignored for regulatory purposes.

The bubble concept was controversial from the time it was first proposed in the early 1970s. Environmentalists generally opposed the bubble because they saw it as locking in the environmental status quo. Suppose a plant consists of four apparatuses, each of which emits 100 tons of pollution per year, for total emissions of 400 tons. A new apparatus subject to new-source controls would emit only 25 tons of pollution. Under the bubble concept, the plant could continue to rebuild itself indefinitely, replacing each uncontrolled apparatus with a new uncontrolled apparatus as the old one wore out. Each replacement would result in no net addition of pollution from the plant, and so the tough technology-based standards would never be triggered. After a while, the plant would consist of nothing but new apparatuses, and yet it would still be emitting 400 tons of pollution, rather than the 100 tons it would emit if each apparatus had been regulated. The objectives of the new source provisions would be evaded, and no further progress would be made in cleaning up the air.

Industry representatives and economists countered with a different example. Suppose, as before, a plant with four apparatuses, each emitting 100 tons in an unregulated state. Now suppose that the plant wants to expand output by adding a fifth apparatus. Under the narrow single-apparatus definition of source, the new apparatus would be subject to controls, and would emit 25 tons. So the plant would now emit a total of 425 tons. Under the bubble policy, however, the plant could escape technology-based controls if it could somehow hold total emissions from the plant to 400 tons or less. Suppose it could do this relatively cheaply by retrofitting the existing apparatuses with a device that reduces emissions from 100 to 75 tons and by installing the device on the new apparatus. The result would be to reduce total emissions from the plant from 400 (4 x 100) to 375 tons (5 x 75). Application of the bubble in this example could save the plant considerable money *and* would also result in a better outcome for the environment—375 tons of pollution per year versus 425 tons of pollution.

As with other attempts to resolve policy disputes by hypothetical example, we can see that the outcome depends on the assumptions built into the example. The case for the single-apparatus definition turns on the assumption that there is a sharp discontinuity between old equipment and new equipment. Old equipment is highly polluting, too costly to retrofit, and will inevitably be replaced by new equipment because of technological obsolescence. Thus, the best policy is hang tough in insisting that technology-based standards apply to each apparatus, because over the long run this will do the most to improve air quality. The case for the bubble concept rests on the assumption that there is more of a continuous function between the costs and benefits of retrofitting existing equipment versus installing new equipment. Sometimes retrofitting old equipment might yield more environmental benefits at lower costs than scrapping old equipment and replacing it with new. Thus, the best policy is to give firms general pollution-reduction goals combined with considerable flexibility in determining how to go about meeting those goals.

EPA's first encounter with the bubble debate came in connection with the administration of the New Source Performance Standards (NSPS) established by Section 111 of the Clean Air Act of 1970. The NSPS applied to "new sources," which were defined as "any stationary source, the construction or modification of which" begins after a NSPS for that category of sources is published.[15] "Stationary source" was defined in turn as "any building, structure, facility, or installation which emits or may emit any air pollutant."[16] "Modification," for its part, was strictly defined to mean any change in a source "which increases the amount of any air pollutant emitted by such source."[17] EPA's initial regulations simply repeated the statutory definitions without clarifying whether "source" means apparatus or an entire plant.[18]

In 1972, representatives of the nonferrous smelting industry, supported by the Department of Commerce, wrote EPA urging it to adopt the bubble concept in determining when a modification of a stationary source has occurred.[19] After initially resisting, EPA endorsed a modest form of the bubble concept in late 1975.[20] EPA acknowledged that there had been some confusion about the meaning of different terms used in the statutory definition of "stationary source." "Generally speaking," EPA explained, " 'sources' are entire plants, while 'facilities' are identifiable pieces of process equipment or individual components which when taken together would comprise a source."[21] EPA therefore decided that "facility" means a single apparatus, and "source" means either a single apparatus or a complex of apparatuses. Consistent with this "dual

---

    15. CAA § 111(a)(2), 42 U.S.C. § 7411(a)(2).

    16. Id. § 111(a)(3).

    17. Id. § 111(a)(4).

    18. See 36 Fed. Reg. 24875, 24977 (December 23, 1971).

    19. See ASARCO Inc. v. Environmental Protection Agency, 578 F.2d 319, 323–24 (D.C. Cir. 1978).

    20. 40 Fed. Reg. 58416 (December 16, 1975).

    21. Id.

definition" of stationary source, EPA amended its regulations to define "source" to mean any "building, structure, facility, or installation" which "contains any one or combination of" facilities.[22] This definition implicitly rejected the bubble, which requires that the entire plant be the "source."

The agency nevertheless went on to endorse a qualified form of the bubble in a separate provision of the regulations dealing with the meaning of "modification." Here, EPA provided that no modification would be deemed to occur when an "existing facility undergoes a physical or operational change" and the owner demonstrates that the "total emission rate of any pollutant has not increased from all facilities within the stationary source."[23] But, EPA cautioned, the bubble would apply only to changes in the operation of existing equipment; if an owner or operator replaced an apparatus, or added a new one, the bubble would not apply.[24]

On cross petitions for review by ASARCO (for the nonferrous smelting industry) and the Sierra Club, a divided D.C. Circuit panel held that the bubble concept must be "rejected in toto."[25] The majority opinion was written by Judge J. Skelly Wright,[26] a staunch liberal who was prone to see industry capture of administrative agencies in many of the regulatory controversies that came before him.[27] Wright's opinion portrayed the controversy as one in which EPA, faced with a concerted lobbying campaign by one industry, had caved in and adopted a position that it knew to be "contrary to both the language and the basic purpose of the Act."[28]

As to the language of the Act, Judge Wright focused on the agency's dual definition of stationary source. He appeared to agree with the Sierra Club that the "plain meaning" of the statutory definition of "source" could not be further defined to mean both "facility" and "combination of facilities." But if "facility" means apparatus (as EPA

---

22.   Id. at 58418, amending 40 CFR § 60.2.

23.   Id .. at 58419, adding 40 CFR § 60.14.

24.   Id. at 58416–17.

25.   *ASARCO*, 578 F.2d at 325; see also id. at 329.

26.   Judge Leventhal joined Judge Wright's opinion but wrote a separate concurrence. Judge MacKinnon wrote a dissenting and concurring opinion.

27.   See Thomas W. Merrill, *Capture Theory and the Courts: 1967–1983*, 72 Chi-Kent L. Rev. 1039, 1065–66 (1997) (citing judicial and extra-judicial writings of Judge Wright exhibiting preoccupation with agency capture).

28.   *ASARCO*, 578 F.2d at 328. See also id. at 329 (stating that EPA had supported the qualified bubble "by examples drawn from circumstances peculiar to the nonferrous smelting industry" which was an improper basis for regulations "setting standards for all industries.").

had decided) and one or more of the other terms ("building," "structure" or "installation") means the entire plant (as EPA also seemed to believe), then facility or combination of facilities is perfectly consistent with the statutory definition. A facility would be a facility and a combination of facilities would be an entire plant. The real problem with EPA's new bubble policy was that it required that "source" be defined solely as "plant" for purposes of "modifications," whereas the agency had adopted the dual definition for all purposes. The problem, in other words, was that EPA was guilty of internal inconsistency, not that it had transgressed the permissible meaning of the statute.[29]

As for the purposes of the Act, Judge Wright thought that the bubble would allow operators to evade their duty to install pollution control systems based on best available technology, as long as they could devise some way to keep total emissions from an entire plant from increasing. As he vividly put it, "[t]reating whole plants as single sources would grant the operators of existing plants permanent easements against federal new source standards and the worst polluters would get the largest easements."[30] Thus, the bubble was incompatible with the central purpose of Section 111, which Judge Wright said was to enhance air quality. Neither ASARCO nor the EPA petitioned for certiorari, so the bubble was dead for purposes of Section 111.

The 1977 Amendments to the Clean Air Act added two additional new source provisions to the Act. These provisions were applicable depending on whether air quality in a particular region is better than or worse than required by the National Ambient Air Quality Standards (NAAQS) established under the 1970 Act. New Part C, called Prevention of Significant Deterioration (PSD), was designed to impose limits on the ability of states to allow clean air to deteriorate downward toward the NAAQS level. New Part D, called Plan Requirements for Nonattainment Areas (nonattainment program or NAP), was designed to prod states to bring dirty air areas into compliance with the NAAQS.

Each of these new Parts included, among its regulatory instruments, new source review provisions requiring states to adopt technology-based standards for certain new and modified sources. Neither of the new provisions made any further attempt to define "facility" or "source,"[31]

---

29. It is possible that Judge Wright wanted to suggest that the dual definition violates the Act because this might force EPA to adopt the single-apparatus definition of source for all purposes. This would reduce the agency's wiggle room to adopt any kind of bubble in the future.

30. Id. at 329 n. 40.

31. The PSD provisions define major emitting facility to mean any "stationary source" on a list of 28 categories of sources with the potential to emit 100 tons of any pollutant per year, or any other type of source with the potential to emit 250 tons of any pollutant per year. CAA § 169(1), 42 U.S.C. § 7479(1). The term "major stationary source"

nor was there any cross reference in either Part to the definition of "stationary source" in Section 111. Both Parts, however, expressly incorporated the definition of "modification" set forth in Section 111.[32]

The 1977 Amendments were enacted after EPA had adopted the qualified bubble under Section 111, but before that policy had been struck down by *ASARCO*. Although *ASARCO* had been decided by the time EPA issued regulations implementing the new PSD program,[33] EPA nevertheless adopted for that program virtually the same qualified bubble concept that had been invalidated by *ASARCO*.[34] The agency reasoned that Congress, in adopting the 1977 amendments, had been made aware of the definition of "modification" EPA had adopted under Section 111. Thus, when Congress directed that "modification" have the same meaning for PSD purposes as under Section 111, it implicitly ratified EPA's qualified bubble under PSD. EPA's PSD regulations implemented the qualified bubble by defining "facility" to mean apparatus, "source" to mean an entire plant, and by making the definition of "major modification" applicable to "sources" rather than "facilities."[35]

The PSD regulations were challenged in the D.C. Circuit in *Alabama Power Co. v. Costle*,[36] a massive judicial review proceeding that entailed dozens of issues besides the legality of the bubble policy. The panel issued a per curiam opinion summarizing its conclusions in June 1979, and issued its final opinion in April 1980. The final opinion, which had 135 headnotes spread over 88 pages of text, was divided up by the three judges who heard the matter,[37] each judge writing a separate section.

---

for NAP purposes is defined to mean "any stationary facility or source" with the potential to emit 100 tons of any pollutant per year. CAA § 302(j); 42 U.S.C. § 7602(j).

32. CAA § 171(4), 42 U.S.C. § 7501(4) (NAP). The incorporation of the definition of "modification" in the PSD program was added by a subsequent technical corrections amendment. See Pub. L. No. 95–190, § 14(a)(54), 91 Stat. 1393, 1402 (1977). It is codified as a parenthetical in CAA § 169, 42 U.S.C. § 7479(2)(C) (definition of "construction").

33. 43 Fed. Reg. 26380 (June 19, 1978).

34. Id. at 26394.

35. See 43 Fed. Reg. 26403 (June 19, 1978), amending 40 CFR §§ 52.21 (b)(2), (b)(4), (b)(5). This was potentially perilous, since the statute made the new source review provisions in the PSD program applicable to "major emitting *facilities*." Although the D.C. Circuit was to invalidate part of the definition of "source" (as going beyond the Section 111 definition), and part of the definition of "modification" (for including a 100 ton-per-year threshold not found in the Section 111 definition), it allowed this potential anomaly pass without remark. See Alabama Power Co. v. Costle, 636 F.2d 323, 394–98, 399–400 (D.C.Cir. 1979).

36. 636 F.2d 323 (D.C. Cir. 1979).

37. Judges Leventhal, Robinson, and Wilkey. Judge Leventhal, who had joined Judge Wright's opinion in *ASARCO*, died before the final opinion was issued. Although the opinion notes that the portion of the opinion written by Judge Leventhal had been concurred in by the other judges prior to his death, see 636 F.2d at 343 n. 1, it did not state

The challenge to the bubble, along with other issues involving the definition of source and modification, was assigned to Judge Malcolm Wilkey, one of the court's more conservative and pro-business members.

In his discussion of general issues regarding the meaning of "source" and "modification," Judge Wilkey announced a number of significant conclusions. He concluded, for example, that the statutory definition of "stationary source" in Section 111 ("any building, structure, facility, or installation") was the meaning Congress intended EPA to apply under the PSD provisions.[38] Accordingly, to the extent EPA had sought to expand the definition of major stationary source to include other terms (including "combination thereof"), it was invalid under *ASARCO*. Similarly, since Congress had specifically incorporated by reference the definition of "modification" under Section 111, EPA's attempt to limit modifications to "major modifications" of 250 or 100 tons per year or more was invalid.[39]

Judge Wilkey recognized that these rulings might impose regulatory burdens on industry and EPA. He sought to soften the blow by indicating that EPA had broad discretion to define the component terms of the statutory definition of "source" (building, structure, facility, or installation) in different ways in order to advance the purposes of different new source programs.[40] He also suggested that EPA would have authority to exempt "de minimis increases" from the definition of modification. Finally, Judge Wilkey noted that the occasions for review of modifications would be reduced because the bubble definition of source would be used for these purposes.[41]

Judge Wilkey spent little time considering the text of the statute in reaching the conclusion that the bubble was a permissible definition of "source" in the context of the PSD program. Instead, the focus was on policy. He made two principal points. First, in the dynamic American economy, "alterations of almost any plant occur continuously." To apply the definition of "modification" to any individual apparatus would result in burdensome and repetitious PSD review of many "routine alterations of a plant."[42] Second, the PSD program was designed to prevent deterioration of air quality, not enhancement of air quality. Thus, any definition other than the bubble "would be unreasonable and contrary to the

---

whether Judge Leventhal had concurred in the portion written by Judge Wilkey prior to his death.

38. Id. at 395; 396.

39. Recall that the statutory definition of modification in Section 111 includes any "increase" in any pollutant. CAA § 111(a)(4); 42 U.S.C. § 7411(a)(4).

40. Id. at 397.

41. Id. at 400.

42. Id. at 401.

expressed purposes of the PSD provisions of the Act."[43] Whereas Judge Wright had implied that the bubble was unlawful in any form under Section 111, the Wilkey opinion seemed to say that the bubble concept was mandatory under the PSD program.

The third leg of the new source review stool was the nonattainment program, also added by the 1977 amendments. This was not really a new program, since EPA had by regulation imposed many of the elements of new Part D in its "Offset Ruling" which applied to States in dirty air areas. The original Offset Ruling required states to adopt tough technology-based standards on "major sources" in noncompliance areas, but was ambiguous as to whether the bubble would be permitted in defining major sources.[44]

After the 1977 Amendments were passed, EPA embarked on a series of zig-zag efforts to clarify whether the bubble should apply under the new Part D Program. In a rulemaking concluded in early 1979, EPA offered up a confusing discussion of the issue, part of which seemed to disapprove of the bubble, part of which seemed to say that a qualified bubble restricted to physical and operational changes was permissible.[45] Then, in a Notice of Proposed Rulemaking issued in response to the June 1979 per curiam order in *Alabama Power*,[46] EPA proposed an intermediate position: a qualified bubble definition of source could be used by States in full compliance with Part D requirements, but laggard States would have to use the apparatus definition.[47]

Final rules were not issued until August 1980, after the D.C. Circuit's full opinion in *Alabama Power* had issued.[48] In its most exhaustive consideration of the issue to date, EPA determined that, given the D.C. Circuit's decisions in *ASARCO* and *Alabama Power*, the bubble had to be prohibited for all purposes under the Part D program. The circuit court had ruled that that the bubble was inappropriate under programs designed to improve air quality, and the nonattainment program was designed to improve air quality. Accordingly, EPA defined "stationary source" for NAP purposes to mean "building, structure, facility *or installation*," with "installation" now standing in for single apparatus, rather than "facility" as under the NSPS regulations invalidated in

---

43. Id. at 401.

44. See 41 Fed Reg. 55524 (December 21, 1976).

45. 44 Fed. Reg. 3274, 3276–77 (January 16, 1979).

46. The *Alabama Power* panel released an order with a summary of its ruling in June, 1979, but released its full opinion only December, which was then further revised in April, 1980.

47. 44 Fed. Reg. 51924, 51934 (September 5, 1979).

48. 45 Fed. Reg. 52676 (August 7, 1980).

ASARCO, and the other terms defined to mean plant.[49] In other words, the agency again adopted the dual definition, under which the bubble was prohibited.

Six months later, Ronald Reagan, who had campaigned on a platform of reducing regulatory burdens, was sworn in as the new President. Shortly thereafter, EPA announced that it had decided to reconsider issues related to the definition of "source" under the nonattainment and PSD new source review programs, as part of "a Government-wide reexamination of regulatory burdens and complexities that is now in progress."[50] The Notice of Proposed Rulemaking proposed to permit the States, at their election, to adopt an *unqualified* bubble definition of source for both PSD and nonattainment purposes. The change would be executed by defining all statutory definitions of "source" (building, structure, facility, or installation) to mean plant rather than apparatus.

The Final Rule released in October 1981 adhered to the proposed rule in all respects.[51] The change was justified on the ground that regulatory complexity would be reduced by using the same definition of source for both PSD and NAP purposes. Moreover, allowing the States to choose the bubble definition would give them "much greater flexibility in developing their nonattainment ... programs."[52] Giving States the option to adopt the bubble definition of source would not undermine the purposes of the nonattainment program, the agency opined, because any State adopting the bubble would still have to demonstrate that it was making reasonable further progress to reach attainment.

The October 1981 regulations were challenged in the D.C. Circuit by three environmental groups, led by the Natural Resources Defense Council. The case was assigned to a panel composed of Judges Abner Mikva, Ruth Bader Ginsburg, and a visiting senior district judge from Montana. Judges Mikva and Ginsburg were both relatively liberal Carter appointees. Judge Mikva would later resign to serve as White House Council to President Clinton, and Judge Ginsburg would later be appointed to the Supreme Court by Clinton.

The decision was unanimous to vacate EPA's regulations. Judge Ginsburg's opinion for the court, stripped of details about the statutory and regulatory background, reduced to a syllogism.[53] First, *Alabama Power* and *ASARCO* "establish as the law of this Circuit a bright line

---

49. Id. at 52746.

50. 46 Fed. Reg. 16280 (March 12, 1981). EPA did not propose to revisit the definition of source under the NSPS, apparently on the ground that this would contravene the judgment in *ASARCO*.

51. 46 Fed. Reg. 50766 (October 14, 1981).

52. Id. at 50767.

53. Natural Resources Defense Council v. Gorsuch, 685 F.2d 718 (D.C. Cir. 1982).

test for determining the propriety of EPA's resort to a bubble concept."[54]
Second, this test provided that the bubble "is mandatory for Clean Air
Act programs designed merely to maintain existing air quality," but is
inappropriate "in programs enacted to improve the quality of the ambient air."[55] Third, "[t]he nonattainment program's raison d'etre is to
ameliorate the air's quality in nonattainment areas sufficiently to
achieve expeditious compliance with the NAAQS."[56] It followed that the
bubble could not lawfully be used under the nonattainment program.

Judge Ginsburg made no attempt to determine whether the bubble
concept could be squared with the statutory meaning of "stationary
source," and she agreed with EPA that the legislative history was "at
best contradictory."[57] The opinion also gave short shrift to EPA's judgment that application of the bubble, at least in the context of the
nonattainment program, would not interfere with efforts to achieve
further improvements in air quality. This was dismissed with the observations that it was inconsistent with the agency's view a year earlier,
and the agency had not cited "any study, survey, or support" for its new
position.[58] Ordinarily, this would be an appropriate judicial response to a
change in agency policy.[59] Here, however, since EPA's previous position
had been justified largely on the ground that it was required by the D.C.
Circuit's decisions in ASARCO and Alabama Power, the demand for
consistency amounted to privileging policy judgments previously reached
by the D.C. Circuit.

Still, it is ironic in retrospect that Judge Ginsburg's opinion was the
one to be singled out for further review by the Supreme Court. Of the
three D.C. Circuit decisions dealing with the bubble controversy, the
Ginsburg opinion is most restrained, in the sense of attempting to
resolve the issue through a good faith reading of existing legal authorities (in this case, circuit precedent). The result reached—invalidation of
the bubble in dirty air areas—was no doubt one that was congenial to
Judge Ginsburg and her panel relatively liberal colleagues. But one does
not get the impression that Ginsburg was actively manipulating to reach
this result. In contrast, both Judge Wright's opinion in ASARCO, and

---

54. Id. at 726.

55. Id.

56. Id. at 726–27.

57. Id. at 727 n 39. Indeed, the opinion "express[ed] no view on the decision we
would reach if the line drawn in Alabama Power and ASARCO did not control our
judgment." Id. at 720 n.7

58. Id. at 727 n.41.

59. Courts frequently respond to agency deviations from prior policy by requiring an
explanation or new evidence in support of the change, a requirement sometimes called the
"swerve doctrine." See, e.g., Shaw's Supermarkets, Inc. v. NLRB, 884 F.2d 34 (1st Cir.
1989).

Judge Wilkey's opinion in *Alabama Power*, reflected transparent attempts to reach ends consistent with the author's views of appropriate policy. The bubble controversy suggests that D.C. Circuit judges were prone to substitute their own preferences for those of EPA. But the most flagrant practitioners of this activism were not directly implicated in the case that eventually went before the Supreme Court.

II. AN INAUSPICIOUS DEBUT

In tracking the progress of *Chevron* in the Supreme Court there are a number of sources to draw upon. The petitioning papers and merits briefs are of course available, as is the transcript of oral argument. Robert Percival has previously reported on information gleaned from Justice Thurgood Marshall's papers, which include the internal memos exchanged by the Justices about Justice Stevens' draft opinion.[60] Perhaps most importantly, we now have available Justice Harry Blackmun's papers, which shed significant new information on the Court's internal deliberations. Unlike Marshall, who did not participate in either the argument or decision in *Chevron*, Blackmun was involved from beginning to end. More importantly, Blackmun was probably the most meticulous note-taker among the Justices during the time he sat on the Court.

After the D.C. Circuit denied petitions for rehearing en banc, Chevron U.S.A. Inc. filed a petition for certiorari in December 1982, thereby securing its name on the caption of the decision. The American Iron and Steel Institute filed a separate petition in January 1983. The Solicitor General, who controls litigation by the executive branch (including EPA) in the Supreme Court, took considerably longer to decide what to do. A critical factor no doubt was the large controversy then brewing in Washington about how reviewing courts should respond to administrative deregulation orders.[61] The Supreme Court had pending before it *Motor Vehicle Manufacturers Ass'n v. State Farm Mutual*,[62] where the Reagan Administration, citing costs and uncertain benefits, had rescinded a mandatory automobile passive restraints rule adopted by the Carter Administration. The order had been set aside by the D.C. Circuit because the agency had failed to consider alternatives to rescission. In the Supreme Court, the Administration was arguing that courts should give greater deference to agencies when they deregulate than when they regulate, and that under the more lenient standard, the air bag rescission should be upheld.

---

60. Robert V. Percival, *Environmental Law in the Supreme Court: Highlights From the Marshall Papers*, 23 ELR 10606, 10613 (1993).

61. For scholarship reflecting the controversy, see Cass Sunstein, *Deregulation and the Hard Look Doctrine*, 1983 Sup. Ct. Rev. 177; Merrick Garland, *Deregulation and Judicial Review*, 98 Harv. L. Rev. 505 (1985).

62. 463 U.S. 29 (1983).

The bubble controversy presented another example of an agency deregulation initiative invalidated by the D.C. Circuit. No doubt the proponents of deregulation within the Administration pressed the Solicitor General to seek further review in *Chevron* in order to press ahead in the campaign for deregulation. This advocacy may have tipped the balance in favor of filing a government petition in *Chevron*, even though there was no circuit conflict and the decision below simply followed two previous decisions of the D.C. Circuit, neither of which the government had seen fit to challenge.

For whatever reasons, the Solicitor General did not file the petition on behalf of EPA until March 1983. Given the lateness of the government's filing, *State Farm* was decided before the Court could act on the petitions in *Chevron*. As it turned out, *State Farm* rejected the Administration's appeal for greater deference to deregulation orders, and affirmed the D.C. Circuit's decision invalidating rescission of the passive restraints rule, providing a significant setback to the Administration's deregulation campaign. It is hard to say how this outcome influenced *Chevron*, which was then briefed and argued the following term. The setback in *State Farm* may have tempered some of the arguments that the Solicitor General and the other petitioners advanced in support of reversal. It is also possible—although there is no direct evidence for this—that it may have caused some of the Justices to tilt more toward the government in *Chevron*, if only to avoid the impression that the Court was taking sides in the deregulation debate.

In all events, there is nothing in the three petitions suggesting that the parties were asking the Court to reconsider basic questions of administrative law. The focus was on the practical significance of the bubble concept, the confusion produced by the three D.C. Circuit decisions, and the claim that the D.C. Circuit had overstepped established bounds of judicial review. For example, the Solicitor General's petition for certiorari said, "The decision of the court of appeals is contrary to well established limits upon the scope of judicial review of administrative action."[63]

Similarly, there is nothing in the merits briefs to suggest that the case was seen as a vehicle for a major statement about administrative law. The Solicitor General's brief was prepared under the supervision of Paul Bator, who had just arrived from Harvard Law School as the first "political" Deputy Solicitor General.[64] The Bator brief advanced two themes that appear to have influenced Justice Stevens. First, the brief

---

63. Petition for Certiorari, Administrator, Environmental Protection Agency v. Natural Resources Defense Council, Inc., 1982 LEXIS U.S. Briefs 1591 (March 25, 1983).

64. For more on the background of the Bator appointment, see CHARLES FRIED, ORDER AND LAW: ARGUING THE REAGAN REVOLUTION—A FIRSTHAND ACCOUNT 28–30 (1991).

hammered on the idea that the 1977 Amendments had not one purpose—improving air quality in dirty air areas—but two purposes: improving air quality and accommodating further economic growth in dirty
air areas. This "two purposes" idea was to become the linchpin of
Justice Stevens' argument that Congress had left the definition of source
to be resolved by the agency in light of these somewhat conflicting
objectives.[65] Second, the Bator brief planted the idea that "implied
delegations" to agencies to fill gaps in statutes should be treated no
differently than express delegations of gap-filling authority. This idea,
which was quite novel in the context of determining the standard of
review of agency legal determinations, was presented by the brief as a
faithful representation of existing law.[66] Justice Stevens took the bait
and offered a similar depiction of the law in his *Chevron* opinion. In
other respects, however, Justice Stevens largely ignored the government's brief.[67]

The brief filed by respondent NRDC may have been more significant, given what it did *not* say. NRDC's position in the D.C. Circuit had
been a strong one. Circuit precedent—*ASARCO* and *Alabama Power*—
made the legality of the bubble turn on whether the Clean Air Act
program in question was designed to enhance or maintain air quality,
and the nonattainment program was designed to enhance air quality.
But when the case moved up the judicial hierarchy to the Supreme
Court, the bottom fell out from under NRDC's position. The Supreme
Court was not bound by *ASARCO* or *Alabama Power*, and would
consider the legality of the bubble in terms of the primary statutory
sources—the language and legislative history of the Clean Air Act. To

---

65. See *Chevron*, 467 U.S. at 851–53.

66. Both the Bator brief and Justice Stevens quoted the following line from Morton v.
Ruiz, 415 U.S. 199, 231 (1974): "The power of an administrative agency to administer a
congressionally created ... program necessarily requires the formulation of policy and the
making of rules to fill any gap left, implicitly or explicitly, by Congress." This statement,
however, was addressed to agency authority to issue regulations, not the standard of review
of questions of law. In the context of determining the standard of review of agency
interpretations of law, the Court had previously applied the arbitrary and capricious
standard only in cases in which Congress had *explicitly* delegated authority to the agency to
define a statutory term or prescribe a method of executing a statutory provision. See, e.g.,
United States v. Vogel Fertilizer Co., 455 U.S. 16, 24 (1982); Batterton v. Francis, 432 U.S.
416, 424–26 (1977).

67. For example, one of the major themes of the government's presentation was
federalism. EPA's regulations, the Bator brief repeatedly stressed, simply gave States the
choice whether to adopt the narrow ("apparatus") definition of source, or the broad
("bubble") definition in their implementation plans. In contrast, said the brief, the
respondents and the D.C. Circuit wanted to put the States in federal straitjacket. Justice
Stevens barely touched on federalism in his opinion, however, and instead developed a
powerful separation of powers theme which was not foreshadowed in the government's
presentation.

make matters more difficult, EPA's 1981 regulations avoided the internal inconsistency in the regulatory definition of "source" that Judge Wright had exploited in *ASARCO*. Accordingly, the only argument left to NRDC was that the statutory term "source" must always mean apparatus, and can never mean plant. Its brief gamely attempted to support this claim through a laborious reconstruction of the legislative history of the new source programs, interwoven with the administrative history of the bubble. But NRDC made no attempt to defend the court of appeals' decision—usually a telltale sign of weakness.

The most striking aspect of the briefs is the absence of any direct antecedent for the two passages for which *Chevron* is most famous, namely the "two-step" approach to review of questions of law, and the justification of deference to agencies in terms of their relationship to the President. Justice Stevens apparently came up with these innovations on his own.

Nor does the transcript of oral argument reveal much of significance. Justices Thurgood Marshall and William Rehnquist were both absent from the bench because of health problems. Bator argued for the petitioners, David Doniger, a seasoned environmental lawyer, for the respondents. The questioning was dominated by Justices White, Stevens, and Brennan, and was directed more toward Bator than Doniger. Justice Blackmun's notes taken at argument suggest that the colloquy left little impression on him. He observed at the end of Doniger's presentation: "Few questions—no one wishes to venture out."

Two days after the argument, on March 2, 1984, the Justices assembled to conference about the case. We learn the following from Justice Blackmun's notes. Although the decision would ultimately be unanimous, the vote at conference was 4–3 to reverse the D.C. Circuit's decision. Justices White, Blackmun, Stevens and Powell voted to reverse. Chief Justice Burger and Justices Brennan and O'Conner voted to affirm. This unusual lineup is confirmed by the fact that Justice White assigned the opinion to Justice Stevens.[68] White would have the power of assignment only if he were the most senior Justice in the majority at conference, which would require that both Burger and Brennan be in dissent.

Blackmun's notes further reveal that each of the Justices voting to reverse was tentative or doubtful about this disposition. Blackmun put a "?" after the "—" sign beside the name of each of the Justices voting to reverse, presumably indicating that each of these Justices expressed some hesitancy about his vote.

---

68. See infra for a discussion of the evidence for this.

As best I can make out from Blackmun's notes, the conference discussion went something like this.[69] Chief Justice Burger started things off with a speech about how the D.C. Circuit was going "pretty far" in environmental cases, and the Supreme Court was going to have "to settle" this. He suggested the way to do so was by affirming. Blackmun expressed his puzzlement with this reasoning by putting "??" next to the Chief Justice's proposed disposition. Burger's comments, as recorded by Blackmun, suggest that the Chief Justice had only the most tenuous grasp of the issues in the case.

Justice Brennan spoke next. Blackmun's notes suggest that Brennan was much more on top of things, and did his best to convince the conference to affirm. He gave a crisp summation of the bill of indictment against the bubble, consistent with the views expressed by his friend, Judge Wright, in *ASARCO*. The dual definition of source was troublesome because it allowed EPA to "have it both ways;" the result might not be "what Congress intended;" the bubble would grant a plant a "perpetual" right to "pollute at achieved level;" EPA had changed directions and hence was not entitled to much deference.

The discussion then turned to Justice White. Blackmun's notes indicate White started out by saying he was "very shaky" but inclined to reverse. He indicated that he had been persuaded by *Alabama Power*. Blackmun's notes do not elaborate on what White meant by this. On its face, the comment is puzzling, since Judge Ginsburg writing for the D.C. Circuit had relied on *Alabama Power* in holding the bubble unlawful in the context of the nonattainment program. Perhaps White was referring to Judge Wilkey's more general discussion in *Alabama Power* about the definition of "source," and to his conclusion that the language was broad enough to allow EPA to define source differently under different programs, but this is speculation. In any event, after White spoke, Blackmun's notes indicate that Chief Justice Burger interjected: "& I might join;" in other words, Burger might join an opinion to reverse.

With Marshall absent, the next speaker was Justice Powell. Although Blackmun also marked Powell down as voting to reverse with a question mark, Powell's comments seemed to follow fairly consistently the line taken in the industry briefs. He said the statute was "complicated" and deference was due to an agency "redetermination" of its policy. He too cited *Alabama Power* as supporting reversal, without recorded elaboration. Powell also observed that the States have primary responsibility for the nonattainment program. "On policy," he said, the decision

---

69. I clerked for Justice Blackmun in the 1978–79 Term, but cannot claim any expertise in deciphering his notes about conference, since he ordinarily provided his clerks with an oral summary of the conference, and did not share the notes themselves.

below would pose a problem for "economic growth" and serve as a "disincentive" (presumably he meant to plant modernization).

Justice Rehnquist ordinarily would go next, but in his absence the next speaker was Justice Blackmun himself. Blackmun naturally did not take notes about his own comments, but his notes on the case written shortly before the conference reveal that he had had trouble making up his mind. Although he marked "—"at the bottom of his notes, meaning reverse, one can clearly see beneath this mark that he had originally written and later erased " + ?"—suggesting that his initial disposition was to affirm, although he had doubts about this. There is no way to tell from the notes when Blackmun erased the " + ?" and wrote "—" over the top, although presumably it was sometime after his initial preparation for the argument and before he spoke at conference. Blackmun's law clerk had written a bench memo urging affirmance, and possibly this influenced the Justice's initial response, but he must have changed his mind while giving the matter further consideration.

After Blackmun came Justice Stevens. Blackmun's notes record the following interesting remarks. Stevens began by saying he was "not at rest." Ideally, he observed, the definition of source ought to be the same throughout the statute. In a mild rebuke to Justices White and Powell, Stevens said he was not sure that *Alabama Power* was completely controlling. The agency interpretation, however, was a "permissible reading" of the statute. The House Report (by which he presumably meant the House Conference Report) was "confusing!" He concluded: "When I am so confused, I go with the agency."

Justice O'Connor, the newest Member of the Court, spoke last. Her remarks betray a certain lack of sophistication about administrative law. After voting to affirm the lower court, she nevertheless indicated that the "bubble made sense as a concept." The stumbling block for her seemed to be that the legislative history provided no support for the EPA position. She concluded: "Industry is suffering" and said the matter was "very painful for me."

What is one to make of this? Perhaps the most obvious point is that there is nothing in the conference notes to suggest that the Justices regarded *Chevron* as a watershed case about the standard of judicial review. The case presented nothing more than a puzzle about the legality of the bubble concept. It is also interesting to note that the Justices were quite focused on what the legislative history did or did not say, and seemed quite conscious of the lower court opinions. In contrast, Justice Blackmun's notes record no comment from any Justice about the specific language of the statute. *Chevron* was decided at a time when the Court's statutory interpretation opinions were devoted primarily to a search for legislative intentions as revealed by legislative history. The conference notes suggest that the Justices thought about statutory interpretation questions the same way in their deliberations.

What we did not know before, and is potentially significant in explaining what happened, is that the conference vote was closely divided (4–3) and that the Justices, with the possible exception of Justice Brennan, all expressed uncertainty or ambivalence about the proper outcome. This meant that the assignment to write the majority opinion was an especially challenging one. In order to hold a majority, the opinion writer would have to unravel the legal complexities about the bubble concept in a persuasive way, and would have to devise some way of framing the issue that the doubters would find compelling.

One especially valuable document in the Blackmun papers is something he called his "Opinion Log Sheet" which he kept for each argued case. It is from this document that we learn Justice White, the senior Justice voting with the majority, assigned the opinion to Justice Stevens. The assignment came on March 2, 1984, the same day as the conference, suggesting that White may have acted quickly to assert his prerogative, perhaps to forestall any attempt by the Chief Justice to assign the case (on the ground that he had changed his mind and had decided to join the majority to reverse).[70]

Justice Stevens' took over three months to prepare his opinion. This was not an unusually long period of time, but in the context of a case argued at the end of February, it meant that the draft opinion was not circulated until June 11, only about three weeks before the Justices were scheduled to adjourn for the year. By this time in the annual opinion-writing cycle, the Justices were immersed in a frenzy of effort to get the last, most difficult decisions out the door.[71] In effect, the other Justices were given virtually no time to consider drafting concurring or dissenting opinions, or even to suggest modifications to the Stevens' draft.

The official paper trail of memos following circulation of the draft reveals the following. Justices Marshall and Rehnquist responded with memos on June 12th confirming that they should be shown as taking no part in the decision in the case. Justice White, the assigning Justice, responded on the 13th with a memo designed to give the Stevens' effort a boost: "Please join me in your very good opinion in this case." On the 14th, Stevens circulated a revised draft. Justice O'Connor then circulat-

---

70. Stories abound that Chief Justice Burger would occasionally switch his vote after conference in order to control assignment of the majority opinion. See BOB WOODWARD AND SCOTT ARMSTRONG, THE BRETHREN 64–66, 171 (1979).

71. *Chevron* was part of an avalanche of opinions handed down at the end of the 1983 Term—a total of 39 decisions from June 25 (when *Chevron* was released) to July 5 (when the Term finally ended). A fair number of these cases had been sitting on the docket longer than *Chevron*.

ed a memo indicating that after the argument, she had inherited a remainder interest in trust in one of the companies in the case, and she was therefore recusing herself. The Court was down to a bare quorum of six participating Justices. That same day, Justice Brennan circulated a memo stating tersely: "Please join me." He offered no explanation for his change of position from conference, where he had voted decisively to affirm. Then, on June 18, Justice Blackmun, the Chief Justice, and Justice Powell joined in quick succession. The only comment beyond the perfunctory was from the Chief Justice, who declared with typical sangfroid: "With others, I am now persuaded you have the correct answer to this case." Another Stevens draft, with further minor changes, was circulated on June 19. The decision was released June 25.

This record of correspondence as preserved in the Blackmun papers strongly suggests that no Justice made any recommendations for modifications in the Stevens opinion. Certainly, no recommendations were made by formal memorandum addressed to the whole conference. It is conceivable that informal suggestions were made, either by private memo or via law clerks. But if any such suggestions were made, they had only the most modest impact. The draft opinion circulated on June 14 indicates that it differs from the original draft only in terms of minor stylistic changes and one new footnote.[72] And the June 14 draft is virtually identical to the opinion as released on June 25. If any Justice harbored reservations about Stevens' effort, those reservations were obviously suppressed in light of all the other tasks that had to be completed to get to the end of the Term.

Of the three preliminary drafts circulated by Justice Stevens, only the draft of June 14, which was the one reviewed by Justice Blackmun, is preserved in his papers. As was his custom, Justice Blackmun marked in pencil throughout the draft, indicating by small circles what he regarded as errors in spelling, grammar, and citation style. There are three arguably more revealing marginal comments.

In the margin opposite footnote 34, Justice Blackmun has written "footnotes!" The opinion is more than ordinarily loaded down with footnotes, and the remark may reflect a sense tedium in having to forge through these complex materials. In the margin opposite the concluding sentence of the section of the opinion devoted to legislative history, Justice Blackmun has written "yes." That sentence reads: "We conclude that it was the Court of Appeals, rather than the Congress or any of the decisionmakers who were authorized by Congress to administer this legislation, that was primarily responsible for the 1980 position taken by

---

72. The new footnote is number 22 in the opinion. It is simply reports that the dispute in the case concerns the meaning of the term "major stationary source," not the term "proposed source." See 467 U.S. at 849 n. 22.

the agency."[73] It is possible this may have been the point in reading when Justice Blackmun became fully convinced by Stevens' argument.[74] And on the first page of the opinion, in the top left hand corner, Justice Blackmun has written simply: "Whew!" In context, it is safe to say that this was an expression of admiration for Justice Stevens' handiwork, and perhaps also a sense of relief that the opinion handled the complicated issue in a way that absolved Justice Blackmun of any further engagement with the matter.

"Whew!" may in fact provide the best clue as to how the Court came to render such an emphatic and unanimous opinion in *Chevron*. Given that he thought he had precarious support, Justice Stevens presumably worked extra hard to produce a persuasive opinion. The result is impressive in its craftsmanship. The opinion frames the standard of review in a bold new way designed to maximize the strengths and minimize the weaknesses of the disposition for which Stevens was arguing. It meticulously dissects the statutory and legislative history arguments. It ends on a high note designed to carry the reader away with a paean to democracy and judicial restraint. Circulated to his colleagues in the midst of the end-of-Term crunch, this over-achieving opinion more than carried the day—it swept the field.

III. THE CONSTRUCTION OF A LANDMARK

There is no evidence that Justice Stevens understood his handiwork in *Chevron* as announcing fundamental changes in the law of judicial review. Both before and after *Chevron* was decided, Justice Stevens authored opinions that analyzed administrative interpretations using the traditional factors approach that pre-dated *Chevron*, and that many believe were superseded by *Chevron*.[75] In later years, when asked about his most famous opinion, Justice Stevens would respond that he regarded it as simply a restatement of existing law, nothing more or less.[76]

---

73. *Chevron*, 467 U.S. at 864.

74. Justice Blackmun recorded no reaction to the passages in the next section of the opinion about the illegitimacy of judges resolving contested policy questions.

75. See Connecticut Dep't of Income Maintenance v. Heckler, 471 U.S. 524 (1985) (Stevens, J.); Aluminum Co. of Am. v. Central Lincoln Peoples' Util. Dist., 467 U.S. 380, 402–03 n. 3 (1984) (Stevens, J. dissenting).

76. Justice Stevens is a graduate of Northwestern Law School, where I formerly served as the John Paul Stevens Professor of Law. In that capacity, I was occasionally invited to attend public events at which Justice Stevens agreed to speak when he came to Chicago. I recall at least two occasions when someone in the question-and-answer session after the speech asked him a version of the "what did you intend when you wrote *Chevron*?" question. The answer was always that he regarded it simply as a restatement of established law.

The most striking evidence that Justice Stevens had no desire to modify the status quo is provided by the remarkable *Cardozo-Fonseca* episode that occurred less than three years after *Chevron* was decided.[77] *Cardozo-Fonseca* was an immigration case, in which the Justice Department sought *Chevron* deference for its interpretation of the legal requirements for establishing asylum in the United States. Writing for the Court, Justice Stevens stated that no deference was appropriate, because the issue was a "pure question of statutory construction for the courts to decide."[78] The discussion strongly implied that *Chevron*-style deference was limited to questions of "law-application," with "pure questions of law" being reserved for independent judicial determination. There was support for such a distinction in pre-*Chevron* case law.[79] But the distinction is in apparent conflict with *Chevron*, which drew no such dichotomy, and the issue in *Chevron* itself should probably be regarded as a pure question of law—whether "source" should be defined as apparatus or plant. That Stevens would seek to deflate his *Chevron* opinion in this manner strongly suggests that he had no design to change the multi-faceted approach to judicial review of questions of law. Certainly he had no intention to restrict his own discretion in future cases to call upon aspects of the traditional approach that were downplayed in *Chevron*.

Nor is there any evidence that Justice Stevens' colleagues on the Court perceived *Chevron* as some kind of watershed decision, either when it was decided or for some time afterwards. We have already seen that the opinion generated no substantive comment from any Member of the Court when it was circulated in June of 1984. Further evidence that the Justices regarded *Chevron* as just another case is provided by the next Term's decisions. Although there were nineteen argued cases in the next Term that presented some kind of question about whether the Court should defer to an agency interpretation of statutory law, *Chevron* was cited in only one of those cases.[80] Based on its initial trajectory as a precedent in the Supreme Court, *Chevron* seemed destined to obscurity.

But *Chevron* was not to be relegated to obscurity, quite the contrary. We can trace the ascendancy of the *Chevron* "two-step" approach to judicial review in the Supreme Court's own body of decisional law. Beginning with the 1985–86 Term, *Chevron* began to appear with increasing frequency in the Court's opinions. Six cases applied the *Chevron* framework in 1985–86, two the next term, and five the term

---

77. See INS v. Cardozo-Fonseca, 480 U.S. 421 (1987).

78. Id. at 446.

79. See GARY LAWSON, FEDERAL ADMINISTRATIVE LAW 428–430 (3d ed. 2004).

80. Chemical Mfrs. Ass'n v. Natural Resources Defense Council, 470 U.S. 116 (1985). For overall data on the 1984 Term, see Merrill, supra note 10 at 1038–39.

following that.[81] By the end of the 1980s, the percentage of deference cases in the Supreme Court adopting the *Chevron* framework had risen to around 40%; by the early 1990s it was up to around 60%.[82] Soon the Court began to debate, in the course of resolving particular stationary questions, whether the *Chevron* approach should apply or not. Thus, questions arose as to whether *Chevron* applies to pure questions of law, whether *Chevron* applies to legal issues that arise in judicial rather than administrative proceedings, and whether *Chevron* trumps statutory interpretation precedents established in previous court cases.[83] Eventually, the Court was granting certiorari and devoting entire cases to questions about the scope of "the *Chevron* doctrine," such as whether it applies to interpretations announced in agency adjudications or opinion letters.[84]

How did *Chevron*, after such an inauspicious beginning, acquire this status as a core precedent of administrative law? Two explanations seem most plausible. The first focuses on the D.C. Circuit, and posits that *Chevron* became a leading case initially in the D.C. Circuit, and then migrated back to the Supreme Court along with personnel who had previously served in the D.C. Circuit. The second focuses on the role of the executive branch, and posits that Justice Department lawyers, perceiving the advantages of *Chevron*'s expanded rule of deference to administrative interpretations, became persistent and eventually successful proselytizers for use of the *Chevron* standard in reviewing agency interpretations of law.

The role of the D.C. Circuit in establishing *Chevron* as a landmark has been suggested by others,[85] and is broadly consistent with much of the data about *Chevron*'s rise from obscurity. The D.C. Circuit is the court that hears the highest percentage of cases involving judicial review of agency action. Many of these cases involve disputes over whether to defer to agency interpretations of law. If the D.C. Circuit were to adopt *Chevron*'s "two-step" formula as the dominant standard for judicial review of questions of law, it could then have been transplanted back to the Supreme Court by employees of D.C. Circuit who were promoted to service on the Supreme Court. The most prominent of these promoted employees, of course, was Antonin Scalia, who was a judge on the D.C.

---

81. Merrill, supra note 10 at 1036–38.

82. See data presented in Thomas W. Merrill, *Textualism and the Future of the* Chevron *Dcotrine*, 72 Wash. U. L. Q. 351, 359–60 (1994).

83. See Cardozo-Fonseca, supra (pure questions of law); Adams Fruit Co. v. Barrett, 494 U.S. 638 (1990) (judicial proceedings); Maislin Indus., U.S., Inc. v. Primary Steel, Inc., 497 U.S. 116 (1990) (judicial precedent). For an overview of these and other issues about the scope of Chevron that have arisen, see Thomas W. Merrill and Kristin E. Hickman, Chevron's *Domain*, 89 Geo. L. J. 833 (2001).

84. See United States v. Mead Corp., 533 U.S. 218 (2001) (opinion letters); INS v. Aguirre-Aguirre, 526 U.S. 415 (1999) (agency adjudication).

85. See Lawson, supra note 79 at 449.

Circuit when *Chevron* was handed down in 1984, and was elevated by President Reagan to the Supreme Court in 1986, where he promptly became the Court's foremost champion of *Chevron*. In addition, a disproportionately large number of Supreme Court law clerks serve as clerks to D.C. Circuit judges before they go on to clerk for Justices on the Supreme Court. They too would be familiar with *Chevron*, and would be expected to turn to its two-step formula in drafting opinions for Supreme Court Justices dealing with judicial review of questions of law.

Some evidence tending to support this reverse-migration hypothesis is provided by the previously-mentioned *Cardozo-Fonseca* episode. The case was decided in Justice Scalia's first year on the Supreme Court, and the junior Justice took it upon himself to write a concurring opinion chastising Justice Stevens for his "eagerness to refashion important principles of administrative law in a case in which such questions are completely unnecessary to the decision and have not been fully briefed by the parties."[86] Justice Scalia objected to Justice Stevens' suggestion that *Chevron* concerned only questions of law application, observing that *Chevron* "has been an extremely important and frequently cited opinion, not only in this Court but in the Courts of Appeals."[87] In effect, the newly-arrived Justice from the D.C. Circuit was telling his colleagues that *Chevron* was already entrenched in the practice of judicial review in the D.C. Circuit, and major revisions could be destabilizing.

In order to shed further light on the reverse-migration hypothesis, I examined all decisions of the D.C. Circuit citing to *Chevron* during the first three years after the decision was handed down. The survey provides further evidence confirming the broad outlines of the hypothesis. The D.C. Circuit picked up on the *Chevron* two-step framework for reviewing agency determinations of law very quickly. One early decision, *Rettig v. Pension Benefit Guaranty Corp.*,[88] provided an elaborate paraphrase of the two-step idea, in effect adopting it as the law of the circuit. In all, the D.C. Circuit handed down 23 decisions citing to *Chevron* in the first year after the decision was announced. This grew to 40 in the second year, and 64 in the third year after the decision was announced. This is a disproportionately large percentage of *Chevron* citations relative to other courts of appeals.[89] By the end of the second year, *Chevron* was already regarded as boilerplate doctrine in the Circuit. One finds

---

86. *Cardozo-Fonseca*, 480 U.S. at 455 (Scalia, J., concurring in the judgment). There is irony in this accusation, given that *Chevron*, the "important principle of administrative law," was itself less than three years old and had been "established" in a decision in which the issues it dealt with had also not been briefed by the parties.

87. Id. at 454.

88. 744 F.2d 133, 150–51 (D.C. Cir. 1984).

89. The D.C. Circuit citations represent about 40% of all citations to *Chevron* at the court of appeals level during the first three years. Today, by contrast, D.C. Circuit citations to *Chevron* have fallen to about 17% of all court of appeals citations.

statements from this period describing *Chevron* as the "now familiar framework," the "familiar two-step framework," the "familiar dictates," or the standard that applies "as always" in reviewing agency interpretations.[90]

There has occasionally been speculation that *Chevron* was embraced with particular fervor by the newly-appointed Reagan judges on the D.C. Circuit.[91] One can tell a plausible story in support of this surmise. The D.C. Circuit was during these years closely divided between Republican and Democratic appointees. The Democratic judges were likely somewhat hostile to the deregulatory initiatives of the Reagan Administration, and would seek some way to strike them down. The newly-appointed Republican judges, in contrast (who were gradually growing in number), would be eager to find some way to uphold these initiatives. Perhaps these Republican judges seized upon *Chevron* as the most effective weapon at hand for upholding controversial administrative decisions.

The data, however, provide no support for such a supposition during the first two years after *Chevron* was decided. The judge who cited *Chevron* most frequently during these years was Judge Patricia Wald, a Carter appointee. She was the author of *Rettig*, and is perhaps the judge most responsible for the rapid assimilation of the two-step framework in the D.C. Circuit. Judge Wald cited *Chevron* in 13 opinions in the first two years, easily outdistancing the top Republican citer, Judge Kenneth Starr, who cited the case in 8 opinions. Indeed, Democratic appointees out-cited *Chevron* relative to Republican appointees 38 to 21 in the first two years, and out-cited Republicans 62 to 53 over all three years.

There are some interesting variations in citation patterns among the judges in these early years, but they appear to have more to do with age and energy level than with politics. Thus, Judge Spottswood Robinson, the most senior Democratic appointee, made relatively little use of *Chevron*, citing it only once the first two years. He tended to stick to the traditional factors, and even after *Chevron* became established referred to it mostly in string citations. Similarly, Judge Mikva never showed

---

90. See Natural Resources Defense Council v. Thomas, 805 F.2d 410, 420 (D.C. Cir. 1986) (Wald, C.J.) ("dictates"); International Brotherhood of Teamsters v. ICC, 801 F.2d 1423, 1426 (D.C. Cir. 1986) (Starr. J.) ("familiar two-step"); Transbrasil S.A. Linhas Aeras v. DOT, 791 F.2d 202, 205 (D.C. Cir. 1986) (Wald, C.J.) ("always"); Investment Co. Institute v. Conover, 790 F.2d 925, 932 (D.C. Cir. 1986) (Starr, J.) ("familiar framework").

91. For evidence that Democratic and Republican judges on the D.C. Circuit respond differently to cases in ways that match their party affiliation, see Richard L. Revesz, *Congressional Influence on Judicial Behavior? An Empirical Examination of Challenges to Agency Action in the D.C. Circuit*, 76 N.Y.U.L. Rev. 1100, 1106–09 (2001) (summarizing studies). Interestingly, one study finds less political influence in *Chevron* cases than in cases presenting procedural challenges to agency decisions. Richard L. Revesz, *Environmental Regulation, Ideology, and the D.C. Circuit*, 83 Va. L. Rev. 1717 (1997).

much affinity for *Chevron*. Judges Wald and Harry Edwards, in contrast, who were younger and arguably more energetic, made greater use of *Chevron*. On the Republican side, Judge Starr, who was the youngest judge on the circuit, was the most frequent user of *Chevron*. In contrast, Judge Robert Bork, who was more senior, made little reference to *Chevron* until the third year after it came down (he cited it in only two opinions the first two years). Interestingly, Judge Antonin Scalia, who was to become identified as *Chevron*'s champion after he was named to the Supreme Court, cited *Chevron* in only three opinions while he sat on the D.C. Circuit.

In the third year of *Chevron*'s existence, the picture begins to change slightly, although this may be due to the fact that the Republican appointees, with their increasing numbers, were getting more of the opinion-writing assignments in major regulatory decisions. Republican appointees in 1986–87 used *Chevron* slightly more than Democratic appointees (32 to 25 citations in majority opinions). Judge Starr became the leading user of *Chevron* that year (11 citations), slightly eclipsing Judge Wald (9 citations). Judge Bork discovered *Chevron* (8 citations), as did Judge Laurence Silberman (6 citations). On the other side of the aisle, after *Cardozo-Fonseca* was decided late in the year, Judge Edwards mounted a short-lived campaign to limit *Chevron* to cases involving "law application."[92] So there is some evidence that *Chevron* was becoming more of a Republican-favored doctrine, and the Democrats were having second thoughts. But the evidence is at most suggestive on this point.[93]

I should add that there is little evidence, from these three years, that *Chevron* caused the judges of the D.C. Circuit to become more deferential toward administrative agencies.[94] In terms of cases citing

---

92. See International Union v. Brock, 816 F.2d 761, 764 (D.C. Cir. 1987) (Edwards, J.); Regular Common Carrier Conf. v. United States, 820 F.2d 1323 (D.C. Cir. 1987) (Edwards, J.). Early the next Term, Justice Scalia announced in another concurring opinion that *Cardozo-Fonseca*'s "law application" interpretation of *Chevron* had been abandoned by the Court (properly enough in his view). NLRB v. United Food & Commercial Workers Union, 484 U.S. 112, 133–34 (1987) (Scalia, J., concurring). The pure question of law/law application distinction quickly and quietly disappeared. See Merrill, *supra* note 10 at 986 n. 74.

93. About this time, a number of Republican-appointed judges took to writing about *Chevron* in the law reviews. See Kenneth W. Starr, *Judicial Review in the Post-Chevron Era*, 3 Yale J. on Reg. 283 (1986); Antonin Scalia, *Judicial Deference to Administrative Interpretations of Law*, 1989 Duke L. J. 511; Laurence H. Silberman, Chevron —*The Intersection of Law & Policy*, 58 Geo. Wash. L. Rev. 821 (1990). Although this confirms that the D.C. Circuit judges attributed great significance to *Chevron*, it would be difficult to characterize these efforts as advocacy pieces. Judge Starr's article presented a carefully balanced view of *Chevron*, and Justice Scalia's article took pains to point out that the *Chevron* standard did not necessarily mean more deference to agencies.

94. In a widely cited study, Peter Schuck and Donald Elliott claimed that *Chevron* caused an increase in deference to agency policy decisions in the lower courts. See Peter H.

Chevron in which there was a clear disposition affirming or reversing the agency, affirmances barely outnumbered reversals (64 to 52). If we look only at those cases that expressly frame the inquiry in terms of *Chevron*'s two-step formula, the ratio of affirmances to reversals improves slightly (30 to 20). Of course, all this could be due to selection effects: judges are more likely to select a deference-promoting framework when they have decided to affirm (and need to justify this result) than we they have decided to reverse. Still, the D.C. Circuit took virtually no time at all to learn how to reverse agency interpretations at step one or step two of the *Chevron* framework.[95] The much-debated question whether *Chevron* has had any impact on the degree of deference judges actually give to agencies remains unresolved.

The second plausible explanation for *Chevron*'s rise to fame is that this was due to aggressive promotion by the executive branch lawyers. *Chevron* was regarded as a godsend by executive branch lawyers charged with writing briefs defending agency interpretations of law. Not only did the two-step standard provide an effective organizing principle for busy brief-writers, the opinion seemed to say that deference was the default rule in any case where Congress has not spoken to the precise issue in controversy. Since this describes (or can be made to seem to describe) virtually every case, *Chevron* seemed to say that the government should nearly always win. *Chevron* may have meant little to the Justices when it was decided, and it may have taken time for courts other than the D.C. Circuit to accept it as orthodoxy. But it was quickly seized on as a kind of mantra by lawyers in the Justice Department, who pushed relentlessly to capitalize on the perceived advantages the decision presented.[96]

Enthusiasm for *Chevron* among government lawyers is one thing; acceptance by courts is another. But here it is plausible to suppose that the Justice Department role as the ultimate institutional litigant is relevant. The Department urged that *Chevron* serve as the relevant standard of review at nearly every turn, and the Department appeared in court much more frequently in cases raising questions about review of

Schuck & E. Donald Elliott, *To the* Chevron *Station: An Empirical Study of Federal Administrative Law*, 1990 Duke L. J. 984 (1990). But their methodology did not single out for study cases that actually cited or relied on *Chevron*.

95. See, e.g., Rettig v. Pension Benefit Guaranty Corp., 744 F.2d 133, 156 (D.C. Cir. 1984) (Wald, C.J.) (reversing agency interpretation as unreasonable at step two of *Chevron*); FAIC Secur., Inc. v. United States, 768 F.2d 352 (D.C. Cir. 1985) (Scalia, J.) (reversing agency interpretation as contrary to statute at step one of *Chevron*).

96. From 1987 to 1990 I served as Deputy Solicitor General in the Justice Department, overseeing appeal authorization and Supreme Court litigation in civil cases. After only a few months on the job, I joked to friends that I was the Deputy Solicitor General for *Chevron*, since it seemed that virtually every request from the Civil Division for appeal authorization or for Supreme Court participation was based on the need to expand or defend the *Chevron* doctrine.

questions of law than any other category of litigant. It is not difficult to imagine that over time the Department persistence would pay off, and courts would start to regard *Chevron* as the accepted standard.[97]

These two explanations for *Chevron*'s delayed investiture as a landmark decision—migration from the D.C. Circuit and executive advocacy—are by no means inconsistent. To the contrary, they are mutually supportive. The Justice Department's impact as an institutional litigant might well be the strongest in the D.C. Circuit, given the very high concentration of administrative law cases in that circuit. So executive advocacy may help explain why *Chevron* caught on first in the D.C. Circuit. Moreover, the Justice Department, through the Office of Solicitor General, is by far the most important institutional litigant in the Supreme Court. So executive advocacy may have played a reinforcing role in *Chevron*'s migration back to the Supreme Court. Perhaps most importantly, vigorous advocacy of executive branch prerogatives served the interests of both D.C.Circuit judges seeking promotion to the Supreme Court—such promotions being controlled by the White House—and Justice Department lawyers seeking victories in court. Both sets of aspirants had a stake in supporting an expansion of executive power, making *Chevron*'s rhetoric of implied delegations of executive authority congenial to both.

CONCLUSION

Chevron presents a striking instance of a case that became great not because of the inherent importance of the issue presented, but because the opinion happened to be written in such a way that key actors in the legal system later decided to make it a great case. *Chevron* became a landmark decision due to the cumulative effect of a series of fortuitous events, among them Justice White's assignment of the case to Justice Stevens, Justice Stevens' creative restatement of certain principles of administrative law, the lack of scrutiny given the Stevens opinion by other Justices, Judge Patricia Wald's quick embrace of the two-step formula in the D.C. Circuit, Justice Scalia's elevation to the Supreme Court from the D.C. Circuit two years later, and the Justice Department's unrelenting campaign to make *Chevron* the universal standard for judicial review of agency interpretations of law. Individually, each of these events is readily explicable; cumulatively, they would have to be described as an accident.

How often a case becomes great because of a series of fortuities is unclear. Conceivably it happens in administrative law more often than in

---

97. The classic study of the advantages of being an institutional litigant is Marc S. Galanter, *Why the "Haves" Come out Ahead: Speculations on the Limits of Legal Change*, 9 L. & Soc'y Rev. 95 (1974).

other fields. Supreme Court opinions play a critical role in administrative law, yet the Court decides relatively few administrative law decisions, and most of the Justices are not particularly conversant with that law. Consequently, the Justices may have more room to "free lance" when assigned to write administrative law opinions than when they write in areas more thickly populated with precedents or subject to closer oversight by other Justices. This freedom, in turn, may generate occasional mutations in the law in the form of idiosyncratic expressions by opinion writers. Most of these mutations probably disappear quickly. But occasionally one strikes a responsive cord and begins to replicate. As *Chevron* suggests, it is even possible for the mutation to replicate initially primarily in one lower court, then return to the Supreme Court, whereupon it receives a new imprimatur and proceeds to spread vigorously throughout the legal system.

Chevron therefore may be seen as a particularly dramatic example of a more general characteristic of administrative law, namely, that unanticipated judicial innovations play an especially large role in its development.[98] To a much greater extent than, say, civil procedure, administrative law is judge-made law. The most important judges who make that law—the Justices of the Supreme Court—are less than fully engaged in the topic, and are therefore capable of producing surprises. *Chevron* is one of the biggest surprises of all, and legal system has only begun to comprehend the full measure of its significance.

---

98.   Other possible examples of this phenomenon might include Abbott Laboratories v. Gardner, 387 U.S. 136 (1967) (suggesting that preenforcement review of rules is available without regard to whether the rules are interpretive or legislative); Association of Data Processing Service Organizations v. Camp, 397 U.S. 150 (1970) (reading the "legal interest" test for standing out of the APA and creating in its place the "zone of interests" test); Vermont Yankee Nuclear Power Corp. v. Natural Resources Defense Council, Inc., 435 U.S. 519 (1978) (holding that courts have no authority to prescribe rulemaking procedures in addition to those set forth in the APA); Citizens to Preserve Overton Park v. Volpe, 401 U.S. 402 (1971) (transforming the arbitrary and capricious standard of review into "searching inquiry"). For the exasperated response of an administrative law specialist to another mutation, see Kenneth Culp Davis, *Administrative Law Surprises in the* Ruiz *Case*, 75 Colum. L. Rev. 823 (1975) (cataloguing misstatements of law in Morton v. Ruiz, 415 U.S. 199 (1974)).

430

The *Abbott Labs* trilogy, prescribes a famous formula for determining whether an agency rule is "ripe" for immediate judicial review. This formula becomes easier to understand in the context of the substantive controversies involved, which concerned the Food and Drug Administration's authority over prescription drug labeling and color additives. In this chapter, Professor Levin traces the development of each case, from passage of the enabling legislation, through rulemaking and judicial review proceedings, to subsequent regulatory action by the FDA. He finds the Court's ripeness holdings reasonable in relation to the specific regulatory issues presented. At the same time, he contends that the Court, initially deadlocked in all three cases, gave only limited endorsement to the pre-enforcement review of rules. Thus, the broad prevalence of that practice today is chiefly the product of evolving features of the administrative law system, especially the increased use of rulemaking and the emergence of new criteria for judicial review of the merits.

11

Ronald M. Levin[*]

The Story of the *Abbott Labs* Trilogy: the Seeds of the Ripeness Doctrine

If the story of *Abbott Laboratories v. Gardner*[1] and its companion cases were produced for the theater, the list of stage properties would contain a variety of objects that can be found in the medicine cabinet of a typical American household, including a tube of lipstick, a compact of rouge, and a bottle of hair dye. Also on the list would be a bottle of prescription medicine—but the story would focus on the design of the labeling on the outside of the bottle, not on the drugs themselves. For several reasons these prosaic items received close scrutiny from the federal Food and Drug Administration (FDA) during the early 1960s. The litigation that resulted from this scrutiny provides the story line for a narrative that also illuminates one of the key turning points in the development of administrative law.

That turning point should be understood in the context of a much larger transformation: the burgeoning of administrative rulemaking during the 1960s and 1970s.[2] Agencies' increased reliance on rules forced

 * Henry Hitchcock Professor of Law, Washington University School of Law. Of invaluable assistance in the writing of this chapter were the extraordinary cooperation of Michelle Bigesby of the FDA Dockets Management Office and John Swann and Cindy Lachin of the FDA History Office; the patient helpfulness of many interviewees cited herein; the archival research contributions and suggestions of colleagues Lee Epstein and Neil Richards; the expert perspective of Jim O'Reilly; and the diligent research assistance of Courtney Brunsfeld. All are warmly thanked, and all are absolved of responsibility for any remaining errors.

1. 387 U.S. 136 (1967) (*Abbott Labs*).

2. See Reuel E. Schiller, *Rulemaking's Promise: Administrative Law and Legal Culture in the 1960s and 1970s*, 53 ADMIN. L. REV. 1139, 1148–49 (2001). (summarizing this trend).

them, as well as the courts, to rethink a host of procedural norms that had worked well enough as applied to case-by-case adjudication but were inadequate for an age of pervasive rulemaking.

One problem that had to be reassessed was the question of *when* a regulated entity would be permitted to go to court to challenge an agency action to which it objected. Prior to the rulemaking revolution, the question was not very troublesome. Courts commonly refrained from allowing judicial review at any but the final stage of the regulatory process, when a statute or rule was enforced against an individual or company in a formal decree. The prospects for judicial review of a rule at the time of its promulgation (often called "direct" or "pre-enforcement" review) were uncertain at best, except in a few situations governed by statute. In an environment in which agencies used rulemaking mainly for procedural and housekeeping matters, postponement of review was a plausible answer. But as the sphere of rulemaking expanded to encompass weighty and expensive regulatory requirements, that solution came to look too restrictive. The courts responded by introducing a more accommodating, yet flexible, approach to rationing the availability of judicial review, known as the doctrine of "ripeness."

The Supreme Court set forth a classic exposition of ripeness in a trio of cases decided on May 22, 1967.[3] These cases have come to be known as the *Abbott Labs* trilogy. The following pages tell the story of the controversies underlying these cases and some of the people who were caught up in it. It has two distinct plot lines, which converged only at the Supreme Court level. We will examine them separately.

The *Abbott Labs* Litigation

Senator Kefauver's legislation

Our first story begins with the Kefauver–Harris Drug Amendments of 1962, an outgrowth of the so-called Kefauver hearings.[4] Their namesake, Senator Estes Kefauver of Tennessee, was a charismatic politician who had a gift for the uses of publicity as an instrument of congressional influence. He made a national reputation as a result of his investigative hearings in 1950 and 1951 on organized crime in America. Later, in

---

3. In addition to *Abbott Labs*, they included *Toilet Goods Ass'n v. Gardner*, 387 U.S. 158 (1967), and *Gardner v. Toilet Goods Ass'n*, 387 U.S. 167 (1967).

4. The following account of the history of the Kefauver–Harris Amendments is digested from several sources, including: RICHARD HARRIS, THE REAL VOICE (1964) (a book-length treatment); CHARLES L. FONTENAY, ESTES KEFAUVER: A BIOGRAPHY 379–93 (1980); JOSEPH BRUCE GORMAN, KEFAUVER: A POLITICAL BIOGRAPHY 351–59 (1971); and Julie A. Grow, *The Legislative History of the 1962 Drug Amendments: A Failure to Forget or A Lesson to Learn From?* (1997), *available at* http://leda.law.harvard.edu/leda/data/189/grow.html. For the industry's perspective, see WILLIAM C. CRAY, THE PHARMACEUTICAL MANUFACTURERS ASSOCIATION: THE FIRST 30 YEARS 7–37 (1989).

1954, he became chairman of a subcommittee on juvenile delinquency and held splashy hearings on sex and violence in comic books.[5]

Kefauver ran for President in 1952 and 1956, losing the Democratic nomination each time to Adlai Stevenson, the governor of Illinois. In 1956, however, Stevenson left the choice of a running mate to the Democratic convention. The delegates chose Kefauver for the vice presidential nomination, passing over another rising politician, John F. Kennedy of Massachusetts. The Stevenson-Kefauver ticket went down to defeat in the general election, losing to the incumbents, President Dwight Eisenhower and Vice President Richard Nixon. After 1956 Kefauver exited from national electoral politics and concentrated his attention on legislative matters.

Beginning in 1959, Kefauver conducted hearings on the pharmaceutical industry as chairman of the Antitrust and Monopoly Subcommittee of the Senate Judiciary Committee.[6] A dominant theme of the hearings was that prescription drug prices were exorbitant. He produced dramatic examples of high markups. For example, he took the president of Schering Corporation to task for selling a bottle of the pain reliever prednisolone for about $18.00, although the company's cost (which did not include research, because the tablets were acquired from an independent supplier) was about $1.50. Kefauver became convinced that one of the main reasons for the ability of drug marketers to charge such high prices was physician ignorance. Doctors often failed to realize that the expensive drugs sold under familiar brand names were chemically the same as the cheaper generic drugs the patient could have bought instead. More informative labels and advertising would ameliorate this confusion, he thought.

Kefauver introduced a bill on April 12, 1961, to follow up on his hearings. The bill, which was assigned the number S. 1552, contained a variety of proposed amendments to the Food, Drug, and Cosmetic Act (FD&C Act), the regulatory charter of the FDA.[7] For example, testimony had suggested that the generic names associated with various pharmaceuticals were often cumbersome and confusing (having been selected by manufacturers themselves). Thus, the bill provided that the FDA Commissioner should maintain a list containing an official name for each generic drug, so as to simplify and standardize the terminology. Under

---

5. AMY KISTE NYBERG, SEAL OF APPROVAL: THE HISTORY OF THE COMICS CODE 53 (1998).

6. The subcommittee's counsel, Paul Rand Dixon, later became the chairman of the Federal Trade Commission and the subject of a well-known administrative law case. A court disqualified him from participating in FTC antitrust proceedings involving the drug tetracycline because of the appearance of partiality created by his active role in the highly adversarial Kefauver hearings. American Cyanamid Co. v. FTC, 363 F.2d 757 (6th Cir. 1966).

7. S. 1552, 87th Cong., 1st Sess. (1961).

other provisions, drug companies would have to disclose possible side effects in their advertising and would have to send information directly to physicians. Pharmaceutical manufacturers would be required to demonstrate affirmatively that their drugs were not only safe (as under prior law) but also effective. In addition, the bill would have required holders of drug patents to grant licenses to their competitors, at a fixed royalty rate, following three years of exclusive rights under the patent.

One further provision, which ultimately set the stage for the *Abbott Labs* litigation, required that a drug's "official" or generic name be "printed in type at least as large and as prominent as that used for any trade or brand name." Senator Kefauver asserted, in introducing the bill, that this requirement would "help the physician to identify the family to which the drug belongs by showing clearly the official name of the product."[8] As his subcommittee's report later noted, "[a] common device in [prescription drug] promotion material is printing the trade name in large letters while the generic name is shown in such small letters as to be virtually unreadable. Other devices employed are placing the generic name in an unlikely spot on the ad where it cannot be discovered without careful examination, or omitting the generic name entirely...."[9]

The main representative of the drug industry during the debates over S. 1552 was the Pharmaceutical Manufacturers Association (PMA). It was a young organization at that time, having been incorporated in 1958. Actually, though, PMA was created through a merger of two rival trade groups that had been founded in 1907 and 1912.[10] During those groups' initial years, most of the member companies were family-owned, but by the time of the Kefauver hearings PMA comprised 140 members, many of them giant corporations, which accounted for ninety percent of pharmaceutical sales in America.[11] During negotiations on S. 1552, PMA was represented by Lloyd N. Cutler, who later served as White House counsel to Presidents Carter and Clinton and became known as one of the most distinguished lawyers in America.[12]

After additional hearings, Kefauver's subcommittee reported out S. 1552 on March 8, 1962, but prospects for its enactment did not look auspicious. Republican opposition was strident. Moreover, the administration of President Kennedy did not share Kefauver's reformist zeal.

---

8. 107 CONG. REC. 5640 (1961).

9. S. REP. NO. 87–448, at 234 (1961).

10. CRAY, supra note 4, at 1–4.

11. The organization's current name is the Pharmaceutical Research and Manufacturers of America (PhRMA).

12. Stuart Taylor, *Last of the Superlawyers*, LEGAL TIMES, May 16, 2005, at 62 (calling Cutler, upon his recent death, "the pre-eminent lawyer-statesman of his generation").

The administration drafted a milder bill, which was soon introduced in the House by Representative Oren Harris. Later, the administration worked with Senator James Eastland, the chairman of the Judiciary Committee (of which Kefauver's subcommittee was a component), to weaken the Kefauver bill. The critical language was worked out on June 8 at what came to be known as the "secret meeting." Eastland, Republican senators, and Cutler and other PMA representatives participated in this meeting, but Kefauver was unaware of it. He found out about it three days later, at a meeting of the Judiciary Committee, when Eastland offered his provisions as amendments to S. 1552. Furious, Kefauver strode to the Senate floor that afternoon and publicly denounced the Eastland substitute as a betrayal of the American consumer. In the wake of this extraordinary departure from the Senate's usual collegiality, the general impression was that Eastland's proposal would not move forward, but neither would Kefauver's original version. Nevertheless, when the Eastland version came to a committee vote on July 12, Kefauver voted in favor of it, hoping that he could get it strengthened later.

The pending legislation might never have overcome the inertia of the congressional process had it not been for a medical calamity of international dimensions involving a tranquilizer and morning sickness remedy called thalidomide. The drug had become freely available in many countries, and its American licensee, Wm. S. Merrell Co., had sent limited quantities to American doctors for testing on patients. However, Merrell's application to market thalidomide in the United States was blocked by an FDA medical officer, Dr. Frances Kelsey. Suspicious about possible side effects and the lack of test results, she repeatedly returned Merrell's application in early 1961 as "incomplete." Dr. Kelsey's caution turned out to be justified. An epidemic of severe birth defects was occurring in several nations, particularly West Germany. Thousands of babies were being born without limbs. In late 1961 the babies' deformities were traced to their mothers' use of thalidomide during pregnancy, and the manufacturer abruptly withdrew the drug from distribution.

These events were described at House hearings in April 1962 but did not receive public notice at that time. However, on July 15—three days after the committee vote on S. 1552—the *Washington Post* published a front-page story by investigative reporter Morton Mintz entitled "Heroine of FDA Keeps Bad Drug Off the Market." The article, which detailed the thalidomide tragedy and Dr. Kelsey's role, captured nationwide attention.

Kefauver acted promptly to turn this controversy to his advantage in promoting his bill. He urged President Kennedy to award a Distinguished Federal Civilian Service Medal to Dr. Kelsey for her service to the nation. (From the PMA point of view, this move simply confirmed that Kefauver was an "opportunist."[13]) The White House accepted the suggestion but kept Kefauver's share of the publicity to an absolute minimum. At the awards ceremony, according to columnist Doris Fleeson, "Dr. Kelsey wore a radiant smile as the President paid her honor.... The President smiled, too, and so did Majority Whip Humphrey.... In the background, somewhere, there was even Senator Kefauver, who first suggested the medal to the President, though he did not seem to make the pictures."[14]

The uproar over thalidomide propelled S. 1552 forward, with newfound support from the administration. In a way this development was ironic. The FDA already had the legal authority to regulate new drugs in the interest of public safety. Moreover, although the Kefauver bill did propose a more complex approval process for new drugs, the main thrust of this reform was to induce the FDA to take steps that would better ensure the *effectiveness* of the drugs. The Senator's original idea had been that FDA assurances of the efficacy of generic drugs would help induce physicians to prescribe those drugs rather than the higher-priced equivalents.

But the dynamics of the legislative process are not always logical. The thalidomide controversy gave rise to a general sense that the government had been lax, manufacturers were not to be trusted, and the public was at risk of hideous injury. That perception made the Kefauver initiative unstoppable. The Senate Judiciary Committee convened on August 20 and reported out a much stronger bill than the version that had emerged from the "secret meeting." The Senate then passed the bill by a vote of 78–0. Still buoyed by the thalidomide scandal, the bill passed the House, and a conference committee worked out differences between the House and Senate versions. President Kennedy signed the amended bill into law on October 10, 1962.[15]

During this complex series of legislative maneuvers, Senator Kefauver's provision on the display of generic names on drug labels underwent repeated revisions, although all versions rested on the same basic idea. The final, enacted version of the provision came from the Senate Judiciary Committee's August 20 draft. Framed as part of a new section 502(e) of the FD&C Act, it stated that a drug would be deemed misbranded unless,

> for any prescription drug, the established name of such drug or ingredient ... on such label (and on any labeling on which a name for such drug or ingredient is used) is *printed prominently and in*

13. CRAY, supra note 4, at 31.

14. FONTENAY, supra note 4, at 387–89 (quoting Fleeson).

15. Pub. L. 87–781, 76 Stat. 780 (1962).

*type as least half as large as that used thereon for any proprietary
name or designation for such drug* . . . .[16]

Note that the statute now used the term "established name" to refer to
a drug's generic name, which usually would be set by the FDA Commissioner. The requirement that labels must use lettering *half as large* as
that of the brand name was a middle ground between the Eastland
version of the bill, which had merely said that the established name had
to be displayed prominently and conspicuously, and Kefauver's original
bill, which had said that the typeface of the official name had to be *as
large as* the brand name. Furthermore, the final text applied not only to
prescription drug *labels*, but also to *labeling*. (In the jargon of the FD&C
Act, these two terms are not synonymous. "Labeling" means "all labels
and other written, printed or graphic matter upon [or] accompanying" a
drug,[17] such as brochures and package inserts.) In addition, section
502(n) of the Act applied the same display requirements to prescription
drug *advertising* as section 502(e) applied to *labeling*.[18]

An important detour occurred during the final stages of legislative
consideration. The House voted to phrase the labeling obligation differently, so that the established name would have to be "printed at the first
place, and at the most conspicuous place if other than the first place, at
which such proprietary name ... is used." Nevertheless, the House-
Senate conference committee decided to stick with the Senate version of
section 502(e). When the negotiated agreement returned to the Senate
for a final vote, Kefauver told his colleagues that the conference committee had not accepted the House's "limitation upon the frequency with
which the established name should appear." Thus, he continued, "the
established name of a prescription drug must appear in type at least half
as large as the trade name *wherever* the latter is used in drug promotional matter, including package inserts, and so forth."[19]

What did Kefauver mean by saying that the established name had to
be printed "wherever" the trade name was used? Did he mean *every time*
the trade name was mentioned? Or did he simply mean that the
established name would have to be "prominently" displayed *on any piece
of labeling* on which the trade name appeared? And how authoritative
was Kefauver's comment, anyway? These questions formed the crux of
the dispute that blossomed into the *Abbott Labs* litigation.

---

16. 21 U.S.C. § 352(e)(1)(B) (emphasis added). Except where otherwise indicated,
statutory citations in this chapter refer to the United States Code as it stood at the time of
the trilogy cases.

17. 21 U.S.C. § 321(m).

18. 21 U.S.C. § 352(n).

19. 108 CONG. REC. 22,039 (1962) (emphasis added).

The rulemaking proceeding[20]

Almost two months after the enactment of the Drug Amendments, a delegation of representatives of PMA and individual drug companies met with FDA officials. A memorandum by M. L. Yakowitz, the director of the agency's Division of Advisory Opinions, summarized this meeting. The visitors "stated that they are most anxious to start printing new labeling in compliance with section 502(e) and to prepare advertising that will be in compliance with 502(n), but are waiting for FDA interpretation of what is required by the new law." The first question they raised was whether the established (generic) name of a drug must accompany *every* use of a brand name in labeling. The FDA officials said that their "present feeling" was that, based on the legislative history, the answer to this question was yes. The visitors called this an "extreme position" and objected strenuously to it, arguing that a "very prominent presentation of the combination of proprietary name and established name on each page of a brochure" ought to suffice. A "lengthy discussion" of this point failed to produce a meeting of the minds.

On February 14, 1963, the agency published in the *Federal Register* a "Notice of Proposed Rulemaking" to implement the Kefauver-Harris amendments.[21] If adopted, the proposed regulations were to be codified as sections 1.104 and 1.105 of the *Code of Federal Regulations*. Most of the proposed provisions were acceptable to the industry, but the FDA had not altered its "extreme" position. Section 1.104(g) provided that "[i]f the labeling of a prescription drug bears a proprietary name or designation for the drug or any ingredient thereof, the established name, if such there be, corresponding to such proprietary name or designation, shall accompany each appearance of such proprietary name or designation."[22] Because of the requirement that the established (generic) name of a drug must accompany "each" appearance of the proprietary (brand) name, this sentence came to be known as the "every time" requirement. Section 1.105(a) applied the same obligation to advertisements for prescription drugs.

Because these were only proposed rules, lobbying for a relaxed version continued. The C.V. Mosby Company, a medical publishing house in St. Louis, prepared a forceful statement on behalf of the Association of Medical and Allied Publications. The memo called the "every time" requirement "impractical and redundant, and of no useful purpose," and

---

20. Documents underlying the discussion in this section were obtained from the FDA archives, Accession No. 88–78–36, box 50, and are on file with the author.

21. 28 Fed. Reg. 1448 (1963).

22. Except where otherwise indicated, citations to regulations in this chapter refer to versions found in the *Federal Register* notices in which they were promulgated, not to their current versions.

suggested various milder alternatives. Representative Thomas B. Curtis, a St. Louis congressman who had worked for years on drug regulation matters, forwarded the statement to the FDA, presumably to ensure that it would get attention. But the agency was not moved by this appeal, nor by an additional PMA–FDA conference in April. On June 20, the agency published the rules in final form, having made minor changes in response to the public comments, but no change in the basic "every time" approach.[23]

To say that the industry was not in the habit of seeking judicial redress from FDA actions would be an understatement. A court challenge to the new rules would represent "the first time in the 25-year history of the Food, Drug, and Cosmetic Act that the makers of prescription drugs [would] have taken concerted action against a regulation of the" FDA.[24] In an article written at about this time, Cutler attributed the industry's avoidance of the courts to the "terrifying armory of legal weapons that the FDA possesses," as well as to "the utter hopelessness of invoking the formal hearing and review procedures with any degree of success." He continued: "[A]ny lawyer who is honest with himself and his client knows that the chances of prevailing in the administrative hearing or in the courts are virtually nil.... [H]earing examiners and judges are laymen and are loath to reverse the judgments of the FDA's medical and scientific experts where the safety and effectiveness of drugs are involved."[25] This assessment may sound like hyperbole to modern ears, but it was a common claim among industry counsel of that era.[26]

But Cutler suspected that the agency had gone too far this time. At a briefing at the Federal Bar Association, he declared: "I am so convinced that major provisions of the new regs exceed FDA's statutory authority that I hope the industry will seek its remedy in the courts."[27] PMA's willingness to seek direct review of the new rules was reportedly also based on a tactical objective: "to avoid review in a context selected

---

23. 28 Fed. Reg. 6375 (1963). Section 1.104(g) was amended to apply to the "label or labeling," and the advertising obligation was moved to section 1.105(b).

24. Robert C. Toth, *Drug Suit Fights U.S. Label Rule*, N.Y. TIMES, Sept. 6, 1963, at 1.

25. Lloyd N. Cutler, *Practical Aspects of Drug Legislation*, in DRUGS IN OUR SOCIETY 149, 153–54 (Paul Talalay ed. 1964).

26. Another leading FDA practitioner told an Association of American Law Schools panel in 1962: "[E]very experienced food and drug lawyer will tell you that in 999 out of 1000 cases, even the most sanguine counsel—egged on by an outraged client whose long-standing product has become outlawed—knows that he hasn't a prayer of persuading an appellate court to second-guess the FDA.... The FDA rule-making process, by and large, has virtual immunity from judicial intervention or correction." H. Thomas Austern, *Expertise in Vivo*, 15 ADMIN. L. REV. 46, 54 (1963).

27. CRAY, supra note 4, at 41.

by the Agency which would involve the most favorable set of facts it could find."[28]

The initiation of litigation

On September 5, 1963—about two and a half months after the final regulations had been issued—the PMA and thirty-seven individual drug companies filed a complaint in the federal court in Wilmington, Delaware, to challenge the "every time" interpretation. The named defendants in the suit were George Larrick, the Commissioner of the FDA, and Anthony Celebrezze, the Secretary of the FDA's parent agency, the Department of Health, Education, and Welfare (HEW). (Thus, the case was originally called *Abbott Laboratories v. Celebrezze*, but it eventually became *Abbott Laboratories v. Gardner* when a new Secretary of HEW, John W. Gardner, took office.) The case was assigned to Judge Caleb Wright.

A front-page story about the suit in the *New York Times* summarized the plaintiffs' objections to the "every time" regulation:

> The suit said . . . that the regulation would result in labels and ads that would confuse the physician.

> It will also cost the companies large sums to destroy present printed matter and the printing plates and to make up new ones. An industry source estimated the cost at "far more than $1,000,000."

> The manufacturers also revived their original complaints against the amendment. They contended that brand names indicate the manufacturers' willingness to stand behind the quality and purity of their products. They also said that drugs with the same generic names might differ in their effect on the patient because of varying inactive ingredients and manufacturing methods.[29]

The plaintiffs' complaint asked for a declaratory judgment that the regulation was invalid and for an injunction forbidding its enforcement.

Although Cutler remained as counsel for PMA in this litigation, the lead counsel for the plaintiffs was Gerhard Gesell, who represented Abbott Laboratories and most of the other individual company plaintiffs. (Gesell, a partner at the Covington & Burling law firm in Washington, was appointed a few years later to be a judge on the federal district court for the District of Columbia.) The government's defense was led by William W. "Billy" Goodrich, the FDA's head counsel, who served the agency for many years and had a reputation for forceful advocacy and aggressive interpretations of the FDA's statutory mandates. He report-

---

28. Richard A. Merrill, *FDA and the Effects of Substantive Rules*, 35 Food Drug Cosm. L.J. 270, 276 (1980).

29. Toth, supra note 24, at 28.

edly "used to quip . . . that there were only three kinds of food and drug law cases: ones the agency won; ones on appeal; and ones decided incorrectly."[30]

Following its common litigating practice, the government deployed an array of technical defenses in an attempt to derail the suit at the outset: (1) that the suit was barred by sovereign immunity; (2) that the Attorney General was an "indispensable" party who had not been joined as a defendant; (3) that the PMA lacked standing to sue; (4) that twenty-six of the thirty-seven plaintiff corporations were suing in the wrong venue because they were not incorporated in Delaware; and (5) that the merits were not yet justiciable. In his decision,[31] Judge Wright easily brushed aside the first three of these arguments, which were weak by 1963 standards (and would be even weaker, if not frivolous, under today's law[32]). The venue defense was stronger—in fact, Judge Wright upheld it.[33] That government victory was, however, completely hollow, because PMA and the Delaware-based companies could and did carry on with the suit, pressing exactly the same issues on the merits that the excluded companies would have raised.

We, of course, are most concerned with the FDA's defense of lack of justiciability or ripeness. In order to put that defense into perspective, we must pause for a bit of doctrinal background.

---

30. Suzanne White Junod, *A Tribute to William H.* [sic] *Goodrich: Legal Counsel Extraordinaire, at* http://www.fda.gov/oc/history/makinghistory/goodrich.html. Goodrich's actual title was Assistant General Counsel, which signified that he was subordinate to the general counsel of the FDA's parent agency, HEW. His successors have borne the less misleading title "Chief Counsel."

31. Abbott Laboratories v. Celebrezze, 228 F. Supp. 855 (D. Del. 1964).

32. In 1976 Congress abolished the defense of sovereign immunity, except in suits for money damages. *See* Pub. L. No. 94–574, 90 Stat. 2721 (1976) (now codified at 5 U.S.C. § 702). The same legislation also abolished for such cases the defense "that the United States is an indispensable party," *id.*, effectively terminating the government's ability to argue in future cases like *Abbott Labs* that the Attorney General must be joined. Finally, under today's law PMA would undoubtedly have standing to sue on behalf of its members. See Hunt v. Wash. State Apple Advertising Comm'n, 432 U.S. 333 (1977).

33. The venue question was a close one. The federal venue statute provided (and still does) that a suit against a federal agency could be brought in any judicial district in which the plaintiff "resides." 28 U.S.C. § 1391(e). At that time, the statute also provided that "[a] corporation may be sued in any judicial district in which it is incorporated or licensed to do business or is doing business, and *such judicial district shall be regarded as the residence of such corporation for venue purposes.*" 28 U.S.C. § 1391(c) (emphasis added). The issue in *Abbott Labs* was whether the latter half of the quoted sentence referred to corporations suing as plaintiffs, or only (like the first half of the sentence) to corporations being sued as defendants. Judge Wright took the narrower view of this language, meaning that the non-Delaware plaintiffs could not qualify for venue under section 1391(e). See generally CHARLES ALAN WRIGHT, THE LAW OF FEDERAL COURTS 247 (4th ed. 1983) (explaining that early cases tended to construe the clause broadly, but eventually the narrow interpretation prevailed). The disputed language was repealed in 1988.

A few doctrinal digressions

1. The FDA's defense was inspired by a body of earlier case law in which notions of judicial restraint had often prompted courts to dismiss suits against administrative agencies as premature. For practitioners of food and drug law, an important case exemplifying the judicial restraint policy was *Helco Products Co. v. McNutt*.[34] Helco planned to sell poppy seeds that had been artificially colored with blue dye, but the Commissioner of Food and Drugs advised the company by letter that he would consider such seeds adulterated. Seeking to contest the Commissioner's determination, Helco sued for a declaratory judgment, but the D.C. Circuit ordered the case dismissed as nonjusticiable. The court noted that the power to enforce the adulteration provisions rested with the Attorney General, who might neither share the Commissioner's view nor be inclined to prosecute on the basis of it. As Professor Louis Jaffe pointed out, the problem with *Helco* was that, although the court based its decision on the absence of a threat of enforcement proceedings, it did not venture any opinion about the actual magnitude of the legal risks facing Helco. Jaffe suggested that a more flexible approach was needed, entailing at least the possibility of judicial intervention through a declaratory judgment action.[35]

The pattern of judicial restraint was by no means uniform. For example, in *Columbia Broadcasting System, Inc. v. United States*,[36] the Federal Communications Commission issued regulations to govern the relationships between radio networks and their station affiliates. The Court, instead of insisting that the rules could be challenged only in a licensing proceeding involving one of the stations, allowed CBS to contest these regulations directly. Similarly, in *United States v. Storer Broadcasting Co.*,[37] the Court permitted Storer to seek direct review of FCC regulations that limited the number of stations it could own. The company did not need to apply for a new station and be turned down. These cases suggested the possibility that the Court was moving toward a more liberal attitude, although they could also be read narrowly as resting on the meaning of the specific statute under which the broadcasters sought review (the Urgent Deficiencies Act of 1913). As we have seen, however, food and drug lawyers tended to believe during the early 1960s that, doctrinal niceties aside, courts would usually bend over backwards to accommodate the FDA and would be loath to enjoin it in a pre-enforcement suit.

In *Abbott Labs*, Goodrich argued that, under the case law, the FDA regulation would become open to review only when "applied to a specific

---

34. 137 F.2d 681 (D.C. Cir. 1943).

35. LOUIS L. JAFFE, JUDICIAL CONTROL OF ADMINISTRATIVE ACTION 414–15 (1965).

36. 316 U.S. 407 (1942).

37. 351 U.S. 192 (1956).

fact situation in an enforcement case." To adjudicate now would be to render an advisory opinion. Responding to Gesell's assertion that the "every time" requirement "absolutely will drive physicians, companies, readers, and everyone else to distraction," Goodrich argued that "in order for you to pass on the validity of what Mr. Gesell has just said, you will have to look at the promotional pieces. That is why we think it is so essential that the application of this regulation await the actual presentation of promotional pieces."[38]

2. Another part of the FDA's argument for lack of ripeness was that the regulations were "interpretive." Some authorities had distinguished for ripeness purposes between rules that had the force of law and rules that did not. According to this argument, the former (so-called "legislative" rules) might be reviewable immediately upon being promulgated, but the latter (so-called "interpretive" rules) should not be. Just a few months before the trilogy lawsuits began, the D.C. Circuit had summed up this position in *American President Lines, Ltd. v. Federal Maritime Commission*:[39] a rule that simply stated an agency's interpretation of a statute and was not binding on anyone was not presently reviewable, "[w]hatever practical or psychological effect [the] rule may have on the conduct of petitioners."

Again, however, the case law was not uniform on this point. The Supreme Court took a more lenient approach in *Frozen Food Express v. United States*.[40] The Interstate Commerce Commission issued what was essentially an interpretive rule, declaring that certain types of frozen foods were not "agricultural" products and thus were not exempt from the Commission's regulatory jurisdiction. Thus, motor carriers that shipped these commodities would have to meet the ICC's licensing requirements or risk criminal penalties. The Court allowed one such carrier to go to court immediately to contest this ruling. Yet the precedential value of this case was debatable. It too could be seen as merely an outgrowth of the Urgent Deficiencies Act, under which it had been decided. On that reading, it would be distinguishable when judicial review of an interpretive rule was sought under more general legislation such as the Administrative Procedure Act (APA)[41] or the Declaratory Judgment Act.[42]

3. Although the *American President Lines* reasoning looked helpful to the FDA's ripeness defense, Goodrich needed to make some delicate

---

38. Transcript of oral argument in district court (excerpted in Joint Appendix at 34, 35, 39–40, Abbott Laboratories v. Gardner, 387 U.S. 136 (1967)).

39. 316 F.2d 419, 421–22 (D.C. Cir. 1963).

40. 351 U.S. 40 (1956).

41. The APA's judicial review provisions were then codified at 5 U.S.C. § 1009 (1958) and are currently found at 5 U.S.C. §§ 701–06 (2000).

42. 28 U.S.C. § 2201.

strategic calculations in deciding how to present this argument. He needed to be mindful of competing considerations that bore more generally on the FDA's rulemaking authority. The "every time" rule had been issued under section 701(a) of the FD&C Act,[43] and this section simply granted the Secretary of HEW (and his delegate the FDA Commissioner) "the authority to promulgate regulations for the efficient enforcement of this [Act]." For many years the conventional wisdom had been that section 701(a) was intended for interpretive and minor housekeeping matters only.[44] When Congress had explicitly conferred legislative rulemaking authority over certain specific matters, in section 701(e) of the Act, it had required the FDA to resort to an elaborate, trial-type hearing in connection with such rules.[45] Now, Goodrich thought the Supreme Court's recent case law might open the door to expanded FDA rulemaking outside this procedural straightjacket. As he later explained,[46] he noticed that in cases such as *Storer Broadcasting*[47] the Court had upheld FCC power to adopt regulations that had significant substantive effect, using a general rulemaking clause that looked a great deal like section 701(a) of the FD&C Act. If section 701(a) were construed in the same fashion, the FDA's powers would be considerably enhanced in the long run. It would mean that the agency could, without having to engage in the cumbersome and burdensome hearing process of section 701(e), adopt across-the-board edicts that would bind an entire industry at once with provisions that would be controlling unless they proved in later litigation to be arbitrary, procedurally flawed, or beyond the agency's statutory authority.[48]

Thus, although Goodrich did call the labeling regulation interpretive for purposes of his ripeness argument, he did not press that characterization very forcefully. As he later explained:

---

43. 21 U.S.C. § 371(a).

44. See Nat'l Ass'n of Pharm. Mfrs. v. FDA, 637 F.2d 877, 880, 886–87 & n.12 (2d Cir. 1981) (Friendly, J.) (citing to sources that had taken this view).

45. 21 U.S.C. § 371(e).

46. Interview with William W. Goodrich, FDA Oral History Program, *at* http://www.fda.gov/oc/history/oralhistories/goodrich/part4.html#701(Oct. 15, 1986).

47. United States v. Storer Broadcasting Co., 351 U.S. 192 (1956), discussed supra note 37 and accompanying text.

48. In a case like *Abbott Labs*, where the disputed regulation was adopted and defended solely on the basis of perceived congressional intent, the difference between an interpretive and a legislative rule might not have been consequential. Either way, courts tend to be fairly independent in their analyses of such contentions. Nevertheless, if the *power* to promulgate legislative rules under section 701(a) were to become established, the FDA would thereafter be able to promulgate numerous other rules that would rest squarely on discretionary determinations that regulated parties would have little hope of challenging successfully.

In arguing this case in Wilmington before the judge, he said to me, "You adopted this as a binding rule, and you have every intention to enforce it?" I said, "Yes, that's true." And he says, "Sounds like it has the force and effect of law." I said, "Judge, if you'll rule that, I'll take my hat, leave, thank you, and be satisfied with it." Well, he then hemmed and hawed, and so did the other side. That was a case [in] which I had nothing to lose. If I got a ruling that the 701(a) rules were binding [and had the] force and effect of law, it was beyond my wildest dream. And so, having said that to the judge—and Judge Gesell was their lawyer again—they about flipped that I would say that. But anyhow, he ruled against me, and didn't touch that issue.[49]

The district court's decision

Judge Wright rejected the government's ripeness defense in a brisk three-paragraph discussion (compared with twenty paragraphs disposing of the other threshold defenses). His main point was that the manufacturers were in a dilemma. "Either they must comply with the every time requirement and incur the costs of changing over their promotional material and labeling or they must follow their present course and risk prosecution." He dismissed the FDA's argument that the government had not taken tangible steps toward enforcement, nor openly threatened it: "Surely, the Commissioner does not announce regulations which he does not intend to enforce by any and every lawful means." And, as the Goodrich quotation indicates, the court bypassed the question of what kind of rule the FDA had issued. Apparently accepting at face value the government's characterization of the rule as "interpretive," Judge Wright cited *Frozen Food*[50] (and a similar court of appeals case) for the proposition that "[p]laintiffs may have judicial review of interpretive regulations upon their promulgation without awaiting some ultimate enforcement."

Judge Wright then turned to the merits, which, he remarked, did "not require as lengthy discussion as [did] negotiation of the procedural maze leading to the merits." Indeed, his reasoning was straightforward. Congress had specified in section 502(e) of the 1962 drug amendments that the established or generic name of a prescription drug on any label must be "printed prominently and in type as least half as large as that used thereon for any proprietary name. . . ." The judge reasoned that if Congress had intended to adopt an "every time" requirement, as the FDA claimed, it could have said so, but it had not. Indeed, if that had

49.   Goodrich oral history interview, supra note 46.

50.   See supra note 40 and accompanying text.

been Congress's intention, "there would be no reason to use the word 'prominently.' "

Nor was the court persuaded by the FDA's reliance on Senator Kefauver's statement to the Senate that, because the Senate language had been retained rather than the House's, "the established name must appear in type at least half as large as the trade name *wherever* the latter is used. . . ."[51] Judge Wright considered the word "wherever" ambiguous, but perhaps his principal point was that the Senator's position was not determinative anyway: "Apparently Kefauver favored the every time requirement. But nowhere in the legislative history is there evidence to show that other members of the Congress favored the every time requirement or that they were aware that 'prominently' should have a special meaning." Although he did not discuss the history of the 1962 legislation in detail, Judge Wright was probably at least generally aware that Kefauver was something of a maverick and not necessarily representative of the entire range of members of Congress who had voted for the Act. Even though the Senator had been the activist who had goaded Congress into adopting the legislation that bore his name, the final product had involved hard-fought compromises and had required the concurrence of numerous members who were, by and large, less zealous than he was.

For better or worse, Judge Wright's ruling turned out to be not only the first judicial decision on the merits of the "every time" regulation, but also the last.

The Third Circuit decision

The government took an appeal to the U.S. Court of Appeals for the Third Circuit, which reversed Judge Wright's decision on the ground that the pharmaceutical companies were not entitled to pre-enforcement judicial review.[52] The appellate court's opinion was written by Gerald J. Weber, a district judge who was sitting by designation on the Third Circuit. He was a relative newcomer to the bench, having taken a seat on the district court for the Western District of Pennsylvania about six months prior to the oral argument of this appeal.

Judge Weber set forth two reasons for withholding judicial review in this case. The first was that Congress had intended to preclude judicial review prior to the enforcement stage. He noted that Congress had created a specific judicial review procedure for rules issued under section 701(e) of the FD&C Act, but it had created no corresponding provision for review of rules issued under section 701(a), such as the prescription

---

51.   108 Cong. Rec. 22039 (1962) (emphasis added); see supra note 19 and accompanying text.

52.   Abbott Laboratories v. Celebrezze, 352 F.2d 286 (3d Cir. 1965).

drug labeling regulation. Second, the case was not appropriate for judicial resolution because of the lack of a "case or controversy." According to Judge Weber, "[t]here must be proof of threatened enforcement action that would cause irreparable harm," and no such threat had been made here.

The court's ripeness analysis left a good deal to be desired. Judge Weber did not attempt to show that there was, in fact, a good chance that the companies would be allowed to violate the rule and get away with it. He simply relied on the absence of an overt "threat" of enforcement. Moreover, although he referred to the pervasive " 'duty of a court of equity to strike a proper balance between the needs of the plaintiff and the consequences of giving the desired relief,' " his evaluation of the "needs of the plaintiff" amounted to little more than pointing out that the companies would be entitled to be heard in full at the enforcement stage.

PMA and the drug companies filed a petition for certiorari with the Supreme Court, which promptly granted it. Our examination of events at that level must, however, await the unfolding of the second plot line in the narrative.

The *Toilet Goods* Litigation

The color additives legislative framework

The two remaining cases in what eventually became known as the *Abbott Labs* trilogy stemmed from a totally separate area of the FDA's regulatory jurisdiction: oversight of color additives.[53] The dyes that manufacturers use to impart pleasing colors to consumer products have been subjects of official scrutiny for more than a century. An early milepost in the federal government's regulatory control was the enactment of the Pure Food and Drugs Act of 1906. It empowered the Secretary of Agriculture to ban unsafe use of synthetic dyes known as coal-tar colors, so-called because they were made from bituminous coal and other petroleum products. The agency now known as the FDA took over the Agriculture Department's regulatory responsibilities in 1927.

In the Food, Drug, and Cosmetic Act of 1938, the FDA's jurisdiction over coal-tar colors was extended to cosmetics, in part because of the "Lash Lure" scandal, in which the public's sympathy was aroused by

---

53. Helpful resources on the development of FDA colors regulation include: Julie N. Barrows et al., *Color Additives: FDA's Regulatory Process and Historical Perspectives*, Food Safety Mag., Oct–Nov. 2003, *available at* www.cfsan.fed.gov/~dms/col-regu.html; Raymond D. McMurray, *Recent Developments Under the Color Additives Amendment*, 19 Food Drug Cosm. L.J. 79 (1964); *Color Additive Amendments of 1960*, 15 Food Drug Cosm. L.J. 432 (1960).

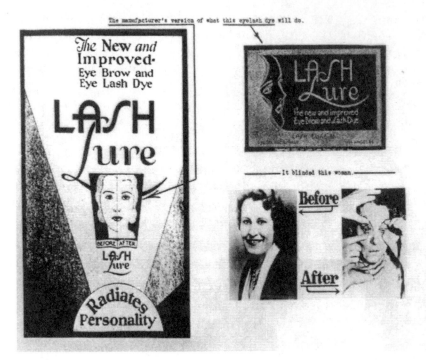

The manufacturer's version of what this eyelash dye will do.

It blinded this woman.

Photo courtesy of FDA History Office

affecting stories of women who had been blinded by an eyelash dye.[54] Moreover, the Act shifted a burden of proof from the government to the manufacturers. Under prior law, the agency could ban a color only by demonstrating that it was unsafe. The 1938 law set up a regime in which manufacturers would need to come forward with proof that their ingredients were safe. A product containing a coal-tar color would be deemed "adulterated" (and thus subject to seizure) unless (1) the FDA had "listed" the relevant color as safe for the purposes for which the manufacturer used it, and (2) FDA inspectors "certified" the particular batch of dye as having been prepared in conformity with the approved listing. The manufacturer's task of arranging for the necessary tests and pursuing a petition to get an ingredient listed was an elaborate and expensive one.[55] (In fact, the FDA used the trial-type hearing processes of section 701(e) of the FD&C Act—the procedures that the agency did *not* use in the *Abbott Labs* rulemaking proceeding.)

---

54. See GWEN KAY, DYING TO BE BEAUTIFUL: THE FIGHT FOR SAFE COSMETICS 1–2, 71–73 (2005); RUTH deFOREST LAMB, AMERICAN CHAMBER OF HORRORS: THE TRUTH ABOUT FOOD AND DRUGS 18–19, 22–23, 37–38 (1936) (discussion of Lash Lure in a muckraking tract published under FDA auspices).

55. McMurray, supra note 53, at 80–81.

It is important to note that the 1938 Act was permissive in its treatment of coal-tar colors used in hair dyes (but not, of course, eyelash dyes). As one author has explained:

> While Congress haggled over the Act, hair-dye manufacturers insisted that they couldn't produce satisfactory dyes without the admittedly dangerous coal-tar colors. They warned Congress that if hair dyes were not exempted, not only would a thriving business that employed many voters be ruined but the hair-dyeing women of America would storm the Capitol. Congress capitulated and coal-tar hair dyes were exempted from all controls, provided they bore a label warning that the product was not to be used on eyelashes or eyebrows, and that a preliminary test was to be made to determine the user's sensitivity to skin irritation from the ingredients.[56]

In the 1950s, pressures for new legislation again became prominent. Consumer advocates particularly noticed several incidents in which children became ill from eating popcorn or Halloween candy containing excessive quantities of dye. Following a party for employees of a chemical company in California in 1955, one hundred fifty-five children experienced nausea, vomiting and headache. An FDA investigation attributed the illness to their having eaten orange-colored popcorn containing the so-called Red Dye No. 32.[57]

In contrast with the pharmaceutical companies' resistance to the Kefauver-Harris Amendments, the colors industry itself also began lobbying for new legislation—for understandable reasons. An important element of the 1938 scheme was the need for the FDA to find a coal-tar color "harmless" in order to list it. The agency might have chosen to apply that term flexibly to prescribe "tolerance" levels. In the Halloween candy situation, for example, the agency might have ruled that the dye was "safe for use" in specified low concentrations, even though excessive use would be unhealthy. Instead, however, the agency interpreted the 1938 Act to mean that *any* toxicity in a coal-tar color, even if detected solely in test animals rather than humans, was enough to foreclose the finding of "harmlessness" and prevent the color from being listed. Much to the industry's consternation, the Supreme Court upheld this position in 1958.[58] Because the FDA had no process for listing colors for limited uses only, it began decertifying various colors entirely. The industry could not accept continuation of this situation and sought legislative relief.

---

56. Toni Stabile, *Adventures in the Skin Trade*, The Nation, Jan. 1, 1968, at 16, 17.

57. This information appears in an attachment to a 1956 letter by Goodrich, which was obtained from the FDA archives. *See infra* note 61.

58. Flemming v. Florida Citrus Exchange, 358 U.S. 153 (1958).

In the Color Additives Amendments of 1960,[59] the industry got the principle of tolerances restored, but it had to accept expansion of the FDA's authority in other ways. The new statutory scheme covered not only coal-tar colors but all synthetic colors. Indeed, the term "coal-tar colors" disappeared from the FD&C Act and was replaced by the broad term "color additives." The industry was allowed to continue using color additives that were already "commercially established," but only on a provisional basis. After a transitional period, manufacturers would be prohibited from using any of these established colors as well, except pursuant to specific approval of that additive by the FDA.

Probably the most controversial feature of the 1960 law was its extension of the so-called Delaney Clause. The clause, which had been added to the Food Additive Act of 1958 at the instance of Representative James Delaney of New York, prohibited the FDA from listing any food additive that was found to induce cancer in humans or animals. The debate in 1960 was whether to extend the Delaney Clause to cosmetics (other than hair dyes). The Senate's bill did not go that far, but proponents of the clause found greater support in the House. One focus of debate was the finding that lipsticks had caused cancer in rats. An industry chemist testified that a woman would have to eat 100 lipsticks per day to be exposed to an equivalent risk. But the argument that one cannot take chances with carcinogens won the day in the House. Among the proponents was Representative Leonor Sullivan of Missouri, a long-time consumer advocate, who wore "a light, bright shade of lipstick" and remarked that she didn't know whether it was safe.[60] Ultimately, the Senate yielded. The bill, including the Delaney Clause, was signed into law on July 12, 1960.

The rulemaking proceeding[61]

Six months later, in January 1961, the FDA published and invited comment on proposed rules to implement the color additives legislation.[62] Again it used its rulemaking authority under section 701(a), rather than the more cumbersome procedures of section 701(e). Filling nearly ten pages in the *Federal Register*, the rules spelled out the agency's tentative understanding of the scope of the new statute, as well as detailed procedures for submitting petitions for obtaining FDA approval of color additives. Apparently some features of the rules were not directly re-quired by the recent amendments but were instead prompted by a desire

---

59. Pub. L. No. 86–618, 74 Stat. 397 (1960).

60. William M. Blair, *Cancer Guard Due in Additives Bill*, N.Y. TIMES, Jan. 28, 1960, at 1.

61. Documents underlying the discussion in this section were obtained from the FDA archives, Accession No. 88–78–36, box 47, and are on file with the author.

62. 26 Fed. Reg. 679 (1961).

to modernize and strengthen the agency's color additives regulatory regime. Perhaps because of the numerous issues the new proposals raised, the agency did not publish its final rules until two and a half years later, in June 1963.[63] (Indeed, those rules came out a few days after the prescription drug labeling regulation that was at issue in *Abbott Labs*, even though the Color Additives Amendments had been enacted in 1960 and the Kefauver law in 1962.)

During the rulemaking process, comments from various users of color additives flowed in. In some instances the agency and manufacturing interests were able to resolve or narrow their differences. An attorney for the Grain Processing Corporation protested a paragraph in which the FDA contemplated defining "color additive" to include "an ingredient of an animal feed which by its action through the biological process of the animal is capable of imparting color to the meat, milk, or eggs of the animal."[64] Did this mean, he asked, that grain that is fed to chickens (sometimes imparting a yellow color to the eggs) would be a "color additive"? If so, the live chicken to which the grain was "added" might be a "food" that would be subject to seizure by FDA inspectors, along with other poultry, beef cattle, etc. Yet, he argued, the duty of setting standards of quality for live animals was far outside the FDA's historic mission and would invade the turf of the Agriculture Department, a result that Congress surely had not contemplated. The FDA was apparently persuaded. It narrowed this portion of its definition to encompass only animal feed ingredients that were *intended* to induce color.

The draft regulations also provided that the hair dye exemption would not apply (and therefore the color additive requirements *would* apply) to dual purpose hair products such as color shampoos.[65] An attorney for Clairol met with Goodrich and maintained that his client could not produce such products on those terms. On a return visit, he presented Goodrich with copies of magazine advertisements for Clairol multiple purpose products, published in 1937. The ads proved, he claimed, that Congress was aware of these products when it passed the hair-dye exemption in the FD&C Act and could not have wanted to ban them. Heeding this critique, the FDA modified the regulations so that dual purpose shampoos would be governed by roughly the same principles as other hair dyes.[66]

---

63.   28 Fed. Reg. 6439 (11963).

64.   21 C.F.R. § 8.1(f). The attorney's letters were dated November 21 and 23, 1960, almost two months *before* the FDA published its proposed rules. He had evidently been given access to a working draft.

65.   21 C.F.R. § 8.1(v) (as proposed).

66.   21 C.F.R. § 8.1(u) (as adopted).

Another issue, however, proved less tractable. An attorney for Helena Rubinstein, Inc., filed rulemaking comments on February 21, 1961, protesting the FDA's proposed definition of "color additives" as far too broad.[67] In that definition, the term color additives did not refer only to "straight colors"—the dyes and pigments that actually imparted color. It also included "diluents." That term was commonly used to mean an ingredient, such as talc or chalk, that was combined with a color to dilute it or add volume to a cosmetic product. Furthermore, the definition provided that a finished product itself could be classified as a color additive if "intended" to color the human body. Rubinstein's lawyer acknowledged that the FDA should be able to ban diluents, or for that matter cosmetic products, that turned out to be unsafe. She insisted, however, that manufacturers should not have to subject these materials to the elaborate premarketing clearance procedures that Congress had designed for "straight colors."

David J. Miller, a staff lawyer in the Commissioner's office, had been the principal draftsman of the color additive regulations. He was inclined to agree with the Rubinstein critique and prepared a redraft to accommodate it. Goodrich, however, was dissatisfied with Miller's new position. He wrote a memorandum to Commissioner Larrick on September 7, 1962, to argue that "this is not near enough." It would mean that FDA inspectors who encountered colors in mixtures would have a more complicated task of determining whether the ingredients were properly listed as safe. He pointed out that the statutory definition of "color additive" referred to a "substance" intended for coloring the human body. "Literally," he said, "this applies to lipstick and rouge," and "we have both the right and responsibility to regulate that class of cosmetics now." (The details of the interpretive questions raised in this jurisdictional dispute will be covered later;[68] for now, suffice it to say that Goodrich's position was a good example of his characteristic boldness.)

Two weeks later, on September 20, a group of FDA officials met to discuss the issue. Deputy Commissioner John Harvey agreed with Goodrich that Miller's solution was too narrow. He argued that if, in the final stages of producing a "soda pop," a manufacturer added a color mixture consisting of a color, propylene, and an emulsifier, the entire mixture would be a "color additive." Despite a "sharp difference of opinion" at the conference, as Miller later reported to Larrick, the officials ultimately followed Goodrich's lead. In the final published regulations, the agency left no doubt about its rejection of the modification requested by Helena Rubinstein. It even added a new sentence to the rules: "Lip-

---

67. 21 C.F.R. § 8.1(f) (as proposed).

68. See infra notes 118–21 and accompanying text.

sticks, rouge, eye makeup colors, and related cosmetics intended for coloring the human body are 'color additives.' "[69]

Accompanying the final rules was an FDA press release, which included the following passage:

Commissioner of Food and Drugs George P. Larrick pointed out the following specific changes in existing procedures and interpretations which he said would strengthen consumer protection from possibly unsafe colors:

1. Additional safety precautions are provided for lipsticks, rouge, eyebrow and lash color and other substances that apply to the human body. Under the new regulations, FDA will require that an entire product—not just the color ingredient—be shown by the manufacturer to be safe before it is released for sale.

Previously only color of the coal tar type ingredients had been subject to the requirement for pre-marketing proof of safety.

Commissioner Larrick said the new requirement is based on the language in the law and the legislative intent to insure that the entire formulation of a "color additive" is safe for the consumer.

2. The language of the regulation dealing with exemption of hair dyes from the safety clearance and certification requirement has been clarified to show that the "patch test" requirement applies only to hair dyes which are dangerous because the user may be sensitive to them.[70]

Commissioner Larrick said that the exemption in the 1938 law was conditioned on a labeling requirement calling for the use of a patch test to determine whether the user is sensitive to the color before hair dye is applied. The patch testing requirement offers no protection from other types of toxicity, Commissioner Larrick said, and the purpose of the new regulation is to close this gap. Hair dyes that do not cause a reaction with the patch test must now be demonstrated to be safe before they can be marketed.

3. The regulations provide that FDA may refuse to certify a color additive—and thus in effect ban it from the market—if the manufacturer refuses FDA inspectors access to manufacturing facilities, processes, and formulas involved in manufacture of the additive.[71]

This provision does not represent a change in policy, Commissioner Larrick said, but the new regulations spell out the policy

69. 21 C.F.R. § 8.1(f) (as adopted).

70. See 21 C.F.R. § 8.1(u).

71. See 21 C.F.R. § 8.28(a)(4).

more specifically. He said that the FDA cannot determine whether the conditions for safe use of color additives, including products exempt from certification, are being met unless a complete inspection of the plant and formulas can be made.[72]

Although the press release went on to highlight other features of the new rules, the excerpt just quoted was an apt summary of the provisions that were about to become embroiled in litigation.

The district court proceedings

Toilet Goods Ass'n v. Celebrezze[73] was filed on November 15, 1963, in the federal court for the Southern District of New York, which sits in Manhattan. The lead plaintiff, the Toilet Goods Association (TGA), was the trade organization of the cosmetics industry. The organization had been founded as the Manufacturing Perfumers' Association in 1894.[74] Its initial function was to resist the enactment of tariffs on substances that the cosmetics industry used to make perfumes and toilet goods, but its lobbying role soon expanded. One of its early successes came during the Prohibition era. By persuading Congress to exempt products "unfit for use of beverage purposes" from the legislation that enforced the Eighteenth Amendment, the association protected its members' ability to use alcohol as a raw material. The association also arranged for exhibits at the Cosmetics Pavilion at the New York World's Fair in 1939 and organized a committee during World War II to develop substitutes for scarce materials. At the time of the *Toilet Goods* suit, the membership of TGA included manufacturers that accounted for more than ninety percent of sales of cosmetics in the United States.[75]

TGA's lawyers foresaw (accurately, as it turned out) that the government might contest the association's standing to sue on behalf of its members. Out of an abundance of caution, therefore, they arranged for forty individual manufacturers of cosmetics to join the suit as co-plaintiffs.[76] These companies' ranks included such well known names as Avon Products, Inc.; Christian Dior Perfumes Corp.; Clairol Incorporated; Fabergé Inc.; the Gillette Company; Helena Rubinstein, Inc.; Helene Curtis Industries, Inc.; John H. Breck, Inc.; Max Factor & Co.; Maybelline Co., and Revlon, Inc. For simplicity's sake, however, the following narrative discusses the suit as though TGA had been the only plaintiff.

---

72. Joint Appendix at 106–07, Toilet Goods Ass'n v. Gardner, 387 U.S. 158 (1967).

73. 235 F. Supp. 648 (S.D.N.Y. 1964).

74. The historical material in this paragraph is taken from *A Centennial History of CTFA, at* www.ctfa.org/Content/NavigationMenu/About_CTFA/History/History.htm.

75. The organization remains active today under its current name, the Cosmetic, Toiletry, and Fragrance Association.

76. Telephone interview with Stephen R. Lang (counsel for TGA), April 21, 2005.

    TGA argued in its complaint that the extensions of FDA authority
that were outlined in the portions of the press release quoted above were
all unauthorized.[77] The premarketing clearance envisioned by the 1960
law was required only for "color additives." Echoing Helena Rubinstein's position during the rulemaking proceeding, TGA alleged that this
term referred only to the specific ingredient that added color to the
product. If, as the FDA claimed, diluents or finished products were
themselves "color additives," the manufacturer would have to present
studies and applications for a much wider range of substances, at great
expense. TGA also contended that the FDA had misread the hair dye
exemption. The 1938 Act provided a flat exemption for coal-tar hair dyes
if the manufacturer provided the label warning spelled out in the statute
itself; the agency had no authority to limit that exemption. Finally, the
complaint sounded alarm bells about the inspection provisions of the
regulation. They would force manufacturers to provide their processes
and formulas to FDA inspectors or face the great inconvenience of
having their certification services suspended. Since any batch of dye had
to be certified before it could be used, this would effectively bring
significant manufacturing operations to a halt. To avoid such a fate,
manufacturers would have to risk exposure of their secret formulas if
the FDA disclosed them—a prospect that could result in great competitive disadvantages. TGA's complaint sought a declaratory judgment and
injunction against all of these violations.

    Handling the *Toilet Goods* case for the government was Arthur S.
Olick, who was then the chief of the Civil Division in the U.S. Attorney's
Office for the Southern District of New York. He recalls the broad
independence that the Department of Justice typically accorded to lawyers from that office.[78] Indeed, in this particular case, Goodrich sought to
manage the litigation, as he was accustomed to doing in FDA cases, but
senior Department officials backed up Olick's prerogatives.[79] It may not
have mattered, however. Olick presently filed a motion to dismiss the
TGA complaint, deploying almost exactly the same set of defenses that
the government had invoked in *Abbott Labs*: improper venue, sovereign
immunity, failure to join the Attorney General as a defendant, lack of
standing, and lack of justiciability or ripeness.

    The judge assigned to the case was Harold L. Tyler, Jr. Before his
appointment he had been a colleague and friend of Olick's in the U.S.
Attorney's Office for the Southern District. But any supposition that the

---

    77. The complaint is reprinted in Joint Appendix at 1, Toilet Goods Ass'n v. Gardner,
387 U.S. 158 (1967).

    78. Telephone interview with Arthur S. Olick, April 15, 2005.

    79. Lang interview, *supra* note 76.

government might get favored treatment in this case was wholly dispelled by the court's ruling on the motion.

On the specific issue of justiciability, Judge Tyler followed the lead of the district court opinion in *Abbott Labs*, which had been handed down several months earlier. He reasoned that the key issue, for purposes of the Declaratory Judgment Act, was whether or not the plaintiffs were threatened with irreparable injury that a declaration of rights could alleviate. That criterion was satisfied by the fact that the "regulations force manufacturers to choose between complying with them, at a cost that may prove to be prohibitive for some of the plaintiffs, or ignoring them at the risk of incurring the statutory penalties should the regulations later be held valid." He found that the defendants' "technical distinction" between legislative and interpretive regulations was "difficult and indeed inappropriate" as a basis for resolving the issue.

Judge Tyler went on to reject all of the government's other threshold defenses. He even rejected the venue objection, which had been sustained in *Abbott Labs*; the courts in the Southern District had consistently construed the venue statute more broadly. Accordingly, he directed the parties to prepare for trial.

About a year later, when those preparations were nearly complete, the Third Circuit announced its decision ordering the *Abbott Labs* suit dismissed as nonjusticiable. Olick filed a motion asking Judge Tyler to reconsider his earlier ruling in *Toilet Goods* in light of that decision. The judge reaffirmed his prior position but agreed to certify the case for interlocutory appeal to the Court of Appeals for the Second Circuit.[80]

The Second Circuit decision

The court of appeals affirmed Judge Tyler's decision in most but not all respects.[81] Indeed, the Second Circuit's opinion, which was written by Judge Henry Friendly for a three-judge panel, was a critical step in the development of the ripeness doctrine. It set forth most of the intellectual framework that would later be incorporated into the Supreme Court's decisions in the *Abbott Labs* trilogy. With one notable exception,[82] authorities on administrative law do not seem to have noticed this connection. One could read a host of modern commentaries on the trilogy without encountering a single acknowledgment of the extent to which Justice Harlan, the Court's spokesman, borrowed his reasoning from the opinion of the court of appeals in *Toilet Goods*.

---

80. See 28 U.S.C. § 1292(b) (authorizing interlocutory appeal on a controlling legal issue if the district court and court of appeals both agree to permit it, in their discretion).

81. Toilet Goods Ass'n v. Gardner, 360 F.2d 677 (2d Cir. 1966).

82. A. Raymond Randolph, *Administrative Law and the Legacy of Henry J. Friendly*, 74 NYU L. Rev. 1, 8–11 (1999).

That Judge Friendly was the jurist who became an intellectual guide for the Court on this issue is not very surprising, however. His insights and scholarship made him one of the most widely admired figures in the federal judiciary during the 1960s and 1970s. He also had a strong interest in administrative law and made a number of enduring contributions to the field.[83] More specifically, he became one of the most influential voices encouraging agencies to make broader use of rulemaking in their work.[84] Indeed, his *Toilet Goods* opinion framed the ripeness problem in exactly that context: "The current healthy trend toward implementing agency policy by rule-making cuts both ways with respect to declaratory relief—increasing the need for this sort of assistance on the part of those subjected to such rules, but also creating a danger that, unless the courts are circumspect, administration may be improperly halted, at least temporarily, before it has gotten the slightest start."

In this case, Judge Friendly set forth his analysis of pre-enforcement review of regulations in several steps. First, he considered the statutory context and rejected the conclusion of the Third Circuit in *Abbott Labs* that the FD&C Act itself indicated that Congress had foreclosed pre-enforcement judicial review of a regulation issued under section 701(a) of the Act. Next, he argued that the issue of ripeness or justiciability "is not to be solved ... by applying some readily procurable litmus paper," but instead calls for "a reasoned evaluation of 'both the appropriateness of the issues for decision by courts and the hardship of denying judicial relief.'" He derived this latter formula from a 1951 opinion of Justice Felix Frankfurter,[85] as elaborated in the writings of Professor Jaffe.[86] The "appropriateness" of immediate judicial review depends, he continued, on "such factors as how far the rule represents the definitive position of the agency and the extent to which the challenge raises a clearcut legal issue susceptible of judicial solution without reference to fact variables arising in its implementation." All of this language soon found its way into Justice Harlan's opinion, barely revised.

Applying these principles to the facts of *Toilet Goods*, Judge Friendly said that the FDA's elaborate rulemaking procedure demonstrated that the agency had reached a definitive position. Moreover, it seemed likely that the question of whether the premarketing requirements in the regulations were consistent with the Act, as applied to broad categories like finished products, diluents, and hair dyes, could be analyzed just

---

83. See id. at 4–5, 8–15.

84. See HENRY J. FRIENDLY, THE FEDERAL ADMINISTRATIVE AGENCIES: THE NEED FOR BETTER DEFINITION OF STANDARDS (1962).

85. Joint Anti–Fascist Refugee Committee v. McGrath, 341 U.S. 123, 156 (1951) (Frankfurter, J., concurring).

86. See JAFFE, supra note 35, at 397, 410, 423.

as reliably in the district court proceedings in this case as in a subsequent individualized proceeding. The issues "appear, *prima facie*, to be susceptible of reasoned comparison with the statutory mandate without inquiry into factual issues that ought to be first ventilated before the agency." This conclusion was, however, only provisional: if such fact issues did emerge, the court would not have to proceed to judgment.

When he turned to the issue of the degree of hardship impinging on the plaintiffs, warranting declaratory relief, Judge Friendly's analysis was not very different from the arguments that Judges Wright and Tyler had made earlier. He recognized that, realistically speaking, the regulations had an immediate impact on the companies, forcing them to comply or face possible penalties. He saw no reason to debate whether the rules were legislative or interpretive, because the rules would have this sort of impact even if they were deemed interpretive. Early clarification of the rules' legality would serve both the public's interest and that of the companies.

Finally, Judge Friendly reached a contrasting conclusion with regard to the part of the rule that required manufacturers to open their facilities to FDA inspectors or face a possible suspension of certification services. The risks to the plaintiffs seemed highly remote, the court said, for no one could say whether the FDA would actually demand access to formulas, whether manufacturers would resist, or what sanction the FDA would pursue under those circumstances. Moreover, the court said that it was unwilling to assume that the agency could never have authority to suspend certification to force a manufacturer to reveal its processes. Therefore, a judgment as to the circumstances in which the agency could permissibly exercise such power would require a factual record and should await further experience. Judge Friendly's isolation of the access portion of the regulation for discrete treatment was entirely original with him—neither of the parties had raised such a possibility.[87] At the Supreme Court level, this separate treatment would prove crucial.

Because TGA and the FDA had each won in part and lost in part in the Second Circuit, both filed certiorari petitions in the Supreme Court. As a result, the *Toilet Goods* proceeding fissioned into two cases. The government's appeal from the Second Circuit's decision to allow immediate judicial review of the rules on the color additives definition and the hair dye exemption acquired the caption *Gardner v. Toilet Goods Association*. In the remainder of this narrative, it will be called the *Gardner* case. Meanwhile, industry's appeal from the Second Circuit's refusal to reach the merits of the access regulation was designated *Toilet Goods Association v. Gardner* and will be called the *Toilet Goods* case here. The

87. Lang interview, supra note 76.

Court granted both petitions and scheduled the cases to be argued together with *Abbott Labs.*

The Supreme Court Proceedings

The oral argument

The Court held oral argument on the ripeness cases on January 16, 1967. Justice Abe Fortas knew the drug industry well from years of private practice, and the questions he posed dominated the argument.[88] He was evidently troubled by the problem of how to "draw the line between administrative actions reviewable in an injunction suit and administrative actions not so reviewable." In fact, he posed variations on this question to all of the participating counsel. He suggested that a ruling for the plaintiffs would, for example, open the door to immediate judicial review whenever the FDA decided that a specific drug was dangerous. Nathan Lewin, the lawyer from the U.S. Solicitor General's office who was arguing the government's side, was quick to encourage this apprehension: "There would be nothing to prevent any drug company from bringing proceedings against any other ruling of the Food and Drug Administration." Edward J. Ross, counsel for TGA, was apparently not sure how to respond to Fortas's concerns. He acknowledged that, in Fortas's hypothetical case, the court would need the expertise of the agency.

Gesell fielded Fortas's question somewhat more successfully. He had to concede, when pressed, that his complaint did "raise a question of reasonableness of the regulation." However, he went on to say, the Commissioner considered his own regulation to be "the only possible interpretation of the statute." Here Gesell had arrived at the crucial point by which Fortas's hypothetical had to be distinguished. The gist of his case was an attack on the "reasonableness" of the FDA's understanding of *what Congress had meant.* This line of argument set the stage for the Court's ultimate holding that the drug companies' suit was susceptible of immediate review because it would turn exclusively on questions of congressional intent.

After the argument, Lewin felt confident.[89] Initially, when he had assumed responsibility for the briefing of the cases, he had thought that the FDA was likely to lose. After working on the briefs and speaking with lawyers from the FDA and Justice Department, however, he had come to believe in the merit of his case, as advocates often do. Now he expected the Court to agree with him. Stephen Lang, one of the lawyers for TGA, read the Court differently. It looked to him as though the

---

88. See *Arguments Before the Court*, 35 U.S.L.W. 3249 (1967).

89. Telephone interview with Nathan Lewin, April 11, 2005.

Court was poised to rule in his clients' favor.[90] Actually, however, the situation was more fluid than either of these adversaries supposed.

Behind the scenes

The Justices met in conference to discuss the cases on January 20 and found themselves deeply divided.[91] Justice William O. Douglas's handwritten notes from the conference discussion of *Abbott Labs* have survived and are particularly interesting for the light they shed on the reasons why some of the Justices favored the government's side. The notes suggest that these Justices' main concern was that the FDA should be free to pursue a worthy initiative. Justice Fortas thought that "if we hold there is standing FDA will not be able to put into effect any regulation for 5 to 10 years."[92] Chief Justice Earl Warren, by Douglas's account, was also disposed to support the FDA: "very vital area— delegation to Bureau is not unreasonable—it has the right to do this— medical ads need regulation." Justice Byron White "agrees with CJ [Chief Justice Warren]." A more legalistic argument was that of Justice Tom C. Clark, a former Attorney General, who minimized the companies' problems: "to reverse forces US behind the 8 ball—resp [FDA] does not sue—only the AG [Attorney General] and when he does all these questions can be answered."

On the other side were four Justices who favored reversing the Third Circuit's judgment and allowing pre-enforcement review. Among them was Justice Harlan, who said that this result followed "a fortiori [from] *Frozen Food*."[93] What makes this comment especially intriguing is that Harlan had filed a solitary dissent in *Frozen Food*. Now, instead of staging a rear-guard action to regain lost territory, he was accepting the case and trying to build on it. Justices Hugo Black, Potter Stewart, and Douglas himself also voted to reverse, although Douglas's notes do not explain their reasons. The lineup on each side in the two color additives cases was identical. The ninth Justice, William J. Brennan, Jr., did not

---

90. Lang interview, supra note 76. Lang thought, however, that Justice Fortas had questioned his co-counsel, Ross, with particular vigor during the argument. The interrogation amused those in the courtroom who were aware that Fortas and Ross had known each other for many years, having been colleagues as student editors on the *Yale Law Journal*. The aggressiveness of Fortas's questioning looked as though it might reflect the continuation of an old law school rivalry. Id.

91. The discussion in this section is based on papers on the trilogy cases in the William O. Douglas and Earl Warren manuscript collections in the Library of Congress. Relevant documents are on file with the author.

92. "Standing" was an imprecise term here, but it is impossible to know whether the imprecision was committed by Fortas or Douglas.

93. He added, according to Douglas's notes, that the venue question was very difficult, and the Court should refrain from deciding it. His ultimate opinion for the Court adopted that solution.

participate in any of the three cases because his son worked at Breed, Abbott & Morgan, the New York City law firm that represented the Toilet Goods Association.[94]

The 4–4 split in each of the three cases created a highly unsatisfactory situation. The Supreme Court's consistent practice in the event of an evenly divided vote is to affirm the judgment below, with no opinion being written either supporting or opposing the merits of that outcome. This disposition is always frustrating, because the Court becomes unable to speak in a case that was originally deemed worthy of its consideration, and also because a great deal of effort will have been expended on all sides to no effect. In this instance the standard practice would have had a much worse result than usual, because it would have meant affirming the *mutually incompatible* decisions of the Second and Third Circuits. The mixed judicial signals regarding the availability of pre-enforcement review of agency regulations would have persisted indefinitely. The need for some sort of compromise or accommodation must have been evident.

One aspect of the impasse was resolved during the conference, or perhaps just after it. Justice Harlan switched his position and voted to affirm in *Toilet Goods*.[95] By supporting the Second Circuit's denial of immediate review of the portion of the color additives rule that required FDA access to factories, he became the first Justice to endorse treating any of the cases in the trilogy differently from the other two cases. Undoubtedly, Judge Friendly's careful discussion in the court of appeals made clear to him how he could arrive at such a position notwithstanding his views on *Abbott Labs* and *Gardner*. The following Monday, Warren assigned to Harlan the task of writing for the Court in *Toilet Goods*. That choice was what one would expect—Chief Justices often assign a case to the "least persuaded" Justice in order to help ensure that the ensuing opinion will be one that all members of the majority can support. Accordingly, Harlan got to work and circulated a draft of *Toilet*

---

94. The reasons for a Justice's recusal are generally not publicly announced, but Douglas's conference notes on *Toilet Goods* and *Gardner* state that this was the reason. Indeed, William J. Brennan III did practice with the Breed Abbott firm for several years following his graduation from Yale Law School in 1962.

95. Harlan's change of vote can be inferred from Douglas's docket sheet in *Toilet Goods*. (The docket sheets were printed forms that listed the names of each Justice and provided columns in which a member of the Court could tabulate colleagues' votes on his own copy for any given case.) Across from Harlan's name, an arrow has been used to move a check mark from the "REV" column to the "AFF" column. Moreover, in Douglas's handwritten notes of the Justices' tentative votes, the word "reverses" next to Harlan's name is crossed out and the word "affirms" written above it. Warren's docket sheet provides further confirmation. A check mark for Harlan in the REV column is erased and a check for AFF inserted. Above the tabulation, the words "4 to 4" are crossed out and "affirm" written above them, reflecting the changed disposition permitted by Harlan's switch.

Goods on February 8. The draft stated, without elaboration, that the other two cases were being affirmed by an equally divided Court. It then went on to justify dismissal on ripeness grounds of the portion of TGA's complaint that dealt with the access rule.

The Justices must have been aware, however, that this resolution was still very awkward. From the parties' standpoint, the access provision of the color additives regulation was by far the least important issue in the cases—indeed, little more than an afterthought. It had not been particularly controversial during the FDA's rulemaking proceedings, nor had it gotten much attention in the briefs. The rules involved in the other two cases, *Abbott Labs* and *Gardner*, were not only more consequential, but also more typical of the kinds of regulations that would be likely to trigger efforts to obtain pre-enforcement review. The pressure to find a more definitive solution must still have been strong.

The logjam was broken at the Court's conference on February 10. Justice White, who had previously supported the government's side, now voted with the companies in *Abbott Labs* and *Gardner*, creating a five-Justice majority in favor of immediate judicial review in those cases.[96] Because Chief Justice Warren was now in the minority, the task of assigning the opinions in these two cases fell to the senior Justice in the majority, Justice Black. He assigned the cases to Harlan on February 13.

By March 10 Harlan circulated drafts in *Abbott Labs* and *Gardner* as well as a revised *Toilet Goods* opinion. These drafts underwent no significant further evolution before the Court announced its final opinions the following May. The dissenters, however, had to decide how to respond. Justice Fortas wrote an extensive opinion for the pro-FDA bloc of Justices, and Justice Clark wrote a brief dissent as well. But no dissenting opinion expounding the opposite perspective ever materialized. Stewart and Black eventually switched their votes in *Toilet Goods* and joined Harlan's opinion for the Court. Douglas, the sole remaining dissenter in that case, simply asked Harlan to append a statement noting that he agreed with the reasoning of Judge Tyler's opinion in the district court.[97]

The majority opinions

Because Justice Harlan's opinions for the Court in the trilogy cases are well known to practitioners and students of administrative law, a

---

96. This switch is borne out by Warren's docket sheets in the two cases. On each of them, a check mark in the AFF column for White is erased, and a check mark in the REV column is annotated with the date "2/10." Similarly, the notes on Douglas's docket sheets use arrows to indicate White's changed votes.

97. Douglas's one-sentence memo requesting this explanation is in his file on *Toilet Goods*.

brief summary of their contents should suffice here. In the main opinion, *Abbott Labs*,[98] Harlan set forth a concise formula for assessing ripeness in the absence of congressional guidance: "The problem is best seen in a twofold aspect, requiring us to evaluate both the fitness of the issues for judicial decision and the hardship to the parties of withholding court consideration." As we have seen, this "twofold" test was drawn almost verbatim from Judge Friendly's opinion in *Toilet Goods*, which in turn relied on the work of Justice Frankfurter and Louis Jaffe. It signaled the Court's endorsement of a basically discretionary and pragmatic approach to the matter of justiciability or ripeness, without reference to any general predisposition to avoid judicial review if possible.

Applying these criteria to *Abbott Labs* and *Gardner*,[99] Harlan found that the issues presented were "fit" for judicial decision and that the impact of the rules on the parties warranted immediate judicial consideration of those issues. The companies' need to choose between costly compliance and the risk of significant penalties placed them in a "dilemma" that satisfied the "hardship" component of the formula. In *Toilet Goods*[100] Harlan reached the opposite conclusion on both criteria. The companies' "dilemma" was less compelling in this context because they were not obliged to do anything immediately.

The legal literature contains many critiques of the trilogy on a doctrinal level,[101] and this chapter, with its storytelling emphasis, is not an appropriate place for another such effort. However, the above discussion of the Court's internal deliberations does lead naturally to a few observations about the scope of the opinions. The difficulty that the Court experienced in assembling a majority in favor of ripeness in *Abbott Labs* and *Gardner* would lead one to expect narrowly written opinions in those cases. And, sure enough, the Court's treatment of "fitness" in those opinions was consistent with such an expectation. In *Abbott Labs*, Harlan stated that the "fitness" criterion for ripeness was satisfied in view of the "purely legal" nature of the issue tendered by the parties. By this he did not mean that *any* "purely legal" issue would satisfy the fitness criterion. The controlling factor in *Abbott Labs* was that "both sides have approached this case as one purely of congressional intent,

---

98. Abbott Laboratories v. Gardner, 387 U.S. 136 (1967). The *Abbott Labs* opinion is also famous in administrative law circles for its broad language ascribing a "basic presumption of judicial review" to the Administrative Procedure Act and announcing that "only upon a showing of 'clear and convincing evidence' of a contrary legislative intent should the courts restrict access to judicial review." In order to keep the focus of this story on ripeness, the Court's teachings on the issue of preclusion of judicial review will not be discussed in this chapter.

99. Gardner v. Toilet Goods Ass'n, 387 U.S. 167 (1967).

100. Toilet Goods Ass'n v. Gardner, 387 U.S. 158 (1967).

101. For a sampling, see sources cited infra at notes 152–54.

and ... the Government made no effort to justify the regulation in factual terms." Similarly, in *Gardner*, Harlan declared that the issues were susceptible of judicial review because they *apparently* could be answered on the basis of the statute and without factual investigation from an enforcement proceeding. To be on the safe side, however, he added in a footnote that this conclusion was only provisional, inasmuch as the case had arisen on a motion to dismiss. A "different question" would arise if such a fact issue did emerge later.

Attention to the precise reasoning by which the Court found "fitness" in two of the cases has the incidental benefit of helping to explain the Court's contrasting conclusion in the third. In *Toilet Goods*, Harlan acknowledged that in a sense the companies were raising a "purely legal" question about the access regulation, namely, "whether the regulation is totally beyond the agency's power under the statute." Nevertheless, he continued, the statute involved was the general rulemaking clause, section 701(a), which authorized the FDA to issue regulations "for the efficient enforcement" of the FD&C Act. To decide whether the access regulation violated this statute, the Court would need to know more about "what types of enforcement problems are encountered by the FDA, the need for various sorts of supervision in order to effectuate the goals of the Act, and the safeguards devised to protect legitimate trade secrets." That information was not now before the Court but presumably could be assembled in an evidentiary record during an enforcement proceeding. Justice Harlan did not clearly articulate the relevance of this information to the present case. Judge Friendly, in the opinion below, had been more explicit: The proposition that the Act on its face foreclosed the FDA from instituting inspection measures, including sanctions for lack of cooperation, was simply not credible. Thus, the plaintiffs' only real hope of prevailing on their challenge would lie in their building a record that would demonstrate an abuse of power by the agency—a line of attack that could be loosely called "interpretation" but would in substance amount to assessing the reasonableness of the agency's implementation of its authority. Given the problems that had been highlighted during the oral argument, the Court was by no means prepared in 1967 to extend the domain of pre-enforcement review that far.

Strikingly, Justice Harlan's opinion appeared to resolve, and in the FDA's favor, the question about section 701(a) authority that had been so delicately handled below. While describing the pressure that the "every time" regulation exerted on drug manufacturers, he commented in passing that the regulations "have the status of law."[102] This made it appear that, unlike every court that had previously ruled in any of the trilogy cases, the Court had concluded that the labeling regulation was a

---

102. Id. at 152.

"legislative" rule as distinguished from an "interpretive" rule. Neither
party had so characterized the rule. The government's briefs called it
interpretive; the plaintiffs agreed with Judge Friendly and other judges
that the rule did not have to be classified, because either type of rule
could, as a practical matter, create the kind of "hardship" that a proper
ripeness analysis should heed. Probably Justice Harlan's language was
just a slip, and he meant only to follow the plaintiffs' position on this
issue. As written, however, the opinion seemed to be saying, contrary to
the then-conventional wisdom,[103] that the FDA had power to issue
legislative rules under section 701(a), the FD&C Act's general rulemaking clause. This would permit FDA attorney Goodrich, years later, to
claim that the agency had effectively *won* the *Abbott Labs* case:

> [W]e really had more to win ... by making those regulations a
> binding regulation than we had to lose. You know, it wouldn't really
> help us much to open the rules up for challenge at some undefined
> time, when we could get it all settled and have it as force and effect
> of law. So I consider the Abbott and [T]oilet [G]oods case, which was
> on the same principle, as cases that gave us a very strong leg up on
> making our general regulations have force and effect of law. And as
> things turned out later, that, of course, has been an important
> development in administration of the law.... By losing, we won.[104]

Others have interpreted *Abbott Labs* in a similar fashion,[105] but
Goodrich's claim of victory was somewhat exaggerated. The question of
the FDA's legislative rulemaking power under section 701(a) remained
controversial for years. Eventually the courts reached a consensus supporting that power,[106] although doubts about the propriety of this interpretation have not entirely disappeared from the law reviews.[107]

The dissents

In his lengthy and vehement opinion dissenting from the Court's
decisions in *Abbott Labs* and *Gardner*,[108] Justice Fortas took issue with
practically every argument in those decisions. He warned that the Court
had "opened Pandora's Box" and had given lower court judges "a license

---

103. See supra note 44 and accompanying text.

104. Goodrich oral history interview, supra note 46.

105. See, e.g., Margaret Gilhooley, *FDA and the Adaptation of Regulatory Models*, 49
St. Louis U.L.J. 131, 136 (2004); Merrill, supra note 28, at 276.

106. Nat'l Ass'n of Pharm. Mfrs. Ass'n v. FDA, 637 F.2d 877 (2d Cir. 1981) (Friendly,
J.); Nat'l Nutritional Foods Ass'n v. FDA, 512 F.2d 688 (2d Cir. 1975).

107. Thomas W. Merrill & Kathryn Tongue Watts, *Agency Rules with the Force of
Law: The Original Convention*, 116 Harv. L. Rev. 467, 513–16, 558–65 (2002).

108. Gardner v. Toilet Goods Ass'n, 387 U.S. 167, 174–201 (1967) (Fortas., J.,
concurring in part and dissenting in part). The opinion was a partial concurrence because
it also explained why Fortas joined the Court's decision in *Toilet Goods*.

for mischief." Reviewing the history of the FD&C Act and the Court's case law, he emphasized the innovative nature of the majority's holding. Fortas also disputed the majority's belief that the issues were "fit" for review: "It is clear beyond question," he wrote, "merely on the basis of the nature of the agency action, that [the color additive] regulations on their face raise questions which should not be adjudicated in the abstract and in the general, but which require a 'concrete setting' for determination." And he minimized the "dilemma" that the Court said was facing the manufacturers: "The overriding fact here is—or should be—that the public interest in avoiding the delay in implementing Congress' program far outweighs the private interest; and that the private interest which has so impressed the Court is no more than that which exists in respect of most regulatory statutes or agency rules."

Some of Justice Fortas's points were telling, but his dissent also contained some weak spots. For one thing, his insistence that the Court could make a more informed decision by postponing review until enforcement proceedings was too dogmatic. At best, it was *possible* that experience under the new regulations would generate lessons that a reviewing court would consider helpful to its decision. Moreover, Fortas's exposition of the policy consequences of immediate review was entirely one-sided. The public interest in firm enforcement of consumer-protection legislation is surely substantial, but so too is the regulated firm's interest in not having to spend large sums to comply with regulations that might turn out to be unlawful (as, indeed, the district court had already held the *Abbott Labs* rule to be). The value of maintaining checks and balances and holding agencies to the rule of law found no recognition in this dissent.

Possibly the Fortas dissent is most noteworthy when seen from a biographical rather than a doctrinal perspective. As mentioned earlier, he was on familiar ground in this subject area. Only two years prior to the decision in this case, Abe Fortas had been the managing partner of Arnold, Fortas & Porter, one of the premier Washington law firms.[109] The firm had developed an extensive clientele of companies—including, of course, pharmaceutical companies[110]—that regularly came into collision with administrative agencies. No one on the Court had more experience representing private interests in regulatory cases than For-

109. See generally JOSEPH C. GOULDEN, THE SUPERLAWYERS: THE SMALL AND POWERFUL WORLD OF THE GREAT WASHINGTON LAW FIRMS ch. 3 (1971) (devoting an entire chapter to the firm, which is now known as Arnold & Porter). Regarding Fortas's management role within the firm, see NORMAN DIAMOND, A PRACTICE ALMOST PERFECT: THE EARLY DAYS AT ARNOLD, FORTAS & PORTER 39 (1997).

110. See GOULDEN, supra note 109, at 133–38 (discussing drug cases handled during this period by the firm's Stuart Land, whom "people who practice at the FDA rank ... among the top half-dozen specialists in Washington").

tas. In this light, the Justice's warnings about obstruction, delay, and the dangers of yielding to "counsel's ability to marshall and deploy horrible examples which logic may accommodate, but the reality of administration would repel"[111] are certainly striking. Of course, jurists do often acquire new perspectives from serving on the bench. Even so, the dissent's total lack of acknowledgment of any equities on the manufacturers' side is curious. A cynic might suggest that Fortas was simply *all too familiar* with the tactics against which his dissent inveighed.

Remarkable as the Fortas dissent was, however, the brief dissenting opinion of Justice Clark might be considered even more so. The nub of his protest was this:

> The pharmaceutical companies, contrary to the public interest, have through their high-sounding trademarks of long-established medicines deceitfully and exorbitantly extorted high prices therefor from the sick and the infirm. Indeed, I was so gouged myself just recently when I purchased some ordinary eyewash drops and later learned that I paid 10 times the price the drops should have cost. Likewise, a year or so ago I purchased a brand name drug for the treatment of labyrinthitis at a cost of some $12, which later I learned to buy by its established name for about $1.

> . . . Rather than crying over the plight that the laboratories have brought on themselves the Court should think more of the poor ailing folks who suffer under [this] practice. I dare say that the practice has prevented millions from obtaining needed drugs because of the price.

Probably this sort of "proof by personal anecdote" is heard with some frequency in the privacy of judges' and Justices' chambers, but one hardly expects to find it openly deployed in an opinion in the *United States Reports*. Evidently Justice Clark, having taken a stand on the legal issues anyway by joining Justice Fortas's thorough dissent, saw no harm in using a separate opinion to tweak the drug companies a bit, in the wake of his unhappy experiences at the local pharmacy.

The Regulatory Aftermath

Drug labeling

Having handed PMA a victory that even that organization considered "almost startling,"[112] the Supreme Court remanded the *Abbott Labs* case to the Third Circuit for consideration of the merits. Soon after-

---

111. 387 U.S. at 197.

112. CRAY, supra note 4, at 61. As already seen, drug industry lawyers were not very accustomed to winning in court. See supra notes 25–26 and accompanying text.

wards, however, the case ended abruptly. On the eve of reargument in the Third Circuit, the parties reached a settlement. In return for the plaintiffs' dropping their declaratory judgment suit, the FDA replaced the "every time" regulation with a narrower requirement.[113] Under the new rule, the established (generic) name had to appear prominently each time the brand name was "featured," but in the "running text" the restrictions were much looser. The rule is still in effect[114] and has apparently not been controversial during the intervening years.

Political and social controversy about the high prices that Americans pay for prescription drugs has by no means disappeared, of course. Current debates about legalizing the importation of relatively inexpensive drugs from Canada, and about the structure of the Medicare prescription drug benefit program, are only a few examples of the way in which the problem continues to generate front page news. Moreover, American pharmaceutical companies are still exceptionally profitable, compared with other industries.[115] Critics of the industry argue that its ability to charge high prices for prescription drugs is largely attributable to aggressive advertising and promotional practices, as well as legal and business strategies that enable the companies to derive maximum benefit from their patent monopolies and avoid competition from generic-drug manufacturers.[116] These, of course, are simply modern variations on some of the same industry practices that distressed Senator Kefauver in the 1960s. From this long-term perspective, one could argue that the FDA's retreat in the *Abbott Labs* litigation was a step in the wrong direction.

Yet it is hardly clear that drug prices remain high because of a continuing problem of doctors' not being aware of the names of the generic counterparts of various brand-name drugs. On the contrary, intuition would suggest that the revised FDA rule gives generic names the prominence in labeling that most of the supporters of the 1962 legislation would have desired, but without the unwieldiness that the strict "every time" requirement would have entailed. Thus, if we focus on the specific battleground that was at issue in *Abbott Labs*, rather than the wider war, it seems reasonable to argue that judicial review contributed to a beneficial outcome in that case, because it "got the FDA's attention" and forced the agency to negotiate a sensible solution that was more livable from the companies' point of view.

---

113. PETER BARTON HUTT & RICHARD A. MERRILL, FOOD AND DRUG LAW: CASES AND MATERIALS 453 (2d ed. 1991).

114. 21 C.F.R. § 201.10(g) (2004).

115. MARCIA ANGELL, THE TRUTH ABOUT THE DRUG COMPANIES: HOW THEY DECEIVE US AND WHAT TO DO ABOUT IT 10–11 (2004).

116. Id. at 76–80, 115–34, 173–92.

Color additives

The subsequent history of the regulations that the Supreme Court remanded in *Gardner v. Toilet Goods Ass'n* is more complex. At issue, it will be recalled, were the agency's definition of "color additive" and its understanding of the statutory exemption for hair dyes. No settlement was forthcoming in these proceedings, and TGA remained defiant. To rally his allies at a meeting of the Cosmetic Industry Buyers and Suppliers Association, TGA's new executive vice president even borrowed from the cadences of the Gettysburg Address, declaring: "Now we are engaged in a great civil strike to determine whether this industry or any other industry may prosper in these United States."[117]

In the end, the cosmetics industry did not perish from the earth. Indeed, it won considerable vindication during the remand proceedings. District Judge Tyler ruled in TGA's favor on every remaining issue and entered a decree invalidating all portions of the FDA regulations that were still in dispute.[118] In one holding, which bears particular attention here because the FDA never appealed it, Judge Tyler rejected the agency's attempt to define "color additive" broadly enough to include "diluents."[119] Diluents, it will be recalled, are ingredients that dilute a dye or pigment or add volume to the product. Had the FDA's position prevailed, companies would have had to submit applications for FDA listing of any and all diluents in their cosmetics. To Judge Tyler, however, the statutory term "color additive" appeared to refer only to a dye or pigment itself. Indeed, the Act provided for certification of color additives "with safe diluents or without diluents." In addition, he said, diluents had been unregulated prior to the 1960 legislation, and the legislative history indicated that Congress contemplated no significant change in that aspect of the statute's coverage.

The FDA filed an appeal in the Second Circuit, which, for the most part, affirmed Judge Tyler's decision.[120] Judge Friendly again wrote for the court. First, he rejected the FDA's position that a finished product, such as lipstick or rouge, could itself be a "color additive" to which the listing and certification requirements of the Color Additive Amendments would apply. The FDA had arrived at this surprising proposition by what Friendly called an "ingenious parsing" of the statutory definition of "color additive." The statutory definition referred to "a dye, pigment, or other substance ... [that,] when added or applied to a food, drug, or cosmetic, or to the human body ... is capable ... of imparting color

---

117.   The remark is quoted in Stabile, supra note 56 at 19.

118.   Toilet Goods Ass'n v. Gardner, 278 F. Supp. 786 (S.D.N.Y. 1968).

119.   See 21 C.F.R. § 8.1(f).

120.   Toilet Goods Ass'n v. Finch, 419 F.2d 21 (2d Cir. 1969).

thereto...."[121] The FDA definition presupposed that a finished cosmetic can be a color additive if it is a "substance" that imparts color when "applied to the human body."

Judge Friendly recognized that this reading was linguistically possible, although counterintuitive. Acknowledging that the textual arguments cut both ways, he found "more enlightenment in the history and purpose of the Color Additive Amendments." The FDA had never advanced its present interpretation during the era when it was governed by the 1938 Act, and Congress had given no indication in 1960 that it intended to make this kind of major change in the FDA's jurisdiction. Friendly also pointed out that the thrust of the 1960 legislation had been to apply the same requirements to all color additives, whether found in food, drugs, or cosmetics. The FDA regulation, however, "would result in finished cosmetics with coloring ingredients being subject to listing and certification whereas food and drugs bearing such ingredients would not be. Yet, if there is a difference in hazard, foods and drugs, which are ingested, would seem to outrank cosmetics; indeed cosmetics were not brought into the regulatory scheme until 32 years after foods and drugs."

Turning to the FDA's regulation delimiting the scope of the hair dye exemption, the court adopted a more textually based line of argument. Under the statute, the FDA's normal powers to declare a cosmetic adulterated if it contains a poisonous or deleterious substance "shall not apply to coal-tar hair dye, the label of which bears the following legend conspicuously displayed thereon: 'Caution—This product contains ingredients which may cause skin irritation on certain individuals and a preliminary test according to accompanying directions should first be made....' "[122] The FDA's regulation provided that this exemption would not apply "[i]f the poisonous or deleterious substance in the 'hair dye' is one to which the caution is inapplicable and for which patch-testing provides no safeguard."[123] The regulation had an obvious policy justification. The patch test by its nature was designed to alert consumers to short-term skin irritants. If use of a given hair dye were to pose a longer-term danger (such as a risk of cancer), a patch test would not uncover it, and normal FDA remedies should thus be available. But the court concluded that this attractive-sounding provision was simply not an option. Here, Judge Friendly noted, "Congress wrote with great specificity," and "the language is too clear for us to read it as meaning something different from what it so plainly says." Thus, the district

---

121.   21 U.S.C. § 321(t)(1).

122.   21 U.S.C. § 361(a).

123.   21 C.F.R. § 8.1(u).

court's invalidation of this regulation was upheld, with minor modifications.[124]

To bring this discussion back to the issue of ripeness, notice that both the district court and the court of appeals developed their arguments on the basis of pure statutory analysis: text, legislative history, and legislative purpose. At first glance, anyway, hindsight seems to bear out Justice Harlan's prediction that the issues in *Gardner* were "fit" for immediate review. Although the district court did consider some affidavits and other evidentiary submissions, those materials dealt exclusively with the reasons behind FDA's regulations, the understandings of congressional intent on which those reasons rested, and prior administrative interpretations.[125] Postponement of review until an enforcement proceeding would surely not have enabled a court to probe these backward-looking issues more thoroughly.

One could respond, however, that this argument is circular. *Of course* the judges limited their attention to backward-looking evidence such as congressional intent. Since the Supreme Court had told them to proceed to the merits without waiting for experience under the regulations to develop, what else could they do? One should not reject out of hand the possibility that, if TGA's suit had been dismissed as premature, the FDA could have developed a track record that would have enabled it to show that its regulation had proved over time to be a vital bulwark for the public health by reining in bad actors. Such a track record might conceivably have induced the courts, in some future enforcement proceeding, to overcome their reservations about the liberties that the agency had taken with the statutory language.

To come to grips with this possibility, let us take a look at some of the FDA's subsequent experiences with color additives in cosmetics. Because the agency cannot classify a diluent or a finished product as a color additive, its jurisdiction to require listing and certification of a

---

124. The court of appeals did uphold part of the FDA's hair-dye regulation. Judge Friendly pointed out that the statutory exemption did not shield diluents in a hair dye from the FDA's authority merely because they were combined with a coal-tar color. Thus, the FDA regulation was valid insofar as it asserted jurisdiction over these substances. Nor did the exemption apply to color additives that were not coal-tar colors. Although a related provision in the 1960 law did say that the listing and certification requirements applied to a color additive "that is not a hair dye," Judge Friendly refused to read this language literally. He treated the provision as merely a poorly drafted cross-reference to the preexisting hair-dye exemption. The FDA had clearly possessed authority over non-coal-tar colors in hair dyes prior to 1960, and nothing in the purpose of the 1960 legislation suggested that Congress would have wanted to weaken that authority.

125. Lang interview, supra note 76. Today this sort of factual exploration would almost certainly not be allowed. If the court were in doubt as to the agency's reasoning, it would normally be expected to remand the case to the agency for an explanation. Pension Benefit Guar. Corp. v. LTV Corp., 496 U.S. 633, 654 (1990).

given ingredient in a cosmetic depends on whether that ingredient is, in fact, a source of color in the product. An interesting case that highlighted this obligation was *United States v. Roux Laboratories*,[126] in which the question was whether the defendant had marketed an eyebrow tinting product using an unlisted color additive. Contending that the color had actually come from a different ingredient than the agency had alleged, Roux won a jury verdict. According to jurors who spoke with Roux's counsel afterwards, the most impressive testimony in the case came from the company's "expert witness," the wife of its CEO, who applied the cosmetic to herself in front of the jury to demonstrate her confidence in its safety! Despite occasional controversy,[127] however, it is not clear that this gap in its jurisdiction has caused significant problems for the FDA. If the agency can make a case that an ingredient that is not subject to listing and certification renders a cosmetic unsafe, it can still take action to force removal of the cosmetic from the market.[128] FDA officials do not currently view the "gap" in its listing and certification jurisdiction as especially problematic.[129]

In 1979 the FDA did take steps to overcome the regulatory gap attributable to the hair dye exemption in the FD&C Act. It issued a rule under which manufacturers of coal tar hair dyes containing a compound known as "4–MMPD" would be required to include the following statement on their product labels: "Warning—Contains an ingredient that can penetrate your skin and has been determined to cause cancer in laboratory animals."[130] The FDA explained that, although the hair dye exemption deprived the agency of power to prohibit the marketing of hair dyes containing 4–MMPD (assuming that the manufacturer included the patch-test warning on its labeling), the exemption did not limit the agency's separate authority to require truthful labeling of cosmetics.[131] Soon thereafter, the rule was challenged in court. The FDA agreed to a consent order under which it would stay the effectiveness of this

---

126. 437 F.2d 209 (9th Cir. 1971). The cited opinion addressed only threshold issues; the anecdote in the text is based on Lang interview, supra note 76.

127. See generally 1 JAMES T. O'REILLY, FOOD AND DRUG ADMINISTRATION §§ 12.01–.02 (1979 & Supp. 1992).

128. Michelle Meadows, *Heading Off Hair–Care Disasters: Use Caution With Relaxers and Dyes*, FDA CONSUMER, Jan.-Feb. 2001, *available at* www.fda.gov/fdac/features/2001/101_hair.html (discussing FDA's actions to remove a hair relaxer—which was not exempt as a hair *dye*—from the market because it caused temporary hair loss and other problems for consumers).

129. Telephone interview with Dr. Sandra Bell, Director, Color Technology Branch, Office of Cosmetics and Colors, Center for Food Safety and Applied Nutrition, FDA, May 6, 2005. Obviously, statements of this kind are not official agency pronouncements, but they are instructive nevertheless.

130. 44 Fed. Reg. 59,509, 59,522 (1979).

131. Id. at 59,510.

rule until such time as it had conducted a risk assessment study to determine whether 4–MMPD is dangerous to humans, not just animals. The agency has never proceeded with that study, and the stay remains in effect.[132] The agency's inaction on this front for twenty-five years is indicative of the lack of urgency that it discerns in this area. FDA officials do not find the available studies on a possible link between hair dyes and cancer to be convincing enough to warrant stronger action.[133]

In short, the seriousness of the regulatory gaps created by the remand decisions in *Gardner* is debatable. There is little reason to believe, however, that the courts would ultimately have considered the desirability of filling those gaps so compelling as to overcome the significant legal objections that TGA was able to lodge against the regulations considered in those proceedings.

Access to facilities

Because of the Supreme Court's holding in *Toilet Goods Association v. Gardner* that the FDA's regulation on access to facilities[134] was unripe for review, that rule went into effect forthwith. Since then, no reported case has addressed its merits. According to an FDA official who actually conducts inspections pursuant to the regulation, manufacturers do routinely provide the FDA with access to their facilities, including access to proprietary formulas. The agency has not actually had to impose the sanction of curtailment of certification services, but its power to impose that sanction does give the companies an incentive to cooperate. On the other hand, she noted, experience has not borne out industry's fears that secret formulas obtained by the FDA through inspections would be leaked to competitors; the agency handles proprietary information scrupulously.[135] Of course, one should be cautious about accepting administrators' assurances of this kind too readily, and it is hard to know what hidden costs the industry may have absorbed without protest. At least, however, it appears that the inspections facilitated by the access regulation have generated little if any controversy in the years since 1967.

Looking at *Toilet Goods* with the perspective of hindsight, one could perhaps argue that the Supreme Court should have decided that the

---

132. A notice of the stay is still being published with the codified text of the rule. 21 C.F.R. § 740.18 (2004). See generally HUTT & MERRILL, supra note 113, at 908–15 (discussing this episode).

133. *Hair Color and Cancer*, sidebar story in Meadows, supra note 128; Bell interview, supra note 129.

134. 21 C.F.R. § 8.28(a)(4).

135. Bell interview, supra note 129. Another official with compliance responsibilities in the cosmetics area agreed with Dr. Bell on these points. Telephone interview with Jennifer Thomas, Team Leader, Division of Enforcement of Compliance, Center for Food Safety and Applied Nutrition, FDA, May 23, 2005.

access regulation was ripe for pre-enforcement review after all. Evidently the Court's refusal to allow direct review drove up the costs of contesting the rule to such an extent that the companies no longer considered such a contest worthwhile. In other words, the effect of the holding was to prevent judicial review of the rule altogether, not merely to postpone it. But so what? The logic of the ripeness doctrine does not presuppose that every disagreement about regulatory power should eventually reach the courts in some fashion. In this instance, the "dilemma" facing manufacturers apparently proved less onerous than they feared, because the costs of compliance with the regulation have apparently turned out to be modest or at least bearable for the industry. In that respect, at least, the Court's discretionary withholding of review does not seem to have brought about a demonstrable injustice.

* * *

In summary, the Court's holdings in the trilogy cases seem to have worked out reasonably well in relation to the particular facts of those cases. But what about the cases' consequences as precedents? The following section offers some concluding perspectives on that score.

Ripeness Law After the Trilogy

Although it was initially a product of compromise, the *Abbott Labs* formula for ripeness has shown considerable staying power. Over the years, Justice Harlan's analysis (or, if one prefers, Judge Friendly's) has become the standard point of reference for ripeness discussions, in administrative law contexts[136] as well as other contexts.[137] The Court accomplished this by adopting a formula that was relatively simple, yet flexible enough to be used in a wide range of situations.

But the trilogy did more than merely provide a new vocabulary for the exercise of judicial discretion. It also served to reshape the courts' role in the oversight of administrative agencies. Today, pre-enforcement review of rules is a pervasive feature of administrative law practice, though it has not entirely displaced review at the enforcement stage. Indeed, in many regulatory programs, Congress has ordained that judicial review of a newly promulgated regulation must be sought immediately after its issuance or not at all.[138]

---

136. See, e.g., Whitman v. Am. Trucking Ass'ns, Inc., 531 U.S. 457, 479 (2001); EPA v. Nat'l Crushed Stone Ass'n, 449 U.S. 64, 72 n.12 (1980).

137. See, e.g., Texas v. United States, 523 U.S. 296 (1998) (Voting Rights Act claim); Thomas v. Union Carbide Agric. Prods. Co., 473 U.S. 568, 580–82 (1985) (Article III challenge to arbitration scheme); Pac. Gas & Elec. Co. v. State Energy Res. Conserv. & Dev. Comm'n, 461 U.S. 190, 200–03 (1983) (preemption of state law).

138. See Paul R. Verkuil, *Congressional Limitations on Judicial Review of Rules*, 57 Tul. L. Rev. 733, 771–75 (1983); Frederick Davis, *Judicial Review of Rulemaking: New Patterns and New Problems,* 1981 Duke L.J. 279.

In at least some ways, the burgeoning of pre-enforcement review has been a beneficial development. In an age of pervasive rulemaking, the traditional maxims allowing regulations to be tested in court only in enforcement proceedings probably could not have been maintained indefinitely. Today, many agency regulations require large investments, and the need to know whether they are valid is pressing. The agency, too, may have a stake in early settlement of any challenges to its regulatory approach. As Justice Harlan wrote, the pre-enforcement challenge in *Abbott Labs* itself was "calculated to speed enforcement. If the Government prevails, a large part of the industry is bound by the decree; if the Government loses, it can more quickly revise its regulation."[139] As mentioned earlier, even the FDA's Goodrich ultimately came to recognize, in a way, that the *Abbott Labs* approach can benefit the agency and fits naturally into a regulatory regime that relics heavily on rulemaking.[140]

One factor that has contributed to the prevalence of pre-enforcement review is the advent of review of agency rules on the "administrative record." Prior to the era in which *Abbott Labs* was decided, persons who wanted to challenge an agency rule on factual grounds would typically offer evidence supporting that challenge in judicial review proceedings.[141] The suggestion in *Toilet Goods* that facts and circumstances bearing upon the validity of the FDA's access regulation could be developed in an enforcement proceeding should be understood in that light. Such facts had not been aired publicly during the proceedings in which the rule was promulgated. In the 1960s and 1970s, however, the working principles changed. Now the operating assumption is that persons who favor or oppose a rule will submit facts and policy arguments in comments for a publicly available "rulemaking record," the agency will respond in a preamble accompanying the final rule, and the court will look to the record to decide whether the agency's responses were reasonable.[142] Indeed, usually the court limits its consideration of these issues to the record and will not accept additional evidence at the judicial review stage.[143]

To be sure, the closed-record principle is not absolute. Courts do often take judicial notice of the way in which a regulatory regime has

---

139. *Abbott Labs*, 387 U.S. at 154.

140. See supra note 104 and accompanying text.

141. See JEFFREY S. LUBBERS, A GUIDE TO FEDERAL AGENCY RULEMAKING 209–10 (3d ed. 1998).

142. See id. at 210–13, 216–24; Jim Rossi, *Judicial Review of Issues of Fact*, in JOHN F. DUFFY & MICHAEL HERZ, A GUIDE TO JUDICIAL AND POLITICAL REVIEW OF FEDERAL AGENCIES 159, 166–69 (2005).

143. See, e.g., United States v. Nova Scotia Food Prods. Corp., 568 F.2d 240 (2d Cir. 1977).

developed since the promulgation of a rule.[144] The *Toilet Goods* alternative of waiting to see how a rule works out in practice is, therefore, not defunct. Indeed, sometimes those circumstances are essentially undisputed. However, if the impact of a rule involves technical and seemingly contestable factual issues, a court would probably refuse to rely on judicial notice and would require the parties to present evidence about a rule's impact to the agency first.[145]

The effect of the emergence of the closed-record concept has been to widen the range of rules that are "fit" for pre-enforcement judicial consideration under the trilogy's criteria. A "purely legal" issue is not a necessary condition for immediate review, because the parties can often join issue over questions about the factual sufficiency, consistency, or reasonableness of the agency's decision by referring to the administrative record, and the court can resolve these questions on the same basis. The operative question is whether the agency engaged in "reasoned decisionmaking" at the time it promulgated the rule. As a result, some judicial review proceedings that might have been controlled by *Toilet Goods* are instead controlled by *Abbott Labs*. This line of reasoning applies most forcefully, of course, when the factual issue in dispute is a backward-looking question such as the state of present scientific knowledge, as distinguished from a forward-looking question such as how the rule will work out in practice.

A separate explanation for the flourishing of pre-enforcement review relates to another important element of modern administrative law practice: the prevalence of judicial review proceedings in which beneficiary groups claim that a regulation is too weak. A public interest group might, for example, sue the FDA seeking more informative drug labeling[146] or broader protection from color additives.[147] A presumption against direct review would not work well in relation to such claims, because in most circumstances a court could not credibly tell such a group to postpone its appeal until an enforcement proceeding. The agency might never bring such a proceeding; the public interest group might not be entitled to participate in it; and the proceeding might not

---

144. See Verizon Communs., Inc. v. FCC, 535 U.S. 467, 516–17 (2002); 1 KENNETH CULP DAVIS, ADMINISTRATIVE LAW TREATISE § 6:17 (2d ed. 1978).

145. The challenger might, for example, file a petition with the agency to revise the rule. See 5 U.S.C. § 553(e) (authorizing rulemaking petitions). This course of action would facilitate compilation of a new record at the agency level. Then, if the petition were denied, the challenger could appeal the denial to a court. See Auer v. Robbins, 519 U.S. 452, 459 (1997).

146. See Chaney v. Heckler, 718 F.2d 1174, 1178 (D.C. Cir. 1983), rev'd on other grounds, 470 U.S. 821 (1985).

147. See, e.g., Simpson v. Young, 854 F.2d 1429 (D.C. Cir. 1988); McIlwain v. Hayes, 690 F.2d 1041 (D.C. Cir. 1982).

involve issues that are relevant to the ones that the public interest group wants to raise. The need for such groups to have access to direct review is not only manifest but also carries implications for the industry group on the other side of the regulatory fence. Allowing pre-enforcement review to the latter not only looks fair as a matter of symmetry, but also enables the court to consider the claims of both sides in a consolidated review proceeding.

Ironically, as earlier discussion in this chapter's narrative sought to make clear, the *Abbott Labs* trilogy need not have been read to encourage as much broad pre-enforcement review as prevails today. The cases certainly rejected the no-direct-review presumption favored by Justice Fortas, but it is not at all clear that the Court intended to commit itself to a contrary presumption. Of course, the behind-the-scenes information presented above highlights the Court's ambivalence and shows that *Toilet Goods* was by no means an afterthought—on the contrary, it was the first of the three cases to command a majority. Even on their face, however, the opinions offered grounds for a cautious reading. Those grounds included not only the finding against ripeness in *Toilet Goods*, but also the nuanced analysis of "fitness" in *Abbott Labs* and *Gardner*.[148] Caution has not, however, been the order of the day. What seems to have happened is that, once the Court had made clear that there was no presumption *against* pre-enforcement review, a combination of factors, such as the ones that have been discussed in this section, induced courts to find that the *Abbott Labs* balance favors such review in most instances.

Still, the more measured reading of the *Abbott Labs* test should not be forgotten entirely, because it helps to explain why the courts do continue to deny direct review of rules from time to time, following the lead of *Toilet Goods*. Such holdings may occur because the chances of an ultimate collision between the parties over the point at issue look highly unlikely,[149] or because administrative consideration is ongoing,[150] or because the hardship confronting the challenger looks minimal.[151] Cases in this vein remain an important feature of modern administrative practice, even though at present they are somewhat exceptional.

To be sure, despite the dominance of the *Abbott Labs* test in discussions of ripeness, not everyone is satisfied with it. Over the decades, various commentators have criticized the formula as allowing

---

148.   See supra text following note 101.

149.   See, e.g., Texas v. United States, 523 U.S. 296 (1998); State Farm Mut. Auto. Ins. Co. v. Dole, 802 F.2d 474 (D.C. Cir. 1986).

150.   See, e.g., Ohio Forestry Ass'n v. Sierra Club, 523 U.S. 726 (1998).

151.   See, e.g., Nat'l Park Hospitality Ass'n v. Dept. of Interior, 538 U.S. 803 (2003).

either too little review[152] or too much.[153] Still others lament the unpredictability and perhaps inconsistency with which the doctrine has often been applied.[154] To a certain extent, of course, such inconsistency should not be surprising, because the Court intended to enunciate a broadly discretionary doctrine. Flexibility is inherent in the Court's pragmatic method, but for some observers it has been a source of frustration.

Although these critiques have not dislodged the *Abbott Labs* paradigm as a general matter, there is at least one sector of administrative law in which one can detect signs that the trilogy's balancing test might be losing its position of dominance. That sector consists of judicial review proceedings in which the agency action in dispute is a highly informal pronouncement, such as an administrator's advice letter or a posting on an agency web site. In several recent decisions, courts have taken a more categorical approach, holding that a pronouncement is not subject to review because it is not a reviewable "agency action" at all,[155] or because it is not a "final" action.[156] These lines of argument may reflect a degree of discomfort with the open-ended balancing that characterizes the *Abbott Labs* approach. On the other hand, a competing line of cases does apply *Abbott Labs* reasoning more or less faithfully to efforts to obtain judicial review of informal advice.[157] A question for the future, therefore, will be whether and how far the former line of cases will eclipse the latter. For now, the law on this point seems to be in flux.

---

152. John F. Duffy, *Administrative Common Law in Judicial Review*, 77 TEX. L. REV.113, 162–81 (1998); G. Joseph Vining, *Direct Judicial Review and the Doctrine of Ripeness in Administrative Law*, 69 MICH. L. REV. 1445, 1495–500 (1971).

153. Jerry L. Mashaw, *Improving the Environment of Agency Rulemaking: An Essay on Management, Games, and Accountability*, 57 L. & CONTEMP. PROB. 185, 233–38 (Spring 1994). For skeptical reactions to Mashaw's analysis, see Mark Seidenfeld, *Playing Games with the Timing of Judicial Review: An Evaluation of Proposals to Restrict Pre–Enforcement Review of Agency Rules*, 58 OHIO ST. L. REV. 85 (1997); Richard J. Pierce, Jr., *Seven Ways to Deossify Rulemaking*, 47 ADMIN. L. REV. 59, 88–93 (1995).

154. See Brian C. Murchison, *On Ripeness and "Pragmatism" in Administrative Law*, 41 ADMIN. L. REV. 159, 159–60 (1989).

155. Indep. Equip. Dealers Ass'n v. EPA, 372 F.3d 420 (D.C. Cir. 2004) (EPA letter was not reviewable agency action because it simply restated extant policy); General Motors Corp. v. EPA, 363 F.3d 442 (D.C. Cir. 2004) (similar).

156. Air Brake Systems, Inc. v. Mineta, 357 F.3d 632, 640–44 (6th Cir. 2004) (agency chief counsel's letter construing safety standard was nonfinal because it lacked binding legal consequences).

157. Aviators for Safe and Fairer Regulation, Inc. v. FAA, 221 F.3d 222 (1st Cir. 2000) (notice of enforcement policy was ripe for review, at least in part); Barrick Goldstrike Mines, Inc. v. Browner, 215 F.3d 45 (D.C. Cir. 2000) (EPA interpretation of miners' duty to report allegedly toxic releases, articulated through guidances, letters, and rulemaking preambles, was final *and* ripe for review). A classic case in this vein is *Nat'l Automatic Laundry & Cleaning Council v. Shultz*, 443 F.2d 689, 694–97 (D.C. Cir. 1971).

Conclusion

We have seen that the Supreme Court had difficulty deciding the trilogy cases. The Justices saw strong equities favoring and opposing pre-enforcement review of FDA regulations. Instead of choosing one set of arguments over the other, they collectively worked out a compromise. Their solution tries to take account of all of the competing variables and leaves much discretion in the hands of individual reviewing courts. That much indeterminacy is hard to sustain in a legal regime, and a desire for simple working principles may help to account for the courts' usual liberality in accepting pre-enforcement review. Still, many judges are wary (at least sporadically) about trying to decide too much too soon, especially when a plaintiff can show no urgent need for review. The defense of lack of ripeness is thus unlikely to disappear, and it may even be headed for a comeback.[158]

In any event, the *Abbott Labs* formula by its nature invites highly fact-intensive inquiries. In line with that emphasis, this chapter has presented a plenitude of facts with which the reader can make a judgment about whether the particular issues raised in the drug labeling and color additives disputes were, indeed, ripe for judicial review. The chapter's story also provides a starting point for consideration of larger questions about how the ripeness doctrine should be applied to today's changed and changing administrative law environment. Those latter questions, however, are themselves unripe for immediate consideration (at least on the present record) and must await another day.

---

158. See Randolph, supra note 82, at 9–11 (suggesting the possibility that, "since 1967, the pendulum has swung too far in favor of permitting [pre-enforcement] review").

Contributors

Cynthia R. Farina is Professor of Law and Associate Dean of the University Faculty at Cornell University. She received her J.D. summa cum laude from Boston University, and then clerked for Raymond J. Pettine, chief judge of the U.S. District Court for District of Rhode Island, and for Spottswood W. Robinson, chief judge of the U. S. Court of Appeals for the District of Columbia Circuit. She practiced as a litigator with Foley, Hoag & Eliot, Boston, MA. She joined the Cornell faculty in 1985 and was a visiting professor at Harvard Law School in 1991. With Peter Strauss and Todd Rakoff, she is co-author of the leading casebook in administrative law, **Gellhorn & Byse's Administrative Law–Cases and Comments** (Foundation Press 1995 and 2003). Her article, *The Consent of the Governed: Against Simple Rules for a Complex World*, was chosen by the ABA Administrative Law Section as the best administrative law article of the year. Professor Farina has worked extensively with the Administrative Law Section, chairing the committee on Government Affairs & Separation of Powers, serving as for the ABA Special Committee on Government Standards, which produced a comprehensive report and recommendations on reforming government ethics regulation, co-Reporter for Judicial Review (Standing) in the APA Project, and co-Reporter for Transparency in the Administrative Law of the European Union Project. She recently was named a Fellow of the Section. She has also chaired the Administrative Law Section of the American Association of Law Schools. Prof. Farina's scholarship, in the areas of separation of powers, procedural due process, and government ethics, is concerned with the question of how public institutions and processes can best be structured to encourage the responsive and responsible use of government power.

Elizabeth Garrett is the Vice Provost of Academic Affairs at the University of Southern California and the Sydney M. Irmas Professor of Public Interest Law, Legal Ethics, Political Science, and Policy, Planning and Development. She is also the Director of the USC–Caltech Center for the Study of Law and Politics (CSLP). Her primary scholarly interests are legislative process, direct democracy, the federal budget process, study of democratic institutions, statutory interpretation, and administrative law. She is the co-author of the Third Edition of the leading casebook on legislation and statutory interpretation, **Cases and Materi-**

als on Legislation: Statutes and the Creation of Public Policy (West Publishing 2001) and of **Legislation and Statutory Interpretation** (Foundation Press 2000). She is the author of many articles and book chapters, analyzing campaign finance laws, courts and political parties, various congressional procedures, judicial review of regulatory statutes, the initiative process, and the California recall. Before joining the faculty of USC, she was a Professor of Law at the University of Chicago, where she also served as Deputy Dean for Academic Affairs, and she has been a visiting professor at Harvard Law School, the University of Virginia Law School, Central European University in Budapest, and the Interdisciplinary Center Law School in Israel. Before entering academics, she clerked for Justice Thurgood Marshall on the U.S. Supreme Court, and she served as legal counsel and legislative director for Senator David L. Boren (D–Okla.). She appreciates the excellent research assistance of Alex Baskin (USC '05) on her chapter.

Robert A. Kagan is Professor of Political Science and Law at the University of California, Berkeley. From 1993 to 2003, he was Director of UC Berkeley's Center for the Study of Law and Society. His books include **Shades of Green: Business, Regulation, and Environment** (with Neil Gunningham and Dorothy Thornton, 2003); **Adversarial Legalism: The American Way of Law** (2001); **Regulatory Encounters: Multinational Corporations and American Adversarial Legalism** (with Lee Axelrad, 2000); **Going By the Book: The Problem of Regulatory Unreasonableness** (with Eugene Bardach, 1982 and 2002); and **Regulatory Justice: Implementing a Wage–Price Freeze** (1978). He has also published articles based on empirical studies of a wide range of topics, including comparative legal systems, the politics of tobacco regulation, income tax law compliance, corporate responses to environmental law, comparative law and seaport labor relations, and the American legal profession's role in shaping American legal institutions.

Ronald M. Levin is Henry Hitchcock Professor of Law at Washington University in St. Louis. He was the 2000–01 Chair of the Section of Administrative Law and Regulatory Practice of the American Bar Association; he also has chaired both the Section on Administrative Law and the Section on Legislation of the Association of American Law Schools, and has served as a consultant to the Administrative Conference of the United States. He served from 2002–05 on the ABA Standing Committee on Amicus Curiae Briefs.

Professor Levin is the co-author (with Michael Asimow and Arthur Earl Bonfield) of **State and Federal Administrative Law** (2d ed. 1998, with 2005 supplement) and (with Ernest Gellhorn) of **Administrative Law and Process in a Nutshell** (4th ed. 1997), and has frequently contributed to the law reviews on administrative law subjects.

At Washington University, Professor Levin has served as Associate Dean of the School of Law from 1990–93, and as chair of the University Senate Council and the University Judicial Board.

Jerry L. Mashaw is Sterling Professor of Law at Yale Law School, where he teaches courses on Administrative Law, social welfare policy, regulation, legislation, and the designing of public institutions. He formerly taught at Tulane University and the University of Virginia. His many books include **Administrative Law: Introduction to the American Public Law System** (most recent edition 2003, with Richard Merrill and Peter Shane), **Bureaucratic Justice** (1983), awarded Harvard University's Gerard Henderson Memorial prize in 1993, **The Struggle for Auto Safety** (with D. Harfst 1990), awarded the Sixth Annual Scholarship Prize of the ABA's Section on Administrative Law and Regulatory Policy in 1992 and **Greed, Chaos and Governance: Using Public Choice to Improve Public Law** (1997), awarded the Section's Twelfth Annual Scholarship Prize in 1998 and the Order of the Coif Triennial Book Award in 2002 for books published between 1997 and 1999.

Professor Mashaw also has been President of the National Academy of Social Insurance, and is a Fellow of the National Academy of Arts and Sciences, and the founding Co-editor (with O.E. Williamson) of the Journal of Law, Economics and Organization.

Thomas Merrill is the Charles Keller Beekman Professor of Law at Columbia Law School; he was formerly the John Paul Stevens Professor of Law at Northwestern University, where he taught from 1981 to 2003. After Grinnell College, Oxford University and the University of Chicago Law School, he clerked for Chief Judge David L. Bazelon, U.S. Court of Appeals for the District of Columbia Circuit, and Justice Harry A. Blackmun, and was an associate at Sidley Austin Brown & Wood. From 1987 to 1990 he served as Deputy Solicitor General in the Department of Justice, representing the United States before the U.S. Supreme Court. His teaching and research interests include administrative law, property, and environmental law. Recent publications include *Agency Rules with the Force of Law: The Original Convention,* Harvard Law Review (with Kathryn Watts, 2002); **Property: Takings** (with David Dana, 2002); *Chevron's Domain,* Georgetown Law Journal (with Kristin Hickman, 2001); and *The Making of the Second Rehnquist Court,* St. Louis L. J. 2003.

Gillian Metzger is Associate Professor of Law at Columbia Law School, whose faculty she joined in 2001. After studying at Yale, Oxford and Columbia Law School, she was law clerk to Judge Patricia M. Wald of the U.S. Court of Appeals for the District of Columbia Circuit and Justice Ruth Bader Ginsburg of the U.S. Supreme Court. She then served as an attorney in the Democracy Program of the Brennan Center for Justice at NYU School of Law (1998–2001) before coming to Columbia. Her principal areas of teaching and research are constitutional law, administrative law, federalism, and poverty policy; her publications include *Privatization As Delegation* and *Facial Challenges and Federalism*, both published in the Columbia Law Review.

Craig Oren is Professor of Law at Rutgers University–Camden School of Law. Professor Oren has written extensively on the Clean Air Act, including a trio of articles on the *Whitman* case. He received his A.B. and J.D. degrees from the University of California, Berkeley. While in law school, he served as Notes and Comments Editor of the California Law Review. He served as assistant counsel to the Subcommittee on Health and the Environment of the House Commerce Committee. He has been a member of National Academy of Sciences committees on environmental issues. Professor Oren teaches Property, Environmental Law, and Administrative Law.

Roy A. Schotland, is Professor of Law at Georgetown University Law Center, where he teaches Administrative Law & Regulatory Policy and Election Law ("Ballots, Bucks, Maps & Law"). After Columbia College, Oxford and Harvard Law School he clerked for Justice William J. Brennan, Jr., worked at several federal agencies and practiced in New York City. He has also taught at the University of Virginia and visited at the University of Pennsylvania. At the Securities and Exchange Commission he twice helped lead Special Studies. He was co-editor of 8th and 9th editions of **Gellhorn & Byse's Administrative Law**; editor of **Abuse on Wall Street: Conflicts of Interest in the Securities Markets**; and has written about pension regulation and election law, particularly about judicial elections. A Senior Adviser to the National Center for State Courts, he received their Distinguished Service Award for work with the Conference of Chief Justices. He has also served as a consultant to the Federal Reserve Board, legislative committees, state pension systems, the Government of Bermuda, and the ABA on campaign finance. He led a six-year national effort to modernize academe's pension system (TIAA–CREF), founded the largest chess facility outside Russia (teaching inner-city youth), is a director of mutual funds and a bank, and a member of the American Law Institute.

Peter L. Strauss is Betts Professor of Law at Columbia Law School, teaching courses in Administrative Law, Legal Methods, and Legislation. He joined the faculty in 1971, after spending two years in judicial clerkships (with Chief Judge David Bazelon of the D.C. Circuit and Justice William J. Brennan, Jr.), two years teaching criminal law at the national university of Ethiopia, and three years as an attorney in the Office of the Solicitor General, briefing and arguing cases before the United States Supreme Court. During 1975–77, Professor Strauss was on leave from Columbia as the first General Counsel of the United States Nuclear Regulatory Commission. His published works include **Administrative Justice in the United States** (1989 and 2002); **Gellhorn's & Byse's Administrative Law: Cases and Comments** (most recently, 2003, with Rakoff and Farina), **Legal Methods: Understanding and Using Cases and Statutes** (2005), and numerous law review articles, generally focusing on issues of rulemaking, separation of powers, and statutory interpretation. In 1987 the Section of Administrative Law and Regulatory Practice of the American Bar Association awarded Professor Strauss its third annual award for distinguished scholarship in administrative law. In 1992–93, he served as Chair of the Section. He has twice been Vice Dean at Columbia. Professor Strauss has visited at Harvard and NYU Law Schools, and lectured widely on American administrative law abroad, including programs in Argentina, Belarus, Brazil, China, Germany, Italy, Japan, the Netherlands, Mexico, Turkey and Venezuela. He is editor of the Social Science Research Network's Administrative Law Abstracts, and a member of the board of the Center for Computer Assisted Legal Instruction.

Rachel VanSickle–Ward is a Ph.D. candidate in Political Science at the University of California at Berkeley. Her research interests are in public law and public policy, particularly social policy-making and regulation at the state level. Her dissertation, *Explicit Language: Fragmentation and Policy Specificity in the US States*, treats the effects of institutional and political fragmentation on policy construction. Rachel graduated from Pitzer College with a degree in Political Studies and English Literature and served as a legislative consultant for California State Assemblymember Helen Thomson.

David C. Vladeck is the Director of the Institute for Public Representation and Associate Professor of Law at Georgetown University Law Center. He teaches courses in civil procedure, first amendment litigation and federal courts, and co-directs the Institute for Public Representation, a clinical law program at the Law Center handling a broad array of civil rights, civil liberties, first amendment, and open government litigation. Prior to joining the Georgetown faculty in 2002, Professor Vladeck spent over 25 years with Public Citizen Litigation Group, serving as its Director from 1992 to 2002. He has handled a wide range of complex litigation, including first amendment, health and safety, civil rights, class actions, preemption and open government cases. He has argued a number of cases before the United States Supreme Court, state courts of last resort, and over 50 cases before the federal courts of appeal. Professor Vladeck also testifies before Congress, advises Members of Congress on legal matters, and writes on administrative law, first amendment, ethics and access to justice issues. He serves as a Scholar with the Center for Progressive Reform and on the boards of various non-profit organizations. He has also served on the Council of the Administrative Law and Regulatory Practice Section of the American Bar Association and as a Public Member of the Administrative Conference of the United States. Professor Vladeck received his undergraduate degree from New York University, his law degree from Columbia University School of Law, and an LL.M. degree from Georgetown University Law Center. Professor Vladeck would like to thank his long-time colleague, Alan B. Morrison, the founder and his predecessor as director of Public Citizen Litigation Group, and now Senior Lecturer in Law at Stanford Law School, who provided helpful comments, based, in part, on his participation as co-counsel in the ethylene oxide litigation.

†